Lecture Notes in Computer Science   9173

Commenced Publication in 1973
Founding and Former Series Editors:
Gerhard Goos, Juris Hartmanis, and Jan van Leeuwen

More information about this series at http://www.springer.com/series/7409

Sakae Yamamoto (Ed.)

Human Interface
and the Management
of Information

Information and Knowledge in Context

17th International Conference, HCI International 2015
Los Angeles, CA, USA, August 2–7, 2015
Proceedings, Part II

 Springer

Editor
Sakae Yamamoto
Tokyo University of Science
Tokyo
Japan

ISSN 0302-9743   ISSN 1611-3349   (electronic)
Lecture Notes in Computer Science
ISBN 978-3-319-20617-2   ISBN 978-3-319-20618-9   (eBook)
DOI 10.1007/978-3-319-20618-9

Library of Congress Control Number: 2015941499

LNCS Sublibrary: SL3 – Information Systems and Applications, incl. Internet/Web, and HCI

Springer Cham Heidelberg New York Dordrecht London

Printed on acid-free paper

Springer International Publishing AG Switzerland is part of Springer Science+Business Media
(www.springer.com)

Foreword

The 17th International Conference on Human-Computer Interaction, HCI International 2015, was held in Los Angeles, CA, USA, during 2–7 August 2015. The event incorporated the 15 conferences/thematic areas listed on the following page.

A total of 4843 individuals from academia, research institutes, industry, and governmental agencies from 73 countries submitted contributions, and 1462 papers and 246 posters have been included in the proceedings. These papers address the latest research and development efforts and highlight the human aspects of design and use of computing systems. The papers thoroughly cover the entire field of Human-Computer Interaction, addressing major advances in knowledge and effective use of computers in a variety of application areas. The volumes constituting the full 28-volume set of the conference proceedings are listed on pages VII and VIII.

I would like to thank the Program Board Chairs and the members of the Program Boards of all thematic areas and affiliated conferences for their contribution to the highest scientific quality and the overall success of the HCI International 2015 conference.

This conference could not have been possible without the continuous and unwavering support and advice of the founder, Conference General Chair Emeritus and Conference Scientific Advisor, Prof. Gavriel Salvendy. For their outstanding efforts, I would like to express my appreciation to the Communications Chair and Editor of HCI International News, Dr. Abbas Moallem, and the Student Volunteer Chair, Prof. Kim-Phuong L. Vu. Finally, for their dedicated contribution towards the smooth organization of HCI International 2015, I would like to express my gratitude to Maria Pitsoulaki and George Paparoulis, General Chair Assistants.

May 2015

Constantine Stephanidis
General Chair, HCI International 2015

HCI International 2015 Thematic Areas
and Affiliated Conferences

Thematic areas:

- Human-Computer Interaction (HCI 2015)
- Human Interface and the Management of Information (HIMI 2015)

Affiliated conferences:

- 12th International Conference on Engineering Psychology and Cognitive Ergonomics (EPCE 2015)
- 9th International Conference on Universal Access in Human-Computer Interaction (UAHCI 2015)
- 7th International Conference on Virtual, Augmented and Mixed Reality (VAMR 2015)
- 7th International Conference on Cross-Cultural Design (CCD 2015)
- 7th International Conference on Social Computing and Social Media (SCSM 2015)
- 9th International Conference on Augmented Cognition (AC 2015)
- 6th International Conference on Digital Human Modeling and Applications in Health, Safety, Ergonomics and Risk Management (DHM 2015)
- 4th International Conference on Design, User Experience and Usability (DUXU 2015)
- 3rd International Conference on Distributed, Ambient and Pervasive Interactions (DAPI 2015)
- 3rd International Conference on Human Aspects of Information Security, Privacy and Trust (HAS 2015)
- 2nd International Conference on HCI in Business (HCIB 2015)
- 2nd International Conference on Learning and Collaboration Technologies (LCT 2015)
- 1st International Conference on Human Aspects of IT for the Aged Population (ITAP 2015)

Conference Proceedings Volumes Full List

1. LNCS 9169, Human-Computer Interaction: Design and Evaluation (Part I), edited by Masaaki Kurosu
2. LNCS 9170, Human-Computer Interaction: Interaction Technologies (Part II), edited by Masaaki Kurosu
3. LNCS 9171, Human-Computer Interaction: Users and Contexts (Part III), edited by Masaaki Kurosu
4. LNCS 9172, Human Interface and the Management of Information: Information and Knowledge Design (Part I), edited by Sakae Yamamoto
5. LNCS 9173, Human Interface and the Management of Information: Information and Knowledge in Context (Part II), edited by Sakae Yamamoto
6. LNAI 9174, Engineering Psychology and Cognitive Ergonomics, edited by Don Harris
7. LNCS 9175, Universal Access in Human-Computer Interaction: Access to Today's Technologies (Part I), edited by Margherita Antona and Constantine Stephanidis
8. LNCS 9176, Universal Access in Human-Computer Interaction: Access to Interaction (Part II), edited by Margherita Antona and Constantine Stephanidis
9. LNCS 9177, Universal Access in Human-Computer Interaction: Access to Learning, Health and Well-Being (Part III), edited by Margherita Antona and Constantine Stephanidis
10. LNCS 9178, Universal Access in Human-Computer Interaction: Access to the Human Environment and Culture (Part IV), edited by Margherita Antona and Constantine Stephanidis
11. LNCS 9179, Virtual, Augmented and Mixed Reality, edited by Randall Shumaker and Stephanie Lackey
12. LNCS 9180, Cross-Cultural Design: Methods, Practice and Impact (Part I), edited by P.L. Patrick Rau
13. LNCS 9181, Cross-Cultural Design: Applications in Mobile Interaction, Education, Health, Transport and Cultural Heritage (Part II), edited by P.L. Patrick Rau
14. LNCS 9182, Social Computing and Social Media, edited by Gabriele Meiselwitz
15. LNAI 9183, Foundations of Augmented Cognition, edited by Dylan D. Schmorrow and Cali M. Fidopiastis
16. LNCS 9184, Digital Human Modeling and Applications in Health, Safety, Ergonomics and Risk Management: Human Modeling (Part I), edited by Vincent G. Duffy
17. LNCS 9185, Digital Human Modeling and Applications in Health, Safety, Ergonomics and Risk Management: Ergonomics and Health (Part II), edited by Vincent G. Duffy
18. LNCS 9186, Design, User Experience, and Usability: Design Discourse (Part I), edited by Aaron Marcus
19. LNCS 9187, Design, User Experience, and Usability: Users and Interactions (Part II), edited by Aaron Marcus
20. LNCS 9188, Design, User Experience, and Usability: Interactive Experience Design (Part III), edited by Aaron Marcus

Human Interface and the Management of Information

Program Board Chair: Sakae Yamamoto, Japan

- Denis A. Coelho, Portugal
- Linda R. Elliott, USA
- Shin'ichi Fukuzumi, Japan
- Michitaka Hirose, Japan
- Makoto Itoh, Japan
- Yen-Yu Kang, Taiwan
- Koji Kimita, Japan
- Daiji Kobayashi, Japan
- Kentaro Kotani, Japan
- Chen Ling, USA
- Hiroyuki Miki, Japan
- Hirohiko Mori, Japan
- Robert Proctor, USA
- Ryosuke Saga, Japan
- Katsunori Shimohara, Japan
- Takahito Tomoto, Japan
- Kim-Phuong Vu, USA
- Tomio Watanabe, Japan

The full list with the Program Board Chairs and the members of the Program Boards of all thematic areas and affiliated conferences is available online at:

http://www.hci.international/2015/

HCI International 2016

The 18th International Conference on Human-Computer Interaction, HCI International 2016, will be held jointly with the affiliated conferences in Toronto, Canada, at the Westin Harbour Castle Hotel, 17–22 July 2016. It will cover a broad spectrum of themes related to Human-Computer Interaction, including theoretical issues, methods, tools, processes, and case studies in HCI design, as well as novel interaction techniques, interfaces, and applications. The proceedings will be published by Springer. More information will be available on the conference website: http://2016.hci.international/.

General Chair
Prof. Constantine Stephanidis
University of Crete and ICS-FORTH
Heraklion, Crete, Greece
Email: general_chair@hcii2016.org

http://2016.hci.international/

Contents – Part II

Information and Interaction for Driving

Information and Interaction for Learning and Education

Information and Interaction for Culture and Art

Supporting Work and Collaboration

Information and Interaction for Safety, Security and Reliability

Information and Interaction for in Novel Advanced Environments

Contents – Part I

Information Presentation

Knowledge Management

Haptic, Tactile and Multimodal Interaction

Context Modelling and Situational Awareness

Multi-criteria Fusion of Heterogeneous Information for Improving Situation Awareness on Emergency Management Systems

Valdir Amancio Pereira Jr.[1], Matheus Ferraroni Sanches[1],
Leonardo Castro Botega[1,2(✉)], Jessica Souza[1],
Caio Saraiva Coneglian[1], Elvis Fusco[1],
and Márcio Roberto de Campos[2]

[1] Computing and Information Systems Research Lab (COMPSI),
Marília Eurípides University (UNIVEM), Marília, São Paulo, Brazil
{valdir.a.junior,matheussanches531,osz.jessica,
caio.coneglian,elvisfusco}@gmail.com,
leonardo_botega@dc.ufscar.br
[2] Wireless Networks and Distributed Interactive Simulations Lab (WINDIS),
Computer Department, Federal University of São Carlos (UFSCar),
São Carlos, São Paulo, Brazil

Abstract. Information Fusion is the synergic integration of data from different sources for the support to decision-making. The emergency management systems predominance of such application has driven the development to new and better sensors, new methods, for data processing and architectures that promote access, composition, refinement and information handling, with the active participation of specialists as data providers and specialists of the systems. In this scenario of data fusion, uncertainty of diverse natures can be aggregated to both data and information at different levels of the process, creating distorted information to the specialist. As a result the situation awareness and cognitive process can be affected leading to poor quality support to decision-making as a generalization of information quality, uncertainty need to be reduced to improve awareness about the situation of interest. The objective of our work is the mitigation of uncertainty propagated by other quality attributes such as information completeness, so specialists can be able to convey an improved understanding. For such, a new fusion framework fed by multi-criteria parameterization, including information quality measures and its semantics, is depicted as an engine to build more accurate information from diverse sensed possibilities. A case study with a situation assessment application is in course to validate the effectiveness of the generated solution. Preliminary and promising results are discussed as a more valuable tool to support decision-making.

Keywords: Information fusion · Situation awareness · Emergency Management Systems

© Springer International Publishing Switzerland 2015
S. Yamamoto (Ed.): HIMI 2015, Part II, LNCS 9173, pp. 3–14, 2015.
DOI: 10.1007/978-3-319-20618-9_1

1 Introduction

Emergency events require building effective operational responses. Frequently, unexpected incidents arise and demand time-critical decisions from a specialist of the state police, security managers or governmental members. Such decisions involve the deployment of new tactics and the allocation of human resources and equipments.

The assessment systems of emergency events are highly complex due the need of comprehension by specialists about what is going on at the event location. Such comprehension is supported by Data Fusion systems, feed by multiple sources (hard sensors, social networks, databases, etc.) offer a more precise notion but aware about what is happening in an environment [1].

Devices and innovative fusion algorithms are being used for better supporting the assessment process for situation awareness for decision-making. Such assessment systems may have to be used even under informational adverse conditions of uncertainty, demanding that non-explicit information must be inferred. The specialist of an assessment system has a crucial role on the improvement of information that are processed from heterogeneous sources and data fusion engines for the acquisition of situation awareness. Data mining, classification algorithms and information quality are aspects of extreme relevance in this process and present several challenges regarding the determination of synergic information and the definition of fusion criteria [2, 3] and consequently new relations among information.

In the literature, different solutions have been succeeded pro- posed and implemented, reaching information with several data and information quality issues. As a result of recent technological developments e.g., proliferation of diverse algorithms and platforms, such as Nearest Neighbors, Probabilistic Data Association, The Kalman Filter, Semantic Methods extends systems abilities to develop a more precise, complete, consistent and timely information in a minor dimensionality. In a wider view, information fusion aims to provide a richer knowledge to promote the acquisition, maintenance and resumption of situation awareness of specialists in a variety of contexts [4].

However, as far as the authors investigated, there are few studies that deal more specifically with semantic information as input and the construction of an incremental knowledge for the identification of new entities and relations among them.

Intelligent systems to support specialists in critical situations (that could compromise lives and patrimony) can benefit from the diversity of available criteria (including quality) for exhaustive fusion to improve the evaluation of critical situations, reducing imperfections of information and present a reliable selection of integrated possibilities.

To overcome some of these challenges, the contributions of this paper are: (1) An intense relation with a Knowledge Representation phase, by managing knowledge as input and output; (2) The use of customisable multi-criteria parameterization, including information quality indexes and Semantic information (relations among entities) to reveal new objects, attributes and relations among them.

This paper presents a Multi-criteria Fusion of Heterogeneous Data for Improving Situation Awareness on Emergency Management Systems. It is also presented the relevance of information quality issues in the process when imperfect data can be a potential impact factor on the quality of the decision-making.

The paper is organized as follows: Sect. 2 presents the Research Background on Situation Awareness; Sect. 3 describes the applicability of Data Fusion on the Emergency Domain and Sect. 4 presents the Multi-criteria Fusion of Heterogeneous Information, followed by a Case Study and Conclusions.

2 Research Background

Situation awareness systems, specially applications Emergency Management Systems rely on information quality to provide specialists a better view of the analyzed scenario for making quality decisions. If imperfect information is provided to SAW systems, the specialist may be uncertain on what he perceives and understands and the quality of the decision will be compromised. For such, this paper presents a framework for Improving Situation Awareness comprising of a multi-criteria fusion of heterogeneous information to mitigate uncertain information about situations and assets and to use and represent enriched knowledge [5]. Hence, this combination will provide a comprehensive fusion framework for coupling into situation assessment systems for specialists deal with adverse conditions of information quality.

2.1 Situation Awareness in Emergency Management Systems

In the C2 domain, there are some elements of awareness that individual specialists must posses, such as mission goal awareness (knowing the current state of a mission and the goals current being attempted); system awareness (knowing about how the system works and its methods of operation); resource awareness (knowing the available physical and human resources) and in case of workgroup, team awareness (knowing that all team members know the state of current events) [6].

The way in which information is combined by the system and also by the specialist through the interface and embedded visualizations influences human's SAW and consequently the quality of the decision. A suitable SA-oriented fusion should determine which information can be synergically integrated in the event timeline, perform an accurately search for the input information and also be committed to deliver an information that is conformable with the specialist's SAW needs and expectations [7].

Data fusion systems are able to deliver the needed processing to provide information for SAW purposes, however, they still require the human participation on the processes for the interpretation of the results produced by such systems and give meaning and relevance for information [8]. Supported by a user refinement phase present on situation assessment models, opportunities referring to the customisation of fusion criteria became imminent given the need for knowledge about data and produced information, strengthening possibilities of effective contributions to the data fusion process [6, 8, 9].

2.2 Information Uncertainty

Applications of data and information fusion systems are then able to process and present data with the objective of enabling specialists to make effective decisions.

However, such systems can propagate imperfection due to fail data acquisition, processing or even in the representation of the produced information, making user uncertain about what s/he perceives and understands.

To overcome such issue, innovative fusion techniques must be present in the assessment system to provide a truly knowledge representation about situations. Also, quality issues must be always known in order to build a better SAW [10]. In a decision making complex environment, commanders need a clear, concise and accurate assessment of the current situation, what may be degraded by an uncertainty about where the assets are located, what are their capabilities, the nature of their intentions and if there is any kind of risk to people or patrimony.

Often, the specialist does not have confidence on his knowledge about his own forces and much less about the enemies, mostly due information unavailability, the dynamics of real scenarios with ever changing situations and the distributed nature of data sources [6, 11]. In summary, when monitoring assets in a conflict scenario, specialists have to pay attention to all assets parameters they had monitored in the past, how long the assets must be monitored, which assets parameters must be monitored in the present, whether new information about the assets are certain and reliable, how to combine new information with the existing information that the specialist already possesses, what parameters must be shared and how to use new information to make future decisions.

3 Information Fusion and SAW in Emergency Field

SAW is the ability of understanding and project a real monitored environment, in this case by an operator of the emergency system, who based on the SAW developed during the observation of the support system, will make a decision.

According to Endsley, SAW is being aware of what is happening around you and understanding what that information means to you now and in the future [2]. In the emergency field, on a particular situation, SAW is developed by means of an enormous range of information collected from various sources, and for the most part, in real time and presenting quality problems in their composition, thus affecting their representation to the operator. With this huge amount of information to be observed by the operator, the development of SAW is difficult and weak, since it still presents quality problems, and it does not have a system and appropriate interfaces to properly represent all that data.

SAW composition presents different aspects for every need or environment, since the perception of information is made by visual, hearing, and tactile stimuli, among others, and also a by a combination. However, in order to supply and feed a SAW system, especially in a critical and complex system such as emergency decision-making, these systems require quality information in several stages that make up a process for evaluating situations, in several dimensions that determine the scope of application.

The role of information fusion routines is to apply techniques that contribute to mitigate such quality problems. It is known, however, that many of the problems depend on the activity of the human expert, and that its input is extremely valuable for the process. In this manner, the expert should be free and able to propose new fusion processes not provided by the system, with new parameters and attributes, and between objects often considered completely different, but that can still account for a lot of valuable information to process SAW and the decision-making process.

Thus, the present paper proposes a multi-criteria and customizable fusion process, able to merge and link data before tried, with no association or irrelevance to the situation, managed by the system and the expert.

4 Multi-criteria Fusion of Heterogeneous Information

In order to fulfill the objectives proposed in this paper, we propose a framework of activities that organize the process of merging information aiming the SAW for a decision-making system of São Paulo State Police (PMESP), and incidences management, and checking of criminal situations.

This framework can be abstracted into four main processes, each of them with internal mechanisms that play specific roles, but of great contribution to improve the quality of information, and therefore the SAW. The main processes (highlighted in Orange in Fig. 1) are, Acquisition (Sect. 4.1) and the Information Fusion (Sect. 4.2), described in detail below.

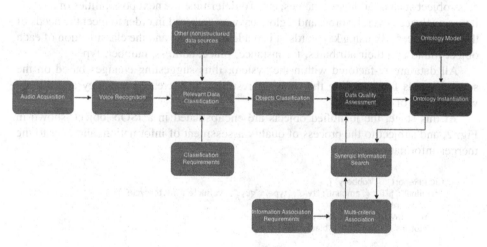

Fig. 1. Framework for multi-criteria fusion of heterogeneous information

4.1 Acquisition of Audio and Pre-processing

In the proposed framework, there are several data sources, such as: audio of a complaint call to the police, social networking posts, databases, and images. Each scope has particularities of the sources adopted for the completion of the evaluation of a situation. In our case study, we will debate how audiotapes, posts, and security camera images can be implemented.

When using audio as input data to the framework, data acquisition is made using the Speech to Text tool. The audio is then captured and transcribed at runtime to a string object. Every word captured is sent to Google's servers that return the spoken words.

At the end of speech, the string containing the transcribed words is sent to the server, which prepares it and insert it into the base, creating a structured information. The string is sent along with the identification metadata of the complaint to a Java server.

A Java server co-running with the PHP server receives the complaint containing the expected identification information and the string containing the transcribed speech. When receiving the data, the string is analyzed using the CoGrOO API, which is a grammar checker developed in Java.

Using the CoGrOO source code alone, it is possible to add Tags such as nouns, number, object, and every other word. We can also join the phrases obtained in the input text. After the classification of words and phrases association, it is made a post to the PHP server using a JSON (JavaScript Object Notation) object containing the analyzed metadata phrase and the classifications made.

In this way, the server can recover the data saved and begins the analysis in search of the elements already defined as important when checking the requirements. By analyzing the classification of a word, it is possible to infer that what comes next may be a class object such as addresses, names, etc. To determine the next possibilities of a word, it was analyzed several words, and a glossary was gathered in order to meet the needs of the occurrences. By using keywords, it is made the linking and the classification of each object found and their attributes, for instance, place, address, number, type.

All data are re-factored within the system, thus suggesting changes based on the several words found during the analysis, resulting in increased accuracy and quality with the use of the system.

At this stage, the identified objects are encapsulated in a JSON object, shown in Fig. 2, and subject to the process of quality assessment of information, and later to the merger information.

```
{ "foundReport": [ "robbery" ],
    "criminal": { "0": { "amount": "two", "type": "guys", "vehucle": "motorcycle" },
        "weapons": [ "gun" ],
        "runaway": [ "klabin subway" ],
        "clothes": [ "red shirt", "black cap" ]
    },
    "stolenObject": [ "car", "black mercedes", "mercedes" ],
    "victim": [ "driver" ],
    "local": { "0": [ "domingos", "setti" ], "address_conter": [ "WITH ], "1": [ "luis", "vives", "dois" ] }
}
```

Fig. 2. JSON after process acquisition

The objects, attributes and properties generated by this stage are then submitted to an evaluation in order to quantify the information according to completeness, timeliness and uncertainty dimension, better discussed by Souza et al. [12]. At this stage quality scores are assigned to information aiming to inform the operator about such measures. Such scores are also used as Fusion criteria to be discussed in the next section.

4.2   Information Fusion from Acquisition

After the acquisition and quality assessment, an object in JSON format (JavaScript Object Notation) is produced. This object corresponds to objects and attributes level L1 of fusion (according to the JDL taxonomy), along with quality scores assigned to each object and attribute, according to the methodology of Souza et al. [12] for quality scores of objects, attributes and situations identified in acquisition time.

From the JSON object decoded, it is instantiated a preliminary ontology with the classes of victim, criminal, robbed object, and place, considering the fundamental classes to define a situation, each with their respective attributes and relationship properties, representing the semantic meaning of the information, as shown in Fig. 3:

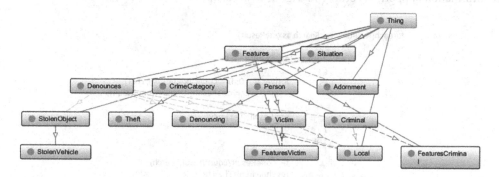

Fig. 3. Ontology of situation

With the instantiated ontology, information set within such ontology is once more transformed into a JSON object, now with the semantic meaning between objects and attributes. These semantic information are related by means of the present properties.

This JSON will be the input of the fusion. In addition, there will be other input parameters, and criteria set by the operator such as: which objects to specifically associate, which external sources to use, which properties must exist, and a new threshold of minimum quality of the information, as shown in Fig. 4:

```
{"inputOperator": {
   "instance": "sit001",
   "multicriteria":{
            "mainQualityIndices":{"uncertainty":"40","completeness":"60",...},
            "object properties":{
                  "has_a":{
                            "criminal":{"completeness":"45","vehicle": "moto",...},
                            "victim":{"completeness":"80","site":"street..."}
                  }
            },
            "sources":{"security camera","hitory of complaints"}
}}}
```

Fig. 4. Input multi-criteria by operator

Once the fusion process is started, there is the search for synergy information among classes, which are already present in the ontology, complaints, posts, and camera metadata, taking into account the objects, attributes, quality scores, and their properties set into the ontology.

After the search for synergy information among the information already stored in the ontology, a search of other sources of data will be carried out in order to obtain new information about the associated objects in each moment, and validate and give greater consistency to the already set information. Considering that the input of this process is isolated information or information already associated among objects (level L2), the result of this process will be a L2 level fusion.

This process will be carried out by an algorithm based on data mining techniques, based on the algorithm a priori [13], which infers the frequency of certain information when analyzed in relation to the rest of an environment (information of the situation and requested other sources), this inference is made from a proposed calculation of the information support, according to Fig. 5, as follows:

```
foreach(resultSinergicSearch as oneResult)
    {
            if(isArray(oneResult))
            {
                    for(var iT = 0; iT < count(oneResult); iT++)
                            fP = oneResult[it]/count(oneResult);

                    oneResult[iT+1] = fP;
            }
            else
            {
                    fP = oneResult/count(resultSearch);
                    resultSearch[fT] += fP;
    }}
```

Fig. 5. Part of the core of data mining algorithm

For the process herein proposed, it will be used the principles of data mining, but some changes will be made in order to analyze the frequency of such information by a single knot or proposed parameter, that is, it will search for the covariance between the data and will calculate this relationship index. It is the calculation of the total of all items related, divided by the total of items found in all the information.

The result of this process is obtained by the initial information plus the new information with their respective attributes, quality scores, properties, and the relationship score among such information.

This result is validated in the next step (multi-criteria association), which deals with the association between the information submitted to the fusion process and the synergy information found. This association meets certain pre-defined criteria such as quality scores and properties pre-defined as satisfactory for each association or type of information. The following process inserts the new information found within the context of the original information submitted to the process, in order to achieve and meet the multi-criteria defined in the previous process. Figure 6 shows part of the core of the multi-criteria association algorithm.

```
foreach(newsInformation as info)
{
        if(isObject(info))
        {
                foreach(info as oh)
                {
                        foreach(multiCriteria as criteria)
                                newInfoOntology = validateInfo(oh, criteria);
}}}
```

Fig. 6. Part of the core multi-criteria association algorithm

Multi-criteria result from two sources as an input of the expert agent entry in times of system operation, or they are based on requirements analysis conducted during the project.

As a result, every initial information submitted to the fusion process is generated, however, with new attributes, properties and even new objects found during the fusion process, thus making results explicitly L2 level (Situation Assessment).

This result can be submitted again to the previous process of search for synergy data, then increasing its capability to find new information and consolidate the information already available. In this manner, information increasingly specializes in the actual current situation, or in a single part of the situation, depending on the input. This cycle will be performed when the result of the multi-criteria Association, objects, attributes, indexes of quality and properties, are not within the parameters required, defined by human input or delimited by the system.

If this second process is not carried out, the resulting information will be submitted to the quality assessment process, now scoring the new information found and reconsidering the general scores of information. After this process, the information re-evaluated by the quality assessment will be re-instantiated in the ontology and represented in the system, according to the request of the operator.

In the primary fusion phase, in the automated process performed immediately after the acquisition and evaluation of the quality of information, it is made the most associations possible between objects, their attributes, properties and their rates of pre-determined quality and quality thresholds, considering the existence of two or more data sets available from the same source or from different sources.

The primary fusion meets informational requirements, that is, the criteria of priorities defined the analysis of requirements, such as minimum levels of quality and main properties between information, which is useful to define what should be built first and consequently shown to the human expert. These informational requirements are based on an analysis questionnaire applied to several police officers of different positions, functions, and career time, thus ensuring a heterogeneous view of the subject, and also managing to validate the most important criteria to a given situation.

In the case of the fusion on the demand of the operator, the algorithm is activated once again, but the criteria for integration are entirely selected by the operator via interface, instead of all possible combinations of automatic objects, attributes and properties identified in the acquisition phase.

This association process, now manual, is operated via interface by the expert, and besides being based on objects and attributes, these associations is strongly supported in related quality scores, and suggest hypotheses about information relating to previously identified objects with other objects identified by other sources related to the real environment.

Since this input process is performed by the operator via interface, the criteria for the data fusion process can be chosen and changed by the same operator, who is able to add new features, as well as removing criteria pre-defined by the requirement analysis. This capability demonstrates the flexibility of the framework to receive and process different criteria for a given situation, and allows the agents to better interact with the system based on their experiences and knowledge, thus ensuring a process of construction and development of SAW very close to the real environment.

5 Case Study

The case study was conducted based on procedures and data of the PEMESP, considering emergency calls in São Paulo, Brazil. From the information collected, It was established the informational requirements which define important standards such as the threshold of information quality, the most relevant information to a situation, and the methodology of the decision-making process.

This information enabled the definition of data acquisition methodology, and the main data to be found within a complaint. From the quality threshold and importance of the relationship between information, it was developed the quality assessment techniques. By using all the information collected, the result is the basic ontology of emergency rule in this particular case for theft situations, but ready to be expanded to other crime scenarios.

From the base of ontology defined and the result of requirements analysis, it was developed the fusion engine algorithm, whose input is information with quality scores and semantic meaning, arising from the quality assessment and the ontology. The algorithm presents customizable features and multi-criteria, that is, it accepts several different inputs made by the operator. The algorithm is prepared to deal with the same process in two different modes: automatically, after the acquisition, with the most associations possible between information, respecting the criteria defined in the requirements analysis and in the process on demand, when the operator selects exactly which objects to fuse and what criteria information must be complied during the process and in the outcome. An example of possible association between two objects by synergy attributes is shown in Fig. 7.

As a result of this process, it is obtained the first information with greater consistency, then proving that information is correct on a given situation. This information may contain new information during the process of synergy search and multi-criteria association, which reached levels of quality and property imposed by the process, thus bringing information to the operator.

Before this resulting information is presented to the operator, they once more can be submitted to the fusing process in case they are not within the related criteria or submitted to the quality assessment, which will re-evaluate the quality scores based on new information found. After the quality re-assessment, this information will be set in a new ontology that represents the current knowledge of the situation, and then it will be presented to the operator via interface, such interface is presented by Botega et al. [14].

"object1":{
        "source":"security camera",
        "attributes":{
                "local":{
                        "street":"avenue Paulista",
                        ...}}},
        "object2":{
                "source":"hitory of complaints",
                "attributes":{
                        "local":{
                                "street":"avenue Paulista",
                                ...}}}}}

Fig. 7. Example association objects

6 Conclusion

This paper presented a framework for Improving Situation Awareness comprising of a process for multi-criteria fusion of heterogeneous information to mitigate uncertain information about situations and their assets. Such framework may be coupled into situation assessment systems for specialists to reason about information of lower dimensionality and better quality. Hence, this work also presented methods for information fusion, natural language processing, information quality assessment and knowledge representation to be employed in such framework to contribute for SAW. The application of the framework and associated methods generated valid results regarding the obtaining of expected information useful for developing SAW, according to the requirements defined by the domain specialists. Such information was successful incrementally built using syntactical and semantical input. The use of multi-criteria information fusion empowers the assessment of situations by generating several integration possibilities of synergic information for the analysis of a specialist. Also, the specialist has the possibility to define the criteria and the information quality threshold for the parametrisation of the fusion algorithm. As future work, the authors intend to expand and optimize the techniques of acquisition and natural speech processing, as well as methods that make fusion engine, expanding the ability to search and synergistic association data. Also, study and improve the data-mining algorithm from semantic data, as well as the power of its association of multiple criteria, increasing the power to process different inputs, given the multitude of criteria, linguistic or quantitative.

References

1. Endsley, M.R.: The challenge of the information age. In: Proceedings of the Second International Workshop on Symbiosis of Humans, Artifacts and Environment, Kyoto, Japan (2001)
2. Kokar, M.M., Endsley, M.R.: Situation awareness and cognitive modeling. IEEE Intell. Syst. **27**(3), 91–96 (2012)

3. Llinas, J., Bowman, C., Rogova, G., Steinberg, A.: Revisiting the JDL data fusion model II. In: 7th International Conference on Information Fusion (2004)
4. White Jr., F.E.: Data fusion lexicon. Technical Panel for C3, Data Fusion Sub-Panel. Naval Ocean Systems Center. Joint Directors of Laboratories, San Diego (1987)
5. Mendoza, G.A., Martins, H.: Multi-criteria decision analysis in natural resource management: a critical review of methods and new modelling paradigms. For. Ecol. Manage. **230**, 1–22 (2006). Elsevier
6. Rogova, G., Bosse, E.: Information quality in information fusion. In: 13th Information Fusion (2010)
7. Batini, C., Cappiello, C., Francalanci, C., Maurino, A.: Methodologies for data quality assessment and improvement. ACM Comput. Surv. **41**(3), 1–52 (2009)
8. Blasch, E.: High level information fusion (HLIF): survey of models, issues, and grand challenges. IEEE Aerosp. Electron. Syst. Mag. **27**(9), 4–20 (2012)
9. Stanton, N., Chambers, P., Piggott, J.: Situational awareness and safety. Saf. Sci. **39**, 189–204 (2001)
10. Salerno, J.: Information fusion: a high-level architecture overview. In: Proceedings of the Fifth International Conference on Information Fusion, vol. 1, pp. 680–686. International Society for Information Fusion (2002)
11. Laskey, K., Ng, G., Nagi, R.: Issues of uncertainty analysis in highlevel information fusion. In: Fusion 2012 Panel Discussion (2012)
12. Souza, J., Botega, L., Segundo, J.E.S., Berti, C.: Conceptual framework to enrich situation awareness of emergency dispatchers. In: Yamamoto (Ed.): HIMI 2015, Part II. LNCS, vol. 9173, pp. 33–44. Springer, Heidelberg (2015)
13. Aggarwal, S., Kaur, R.: Comparative study of various improved versions of apriori algorithm. Int. J. Eng. Trends Technol. (IJETT) 4(4), pp. 687 (2013)
14. Botega, L., Ferreira, L.C.N., Oliveira, P., Oliveira, A., Berti, C.B.: SAW-oriented user interfaces for emergency dispatch systems. In: Yamamoto (Ed.): HIMI 2015, Part II. LNCS, vol. 9173, pp. 537–548. Springer, Heidelberg (2015)

Situational Transformation of Personal Space

Yosuke Kinoe(✉) and Nami Mizuno

Faculty of Intercultural Communication, Hosei University,
2-17-1, Fujimi, Chiyoda City, Tokyo 102-8160, Japan
kinoe@hosei.ac.jp

Abstract. This paper describes an experimental study that investigated how interpersonal distance varied depending on situational factors, as well as postures and gender. The results revealed statistically significant simple main effects of the "task", "combination of bodily directions", and "devices". Interpersonal distances were affected by the differences between: (a) "without task > with a task", (b) "front > lateral", (c) "lateral > side-by-side", and (d) "front > backward" under the conditions except for "typing" task. It was considered that interpersonal space was co-constructed through an interactive process by a dyad.

Keywords: Personal space · Spatial behavior · Nonverbal communication

1 Introduction

This paper describes an experimental study of the flexibility and situational transformation of personal space. The study investigated how interpersonal distance varied depending on tasks, devices, combinations of bodily directions, postures and gender. We propose two types of data correction models for measuring interpersonal distances.

Personal space can be defined as "an area individuals actively maintain around themselves into which others cannot intrude without arousing some sort of discomfort" [14, 24]. Dosey and Meisels [7] interpreted it as a body buffer zone which serves as a protection against perceived threats and emphasized the ownership of personal space. Research on human spatial behavior influenced various design issues not limited to the area of architecture [24] and environmental design [10], but extended to service design, proxemics of social robots [19], and human-robot embodied interaction.

1.1 Flexibility of Personal Space

The dimensions of personal space are not fixed but vary according to internal states, culture, and context [25]. Research findings suggested that the influences upon interpersonal distance were caused by various factors including gender [11], age [4], culture [2], personality traits [10], attractiveness [11], psychological disorders [26], attitudes [20], approach angle [28], eye contact [4], co-operation [27], experimental environment including room size [8], lighting conditions [1] and indoor/outdoor [6].

There is a considerable interaction between personal space and interpersonal distance. It affects the distribution of persons [24]. Interpersonal distance may be outside

© Springer International Publishing Switzerland 2015
S. Yamamoto (Ed.): HIMI 2015, Part II, LNCS 9173, pp. 15–24, 2015.
DOI: 10.1007/978-3-319-20618-9_2

the area of personal space if two unfamiliar persons exist in a spacious room. On the contrary, it may be less than the boundaries of personal space when crowded.

1.2   Our Approach

Tasks and Combination of Bodily Directions. We aim to cover more natural settings, especially of tasks, and of combinations of bodily directions. In addition to a typical experimental setting (face-to-face, with no task), we shed light on an ordinary situation doing such a small task as listening-to-music and e-mailing, and also included alternative combinations of bodily directions such as "side-by-side" and "backward" (Fig. 1).

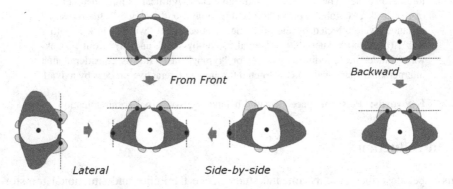

Fig. 1. Personal space and various combination of bodily directions

Validity and Reliability of Measuring Method. Research on personal space has employed diverse methods. Measures of interpersonal distance have typically been used as a dependent variable. Altman [3] distinguishes three classes of methods: simulation, laboratory methods, and field methods. The stop-distance method [7, 16] and unobtrusive observation [9] had been widely used and evaluated as feasible techniques for experimental and naturalistic studies, respectively [14]. In our study, we employed the stop-distance method that yields high test-retest reliability [14, 22]. It controls rate of approach (slow), facial expression (neutral), gestures (arms and hands relaxed at side), conversation (not permitted), and eye contact (absent).

In the use of stop-distance method, the distance is usually measured by the feet positions [14]. It well works when the participants face each other in a sufficient distance. However, a considerable error possibly occurs especially in a close distance or under a sort of situation such as sitting side-by-side. As for the validity, the methodological improvement is a key for investigating the anisotropy and flexibility of personal space.

Re-modeling. Instead of a foot position, we re-considered a starting point of the interpersonal distance by focusing on several landmarks on human body surface including Acromion (summit of the shoulder), Thelion (a bust point), the tip of the nose, Scapula (on back), and Vertex (upper surface of the head) (Fig. 2). In the present study, we developed two different concepts of modeling the interpersonal distances: "surface" model which employs the distance between body surfaces and "center-center" model which employs the distance between the centers of human bodies.

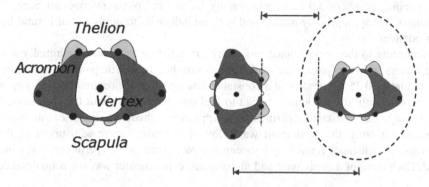

Fig. 2. A plan view of human body and example of the landmarks on body surface

2 Empirical Study

2.1 The Study I

The study I investigated the flexibility of personal space. In particular, the settings were enhanced to include daily tasks and alternative combinations of participants' bodily directions. The experimental design of the study I is shown in Table 1.

Table 1. Experimental Design of the Study I

	Factor		Level
Between subjects	Gender and gender combination	4	male-male, male-female, female-male, female-female
Within subjects	Posture	2	standing, squatting posture
Within subjects	Task	4	seeing ahead (no particular task), writing a memo with a smart phone, enjoying music with an ear-phone and a USB player
Within subjects	Combination of bodily directions	4	from front, backward from front, from a lateral direction(*), side-by-side (facing the same direction from a lateral direction(*))

Note (*): The participant was approached from a lateral of dominant hand.

Participants. Forty four healthy university students including 21 males (ranged in age 19−24 years) and 23 females (ranged in age 18−23 years), who were educated between 13−17 years, participated to the study. Mean stature of male participants was 171.1 cm (SD 5.24) and that of female participants was 157.9 cm (SD 6.96).

Method and Procedure. The data were collected in the time period between November 2014 and January 2015. The participants were recruited individually and were informed that the study dealt with spatial preferences. The data collection was carried out during daytime, in an empty and quiet class room (approx. 6.5 m × 6.3 m with a ceiling height of 3.0 m) of a university located in Tokyo metropolitan area. The brightness was appropriately maintained with an indoor lighting instead of natural light from outside.

According to the stop-distance procedure, an assistant experimenter initially stood three meters from the participant and then approached the participant, in small steps, approximately 0.25 m per step, at a constant slow velocity, approximately one step per two seconds, until the participant began to feel uncomfortable about the closeness. By saying stop, the assistant experimenter's approach halted. In order to minimize a measurement error, the participant was allowed to make fine re-adjustment of their positions. The distance remaining between the participant and experimenter was measured. Each dyad of a participant and an assistant experimenter was not acquaintances.

Data Analysis. There were four factors in the study I. The between-subject factor was "participant's gender and gender combination" (4 levels). The within-subject factors were the "posture" (2), the "task" (3) and the "combination of bodily directions" while approaching (4) (see Table 1). A multiple comparison test was performed. We applied Bonferrroni-Dunn's procedure by using SPSS (ver. 21). It is not necessary to test the null omnibus hypothesis using an ANOVA prior to tD statistic [17, p. 181].

Data Correction by Re-modeling Personal Space. We focused on several landmarks on human body surface: Acromion, Thelion, the tip of the nose, Scapula and Vertex as candidates for a starting point of interpersonal distance (Fig. 2). Data correction on raw data obtained from the stop-distance method was made when needed by using the anthropometric database [18] available from Digital Human Research Center, AIST. Two different models were developed: the *surface* model and the *center-center* model. We applied the surface version in the study I.

Result. Forty four participants were distributed into four groups of different gender combinations: male (participant)-male (assistant experimenter) (13), male-female (8), female-male (9) and female-female (14). Means and standard deviations of all the interpersonal distances obtained under the condition of standing posture are given in Table 2. The observed data (before correction) ranged between 0 cm (F-F, squatting, music player, lateral) and 183.5 cm (M-M, standing, no particular task, backward); M = 54.2 cm, SD = 27.77. According to Hall's classification [13], they widely ranged from the intimate distance (0−18 in.), to the close phase of social distance (4−7 ft.).

Gender. The factor of "gender" had four levels. The result showed a trend similar to a well-known pattern "male pairs > female pairs" [10], however, there was no statistically significant simple main effect of the gender (Fig. 3-a).

Posture. The factor of "posture" had two levels (standing vs. squatting). There was no statistically significant simple main effect of the "posture" (Fig. 3-a). The interaction of the "posture" and the "combination of bodily directions" was statistically significant (p < 0.01). In particular, there were statistically significant differences between

Table 2. Means and standard deviations of interpersonal distances (surface model)

Factors			Task								
			No particular task			Typing w/smart phone			Music player		
Posture	Gender combination (participant-experimenter)	Combination of bodily directions while approaching	n	Mean (cm)	SD	n	Mean (cm)	D	n	Mean (cm)	SD
Standing	M - M	From front	13	89.11	44.02	13	63.85	34.26	13	72.51	37.96
		Lateral	13	42.20	30.68	13	32.84	30.29	13	34.31	25.42
		Backward	13	81.67	44.84	13	58.82	19.80	13	67.17	34.20
		Side-by-side	13	36.95	29.83	13	30.44	25.56	13	28.85	21.68
	M - F	From front	8	78.91	23.49	8	61.38	21.55	8	60.47	22.22
		Lateral	8	62.76	24.55	8	41.79	18.77	8	40.46	18.71
		Backward	8	73.41	28.05	8	58.49	15.43	8	60.32	22.21
		Side-by-side	8	44.67	15.47	8	26.82	15.18	8	30.33	19.80
	F - M	From front	9	78.57	24.12	9	55.17	26.31	9	71.33	18.87
		Lateral	9	52.61	22.49	9	36.88	17.16	9	46.02	17.56
		Backward	9	60.50	17.53	9	60.88	20.50	9	52.70	23.87
		Side-by-side	9	47.08	24.57	9	27.19	19.23	9	35.08	23.83
	F - F	From front	14	71.59	39.98	14	51.71	23.78	14	51.44	28.32
		Lateral	14	47.72	30.45	14	32.23	19.61	14	31.49	28.35
		Backward	14	48.64	35.89	14	47.19	25.80	14	41.57	24.10
		Side-by-side	14	29.29	21.26	14	23.00	19.44	14	22.95	24.98

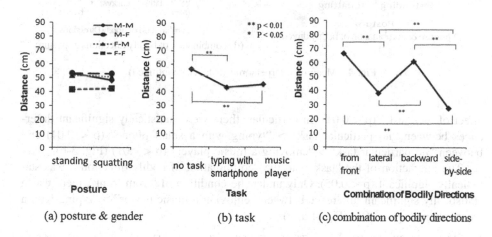

(a) posture & gender   (b) task   (c) combination of bodily directions

Fig. 3. Mean of interpersonal distance

"standing" > "squatting" only under the condition of "side-by-side" ($p < 0.01$), and between "standing" < "squatting" only under the condition of "backward" ($p < 0.05$) (Fig. 4-c, d).

Task. The factor of "task" had three levels (no particular task vs. typing with a smart phone vs. enjoying a music player). There was a statistically significant simple main

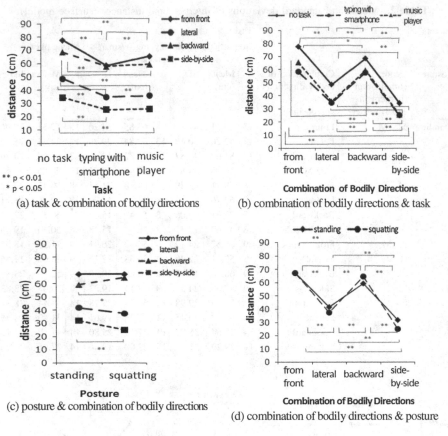

** p < 0.01
* p < 0.05

(a) task & combination of bodily directions

(b) combination of bodily directions & task

(c) posture & combination of bodily directions

(d) combination of bodily directions & posture

Fig. 4. Mean of interpersonal distance (continued)

effect of the "task" ($p < 0.01$). In particular, there were statistically significant differences between "no particular task" > "typing with a smart phone" ($p < 0.01$) and between "no particular task" > "enjoying a music player" ($p < 0.01$) (Fig. 3-b).

The interaction of the "task" and the "combination of bodily directions" was statistically significant ($p < 0.05$). Only under the condition of "from front", there was a statistically significant difference between "enjoying a music player" > "typing with a smart phone" ($p < 0.01$) (Fig. 4-a, b).

Combination of Bodily Directions. The factor of "combination of bodily directions" had four levels (from front vs. backward vs. lateral vs. side-by-side). There was a statistically significant simple main effect of the "combination of bodily directions" ($p < 0.01$). In particular, there were statistically significant differences between "from front" > "lateral" > "side-by-side" ($p < 0.01$), and between "backward" > "lateral" > "side-by-side" ($p < 0.01$) (Fig. 3-c); but the difference between "from front" and "backward" was not statistically significant.

However, the interaction of the "combination of bodily directions" and the "task" was statistically significant ($p < 0.05$). There were statistically significant differences between "from front" > "backward" under all the "task" conditions except for "typing with a smart phone" (Fig. 4-a, b).

2.2   The Study II

In the study II, we aimed to investigate the dynamic characteristics of *interaction distance* between interacting individuals [25]. There were four factors. The within-subject factors were "posture" (2: standing vs. chair-sitting), "combination of bodily directions" (2: face-to-face vs. side-by-side), "task" (5: no particular task vs. holding a device (prior to search) vs. search on a map vs. holding a device (prior to puzzle) vs. puzzle), and "devices" (3: smartphone vs. notebook-PC vs. blackboard).

Participants and Research Settings. Twenty university students including 6 males and 14 females, ranged in age 18-23 years, participated. The stop-distance method was employed to measure interpersonal distances. The data were collected January 2015.

Data Analysis and Initial Results. A multiple comparison test was performed by applying Bonferrroni-Dunn's procedure. Data correction was made by using the center-center version in the study II. There were statistically significant simple main effects of the "task" ($p < 0.01$), the "device" ($p < 0.01$), and the "combination of bodily directions" ($p < 0.01$). The interactions of the "device" and the "task", and the interaction of the "combination of bodily directions" and the "task" were statistically significant.

Initial results revealed interesting findings. For instance, even *before* starting a task, there was a statistically significant difference between "no task" and "holding a device", under the condition of "face-to-face". Furthermore, there was a statistically significant difference between "holding a device" > during the task ("search for a place on a map"), with either devices. The result showed that interaction distance was influenced by the presence of a device and types of co-operation. Further analyses are underway.

3   Discussion

Influence of the Presence of an Eye in Peripheral Vision. The study I revealed not only a well-known anisotropic pattern "from front > lateral" [10] but also an interesting pattern "lateral > side-by-side". After a session of "side-by-side", 16 of 44 participants claimed they didn't notice the presence of an eye. Furthermore, under all the tasks except for "typing while looking-down at a smartphone", there was a significant difference between "from front" > "backward". The result suggested interpersonal distance consciously or unconsciously increased by feeling the presence of eyes even in peripheral vision.

Cognitive Resources and Equilibrium of Interpersonal Distance. The only difference between "without task" (i.e. looking ahead) and "listening-to-music" was the presence of a task "listening-to-music". However, despite this small modification, there was a statistically significant difference between them ($p < 0.01$). There was a considerable relation between the transformation of equilibrium point of comfortable interpersonal distance [2] and a consumption of cognitive resources.

Co-constructing Interpersonal Space by Dyad. Interpersonal distance varies with a complex of multiple causes rather than a single and identifiable cause [13] such as the presence or absence of eye contact. The result also suggested the importance of taking into account various structures of elements another person formed around a body. It is considered that interpersonal space or distance is co-constructed as a result of the cooperative interaction process by two individuals sharing the same environment.

The Third Model. We presented two models of data correction: the "surface" and the "center-center". By taking into account the subjective viewpoints of space perception, we developed the revised versions, "center-to-surface" and "eye-to-surface" models. The modeling of personal space concept was not limited to the issue of measurement. It was closely related to a central theoretical issue on *embodiment* [21].

Reflecting the Complexity of Interaction. Social interactions influence a transformation of personal space [15]. Goffman [12], Birdwhistell [5], and Scheflen [23], for example, pointed out theoretical concern which cut across the areas of nonverbal communication, territoriality, personal space, and phenomenology, and exemplified their interdependence in social interactions. In our study, there were significant interactions of "task" x "device", and also "task" x "combination of bodily directions". It was considered this result reflected not only the flexibility of individual personal space but the complexity of co-operation between persons interacting within an environment.

4   Conclusion

This paper presented an experimental study that investigated how interpersonal distance varied depending on the differences of tasks, devices, combinations of bodily directions, as well as postures and gender.

There were statistically significant simple main effects of the "task" and the "combination of bodily directions". Especially, the study I revealed that interpersonal distance varied depending on the differences between: (a) "without task > with a task" (listening-to-music, typing), (b) {from front, backward} > {lateral, side by side}, (c) "lateral > side by side", and (d) "from front > backward" under all the task conditions except for "typing". On the other hand, however, there was a simple main effect of neither "genders" nor "postures". The results of the study II revealed simple main effects of the "co-operation" and the presence of "devices". The results suggested that: interpersonal distance was influenced by feeling the presence of eyes even in peripheral vision; there was a considerable relation between the transformation of interpersonal distance and a consumption of cognitive resources. By taking into account a significant influence of the structures another person forms around his/her body, it was considered that interpersonal space was co-constructed through an interaction process by a dyad.

In order to grasp dynamic nature of human spatial behavior, it is essential to enhance a methodological framework including re-modeling of personal space concept and the improvement of the validity of a measuring method.

Acknowledgments. This work was supported in part by JSPS Grant-in-Aid for Scientific Research (23300263). We thank all the study participants, and our laboratory members 2013-2014.

References

1. Adams, L., Zuckerman, D.: The effect of lighting conditions on personal space requirements. J. Gen. Psychol. **118**(4), 335–340 (1991)
2. Aiello, J.R.: Human spatial behavior. In: Stokels, D., Altman, I. (eds.) Handbook of Environmental Psychology, pp. 385–504. Wiley, NY (1987)
3. Altman, I.: The Environment and Social Behavior: Privacy, Personal Space, Territory, and Crowding. Brooks/Cole Publishing, Pacific Grove (1975)
4. Argyle, M., Dean, J.: Eye-contact, distance, and affiliation. Sociometry **28**(3), 289–304 (1965)
5. Birdwhistell, R.: Kinesics and Context. University of Pennsylvania Press, Philadelphia (1970)
6. Cochran, C.D., Hale, W.D., Hissam, C.P.: Personal space requirements in indoor versus outdoor locations. J. Psychol. **117**(1), 121–123 (1984)
7. Dorsey, M., Meisels, M.: Personal space and self-protection. J. Pers. Soc. Psychol. **11**, 93–97 (1969)
8. Evans, G.W., Lepore, S.J., Schroeder, A.: The role of interior design elements in human responses to crowding. J. Pers. Soc. Psychol. **70**, 41–46 (1996)
9. Felipe, N.J., Sommer, R.: Invasions of personal space. Soc. Probl. **14**(2), 206–214 (1966)
10. Gifford, R.: Environmental Psychology, 5th edn. Optimal Books, Colville (2014)
11. Gifford, R.: Projected interpersonal distance and orientation choices: personality, sex, and social situation. Soc. Psychol. Q. **45**(3), 145–152 (1982)
12. Goffman, E.: Relations in Public. Basic Books, New York (1971)
13. Hall, E.T.: The hidden dimension. Doubleday, New York (1966)
14. Hayduk, L.A.: Personal space: an evaluative and orienting overview. Psychol. Bull. **85**(1), 117–134 (1978)
15. Kinoe, Y., Hama, T.: A framework for understanding everyday situations through interactions. In: Proceedings of the 16th World Congress of on Ergonomics, International Ergonomics Association, Elsevier (2006)
16. Kinzel, A.F.: Body-buffer zone in violent prisoners. Am. J. Psychiatry **127**, 59–64 (1970)
17. Kirk, R.E.: Experimental Design: Procedures for the Behavioral Sciences. Sage, Los Angeles (2013)
18. Kouchi, M., Mochimaru, M.: AIST/HQL Anthropometric data database, H18PRO-503 (2006)
19. Mead, R., Atrash, A., Matarić, M.J.: Automated proxemic feature extraction and behavior recognition: applications in human-robot interaction. Int. J. Soc. Robot. **5**(3), 367–378 (2013)
20. Mehrabian, A.: Significance of posture and position in the communication of attitude and status relationships. Psychol. Bull. **71**(5), 359–372 (1969)
21. Merleau-Ponty, M.: Phenomenology of Perception (Trans. Smith, C.). Routledge & Kegan Paul, London (1962)
22. Pedersen, D.M.: Development of a Personal Space Measure. Psychol. Rep. **32**, 527–535 (1973)

23. Scheflen, A.E., Ashcraft, N.: Human Territories: How we behave in space-time. Prentice-Hall, Englewood Cliffs (1976)
24. Sommer, R.: Personal Space: The behavioral basis of design Updated. Bosko Books, Bristol (2008)
25. Sommer, R.: Personal Space in a Digital Age. In: Bechtel, R.B., Churchman, A. (eds.) Handbook of Environmental Psychology, pp. 385–504. Wiley, NY (2002)
26. Srivastava, P., Mandal, M.K.: Proximal spacing to facial affect expressions in schizophrenia. Compr. Psychiatry **31**, 119–124 (1990)
27. Tedesco, J.F., Fromme, D.K.: Cooperation, competition, and personal space. Sociometry **37**, 116–121 (1974)
28. Wormith, J.S.: Personal space of incarcerated offenders. Clin. Psychol. **40**, 815–827 (1984)

A Method for Calculating Air Traffic Controller Communication Complexity

Zach Roberts[✉], Blake Arnsdorff, James Cunningham,
and Dan Chiappe

California State University Long Beach, Long Beach, CA, USA
{zach.roberts100, thearnsdorff, ether33}@gmail.com,
dan.chiappe@csulb.edu

Abstract. Verbal communication is currently the primary tool Air Traffic Controllers (ATCos) use to manage traffic and ensure separation [1]. For these verbal communications to be effective they need to be clear, concise, and use proper phraseology. Under increased workload, however, ATCos may issue multiple commands in one transmission. Pilots commonly cite message complexity and length as a potential source of frustration and error [2]. The current study discusses an algorithm for calculating communication complexity values. This algorithm is applied to a simulated environment involving different speeds and numbers of Unmanned Aircraft Systems (UAS), examining the communications between the ATCos and the surrounding conventional aircraft. The findings suggest that the computer program for calculating communication complexity is a helpful tool for examining ATCo-pilot communications and can be used in future studies to analyze communications in dynamic environments.

Keywords: Communication complexity · Unmanned aircraft systems · Air traffic control

1 Introduction

Air traffic controllers (ATCos) manage traffic by issuing verbal commands to pilots. To be effective, these need to be clear, concise, and use proper phraseology. Under conditions of high workload, however, ATCos may compensate by including multiple commands per message. Increasing the complexity of messages is problematic as it can lead to increased pilot read back errors and increased requests for clarification. Pilots have cited complexity and length of ATCo commands as a source of frustration and potential error [2]. The current study presents an algorithm for calculating ATCo communication complexity. It applies this algorithm to communications between ATCos and conventional aircraft in a simulated environment where the number of Unmanned Aircraft Systems (UAS) and their speeds varied.

Although issuing complex, lengthy messages might help to reduce ATCo workload, it can also elevate pilots' working memory load [3]. Increasing demands on pilots' working memory can lead to more pilot requests for clarification (e.g., "say again" or "repeat last transmission") as well as more pilot read back errors. Pilot requests for clarifications congest the radio frequencies and this can be a distraction to

© Springer International Publishing Switzerland 2015
S. Yamamoto (Ed.): HIMI 2015, Part II, LNCS 9173, pp. 25–32, 2015.
DOI: 10.1007/978-3-319-20618-9_3

an ATCo when there is an abundance of radio traffic. Additionally, pilot read back errors can be disastrous if not caught by the ATCo. It may be difficult for ATCos to catch all of these read back errors under high-density traffic situations.

Examining communication complexity is therefore important. Indeed, analyzing message content and structure can help determine the contributing factors that lead to aviation accidents and incidents as well as help describe common practices in ATCo-pilot communications [4]. It is also imperative to address the issue of communication complexity when implementing new technologies. These communication issues, for example, must be examined given the current mandate for UAS to be integrated into the NAS.

The methods described herein were applied to a study examining ATCo command complexity as a function of speed and number of UAS in a simulated environment. ATCo-conventional pilot communications were analyzed for their communication complexity. We predicted that as the number of UAS is increased, ATCo communication complexity would also increase. This is because, with a greater number of UAS present, each with complex routes through the sector, it is likely that ATCos would require more interactions with conventional AC to maintain safe separation. Additionally, we predicted that the faster the UAS the greater the ATCo communication complexity for conventional AC. This is because when UAS are slow, it is easier to for ATCos to structure the flow of conventional aircraft around the UAS. When UAS are faster, geometries become more difficult to predict and would require more communication and coordination. It was also predicted that increased communication complexity would be positively correlated with increased number of Losses of Separations (LOS) and ATCo workload.

2 Method

To extract communication complexity values of ATCo clearances, transmissions were broken down into communication elements. In the context of aviation, communication elements are recognized by their functional purpose or associated action plan (e.g., clearance/instructions, request, etc.) and are limited to specific aviation topics (speed, heading, altitude; [1]). ATCo communications frequently contain multiple commands in one transmission, each being composed of multiple communication elements. To calculate an overall communication complexity value for each ATCo transmission, the sum of all communication elements within each transmission was calculated.

A computer program was written using Visual Basic 2012 to separate ATCo transmissions between conventional pilots. The program analyzed transcribed audio files and extracted ATCo communications. The program cross-referenced ATCo communications against a researcher-defined database of complex and non-complex ATCo phraseology. If a phrase was not found in either database, the program would prompt the researcher with, "Is the presented phrase complex or not"? If the phrase was judged as non-complex the program would add it to the non-complex database. Otherwise the researcher was prompted to decide the phrase's complexity value, number of aviation topics, and specific aviation topics. The complex phrase and its complexity value, number of aviation topics, and specific aviation topics were stored in the corresponding database. The program then calculated complexity values, number of aviation topics, and aviation topic types for each ATCo communication. From these calculations, average complexity, average number of aviation topics, and total word count were calculated for each transcribed file.

The Instruction Complexity Guide and Advisory Complexity Guide from [5] were used to ensure consistency and reliability of coding communication complexity values for ATCo phraseology. Consistent with these documents, each ATCo transmission was broken down into aviation topics (e.g., altitude, heading, speed) and each was assigned a complexity value; the larger the complexity value the more complex the transmission. The complexity guides have a column that consists of ATCo phraseology taken from [6]. The Instruction complexity guide examples can be seen in Table 1.

Table 1. Excerpt from the instruction/clearance complexity guide

AVIATION TOPIC	COMPLEXITY	PHRASEOLOGY EXAMPLE
Altitude	3	*(altitude) two digits* + THOUSAND
	2	*(altitude) one digit* + THOUSAND
	3	*(altitude) two digits* + HUNDRED
	2	*(altitude) one digit* + HUNDRED
	2	*(altitude) two digits*
	1	*(altitude) one digit*
	6	DESCEND/CLIMB & MAINTAIN *(altitude)* THOUSAND *(altitude)* HUNDRED *three* *five*
	5	DESCEND/CLIMB & MAINTAIN *(altitude)* THOUSAND *one zero*
	4	DESCEND/CLIMB & MAINTAIN *(altitude)* THOUSAND *four*
	*4-8	CONTINUE CLIMB/DESCENT TO *(altitude)*
	*4-8	AMEND YOUR ALTITUDE DESCEND/CLIMB AND MAINTAIN *(altitude)*
	*3-7	*(altitude)* AMEND YOUR ALTITUDE MAINTAIN *(altitude)*
	*3-8	DESCEND/CLIMB TO *(altitude)*
	*2-6	MAINTAIN *(altitude)*
	*1-2	*(altitude,* omitted "THOUSAND" "HUNDRED")

The coding scheme of [5] had 2 raters encode the same set of 25 randomly selected messages with an agreement rate of 95 %. A follow up analysis of 125 messages (using Krippendorff's alpha) produced a value of .9898, indicating high inter-rater agreement. The current study's coding scheme was similar to [5] and assigned a complexity value of 1 to every anchor, qualifier, direction, fix, waypoint, etc., as determined by the phraseology in [6]. To ensure consistency of data coding, two raters encoded the same set of 25 randomly selected messages and computed an agreement analysis against the computer program, which exceeded 0.80. For the present study seventy-two, forty-minute, audio recordings were transcribed and analyzed.

3 Results

The complexity coding method was applied to a study examining the influence of number and speed of UAS on ATCo's ability to manage traffic in a simulated environment that included both, conventional aircraft and UAS. ATCos received 9 experimental trials, each lasting 40 min. The trials differed in the number of UAS (1, 2, or 4) in the sector and the relative speed of the UAS (slow, mixed or fast).

A 3 (Speed: slow, mixed, or fast) X 3 (Number of UAS: 1 UAS, 2 UAS, or 4 UAS) ANOVA was conducted on the dependent variable Communication Complexity (calculated by the computer program). Due to the small sample size alpha was set at 0.10 for the current study. The analysis revealed a main effect of the Number of UAS on communication complexity, $F(2,14) = 4.06$, $p = .041$, $\eta2 = .37$ (see Fig. 1). However, contrary to the hypothesis, as the number of UAS increased, communication complexity decreased. Post hoc tests revealed that the 1 UAS scenarios (M = 6.22) had a higher complexity value than 2 UAS scenarios (M = 6.01; p = .026). They also revealed a difference between 1 UAS scenarios (M = 6.01) and 4 UAS scenarios (M = 5.98; p = .067).

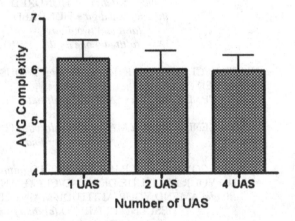

Fig. 1. Main effect of number of UAS on complexity

There was no effect of speed on communication complexity. However, there was a significant interaction between speed of UAS and number of UAS on communication complexity, $F(4,28) = 2.50$, $p = .065$, $\eta^2 = .26$. Simple effects analysis revealed a significant difference in communication complexity for different numbers of UAS when the UAS speed was fast, $F(2,14) = 4.29$, $p = .035$, $\eta^2 = .38$. Post hoc tests revealed communication complexity values significantly decreased as the number of UAS increased from 1 Fast UAS (M = 6.27) to 4 Fast UAS (M = 5.86; p = .07; see Fig. 2). There was no difference between 1 Fast UAS and 2 Fast UAS (p = .401) or 2 Fast UAS and 4 Fast UAS (p = .997). Simple affects analysis revealed no significant effects for number of UAS for Mixed or Slow speed scenarios.

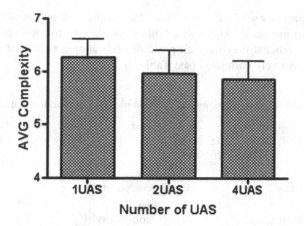

Fig. 2. Simple effect of number of UAS for fast speed

A simple effects analysis also revealed a significant difference in communication complexity for different speeds but only when there was 1 UAS in the sector, $F(2,14) = 4.16$, $p = .038$, $\eta^2 = .37$. Post hoc tests revealed a trend indicating that complexity values increased as the UAS speeds changed from 1 Slow UAS ($M = 5.94$) to 1 Mixed UAS ($M = 6.46$; $p = .16$). Complexity values decreased from 1 Mixed UAS to 1 Fast UAS ($M = 6.27$; $p = .54$). There was no communication complexity difference between 1 Slow UAS and 1 Fast UAS ($p = .338$; see Fig. 3). There were no simple effects of speed for 2 or 4 UAS. There were no other significant differences for number and speed of UAS.

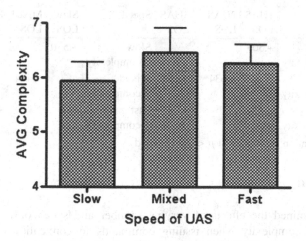

Fig. 3. Simple effect of speed for 1 UAS

Correlations were calculated relating communication complexity to ATCo workload (NASA-TLX) and safety (LOS). Beginning with workload, one significant positive correlation was found when examining communication complexity and workload in the mixed speed scenarios, $r = +.762$, $p = .029$; as the communication complexity increased the workload also increased. Although all other correlations for number and speed of UAS were not significant they were all positive, indicating a trend that workload and complexity are positively correlated (see Table 2).

Table 2. Correlations between communication complexity and workload-number and speed

Number	1 UAS WL	2 UAS WL	4 UAS WL	Speed	Slow WL	Mixed WL	Fast WL
1UAS complexity	+.568			Slow complexity	+.470		
2UAS complexity		+.519		Mixed complexity		+.762*	
4UAS complexity			+.505	Fast complexity			+.494

*Correlation significant at the 0.05 level (2-tailed).

Correlations between communication complexity and LOS were also examined. A significant correlation was found when there were 2 UAS in the sector (see Table 3). Although the remaining correlations for LOS and complexity were not significant, there was a trend toward LOS and complexity being positively correlated; the strongest correlations were for 2 UAS and Slow speed.

Table 3. Correlations between communication complexity and LOS-number & speed

Number	1UAS LOS	2UAS LOS	4UAS LOS	Speed	Slow LOS	Mixed LOS	Fast LOS
1UAS complexity	+.508			Slow complexity	+.530		
2UAS complexity		+.634**		Mixed complexity		+.424	
4 UAS complexity			+.225	Fast complexity			+.381

**Correlation significant at $p < .10$ (2-tailed).

4 Discussion

This study examined the effects of varying number and speed of UAS on ATCo communication complexity when issuing commands to conventional aircraft in a simulated environment. Results indicated that as the number of UAS increased in the sector the communication complexity actually decreased. Regarding workload, for UAS at mixed speeds workload was positively correlated with communication complexity. There was also a trend showing complexity was positively correlated with LOS when 2 UAS were in the sector.

The finding that as the number of UAS increased the communication complexity of ATCo commands to conventional pilots decreased was counter to expectations. One reason this may have occurred is that when there were less UAS in the sector there were more conventional aircraft present. The airspace may therefore have become more complex, and ATCos may have been forced to issue simpler (but more frequent) commands to conventional aircraft.

In support of this claim, [7] examined the same simulation and found there were in fact more ATCo-conventional pilot communications (per aircraft) with 4 UAS in the sector compared to when 1 or 2 UAS were in the sector. Therefore, when there were more UAS in the sector ATCos may be issuing less complex commands at a higher volume to conventional aircraft, simply because they cannot predict what commands should be issued ahead of time.

With respect to effects of UAS speed on communication complexity, there were no main effects, though the effect of speed did interact with number of UAS present. The general lack of significant results may simply reflect the fact that UAS speeds were in general slow compared to conventional aircraft and the fact that the number of UAS in the sector may be the most critical factor, and not speed, at least in terms of affecting communication complexity.

We predicted that number of LOS per scenario and ATCo workload would be positively correlated with communication complexity. We found that the complexity of ATCo commands was in fact positively correlated with workload when the UAS speeds were mixed. The changing UAS speed may thus have posed a challenge to ATCos, compared to when UAS speeds were constantly fast of slow.

Contrary to expectations, there were no statistically significant results relating LOS and communication complexity, possibly due to a small sample size. However, all correlations were positive, indicating a trend that when communication complexity increased the number of LOS also increased. Although further research is required, our findings thus suggest that decreasing communication complexity may help decrease the number of LOS.

To conclude, this study demonstrates that the method of calculating complexity can be a helpful tool for examining the safety and efficiency of the airspace. Moreover, it suggests that communication complexity is an important factor to consider when introducing new technologies, such as UAS, into the air traffic management system.

References

1. Prinzo, O.V., Britton, T.W., Hendrix, A.M.: Development of a coding form for approach control/pilot voice communications. Technical report, DOT/FAA/AM-95/15, Federal Aviation Administration, Office of Aviation Medicine, Washington, D.C. (1995)
2. Cardosi, K.M., Brett, B., Han, S.: An analysis of TRACON (Terminal Radar Approach Control) controller-pilot voice communications. Technical report, DOT/VNTSC-FAA-96-7, John A Volpe National Transportation Systems Center, Cambridge, MA (1996)
3. Morrow, D., Lee, A., Rodvold, M.: Analysis of problems in routine controller-pilot communication. Int. J. Aviat. Psychol. 3(4), 285–302 (1993)

4. Prinzo, O.V.: An analysis of voice communication in a simulated approach control environment. Technical report, DOT/FAA/AM-98/17, Federal Aviation Administration, Office of Aviation Medicine, Washington, D.C. (1998)
5. Prinzo, O.V., Hendrix, A.M., Hendrix, R.: The outcome of ATC message complexity on pilot read back performance. Technical report, DOT/FAA/AM-06/25, Federal Aviation Administration, Office of Aviation Medicine, Washington, D.C. (2006)
6. Federal Aviation Administration: FAA Order JO 7110.65U, Federal Aviation Administration (2012). http://www.faa.gov/documentlibrary/media/order/7110.65ubasic.pdf
7. Vu, K.P.L., Morales, G., Chiappe, D., Strybel, T., Battiste, V., Shively, R.J.: Measured response for multiple UAS in a simulated NAS environment. In: Proceedings of the Human Factors and Ergonomics Society Annual Meeting, vol. 58(1), pp. 59–63 (2014)

Conceptual Framework to Enrich Situation Awareness of Emergency Dispatchers

Jessica Souza[1,2], Leonardo Castro Botega[1,4(✉)],
José Eduardo Santarém Segundo[3], Claudia Beatriz Berti[4],
Márcio Roberto de Campos[4], and Regina Borges de Araújo[4]

[1] Computing and Information Systems Research Lab (COMPSI),
Marília Eurípides University – UNIVEM, Marília, Brazil
{osz.jessica,leobotega}@gmail.com,
leonardo_botega@dc.ufscar.br
[2] São Paulo State University "Júlio Mesquita Filho" – UNESP, Marília, Brazil
[3] São Paulo University – USP, Ribeirão Preto, Brazil
santarem@usp.br
[4] Wireless Networks and Distributed Interactive Simulations Lab (WINDIS),
Computer Department, Federal University of São Carlos – UFSCar,
São Carlos, Brazil
{claudiabberti,marcamposbr}@gmail.com,
regina@dc.ufscar.br

Abstract. Computer-Aided Dispatch (CAD) systems provide powerful resources to support emergency operators (dispatchers) in their activity. However, these dispatchers can work under heavy stress, which can lead to failure to get necessary information, resulting in unsuccessful response to calls. One challenging issue to better support operators in stressing calls is to determine how to generate, score and represent informational quality cues to help them to reason under uncertainties and improve their understanding about an ongoing situation (situational awareness - SAW). In such a context, the poor knowledge about the entities involved in a situation and what is really going on may lead to wrong decision-making. One of the gaps in the state-of-the-art research in this area is the lack of a common ground regarding information quality. This is due to domain-specific demands and the absence of a comprehensive framework of information quality that interface with different levels of knowledge during a situation assessment cycle. Hence, in order to improve dispatchers' situational awareness, we present a new conceptual framework to support decision making in emergency call situations by enriching situations knowledge with reliable metadata and successive reassessments of information quality. The framework's requirements elicitation was carried out with police experts as well as the definition and application of information quality scoring criteria and the representation of such scores along with a semantic knowledge representation model. The framework application on real robbery reporting calls has indicated very positive results.

Keywords: Information management · Data quality framework · Situational awareness · Knowledge management

© Springer International Publishing Switzerland 2015
S. Yamamoto (Ed.): HIMI 2015, Part II, LNCS 9173, pp. 33–44, 2015.
DOI: 10.1007/978-3-319-20618-9_4

1 Introduction

Situation awareness - SAW is a concept widely spread in military and aviation areas (with increasing use in different application areas that require critical decision making), related to the level of consciousness that an individual or team has to a situation. It is a dynamic understanding of an operator about what is happening in the environment and the projection of its status in the near future [1]. According to Endsley [1] SAW is divided in three levels: perception of the elements in the environment, comprehension of these elements status in a situation and the evolution of these in a near future. Achieving complete SAW is a process that takes place in the human mind, which requires cognitive activity. The prior user mental model of situations can assist to reduce the cognitive overload. However, poor understanding of information may not only cause the loss of its global significance, but can also lead to failures while allocating resources.

Mental model and SAW are highly related, since a mental model is formed by the user's understanding of situations. Hence, a poor understanding of a situation affects the user's mental model, which leads to poor comprehension and decision-making jeopardy [1].

One critical service that can benefit from a better SAW-oriented support to decision making is emergency calls. Bad identification, for instance, in a robbery report, can lead to failures in both resource allocation and tactics definition to respond to such calls. Under stress, operators can be provided by informational quality cues to help them to reason under uncertainties and improve their understanding about an ongoing situation. Semantic models have been used, which can adapt to specific contexts and create verbal schemes in order to attach meaning to the information.

The literature registers approaches that aim to enhance and maintain the user's SAW, by employing technologies such cognitive models, ontologies and frameworks based on core ontologies, fuzzy logic, and data fusion models [2–5]. However, to the knowledge of the authors, there is a lack of a common ground regarding information quality in the evaluation of situations.

This paper introduces a conceptual framework for Information Quality that can enrich SAW for emergency dispatchers. A semantic model of the call is devised that can be used to support operator in a real time, to better acquire SAW under call uncertainties. The framework is used for real robbery victims report. However, it can be easily adapted to other crime reporting calls.

The paper is organized as follows: Sect. 2 discusses data quality dimensions for general decision-making systems. Section 3 presents our framework for quality assessment and representation for acquire SAW in robbery report attending followed by a case study that applies our framework in a robbery report in Sect. 4 and Conclusions.

2 Information Quality for the Evaluation of Situations for General Decision-Making Systems

Information quality is one among the crucial factors in decision-making systems. Imperfect information, which do not truly describe real world situations (e.g., incomplete set of necessary data, information which do not fully describe an event or fact, misspelled words, etc.), reduce the effectiveness of the systems, contribute negatively to the mental model formation and, consequently, undermine the SAW process.

According to the literature, there is not a defined pattern to information quality in decision-making systems. Requirements are divided into dimensions or metrics, and their decision-making applications are highly domain dependent, whereas the application defines their respective meanings according to objectives, tasks and associated decisions [6, 7].

For the robbery reporting call in our case study, completeness, uncertainty and timeliness information quality dimensions are addressed. Approaches, descriptions, and different information quality perspectives are described below.

O'Brien [8] defines data quality dimensions required for information systems in three main dimensions: content, time, and shape. Among the quality attributes there are readiness, acceptance, frequency, period, accuracy, relevance, completeness, conciseness, breadth, performance, clarity, detail, order, presentation, and media.

Wang et al. [9] categorize quality dimension attributes in four main classes (intrinsic, contextual, representational and contextual data quality) described as follows:

Intrinsic data quality implies guaranteeing credibility and reputation to data, among the attributes there are credibility, reputation, accuracy and objectivity.

Contextual data quality is comprised by attributes that should be considered and evaluated according to the context of the task to be performed, having as attributes: value-added, relevance, timeliness, completeness, and appropriate amount of data.

As for the quality of representation, the attributes are defined according to the given format-related aspects (such as conciseness and representation), and the meaning in the understanding and interpretation of such data. Finally, the authors classify individual accessibility-related attributes.

It is important to note that in addition to the works cited, most works analyzed presented in their methodology a subjective analysis step performed by experienced users in the field by means of questionnaires, interviews or surveys.

Among the related methodologies in the literature that evaluate data quality and relate to emergency decision-making context, it is noted that most of them are applied after the crime event, during the report recording process in order to prevent spreading low-quality reports in the system [10, 11].

It is evident that there are several applications of quality dimensions both in emergency and other application areas.

3 A Framework to Acquire Situation Awareness for Emergency Dispatchers: Robbery Report Event

In order to help developing SAW (specifically at the Perception level of the elements in the environment), our framework was defined to be coupled in a robbery situation assessment system, in which the operator can deal with information by using a multiple data sources combination (data fusion), as well as perform diverse kinds of refinement to build an incremental knowledge about what is going on in real scenarios. The Fig. 1 presents our conceptual framework and, main components.

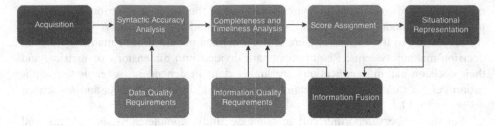

Fig. 1. Framework to Enrich SAW for emergency dispatchers

As part of a complete situation assessment system, our framework is preceded by an acquisition module and followed by information fusion activities. The final objective is to reduce data dimensionality and convey better information about what is going on for a more grounded decision. The Fig. 1 presents how the information quality module relates to the other modules for situation assessment of robbery report events (the framework can be easily adapted to other crime reporting calls).

The quality assessment is performed upon data and information. In data when the primary assessment occurs, Syntactic Accuracy is applied, and information after the ontology is instantiated that is when the data turns into information with its relationships and meaning.

Before performing any information analysis, our framework receives the output of the acquisition phase. Such, acquisition performs a Natural Language Processing (NLP) [12] to identify objects, attributes and properties from audio reported to the PMESP (Military Police of the State of São Paulo) via emergency calls (number 190). As an output, it is produced a JavaScript Object Notation (JSON) object such as shown in Fig. 2.

Then, a Syntactic Accuracy analysis is performed leading a data preparation by checking for misspelled words, which can influence negatively the completeness assessment that will be conducted as follows.

First, it is used an algorithm called Metaphone [13] that generates a keyword as the word is pronounced – consequently, the words with similar sounds generate the same key. Then, the Levenshtein [14] Distance algorithm is applied to compare the words in the robbery report. Such algorithm measures the edit distance between two strings. As result, it discovers the number of operations needed for a string to be equal to another.

The process depends on a dictionary of sound key from words as parameter. If the result of the key comparison equals 0 it means a match is found, which indicates the presence of attributes (words) in an emergency call. Even if there is a misspelled word the evaluation process will happen without errors.

The completeness assessment occurs through examination of attributes that should be present in the call, which were defined by means of a Goal Driven Task Analysis (GDTA) [1]. The assessment results in a quantitative value a percentage of how much the object of the call is complete. Additional priority data and information were obtained through a questionnaire applied to members of PMESP in Brazil.

Timeliness will be assessed according to four requisites, the time of the robbery event, time that the robbery report was made, time spent to process such information

```json
{
  "robberyReport": {
    "criminal": {
      "vehicle": "motorcycle",
      "criminal": "two",
      "armed": "yes",
      "criminalLocation": "Klabin subway",
      "quality": {
        "completeness:""
      }
    },
    "object": {
      "object": "car",
      "model": "Mercedes",
      "color": "black",
      "quality": {
        "completeness:""
      }
    },
    "eventSpot": {
      "street":"Domingos Setti Street with Luis Vives",
      "quality": {
        "completeness:""
      }
    },
    "quality":{
      "uncertainty":"",
      "timeliness":{
        "time":"",
        "percentage":""
}}}}
```

Fig. 2. JSON schema for robbery report to perform quality assessment

while finding objects and attributes, and the current system time. As a result, the elapsed time from the event will be returned.

Later, a score assignment is performed to represent quantitatively the completeness and timeliness measures. Such score is crucial for both the fusion process, to use it as a parameter for information integration, and the operator to analyze them for decision-making. Also, such quality assessment is performed in a local and global fashion, ensuring that objects and situations can be evaluated, to be discussed further.

Therefore, the proposed framework can be summarized into three main steps, which follows: (1) data quality requirements elicitation for the emergency call, (2) definition and application of quantitative metrics and functions for requirements classification, and (3) knowledge representation of the generated knowledge using domain ontology.

3.1 Data Quality Requirements Elicitation

The requirements needed for the understanding of emergency calls were defined with the help of the PMESP. Initially, in order to perform the requirements elicitation, two different but complementary approaches were conducted: a Goal-Directed Task Analysis (GDTA) and a questionnaire. Both with the same objective of gather the necessary information for granting SAW Level 1 and complementary cues about the quality of information needed for emergency dispatchers' decision-making.

In order to define how a robbery report is completed, the definition of a model of objects and attributes for this report is devised. With the information obtained by GDTA (Table 1) it was modelled an attribute tree according to the requirements in a report. Also, from the requirements, it was defined the components present in an event of robbery: the victim, the criminal, the stolen object, and the place and time of the event. The following is a description of each attribute:

- Criminal and Victim, who have similar attributes as individuals: clothing, characteristics, ornaments, and respective descriptions;
- Object: defines characteristics of the stolen object such as color, brand, size, and model. There is also an extension named Vehicle with specific features such as license plate and year, in case such information is provided;
- Event spot: component provided with some type-specification (house, land, apartment, square) and information related to the address such as street, neighborhood, etc.

Table 1. Robbery requirements set thru GDTA

SAW's level 1
Information to stimulate operator's situational awareness
- Victim condition
- Potential start and end of event
- Event spot or surroundings
- Number of suspects
- Object in the suspect's possession
- Perpetrator's physical attributes
- Stolen object and its characteristics
- Quality score and data source (uncertainty, completeness and time)

Four attributes were defined to also assess timeliness dimension: (1) time of the robbery event, (2) time that the robbery report was made, (3) time spent to process such information while finding objects and attributes and the (4) current system time. The Attributes Tree plays an important role in the next steps, since quality evaluation and knowledge representation of the domain take place by means of the objects and attributes defined.

3.2   Quantitative Metrics Elicitation for Data Quality Evaluation

Information Quality assessment will be performed upon a JSON scheme for robbery report with objects and its attributes presented in Fig. 2.

Metrics for quality assessment were defined according two specifics quality dimensions: timelines and completeness. For last, the score from the objects together will form a third quality attribute, uncertainty, which generalizes the other dimensions into a single quality measure for the robbery report (set of objects). Every object has its own completeness score; on the contrary, the timeliness and uncertainty score will be applied to the robbery report as a whole. This means that every report has at least the measures of uncertainty and timeliness dimensions.

The completeness metric were defined with the questionnaire applied to police experts who helped to define priority attributes related to a robbery report, as follows:

- Information if weapons were used
- What kind of weapons were used
- Current location of the criminal
- Location of the crime
- Information about the victim (e.g., condition)
- Information about the vehicle (e.g., if stolen)

The formula (1) defines the completeness calculus, as follows:

$$\frac{\delta \sum \varphi + (10 \sum \beta \times \varphi - \sum \varphi)}{10 \sum \varphi}. \tag{1}$$

To deal with the presence of an object without attributes (e.g., the object is present in the JSON scheme but no attributes were mentioned by in the report) a default value of 10 % was set to such object to perform completeness score assessment. Therefore, where δ represents one of the four objects presence, being equals 0 if is not present in the JSON scheme and 1 if it is present.

Hence, if the object its present it means the completeness is already equals 10 %. To find the remainder score β consists in the presence of the attribute, which has the range of 1 when the attribute it is present and 0 if it is not multiplied by φ that is the weight of the attribute, it can be in a range of 1 if is a normal attribute and 2 if is a prior attribute. The result is divided by the sum of φ and finally multiplied by 100 to find the overall completeness percentage.

The timeliness dimension assessment will result in two kind of information: a quantitative score regarding the existence of the four attributes needed, and how many in minutes have elapsed since the robbery event. The formula (2) was set to perform the timeliness quantitative score:

$$\sum_{\gamma=1}^{4} -\theta. \tag{2}$$

Where θ consists in a successive subtraction of the four attributes in the following order: the time of the robbery event, minus the time that the robbery report was made, minus the time spent to process such information while finding objects and attributes, minus the current time. To find the uncertainty score, the sum of each completeness score from all objects will be divided by the amount of objects found in the report.

3.3   Knowledge Representation

Matheus et al. [15] presents an ontology to improve SAW, for emergency dispatchers, which represents the objects and the relationship among them, besides their respective evolutions over time. Such ontology is used in this work to model robbery report.

The assessment system processes data from heterogeneous sources and also from an information fusion module. The latter information helps mitigating uncertainty locally, in a single report, or globally, when several reports, containing similar objects, have a property that links these objects, such as activities like "stealing, running, screaming, fighting".

When an information fusion occurs, there is a need to re-asses information, considering that now we refer to a situation and uncertainty became a global measure of what is going on.

The ontology describes the relationship between four main classes named Victim, Criminal, *StolenObject* and *RobberySpot*. A class called *RobberyReport* was set do gather information about the report itself. The two classes Victim and Criminal hold some common attributes such as gender, condition, and *physicalAspects*. When some of the main classes are instantiated it must be instantiated together the class *Situation* whose the main attribute is called *updateTime,* to store every time any change happens in the whole situation and its instances' attributes. A reduced example of the classes is shown in Fig. 3.

4   Case Study

This case study presents a situation in which SAW is a paramount factor for decision-making because of the impact on police resources allocation. Given the large amount of criminal events reported to the PMESP, and considering the stress that emergency dispatchers are submitted to, the main objective of this study is to provide a supporting tool to dispatchers that can enhance their SAW, by reducing uncertainties and providing high level abstractions to help decision-making resulting in more efficient emergency call response service and police resource allocation. Additionally, we seek to identify and understand contexts associated with the situation, such as location, criminal, stolen object, presence of weapons and victims. This case study discusses specifically the situation of robbery. The occurrence is initially reported via phone 190, and then applied the functions of quality involving the completeness and temporal aspects of the events data. An example of a call is given below.

```
{"Situation": {
     "instance": "sit001",
     "data properties": {
        "date": "25/02/2015",
        "updateTime":"07:29 pm",
        "uncertainty": "60%"
     },
     "object properties": {
        "has_a": {
           "robberyReport": {
              "instance": "den001",
              " data properties ": {
                 "dataReport": "25/02/2015",
                 "transcribedCall": "good night ... black cap"
              }
           },
           "Criminal": {
              "instance": "crim_001",
              " data properties ": {
                 "vehicle": "moto",
                 "completeness": "70%",
                 " object properties ": {
                    "runaway": {
                       "site": {
                          "instance": "local_001",
                          " data properties ": {
                             "street": "avenue...",
                             " completeness ": "80%"
}}}}}}}}}}}
```

Fig. 3. Example of ontology represented in JSON format

(Phone call): *"Good evening! A carjacking has just happened at Domingos Setti with Luis Vives streets. Two guys riding bikes pointed a gun to the driver of a black Mercedes and made him leave the car without taking anything. They two fled speeding toward Klabin subway station."*

After receiving the robbery report, the system receives the JSON scheme with the objects and attributes present in the report (Fig. 1) with no values in the quality items. The objects identified were *Criminal, StolenObject* and *EventSpot* and its attributes. A report may or not have all the attributes set in the GDTA - it depends on the informer.

So first, the JSON scheme is processed in order to set a completeness score, to the first object detected (*Criminal*). Six attributes presents are identified (being 2 of these a priority attribute being equals 4) divided by the total of attributes defined for the *Criminal* having a total of 0.31 which is going to be multiplied by 100 generating a score of 31,60 %. The same calculation is applied to the second objecte found (*StolenObject*) generating a score of 50 % and to the third object found (*EventSpot*) a completeness score of 25 %.

Assuming that the four time attributes received, via JSON scheme: the event occurrence time (7:21 pm); the reporting time (7:25 pm); the report registration time (0:02 min) and the current time (7:29 pm), the timeliness node will be composed by two information: time elapsed from the event occurrence until the end of the event occurrence registration (8 min ago), and the percentage of these four attributes (100 %).

Finally, to perform the uncertainty calculation the three object completeness was added to the above calculation, resulting in 206.6, divided by the amount of objects

```
{
"robberyReport": {
    "criminal": {
        "vehicle": "motorcycle",
        "criminal": "two",
        "armed": "yes",
        "criminalLocation": "Klabin subway",
        "quality": {
            "completeness:"31.60%"
        }
    },
    "object": {
        "object": "car",
        "model": "Mercedes",
        "color": "black",
        "quality": {
            "completeness:"50%"
        }
    },
    "eventSpot": {
        "street":"Domingos Setti Street with Luis Vives",
        "quality": {
            "completeness:"25%"
        }
    },
    "quality":{
        "uncertainty":"41.32%",
        "timeliness":{
            "time":"8 minutes ago",
            "percentage":"100%"
        }}}}
```

Fig. 4. JSON scheme after quality assessment is performed

defined by the GDTA (5), resulting in 41.32 %. After the quality assessment of each dimension is performed, the JSON scheme will look as shown in Fig. 4.

Considering that an information fusion should occur to automatically mitigate the absence of information in a single report, all the quality scores will be recalculated if new objects and attributes are discovered by the fusion routines - information quality assessment must be performed once again. If fusion provides a relationship among objects, the completeness is calculated based on the presence or not of the objects that compose such relation. In both cases, uncertainty must be recalculated. Figure 3 presents a JSON scheme after a quality assessment is performed, with fusion results.

5   Conclusion

This work introduced a framework to enhance the first level of situational awareness of emergency dispatchers when responding to robbery reports. Because dispatchers may have to make decisions under heavy stress, our framework tackles information quality processing to reduce uncertainty, providing means for a better perception of what is going on during an emergency report. For the requirements elicitation, interviews with

PMESP police experts were carried out with the application of GDTA methodology. As a result, an attribute tree was created with the main robbery objects and its attributes. The metrics to perform quality assessment were defined four quality dimensions: syntactic accuracy, completeness, timeliness and uncertainty.

The weight of objects and attributes set for a robbery were established with the help of PMESP police experts. Also, a domain ontology base on SAW core ontology was set to provide semantic meaning and relationships between objects and attributes while performing data quality evaluation.

The assessments of the data contained in each robbery report provide a full perception of the entities of an event and the necessary information about an ongoing crime event report. The knowledge generated may assist the development of systems that require SAW, since the evaluation of quality tends to improve the representation of both present and absent report information. Since the main objective of the framework was to focus on the perception of the elements, and it does so by identifying elements present in reports of robbery events by highlighting them and setting scores of quality, the framework meet its initial goal. As future work, time and quality dispatchers' response to the calls will be measured (community evaluation and police resources allocation). Another quality dimension that can be considered is consistency. This dimension refers to divergence in a set of data, which breaks semantic meaning, for instance in this case of a robbery report, two different addresses belonging to the same report (it is considered wrong to assume that a robbery report cannot happen in two different places at the same time). This problem may happen after a data fusion process that combines a set of different reports.

References

1. Endsley, M.R.: Designing for situation awareness: An approach to user-centered design, pp. 727–728. CRC Press, Boca Raton (2011)
2. Ciaramella, A., Cimino, M.G., Marcelloni, F., Straccia, U.: Combining fuzzy logic and semantic web to enable situation-awareness in service recommendation. In: Bringas, P.G., Hameurlain, A., Quirchmayr, G. (eds.) DEXA 2010, Part I. LNCS, vol. 6261, pp. 31–45. Springer, Heidelberg (2010)
3. Baumgartner, N., Gittesheim, W., Mitsch, S., Retschitzegger, W., Schwinger, W.: BeAware!— situation awareness, the ontology-driven way. Data Knowl. Eng. **69**(11), 1181–1193 (2010)
4. Jameson, S.M.: Architectures for distributed information fusion to support situation awareness on the digital battlefield. In: 4th International Conference on Data Fusion (2001)
5. Matheus, C.J., Kokar, M.M., Backawski, K., Letkowski, J., Call, C., Hinman, M., Salerno, J., Boulware., D.: SAWA: an assistant for higher-level fusion and situation awareness. In: International Society for Optics and Photonics Defense and Security (2005)
6. Batini, C., Francalanci, C., Maurino, A.: Methodologies for data quality assessment and improvement. ACM Comput. Surv. (CSUR) **41**, 1–52 (2009)
7. Lee, Y., Strong, D., Kahn, B., Wang, R.: AIMQ: a methodology for information quality assessment. Inf. Manag. **40**(2), 133–146 (2002)
8. O'Brien, J.: Sistemas de Informação e as Decisões Gerenciais na Era da Internet. 2. ed. São Paulo: Saraiva. v. 2, p. 431 (2004)

9. Wang, R., Strong, D.: Beyond accuracy: what data quality means to data consumers. J. Manag. Inf. Syst. **12**, 5–33 (1996)
10. Laudon, K.C.: Data quality and due process in large interorganizational record systems. Commun. ACM **29**(1), 4–11 (1986)
11. Bureau of Justice Statistics, U.S. Assessing completeness and accuracy of criminal history record systems: audit guide. Boureal of Justice Statistics. U.S. Deptartment. of Justice, Office of Justice Programs, Ed, Indiana, p. 65 (1992)
12. Junior, V., Sanches, M., Botega, L., Souza, J., Saraiva, C., Fusco, E., Campos, M., Araújo, R.: Multi-criteria fusion of heterogeneous information for improving situation awareness on military decision making system. In: 17th International Conference on Human-Computer Interaction, 2015, Los Angeles. Lecture Notes in Computer Science (LNCS) (2015)
13. Philips, L.: The Double Metaphone Search Algorithm, C/C ++ Users Journal, June 2000
14. Levenshtein, V.I.: Binary codes capable of correcting deletions, insertions, and reversals. Cybern. Control Theor. **10**(8), 707–710 (1966)
15. Matheus, C.J., Kokar, M.M., Baclawski, K.: A core ontology for situation awareness. In: Proceedings of the 6th International Conference on Information Fusion, FUSION 2003. v. 1, pp. 545–552. IEEE Computer Society (2003)

Using Eye Movements to Test Assumptions of the Situation Present Assessment Method

Lindsay Sturre[✉], Dan Chiappe, Kim-Phuong L. Vu, and Thomas Z. Strybel

California State University, Long Beach, Long Beach, CA, USA
lsturre@g.clemson.edu

Abstract. The Situated approach to Situation Awareness (SA) holds that when the immediate task environment is present, an operator will form partial internal representations of a situation and offload detailed information to the environment to access later, as needed. In the context of air traffic control (ATC), Situated SA states operators store general features of the airspace internally, along with high priority information, and offload specific and low priority information. The following describes a method for testing these claims that involves combining the Situation Present Assessment Method (SPAM) with a web camera used to record eye movements to the radar display while probe questions are presented during a simulated air traffic control task. In the present study, probe queries address information specificity and information priority. Images from queries that are correctly responded to are coded for total number of glances and total glance duration. We argue that this technique is reliable for determining whether information is stored internally or offloaded by operators.

Keywords: Situation awareness · SPAM · Situated SA

1 Introduction

Situation awareness (SA) is a major topic in the human factors community. Although many theories claim that operators store internally very detailed mental models of a situation, a new approach called Situated SA holds that operators store very limited representations, offloading much of it and accessing it only when needed [1–3]. In what follows, we outline a method for studying Situated SA in the context of air traffic control (ATC) operations and present some data on its reliability.

The Situated approach to SA is partly motivated by perceptual research on change blindness, where simple changes made to a scene are hard to detect unless they are explicitly the focus of attention [4]. What this research shows is that people do not store internally a complete detailed model of their perceptual world. Instead they represent general scene schemata, consisting of an inventory of objects likely to be in a scene and the location of those objects [4]. People then use this information to guide their fixations when they are in need of more detailed information.

The Situated approach holds that interactions between the operators and their immediate task environment are crucial for maintaining SA [2, 3]. In particular, operators store internally some information and offload that which can be accessed with

© Springer International Publishing Switzerland 2015
S. Yamamoto (Ed.): HIMI 2015, Part II, LNCS 9173, pp. 45–52, 2015.
DOI: 10.1007/978-3-319-20618-9_5

little effort from the environment. They form partial internal representations of a situation, which allows them to free up their working memory, whose resources can be devoted to other tasks. The Situated approach is consistent with recent studies on Google effects on memory that show people are less likely to be able to recall information if they believe they will be able to access it from a computer later on [5].

In the context of ATC operations, the Situated approach hypothesizes that controllers do not store internally a complete picture of the traffic patterns in the sector they are managing. Instead, they are likely to store internally information about general characteristics of their airspace, as well as high priority information – information that they will need to act on presently, like whether two aircraft are currently in conflicting paths. They are likely to offload specific information and low priority information onto their displays including, for example, aircraft call signs and whether two aircraft will be in conflict in five minutes or more.

In this paper we present a method for testing such claims by the situated approach, one that we believe can be generalized to other operational contexts. The method involves using the Situation Present Assessment Method (SPAM). It is an online probe technique for measuring Situated SA [6, 7]. Unlike other SA measurement techniques [1], SPAM queries participants while they are still engage in a task, granting them access to their displays while they are responding to probe queries [6, 7]. Participants are first presented with a ready prompt, as well as an acoustic tone to announce the arrival of the new query. If workload permits, participants respond to the ready prompt and a probe query is presented. When answering queries, participants can either use information represented internally, or they can access offloaded information from their display.

SPAM uses the reaction time (RT) between the presentation of the probe query and the onset of the participant's response (i.e., the "probe latency") to measure SA. SPAM assumes that fast probe latencies indicate good SA, with information being stored internally. Slightly slower probe latencies still indicate good SA, but it is assumed that information is being retrieved from the environment. Thus, if the location of the information in the environment is known, latencies will be longer than if the information is represented internally. However, when the location of the information is not known, probe latencies are assumed to be the slowest and participants are said to have poor SA, as they must then engage in a serial search of the display for the information.

Our method involves supplementing SPAM with a measure of participant eye glances, which allows us to determine whether lengthy SPAM reaction times really do reflect where operators store information. A web camera is used to capture images of participants while they respond to probe queries. This allows us to determine what information was retrieved internally and what was accessed from an external display. Web cameras were determined to be more cost effective than expensive eye tracking equipment, and would provide ample data for a test of the hypotheses outlined by Situated SA. Thus, for offloaded information participants should be more likely to turn to the radar display prior to answering probe questions than for information stored internally.

A key aspect of this method is also varying the type of information queried. We used two categories of information: We varied query specificity (specific vs. general)

Table 1. Sample questions from four categories

	Low priority	High priority
General	In the past 2 min (20 nm), did most AC enter into your sector from the east?	Are any co-altitude AC within 10 nm of each other?
Specific	In the past 2 min (20 nm), did SWA892 exit your sector from the south?	Are any AC that are co-altitude with ASQ4253 within 10 nm of it?

and priority (high vs. low). By combining the levels of these categories, four unique types of information can be examined (see Table 1).

2   Method

2.1   Participants

Participants for this study were 17 students enrolled in an aviation sciences program at Mount San Antonio College, studying for careers in air traffic control. Students completed a 16-week ATC radar internship in the Center for Human Factors in Advanced Aeronautics Technologies (CHAAT) at California State University, Long Beach prior to participating in the study. Over the course of the internship, participants trained on the simulation technology, gaining familiarity with the system.

2.2   Apparatus and Scenarios

Participants managed air traffic on a medium fidelity radar display that is simulated through the Multi Aircraft Control System (MACS) [8]. Participants' experimental stations consisted of two computer monitors, a keyboard, and mouse. One monitor served as an ATC radar screen for managing air traffic in simulated Indianapolis Center (ZID-91) airspace, and contained screen capture software for replaying scenarios for later analyses. The second monitor was a touchscreen probe station. It was used to present participants with SA probe queries as well as capturing pictures in rapid succession of participants responding to these queries.

The MACS simulation software provided participants with NextGen tools that enabled the issuing of commands to an aircraft equipped with NextGen communications. Available tools included Datalink communications, trial planner with conflict probe, and conflict alerting. The latter warned participants when two NextGen equipped aircraft were in conflict with one another for a potential loss of separation (LOS; two aircraft within 5 nautical miles horizontally and 1000 ft vertically of one another). The trial planner provided participants with a means of adjusting flight plans for equipped aircraft, and advised participants of potential conflicts before they implemented changes.

Participants completed a 10-min training scenario and four 40-min test scenarios of 50 % mixed aircraft equipage; half of the aircraft throughout the scenario were equipped with NextGen technology and half were unequipped. The number of aircraft steadily increased through the first 10 min of each scenario, then remained consistent for the duration of the run. Six planned conflicts were built into each trial scenario.

2.3 Probe Queries

A subject matter expert (a retired ATC with 39 years of air traffic management experience) as well as a group of 12 ATC students (not part of this study), assisted in the development and classification of all probe queries. The questions were designed to address the different levels of each of the two information types of interest: specificity (general vs. specific) and priority (high vs. low). Questions topics included past and present conflicts, aircraft position, altitude, direction of aircraft travel, handoff status, and frequency changes. General questions asked about information such as conflicts, altitudes, position, and direction for any or all aircraft in the sector. Specific questions asked about information that related to a single, specified aircraft. High priority questions were related to events or information that required swift action (within 1 min of probe question presentation) to prevent a LOS, collision, or other incident. Low priority questions were those related to events or information that did not require immediate action (within 3 min of probe question presentation), but could be put off until later without incident.

SA measures were collected using the SPAM probe technique on the touchscreen monitor. Each scenario contained 12 queries: two specific/high priority questions, two general/high priority questions, two specific/low priority questions, two general/low priority questions, and four additional questions that were not relevant to this study. Queries began three minutes into a scenario and were asked once every three minutes after that. Query positions were counterbalanced by question category, as well as for predicted number of "yes" or "no" responses for each category, with four orders of probe queries developed for each of the four scenarios, producing 16 total orders. Aircraft call signs, waypoints, and cardinal directions were modified as questions were applied to each scenario. All questions were used an equal number of times, with no identical or similar questions appearing in the same scenario for a given participant. All relevant questions were accompanied by two response buttons marked "Yes" and "No." Participants were instructed to answer probe queries as quickly and as accurately as possible.

2.4 Image Collection

The touchscreen probe station contained a built-in web camera (see Fig. 1). The SPAM software was programmed to activate the camera in conjunction with the presentation of probe queries. Probe stations were positioned to the right of each ATC radar scope and angled precisely at a 45°clockwise rotation from the radar display (see Fig. 2). This angle allowed for the web cameras to capture participant eye glances between the probe screens and the radar scopes.

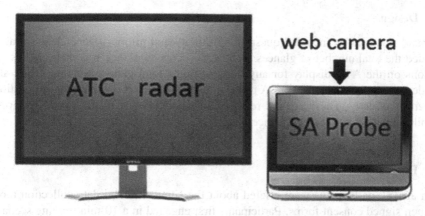

Fig. 1. The ATC view of the radar station monitors. SA probe stations were placed to the right of the ATC radar screen. The camera, represented by a small white dot in the above figure, was located on the top of the SA probe station and was continuously in the on position throughout the simulation.

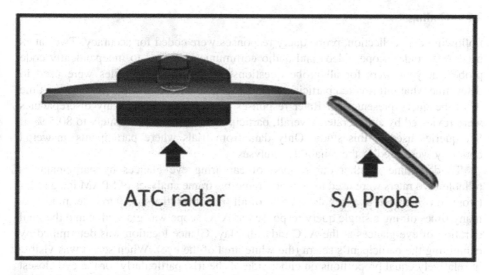

Fig. 2. A view from above of the monitors for the ATC radar station. SA probe stations were positioned to promote head turns and drastic eye glances for retrieval of answers to probe questions not stored in an internal mental model.

The SPAM software was programmed to instruct the camera to take pictures once every 100 ms from the moment the "Ready?" button was pressed, without the use of flash to minimize probe intrusiveness. The program saved image files with the time of image capture and organized them for later analyses. These time stamps allowed researchers to determine total number and duration of eye glance at the ATC display.

2.5   Design

Independent variables included question specificity and priority. Dependent variables included the total number of glances at the ATC scope (a glance was measured as eye fixations on the ATC display for any duration), and total glance duration. They also included reaction time to answer SA probe questions correctly and number of questions answered correctly. These are not reported in what follows. Instead, we focus on a reliability analysis for the eye glance data.

2.6   Procedure

Upon arrival, participants were briefed about the simulation and data collection tools, and then signed consent forms. Participants first engaged in a 10-min training scenario to familiarize themselves with MACS. They then completed four 40-min trial scenarios, which had been counterbalanced for scenario number and probe query order. Participants were given at least a 10 min break after the training and between each trial.

2.7   Coding

Following data collection, probe query responses were coded for accuracy. Two raters used ATC radar scope videos and audio communication files to independently code probe query answers for all probe questions. Video and audio files were used to determine what information participants had access to and commands given at the time of probe query presentation. Rater responses were compared and any discrepancies were reviewed by a third rater. Overall, participants responded accurately to 80.5 % of SA queries used in this study. Only data from trials where participants answered correctly were used in the reliability analyses.

To determine whether our method of capturing eye glances by participants is reliable, two raters were used to conduct frame-by-frame analyses of SPAM image files (from runs included in a sample of 25 % of all trials from the study) to determine how many times during a single query response the ATC scope was glanced at and the total duration of eye glances at the ATC radar display. Glance location was determined by examining the participant's sclera (the white area of the eye). When sclera was visible in relatively equal proportions on either side of the iris, particularly for the eye closest to the probe station, the image was coded as a participant viewing the probe station. When a participant was glancing to the right of the image (toward the location of the ATC display), and sclera was dominant on the left side of the iris in the participant's right eye, with little to no sclera visible on the right side of the iris, the image was coded as a participant viewing the ATC radar scope. The total number of glances for a single probe query was tallied. Timestamps were collected for the images corresponding to each glance onset to the ATC display and glance end, and the duration of each glance was calculated. Durations of all glances for a single probe query were totaled.

Any images that did not meet the criteria for eye glances or that appeared to have participants speaking were examined closely to determine the circumstances for the query response. The image sets for these queries were analyzed with the voice communication files to determine if the participant was managing traffic or engaging in some other activity, despite having indicated that he or she was ready to respond to the probe query. Performing activities in conjunction with responding to probe queries would interfere with the SA measurement, thus these queries were excluded from analyses. A total of 92.4 % of the image sets for queries with accurate responses met the criteria to be usable for analyses.

3 Results

Inter-rater reliability for the coding of total number of eye glances was 95 %. Overall, researchers were consistent with their assessment of what counted as an eye glance. Total glance latency was a little more difficult to get precisely times for, as it could easily be off by one or two SPAM image files; occasionally the program would duplicate an image. The inter-rater reliability for the exact times was low (.14), but the average difference in total eye glance latency between two raters was .57 s without removing any outliers. Once outliers were removed (3 outliers out of 80 total coded questions used for testing rater reliability) the average difference in total glance latency between the two raters dropped to .29 s. When compared to the actual averages of total eye glance latency, these numbers are quite small. Average total eye glance latencies for questions used for analyses ranged from 2.81 to 5.79 s, depending on information type (i.e., general/low priority, general/high priority, specific/low priority, and specific/ high priority), with standard errors ranging from .32 s to .58 s. Inter-rater differences in total eye glance latency for all questions were therefore lower than the smallest standard error for a single information type.

4 Discussion

Combining the SPAM technique and measures of eye glance duration and latency provides a reliable, straightforward means of testing implications of a situated approach to SA. Through this method we will be able to examine whether operators store particular SA-related information internally or offload it onto a display, accessing it only as needed. We will analyze the eye glance data to determine whether operators glance more at displays and for longer when asked about specific information and low priority information than for general and high priority information.

Importantly, we will also be able to validate a key assumption of SPAM, which is that longer latencies to answer probe questions reflect whether operators are answering based on what they represent internally, or whether they are accessing information on a display. Although this claim has been made by proponents of SPAM [6, 7], it has not been validated to our knowledge. We will do so by correlating probe latencies with eye glance frequency and duration.

The method discussed herein is a promising way of addressing broad questions about where operators store SA related information – in internal memory or offloaded onto a display. This can be studied by examining whether or not operators have to look at primary operational display to prior to answering probe questions. However, this eye glance method is likely to be insufficient if more precise details are required as to where on the display they are looking. Indeed, if one wants to determine, for example, whether operators know exactly where on the display to access information or have to look around for it, the present method would likely be insufficient. The number of glances might be telling, but in such circumstances eye tracking technology would likely be most effective, and indeed some research on SA has made use of it [9, 10]. Fortunately, not all questions require that level of precision. This is because eye tracking technology is generally cumbersome to implement, expensive, and the data obtained difficult to process. Whenever it is possible reliable, but low-tech alternatives are desirable.

Acknowledgement. This project was supported by NASA cooperative agreement NNX09AU66A, *Group 5 University Research Center: Center for Human Factors in Advanced Aeronautics Technologies* (Brenda Collins, Technical Monitor).

References

1. Endsley, M.R.: Measurement of situation awareness in dynamic systems. Hum. Factors Ergon. Soc. **37**(1), 65–84 (1995)
2. Chiappe, D.L., Strybel, T.Z., Vu, K.P.L.: Mechanisms for the acquisition of situation awareness in situated agents. Theor. Issues Ergon. Sci. **13**(6), 625–647 (2012)
3. Chiappe, D.L., Strybel, T.Z., Vu, K.P.L.: A situated approach to the understanding of dynamic situations. J. Cogn. Eng. Decis. Making (in press)
4. Rensink, R.A.: The dynamic representation of scenes. Vis. Cogn. **7**(1–3), 17–42 (2000)
5. Sparrow, B., Liu, J., Wegner, D.: Google effects on memory: cognitive consequences of having information at our fingertips. Science **333**, 776–778 (2011)
6. Durso, F.T., Dattel, A.R.: SPAM: The real-time assessment of SA. In: Banbury, S., Tremblay, S. (eds.) A cognitive approach to situation awareness: Theory, measures, and application, pp. 137–154. Ashgate, Burlington (2004)
7. Durso, F.T., Truitt, T.R., Hackworth, C.A., Crutchfield, J.M., Nikolic, D., Moertl, P.M., Ohrt, D., Manning, C.A.: Expertise and chess: A pilot study comparing situation awareness methodologies. In: Garland, D.J., Endsley, M.R. (eds.) Experimental Analysis and Measurement of Situation Awareness, pp. 295–303. Embry-Riddle Aeronautical University Press, Daytona Beach (1995)
8. Prevot, T.: Exploring the many perspectives of distributed air traffic management: the multi-aircraft control system MACS. In: Chatty, S., Hansman, J., Boy, G. (eds.) Proceedings of the HCI-Aero 2002, pp. 149–154. AAAI Press, Menlo Park (2002)
9. Hauland, G.: Measuring individual and team situation awareness during planning tasks in training of en route air traffic control. Int. J. Aviat. Psychol. **18**(3), 290–304 (2008)
10. Moore, K., Gugerty, L.: Development of a novel measure of situation awareness: The case for eye movement analysis. Proc. Hum. Factors Ergon. Soc. Annu. Meet **54**(19), 1650–1654 (2010)

Map-Based Linking of Geographic User and Content Profiles for Hyperlocal Content Recommendation

Steven Verstockt[1]($\boxtimes$), Viktor Slavkovikj[1], and Kevin Baker[2]

[1] ELIS Department - Multimedia Lab Gaston Crommenlaan,
Ghent University–iMinds, 8 Bus 201, 9000 Ghent, Belgium
`steven.verstockt@ugent.be`
[2] Department of Geography, Ghent University–Rotuteyou,
Krijgslaan 281, S8, 9000 Ghent, Belgium

Abstract. In this paper we describe a novel approach for map-based linking of users with content (and vice versa) based on their geographic profiles. The proposed technique facilitates hyperlocal content recommendation targeted to the user's geographic footprint. The generation of the geographic user profiles (GUP) is based on user-logged activity analysis. The result of this analysis is a heat map of the geographic keypoints where the outdoor activities were performed. For the geographic content profiling (GCP), we use the available geotags and perform address geocoding and geographic named entity recognition to extract additional locations from the media objects. In order to link the GCP to the GUP, and to be able to recommend the hyperlocal content that fits the user's current profile, heat map analysis is performed using geographic analyzing tools. The GEOprofiling demonstrator, which is evaluated on real activity profiles and different media types, shows the feasibility of the proposed approach.

Keywords: Recommendation · Geo-profiling · Geocoding · Heat map analysis

1 Introduction

Local media plays an important role in each of our lives. It is both functional, telling us what is going on in our direct environment, and emotional, helping us to feel like we belong to a local community. Furthermore, consuming media on the move has become a mainstream behavior for many of us, and more and more we expect media to be related to our current location. As such, it is not surprisingly that a huge increase is observed in the volume and usage of (online) local media. Traditional media, like newspapers, have observed this tendency, and start to focus more on localized content in their digital environments [1]. A similar evolution is seen on social media platforms, allowing people to connect to timely, relevant information at the hyper local level. Whoo.ly, for example, is a web service that provides neighborhood-specific information based on Twitter posts [2] and Field Trip is Google's hyperlocal recommendation engine for nearby sights and destinations.

© Springer International Publishing Switzerland 2015
S. Yamamoto (Ed.): HIMI 2015, Part II, LNCS 9173, pp. 53–63, 2015.
DOI: 10.1007/978-3-319-20618-9_6

Up till now, however, the way in which media platforms support (hyper)local content is still too much focused on large and static geographic areas/communities, i.e., too 'glocal', and does not take into account the specific and dynamic geographic footprint of the user. Similarly, the geographic description of the content is still too high-level and the annotation is still very often a manually labor-intensive process. Automatic geographic analysis at the micro level of the content, e.g. on scenes in a video or paragraphs in a text, is needed to create more valuable geographic content descriptions, which on their turn lead to more relevant queries.

The higher content scores on the two major dimensions of hyperlocality, i.e., geography and time, the more relevant the content becomes to the individual and the less it becomes to the masses. In order to be successful, hyperlocal content needs to be targeted to a specific user in a well-defined area and a specific time window. Nowadays, however, hyperlocal content recommendation is mostly based on static information from user profiles or device-based localization techniques. Furthermore, geographic annotation on the content level is mostly restricted too some geographic keywords or global geotags, which only marginally support the hyperlocality concept.

Within this paper, we propose a more dynamic and effective approach for hyperlocal content recommendation based on geographic user and content profiling. The idea behind our methodology is based on the criminal investigative methodology of geographic profiling that analyzes the locations of a connected series of crimes in order to identify the likely area where a serial offender resides. In a similar way, location data of a specific user can be analyzed to generate his geographical footprint and geographical media analysis (GMA) can be used to do the same for content items. The user-specific location data can be collected in several ways, e.g., by analyzing GPS activity loggings [3] or social media based events and check-ins [4, 5]. For GMA, both text-based [6] and image-based techniques [7–9] can be used. Due to the generic character of the proposed GEO-profiling architecture, shown in Fig. 1, we do not put any restrictions on the GMA and the geographic user analysis methods. If they are able to produce a geographic content profile (GCP) or geographic user profile (GUP), i.e., a kind of map-based feature layer, they can be integrated in our set-up.

In order to link the GCPs to a particular GUP (and vice versa), our approach makes use of map-based analysis techniques. Firstly, a heat map is created for the GUP and GCPs taking into account several GUP and GCP features, like the trajectory, date and duration of the user activities, and the number of occurrences of a particular place in the media item and its distance to other places in the GCP description. Secondly, we project both heat maps on each other and calculate the heat map score for each of the content items. Finally, the content items with the highest scores are recommended.

The remainder of this paper is organized as follows. Section 2 focuses on the GCP generation and discusses three techniques that we have used to retrieve the geographic content locations. Furthermore, more information is given on the GCP features that are used for the content heat map generation. Subsequently, Sect. 3 proposes our method for GUP generation based on GPS activity logging. As already mentioned before, other techniques for GUP and GCP generation can easily be integrated. Next, Sect. 4 presents the demonstrator of the GEOprofiles-based content recommendations. Finally, Sect. 5 lists the conclusions and points out directions for future work.

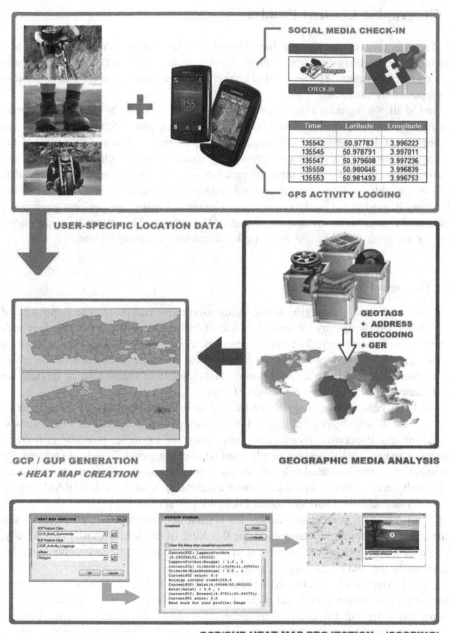

Fig. 1. General architecture of map-based hyperlocal content recommendation using geographic user and content profiling.

2   Geographic Content Profiles

For the generation of the Geographic Content Profiles (GCPs), three different GMA techniques are investigated. Important to remark is that, within this paper, we only focus on textual content. However, also image, video and audio content can be used in the proposed architecture.

First of all, we focus on existing geotagged media. Currently, however, only a small portion of online content is geotagged (mostly pictures and video, and only limited number of text documents and web pages). Furthermore, we observed that most of the geotagged content is only labeled with a geographic tag at the global level, i.e., not within the content itself, which limits its practical applicability in our set-up. Secondly, we focus on address geocoding of available addresses in the content. Some document structuring is needed too easily extract these elements. Finally, we perform geographic named entity recognition on the textual part of the content. This micro-level technique is by far the most valuable one for hyperlocal content recommendation.

2.1   Geotagged Media Content

Over the last decade, geotagging is becoming used more and more. The popularity of the geotag is on the rise by the increased use of Internet capable mobile devices with built-in GPS functionality. The geotag itself is a form of metadata which marks a multimedia object, such as an image, video or text message, with its location information (longitude and latitude coordinates). The majority of recent capture devices are able to automatically assign these kinds of tags.

The huge benefit of geotagged media is that it allows multimedia objects to be browsed and arranged geographically. Photo-sharing websites such as Flickr (www.flickr.com) and Panoramio (www.panoramio.com), for example, provide millions of geotagged images contributed by people from all over the world. In order to retrieve the multimedia data that is related to a specific location, one can choose from several social media web services that support geo-based queries, such as the PANORAMIO geo-picture service and the DBPedia-based FlickrWrappr service [10].

Up till now, the number of geotags for textual documents and web pages is still limited, and the geographic annotation for this kind of content is mostly a manually, error-prone process. However, we expect more and more mechanisms coming soon that will facilitate the textual geotagging process.

A good example of a geotagged webpage is shown in Fig. 2. This webpage of the video archive of Vlaanderen Vakantieland (i.e., a touristic program on Flemish television), has a geotag for each of its episodes. Additional textual information and addresses are linked to each of these geotags, which can be analyzed using the address geocoding and geographic entity recognition that are discussed in the next sections. The set of locations for each episode, i.e. the 'global' geotag, the address location(s) and/or the geographic entities detected in the episode's textual description, will be fed to the GCP generator.

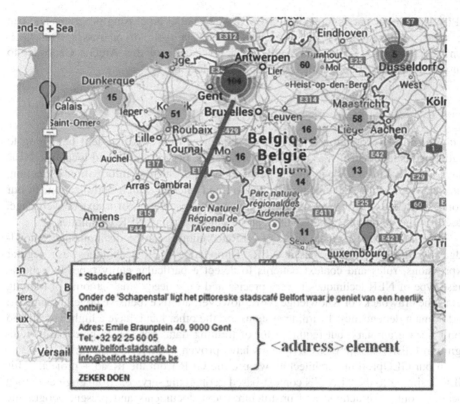

Fig. 2. Geotagged media content – a video archive of a touristic program on Flemish television

2.2 Address Geocoding

Address geocoding is the process of determining an estimated latitude and longitude position for the location of a street address. In the example given in Fig. 2, address geocoding can be used to convert the address element "Emile Braunplein 40, 9000 Gent" into the coordinates (51.053657, 3.723612) of this place.

Address geocoding process. First of all, a parser will break down the address element into a number of components. Then, address standardization identifies each address component (e.g., street number, street name, city and zip code) and places them in order. Finally, the values for each address component are matched to the reference database and an estimate of the spatial location is given. Several matching problems can occur during this process, e.g., misspelled street names, outdated reference data, and incorrect numbers.

In order to automatize the address geocoding process, several address geocoding web services can be used, such as the ArcGis Geocoder[1] and the Mapquest Geocoding

---

[1] http://geocode.arcgis.com/arcgis/index.html.

API.[2] The former one is integrated in ESRI's geospatial processing programs and can be used, for example, to automatically geocode a table of addresses. Our GCP generator, which is scripted in ArcPy, also makes use of this ArcGis Geocoder to convert address elements in their corresponding locations.

2.3   Geographic Entity Recognition (GER)

Named Entity Recognition (NER) labels sequences of words in a text belonging to predefined categories such as the names of persons, organizations, and locations. NER plays a significant role in many application domains, such as information extraction, summary generation, document classification and internet search optimization. In our work, NER is used for creating a geographical representation of a text or web page, based on the geographic entities that can be detected using NER techniques.

In broad terms, two main types of NER techniques can be distinguished: knowledge based and learning based NER. Knowledge NER techniques use regular expressions, rules and context patterns to detect a particular entity type. In general, these type of NER techniques is very precise and only needs small amount of training data. The drawbacks of Knowledge NER, however, are its expensive development cost and domain dependency. Learning systems, on the other hand, have a higher recall and don't need grammars, but require a lot of training data. For Geographic Entity Recognition (GER), learning based systems have proven to perform best [6, 11, 12].

In our GEOprofiling architecture we use the GER from the iRead + project.[3] This GER is similar to the CLAVIN context-based geotagging service.[4] Both engines extract locations out of structured and unstructured text documents and present geographic features with metadata. The geocoding in both systems is done with help of a gazetteer, i.e. an existing list of entities that automatically can be generated from other data sources. In iRead + , we use an Open Street Map (OSM) gazetteer of Flanders and the discovered geographic entities are weighted according to their occurrence frequency. In Fig. 3, an example is shown of our GER.

2.4   GCP Heat Map Generation

For the generation of the GCP heat maps we make use of a base layer with polygons of interest. In our set-up, these polygons are the town/city boundaries in Flanders. However, other types of polygons, and levels of detail, can be used within the proposed architecture. For each of the GCP locations (geotag, address or geographic entity), we update the polygon that holds it coordinates. In the current set-up, we add the number of occurrences of the GCP location in the content item and weight it with its distance to other places in the GCP description. However, more advanced features/weighting can

---

[2] http://www.mapquestapi.com/geocoding/.

[3] http://www.iminds.be/en/projects/2014/03/05/iread.

[4] http://clavin.berico.us/clavin-web/.

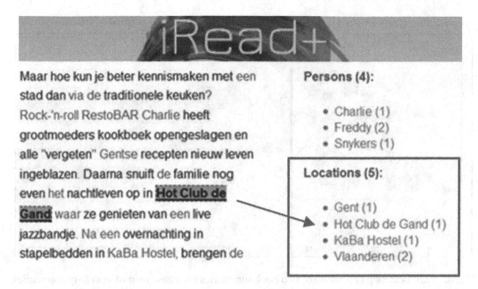

Fig. 3. Geographic entity recognition within iRead + platform. Location entities are detected using an Open Street Map (OSM) gazetteer of Flanders.

easily be integrated. Finally, to benefit the neighborhood of the GCP locations and to make the content recommendation more flexible, adjacent polygons can be updated with a distance-weighted fraction of the GCP location score.

Figure 4 shows an example of our GCP heat map generation. Two book summaries are projected onto the base map of town/city boundaries in Flanders. The first book summary, of which the GCP locations are represented by the white dots, is geographically spread over multiple polygons. The second book ($\sim$ red dots) its locations are fixed at a single polygon. To calculate the heat map score for each of the content items, the resulting GCP heat map will be projected on the heat map of the Geographic User Profile (GUP), which is discussed in the next section.

3   Geographic User Profiles

The generation of the geographic user profiles (GUP) in our GEOprofiles architecture is based on user-logged activity analysis [13, 14]. Several platforms, like Garmin Connect and RouteYou, provide web services to query the activities of a particular user. Figure 5 shows a data table of one of the author's activities performed during a specific time period. Each of the listed features, such as the startTime, distance and duration, can be used in the weighting of the GUP. Currently, only startTime and duration is used.

The data table in Fig. 5 corresponds to the geographic locations shown on top of Fig. 6. For each of the logged activities, a more detailed view of the trajectory can be retrieved. Such a detailed trajectory can be used to weight all the polygons in the base layer that overlap with the trajectory.

Geographic Content Profile (GER-plot of book summaries)

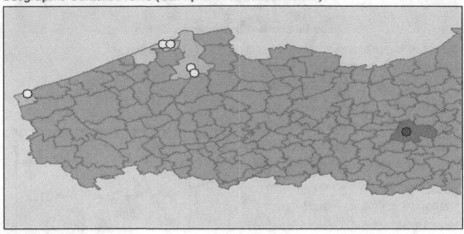

Fig. 4. GCP heat map generation of two book summaries on a base map of town/city boundaries in Flanders.

activityId	startTime	distance	duration	startLat	startLong	calories
253738029	12/15/2012 12:45	45415.94	7670.423	50.97757	3.995826	1589.014
253738039	12/12/2012 13:07	43297.07	8730.193	50.8687	4.174751	1554.885
253738046	12/9/2012 12:12	40000.49	7467.78	51.15179	3.899916	1136.033
253738060	11/25/2012 12:30	40909.83	7280.539	50.9779	3.99608	1351.068
253738078	11/17/2012 9:51	33456.61	5840.738	50.88465	3.892722	1212.882

Fig. 5. Data table of user-specific activity loggings

Fig. 6. Detailed view of a specific activity trajectory

An exemplary GUP heat map, on top of the same base map as used in the GCP creation, is shown in Fig. 7. Important to remark is that similar GUP heat maps can be generated for users' social media based events and check-ins. It is even possible to use geographic entity recognition to analyze a user his status messages. Similarly as for

Geographic User Profile (Duration-Location plot of recent Garmin Activities)

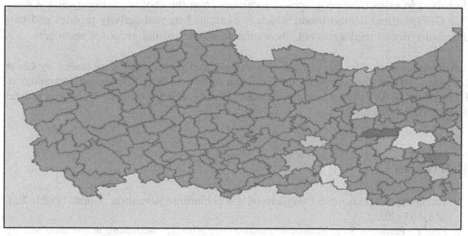

Fig. 7. GUP heat map generation of user-logged activities on a base map of town/city boundaries in Flanders.

the GCP heat maps, adjacent polygons can be updated with a distance-weighted fraction of the GUP location scores.

4 GEOprofiles Demonstrator

In order to evaluate the proposed GEOprofiles architecture for hyperlocal content recommendations, we have developed an ArcPy-ArcGis demonstrator. The demonstrator has been tested on two test cases: the hyperlocal book recommendation (using geographic analysis of book summaries) and hyperlocal recommendation of video episodes from the video archive discussed in Sect. 2.

For both test cases, the heat map score for each content item is calculated by projecting the GCP heat map on the GUP heat map. For each polygon, we multiply the corresponding GCP and GUP polygon values and count them together. Finally, the content items with the highest scores are recommended to the user. The subjective results of both test cases were very positive. Future work will focus on a thorough objective evaluation. Important to remark is that, besides the geographic contextualization of the content, also other contextualization techniques can be added on top of the proposed GEOprofiles architecture.

5 Conclusions

The production and consumption of hyperlocal content is thriving. This paper proposed a novel approach for hyperlocal content recommendation which uses map-based linking of users with content. Key components of the proposed GEOprofiles architecture are the geographic content and user profiles. Several techniques are discussed to extract the geographical locations from the content and user-related data. The GEOprofiling demonstrator, which is evaluated on real activity profiles and two different types of media content, shows the feasibility of the proposed approach.

Acknowledgments. The research activities as described in this paper were funded by Ghent University, iMinds, the Institute for the Promotion of Innovation by Science and Technology in Flanders (IWT), the Fund for Scientific Research-Flanders (FWO-Flanders), the Belgian Federal Science Policy Office, and the EU.

References

1. Paulussen, S., D'heer, E.: Using citizens for community journalism. Journal. Pract. **7**(5), 588–603 (2013)
2. Hu, Y., Farnham, S.D., Monroy-Hernandez, A.: Whoo.ly: facilitating information seeking for hyperlocal communities using social media. In: Proceedings of the SIGCHI Conference on Human Factors in Computing Systems, CHI 2013, pp. 3481–3490. ACM, New York, NY (2013)
3. Biagioni, J., Krumm, J.: Days of our lives: assessing day similarity from location traces. In: Carberry, S., Weibelzahl, S., Micarelli, A., Semeraro, G. (eds.) UMAP 2013. LNCS, vol. 7899, pp. 89–101. Springer, Heidelberg (2013)
4. McKenzie, G., Adams, B., Janowicz, K.: A Thematic Approach to User Similarity Built on Geosocial Check-ins. Lecture Notes in Geoinformation and Cartography - Geographic Information Science at the Heart of Europe, pp. 39–53. Springer International Publishing, Heidelberg (2013)
5. Van Canneyt, S., Van Laere, O., Schockaert, S., Dhoedt, B.: Using social media to find places of interest: a case study. In: Proceedings of the 1st ACM SIGSPATIAL International Workshop on Crowdsourced and Volunteered Geographic Information, GEOCROWD 2012, pp. 2–8 (2012)
6. Martins, B., Chaves, M.S., Silva, M.J.: Assigning geographical scopes to web pages. In: Losada, D.E., Fernández-Luna, J.M. (eds.) ECIR 2005. LNCS, vol. 3408, pp. 564–567. Springer, Heidelberg (2005)
7. Chen, D.M., Baatz, G., Koser, K., Tsai, S.S., Vedantham, R., Pylvanainen, T., Roimela, K., Chen, X., Bach, J., Pollefeys, M., Girod, B., Grzeszczuk, R.: City-scale landmark identification on mobile devices. In: Proceedings of IEEE Conference on Computer Vision and Pattern Recognition, CVPR 2011, pp. 737–744 (2011)
8. Mamei, M., Rosi, A., Zambonelli, F.: Automatic analysis of geotagged photos for intelligent tourist services. In: Proceedings of the 2010 Sixth International Conference on Intelligent Environment, pp. 146–151 (2010)
9. Yeh, T., Tollmar, K., Darrell, T.: Searching the web with mobile images for location recognition. In: Proceedings of the IEEE Computer Society Conference on Computer Vision and Pattern Recognition, CVPR 2004, pp. 76–81 (2004)
10. Becker, C., Bizer, C.: Exploring the geospatial semantic Web with DBpedia mobile. J. Web Semant.: Sci. Serv. Agents World Wide Web **7**(4), 278–286 (2009)
11. Mikheev, A., Moens, M., Grover, C.: Named entity recognition without gazetteers. In: Proceedings of the 9th Conference of the European Chapter of the Association for Computational Linguistics, EACL-1999, pp. 1–8 (1999)

12. Silva, M.J., Martins, B., Chaves, M., Afonso, A.P., Cardoso, N.: Adding geographic scopes to Web resources. Comput. Environ. Urban Syst. **30**, 378–399 (2005)
13. Verstockt, S., Slavkovikj, V., De Potter, P., Vandersmissen, B., Slowack, J., Van de Walle, R.: Automatic GEO-MASHUP generation of outdoor activities. In: Proceedings of 11th International Conference on Advances in Mobile Computing & Multimedia, MoMM 2013, pp. 1–4 (2013)
14. Verstockt, S., Slavkovikj, V., De Potter, P., Van de Walle, R.: Collaborative bike sensing for automatic geographic enrichment. IEEE Signal Process. Mag. **31**(5), 101–111 (2014)

Scene Feature Recognition-Enabled Framework for Mobile Service Information Query System

Yi-Chong Zeng[1(✉)], Ya-Hui Chan[1], Ting-Yu Lin[1], Meng-Jung Shih[1], Pei-Yu Hsieh[1], and Guan-Lin Chao[2]

[1] Data Analytics Technology and Applications Research Institute, Institute for Information Industry, Taiwan, Republic of China
{yichongzeng, yhchan, timlin, mengjungshih, simcoehsieh}@iii.org.tw
[2] Department of Electrical Engineering, National Taiwan University, Taiwan, Republic of China
guanlinchao@gmail.com

Abstract. Aiming at development of intelligent service on mobile device, this paper proposes a new travel information query method, which combines image acquisition device, image recognition, and recommendation technologies. The framework of information query consists of four components, including passive information query, active information query, trip scheduling, and information management. A prototype application is designed to demonstrate the feasibility of smart tourism guidance by mobile device. User can browses stationary information through the application program. Furthermore, the user takes pictures and transmits it to cloud server. The cloud server hosts image recognition and delivers the corresponding information to the user. For trip scheduling, the prototype recommends the proper trips to guide user easily, which is referred to user's preferences with location based service. The resultants will demonstrate that the prototype is implemented by an application program runs on mobile device. It is powerful to search for travel information and to generate trip schedules.

Keywords: Intelligent services · Recommendation · Information query · Recognition · Trip scheduling

1 Introduction

In the tourism domain, mobile and wireless technologies have been pointed out as one of the most influential technological innovation because of the fast growing of intelligent devices are in a huge user base [1]. In the past, tourists got traveling information only from few stationary channels such as tour guide books, television programs, and discussion among friends, so the information retrieving process could be monotonous and time wasting [2]. After the late 1990s, thanks to the popularization of the computer and the developing of the internet, most people can easily search for and get the traveling information by using internet connected computers. In the kind of Internet

© Springer International Publishing Switzerland 2015
S. Yamamoto (Ed.): HIMI 2015, Part II, LNCS 9173, pp. 64–74, 2015.
DOI: 10.1007/978-3-319-20618-9_7

Content Provider (ICP) environment, traveling information were usually shared by formal content provider or website owner, causing the insufficient richness of information. After 2000, wireless communication and smart mobile device technology have grown rapidly, and mobile services have turned into mainstream and changed the traditional information environment from ICP into Wireless Content Provider (WCP). The change not only makes people interact with each other and get the information easily, but also revises the traditional tourists behavior and information service model, allowing the tourists to grasp the real-time and personal information anytime, anywhere [3].

In the era that mobile devices are taking over, more and more tourists search for travel information and make travel plans via mobile devices [4]. Mobile technology with the properties of ubiquity, timely, flexibility and localization frees the tourists from being restricted to passive and fixed-point information gathering [5], dramatically changing the information service model to be directly and personalized. There is a variety of mobile travel information services in the market. The services are categorized into before-travel, during-travel, and after-travel services based on when the users use them listed in Table 1. And the most emphasis is how to enhance the information interactive services, to fulfill tourists' demand at the right place and right time. The smart mobile device is therefore become the most important connecting channel to this purpose [6].

Table 1. Mobile services in tourism domain

Before-travel	During-travel	After-travel
• Point of Interest search	• Nearby information search	• Photo management and sharing
• Restaurant and accommodation reservation	• Route Navigation	• Travel experience editing and sharing
• Transportation check and booking	• Temporary changes in Itinerary	• Budget management
• Weather check	• Bring your own device (BYOD) interactive guide	
• Itinerary planning	• Shopping discount search and push	

The main task that most users perform via mobile devices is information search, especially for those which are in urgently needed. However, restricted by the screen size and the operation mode, searching for and browsing information via mobile devices is not as easy as via the traditional computers [7]. To resolve the difficulties in operating on mobile devices, the user interfaces, including information inputting, should be simple and easy enough [8]. In the past, researches have been focused on optimal design for inputting texts and searching via mobile devices. Recently, as hardware technology to smart mobile devices improves, non-contact inputting (such as, microphone, camera, or NFC wireless sensor technology) is becoming an alternative to text inputting and the new solution for information retrieving on mobile devices [9]. This paper will investigate the new travel information querying method, which combines mobile phone camera, image recognition and recommendation technology.

Almost all mobile phones come with an integrated camera or image acquisition device. Camera is typically used for taking pictures for posterity purposes; however, there are many other applications for which the images may be applied [10]. Instead of typing the key word to search for and get the information on mobile phone, tourists can now use a powerful image-based mobile search service, which functions by sending an image acquired by a phone camera to a server. The server hosts visual-based recognition and personalized recommendation engines, returns the personalized, appropriate search results back to the user, and helps the tourists know the attraction or finishes a suitable itinerary in convenience. The visual input in the real environment is a new and rich interaction modality between a mobile user and vast information [11], and it brings advantages as follows:

- Compared to traditional text searching, the visual input saves a lot of time that typing may cost.
- In most of the traveling conditions, the tourists are not familiar with the searching object. Visual input by camera can solve the main problem that users have no idea to come out an appropriate key word or suffer from the language problem.
- Unique feature of image makes the searching results more precise than ever.

The tourism industry acknowledges that the launch of value-added mobile services is clearly identified as the main factors affecting the competitiveness of the tourism market [12]. Mobile phones with cameras present new opportunities and challenges for mobile information association and retrieval, and it is clear that visual information query will eventually be integrated with other mobile traveler supported services and change the way the tourism industry works today.

In this paper, we propose the framework of information query system, which is implemented by the prototype application (APP). The system consists of passive information query, active information query, trip scheduling, and information management. In the beginning, user browses information on APP. Furthermore, he/she can take a picture to get the corresponding information. Combined user's preferences with location based service (LBS), the prototype recommends the proper trips to guide user easily. The rest of this paper is organized as follows: design and prototype implementation are described in Sects. 2 and 3, respectively. The resultants will be shown in Sect. 4, and the concluding remarks will be drawn in Sect. 5.

2 Design

The proposed prototype implements the framework of information query system for tourism. Figure 1 shows the block diagram of the proposed prototype. The details of functions in the prototype are introduced as follows:

- **Passive Information Query.** In the conventional applications, theme-based query and context menu are common approaches to obtain information. Considerations of user's preference and time consumption, seven types of themes have been set in the prototype. Those themes include "culture & heritage", "gourmet guide", "offshore islands", "ecotourism", "hot springs", "LOHAS", and "night markets". User acquires information by pressing the theme of interest. For instance, when user presses the button of "gourmet guide", he/she can browse the introductions of restaurants in Taiwan. Similarly, user clicks the item in the context menu to acquire the corresponding information.

- **Active Information Query.** In order to provide friendly query, active information query are realized by two approaches, namely LBS-based query and recognition-based query. User clicks the button of "Nearby", then, landmarks, restaurants, and exhibitions around user are marked on Google Map. He/she clicks the icon on the map to acquire the information of the spot. For recognition-based query, user clicks the button of "Scan" to take picture. Cloud server analyzes the shoot picture and then delivers the related information to mobile device.

- **Trip Scheduling.** Pressing the button of "Quick Plan", user picks the dates, the locations, and the themes of interest, and the prototype creates a new trip schedule against different periods. Shaking the mobile device, a new schedule is created. Furthermore, the other way to create trip schedule is referred to the result of recognition-based query. The recognition result is treated as a seed point of interest (POI) to create trip schedule.

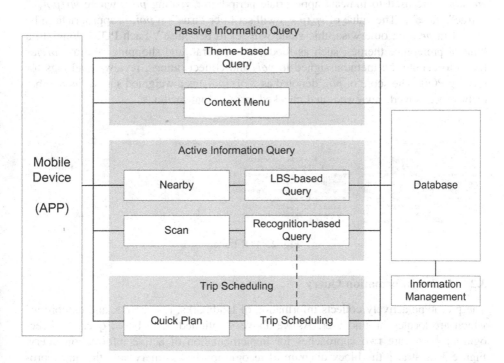

Fig. 1. Block diagram of the proposed prototype

- **Information Management.** The tasks of information management have two: (1) systematically retrieval information via defined metadata, (2) flexibly update information. Especially for implementation of active information query, we flexibly add/delete the reference images and the information without altering the system.

3   Prototype Implementation

3.1   Information Management

For collecting and updating POI related information, a POI table is built and maintained. Figure 2 shows a screenshot of a partial POI table. This table integrates information collected from multiple sources and is used for further analysis and recommendation.

The structure of a record in POI table is shown in Table 2. For the x-th POI (denoted as poi_x), the denotations $id(poi_x)$, $name(poi_x)$, $add(poi_x)$, and $des(poi_x)$ represent the identity, the name, the address, and the description of poi_x, respectively. The denotation $ts(poi_x)$ is the expected number of hours that tourists spend on poi_x, where ts $(poi_x) \in \{1,2,3\}$. Each POI has its own business hours. In this system, a day is divided into three time intervals, i.e., $period_1(8:00 \sim 11:59)$, $period_2(13:00 \sim 16:59)$, and $period_3(18:00 \sim 20:59)$. Three Boolean variables, namely $vp_1(poi_x)$, $vp_2(poi_x)$, and $vp_3(poi_x)$, are used to indicate appropriate periods for visiting poi_x, where $vp_i(poi_x) \in$ {"true","false"}. The value of $vp_i(poi_x)$ will set to be "true", if poi_x is appropriate to be visited in $period_i$; otherwise, this value will set to be "false". Each POI belongs to a kind of preference themes, such as foods, arts, natural, and shopping. We use $prefer$ (poi_x) to denote the theme assigned to poi_x and collect ratings, reviews, and tags for scoring POIs. The score of poi_x denoted as $score(poi_x)$ is a weighted sum of its number of browsed, saved, reviewed, and checked in on social media.

name	address	description	morning	afternoon	night	stayTime	preference	N_score
國父紀念館	臺北市信義區仁愛路4段505號	為紀念國父孫中山先生之革命行誼、人格，並發揚其偉1	1	0		2	PF4	0.832867883
自來水博物館	臺北市中正區思源街1號	位於新店溪與景尾溪之匯流處東水發源地--臺北水源1	1	0		2	PF4	0.763128186
臺北市立美術館	臺北市中山區中山北路3段181號	1983年開館，是當前臺座現代美術館，定期與展品的1	1	0		2	PF4	0.181458318
臺北市當代藝術館	臺北市大同區長安西路39號	臺北當代藝術館為古蹟建築，紅磚教室、木框提釘、臺1	1	0		1	PF3	0.247367807
北投溫泉博物館	臺北市北投區中山路二號	這座早在日治時代就事用最名的溫泉公共浴場，有著當1	1	0		2	PF4	0.9313585
臺北市立天文科學教育館	臺北市士林區基河路363號	你知道天文的奧妙嗎？臺北市立天文科學教育館。半圓1	1	0		1	PF3	0.077399463
台北探索館	臺北市信義區市府路1號1樓	身為臺北人，你知道臺北事嗎？歡迎來到台北探索館。1	1	0		1	PF3	-0.110846117
信義公民會館	臺北市信義區松勤街50號	在臺北信義區的一隅，有座懷著當情與的低矮住宅，這1	1	0		2	PF4	0.390225065
北投文物館	臺北市北投區幽雅路32號	北投文物館具豐的木構建築座落於19204年，幕時臺北北1	1	0		2	PF4	0.192132432

Fig. 2. POI table

3.2   Active Information Query

The prototype actively collects information of landmarks, restaurants, and exhibitions which are located around user. As we above mentioned, LBS-based query and recognition-based are two approaches for implementation of active information query. Figure 3 illustrates the block diagram of recognition-based query, and the query process to mobile device is described as follows:

Table 2. Structure of a record in POI table

ID	Name	Address	Description	Time Spend
$id(poi_x)$	$name(poi_x)$	$add(poi_x)$	$des(poi_x)$	$ts(poi_x)$
Visiting Period			Preference	Social Score
$vp_1(poi_x)$	$vp_2(poi_x)$	$vp_3(poi_x)$	$prefer(poi_x)$	$score(poi_x)$

- User takes a picture which is called as query image, and then the image is transmitted to cloud server.
- After implementing image recognition, the application receives the information with respect to query image from the second database in cloud server.

The objectives of cloud server have two: (1) finding a reference image in database as like as the query image, and (2) delivering the information to the application. The query process to cloud server is described as follows:

- Corner detection is applied to reference images and query image to find key pixels.
- Extract features of key pixels. Histogram of oriented gradient (HOG) is employed to represent feature descriptor of key pixel [13, 14].
- The first database stores feature descriptors of all reference images, and the information corresponded to the reference image are stored in the second database.
- Compute feature similarity between the query image and the reference images. The most similar reference image is found with the maximum feature similarity.
- The identity of the selected reference image (which is denoted as $id(poi_x)$ in Table 2) is an index to acquire the related information in the second database. Then, the information is delivered to the application.

3.3 Trip Scheduling

Given date, location and user's preference, the system recommends schedule of trip with respect to opinions on social media. The structure of schedule of trip is listed in Table 3. Each hour is regarded as a time slot. The three periods, $period_1(8:00 \sim 11:59)$, $period_2(13:00 \sim 16:59)$, and $period_3(18:00 \sim 20:59)$, consist of 4, 4, and 3 time slots, respectively. Let $slot(i,j)$ be the j-th time slot in the i-th period, and $slotnum(period_i)$ be the total number of time slots in $period_i$, where $i \in \{1,2,3\}$ and $j \in \{1,2,3,4\}$. The $rec(i,j)$ denotes the recommendation POI at $slot(i,j)$. In our definition, a recommendation POI crosses one or more time slots. For each period, the seed POI is given by either recognition-based query or user's selection.

For example, the seed POI, "Taipei National University of the Arts", puts into $period_1$, and it derives from the result of recognition-based query. Let tc and TH be, respectively, target county and preference themes, where $TH = \{theme_{k1}, theme_{k2}, \ldots\}$. In $period_2$, given tc and TH, the system selects a seed POI (denoted as poi_s) which

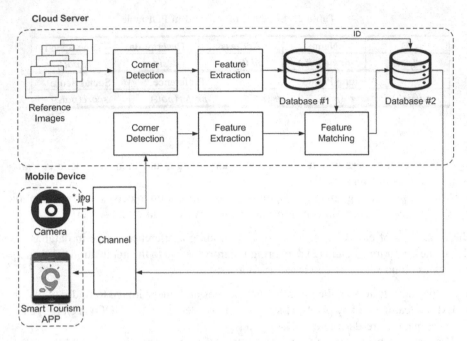

Fig. 3. Flowchart of recognition-based query

belongs to tc and TH with the highest social score. The selection of poi_s follows the four conditions:

(1) $add(poi_s) \subset tc$,
(2) $vp_i(poi_s) = true$,
(3) $\exists\ theme_k \in TH$ such that $theme_k(poi_s) = true$,
(4) $\forall\ poi_x, poi_x$ satisfies (1) $\sim$ (3) $\land\ poi_x \neq poi_s \rightarrow score(poi_x) \leq score(poi_s)$.

Whenever poi_s is selected, $ts(poi_s)$ time slots will become occupied. For example, assuming that "Taipei Water Park" is the seed POI selected for $period_2$ and $ts($"Taipei Water Park"$) = 2$. After selecting "Taipei Water Park" as the seed POI in $period_2$, the time slots $slot_{(2,1)}$ and $slot_{(2,2)}$ become occupied, and the values of $rec_{(2,1)}$ and $rec_{(2,2)}$ become "Taipei Water Park".

The system continues selecting subsequent POIs for filling the schedule. As the last occupied time slot in the schedule of $period_i$ is $slot(i,l)$, and $rec(i,l) = poi_a$. The next POI, denoted as poi_b, is selected according to the following conditions:

(5) $add(poi_b) \subset tc \land distance(poi_a, poi_b) \leq 3$ km,
(6) $vp_i(poi_b) = true$,
(7) $\exists\ theme_k \in TH$ such that $theme_k(poi_b) = true$,
(8) $l + ts(poi_b) \leq soltnum(period_i)$,
(9) $\forall$ other unselected poi_x, poi_x satisfies (5) $\sim$ (8) $\land\ poi_x \neq poi_b \rightarrow score$
     $(poi_x) \leq score(poi_b)$.

Table 3. Structure of schedule of trip

Period	Time	Time slot	Recommendation POI
$period_1$ (morning)	08:00 ~ 08:59	$slot_{(1, 1)}$	$rec_{(1, 1)}$
	09:00 ~ 09:59	$slot_{(1, 2)}$	$rec_{(1, 2)}$
	10:00 ~ 10:59	$slot_{(1, 3)}$	$rec_{(1, 3)}$
	11:00 ~ 11:59	$slot_{(1, 4)}$	$rec_{(1, 4)}$
Lunch	12:00 ~ 12:59		
$period_2$ (afternoon)	13:00 ~ 13:59	$slot_{(2, 1)}$	$rec_{(2, 1)}$
	14:00 ~ 14:59	$slot_{(2, 2)}$	$rec_{(2, 2)}$
	15:00 ~ 15:59	$slot_{(2, 3)}$	$rec_{(2, 3)}$
	16:00 ~ 16:59	$slot_{(2, 4)}$	$rec_{(2, 4)}$
Dinner	17:00 ~ 17:59		
$period_3$ (night)	18:00 ~ 18:59	$slot_{(3, 1)}$	$rec_{(3, 1)}$
	19:00 ~ 19:59	$slot_{(3, 2)}$	$rec_{(3, 2)}$
	20:00 ~ 20:59	$slot_{(3, 3)}$	$rec_{(3, 3)}$

The function $distance(poi_a, poi_b)$ is defined as the geographical distance between poi_a and poi_b. The condition (5) makes sure that the distance between two POIs is acceptable. The condition (8) ensures that the total number of time slots spent by all recommendation POIs will not exceed $slotnum(period_i)$. The system continues selecting subsequent POIs until either all time slots in $period_i$ are occupied or there is no POI satisfying the conditions of (5) ~ (9).

4   The Resultants

The prototype application employed the Qualcomm Vuforia software development kit (SDK) to implement feature extraction and feature matching [15]. The APPs for Android and iOS can be downloaded from [16, 17], respectively. Three resultants were emphasized on and presented in this paper, including LBS-based query, recognition-based query, and trip scheduling. In what follows, the resultants are introduced in detail.

4.1   LBS-Based Query

Pressing the button of "Nearby" in the main frame, the application immediately presented the related information of landmarks, restaurants, and exhibitions around the user, which is realized based on LBS. Figure 4(a) shows the map marked the icons after pressing "Nearby". Figure 4(b) and (c) depict the detailed information of two spots corresponded to the red icon and the blue icon in Fig. 4(a), respectively.

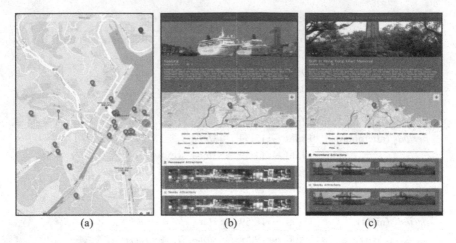

(a)   (b)   (c)

Fig. 4. LBS-based query: (a) the result map marked the icons of landmarks, (b) the information of Keelung corresponded to the red icon in (a), and (c) the information of Memorial Park corresponded to the blue icon in (a) (Color figure online).

4.2 Recognition-Based Query

Pressing the button of "Scan" to shoot a picture, the application transmits the shot picture to cloud sever and then receives the related information after image recognition. Figure 5(a) and (b) show the query image and the corresponding information, respectively. Figure 5(a) is the image shot in the activity handbook. This function was practically verified through the activity of Taipei National University of the Arts in October 2014, and the activity called as "Kuandu Story Guidance".

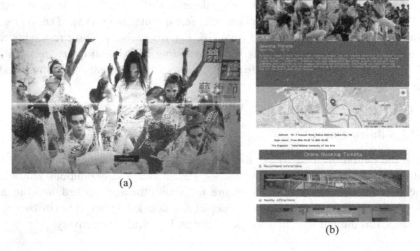

Fig. 5. Recognition-based query: (a) the image shot in the activity handbook of "Kuandu Story Guidance", and (b) the activity information.

4.3   Trip Scheduling

Given date, location, and user's preference theme, the application planned a schedule of trip. Furthermore, the prototype designed to generate another trip schedule by shaking mobile device. In the case of Fig. 6(a), the user set a two-day trip in two locations, and he/she was interested in the theme of gourmet. Figure 6(b) shows two different schedules of trip under the same initial settings. It is obvious that the right-side schedule has one spot more than the left-side schedule has.

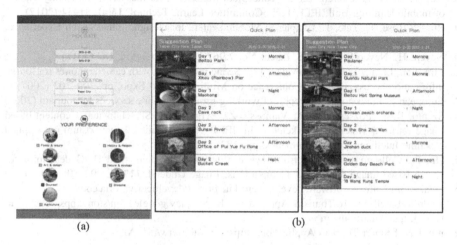

(a)   (b)

Fig. 6.   Trip scheduling: (a) frame of initial setting, and (b) two schedules of trip under the same initial settings.

5   Conclusions and Future Work

This paper introduces the framework of information query system, and it is realized by a prototype application. We propose a new travel information query scheme, which combines image acquisition device, image recognition, and recommendation technology. The resultants demonstrate that four functions run efficiently to provide user travel information, and those functions include passive information query, LBS-based query, recognition-based query, and trip scheduling. The future work will focus on how to actively provide user more appropriate information by analyzing user's query behavior.

References

1. Buhalis, D., Law, R.: Progress in information technology and tourism management: 20 years on and 10 years after the internet—the state of eTourism research. Tour. Manag. **29**(4), 609–623 (2008)
2. Liao, J.-M.: A usability study on a real-time travel information system in 3G mobile phone applications. Master's thesis, National Cheng Kung University, Taiwan (2005)

3. Lu, M.-P.: Market research of taiwan internet social networking system mobilization development. Master's thesis, National Chiao Tung University, Taiwan (2009)
4. Kray, C., Baus, J.: A survey of mobile guides. In: Workshop on HCI in Mobile Guides, 5th International Symposium on HCI with Mobile Devices and Services, pp. 1–5 (2003)
5. Siau, K., Lim, E.P., Shen, Z.: Mobile commerce: promises, challenges and research agenda. J. Database Manage. **12**(3), 4–13 (2001)
6. Carlsson, C., Walden, P., Yang, F.: Travel MoCo: a mobile community service for tourists. In: The 7th International Conference on Mobile Business, pp. 49–58 (2008)
7. Langelund, S.: Mobile travel. Tourism Hospitality Res. **7**(3/4), 284–286 (2007)
8. Ali, A., Ouda, A., Capretz, L.F.: A conceptual framework for measuring the quality aspects of mobile learning. Bull. IEEE Tech. Committee Learn. Technol. **14**(4), 31–34 (2012)
9. Russell-Rose, T., Tate, T.: Chapter 8: Mobile search. In: Designing the Search Experience, pp. 219–251 (2013)
10. Neven, H., Neven Sr., H.: U.S. Patent No. 7,962,128, Washington, DC (2011)
11. Lim, J.H., Li, Y., You, Y., Chevallet, J.P.: Scene recognition with camera phones for tourist information access. In: IEEE Conference on Multimedia and Expo, pp. 100–103 (2007)
12. European Commission. Final report of working group on mobile services for tourism (2003)
13. Szántó, B.M., Pozsegovics, P., Vámossy, Z., Sergyán, S.: Sketch4match - content-based image retrieval system using sketches. In: IEEE 9th International Symposium on Applied Machine Intelligence and Informatics, pp. 183–188 (2011)
14. Hu, R., Collomosse, J.: A performance evaluation of gradient field HOG descriptor for sketch based image retrieval. J. Comput. Vis. Image Underst. **117**(7), 790–806 (2013)
15. Qualcomm Vuforia software development kit. https://developer.vuforia.com/
16. Android-based Smart Tourism Application. https://play.google.com/store/apps/details?id= tw.org.iii.ari.smarttourism
17. iOS-based Smart Tourism Application. https://appsto.re/tw/nE_tM.i

Decision-Support Systems

What Methodological Attributes Are Essential for Novice Users to Analytics? – An Empirical Study

Supunmali Ahangama(✉) and Danny Chiang Choon Poo

Department of Information Systems, School of Computing,
National University of Singapore,
13 Computing Drive, Singapore 117417, Singapore
supunmali@comp.nus.edu.sg

Abstract. Data analytic methodologies proposed to improve the productivity of a data analytic process have failed due to user resistance for changing their existing working practices. Thus, an attempt was made in this paper to determine methodological attributes influencing user acceptance, using literature on software engineering methodology adoption, Theory of Diffusion of Innovation and Technology Acceptance Model. Through a survey carried out among novice users we found that the relative advantage and result demonstrability of the analytical model development process as well as the usefulness of knowledge management are significant attributes affecting usage intention of an analytics methodology. The theoretical and practical implications for effective implementation of data analytic methodologies too are mentioned.

Keywords: Data analytics · Methodology · Survey · Diffusion of innovation · Technology acceptance

1 Introduction

A data analytic methodology is useful in improving the productivity of the data analytic process and quality of the output generated. A process model includes a set of processing steps that should be followed by practitioners and researchers involved with analytics projects. A methodology can be described as an instance of a process model with sets of inputs, outputs, tasks and specifications on 'how to perform' a certain activity [1]. This allows to carry out projects in a systematic manner as it defines the policies, procedures and processes that should be followed by analysts [2]. For example, there are methodologies like CRISP-DM [3] and SEMMA [4] for data mining (DM) and USAM for Health Analytics (HA) [5].

Even though there are visible benefits of using an analytics or a DM methodology, it could be noted that such methods are not dispersed among the practitioners. According to studies carried out related to software engineering (SE) methodologies' it is found that user resistance is the main reason for not using new methodologies [6, 7]. Thus, it is important to understand the essential factors affecting methodology acceptance and this study plans to understand individual's attitude towards using a

© Springer International Publishing Switzerland 2015
S. Yamamoto (Ed.): HIMI 2015, Part II, LNCS 9173, pp. 77–88, 2015.
DOI: 10.1007/978-3-319-20618-9_8

methodology. Since it is considered that the initial decision to adopt will be made at individual user level, this study was performed at individual level rather than at organizational level. Furthermore, most of these projects are usually carried out by one or two individuals at the organization context (with interactions with many stakeholders); the decisions will be made at individual level rather than at organizational level based on their personal preferences. In this paper, the target users will be novice users as they will be new to the analytic process and their learning curve will be steep if there is no methodology to follow. Thus, undergraduate students who will be learning the techniques were used as novice users.

In this study, focus was on the perception of the technical aspect of the methodology (methodological attributes) instead of looking at the actual primary methodological attributes. It was considered that their perception of the artifact will depend on how they perceive these primary attributes [8] and the individual perception about an innovation's potential effect on his/her work will impact the intention to use [6]. Potential individual novice users will adopt the methodology based on their perception [9] of how its attributes fulfill their requirements. The research question (RQ) is, "what methodological attributes affect the novice analyst's decision to use it". Thus this study will make it possible to understand an individual's attitude towards using an analytic methodology that is deemed suitable for its users.

2 Conceptual Background

Even though there are several DM methodologies, there is a dearth of empirical studies related to adoption of such methodologies. The available studies are confined to case studies carried out in organization context on adoption of business intelligence (e.g. [10]). Thus, it was necessary to examine the literature related to SE methodology adoption. Several authors have carried out empirical studies on the adoption of a SE methodology by individual users in an organization. Even among those studies, most are carried out as case studies [11].

Recently, researchers have started to look at methodologies as an innovation, if they are reflected to be new by the potential users [8]. Most of the authors have carried out these user acceptance studies in a technology acceptance and innovation diffusion perspective (as a technology innovation rather than considering as a process) [2, 8]. For example, they have used Technology Acceptance Model (TAM) [12] and Diffusion of Innovation (DOI) [13] to examine technical characteristics of the methods [7, 14]. Also, Raghavan and Chand [15] suggested that DOI is suitable for methodological acceptance studies [6]. However, earlier, it was under the notion that these theories are used to study the acceptance and diffusion of products (not for practices). In a similar sense, Riemenschneider et al. [7] used TAM, TAM2, Theory of Planned Behavior (TPB), Perceived Characteristics of Innovating (PCI), Model of Personal Computer Utilization (MPCU) to examine the acceptance of SE processes and found the relationship between perceived usefulness, voluntariness, compatibility and subjective norm to be significant with intension to use the SE process. Hardgrave et al. [6] reported similar findings using TAM and DOI.

It was decided to draw Roger's DOI Theory with TAM as the theoretical foundation of this study. DOI is selected due to several reasons. First, based on DOI, the innovation's adoption rate is most extensively determined by its characteristics. Second, DOI is applied at individual level. Third, as previously mentioned, DOI had been used in studying methodological characteristics [6]. Thus, it will provide necessary theoretical basis to study the RQ. In previous methodological studies, DOI characteristics had given mixed results relevant to the significance of their influence on adoption [6, 7]. Similarly, TAM also provides a suitable theoretical foundation on intention to use based on ease of use and usefulness of the innovation [12].

On the other hand, some authors have examined the effect of organizational characteristics effect on the acceptance of SE processes. They have shown organizational culture [16], management support, training and external support influencing the acceptance of them [17]. In this study, organizational characteristics were not considered as undergraduate students who do not have prior work experience were used for the study. Johnson et al. [18] identified a list of beliefs underlying intention formation to use object oriented development and it includes several usefulness elements like process usefulness and communication usefulness. According to Nambisan [19], IT plays four roles in new product development (NPD) in IS, namely, process management, project management (PM), communication management (CM) and knowledge management (KM). Latter three can be considered as supporting dimensions on process management. Thus, perceived usefulness of each of these three dimensions can be considered as separate usefulness elements.

3 Research Model and Hypotheses

The proposed research model developed based on the conceptual background outlined above is presented in Fig. 1. The dependent variable is the intention to use a methodology. According to Rogers [13], perceived characteristics of innovations are relative advantage, compatibility, complexity (replaced as ease of use), trialability and observability (replaced as result demonstrability). The variations to the characteristics were made based on the prior literature and according to the context studied. The justifications for the replacement for each construct are given in subsequent sections. Process management (analytical data model development process) is represented by the five model characteristics. The final two constructs represent the usefulness of supporting elements to the main model development process.

Ease of Use. Ease of use refers to 'the degree to which a person believes that using a particular system would be free of effort' [20]. Ease of use has been used to address complexity construct in technology adoption literature [8]. As such, instead of using complexity, ease of use is considered [9]. The decision to use a methodology will depend on whether it is perceived to be easy to understand and use. Therefore, if the users find a methodology is free of mental and physical effort and it is easy to learn, they are likely to use it.

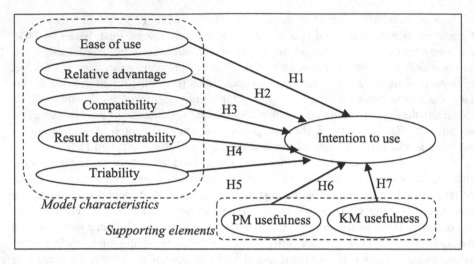

Fig. 1. Research model

HYPOTHESIS 1 (H1): Ease of use has a positive effect on the intention to use a methodology

Relative Advantage. Relative advantage refers to 'the degree to which an innovation is perceived as being better than its precursor' [9]. This is the lead of methodologies like CRISP-DM over using an ad hoc approach. Excellence of a methodology can be measured through improvement of status as well as through improvement of efficiency and productivity [6, 8] or meeting intended purpose [9]. Similarly, perceived usefulness in TAM demonstrates conceptual equivalence to the relative advantage [9]. The expectation of developing a structured process is to improve the application of the analytics techniques to the processed data based on the user requirements and coming up with better results while having a low learning curve which would not have been possible by using an ad hoc approach. Therefore, if the novice users find that using a methodology for analytics will be useful for their work there is a prospect of successful deployment of it.

HYPOTHESIS 2 (H2): Relative advantage has a positive effect on the intention to use a methodology

Compatibility. Compatibility refers to 'the degree to which an innovation has been consistent with existing values, needs, and past experiences of potential adopters' [9]. If an individual is used to certain habits, there may be resistance from users towards a new process. In analytics, if the users are used to their own personal styles of carrying out analytics projects which have been developed based on their experiences, they may find it hard to change their practices. Even for novice users, if there is a certain style learnt earlier, they may find it hard to deviate from it as it is the initial practice that had been engraved in them. Therefore, if the methodology is compatible with past experiences and learning of the users, they will use a new methodology.

HYPOTHESIS 3 (H3): Compatibility has a positive effect on the intention to use a methodology

Result Demonstrability. Result demonstrability refers to 'the degree to which the results of using an innovation are observable by others' [8, 9]. Thus, as indicated by Moore and Benbasat [9], if it is perceived that the methodology provides observable results which can be communicated then it is considered that the results are demonstrable. Poor communication of usage benefits and quantification of results in an analytic method will make it hard for others to see the results as highlighted in any other methodological domain [8]. Particularly, as novice users, they will be more concerned about the quantification of results. Therefore, if the results are demonstrable the novice users will intend on using a methodology.

HYPOTHESIS 4 (H4): Result demonstrability has a positive effect on the intention to use a methodology

Triability. Triability refers to 'the degree to which an innovation may be experimented with before adoption' [9]. Ability of the users to test the method before making the final decision will allow them to make an informed decision about the method. This allows users to understand the un-communicated benefits of the method [8]. Therefore, if the novice users can try out a methodology before adopting, there will be a positive influence on the prospect of using it.

HYPOTHESIS 5 (H5): Triability has a positive effect on the intention to use a methodology

Usefulness. Perceived usefulness is 'the degree to which an individual expects that following a methodology will improve job performance' [6]. Even in analytics projects, PM, KM and CM are playing a key role. Since no (or minimum) attention has been given to CM in existing methodologies, it is not considered in this study even though the result demonstrability focuses on some attributes of CM. As perceived usefulness of the process is evaluated through relative advantage from DOI [9], the process management was not considered here. Thus, only the influence of usefulness of PM and KM on usage intention of the process model will be considered here.

Considering the risk involved in analytic projects, having PM elements in the process model is useful [21]. PM is to establish reasonable plans for performing and managing the project [22] and it includes estimating the work to be performed (milestones), identifying necessary resources and creating schedules. In considering the uncertainty involved in analytic outputs, PM is useful in scheduling the resources and keeping the project on track. Therefore, novice users will find PM useful to plan out and perform their tasks.

HYPOTHESIS 6 (H6): Usefulness of project management has a positive effect on the intention to use a methodology

KM is an important part in a methodology. Chan and Thong [2] considered KM as a strategic perspective to be considered in implementation of agile methodologies in

SE. Similarly, in an analytic methodology too, achieving positive KM outcomes (create, retain and transfer of knowledge) are crucial for learning and in replicating the best practices [23]. Success of an analytic project depends on how knowledge is retained within the project teams and how they are transferred to team members. Therefore, such a suitable means for KM will be useful for novice users in coping with and adopting the organizational context in less time thus increasing their intent to use a methodology.

HYPOTHESIS 7 (H7): Usefulness of knowledge management has a positive effect on the intention to use a methodology

4 Research Methodology

As described earlier, students following two courses relevant to analytics are used for the survey. This was carried out among undergraduate students studying a module related to HA and a module related to business intelligence at a local university having around 30,000 students. Also, as a requirement for the module, they are assigned to read research papers related to analytics every week. Thus, those students were considered to have sufficient understanding of analytics and as they are new to analytic context we considered them as novice users. The survey was carried out at the end of the semester (during the last lecture), with the assumption that the students would have gained a satisfactory idea of their subject through lectures, assignments and reading material (research papers). Even though, both modules are related to analytics, certain differences between those modules increase the generalizing ability of the results. This is made possible as one module deals with analytics in general and the other module is designed specifically for HA.

4.1 Operationalization of Constructs

To develop the survey instrument, existing validated scales were used.[1] To measure, the intention to use a methodology, scales were adapted from Venkatesh et al. [24] by considering the research context of analytics. Items for compatibility and usefulness were adapted from Hardgrave et al. (2003). Items from previous literature were adapted to measure the other perceived characteristics of a methodology [9]. Seven-point Likert scale ranging from 1 (strongly-disagree) to 7 (strongly-agree) was used in the questionnaire for all the constructs expect for usage intention. Usage intention was measured using a scale ranging from 1 (no) to 3 (yes). In addition, gender was used as a control in the model analysis. To ensure the appropriateness of the questions, the questionnaire was reviewed by three IS researchers prior to the actual survey. Then a separate pilot study was conducted among 20 3rd and 4th year undergraduate students to improve the validity and reliability of the instrument.

---

[1] Survey questionnaire is not given in this paper due to page limitation. Please email authors should you require further details.

4.2 Data Collection

As survey participants we used undergraduate students studying analytics in two courses. The questionnaire was given as paper based surveys to students. It was decided to not to use online surveys as the students may not be receptive to them and there is a high chance of them delaying in providing responses to the survey. Even though, online surveys are flexible and one can create and distribute surveys (via emails, social networks) and collect and organize data very swiftly, we decided to use the paper based surveys to ensure participation of all the selected students in the survey. However, the participation in the survey was totally on a voluntary basis. The questionnaire was distributed during the break of the lesson on the last day of the module at the end of the semester with prior permission from the respective lecturers. A three to four minutes verbal explanation on what is an analytic methodology and about the survey was given in addition to the explanations on CRISP-DM given in the front page of the questionnaire.

A total of 114 completed and valid responses were collected. As a general rule, there should be at least 10 times of number of constructs as the minimum sample [25, 26]. As there are only seven constructs, it is reckoned that the sample size of 114 is adequate. The correlations of the sample are given in Table 1. The descriptive statistics indicates that students are between age of 20-28 years (mean 23.75 years and standard deviation of 1.75).

Table 1. Correlations

	I	RA	C	EU	RD	T	KM	PM	CR
I	**0.82**								0.86
RA	0.21	**0.83**							0.92
C	0.22	0.36	**0.88**						0.91
EU	0.14	0.28	0.58	**0.85**					0.89
RD	0.42	0.36	0.42	0.41	**0.77**				0.81
T	0.08	0.20	0.18	0.22	0.13	**0.79**			0.76
KM	0.29	0.25	0.12	-0.11	0.17	-0.01	**0.77**		0.84
PM	0.24	0.36	0.31	0.10	0.18	0.14	0.53	**0.79**	0.85

Notes. Leading diagonal shows the squared root of AVE of each construct,
I = intention, RA = relative advantage, C = compatibility, EU = ease of use,
RD = result demonstrability, T = triability, KM = knowledge management,
PM = project management, CR = composite reliability

5 Data Analysis and Results

The data analysis was performed using the partial least squares (PLS) technique with SmartPLS. PLS was selected as it enables to analyze measurement model (relationship between items and constructs) and structural model (relationship among constructs) [27] with multi items constructs and not restrictive on the sample as covariance based structural equation modeling (SEM) [28]. Since PLS is primarily intended to be used in early stages of theory development [27] and as this is one of the first attempts to do a causal predictive analysis on the behavioral intention to use a methodology for analytics, PLS was considered to be suitable for this study.

5.1   Instrument Validation

The convergent validity and discriminant validity of the constructs were assessed to demonstrate the construct validity. Convergent validity indicating the extent to which two or more items measure the same construct is examined using (1) standardized path loadings of items, (2) composite reliability (CR), and (3) average variance extracted (AVE), [28]. The standardized path loadings are significant (at t-value > 1.96) with a threshold of 0.7. It is considered appropriate to have at least 0.7 for CR and 0.5 for AVE [28]. Thus, based on the results it could be noted that the construct's convergent validity was acceptable. The squared root of AVE of each construct and the CR are shown in Table 1. The discriminant validity indicates the degree to which items that measure different constructs differ [25]. This is satisfied by having a square root of the AVE for each construct greater than its correlation with other constructs (Table 1) [28]. Based on the results discriminant validity is supported.

5.2   Hypotheses Testing

After establishing the instrument validity, PLS was used for hypotheses testing. Gender was used as the control variable as it is expected that the males may be more willing to take advantage of available opportunities [29] and prefer a structured process. Age is not considered as a control variable as all the users are from the same age category. In Fig. 2, path coefficients and significant results are indicated. Perceived relative advantage, result demonstrability, triability and usefulness of KM indicate a significant effect on the intention to use the methodology for analytics. However, the direction of relationship between triability and intention to use is negative (path coefficient = -0.047), and as such the hypothesis H5 is not supported. All the other significant relationships indicate a positive influence and as such H2, H4 and H7 are supported. The explanatory power (R^2) is 0.31 and it is above the threshold of 0.10 as specified by Falk and Miller [30].

6   Discussion

Several important relationships were found from this study. First, characteristics such as relative advantage and results demonstrability are important attributes in a process. Novice users may also like to get a relative advantage over others by using a methodology. They will see that using a method will enable them to kick start the project rather than going in ad hoc directions. Similar results could be observed in considering the previous studies related to methodology adoption too. Consistently, relative advantage is the only attribute that is significant in those studies while other attributes are insignificant [8]. Even through the study carried out by Riemenschneider et al. [7]

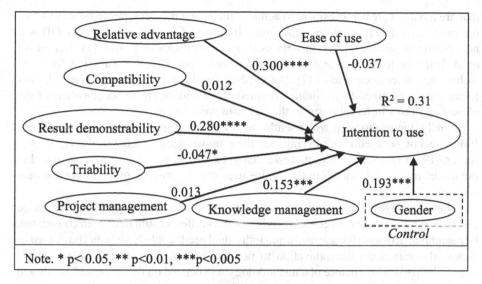

Fig. 2. Results of hypothesis tests

using five theoretical models this is justified as perceived usefulness (referred as relative advantage in DOI) was the only construct significant in all models. Novice users will like to see if the progress of their performance is shown or demonstrated and also giving them the possibility of showing their progress even to their seniors. Specially, this will be a motivator and will allow getting further assistance from the senior analysts.

Second, it is noted that novice users find KM components in a methodology as useful. Thus, having documentation will be useful in managing the creation and transfer of knowledge. In their study, Chan and Thong [2] also indicate the usefulness of KM in SE methodology usage. However, it is important to explore how KM is used in successful data analytic teams.

Third, it is interesting to note that triability is showing a negative relationship. It is a negative relationship of low significance. Nevertheless, individuals might not try out a new innovation if they perceive risks in doing so or if there is no continued accessibility [31]. Accessibility should be provided through proper information management (access to specific information on usage, e.g. user manual). Furthermore, it is hard to explore a process without actually using in a real context. Thus, this may be indicating a negative relationship. However, this can be explored further with KM.

Fourth, compatibility and ease of use are not proving significant relationships. Hardgrave et al. [6] found the relationship between compatibility and SE methodology usage to be significant but weak. CRISP-DM like methodologies are introduced independent of the data, analytic tools or analytic algorithms that are being used. As such compatibility may not be a relevant issue. However, if a practice is more compatible with the type of projects that are been carried out and if they are compatible with existing work practices, the users will be more willing to use a process model [6]. As such, when developing new methodologies it is important to look into components that are having a greater alignment to actual settings and project types to be included in the process model. It is interesting to note that ease of use (complexity in DOI) was not significant among all five models used by Riemenschneider et al. [7]. Hardgrave et al. [6], also found similar results in their study too. This is a variation from the technology acceptance studies [2]. Rather than considering the ease of use, a higher focus should be given to providing comprehensive and complete specification of the phases and tasks to be followed in the full data analytic process.

Finally, the relationship with usefulness of PM is not significant. For novice users, PM may not be useful in carrying out their university projects. However, in real settings PM is important. Thus, it is essential to explore how PM can be incorporated in the model in a useful manner to the novice user starting projects in real organizational settings.

There are several limitations encountered in this study and suggestions for future research. First, additional antecedents and interaction effects could have been considered. For example, personal characteristics and individual needs could have been considered as factors that can affect the motivation to use the method. Mohan and Ahlemann [8] conceptualize that acceptance of a methodology will depend on the individual needs and it will motivate them to use the methods. They had considered individual needs as moderators. Second, a large sample size could be used to further test the robustness of the results and study could be further extended to other user groups, such as very fresh employees in an analytics organization.

7 Conclusion

In this paper, it is elaborated on how a survey is used to explore methodological attributes that are important for adoption of a data analytic methodology by novice users. The conceptual model used for hypothesis testing was developed based on DOI and TAM. The survey data showed that the relative advantage and result demonstrability of the analytical model development process as well as the usefulness of knowledge management are the attributes affecting the usage intention of an analytics methodology. Usage of these findings in developing a methodology will help in reducing the user resistance for its adoption.

References

1. Mariscal, G., Marbán, Ó., Fernández, C.: A survey of data mining and knowledge discovery process models and methodologies. Knowl. Eng. Rev. **25**, 137–166 (2010)
2. Chan, F.K., Thong, J.Y.: Acceptance of agile methodologies: a critical review and conceptual framework. Decis. Support Syst. **46**, 803–814 (2009)
3. Chapman, P., Clinton, J., Kerber, R., Khabaza, T., Reinartz, T., Shearer, C., Wirth, R.: CRISP-DM 1.0 Step-by-step data mining guide (2000)
4. SAS Enterprise Miner: SEMMA (2008, 27 February 2014). http://www.sas.com/technologies/analytics/datamining/miner/semma.html

5. Ahangama, S., Poo, D.C.C.: Unified structured process for health analytics. Int. J. Med. Health Pharm. Biomed. Eng. **8**, 744–752 (2014)
6. Hardgrave, B.C., Davis, F.D., Riemenschneider, C.K.: Investigating determinants of software developers' intentions to follow methodologies. J. Manage. Inform. Syst. **20**, 123–152 (2003)
7. Riemenschneider, C.K., Hardgrave, B.C., Davis, F.D.: Explaining software developer acceptance of methodologies: a comparison of five theoretical models. IEEE Trans. Softw. Eng. **28**, 1135–1145 (2002)
8. Mohan, K., Ahlemann, F.: What methodology attributes are critical for potential users? understanding the effect of human needs. In: Mouratidis, H., Rolland, C. (eds.) CAiSE 2011. LNCS, vol. 6741, pp. 314–328. Springer, Heidelberg (2011)
9. Moore, G.C., Benbasat, I.: Development of an instrument to measure the perceptions of adopting an information technology innovation. Inf. Syst. Res. **2**, 192–222 (1991)
10. Catley, C., Smith, K., McGregor, C., Tracy, M.: Extending CRISP-DM to incorporate temporal data mining of multidimensional medical data streams: a neonatal intensive care unit case study. In: 22nd IEEE International Symposium on Computer-Based Medical Systems, CBMS 2009, pp. 1–5 (2009)
11. Dybå, T., Dingsøyr, T.: Empirical studies of agile software development: a systematic review. Inf. Softw. Technol. **50**, 833–859 (2008)
12. Davis, F.D., Bagozzi, R.P., Warshaw, P.R.: User acceptance of computer technology: a comparison of two theoretical models. Manage. Sci. **35**, 982–1003 (1989)
13. Rogers, E.M.: Diffusion of innovations. Simon and Schuster, New York (2010)
14. Fichman, R.G., Kemerer, C.F.: Adoption of software engineering process innovations: the case of object-orientation. Sloan Manag. Rev. **34**, 7–22 (2012)
15. Raghavan, S.A., Chand, D.R.: Diffusing software-engineering methods. IEEE Softw. **6**, 81–90 (1989)
16. Iivari, J., Iivari, N.: The relationship between organizational culture and the deployment of agile methods. Inf. Softw. Technol. **53**, 509–520 (2011)
17. Roberts, T.L., Gibson, M.L., Fields, K.T., Rainer Jr., R.K.: Factors that impact implementing a system development methodology. IEEE Trans. Softw. Eng. **24**, 640–649 (1998)
18. Johnson, R.A., Hardgrave, B.C., Doke, E.R.: An industry analysis of developer beliefs about object-oriented systems development. ACM SIGMIS Database **30**, 47–64 (1999)
19. Nambisan, S.: Information systems as a reference discipline for new product development. MIS Q. **27**(1), 1–18 (2003)
20. Davis, F.D.: Perceived usefulness, perceived ease of use, and user acceptance of information technology. MIS Q. **13**, 319–340 (1989)
21. Marban, O., Segovia, J., Menasalvas, E., Fernández-Baizán, C.: Toward data mining engineering: a software engineering approach. Inf. Syst. **34**, 87–107 (2009)
22. Weber, C.V., Paulk, M.C., Wise, C.J., WitheyKey, J.V.: Practices of the capability maturity model, DTIC Document (1991)
23. Argote, L., McEvily, B., Reagans, R.: Managing knowledge in organizations: an integrative framework and review of emerging themes. Manage. Sci. **49**, 571–582 (2003)
24. Venkatesh, V., Morris, M.G., Davis, G.B., Davis, F.D.: User acceptance of information technology: toward a unified view. MIS Q. **27**, 425–478 (2003)
25. Kankanhalli, A., Lee, O.-K.D., Lim, K.H.: Knowledge reuse through electronic repositories: a study in the context of customer service support. Inf. Manag. **48**, 106–113 (2011)
26. Hair, J.F., Tatham, R.L., Anderson, R.E., Black, W.: Multivariate Data Analysis, Pearson Prentice Hall, Upper Saddle River (2006)

27. Kankanhalli, A., Tan, B.C., Wei, K.-K., Holmes, M.C.: Cross-cultural differences and information systems developer values. Decis. Support Syst. **38**, 183–195 (2004)
28. Kim, H.-W., Chan, H.C., Kankanhalli, A.: What motivates people to purchase digital items on virtual community websites? the desire for online self-presentation. Inf. syst. Res. **23**, 1232–1245 (2012)
29. Arch, E.C., Cummins, D.E.: Structured and unstructured exposure to computers: sex differences in attitude and use among college students. Sex Roles **20**, 245–254 (1989)
30. Falk, R.F., Miller, N.B.: A primer for soft modeling. University of Akron Press, Akron (1992)
31. Agarwal, R., Prasad, J.: The role of innovation characteristics and perceived voluntariness in the acceptance of information technologies. Decis. Sci. **28**, 557–582 (1997)

What Should I Read Next? A Personalized Visual Publication Recommender System

Simon Bruns[1], André Calero Valdez[1]([✉]), Christoph Greven[2],
Martina Ziefle[1], and Ulrik Schroeder[2]

[1] Human-Computer Interaction Center, RWTH Aachen University,
Campus Boulevard 57, Aachen, Germany
{bruns,calero-valdez,ziefle}@comm.rwth-aachen.de
[2] Learning Technologies Research Group, RWTH Aachen University,
Ahornstr. 55, Aachen, Germany
{greven,schroeder}@cs.rwth-aachen.de

Abstract. Discovering relevant publications for researchers is a non-trivial task. Recommender systems can reduce the effort required to find relevant publications. We suggest using a visualization- and user-centered interaction model to achieve both a more trusted recommender system and a system to understand a whole research field. In a graph-based visualization papers are aligned with their keywords according to the relevance of the keywords. Relevance is determined using text-mining approaches. By letting the user control relevance thresholds for individual keywords we have designed a recommender system that scores high in accuracy ($\bar{x} = 5.03/6$), trust ($\bar{x} = 4.31/6$) and usability (SUS $\bar{x} = 4.89/6$) in a user study, while at the same time providing additional information about the field as a whole. As a result, the inherent trust issues conventional recommendation systems have seem to be less significant when using our solution.

Keywords: Recommender systems · Visualization · User-study · Trust · Usability

1 Introduction

The rapid growth of information on the world wide web enables users to get information from multiple sources. However, it can still be difficult to evaluate which sources are trustworthy [1]. This phenomenon is not only limited to standard users, but also influences specialists such as researchers. Researchers are required to be up to date on any recent technology or research that is relevant to their own work. The main source to find information on current research projects are scientific publications. However, this is getting more and more difficult, due to the sheer amount of publications released every year. The underlying problem of this development is addressed by Bradford's law [2]. Bradford states that the effort to find relevant publications for oneself increases exponentially over time and the number of available publications. As a result, the chance to miss useful research information is very high.

© Springer International Publishing Switzerland 2015
S. Yamamoto (Ed.): HIMI 2015, Part II, LNCS 9173, pp. 89–100, 2015.
DOI: 10.1007/978-3-319-20618-9_9

The miss rate is even further increased, due to the fact that not enough publications are taken into account. Most researchers mainly focus on publications that have been published in their own research field. By also considering publications with different research backgrounds, new aspects or questions for already well known problems can arise [3].

In a large research cluster Social Portals are used as an approach to assist interdisciplinary collaboration in order to increase the awareness of research generated within an organization [4]. Publications and their relationships can be visualized [5,6] in order to improve access to research results from within an organization. Nonetheless, this requires researchers to put their own effort into searching for relevant publications.

In order to provide researchers with the necessary means to increase their finding rate, a recommender system can be utilized. However, to be beneficial to the researcher not only is it necessary to generate good recommendations, but also to convince the users that the system is trustworthy and beneficial for them. The success of both aspects greatly depends on the recommendation algorithm, visualization of its results and the systems look and feel [7]. A recommender system that provides valuable suggestions most of the time may still be perceived poorly if its results are difficult to access or understand [8]. Web-based recommender system also require to appeal to the hedonic needs of the user to be successful [9], thus overall visual appeal is highly important.

2   Related Work

Several approaches have been used in recommender systems to improve their outcome on different aspects. The initial aim for our system was to create a highly transparent recommender system, where the user himself explores the data graph to find appropriate content. In order to ensure that the system meets user requirements, we identified two critical aspects for our project: visualization and recommender logic.

Telling Stories with Visualizations. Visualizations for data exploration or recommender systems have recently started to employ techniques that tell stories with data. For example, Wu et al. [10] have used a tree branch visualization to show the development of career paths of researchers. By visualizing which topics were published in which year, the development and shift of interest of researchers can be seen. A similar approach has been tried by Liu et al. [11], who using co-word analysis have used a visualization to track the change of research topics over time.

Segel and Heer [12] propose the use of so-called narrative visualization for recommender systems. The main focus is put on the data itself and its arrangement. Depending on the query and the user's preferences, the system generates a result screen, which consists of multiple items connected to the initial query. The items are aligned so the user does not perceive them as simple facts, but more as a story told to him.

The project Bohemian Bookshelf [13] shows the potential of creating explorative interfaces. It emulates a digital book shelf. Instead of using the hard covers as visualization means, the user can choose between multiple styles of visualization. One of these styles is a clustered bubble graph. When a user inspects a bubble, he is not only shown the referenced book, but also all books aligning to this bubble. In a case study, it was shown that users were highly motivated and genuinely excited to use the system, since they felt more integrated.

Since data arrangement in graphs are not arbitrary, but contextual, graphs themselves provide information. For this purpose Miller et al. [14] developed a cluster graph. The graph was accumulated of numerous papers, which were analyzed in respect of meaningful words. The whole corpus of papers was then rearranged into word clusters, which consisted of their respective papers. The goal was to give users an overview of possible current trends, but also to motivate them to work interdisciplinary with other facilities.

Integrating the User in Recommender Logic. Another trend in recommender systems is to integrate the user in the recommender logic. The user gets control over various aspects of the system or his behavior is analyzed to optimize recommendations. Loepp et al. [15] base the recommendations on user choices that have been done previously, thus applying a mix of collaborative filtering and user analysis. But analyzing the users choices his preferences are elicited by factor analysis.

The other approach is to implement the user as the recommender logic. Mühlbacher et al. [16] found that the main challenge is to identify significant steps in the system and to visualize them in a understandable form. While such systems provide high level of interaction, it is difficult to select the right steps for the user to influence according to Yi et al. [17].

In other projects, we have also encountered the idea of parametrization of the recommender process. However, the parametrization is rather limited and the results are only shown as a list. Examples of this approach are existing in team recommender systems. T-Recs [18] is a system, which suggests developing teams for upcoming projects. Thereby, the user can influence the importance of specific requirements. Another team recommender HR Database for team recommendation [19] also generates suggestions, however it requires the user to input their requirements at the start of each query.

For our approach we decided to use a combination of both ideas. On one hand enabling the user to explore the data, on the other hand giving him the ability to directly influence the query parameters and the result visualization.

3 The Recommender System - TIGRS

In this paper we propose a user-centered recommender system for researchers. The recommender system supports the user in identifying publications suited for his research interests. In addition, it enables him to explore the set of publications on his own (see Fig. 1).

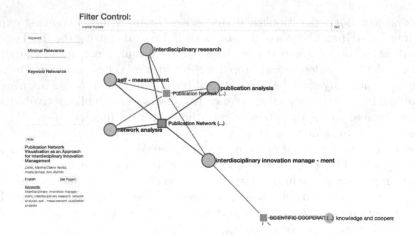

Fig. 1. Exemplary visualization of a user selecting a publication.

In contrast to conventional recommender systems, the proposed one has a user-centered interaction model. Thereby, the system provides the user with an interface that allows to directly influence the behavior of the recommender algorithm and thus immediately observe the impact of adjustments. Therefore, the system is separated into two parts, the first one is responsible for the adjustment of the algorithm behavior and the second part deals with the results and their visualization.

The behavior adjustments range from influencing the topic weighting in the filtering process to focusing on content-based recommendations. In addition the system also enables the user to filter for only keywords but also for specific authors and their respective research fields.

3.1 Text-Mining for Keyword Relevance

For our recommendations we use a keyword based approach. All full-text PDF files are required for the text mining approach. Furthermore we have access to our institutional library that allows API based access to meta data (when available) to ensure correctness of data. Similar APIs are provided by arXiv[1] and Mendeley[2]. When no meta-data is available TIGRS scans the PDF for keywords in the document header.

We then use Apache OpenNLP[3] to mine the full text of the PDF. Using language and noun phrase detection we reduce the amount of words considered for further data processing. To ensure, that words have no duplicates, the system calculates the Levenshtein-Distance for the potential duplicate pairs. If the resulting value exceeds a predefined tolerance level, the respective words are

---

[1] http://arxiv.org/help/api/index.
[2] http://dev.mendeley.com/.
[3] http://opennlp.apache.org/.

merged together. For the remaining words we perform term frequency-inverse document frequency (TF*IDF) to establish the words relevance for the document in contrast to the corpus.

For every keyword that we find, we gather the distinctive words from all documents that refer to that keyword in a global category. Then we use an iteration of TF*IDF, term frequency-inverse category frequency (TF*ICF), where we calculate the relevance of a word in a category in contrast to the whole category-corpus. The resulting word sets do not only describe, how distinctive a word is for a paper, but also the word's relevance as a representative of its category. Finally, the keyword relevance for each paper is calculated by adding up all TF*ICF values. Using this approach we can identify the relative importance of each keyword for each document.

3.2 Visualizing Results

The adjustments and recommendations are accessible from the visualization UI. The visualization UI consists of a responsive graph. Each node within the graph represents either a keyword or a publication that match the users' research profiles or their interests. The graph reacts to every interaction of the user, thereby immediately displaying the consequences of the user's actions. Additionally, the graph acts as a substitute for the conventional ranking visualization of results. Because of that, the user is able to better distinguish between the recommended items in respect of their value to the user and also their discerning factors between one another [20].

Besides the graph, the system allows the user to explore the whole database on his own by traversing the links of the graph. In doing so, the connection between publications and topics are further clarified. Furthermore, the publications are put into context to one another.

Our graph based visualization has two type of nodes (see Fig. 2). The first type of nodes are publication nodes. For them shortened titles are displayed. Publication nodes are connected to keyword nodes, when the keyword is listed on the publication. Node size of keywords depends on node degree. This makes keywords that are used in multiple documents larger than less frequently used keywords (see Fig. 3). For each edge a relative importance is stored as a double value indicating the relative relevance of the keyword for the document.

The UI has a filter that allows auto-complete assisted selection of keywords. Furthermore from any given node all its meta descriptors such as keywords or authors can be added by a single click. Adding a keyword to the filter adds a relevance selector to the left part of the screen. By moving the selector the user can select a minimum threshold of relevance of a keyword. The author filter retrieves the research profile of the selected author and adds it, similar to the keyword filter, as a unique filter with a relevance selector. This limits the amount of publications displayed and allows to dynamically adjust weighing of filter keywords by the user.

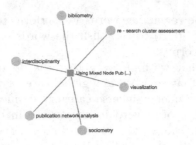

Fig. 2. Publications are displayed as blue squares and keywords as gray boxes, using [6] as an example.

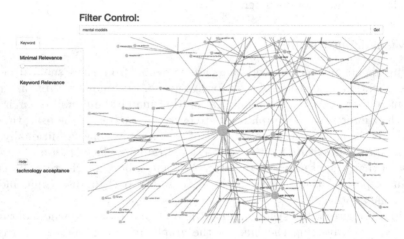

Fig. 3. By visualizing all research of a group prominent topics become more apparent

4 Evaluation

The recommender system was tested in an interdisciplinary research facility with a sample of 16 members from different fields. In a user study we evaluated usability [21](SUS) in respect to user factors (e.g. age, gender, track record). We particularly evaluated the effectiveness of recommendations by measuring trust and accuracy for recommendations [22]. Additionally, we evaluated supplemental factors of relevance of the visualization (i.e. structure and overview, topic discovery, information about colleagues) and compared the visualization to a list-based recommendation. At last we evaluated the visualization using the NPS [23] (NPS).

4.1 Method

First participants were handed a questionnaire to elicit user factors. They were given access to the visualization and given a short introduction into the general mechanics of the visualization (What are node types? What do mouse gestures do? etc.). Then they were given two tasks. First they were asked to play around with the visualization until they felt comfortable using the visualization. Then they were asked to look for a publication in the recommender system that was relevant to them and previously unknown. The whole process was recorded by video and later analyzed. After the interaction users were given another questionnaire to evaluate the prototype.

The assessed metrics for the prototype are partially taken from ResQue, [22] accuracy (A.1.1, $\alpha = .745$), relative accuracy (A.1.2, $\alpha = .362$) and generated from own items (see Table 1). All were measured on six-point Likert scales. For all used scales we assessed the Cronbach's α when more than one item is used. The SUS had a reliability of $\alpha = .731$.

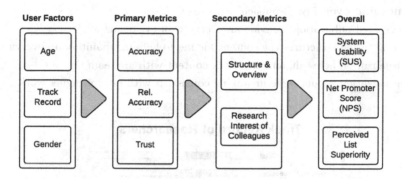

Fig. 4. Research model overview

Additionally, we assessed whether our visualization was seen as superior to a list based presentation in regard to four aspects. Does the visualization help when one is looking for *new content*? Does it help in *understanding the research group*? Does it provide more *overview* and provide *more information* in general than a list based presentation? Those were assessed on a six-point Likert scale (1=disagree completely, 6=agree completely). The investigated relationships can be seen in Fig. 4.

4.2 Sample Description

As a sample of $N = 16$ researchers from an interdisciplinary research facility were selected at random. The average age of the researchers was $\bar{x} = 33.6$ years ($\sigma = 6.14$, range= $23 - 52$) and 56% of the participants were female. 10 had finished their Masters (or similar) while 5 already had a Ph.D. In total we had six communication scientists, five psychologists, four computer scientists, three sociologists and one architect in our sample (multiple selections allowed). When looking at the track record distribution of experience was mixed ($\bar{x} = 4.25$, $\sigma =$, 0=no publications, 7=more than 30 publications). Although most researchers had a focus on conference proceedings ($\bar{x} = 4.0$, $\sigma = 2.0$). Journal articles ($\bar{x} = 2.57$, $\sigma = 1.55$) and book chapter contributions were less frequent ($\bar{x} = 1.93$, $\sigma = 1.54$, see also Fig. 5).

Table 1. Scales and their item texts. *=inverted items.

Scales and Items
Research interest of colleagues Cronbach's $\alpha = .858$
- The suggested publications help me understanding my colleagues research interests
- The research interests of my colleagues can be derived from the visualization
- The visualization helps to understand my colleagues research interests
Trust Cronbach's $\alpha = .808$
- I believe that the system can give sensible recommendations
- I trust that the system gives me sensible recommendations
- I would rather trust my colleagues to give me recommendations than the system.*
Structure and overview Cronbach's $\alpha = .594$
- The suggested publications provide an overview of my teams work
- The visualization structures the content for me to help me maintain an overview
- The visualization helps aligning my work content with my team
- The visualization supports me in staying consistent with my colleagues work

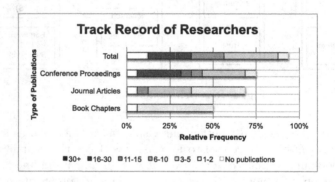

Fig. 5. Overview of the track records of the individual researchers

4.3 Descriptive Results

When looking at the results descriptively, we can say that the *accuracy* of the system is very high ($\bar{x} = 5.03$, $\sigma = 0.15$), while the *relative accuracy* is relatively low ($\bar{x} = 3.13.$, $\sigma = 0.19$). This means that the system does give good recommendations, but colleagues recommendations are still seen as superior to the visualization. Interestingly the relative accuracy showed a very low reliability, indicating that the phrasing of the items leads to differing answers between the items.

The *trust* in the given recommendations is relatively high ($\bar{x} = 4.31$, $\sigma = 0.20$). Users were able to get the impression that the given recommendations were actually sensible. When looking at the secondary metrics *structure and overview* showed a high agreement ($\bar{x} = 4.72$, $\sigma = 0.22$) and *colleagues research interest* as well ($\bar{x} = 4.69$, $\sigma = 0.22$). This means besides giving adequate recommendations the system was able to inform the user about the structure of the research group and the research interests of their colleagues. Overall *SUS* was high ($\bar{x} = 4.89/6$, $\sigma = 0.13$) indicating a good usability of the system. Nonetheless the *NPS* was relatively low (-7). This means further development of the system needs to be performed to align with user requirements. In regard to a *comparison over lists* our visualization was considered superior in all four aspects (see Fig. 6).

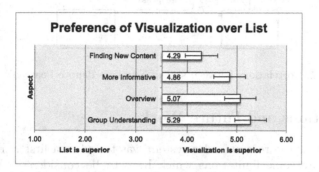

Fig. 6. Perceived preference of our visualization over lists in four aspects. Error bars denote standard errors. A value of 3.5 would indicate a neutral judgement.

4.4 Interaction Effects

When looking at age, gender and track record no interaction with any measured scale could be found ($p > .05$). This means that all our users were able to use the system and evaluated it independently from our user factors.

Trust was a factory correlating with most other evaluated metrics. Trust and accuracy showed a high correlation ($r = .761, p < .01$), similar as trust and overview ($r = .825, p < .01$). The SUS only correlated with accuracy and *research interest of colleagues*, while NPS correlated with trust directly (see also Fig. 7).

4.5 Summary

Overall we can say that our visualization and recommender approach was evaluated quite positively. The usability was rated as good and the visualization was judged superior over list based presentations. Interestingly the NPS was relatively low indicating the need for further improvements.

Our visualization is particularly good at assisting in understanding the research group while giving the user information on the research structure and an overview of the institute. Trust seems to be a major factor in influencing adoption by the user because it correlates with secondary metrics and the perceived accuracy of the recommendations.

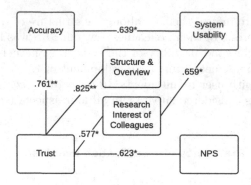

Fig. 7. Correlations between scales. Numbers denote Pearson's r

5   Limitations and Future Work

The prototype of the recommender system was tested in a first iteration. Naturally, there are some limitations which have to be considered when further developing the tool. A technical limitation regards the fact that the system is limited to visualizing publications to which non-encrypted PDF files are available for the text-mining to work. This might work in a research setting in which all relevant publications are available, as e.g. within research groups that might work together for an extended period of time. Further limitations of the current version of the prototype are directed to usability. During the user studies some improvements were mentioned, mostly with respect to the interaction possibilities. Users should be able to change the graph density and the amount of recommendations directly (in order to prevent visual overload and cognitive complexity). Furthermore, we want to improve on the transparency of the relevance thresholds. Changes on the slider should directly highlight changes in the graph to improve the understanding of how the relevance slider works. Finally, functions scope was quite narrow. It could be helpful to add filtering based on article source (outlet) and publication date, in order to support the search process and to match user expectations. This also reflects the nature of the approach here: It was a computer science approach (to automatize the search for publications) that was then tested and evaluated with users. Another way to improve the tool would be the vice versa approach: observing natural users during academic work, what they are looking for, and why and how the keywords are connected semantically. The findings then could be matched with the recommendation systems finding.

Future work might be directed to the understanding of different search scenarios. One could be to examine different levels of domain knowledge and to study the perceived usefulness of the system. Here we could expect that the system should be extremely helpful for getting a fast overview for novices, while it could be even detrimental for experts with an elaborated mental model. Also it seems worth to study different search approaches across different target scenarios: looking up information in a quick and dirty style (searching for a specific information), or, getting an overall picture of a sample of papers (learning about major research topics of a group), or just looking for interesting papers within a given field.

Acknowledgments. We would like to thank the anonymous reviewers for their constructive comments on an earlier version of this manuscript. The authors thank the German Research Council DFG for the friendly support of the research in the excellence cluster "Integrative Production Technology in High Wage Countries".

References

1. Beaudoin, C.E.: Explaining the relationship between internet use and interpersonal trust: taking into account motivation and information overload. J. Comput.-Mediat. Commun. **13**(3), 550–568 (2008)
2. Hjorland, B., Nicolaisen, J.: Bradford's law of scattering: ambiguities in the concept of "subject". In: Crestani, F., Ruthven, I. (eds.) CoLIS 2005. LNCS, vol. 3507, pp. 96–106. Springer, Heidelberg (2005)
3. Maglaughlin, K.L., Sonnenwald, D.H.: Factors that impact interdisciplinary natural science research collaboration in academia. In: Proceedings of the ISSI, pp. 24–25 (2005)
4. Calero Valdez, A., Schaar, A.K., Ziefle, M., Holzinger, A.: Enhancing interdisciplinary cooperation by social platforms. In: Yamamoto, S. (ed.) HCI 2014, Part I. LNCS, vol. 8521, pp. 298–309. Springer, Heidelberg (2014)
5. Schaar, A.K., Calero Valdez, A., Ziefle, M.: Publication network visualization as an approach for interdisciplinary innovation management. In: 2013 IEEE International Professional Communication Conference (IPCC), pp. 1–8. IEEE (2013)
6. Calero Valdez, A., Schaar, A.K., Ziefle, M., Holzinger, A., Jeschke, S., Brecher, C.: Using mixed node publication network graphs for analyzing success in interdisciplinary teams. In: Huang, R., Ghorbani, A.A., Pasi, G., Yamaguchi, T., Yen, N.Y., Jin, B. (eds.) AMT 2012. LNCS, vol. 7669, pp. 606–617. Springer, Heidelberg (2012)
7. Knijnenburg, B., Willemsen, M., Gantner, Z., Soncu, H., Newell, C.: Explaining the user experience of recommender systems. User Model. User-Adap. Inter. **22**(4–5), 441–504 (2012)
8. Ortega, F., Bobadilla, J., Hernando, A., Rodríguez, F.: Using hierarchical graph maps to explain collaborative filtering recommendations. Int. J. Intell. Syst. **29**(5), 462–477 (2014)
9. Alagöz, F., Calero Valdez, A., Wilkowska, W., Ziefle, M., Dorner, S., Holzinger, A.: From cloud computing to mobile internet, from user focus to culture and hedonism - The crucible of mobile health care and wellness applications. In: ICPCA 2010 - 5th International Conference on Pervasive Computing and Applications, pp. 38–45 (2010)
10. Wu, M.Q.Y., Faris, R., Ma, K.L.: Visual exploration of academic career paths. In: Proceedings of the 2013 IEEE/ACM International Conference on Advances in Social Networks Analysis and Mining, pp. 779–786. ACM (2013)
11. Liu, Y., Goncalves, J., Ferreira, D., Xiao, B., Hosio, S., Kostakos, V.: Chi 1994–2013: mapping two decades of intellectual progress through co-word analysis. In: Proceedings of the 32nd Annual ACM Conference on Human Factors in Computing Systems. ACM (2014)

12. Segel, E., Heer, J.: Narrative visualization: telling stories with data. IEEE Trans. Vis. Comput. Graph. **16**(6), 1139–1148 (2010)
13. Thudt, A., Hinrichs, U., Carpendale, S.: The bohemian bookshelf: Supporting serendipitous book discoveries through information visualization. In: Proceedings of the SIGCHI Conference on Human Factors in Computing Systems, CHI 2012, pp. 1461–1470. ACM, New York (2012)
14. Miller, L.J., Gazan, R., Still, S.: Unsupervised classification and visualization of unstructured text for the support of interdisciplinary collaboration. In: Proceedings of the 17th ACM Conference on Computer Supported Cooperative Work and Social Computing, CSCW 2014, pp. 1033–1042. ACM, New York (2014)
15. Loepp, B., Hussein, T., Ziegler, J.: Choice-based preference elicitation for collaborative filtering recommender systems. In: Proceedings of the 32nd Annual ACM Conference on Human Factors in Computing Systems, pp. 3085–3094. ACM (2014)
16. Mühlbacher, T., Piringer, H., Gratzl, S., Sedlmair, M., Streit, M.: Opening the black box: strategies for increased user involvement in existing algorithm implementations. to appear in IEEE Transactions on Visualization and Computer Graphics? Proceedings IEEE VAST 2014 (2014)
17. Yi, J.S., Kang, Y., Stasko, J., Jacko, J.: Toward a deeper understanding of the role of interaction in information visualization. IEEE Trans. Vis. Comput. Graph. **13**(6), 1224–1231 (2007)
18. Datta, A., Tan Teck Yong, J., Ventresque, A.: T-recs: Team recommendation system through expertise and cohesiveness. In: Proceedings of the 20th International Conference Companion on WWW, WWW 2011, pp. 201–204. ACM, New York (2011)
19. Brocco, M., Hauptmann, C., Andergassen-Soelva, E.: Recommender system augmentation of HR databases for team recommendation. In: 2011 22nd International Workshop on Database and Expert Systems Applications (DEXA), pp. 554–558 (2011)
20. Cramer, H., Evers, V., Ramlal, S., van Someren, M., Rutledge, L., Stash, N., Aroyo, L., Wielinga, B.: The effects of transparency on trust in and acceptance of a content-based art recommender. User Model. User-Adap. Inter. **18**(5), 455–496 (2008)
21. Brooke, J.: SUS - a quick and dirty usability scale. Usability Eval. Indus. **189**, 194 (1996)
22. Pu, P., Chen, L., Hu, R.: A user-centric evaluation framework for recommender systems. In: Proceedings of the Fifth ACM Conference on Recommender Systems, pp. 157–164. ACM (2011)
23. Reichheld, F.F.: The one number you need to grow. Harvard Bus. Rev. **81**(12), 46–55 (2003)

The Effect of Timing When Introducing a Decision Aid in a Decision Support System for Supply Chain Management

Nirit Gavish$^{(\boxtimes)}$ and Hussein Naseraldin

Ort Braude College, Karmiel, Israel
{Nirit,nhussein}@braude.ac.il

Abstract. In the current research, we evaluated the effect of previous experience with a task on users' willingness to accept a suggested decision aid and their performance in a supply chain management system. Participants were randomly assigned to one of three between-participants groups: the No Aid Group, which did not receive any decision aid during the interaction; the Aid Group, which was offered an algorithm, at the beginning of the first session, to help members improve their decisions; and the Mid-term Aid Group, which received, at the beginning of the second session, the same algorithm that was offered to the Aid Group. The results demonstrated that in the second session the performance of the Aid Group was significantly better in comparison to the No Aid Group. The Mid-term Aid Group's performance did not show any gain, although both the Aid and Mid-term Aid Groups made similar use of the aid in this session. We concluded that in a decision support system, previous experience with the task before introducing the decision aid is not always helpful.

Keywords: Decision aid · Decision support system · Experience · Algorithm · Compliance · Reliance

1 Introduction

Decision support systems (DSSs) in the domain of Industrial Engineering and Management (IE&M) can be very powerful tools, but how much do we know about the way users utilize these systems? Do they exploit the systems' strengths or do they hamper the system from maximizing its effectiveness? More specifically, what are the factors that cause users to adopt the system's decision aids so that they can improve their performance? In the current study we focused on the issue of previous experience: What is the impact that a decision aid has on the performance of a user who has past experience with a task, but without the decision aid?

When developing DSS for IE&M, special care should be given to the user's willingness to use the decision aid. Past studies have shown that this willingness is affected by several factors. For example, Rice and Keller [1] demonstrated that time pressure increased willingness to accept the system's recommendations. Dzindolet et al. [2] showed that information about the possible reasons behind the system's incorrect decisions increased reliance on the system. Lacson et al. [3] showed that

© Springer International Publishing Switzerland 2015
S. Yamamoto (Ed.): HIMI 2015, Part II, LNCS 9173, pp. 101–108, 2015.
DOI: 10.1007/978-3-319-20618-9_10

willingness to rely on the system is affected by presenting its reliability in terms of correct or incorrect diagnoses. Systems, however, may be as fallible as humans and users must also exercise judgment when accepting the system's help. They should consider when and how the decision aid helps increase performance levels. Several examples in the literature present both under-reliance on the system's aid, when users ignored the aid that could assist their performance [4, 5, 6], and overreliance, when users accepted bad decisions offered by the system [7, 8]. A successful DSS, accordingly, is one that is both utilized efficiently and improves performance.

In the current study, we focused on the effect on users' willingness to accept the aid when they had previous experience with the task, and on their performance. It is important to examine whether a decision aid should be introduced to the user very early in her interaction with the system or later on. We questioned whether previous training on performing the task, without the decision aid, result in a higher or a lower acceptance level of the decision aid when the decision aid is given, and does it result in better or worse performance measures then?

We evaluated the effect of previous experience on users' willingness to accept the support of a simple decision aid and their performance operating a supply chain management system. Participants were invited to a computer lab and had two successive sessions interacting with a simulation-based supply chain game. The decision aid we adopted in this research is a simple aid that is not automatically produced by the system. We offered participants a simple algorithm and a formula that could help them make a better decision; yet, the aid can shed some light on the way users accept and utilize decision aids in general. Our hypotheses were that since the task is difficult to perform, having had previous experience with the task, users know the task is difficult and hence will be more inclined to accept the decision aid when the decision aid is given. Previous experience should, theoretically, lead to better performance.

2 Method

2.1 Design

Participants were randomly assigned to one of three between-participants groups: the No Aid Group, which did not receive any decision aid during the interaction; the Aid Group, which was offered an algorithm at the beginning of the first session, to help members improve their decision making; and the Mid-term Aid Group, which received, at the beginning of the second session, the same algorithm that was offered to the Aid Group. The randomized assignment was achieved by letting participants choose their preferable date and hour for the experiment, and then assigning each hour randomly to one experimental condition, but controlling for an equal proportion of genders among the groups. The design was mixed, with the session as the within-participants repeated measure independent variable, and the group (No Aid Group, Aid Group and Mid-term Aid Group) as the between-participants independent variable, and two dependent variables: mean total cost and mean deviation from the algorithm.

2.2 Participants

One hundred undergraduate students (66 % males, 34 % females) from ORT Braude College, Israel, participated in the experiment. Participants' average age was 25.2, with a range of 18–51. Ten percent of the participants (19 % in the No Aid Group, 3 % in the in Aid Group, and 9 % in the Mid-term Aid Group) were from the Department of Industrial Engineering and Management at ORT Braude, and the others were from several other engineering departments. Note that in courses given in the Department of Industrial Engineering and Management students are exposed to the topic of supply chain management. It is important that only ten were from this department, and that they were assigned to all experimental groups.

Participants were paid a fixed amount of NIS 40 (about USD 10) for their participation, and given bonuses, which depended on their performance (minimum total cost): The best performer in the respective condition (out of the three groups) received a bonus of NIS 100, and four runner-ups got a bonus of NIS 50 each.

2.3 Apparatus

The experiment took place in a computer lab at the college. Sixteen desktop computers were used, each having a 19-inch monitor. The dedicated program for this experiment was downloaded for each computer; see Experimental Task section. Papers, pencils and calculators were provided to participants.

2.4 Experimental Task

The experimental task was a variation of the Beer Distribution Game, which was developed at MIT in the 1960s and has been widely used to educate graduate students and business managers about supply chain dynamics [9–12]. The version used in the current study was downloaded from the site http://www.runthemodel.com/models/run. php?popup=1&id=507 and was developed by XJ Technologies©, www.anylogic.com; see the experimental task screen layout in Fig. 1. Participants were assigned the role of Retailer, and the computer played the roles of Wholesaler, Distributer, and Factory. For all four roles, the Initial inventory was set at 100.

The experimental task required participants to determine the daily amount to order from their supplier so as to reduce their total costs. The costs for each day included storage costs (for the inventory) and backlog costs (in case a participant could not satisfy customer demand on the same day – negative inventory). Each of the two sessions included 60 days of running the simulation. Participants' goal was to reach the minimum cumulative costs at the end of each session of 60 runs. The inventory was updated every day. Participants could also see, for each day, the following data:

- Expected: The amount ordered and not yet arrived.
- Shipped: The amount shipped the same day to the customer.
- Ordered: The amount that the customer ordered that day. If the amount was in the inventory, it was supplied to the customer—in which case, the shipped amount was

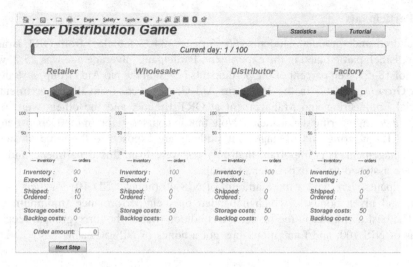

Fig. 1. The experimental task screen layout.

identical to the order amount. If the inventory was smaller than the ordered quantity, the customer was provided with the available inventory and the remainder was provided later when the inventory became available.

The cumulative holding cost was given in the Storage costs. Each unit held in inventory on a particular day cost participants 0.5. For example, if a participant had 3 units in stock on a particular day, that day's storage cost was 1.5. The cumulative cost of holding stock accrued daily. The cumulative backlog cost was given in Backlog costs. This is the cost incurred when a customer ordered merchandise that could not be provided. Each unit missing on a particular day cost 1. For example, if the inventory on a particular day was (−3), the backlog cost for that day was 3. The cumulative backlog cost accrued from day to day. When a certain amount was lacking, participants paid for it until the shortfall was filled. Since the cost of a backlog unit was twice as much as an inventory unit, it was rational to pay more attention to decreasing the backlog than to decreasing the inventory. However, no formal instructions about this were given to participants.

The lead time of each order was four days. For example, if on day 10 participants ordered 20 units, they would receive them on day 14. Once participants decided on the Order amount, they clicked "Next Step" to move to the next day.

The customer orders in each session were, in fact, identical. However, this information was not given to participants. All participants were exposed to the same demand scenarios.

2.5   Procedure

Ten participants at a time sat in the lab but each participant worked individually at his desktop. Each group was assigned randomly to one experimental condition and was blind to the other conditions. On average, the entire experiment took about 45 min and no more than 75 min. An experimenter remained in the lab, instructed the participants, and presented the algorithm to the relevant groups at the relevant stage.

Participants received a consent form to sign and completed a personal details questionnaire. Following this, the experimenter read aloud an explanation about the experiment and the game. The game, its menus, screens, etc. were explained to participants as they sat in front of their computers. They also received a written manual about the game to assist them during the experiment. Thereafter, participants practiced playing the game for three periods (days) with a self-tutorial, lasted about 5 min. Once this stage was completed, the experimenter confirmed that the participants successfully followed the practice's instructions. Then, participants from the Aid Group received a written explanation about the algorithm, and had it read aloud to them by the experimenter. Participants played the game over one session equaling 60 days, each at his or her individual pace. They were instructed to write down in a table their data and decisions for each day. The data and the decisions (orders) were analyzed. When they finished, participants from the Mid-term Aid Group received the explanation about the algorithm in writing and had it read it aloud to them by the experimenter. Participants from the Aid Group and from the No Aid Group did not receive any additional instructions. Participants again played the game over one session equaling 60 days. When completed, participants were thanked and paid for their participation.

3   Results

Participants' performance and decisions in the first and in the second session were analyzed using a multivariate analysis. In the first session, the results of the No Aid Group and the Mid-term Aid Group were combined (and the combined group was termed "No Aid - First Session Group"), because at this stage of the experiment the manipulation they were exposed to was identical. Two measures were analyzed for evaluating the performance and acceptance level. These measures were mean total cost (sum of storage and backlog costs for each day) and the mean deviation from the algorithm (measured as the absolute value of the order amount recommended by the algorithm minus the participant's order amount for each day). Although the mean deviation from the algorithm was not a perfect indicator of the acceptance level, it reflected how much the participant's decisions were close to the suggestion of the algorithm. As was demonstrated, this later measure did not have to be connected to better performance since the algorithm was not ideal to achieve the best score possible.

3.1   First Session Analysis

In the multivariate analysis, the group (No Aid - First Session Group and Aid Group) was the independent variable; the mean total cost and the mean deviation from the algorithm were the dependent variables.

The multivariate analysis demonstrated that the effect of group was not significant (Wilks' Lambda test on the combined variable: $(F(2,97) = 2.5, p = 0.08, Partial Eta Squared = 0.05)$. A positive significant correlation was found between the two dependent variables ($Pearson\ r = 0.6, p < 0.001$). A univariate analysis was performed for each of these variables, and demonstrated that for the mean total costs, the effect of group was not significant ($F(1,98) = 3.6$, $p = 0.06$, *Partial Eta Squared* = 0.04). For the mean deviation from the algorithm, the effect of group was significant ($F(1,98) = 4.4$, $p = 0.04$, *Partial Eta Squared* = 0.04), with higher deviation from the algorithm to the No Aid – First Session Group ($M = 30.0$, $SD = 46.1$) compared to the Aid Group ($M = 12.5$, $SD = 17.9$).

3.2 Second Session Analysis

The multivariate analysis demonstrated that the effect of group was significant (Wilks' Lambda test on the combined variable: ($F(4,192) = 4.3$, $p = 0.002$, *Partial Eta Squared* = 0.08). A positive significant correlation was found between the two dependent variables (*Pearson r* = 0.7, $p < 0.001$). Reported below are the univariate results of these variables.

For the mean total costs, the effect of group was significant ($F(2,97) = 4.0$, $p = 0.021$, *Partial Eta Squared* = 0.08). Post hoc Tukey HSD test showed that No Aid Group had a significantly higher mean total cost ($M = 45.5$, $SD = 27.7$) compared to the Aid Group ($M = 26.1$, $SD = 27.7$; $p = 0.015$), while the other contrasts were not significant (No Aid Group compared to the Mid-term Aid Group ($M = 34.3$, $SD = 27.7$): $p = 0.2$; Aid Group compared to the Mid-term Aid Group: $p = 04$).

For the mean deviation from the algorithm, the effect of group was significant ($F(2,97) = 6.1$, $p = 0.003$, *Partial Eta Squared* = 0.1). Post hoc Tukey HSD test showed that No Aid Group had a significantly higher mean deviation from the algorithm ($M = 20.3$, $SD = 15.2$) compared to both the Aid Group ($M = 10.0$, $SD = 15.2$; $p = 0.02$) and the Mid-term Aid Group ($M = 8.1$, $SD = 15.2$; $p = 0.004$). The difference between the Aid Group and the Mid-term Aid Group was not significantly different ($p = 0.9$).

4 Discussion

The results demonstrated that generally, when exposed to the algorithm, participants tended to use it. In the first session, the Aid Group's decisions were closer to the algorithm than these of the No Aid - First Session Group; in the second session, there was a significant difference in the deviation from the algorithm between the two groups (Aid Group and Mid-term Aid Group) in comparison to the No Aid Group. In addition, it seems that using the algorithm was intuitive and participants did not need to gain experience in learning how to use it, as both the Mid-term Aid Group, which was exposed to the algorithm in the second session, used it in that session no less often than did the Aid Group, which had previous experience with it.

The Aid Group had significantly better performance compared to the No Aid Group in the second session, while no significant difference was demonstrated between the Mid-term Aid Group and the No Aid Group. In contrast, the degree of utilization of the decision aid was similar in both groups that were exposed to it in the second session. Only the group that received the algorithm at the beginning of its first session of interaction with the system improved its performance better. The contrast between the acceptance level and performance results is especially interesting since the two measures were correlated: Using the algorithm indeed can lead to better performance, but it seems that mere using it is not enough, and it should be done carefully.

Our hypotheses that previous experience with the task without the decision aid will result in higher acceptance level of using the decision aid and lower total costs compared to experience with the decision aid only were not confirmed. The two groups that received the aid demonstrated a similar acceptance level, and the group that had previous experience with the aid performed better. We conjectured that the previous experience with the decision aid did not change the mean acceptance levels, but did change their nature: Since the decision aid was not optimal, participants learned how to utilize it better, to use it more when it is constructive and less when it led them to poorer performance.

The conclusions from the current study are that in a decision support system, previous experience performing a task without decision aids is not only not necessary, but can also delay the process of learning how to best utilize the decision aids—most importantly, avoiding both under-reliance [4–6] and overreliance [7, 8].

Acknowledgments. This research was supported in part by ORT Braude Research Committee, Israel.

References

1. Rice, R., Keller, D.: Automation reliance under time pressure. Cogn. Technol. **14**, 36–44 (2009)
2. Dzindolet, M.T., Peterson, S.A., Pomranky, R.A., Pierce, L.G., Beck, H.P.: The role of trust in automation reliance. Int. J. Hum. Comput. Stud. **58**, 697–718 (2003)
3. Lacson, F.C., Wiegmann, D.A., Madhavan, P.: Effects of attribute and goal framing on automation reliance and compliance. In: Proceedings of the Human Factors and Ergonomics Society 49 h Annual Meeting, pp. 482–486. Human Factors and Ergonomics Society, Santa Monica (2005)
4. Dzindolet, M.T., Pierce, L.G., Beck, H.P., Dawe, L.A.: The perceived utility of human and automated aids in a visual detection task. Hum. Factors **44**, 79–94 (2002)
5. Parasuraman, R., Riley, V.: Human and automation: use, misuse, disuse. Abuse. Hum. Factors **39**, 230–253 (1997)
6. Riley, V.: Operator reliance on automation: theory and data. In: Parasuraman, R., Mouloas, M. (eds.) Automation and Human Performance: Theory and Applications, pp. 19–35. Lawrence Erlbaum, Mahwah (1997)
7. Layton, C., Smith, P.J., McCoy, C.E.: Design of cooperative problem-solving system for en-route flight planning: an empirical evaluation. Hum. Factors **36**, 94–112 (1994)
8. Parasuraman, R., Molloy, R., Singh, I.L.: Performance consequences of automation-induced complacency. Int. J. Aviat. Psychol. **3**, 1–23 (1993)
9. Jackson, G.C., Taylor, J.C.: Administering the MIT beer game: lessons learned. Dev. Bus. Simul. Exp. Learn. **25**, 208–214 (1993)
10. Liu, H., Howley, E., Duggan, J.: Optimisation of the beer distribution game with complex customer demand patterns. In: IEEE Congress on Evolutionary Computation, 2009, CEC 2009, pp. 2638–2645. IEEE (2009)

11. Ravid, G., Rafaeli, S.: Multi player, Internet and java-based simulation games: learning and research in implementing a computerized version of the "beer-distribution supply chain game". Simul. Ser. **32**, 15–22 (2000)
12. Sterman, J.: Instructions for Running the Beer Distribution Game. Systems Dynamics Group. Sloan School of Management, Cambridge, Massachusetts 02139 (1984)

Design of Framework for Students Recommendation System in Information Technology Skills

Thongchai Kaewkiriya[✉]

Faculty of Information Technology, Thai-Nichi Institute of Technology,
1771/1, Pattanakarn Road, Suanluang, Bangkok, Thailand
thongchai@tni.ac.th
http://www.tni.ac.th/

Abstract. One of the problems of learners is learners do not know their own skills. Especially learners who study IT field will have different aptitudes. If learners do not know their aptitude will affect themselves such as learning without a goal, and so on. The objective of this research is to design of conceptual framework for students recommendation for Information Technology skills. The concept framework consists of five modules. (1) to introduce the pattern base module which is an analysis by data mining. (2) to explain the mapping module for students. (3) to present the forecasting module which connect to the mapping module. (4) to present the web portal module. Web portal module is the User interface (UI) to connect user with system application. (5) to describe the Information Technology skills. This module consists of four parts; (1) programming skills (2) System engineering and network engineering (3) Graphic designs (4) other skills. Information Technology skills are mapped by using Multiple Intelligence theory. The process of selection pattern base, is use to compare the algorithm which is consisted of three algorithms (1) ID3 algorithm (2) J48 algorithm (3) Bayes Net algorithm. J48 algorithm is the highest percentage of prediction. Percentage of prediction for J48 algorithm is 78.267 % which base on pattern base for recommendation systems.

Keywords: Recommendation system · Data mining · Multiple intelligence · Information technology skill

1 Introduction

The amount of data in each field has been increased every year, such as the amount of business data, industry data or education data. At present, data is increasing in the education institute, such as data of students who take exam for entrance or data of students who graduated each year and so on. As for the amount of data has been increasing how to get the benefit from data used. Currently, there are a lot of institutions especially, some problems occur with students' enrollment and retire. In particular, engineering faculty and information technology faculty due to; (1) Each student who graduated from high school enrolls to the university without concerning what their expertise is. (2) The students enroll by following their friends who graduated from the same high school. (3) Students enroll under the guidance of their parents or guardian, etc.

© Springer International Publishing Switzerland 2015
S. Yamamoto (Ed.): HIMI 2015, Part II, LNCS 9173, pp. 109–117, 2015.
DOI: 10.1007/978-3-319-20618-9_11

From the problems mentions above, so the statistics of students who cannot graduate will be higher each year. These problems effect to the country's economic and social issue because of high cost, and waste time. Therefore, before students enroll to the faculty of the information technology, they have to know their abilities or skills which can be encouraged in the appropriated way.

As the mentioned problems and the effects that has been previously described, so this research presents the design of framework for students recommendation system with Information Technology skills. The research focuses on the system of student recommendation in the Information Technology by divided skills into 3 aspects; programming skills in system, engineering/network skills and graphic design skills.

2   Previous Work

The previous work [1] proposed the recommendation system to choose a study program based on the repertory grid. This paper will present the recommendation system by analyzing the old knowledge of students. But do not take other profiles from learners to consider. In addition the result of the recommendation system has minimal distortion and does not match with reality.

Furthermore, the research [2, 3] presented the recommendation system of e-learning by focusing on lessons not students of e-learning system. Therefore, learners with different abilities will get different contents. This learning and teaching has not good in performance. However, this research is still limited in using only recommendation on e-learning.

The research [4] presented a comparison of decision tree and support vector machine techniques for classifying students for e-Learning in Information Technology course. The research [4] analyses only profile of students. But this research did not analyze other factors such as ability or IT skills. As the result, the performance of the system has not been good.

The research [5] found the way to separate learners by following each learning form and managed learning and teaching to relate with learners. The experiment started with computer programming topics. However, there are the same contents for learners although there are separate groups by following learning forms. The research [6] found that there is some creating of learning paths for each learner and lessons for learners. Creating of learning path came from learner's profile (Log file). Moreover, there is the adjustment of learning for learner, as well. However, the research [5, 6] had promoted the appropriate learning and teaching, but not focus on the recommendation form to students with the ability of Information Technology skills.

3   Background

Howard Gardner from Harvard University who was the founder of the theory of Multiple Intelligences [7], said that each student has different learning methods, teachers and parents need to realize and recognize the value of the difference. They found that students have learning natures and abilities to learn in order to continue the activities to fulfill their potential. Human cognitive abilities by multiple intelligences theory is divided into nine areas: (1) Verbal/Linguistic Intelligent (2) Logical/Mathematical Intelligent (3) Musical/Rhythmic Intelligent (4) Body/Kinesthetic Intelligent (5) Visual/Spatial Intelligent (6) Interpersonal Intelligent (7) Intrapersonal Intelligent (8) Naturalist Intelligence (9) Existential Intelligence.

Considering all nine areas, it has been discovered that many have a different dominant intellectual parts. The most important thing is that all areas are stimulated to encourage development. In addition, some dominated areas can be used to help weaker parts. The Multiple Intelligence model is depicted in Fig. 1.

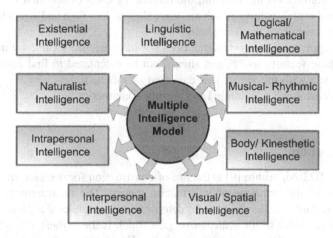

Fig. 1. Multiple Intelligence model

This research uses Multiple Intelligence to apply for mapping with IT skill. Figure 2 shows the framework of an adaptive e-Learning guidance system which consists of 5 modules. It divided into 3 groups; (1) programming skills (2) Graphic design skills (3) System engineering and network skills. Figure for mapping shown as Fig. 2.

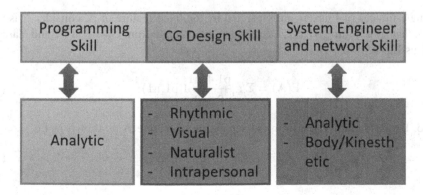

Fig. 2. Mapping model

3.1 J48 Algorithm

Algorithm J48 Decision Tree (C4.5) is the algorithm that constructed a decision tree. Algorithm J48 was developed by Ross Quinlan [8] which C4.5 additionally extended from ID3 Decision tree. This structure can be used for classification. The concept of C4.5 is the use of construction for a decision trees to classify information. The use of the gain value (Gain) and estimates data of (Entropy), as well as ID3, but there will be additional significant functions form ID3 algorithm as follows.

1. Be able to use for both the continuous information and discrete information. On the part of the continuous information, the method of C4.5 established the Threshold and extracted into 2 features which are more than or less than and equal to the value used in the creation of the Threshold.
2. Be able to apply to training data that does not have feature's value by marking the signal in these features as "?" and should not be calculated to find entropy.
3. Be able to use with the values that damaged or infected.
4. Be able to customize a Pruning Trees during construction.

3.2   ID3 Algorithm

The process of ID3 Algorithm [9] is the use of construction for decision trees by using the application of the principle of information theory. The measurement is used to decide which variables to divide data. To determine the structure of a decision tree will choose data in sequence of the indicator or gain which is the highest as beginning data and the lower gain as the next data, respectively. For example, the consideration two group data of P and N, which the sample number in P is P numbers and the sample number in N is N numbers. The value of group data is the prediction of sample group which required numbers of bits to separate classes of P and N, defined as Eq. 1.

$$I(p,n) = -\frac{p}{p+n}\log 2(\frac{p}{p+n}) - \frac{n}{p+n} - \log 2(\frac{n}{p+n}) \tag{1}$$

The estimates of Entropy are separated by the fixed feature of A, consider A is the feature that split S into {S1, S2,.., Sv}. S1 is an example from class P at P1 and class N at N1 as Eq. 2

$$E(A) = \Sigma_{i=1}^{v}\frac{p1+n1}{p+n}I(p1,n1) \tag{2}$$

So, the Data Gain value from the separation of feature A as shown in Eq. 3.

$$Gain(A) = I(p,n) - E(A) \tag{3}$$

3.3   Bayesian Network Algorithm

The Bayesian Network is a simulation graph's model that was invented by a British scientist, Thomas Bayes [10]. This model is a simulation's graph which has the Joint Probability Distribution that shown the relationship between the Node and each node in the graph. Storages of Probability Distribution used the conditional probability distribution which depended on Parents node within each node. Inside data in each node can be calculated the probability for any status of the systems.

Bayesian Network consists of;

1. Node is the set of random variables.
2. Directed Link, the connection between nodes used by the lines which has exactly direction and came from which direction. For example, Y means that X is directed influence to Y.
3. Directed acyclic graph: DAG will not occur within a stimulation graph's model.
4. The Conditional Probability Table: CPT, the construction of Joint Probability

Distribution has to create table in all possible cases such as 2Node. In some cases, we cannot find the possibility of all cases or even the possibility of the same case is also difficult. So that we can reduce table size down if there is more possibility of the Joint distribution probability. The smaller table called Conditional Probability Table: CPT which is available in every node. Also, identify the impact of Parent's node to Child node. So that Child node will be able to answer all the questions that are allowed to enter and reduce to smaller table. This is the concept of Conditional Independency.

4   Conceptual Framework

4.1   Pattern Base Module

The pattern base module is the module that keeps track of each student's IT skill by creating a pattern base. Creating a pattern base consists of 3 processes which are (1) creation of a query which contains two further sub parts: (1). Testing of Multiple intelligence exams according to the pattern of mapping model. The MI exam is designated as the dependent variables. (2). Leaner's profile which is the set of independent variables. This variable came from the interview of 5 Multiple Intelligence experts and the past research. (2) Surveyed sample group of 1,000 students (IT) from Thai Nichi Institute of Technology. (3) Result of the analysis survey creates a pattern base which can use 3 methods of analysis to compare the accuracy (Decision Tree J48, ID3, Bayes net) (Fig. 3).

4.2   Mapping Module

Mapping module is a module that is responsible on the mapping data between student's profiles and the pattern base. Mapping process will compare student profiles and the pattern base. If the comparison result matches to any pattern, it will show results.

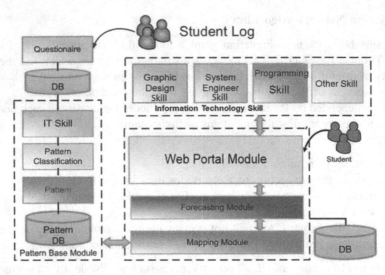

Fig. 3. Conceptual framework

4.3 Forecasting Module

Forecasting module is a module that is responsible in forecasting data which has been mapping from Mapping Module. Therefore, the main responsibility of this module shows the results of the prediction and sends the result to Web portal Module. The part of Web portal Module will directly connect to User Interface and will display the results, so learners will know which their expertise in IT field is.

4.4 Web Portal Module

The web portal module is the module that's responsible the medium between the students and the entire system since the part of web portal module will connect to 2 modules as follows; (1) Web portal module is connected to the forecasting module, mapping module and pattern base module in order to send data of the learner profile when the student logs in. The next process is mapping with the pattern base module. The forecasting module then sends the data content back to the web portal module so the student can begin. (2) The web portal module is connected to the Information Technology skill module in order to retrieve result and forward it to the student.

4.5 Information Technology Skill Module

The Information Technology skill module is a module that acts as storage which derives from the IT skill analysis by Multiple Intelligences 4 groups (1) Programming skills for the students who prefer analysis and mathematic calculation. (2) Graphic design skills that applies to the students who prefer imagination, arts and so on. (3) System engineering and network skills for the students that prefer analytic skills and kinesthetic skills.

4.6   Example of Process for Framework Working

The process starts when learner login to the system. Then, the system will input learner's profile, such as sex, age, year of studying, GPA to match with the rule of data classification from pattern base module. Then, the system stores learner profile Database. The result of the matching is to note that students who login into the system have aptitudes in the field. The next step is the recommendation module that will be responsible for getting the result of IT skill that matches to student's aptitudes which comes from Information Technology skill module and recommendation for the students.

5   Design of Pattern Base

5.1   Process for Pattern Base Design

The steps of creating pattern base divided into 4 steps. (1) First step is a survey of variables that affects the ability of IT skill for students. This process can be studied from previous research to study variables that have an impact on the ability of multiple intelligences. Moreover, there also was the interview to multiple intelligence's experts. For the interview, the researcher used the specific method for 5 people. (2) The second step is a creation of questionnaires to survey data from sample group. The question of questionnaires consists of two parts. One is question for general information of respondents (defines as a main variable) such as name, year, field, faculty, etc. Next part is the question to separate the ability of Information Technology skills (defines as a prediction variable). (3) The third step is an information survey by sample of students to answer the questionnaires which created from last part. This paper uses the sample of

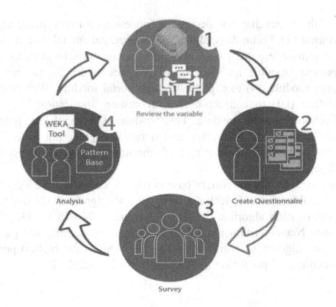

Fig. 4. Process of pattern base creation

1,000 TNI students. (4) The fourth step is using the survey's information from the third step to analyze by using Data Mining. This paper uses three algorithms to analyze. (1) ID3 algorithm (2) J48 algorithm (3) Bayes net algorithm. Process for selection algorithm is used to compare 3 algorithms for choosing for the most prediction. Figure 4 shows the process of pattern base design.

5.2   Comparison of Algorithm

This part presents the evaluation in creating pattern base to guide students by considering the percentage for the precision of student's abilities. I can compare the evaluation of creating pattern base by using 3 methods; (1) ID3 algorithm (2) J48 algorithm (5) Bayes Net algorithm. The result of the comparison is shown in Table 1.

Table 1. The comparison of creating the pattern base. The result of each algorithm is, ID3 algorithm is 74.618 %, J48 algorithm is 78.267 %, Bayes Net algorithm is 68.352 %. This paper focuses on the percentage of the prediction for each algorithm. J48 algorithm is the highest percentage of prediction. Percentage of prediction of J48 algorithm is 78.267 %.

Algorithm	% Prediction
1. ID3 algorithm	74.618
2. J48 algorithm	78.267
3. Bayes net algorithm	68.352

6   Conclusion

The objective of this research was to design the framework for student recommendation system for Information Technology skill. The conceptual model was divided into 5 sections; (1) to introduce pattern base module is an analysis by data mining. (2) to explain the mapping module for students. (3) to present the forecasting module to connect mapping module. (4) to explain the web portal module. Web portal module was User interface (UI) to connect user with system application. (5) to describe Information Technology skills module. This module consists of four parts; (1) programming skills (2) System engineering and network engineering skills (3) Graphic design skills (4) other skills. Information Technology skills are mapped by using Multiple Intelligence principle.

The process for selection the pattern base is used to compared the algorithm which is consists of five algorithms (1) ID3 algorithm (2) J48 algorithm (3) Bayes Net algorithm. The result of each algorithm is, ID3 algorithm is 74.618 %, J48 algorithm is 78.267 %, Bayes Net algorithm is 68.352 %. When considering the percentage of prediction for each algorithm, it shows that J48 algorithm is the highest percentage of prediction. Percentage of prediction of J48 algorithm is 78.267 %.

References

1. Wanissan, D.: A recommendation system to choose a study program based on repertory grid. In: NCCIT, Bangkok, pp. 780–785 (2014)
2. Firte, A.: Intelligent component for adaptive E-learning systems. In: IEEE 5th International Conference on Intelligent Computer Communication and Processing, pp. 35–38 (2009)
3. Kaewkiriya, T., Utrakrit, N., Tiantong, M.: A conceptual framework of synthesize on an adaptive e-learning guidance system base on multiple intelligence. Int. J. Inf. Electron. Eng. 3(6), 622–625 (2013)
4. Ployong, N., Porrawatpreyakorn, N.: A comparison of decision tree and support vector machine techniques for classifying students for e-learning in information technology course. In: NCCIT, Bangkok, pp. 127–132 (2013)
5. Norwawi, N.: Classification of students' performance in computer programming course according to learning style. In: IEEE-DMO 2009, pp. 37–41 (2009)
6. Kolekar, S.: Learning style recognition using artificial neural network for adaptive user interface in e-learning. In: Proceedings of IEEE-Computational Intelligence and Computing Research, pp. 1–5 (2010)
7. Gardner, B., Korth, S.: A framework for learning to work in teams. J. Educ. Bus. 74(1), 28–33 (2010)
8. Quinlan, J.R.: C4.5 Programs for Machine Learning. Morgan Kaufmann Publishers, San Francisco (1993)
9. Qui, R.: Ductio of decisio trees. Mach. Learn. 1(1), 81–106 (1986)
10. Bayesian Network. http://en.wikipedia.org/wiki/Bayesian_network. Accessed 15 January 2015

Improving Knowledge Management in Patient Safety Reporting: A Semantic Web Ontology Approach

Chen Liang and Yang Gong[(⊠)]

The University of Texas Health Science Center at Houston,
Houston, TX, USA
{Chen.Liang,Yang.Gong}@uth.tmc.edu

Abstract. Patient safety reporting system is in an imperative need for reducing and learning from medical errors. Presently, a great number of the reporting systems are suffering low quality of data and poor system performance associated with data quality. For improving the quality of data and the system performance towards reducing harm in healthcare, we introduce an ontological approach with the scope of establishing a comprehensive knowledgebase. A semantic web ontology plays a crucial role to facilitate the knowledge transformation ranging from human-to-computer data entry to computer-to-human knowledge retrieval. The paper describes the theoretical foundation, design, implementation, and evaluation of the prototype ontology. Based on W3C open standard Web Ontology Language (OWL), the proposed ontology was designed and implemented in Protégé 4.3. We envision that utilizing semantic web ontology would serve as a uniformed knowledgebase facilitating information retrieval and clinical decision making.

Keywords: Knowledge management · Ontology · Clinical information system · Patient safety

1 Introduction

In the effort of improving patient safety, much attention has centered on the importance, benefits, and challenges of developing well-functioning patient safety reporting systems. Among many other research aspects in patient safety, the knowledge management under human-computer interaction (HCI) was identified as one crucial research objective to address the challenges, including data types to report [1], means to minimize reporting costs [2], and means to conduct evaluation [3], which present weak links to the reporting systems. A pivotal role of knowledge in patient safety embodies in bridging patient safety data and healthcare quality. The development and application of knowledgebase is prominent in sharing and learning from safety events. High quality data can provide invaluable insights into potential safety concerns and benefit root cause analysis for further intervening measures. Therefore, its importance has been increasingly recognized [1, 4, 5].

© Springer International Publishing Switzerland 2015
S. Yamamoto (Ed.): HIMI 2015, Part II, LNCS 9173, pp. 118–128, 2015.
DOI: 10.1007/978-3-319-20618-9_12

A great number of reporting systems are suffering low quality of data, such as inefficiency and ineffectiveness of data entry, inconsistency in data formats, and technical challenges in processing text data [1, 6, 7]. The increase in quantity generated by reporting systems does not guarantee an improvement of performance in reporting systems, on the contrary gradually becomes a burden for data processing. This is primarily because the majority of patient safety data is recorded in free text. Although free text might be an efficient and natural means for users to deliver informative cases, it could be costly to turn the raw information into a cognitively organized and manageable format for professionals to use. The usage of pre-defined reporting categories was proposed as a key component in patient safety reporting [1]. However, structured data entry as such could be limited on both timeliness and accuracy [8]. Natural language provides the richest information that conveys details of patient safety events [9, 10], yet on the other hand, it prevents traditional computerized system from effectively processing the data. It is generally agreed that manually categorizing large scale dataset is not practical. Due to these barriers, the data quality has hindered the development of patient safety reporting.

Taxonomies can be used to solve these problems, as they are capable of managing patient safety events as a knowledgebase. The use of taxonomies for documenting and classifying patient safety reports can be traced back to 1987 when the Australian Patient Safety Foundation (APSF) originally employed a taxonomy in the Australian Incident Monitoring System [11]. Later on, many other taxonomies were developed to perform the similar function. Most of them serve a variety of purposes from one hospital to another and vary in structures and terminologies. Nevertheless, the taxonomies developed for organizing patient safety events yield limited values for healthcare providers and patients. A notable barrier to learning from safety events was known as the lack of comprehensive architecture and sharable format for the taxonomy [12]. Clear and consistent definitions and terms are a core in describing a full spectrum of patient safety. The World Health Organization (WHO) World Alliance for Patient Safety launched a project which described a conceptual framework for International Classification for Patient Safety (ICPS) [13]. A drafting group of WHO intended to construct a standardized collection of concepts in a hierarchy. The ICPS serves as a taxonomy of patient safety and an underlying knowledgebase supporting any types of patient safety reporting. However, clinical practice in patient safety reporting still needs a transformation from ICPS to a localized patient safety classification. For example, the Common Definitions and Reporting Formats (a.k.a., Common Formats) (CFs) promulgated by The Agency for Healthcare Research and Quality (AHRQ) were made compatible with ICPS and used for patient safety reporting in US hospitals [1]. ICPS and CFs, working as a combination, benefit reporting, managing, and improving of patient safety reports from the perspectives of both academic research and clinical practice. Unfortunately, they show limited advantages in handling ever-growing concepts, terms, and real-world data cooperated into reporting systems.

2 Background

2.1 Semantic Web Ontology

Ontologies are explicit specifications of conceptualizations where these specifications define a taxonomy of the knowledge [14]. In medical error reporting, a taxonomy is served as a controlled vocabulary represented in a hierarchical structure. In general, an ontology provides a broader scope to describe domain information than a taxonomy. In specific, an ontology models real-world knowledge by encoding entities and relationships between them.

A semantic web describes information with explicit meanings and supports machine interpretable web content [15]. The semantic web ontology has been used in biomedical domain for various purposes in terms of facilitating biomedical data integration, managing biomedical concepts, and supporting ontology-driven biomedical natural language processing (NLP), disambiguation and named-entity recognition (NER) [16, 17]. Semantic web ontology was employed in our project because it captures both a hierarchical structure of patient safety concepts and relations among related concepts [18]. In addition, semantic web technologies are made compatible with descriptive logic reasoning and other data mining processes. In the project, we build a semantic web ontology using W3C open standard Web Ontology Language (OWL), through which we are able to (1) identify unique concepts/terms that appear in different sources or in different terms; (2) encode all the relations between concepts/terms in a certain domain; and (3) perform semantic reasoning.

2.2 Source Taxonomy

WHO International Classification for Patient Safety. The ICPS conceptual framework contains approximately 600 patient safety concepts across the existing classifications. The concepts are organized under ten top-level categories, which are incident type, patient characteristics, incident characteristics, detection, mitigating factors, patient outcomes, organizational outcomes, ameliorating actions, actions taken to reduce risk, and contributing factors/hazards. Each category may contain subcategories for organizing substantial concepts. The ICPS provides a supportive structure, which helps the transformation into an ontology. For this reason, we used ICPS conceptual framework as the cornerstone of our proposed ontology. In specific, we kept the hierarchical structure and the concepts and terms used in ICPS as a founding stone for the subsequent design and revision.

AHRQ Common Formats. The Common Formats (v1.2) developed by AHRQ are primarily designed for clinical purposes. Recognized as a unified standard of reporting patient safety events, the CFs are designed to specify and collect event information, which range from general concerns to frequently occurring and serious types of the events. The complete forms are comprised of generic formats and event-specific formats. The generic formats are designed for collecting incidents, near misses, and unsafe conditions that occur in all patient safety events. Types of information being collected are organized into the following subcategories: types of event, circumstances of event, patient information, and reporting/reporter/report information. The event-specific formats are particularly used for collecting patient safety concerns that occur in a high frequency and/or in severe events. These formats collect information such as definitions of the event, scope of reporting, risk assessments and preventive actions, and circumstances of the event. We employed CFs as the additional data source where we extracted and encoded semantic knowledge into our ontology.

3 Design and Implementation

3.1 The Framework

The main component in an ontology statement is a set of triples, which constitute what are assumed to be true in certain domain [15]. A simple triple declares entities in the domain and the relations between them. For example,

Cellular products has Red blood cells

"*Cellular products*" and "red blood cells" plasma are entities we assume to be true in the domain that an ontology models. Whereas "has" is a type of relations that links the two entities. This triple is assumed to be true in the ontology and must pass the semantic reasoning so that it contains meanings.

Similarly in ICPS, the concepts and terms being used are true assumptions and fundamental in our ontology. As a result, we imported the concepts and terms from ICPS and the CF concepts originated from ICPS. For the differences between ICPS and CFs, we adopted the CFs concepts with a prioritized consideration of the practical needs in patient safety reporting in US hospitals. For example, patient fall is one of the frequently occurred events that has been reported to AHRQ Patient Safety Organization. Nevertheless, there is no definition or individual category in ICPS. It is assured that ICPS is still under development and evaluation by WHO experts from various disciplines. Therefore, we believe it is beneficial to the design and implementation of the ontology when keeping a flexible consideration of using combined concepts, and/or the knowledge structure. To help understand the framework, we visualize of the top-level concepts of the ontology shown in Table 1.

Table 1. List of concepts and terms for top-level ontology

Incident type:
Clinical administration:
Clinical process/procedure:
Documentation:
Healthcare associated infection:
Type of organism:
Bacteria
Virus
Fungus
...
Type/site of infection:
Bloodstream

```
                            Surgical site
                            Abscess
                            ...
        Medication/IV fluids:
        Blood/blood products:
        Nutrition:
        Oxygen/gas/vapour:
        Medical device/equipment:
        Behavior:
        Patient accidents:
                Blunt force:
                Piercing/penetrating force:
                ...
                Fall:
                            Type of fall:
                            Fall involving:
                            Patient activity immediately prior to the fall:
                                    Navigating bedrails
                                    Toileting
                                    Changing position
                                    ...
        Infrastructure/building/fixtures:
        Resources/organizational management:
Patient outcomes:
        Type of harm:
        Degree of harm:
        Social and/or economic impact:
Patient characteristics:
        Patient demographics:
        Reason for encounter:
        Diagnosis/procedure:
Incident characteristics:
        Origin of incident:
                People involved:
                        Who:
                        Discipline/specialty
                When:
                Where:
                Medication identifier:
                Risk assessments and preventive actions:
                Processes of care:
                Device/HIT device:
        Discovery of incident:
        Reporting of incident:
Contributing factors:
Mitigating factors:
Detection:
Organizational outcomes:
Ameliorating actions:
Actions to reduce risk:
```

3.2   Data Transformation

Although the entities implemented in our ontology were initially exported from ICPS and CFs, the data cannot be directly used for ontology constructing without a translation. This is because ontology breaks a triple down into entities and relations, whereas the concepts and terms used in ICPS and CFs were not designed in this fashion. The translational processes were comprised of two steps.

First, we followed a set of principles towards a comprehensible ontology to obtain high-quality data from ICPS and CFs [19]. Most concepts and terms from ICPS are semantically clear, and are ready to be imported to our ontology. Since CFs are used as a guideline for real-world patient safety data entries, the concepts and terms do not fit for the ontology without a transformation. Three coders, including two Doctors of Medicine (YG and XW) and one ontology developer (CL), participated in the translational process.

Second, we manually extracted the relations that link concepts and terms in ICPS and CFs, and implemented them into the ontology. The relations in ICPS have a clear schema since ICPS was developed as a uniform classification where the hierarchical relations between concepts/terms have been well defined. Following ICPS structure, we linked the selected concepts and terms in CFs with those in ICPS by utilizing the existing relations extracted from ICPS and/or defining appropriate relations. Four reviewers (YG, XW, CL, and KA) discussed the effectiveness of the relation implementation and performed revisions until a consensus was reached.

3.3   Ontology Implementation

We imported the corresponding data into the ontology implemented in Protégé 4.3.0. Then, we performed consistency checking, classification, and semantic reasoning for the ontology once the implementation was completed [20, 21]. The ontology constructed a uniform knowledge representation that links the entities and relations of patient safety reports.

3.4   Evaluation

We performed an evaluation intended to demonstrate the effectiveness and validity of the ontology. The evaluation was designed to assess two portions, (1) user experience of domain experts and, (2) effectiveness and validity of the ontology. A questionnaire in a 5-point Likert scale was designed for the evaluation. An example of the draft questionnaire is shown in Table 2.

The questionnaire is subject to a pre-assessment prior to domain experts' evaluation on the ontology. The pre-assessment was intended for measuring the content validity and inter-rater reliability of the questionnaire and revising of the questionnaire as needed. The content validity measures to what extent the designed questions subjectively reflect the tasks they purpose to measure. The inter-rater reliability measures the degree of agreement among the raters. Table 3 enumerates a set of scales that were used for content validity in the pre-assessment. The measurement for inter-rater reliability is gained by using the questions shown in Table 2.

Table 2. A set of questions listed in the questionnaire for ontology evaluation

1. The phrases used in the vocabulary are well-formed and the words are well-arranged.
2. The terms used in the vocabulary can explain the meanings of real-world concepts.
3. The terms that appear in the vocabulary are clear. For example, if a vocabulary claims that class "Chair" has the property "Salary", an agent must know that this describes academics, not furniture.
4. The vocabulary provides sufficient knowledge in the designated domain to the user.
5. The information the vocabulary provides is clear.
6. The vocabulary can satisfy your requirements when you use it to categorize the case you are reviewing.
7. Please rate the overall satisfaction based on your experience using the vocabulary.
Note: We use a 5-point scale for the measurement (1 = strongly disagree; 2 = disagree; 3 = neither agree nor disagree; 4 = agree; 5 = strongly agree).

Table 3. Questions for measuring content validity

1. "The phrases used in the vocabulary are well-formed and the words are well-arranged." Does the scale purport to measure "The correctness of syntax."?
2. "The terms used in the vocabulary can explain the meanings of real-world concepts." Does the scale purport to measure "The meaningfulness of terms."?
3. "The terms that appear in the vocabulary are clear. For example, if a vocabulary claims that class "Chair" has the property "Salary", an agent must know that this describes academics, not furniture." Does the scale purport to measure "The clarity of terms."?
4. "The vocabulary provides sufficient knowledge in the designated domain to the user." Does the scale purport to measure "The comprehensiveness of the vocabulary in a certain domain."?
5. "The information the vocabulary provide is accurate." Does the scale purport to measure "The accuracy of information."?
6. "The vocabulary can satisfy your requirements when you use it to categorize the case you are reviewing." Does the scale purport to measure "Whether the vocabulary specifies agent's specific requirements."?
7. "Please rate the overall satisfaction based on your experience using the vocabulary." Does the scale purport to measure "The overall satisfaction to the vocabulary."?
8. "Please select the types of event. (You may select one or more items.)" Does the scale purport to measure "The event type of the report."?
9. "Please select the types of error. (You may select one or more items.)" Does the scale purport to measure "The error type of the report."?
10. "Please select the contributing factors of the reported event. (You may select one or more items.)" Does the scale purport to measure "The contributing factors of the report."?
11. "Please select the risk factors of the event. (You may select one or more items.)" Does the scale purport to measure "The risk factors of the report."?
12. "Please rate the value of the present event for preventing similar events in the future." Does the scale purport to measure "The value of the report for preventing similar events in the future."?
13. "Please rate the education value of the reported event." Does the scale purport to measure "The educational value of the report."?
Note: We use a 4-point scale for the measurement (Not relevant; Somewhat relevant; Quite relevant; Highly relevant).

4 Discussion and Future Work

Patient safety research has shown a rapid growth in the past decade. However, the depth on research and a broader application of patient safety system have been constrained by road blocks such as redundant volume of data, inconsistency in data formats, and technical challenges in processing semantic data [1, 6]. We proposed an ontology to represent the concepts/terms and the relations towards a knowledgebase for representing patient safety data and information. The goal of this ontological knowledgebase is to facilitate data entry, information retrieval and data management in the patient safety reporting system. The present work employing an ontological method holds promise to address the challenges in patient safety research.

The present work is a part of the effort to build a uniformed knowledgebase, which is identified as a significant contribution in patient safety report. Redundant volume and low quality of patient safety data reveal a pressing need for a comprehensive knowledgebase, which could aid data entry and storage towards clinical usage and research. Ironically, there is no lack of well-defined taxonomies over decades. As shown in Table 4, a list of patient safety taxonomies/ontologies that were previously used or being presently in use.

Table 4. A review of taxonomies/ontologies used for specific domains

Taxonomies	Usages
Australian Patient Safety Foundation (APSF) [11]	Incident monitoring
A cognitive taxonomy of medical errors [22]	Categorize major types of human error contributing to medical errors
JACHO patient safety event taxonomy [23]	–
National coordinating council for medication error reporting and prevention (NCC MERP)'s taxonomy of medication errors [24]	–
Neonatal Intensive Care system (NIC) [25]	–
Pediatric Patient Safety taxonomy (PED) [26]	Pediatrics
Preliminary Taxonomy of medical errors in Family Practice (PTFP) [27]	Family healthcare
Taxonomy of Nursing Errors (TNE) [28]	Nursery
Adverse Event Reporting Ontology (AERO) [29]	Vaccine adverse event reports

While these taxonomies/ontologies served primarily as standards of domain specific taxonomies, the rapid increase in medical information calls for a uniformed knowledgebase that can be used across patient safety reporting systems. ICPS and CFs are two remarkable milestones to represent patient safety events. They significantly contribute to disambiguation of concepts and terms by defining the uniformed concepts and preferred terms. In particular, ICPS lays particular emphasis on defining uniformed concepts and preferred terms, which holds promise to increase the data quality for patient reporting systems [13]. CFs received a nationwide acceptance in US hospitals because CFs provide a standard to record a wide range from general concerns to frequently occurred patient safety events and serious types of the events. These features bought by CFs hold critical meanings in practical use. For example, Patient fall as an incident type takes a large portion in hospital statistics in the US. CFs count 'patient fall' as a type of frequent occurrence in hospital, whereas in ICPS this concept and/or term has not been defined or not shown the significance. From this viewpoint, CFs play an important role in the practical use of patient safety knowledgebase. Towards integrating the advantages of ICPS and CFs, our ontology may provide better standardization and flexibility for nation-wide usage in US hospitals.

The present work endeavors to meet the challenges of data consistency and semantic data processing, therefore provides a different angle to improving data quality in patient safety reporting. Among many factors that are fundamental for high quality data in patient safety reporting, the incompleteness and inaccuracy of data were identified as two major concerns [1, 30]. Our strategy for addressing these concerns is focusing on data entry, a critical step in the reporting system [8, 31, 32]. Meanwhile, the capability of system to deal with semantic data has largely drawn our attention since the majority of patient safety data are recorded in free text. Our ontological approach helps improve the system performance in terms of data entry and semantic data processing. It is a reasonable yet technically challenging approach in data management and information retrieval that a data entry combining both structured format and unstructured format. The ontology used as a conceptual map would help annotate unstructured data mapping to a domain conceptual map where concepts, terms, and relations are contained. For the semantic data processing, the ontology serves as a thesaurus to support NLP for information extraction tasks. The ontology also helps disambiguation when terms (i.e., acronym) used in patient safety may represent different things. Therefore, there is a pressing need in developing a domain ontology.

During the development of the ontology, we need to continuously evaluate its effectiveness, confidence, and acceptance in multiple dimensions. We are currently evaluating whether our ontology is valid in a broad scale and how compatible it would be when it works under various reporting systems across healthcare settings. In the future, we will design and implement a pipeline to collect, manage, analyze, and retrieve patient safety data supported by the ontology. The pipeline functions as modules of sharing the domain knowledge and supporting date entry, semantic data annotation, document similarity and so forth.

Acknowledgement. We thank Drs. Khalid Almoosa, Xinshuo Wu, and Jing Wang for their expertise and participation in data translation and code review. This project is in part supported by a grant on patient safety from the University of Texas System and a grant from AHRQ, grant number 1R01HS022895.

References

1. Gong, Y.: Data consistency in a voluntary medical incident reporting system. J. Med. Syst. **35**, 609–615 (2011)
2. Thompson, D.A., et al.: Integrating the intensive care unit safety reporting system with existing incident reporting systems. Jt. Comm. J. Qual. Patient Saf. / Jt. Comm. Resour. **31**, 585–593 (2011)

3. Itoh, K., Andersen, H.B.: Analysing medical incident reports by use of a human error taxonomy. In: Spitzer, C., et al. (eds.) Probabilistic Safety Assessment and Management Probabilistic safety assessment and management, pp. 2714–2719. Springer, London (2004)
4. Zhan, C., Miller, M.R.: Administrative data based patient safety research: a critical review. Qual. Saf. Heal. Care **12**, ii58–ii63 (2003)
5. Miller, M.R., Elixhauser, A., Zhan, C., Meyer, G.S.: Patient safety indicators: using administrative data to identify potential patient safety concerns. Health Serv. Res. **36**, 110–132 (2001)
6. Gong, Y.: Terminology in a voluntary medical incident reporting system: a human-centered perspective. In: Proceedings of the 1st ACM International Health Informatics Symposium. ACM, pp. 2–7 (2010)
7. Pronovost, P.J., Morlock, L.L., Sexton, J.B., Miller, M.R., Holzmueller, C.G., Thompson, D.A., Lubomski, L.H., Wu, A.W.: Improving the value of patient safety reporting systems. In: Advances in Patient Safety: New Directions and Alternative Approaches. Assessment vol. 1, pp. 1–9 (2008)
8. McDonald, C.J.: The barriers to electronic medical record systems and how to overcome them. J. Am. Med. Inform. Assoc. **4**, 213–221 (1997)
9. Sager, N., Friedman, C.: M.S.L.: Review of "medical language processing: computer management of narrative data". Comput. Linguist. **15**, 195–198 (1989)
10. Friedman, C., Johnson, S.B.: Natural language and text processing in biomedicine. In: Shortliffe, E.H., Cimino, J.J. (eds.) Biomedical Informatics: Computer Applications in Health Care and Biomedicine. Health Informatics, pp. 312–343. Springer, New York (2006)
11. Spigelman, A.D., Swan, J.: Review of the Australian incident monitoring system. ANZ J. Surg. **75**, 657–661 (2005)
12. Battles, J.B., Kaplan, H., Van der Schaaf, T., Shea, C.: The attributes of medical event-reporting systems. Arch. Pathol. Lab. Med. **122**, 132–138 (1998)
13. Sherman, H., et al.: Towards an international classification for patient safety: the conceptual framework. Int. J. Qual. Health Care **21**, 2–8 (2009)
14. O'Leary, D.E.: Using AI in knowledge management: knowledge bases and ontologies. IEEE Intell. Syst. Their Appl. **13**, 34–39 (1998)
15. McGuinness, D.L., van Harmelen, F.: OWL Web Ontology Language Overview
16. Maynard, D., Li, Y., Peters, W.: NLP techniques for term extraction and ontology population. In: Proceeding of the 2008 conference on Ontology Learning and Population: Bridging the Gap between Text and Knowledge, pp. 107–127 (2008)
17. Ananiadou, S., McNaught, J.: Text Mining for Biology and Biomedicine. Artech House, London (2006)
18. Gilchrist, A.: Thesauri, taxonomies and ontologies – an etymological note. J. Doc. **59**, 7–18 (2003)
19. Burton-Jones, A., Storey, V.C., Sugumaran, V., Ahluwalia, P.: A semiotic metrics suite for assessing the quality of ontologies. Data Knowl. Eng. **55**, 84–102 (2005)
20. Sirin, E., Parsia, B., Grau, B.C., Kalyanpur, A., Katz, Y.: Pellet: a practical owl-dl reasoner. Web Semant. Sci. Serv. Agents World Wide Web. **5**, 51–53 (2007)
21. Tsarkov, D., Horrocks, I.: FaCT++ description logic reasoner: system description. In: Furbach, U., Shankar, N. (eds.) IJCAR 2006. LNCS (LNAI), vol. 4130, pp. 292–297. Springer, Heidelberg (2006)
22. Zhang, J., Patel, V.L., Johnson, T.R., Shortliffe, E.H.: A cognitive taxonomy of medical errors. J. Biomed. Inform. **37**, 193–204 (2004)
23. Chang, A., Schyve, P.M., Croteau, R.J., O'Leary, D.S., Loeb, J.M.: The JCAHO patient safety event taxonomy: a standardized terminology and classification schema for near misses and adverse events. Int. J. Qual. Heal. Care. **17**, 95–105 (2005)

24. Brixey, J., Johnson, T.R., Zhang, J.: Evaluating a medical error taxonomy. In: Proceedings AMIA Symposium, pp. 71–75 (2002)
25. Suresh, G., et al.: Voluntary anonymous reporting of medical errors for neonatal intensive care. Pediatr. **113**, 1609–1618 (2004)
26. Woods, D.M., Johnson, J., Holl, J.L., Mehra, M., Thomas, E.J., Ogata, E.S., Lannon, C.: Anatomy of a patient safety event: a pediatric patient safety taxonomy. Qual. Saf. Health Care. **14**, 422–427 (2005)
27. Dovey, S.M., Meyers, D.S., Phillips, R.L., Green, L.A., Fryer, G.E., Galliher, J.M., Kappus, J., Grob, P.: A preliminary taxonomy of medical errors in family practice. Qual Saf Health Care **11**(3), 233–238 (2002)
28. Woods, A., Doan-Johnson, S.: Executive summary: toward a taxonomy of nursing practice errors. Nurs. Manage. **33**, 45–48 (2002)
29. Greens, R.A.: Clinical Decision Support: The Road Ahead. Academic Press, San Diego (2006)
30. Tuttle, D., Holloway, R., Baird, T., Sheehan, B., Skelton, W.K.: Electronic reporting to improve patient safety. Qual. Saf. Health Care. **13**, 281–286 (2004)
31. Kaplan, B.: Reducing barriers to physician data entry for computer-based patient records. Top. Health Inf. Manage. **15**, 24–34 (1994)
32. Walsh, S.H.: The clinician's perspective on electronic health records and how they can affect patient care. BMJ **328**, 1184–1187 (2004)

Human Error and e-Navigation: Developing the Nautical Chart as Resilient Decision Support

Thomas Porathe(✉)

Norwegian Universality of Science and Technology,
Trondheim, Norway
thomas.porathe@ntnu.no

Abstract. Recent development of HCI on the ship bridge has led to a discussion of deskilling and out of the loop syndrome; of the "navigating navigator" versus the "monitoring navigator". In this paper work done on some new design concepts for decision-support systems on the ship's bridge is presented. The work has focused on keeping the navigator in the loop while sharing information to the wider maritime system: route exchange.

The paper offers an overview of the route exchange concept developed in the ACCSEAS and MONALISA projects as well as the results of recent tests done in a ship handling simulator at Chalmers University of Technology and in ship trials in Korea.

The results of the concept development have so far been mostly positive and professional actors participating in user tests have mainly been positive.

Keywords: e-navigation · MONALISA · ACCSEAS · Human error · ECDIS · Route exchange

1 Introduction

The maritime world entered the world of electronics more than a century ago with Marconi and the radio telegraph. With the sinking of Titanic the radio became an important safety device and soon it became evident that it could also be used in navigation (Radio Direction Finding). From there on RADAR, autopilot, DECCA, GPS, ECDIS, and AIS has become familiar maritime acronyms on the road to safer shipping. Presently the International Maritime Organization (IMO) is working on what has been termed an "e-Navigation" concept defined as "the harmonized collection, integration, exchange, presentation and analysis of maritime information onboard and ashore by electronic means to enhance berth to berth navigation and related services, for safety and security at sea and protection of the marine environment" [1]. The development of advanced computerized navigation has for many years keep a discussion about the "navigating navigator" versus the "monitoring navigator" alive, up to a point where IMO's Sub-Committee on Radio Communications and Search and Rescue (COMSAR) in 2011decided that the navigator should be kept in the loop as a "navigating navigator" [2].

© Springer International Publishing Switzerland 2015
S. Yamamoto (Ed.): HIMI 2015, Part II, LNCS 9173, pp. 129–139, 2015.
DOI: 10.1007/978-3-319-20618-9_13

Deskilling is, as in many other walks of professional life, a companion to modern development. Few mariners would today be able to handle astronomical navigation should the automated satellite systems go down. The accident with Air France 447 that crashed in the Atlantic Ocean in 2009 because the automatic flight management system failed and handed the aircraft over to an unexperienced pilot that could not fly - to put it bluntly [3].

How can we ensure that modern technology is used for safety improvement while still keeping the navigator in the loop, practicing skills that allow him or her to step in and perform professionally in times when automation fails? Hollnagel [4] called "the intrinsic ability of a system to adjust its functioning prior to, during, or following changes and disturbances, so that it can sustain required operations under both expected and unexpected conditions," for Resilience Engineering.

This paper presents the development of "route exchange", a decision-support function for ship navigation, within two EU projects. However, let us first give an example of the problem.

1.1   The Trans Agila Accident

In the dark hours of the morning the 29 November 2012 the Antigua registered container vessel Trans Agila grounded in the Strait of Kalmar on the Swedish east coast. The second mate was alone on the bridge at the time of grounding as the lookout had gone down to prepare for embarking the pilot, who was shortly due. As he negotiated the final turn before the stretch down to where the pilot boat waited he passed on the wrong side of Bredgrund lateral red light-buoy, failing to enter into the white sector of Masknaggen sector light, instead approaching in the green sector and passing it on the ship's port instead of starboard side, subsequently grounding. The grounding resulted in a flooded engine room and a total loss of the hull, however no personal injuries.

The accident investigation reported that the track of the voyage plan that had been entered into the Electronic Chart Display and Information System (ECDIS) was wrong, leading right over Bredgrund buoy and on the wrong side of Masknaggen light, bringing the ship with a draught of 4.8 m over several shallow areas (see Fig. 1). On a paper chart carried onboard the crucial waypoint had been correctly marked, but in the electronic chart system the way-point had been misplaced. Voyage plans are mandatory parts of the preparations for a voyage by regulations from the IMO. The second officer, who was the watch officer this nigh, was also the one responsible for the voyage planning onboard.

The accident report [5] suggest considering moving the mandatory pilot pick-up point further out to make sure ships get assistance also for the section of the fairway where the accident occurred. But the accident report leaves several questions unanswered: How could an obviously faulty voyage plan remain unnoticed? And during the actual voyage, why did the watch officer not notice that the ship was sailing on the wrong side of both the buoy and the sector light into waters that was obviously too shallow for the ship?

This was a minor accident, leading to economic loss, but no loss of lives. But we could continue to list accidents with fare worse outcomes. The Exxon Valdes and the

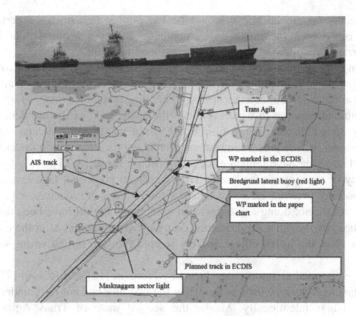

Fig. 1. Top. Trans Agila with flooded engine room is re-floated and moved to safety. Bottom: Planned track, actual route as well as the correct waypoint (WP) from the paper chart.

Sleipner ferry accident, both belong to this category of accidents. I have chosen this accident because it is recent; it occurred in waters well-known to Scandinavian mariners and happened under normal, almost perfect conditions: darkness, but good visibility in well-lit fairways and calm weather. It is an illustration of an accident that, when we ask for the reason, we get the unsatisfying answer: human error.

1.2 Human Error

In 1997, IMO adopted a resolution setting out the organizations vision, principles and goals for what it called the human element. "The human element is a complex multi-dimensional issue that affects maritime safety, security and marine environmental protection involving the entire spectrum of human activities performed by ships' crews, shore based management, regulatory bodies and others" [6].

Working with the human element often means working with imprecise and varying behaviour, with mistakes, slips and lapses. In short: working with human error. But it also means working with human ingenuity, with creativity and miraculous recovery, in short; with human error resilience. And one has to remember that while human error is always recorded in accident statistics, human recovery is seldom mentioned, let alone accounted for in statistics.

Most accidents are the result of a chain of minor mishaps. James Reason [7] introduced the "Swiss cheese model" and the notion of safety barriers that would prevent a potential unsafe act to promulgate into an accident. Examples of such barriers in the accidents mentioned above would be the pilot which brings experience and second pair of eye on to the bridge, or the mandatory look-out during dark hours – both of these barriers was missing in the aforementioned accident.

But even if the accident can be seen as a chain of events where safety barriers have been breached, there is most often an unsafe act somewhere that triggers it all. It could be a technical breakdown, but as technology becomes more and more robust, it is ever so often a human operator in what is called "the sharp end" of the accident pyramid; and many studies indicates figures from 60–90 % of major accidents and incidents in complex systems such as process industries, medicine or transportation systems such as aviation and shipping have human error as a primary cause [8–11].

A variety of taxonomies for human error has been proposed. One example is the simple dichotomy between *errors of omission* and *errors of commission* [12]. Errors of omission mean: not doing anything when something should have been done. Error of commission, on the other hand, means: doing the wrong thing, as in the example of Trans Agila when the watch officer actively steered the ship on the wrong side of the lighthouse.

A more elaborated taxonomy developed by Norman [13] and Reason [7] involves *mistakes*, *slips* and *lapses*. Mistakes are when the operator has not fully understood the situation and acts intentionally. Maybe the second mate of Trans Agila had not understood the fact that he was heading into danger, in such a case the mistake was due to lack of situation awareness.

Slips, on the other hand, are when the intention is right but the action is carried out wrong. Maybe the wrong button is pressed although the intention was to press the right one. Because humans monitor their own actions, slips are often noticed and corrected before any harm has been done.

Lapses, finally, are a failure of making any action at all, i.e. an error of omission. Often they are lapses of memory, forgetfulness. Humans forget, we become distracted or think about other things. This is all part of the human condition; the abovementioned accident could have a laps. Lapses are sometimes easy to prevent by technical solutions.

1.3 Technical Solutions

A common solution for lapses is technical solutions, e.g. checklists: whenever we start a procedure that involves many steps, and where forgetting to execute a step might be hazardous, a checklist can be used. A common example is the checklists pilot's use when doing the pre-flight checks of the airplane's systems.

Technical checks can also be built into systems to prevent faults to be made. In the case of the Trans Agila above a waypoint had been placed on the wrong side of a lighthouse resulting in a track that went over areas too shallow for the ship. Most ECDIS has technical provisions to make sure the planned track is validated against a set depth value. And without such validation the ECDIS should not be able to feed the ship's autopilot with the course from the chart system. If such a system was properly used and the draught of the ship was correctly fed into the system, the validation procedure should have warned about the lack of under keel clearance. The accident report does not give any answer to whether a validation had been done before the ship left port, or not. Most ECDIS also allows the operator to set a cross-track-error, a distance the ship is allowed to deviate from its planned track before an alarm is triggered. Many times there are also some kinds of "safety sector" function, a sector that is stretched out in front of the ship and which sets off an alarm if the water in front of the ship becomes too shallow. Unfortunately both of these functions is often deactivated by bridge officers during transits in confined waters because the alarm go off constantly because of narrow passages and close turns.

Technical solutions like this can, and are, constantly developed by equipment manufacturers. The problem is only that they are context insensitive and "stupid" giving frequent false alarms and therefore often disconnected by the mariners. If they even know they exist, because elegant technical solutions often tend to make systems even more complex (known as the problem of *complexity creep*), and one big problem in shipping is the lack of standards in ECDIS and other complex systems. An officer trained in one system might get very little for free when encountering another system at another ship.

So how can we deal with this situation? One way is to make use of human adaptivity and resilience. By sharing intentions with other actors, the chance is that a shared effort discover anomalies missed on the own ship. One such feature is the proposed *route exchange*.

1.4   Route Exchange

As mentioned before, every ship is by regulations forced to do a berth-to-berth voyage plan before leaving port. This intended route resides in the navigation system of each ship. By enabling vessels to send and receive each other's routes, and display them on their own ECDIS, other eyes in the maritime domain might detect anomalies. The pilot boat waiting further down the fairway for Trans Agila in the example above might have noted the faulty intentions and warned the watch officer. Such show of intentions could be made by transmitting a few waypoints ahead of each ships present position using the ships transponder system. And the track could, on request, be made visible on the ECDIS of ships within range.

A more elaborate system could involve sending the entire voyage plan from berth to berth to a coordination centre where a second validation for under keel clearance could be made. With careful consideration of the planned time schedule, dynamic separation like in air traffic control could be achieved, making sure no two ships are at the same place at the same time.

The same system of transmitting routes might further make it possible for shore-based services to send routes to vessels. Pilots and VTS operators could then assist ships by sending out route suggestions when they notice that bad route choices have been made. In this way it might be possible to create greater system resilience by integrating ship and shore teams through information sharing.

2   Method

In three recent and on-going EU projects, EfficienSea (2009–2013) [14], MOANLISA 1 + 2 (2011–2015) [15] and ACCSEAS (2012–2015) [16], the route exchange idea has been investigated. The E-navigation Prototype Display (EPD), an ECDIS-like chart experiment platform, has been developed by the Danish Maritime Authority. This prototype display have the ability to show other ships route intentions and to send entire voyage plans to a shore-based Ship Traffic Coordination Centre for checks and optimization.

2.1   Intended Route

Tactical route exchange (route intentions and route suggestions) was developed in the EfficienSea and ACCSEAS projects. In the prototype system a configurable number of waypoints ahead of the ships present position were transmitted. The intended route could then be received and displayed on other ships with the same prototype software (see Fig. 2).

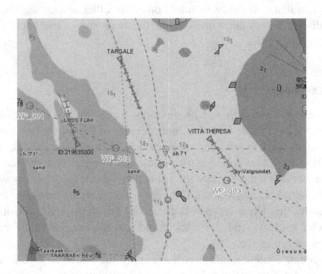

Fig. 2. A screen dump from the prototype software. By right clicking on the target ship *Targale* and choosing "Show intended route" in a context menu the green dotted line becomes visible (Color figure online).

2.2   Route Suggestion

The EPD exists as a ship-side and a shore-side platform. From the shore-side platform route segments can be created and send to addressed vessels (see Fig. 3).

A route suggestion could for instance have been sent out from the pilot boat to Trans Agila if the pilot had spotted the intention to pass on the wrong side of the beacon. Every year there are dozens of occasions where the Sound VTS have to call up

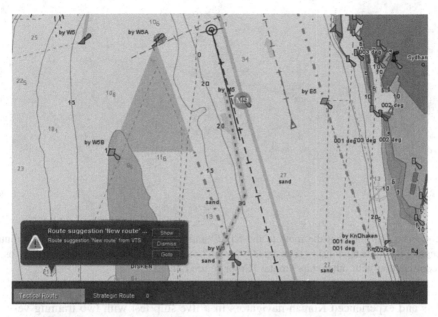

Fig. 3. A route segment (yellow backdrop) has been sent from shore to the own vessel (black circle top center). It appears together with a text message from the VTS and gives the watch officer an option to reject or accept the suggestion, or start a text message conversation with the VTS (Color figure online).

ships on a faulty course in the Sound between Sweden and Denmark asking them to check their navigation (personal communication with VTS operators).

2.3 Route Coordination

In the MONALISA project the idea of strategic route exchange has been investigated. In this project ships approaching a coordination area sends their voyage plans to a Shore Traffic Coordination Centre (STCC). The centre checks the routes for under keel clearance, violations of NoGo areas and for separation to other ships. The route is then either "recommended" or "not recommended." If the route is recommended the captain on the ship has the final word on whether to accept or reject the route. If he accepts the route it becomes a "green" agreed route (see Fig. 4).

If the STCC finds some problems in the route sent in by a vessel, they may "not recommend" the route and send a suggested change, which then in turn can be accepted or taken as a starting point for a new round of negotiations with the STCC.

2.4 User Tests

The EPD with the abovementioned functionality has been tested with cadets and experienced navigators in the full mission bridge simulator it Chalmers University of Technology in Gothenburg, Sweden in May and September 2013, as well as with

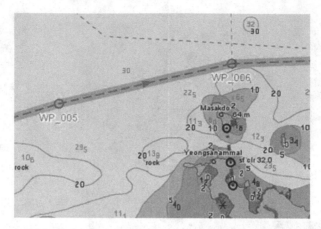

Fig. 4. The ship has sent the route to the STCC and got it back as a "recommended" route. Accepting the route then makes is an agreed, "green" route, signifying that this route will be used for coordination with other ships' routes (Color figure online).

cadets and experienced Korean navigators in a live ship test with two training vessels from Mokpo National Maritime University and Korean Maritime University in Busan in Korea in April 2014. In the Swedish simulator tests participated 12 experienced officers, 11 maritime academy 4th year cadets, and 5 VTS operators. This gave a sample of subject matter experts: 25 male, 3 female; ages 27–66, mean age 42; professional experience from none (cadets) to 40 years, the mean being 15.7 years of professional experience (cadets excluded). In the Korean test participated 9 experienced navigators (mean experience as navigators 11.3 yrs.) and 10 4th year cadets (12 male and 6 female). The collected mean age was 28 years. In both the Swedish and Korean tests the participants where a sample of convenience selected by volunteering cadets and navigators available at the time of the experiment.

On all occasions the users were asked to make a voyage plan, send the voyage plan to the STCC for validation and then accept the returned route. They were also asked to make changes to an already accepted route, and also to accept changes initiated from the shore centre.

The studies were explorative and qualitative. Users were asked to think aloud and afterwards interviewed on four levels: conceptual, procedural, functional and details of the user interface. The users were also asked to grade the concept on an acceptance scale.

3 Results and Discussion

In early stages of testing design concepts for new navigational services the question of professional acceptance becomes very crucial. If the professional users does not accept, or see any benefits with the suggested concept, the designers need to make a new approach. Therefore the tests so far have used qualitative methods. Also the prototype software has been in constant development why close comparison between results should not be made.

3.1   Conceptual Level

The hypothesis was that ship-board participants should be negative to the route exchange concept (based on earlier experiences of ship masters being negative because of surrendered sovereignty) but instead all participants were in general positive to the concept of voyage plan coordination; younger somewhat more than older (this was true also for the Korean participants). But even if older participants were more concerned with issues like deskilling they still accepted the system. A pensioned Swedish captain with 40 years of experience said: "I don't like this, but I see it coming, and I guess it is all right."

For the Korean study we expected to find cultural differences but found instead a similar high degree of acceptance.

The most discussed issue in the Swedish tests was about control; if voyage plan coordination would lead to control being shifted from the ship to the shore. Most bridge officers pointed out that it was important that the captain still had the last word, being on the scene and experiencing the situation first hand. Several participants saw a likelihood of conflicts between the STCC and vessel on the issue of control, and between the STCC and ship owners on the issue of costs [17].

From a VTS perspective, the ability to check routes and see vessels' intentions was welcomed but concerns were raised about the workload when dealing with several vessels in a heavy traffic or emergency situation. On the question of whether a route exchange system has a future, comments ranged from that it is inevitable, to that it may have a positive effect on the quality of navigation if captains can learn to trust it, to that it will never be accepted by captains and ship owners. The Korean participants were more positive that the Swedish.

3.2   Procedural Level

Participants in both vessel and STCC felt that new routines were involved in operating the system, but within a familiar environment so that once they understood what was expected of them and how to do it, it was easy to get accustomed.

With regard to work load, some of the Swedish participants felt that an extra person may be needed on the bridge in heavy traffic situations to leave the watch officer free to navigate and avoid collision. It was also felt by some that, depending on the degree of freedom allowed to deviate from the planned course, implementation of such a system would result in extra workload for the captain, who would be required to approve all changes made. The Koreans participating in the sea trial also made this comment on that the need for keeping close look-out was compromised by the need for working the computer system.

3.3   Survey

In a survey that was sent to the Swedish participants several weeks after they participated in the study the question "What is your opinion about the tested route exchange concept?" was asked. 18 answers where received out of 28 and from them 14 were "positive" or "very positive" and 4 "did not know". No one was negative. On the question "Do you think a similar route exchange concept will become reality in the future?" 17 answered "probably" or "most probably" and only 1 answered "probably not".

The same survey was put to the Korean participants after the sea trials. It gave that result that all 19 of the participants gave a "positive" or "very positive" answer to the question: "What is your opinion about the tested route exchange concept?" On the question "Do you think a similar route exchange concept will become reality in the future?" 18 answered "probably or most probably" and 1 answered "I do not know".

3.4   Validity

The validity of these tests is of course limited due to the low number of participants. However, the professional background and, particularly in the Swedish case, the long experience, gives some credit to the results. It is also interesting to see the similarity in opinions of both Swedish and Korean mariners.

4   Conclusions

The example in the beginning illustrated a "monitoring navigator" slavishly following the programmed track, bypassing the technical barriers that the system engineers had added to avoid accidents. The idea by the proposed new inventions presented in this paper is that by widening the system definition to include not only the human-computer interaction on the individual bridge, but also fellow mariners and shore services in the area, resilience will increase. By sharing intentions, the chance that someone will detect anomalies and warn will increase; technical barriers turned off onboard might still be working elsewhere, thus avoiding so called "single person failures".

The result of this process has been the concept of tactical and strategic route exchange. The concept was prototyped and tested both in simulators and at sea trials with good results, showing professional acceptance to the concept.

Continued work within several is ongoing projects to further refine and test the concept and to work with the regulating authorities to make the concept come true.

Acknowledgements. This research has been possible thanks to funding from the European Union's Seventh Framework program for infrastructure TEN-T (the MONALISA project), and the InterReg IVB North Sea Region program and the Swedish Region of Västra Götaland (the ACCSEAS project).

References

1. IMO: e-Navigation. http://www.imo.org/ourwork/safety/navigation/pages/enavigation.aspx
2. IMO: COMSAR 15/16. Report to the Maritime Safety Committee, 25 March 2011
3. BEA: Final report on the accident on 1st June 2009 to the Airbus A330-203 registered F-GZCP operated by Air France flight AF 447 Rio de Janeiro – Paris, 5 July 2012

4. Hollnagel, E., Pariès, J., Woods, D.D., Wreathall, J.: Resilience Engineering Perspectives. Resilience Engineering in Practice, vol. 3. Ashgate, Farnham (2011)
5. Statens Haverikommision: Slutrapport RS 2014:05: Trans Agila – grundstotning i Kalmarsund den 29 November 2012, Stockholm (2014)
6. IMO: Resolution A.850(20). http://www.imo.org/OurWork/HumanElement/Pages/Default.aspx
7. Reason, J.: Human Error. Cambridge University Press, Cambridge (1990)
8. Rouse, W.B., Rouse, S.H.: Analysis and classification of human error. IEEE Trans. Syst. Man Cybern. **SMC-13**, 539–554 (1983)
9. Blanding, H.C.: Automation of ships and the human factor. In: SNAME Ship Technology and Research Symposium, Philadelphia (1987)
10. Sandquist, T.F.: Human factors in maritime applications: a new opportunity for multi-modal transportation research. In: Human Factors 36th Annual Meeting (1992)
11. Rothblum, A.M.: Human Error and Marine Safety, USCG. (n.d.) http://www.bowles-langley.com/wp-content/files_mf/humanerrorandmarinesafety26.pdf
12. Wickens, C.D., Hollands, J.G., Banbury, S., Parasuraman, R.: Engineering Psychology and Human Performance, 3rd edn. Pearson, New York (2013)
13. Norman, D.A.: The Psychology of Everyday Things. Basic Books, New York (1988)
14. EfficienSea. http://efficiensea.eu/
15. MONALISA. http://monalisaproject.eu/
16. ACCSEAS. http://www.accseas.eu/
17. Porathe, T., de Vries, L., Prison, P.: Ship voyage plan coordination in the MONALISA project: user tests of a prototype ship traffic management system. In: De Waard, D., Brookhuis, K., Wiczorek, R., Di Nocera, F., Barham, P., Weikert, C., Kluge, A., Gerbino, W. Toffetti, A. (eds) Proceedings of the Human Factors and Ergonomics Society Europe Chapter 2013 Annual Conference (2014)

Dealing with Data Deluge at National Funding Agencies: An Investigation of User Needs for Understanding and Managing Research Investments

Mihaela Vorvoreanu[1](✉), Ann McKenna[2], Zhihua Dong[3],
and Krishna Madhavan[4]

[1] Computer Graphics Technology, Purdue University West Lafayette,
West Lafayette, IN, USA
mihaela@purdue.edu
[2] Ira A. Fulton Schools of Engineering, Arizona State University,
Tempe, AZ, USA
Ann.McKenna@asu.edu
[3] Microsoft Corporation, Redmond, WA, USA
zhdong@microsoft.com
[4] Engineering Education, Purdue University West Lafayette,
West Lafayette, IN, USA
cm@purdue.edu

Abstract. This paper provides in-depth, applied and contextualized insights about the particular challenges members of federal government funding agencies face when dealing with data deluge. We present the findings of qualitative research conducted with members of a federal US funding agency. The findings point out specific needs for understanding investment portfolios broadly and tracking the evolution and impact of ideas. They show limitations of existing solutions and their negative effects on labor, time, and personal stress. Based on these findings, we make specific suggestions for the design of automated tools that can help funding agencies understand and manage their portfolios.

Keywords: Understanding users · User research · Knowledge management · Data deluge · Funding agencies · Research investments · Portfolio mining

1 Introduction

Government funding agencies play an important role in both knowledge advancement and economic development in the United States and elsewhere. They set the agenda and make investments that stimulate research in areas that are considered of strategic importance for the country. As is the case with any kind of investment, it is important for government funding agencies to be able to understand investments, track their impact, and assess ROI. However, given the nature of the output of such investments (knowledge and knowledge products), results are often hard to quantify and assess. As a result, many government funding agencies in the United States struggle with

© Springer International Publishing Switzerland 2015
S. Yamamoto (Ed.): HIMI 2015, Part II, LNCS 9173, pp. 140–151, 2015.
DOI: 10.1007/978-3-319-20618-9_14

understanding their large investment portfolios. The National Science Foundation charged a subcommittee with investigating this problem. A report released in 2010 [31] pointed out that portfolio management is done mostly manually, which requires tremendous amounts of time and effort, that are only increasing as the quantity of information grows. The report called for the development of automated tools to help funding agencies understand and manage their investment portfolios. This paper contributes to addressing this need by presenting data about the users of such portfolio management tools. The goal of this research is to provide a better understanding of the environment and problems decision makers who work inside governmental funding agencies struggle with on a daily basis. This user research leads to guidelines and requirements that can inform the development of effective, user-centered [4, 12] portfolio management tools.

The importance of being able to understand, manage, and assess knowledge about investment portfolio cannot be understated. In the United States alone, the investment in research and development is measured in billions (about \$140 billion annually for the past five years) [32]. Government funding agencies need to be accountable to taxpayers and to demonstrate the impact of these investments. Moreover, understanding the impact of investments is necessary for future decision-making and strategic planning about what areas of research to stimulate through funding.

The intellectual products that result from federal funding present a particular type of challenge for portfolio management. The sheer quantity and diversity of these products (research papers, tools, patents, learning materials, etc.) that result from more than 10,000 awards a year that the National Science Foundation alone [19] funds, makes it very difficult to systematically assess and quantify impact. As more and more data is being generated, agencies face the need to manage knowledge generated from this data: insights about the nature of intellectual properties being produced, the social and community processes of producing these intellectual properties, their adoption and practical applications. Governmental agencies are not alone in this struggle. The problem of too much data and information is known as data deluge and has been documented widely. Knowledge management can provide a solution to this problem.

2 Related Work

2.1 The Problem of Data Deluge

With computer hardware development following Moore's law and the rapidly growing adoption and speed of the Internet, a huge influx of data is being generated from various sources. Not only is this a problem in the scientific-research field or business world, where overflow of data is not news, but also federal funding agencies face the challenge of spectacular increases in data volume. For federal funding agencies, the data deluge comes from the growing body of historical and continuously incoming funding documents - including funding solicitations, submitted proposals, awarded project information, published papers, project evaluations, etc. This data requires aggregation and interpretation, which forms knowledge to help with agencies' decision making.

In the knowledge pyramid, knowledge is formed through integration and making sense of data and information [6, 7, 17]. In this view, data refers to raw and objective entities collected directly; information is data processed into meaningful patterns; while knowledge is an aggregation of information that can become a guide for people to take actions in certain work conditions [7, 13, 16, 17]. Tuomi [26] suggested an inverse view of this hierarchy claiming that knowledge influences the process of collecting and processing data.

Ideally, more data can improve decision making as data-supported insights rather than intuition can bring more rationality into the decision-making process. However, as the cost of collecting data decreases, many organizations find that the overwhelming quantity of available data makes it difficult to process it into information and knowledge. With the unprecedented growth of data that cannot be managed, accessed, analyzed, and integrated into actionable knowledge, the availability of even more data can cause the "file-drawer" issue. Large amounts of data remain in virtual "file drawers" and are never seen or used [8]. Opportunities from deriving actionable insights from these data are missed. In a world where knowledge has been recognized as a core competence for an organization [3, 14, 15, 21], the difficulty of transforming knowledge into data can be a serious liability. Knowledge is recognized as an important organizational asset that influences an organization's strategies and decision-making processes. So, how can organizations such as national funding agencies address this problem? In the next section, we review existing knowledge management systems (KMS) and evaluate their fit for large governmental funding agencies.

2.2 Knowledge Management in Organizations

As discussed in the previous section, data deluge in an organization is actually becoming a knowledge management (KM) problem. To address the problem, researchers have studied knowledge management systems (KMS) intensively.

Knowledge management is defined as "the generation, representation, storage, transfer, transformation, application, embedding and protecting of organizational knowledge" (p. 218) [23]. It aims to increase the ability of innovation and responsiveness of an organization [11].

Knowledge management nowadays needs to do much more than just provide storage and access to data. It is expected to provide more exploration and easier distribution, to help with organizational problem solving, decision-making and strategic planning. The environment of organizational decision-making has been recognized as complex and ill structured due to high volume of data, with many semi-structured problems occurring at the strategic planning stage of decision-making [5, 20, 25]. This situation requires a solution that existing search technologies do not address. The challenge posed by the data deluge and failure of knowledge management is not that of finding a particular item; rather, the challenge is to make sense of knowledge developments, to be able to characterize the field of knowledge - its growth, evolution, and impact. Researchers have pointed out the need to make sense of the body of knowledge and to derive actionable insights by investigating the knowledge that is buried in the overflow of data in order to know more about "what is known, how, and by whom"

(p. 721) [8]. In this context, knowledge management tools should offer exploitation of the known as well as exploration of the unknown, which could help maintain the mental model as well as encourage building new mental models for organizational members [27].

Within this framework, researchers have studied the inclusion of knowledge management into decision support systems [5, 27, 29]. For example, KMS was found to cater to high-level executive decision-making [29], and to promote sharing and amplifying individual knowledge [30]. However, despite all these efforts for different business organizations, federal funding agencies are left out on the battlefield: they are for the most part still buried in massively abundant data and lack tools for exploring their own funding portfolios [18]. Funding agencies might require different approaches to knowledge management and they have called for solutions customized to their own organizations' complex needs [31].

One notable example of a project that undertakes knowledge management for funding agencies is Science and Technology for America's Reinvestment (STAR) Metrics [33]. Development and adoption of the ambitious STAR Metrics project has been difficult and slow, and at the time of data collection for this research project it was yet to meet the needs of decision makers at funding agencies.

System adoption often depends on multiple factors such as perceived value and usability [22]. Designing usable systems that provide meaningful and pleasant user experiences and help users achieve their goals requires not only a theoretical understanding of the problem of data deluge and knowledge management, but also applied, nuanced, and local understandings of the people who struggle with this issue on a daily basis and of their work environment [3, 6]. Design of KMS especially needs insights of operations and structures of the target organization. According to Gold et al. [10], there are three major infrastructures of an organization that influence the capability and efficiency of creating and utilizing new knowledge: the technical, structural, and cultural. Thus, examination of the existing technical solutions, and organization norms and contexts could help with the system design. Furthermore, as pointed out by Yim et al. [29], positions at different hierarchical levels might require different categories and representations of knowledge. As suggested by Faniel and Zimmerman [9], in-depth investigation of how researchers manage their data can provide useful insights for improving the design of systems to share and reuse data. User research needs to be carried out first in order to understand federal funding agencies' difficulties of dealing with big data. To the best of our knowledge, there is no similar user study addressing funding agencies' perspectives, however, we did find one reflecting researchers' consideration of building infrastructure to manage large data. Beagrie and Rowlands conducted a qualitative study with online surveys and interviews in 2008 [1]. This study revealed the importance of local data management for researchers as well as the concern regarding secure storage and access control to research data. While members of funding agencies may share these needs and concerns, more research is needed to understand their particular situation before designing technical solutions that will be both useful and usable. To address this need, we conducted user research inside a federal US funding agency. The methods and results of this research effort that benefited from unprecedented access to decision makers inside a federal funding agency are presented next.

3 Method

We conducted in-depth focus group interviews with decision makers and support staff at a US federal funding agency. Data was collected during two months in the fall of 2011. A total of 31 participants, including five members of the higher administration, 19 program officers, and seven support staff (science analysts) from different parts of the organization participated in the focus groups. The participants were selected through key informant sampling facilitated by a member of the organization who invited selected colleagues to participate in this effort. The selection was based on the participants' likelihood of being information rich cases who could share rich insights on the issue at hand. The focus group discussions resulted in 476 min of data, which was transcribed under confidentiality contract by a professional transcription service. All research abided by the strict confidentiality guidelines of the funding agency and was approved by the Institutional Review Boards of the authors' institutions.

3.1 Analysis

Focus group transcripts were subjected to thematic analysis [2]. Four researchers read through the transcripts repeatedly in order to identify recurring codes in the data and organize them into themes. Findings were discussed until agreement was reached upon a set of major themes, presented next.

4 Results

We organize the results around three major themes that describe how decision makers at this federal agency cope with the problem of data deluge. The first major theme focuses on users' information needs. The second one discusses the inadequacy of existing systems to meet information needs. The third theme addresses the personal and institutional stress associated with the need to derive actionable insights from large data.

4.1 Theme 1. Information Needs: Beyond Search

We found that the most pressing information needs were not for individual items that could be retrieved through search. They were for qualitative, contextual, or historical knowledge that would describe and characterize the existing state of the institution's investments and thus provide a foundation for strategic decision-making.

During focus group discussions, agency members mentioned repeatedly the need to visualize and understand the current state of their funding portfolios. They expressed the desire to be able to quickly grasp the big picture of funding portfolios in order to understand the distribution of institutional funds across geographic districts, institution types, research problems, and so on.

And so being able to both get a 40,000-foot view of what a portfolio is, to understand it in broader terms, and then to be able to dig down very deeply… is something that program officers need, but cannot currently do with available tools.

And we don't have that. We have no way of aggregating data, we don't even have similar measures across projects, or any way of determining equivalencies so you can begin to aggregate.

This need was even more pressing for organization members who held short-term positions with the institution. As opposed to the permanent employees who had historical knowledge by virtue of their long tenure, short-term employees struggled with understanding the portfolios they had taken over and were in charge of managing for a limited period of time. They mentioned spending a lot of time and effort trying to gain an overall understanding of their portfolios before they felt they could make informed decisions as to future research agendas the institution should encourage. Short-term employees relied on conversations with their colleagues for historical information on funding trends, as this quote from a program officer illustrates:

But I think, too, as a [short-term employee], *I mean, I rely very heavily on permanent staff. You know, because from a historical perspective, they have the most knowledge about sort of the trends and what's been funded and where, you know, where they see things going. So that's a critical resource for me.*

Both short-term and permanent employees provided similar reasons why they thought big-picture portfolio characterization was needed. One of the reasons was the need to understand funding trends and to ensure portfolio diversification by avoiding repeated funding of the same topic or idea. Another reason was the need to be able to assess impact efficiently. The agency officers hoped that a global understanding of funding portfolios could help them ascertain what projects, topics, practices, and ideas were successful and made an impact. In other words, they needed better methods to evaluate the return on funding investments. This impact data is used for institutional evaluation, reporting, and public accountability, but also for informing strategic directions for future growth, as this quote from a program officer shows:

I think it would help us to be able to reflect a little bit on, you know, getting back to what are some of the big changes that [this organization] *has helped push and sort of having a better version of those stories and what really was it that started it and maybe to realize that $100,000 and $150,000 proposal was maybe what got something started, but that there were several more steps and several other things that had to line up. And so what are realistic expectations for how transformative one funding decision might be or how does that fit into the context of what else is going on. That would sort of help us think about the impacts of our decisions.*

In summary, the greatest information needs of decision makers at this federal agency were actionable knowledge: clear, insightful analyses of existing data that would showcase trends and provide an easy to grasp description of the overall current state of affairs. The institution employs several analysts who are in charge of producing such insights manually, since automated solutions do not exist at the moment. However, because of the inadequacy of existing systems, the analysts end up spending their time inefficiently instead of focusing on higher-level tasks. The inadequacy of existing systems is the second major theme we identified.

4.2   Theme 2. Inadequacy of Existing Systems

Currently, the federal agency we studied houses information in several databases accessible through various user-facing systems. The databases are accessible by decision makers, but because they are cumbersome and time-consuming, program officers usually ask analysts to pull up information and prepare reports for them. The analysts' usual work process consists of several time-consuming stages that require a lot of manual processing and filtering of results before any analysis can be performed. This is explained by some major inadequacies we identified with existing systems, as follows:

Existing systems support search and filtering of results, but not analytics and visualizations. Those need to be performed manually. Even though manual analysis should address difficult, sophisticated problems that machines cannot solve reliably, a lot of the analysts' time is spent refining search results. This problem stems from the second inadequacy we identified.

Existing systems cannot cope with growing data, shifting categories, and ambiguous concepts. In most of these systems, information is stored and retrieved according to predefined database categories. As the types of information change, they may not fit existing categories. Also, the limited number of categories includes only major characteristics that database designers identified as relevant when they planned the system. The system is incapable of automatically adapting to growing data and data types and to new categories that may become relevant. Also, the system is not designed to reconcile linguistic differences between similar concepts, thus producing either repetitive or incomplete search results. Interviewees made several comments about the difficulty of capturing shifting categories in taxonomies:

What happens is that you don't have a specific category because that thing is something that is just arising and you don't know if it's going to be anything of importance, so you don't have that. So then like remote, use of remote instruments, so you don't bother to put it down because you think this guy is doing it, but then all of the sudden you have 20 of them or 10 of them, so do you go back and comb the old ones to see if any of them did it.

The consequences of these limitations are that a lot of manual filtering is required before analysts can obtain a reliable and complete list of search results they can later run analyses on. Besides being time consuming, the system displays a third inadequacy: it is difficult to use.

Manual filtering of search results is difficult and requires both topic expertise and institutional knowledge. Therefore, analysts who are not topic experts need to spend a lot of time communicating with decision makers in order to gain an understanding of the key terms and concepts they should search for, and be able to make judgment calls about the relevancy of search results. In addition to topic knowledge, analysts also need institutional knowledge. They need to understand the institution's processes and procedures and the way these are coded and recorded into the various databases. Without such understanding, they run the risk of producing unreliable search results. For example, when calculating a funding rate, they need to know how to address the situation of a principal investigator transfer. In the absence of solid institutional knowledge, proposals that were transferred to a different investigator could be counted twice, thus producing incorrect funding rates. Many such cases need to be filtered manually, and often times analysts spend days reviewing search results one by one and deciding whether to include them in the list of valid search results they will perform analyses on. In the next quote, an analyst explains how long it took to filter thousands of research proposals in order to identify the 250 documents that were needed for an analysis:

For that specific dataset that I pulled up because of the limitations I have in being able to filter out proposals I had to do it broadly. Like I searched by program code, which pulls up a lot of unnecessary proposals that are false hits, so that took me about two and a half weeks of just searching through.

The extent of manual labor needed to track down impact for a particular topic is illustrated by this analyst's story:

It's just getting us a list of 2,000 proposals or awards that could potentially implement best practices and have good outcomes. The next step would be to separate out all these 2,000 proposals I've pulled out by program manager and then beg each program manager to look at this 20 that they get to see if they remember these proposals coming in and if they know what has been done subsequently with what they've researched.

The difficulties posed by working within the limitations of existing systems create personal and institutional stress, as explained in the third major theme we identified.

4.3 Theme 3. Personal and Institutional Stress

As a result of these difficulties, decision makers state that they often forego information requests. They understand how time-consuming they are for analysts, and that they have to be very judicious with their requests in order to avoid overloading the analysts and allow them time for high priority tasks. Decision makers employed by this federal agency either short or long term are highly capable, well-trained individuals who have demonstrated expertise in their own areas of scholarly research. Yet, they depend upon analysts even for relatively simple reports, and this presents a cause of stress and dissatisfaction.

Another major cause of stress and dissatisfaction is captured by a phrase research participants used repeatedly during focus group discussions: "firefighting mode." Decision makers felt that a lot of their time was spent solving problems rapidly, on an emergency basis. The fact that producing reports and analyses is so time-consuming compounds this problem and leaves little to no time for reflection and achieving broad, contextual understanding that participants wished for, as this quote from a program officer illustrates:

We don't really even have time to anticipate, kind of think about and anticipate the kinds of questions we might be asked or the kinds of things we would like to know because we – there really isn't that time set aside that we can spend really doing that self-reflection.

5 Discussion and Design Implications

The fundamental insights emerging from our study point to the urgent need for a system that is designed primarily with these constituents in mind. A simple search engine that will provide a list of search results is just not sufficient to meet these users' needs, as

Theme 1 shows. Clearly, our own analyses have shown that there are existing efforts at the national level that attempt to characterize the portfolio of projects that form the research ecosystem of federal agencies. Yet – these tools are not used daily by decision makers at funding agencies (as reflected in Theme 2 of our results section). The results presented in the previous section point to several fundamental design implications:

First, regardless of how sophisticated a tool for knowledge management and portfolio analysis may be, the user-facing interface needs to be simple and easy enough to use that decision makers will actually consider its affordances. The design of the tool itself needs to make affordances obvious while shielding end-users from the complexities of data mining and visualization. One of the core problems with many of the current generation of knowledge management tools is that they are designed by experts in data mining with minimal consideration of how complex it may be for users to operate on a daily basis. Therefore they create decision makers' dependency upon research analysts. As our results show, this is a source of stress and organizational inefficiency.

Theme 3 that was raised in our analyses also supports this requirement. Potential users of knowledge management and analysis systems are constantly in "firefighting mode." The results show that they are hard-pressed for time and are under constant pressure to deliver. Adding a tool or a set of tools that will require them to spend an enormous amount of time learning the systems and their functionalities will not allow rapid diffusion. Therefore, the tools themselves need to feed into the users' day-to-day workflow. If the users have to visit yet another site and go through extensive training (or other time consuming activities) before the tools become valuable to them, the portfolio mining tools would have failed in their design.

In many instances, current tools make the assumption that providing a search box is sufficient to allow exploration by the end users. Our study reveals that in most cases potential users of knowledge management systems do not even understand where to begin their exploration process. Theme 2 in our analyses also showed that current data mining systems used in the funding agencies are inefficient in a way that the organization depends highly on tacit knowledge (i.e., personal knowledge, which is hard to communicate and spread) rather than explicit knowledge [5, 24]. Collecting and codifying tacit knowledge into explicit knowledge has been recognized as a core step for an organization to lower the cost of creating new knowledge. A good knowledge management system should be able to facilitate this process and leverage tacit knowledge within an organization. Therefore, the second equally significant design direction that emerges is that not only does the tool need to be simple for users to understand, but it also needs to provide suitable explorative vantage points for the end users as well as learn over time from patterns of usage.

Third, results from our analyses point out that these users need tools that not only capture current information in usable forms, but also engage in historical time-slice based exploration. In essence, they look for a more epistemic approach to their portfolios rather than a static view of their research ecosystem as it exists currently. A successful tool would have to support dynamic exploration of historical data in order to enable the identification of trends and assessment of impact.

Impact assessment and evaluation of ROI emerged as important topics in focus group discussions and they lead to a fourth design implication: Users at funding agencies need tools that show the connections between knowledge products and can trace the development of a funded proposal into papers, publications, patents, materials, commercialization, as well as their citation and adoption rates. These are some of the ways that the tool could help assess impact and ROI, although the operational definition of these concepts is still in need of more research.

Implicit in the results is also the need for the stakeholders to have an open discourse about the characteristics of their portfolios with each other, which points to a fifth design implication: A community aspect is needed for these tools. As much as the design would allow, the tools need to provide venues for co-construction of vocabulary and knowledge artifacts among the community of users. It is in this context that folksonomies [28] play a critical role. Traditionally, portfolio-mining systems provide or have constructed static taxonomies for end users to consider. This approach works to a certain degree in certain scientific contexts. For example, medical research renders itself better to rigid classification. However, research in other fields can be much more fluid and therefore far more difficult to categorize and classify. Therefore, a tool needs to consider these complexities carefully in its design. One of the best ways to approach this scenario is to allow human expertise to play a significant role in shaping and evolving the vocabulary and terminologies that are part of the toolsets, which points to the sixth design implication we identify: Portfolio mining tools need to be intelligent enough to evolve folksonomies bottom-up from existing information and to continuously learn from users in order to improve categorization of knowledge products. The system developed based on these design requirements is discussed in [34, 35].

5.1   Conclusion

This paper set out to provide in-depth, applied and contextualized insights about the particular challenges members of federal government funding agencies face when dealing with data deluge. We presented the findings of qualitative research conducted with members of a funding agency. The findings point out specific needs for understanding investment portfolios broadly and tracking the evolution and impact of ideas. They show limitations of existing solutions and their negative effects on labor, time, and personal stress. Based on these findings, we make specific suggestions for the design of automated tools that can help funding agencies understand and manage their portfolios.

Further research is needed to explore creative technical solutions that would address these challenges and to evaluate their viability and potential utility for solving the particular problems of decision makers at funding agencies. Further research can investigate the difficulties scholars who do not make funding decisions encounter as they make sense of growing amounts of knowledge in their respective fields. That information would inform the development of similar knowledge mining tools for researchers.

Acknowledgements. This research is supported by NSF awards TUES-1123108, TUES-1122609, TUES-1123340, TUES-1122650.

References

1. Beagrie, N., Beagrie, R., Rowlands, I.: Research data preservation and access: the views of researchers. Ariadne (2009). http://www.ariadne.ac.uk/issue60/beagrie-et-al/
2. Boyatzis, R.E.: Transforming Qualitative Information: Thematic Analysis and Code Development. Sage Publications, Inc., New York (1998)
3. Conner, K.R., Prahalad, C.K.: A resource-based theory of the firm: knowledge versus opportunism. Organ. Sci. 7(5), 477–501 (1996)
4. Cooper, A., Reimann, R., Cronin, D.: About Face 3: The Essentials of Interaction Design. Wiley, Hoboken (2007)
5. Courtney, J.F.: Decision making and knowledge management in inquiring organizations: toward a new decision-making paradigm for DSS. Decis. Support Syst. 31(1), 17–38 (2001)
6. Davenport, T.H., Prusak, L.: Working Knowledge: How Organizations Manage What They Know. Harvard Business Press, Boston (2000)
7. Dretske, F.: Knowledge and the Flow of Information. MIT Press, Cambridge (1983)
8. Evans, J.A., Foster, J.G.: Metaknowledge. Science 331(6018), 721–725 (2011)
9. Faniel, I.M., Zimmerman, A.: Beyond the data deluge: a research agenda for large-scale data sharing and reuse. Int. J. Digit. Curation 6(1), 58–69 (2011)
10. Gold, A.H., Malhotra, A., Segars, A.H.: Knowledge management: an organizational capabilities perspective. J. Manage. Inf. Syst. 18(1), 185–214 (2001)
11. Hackbarth, G.: The impact of organizational memory on IT systems. In: Proceedings of the Fourth Americas Conference on Information Systems, pp. 588–590 (1998)
12. Hartson, R., Pyla, P.: The Ux Book: Process and Guidelines for Ensuring a Quality User Experience. Morgan Kaufmann, San Francisco (2012)
13. Hemsley, J., Mason, R.M.: Knowledge and knowledge management in the social media age. J. Organ. Comput. Electron. Commer. 23(1–2), 138–167 (2013)
14. Kogut, B., Zander, U.: Knowledge of the firm, combinative capabilities, and the replication of technology. Organ. Sci. 3(3), 383–397 (1992)
15. Kogut, B., Zander, U.: What firms do? coordination, identity, and learning. Organ. Sci. 7(5), 502–518 (1996)
16. Lee, C.C., Yang, J.: Knowledge value chain. J. Manage. Dev. 19(9), 783–794 (2000)
17. Maryam, A., Leidner, D.E.: Review: knowledge management and knowledge management systems: conceptual foundations and research issues. MIS Q. 25(1), 107–136 (2001)
18. Mervis, J.: Agencies rally to tackle big data. Science 336(6077), 22 (2012)
19. NSF. NSF FY 2013 Budget Request to Congress (2012)
20. Pirolli, P.: Rational analyses of information foraging on the web. Cogn. Sci. 29(3), 343–373 (2005)
21. Prahalad, C.K., Hamel, G.: The core competence of the corporation. In: Hahn, D., Taylor, B. (eds.) Strategische Unternehmungsplanung—Strategische Unternehmungsführung, pp. 275–292. Springer, Heidelberg (2006)
22. Rogers, E.M., Rogers, E.: Diffusion of Innovations, 5th edn. Free Press, New York (2003)
23. Schultze, U., Leidner, D.E.: Studying knowledge management in information systems research: discourses and theoretical assumptions. Manage. Inf. Syst. Q. 26(3), 213–242 (2002)
24. Schultze, U.: A confessional account of an ethnography about knowledge work. MIS Q. 24 (1), 3–41 (2000)
25. Simon, H.A.: The structure of ill structured problems. Artif. Intell. 4(3–4), 181–201 (1973)

26. Tuomi, I.: Data is more than knowledge: implications of the reversed knowledge hierarchy for knowledge management and organizational memory. In: Proceedings of the 32nd Annual Hawaii International Conference on System Sciences, HICSS-32, p. 12 (1999)
27. Vandenbosch, B., Higgins, C.: Information acquisition and mental models: an investigation into the relationship between behaviour and learning. Inf. Syst. Res. 7(2), 198–214 (1996)
28. Weinberger, D.: Everything Is Miscellaneous: The Power of the New Digital Disorder. Times Books, New York (2007)
29. Yim, N.H., Kim, S.H., Kim, H.W., Kwahk, K.Y.: Knowledge based decision making on higher level strategic concerns: system dynamics approach. Expert Syst. Appl. 27(1), 143–158 (2004)
30. Zack, M.H.: Managing codified knowledge. Sloan Manage. Rev. 40(4), 45–58 (1999)
31. NSF. Discovery in a Research Portfolio: Tools for Structuring, Analyzing, Visualizing and Interacting with Proposal and Award Portfolios (2010)
32. NSF. NCSES Proposed Federal R&D Funding for FY 2011 Dips to $143 Billion, with Cuts in National Defense R&D - US National Science Foundation (NSF). http://www.nsf.gov/statistics/infbrief/nsf10327/
33. STAR METRICS. https://www.starmetrics.nih.gov/
34. Liu, Q., Vorvoreanu, M., Madhavan, K.P.C., McKenna, A.F.: Designing discovery experience for big data interaction: a case of web-based knowledge mining and interactive visualization platform. In: Marcus, A. (ed.) DUXU 2013, Part IV. LNCS, vol. 8015, pp. 543–552. Springer, Heidelberg (2013)
35. Madhavan, K., Elmqvist, N., Vorvoreanu, M., Chen, X., Wong, Y., Xian, H., Dong, Z., Johri, A.: DIA2: web-based cyberinfrastructure for visual analysis of funding portfolios. IEEE Trans. Vis. Comput. Graph. 20(12), 1823–1832 (2014)

Dot Matrix Analysis of Plant Operation Data for Identifying Sequential Alarms Triggered by Single Root Cause

ZheXing Wang and Masaru Noda[✉]

Department of Chemical Engineering, Fukuoka University, Fukuoka, Japan
{td133003,mnoda}@fukuoka-u.ac.jp

Abstract. Sequential alarms are alarms triggered in succession by a single root cause in a chemical plant. In general, they occur sequentially with specific time lags within a short period of time and, if they are numerous, they reduce the ability of operators to cope with plant abnormalities because critical alarms can become buried under numerous unimportant alarms. In this paper, we propose a method for identifying sequential alarms hidden in plant operation data by using dot matrix analysis. Dot matrix analysis is one of the sequence alignment methods for identifying similar regions in a pair of DNA or RNA sequences, which may be a consequence of functional, structural, or evolutionary relationships. The proposed method first converts plant operation data recorded in a Distributed Control System (DCS) into a single alarm sequence by putting them in order by alarm occurrence time. Then, similar regions in the alarm sequence are identified by comparing the alarm alignment with itself. Finally, the identified regions, which are assumed to be sequential alarms, are classified into sets of similar sequential alarms in accordance with the similarities between them. The method was applied to simulated plant operation data of an azeotropic distillation column. The results showed that the method is able to correctly identify sequential alarms in plant operation data. Classifying sequential alarms into small numbers of groups with this method effectively reduces unimportant sequential alarms at industrial chemical plants.

Keywords: Plant alarm system · Dot matrix analysis · Sequential alarms

1 Introduction

Sequential alarms are alarms that occur in succession with specific time lags within a short period of time [1–3]. Sequential alarms are usually caused by poor alarm rationalization [4, 5]. The grouping of correlated sequential alarms in accordance with their degree of similarity helps to identify their occurrences more effectively than by analyzing individual sequential alarms.

The alarm similarity color map [6] is helpful for assessing the performance of alarm systems in terms of effectiveness and reducing the occurrences of sequential alarms. The alarm similarity color map orders alarms in accordance with their degree of Jaccard similarity [7] with other alarms to identify sequential alarms. A Gaussian kernel method [8] was applied to historical alarm data to generate a pseudo-continuous time

© Springer International Publishing Switzerland 2015
S. Yamamoto (Ed.): HIMI 2015, Part II, LNCS 9173, pp. 152–158, 2015.
DOI: 10.1007/978-3-319-20618-9_15

series to reduce the effect of missed, false, and chattering alarms when visualizing the correlation information from alarms.

Event correlation analysis [9] was proposed to identify sequential alarms in noisy plant operation data. This method uses plant operation data and a cross correlation function to quantify the degree of similarity on the basis of the time lag between two alarms. Sequential alarms are found by grouping correlated alarms and operations in accordance with their degree of similarity. Event correlation analysis was applied to the operation data of an industrial ethylene plant and was able to correctly identify similarities between correlated sequential alarms [10–12]. However, event correlation analysis occasionally failed to detect similarities between two physically related sequential alarms when deletions, substitutions, and/or transpositions occurred in the alarm sequence.

A method for evaluating similarities between sequential alarms by using the normalized Levenshtein distance was proposed [13]. The Levenshtein distance [14, 15] is a string metric for measuring the difference between two sequences defined as the minimum number of edit operations such as insertion, deletion, and substitution of a single character needed to transform one string into another. The Levenshtein distance was applied to the simulation data of an azeotropic distillation column, and the results revealed that the method is able to correctly identify similarities between correlated sequential alarms even when the event correlation analysis failed due to deletions, substitutions, and/or transpositions in the alarm sequence. However, the method is not able to identify sequential alarms hidden in plant operation data.

In this paper, we propose a method that can identify sequential alarms hidden in plant operation data by using dot matrix analysis.

2 Dot Matrix Analysis

Dot matrix analysis [16] is one of the sequence alignment methods for identifying similar regions in DNA or RNA. Figure 1 shows an example of two DNA sequences. Similar regions in DNA or RNA may be a consequence of functional, structural, or evolutionary relationships between the sequences.

In the dot matrix method [17], one sequence S_1 is listed across the bottom of a graph, and the other sequence S_2 is listed down the left side, as illustrated in Fig. 2. Starting with the first character in S_2, the comparison moves across the graph in the first row and places a dot in any column where the character in S_1 is the same. The second character in S_2 is then compared to the entire S_1 sequence, and a dot is placed in row 2 wherever a match occurs. This process is continued until the graph is filled with dots representing all the matches of S_1 characters with S_2 characters. A diagonal row of dots reveals similarity between the two sequences. Dots not on a diagonal row represent random matches that are probably not related to any significant alignment.

The major advantage of the dot matrix analysis for finding sequence alignments is that all possible matches between two sequences are found, leaving the engineers the choice of identifying the most significant matches by examination of the dot matrix for long runs of matches, which appear as diagonals [17].

$$S_1: \text{A G C T A G G A} \qquad (1)$$

$$S_2: \text{G A C T A G G C} \qquad (2)$$

Fig. 1. Example of two DNA sequences

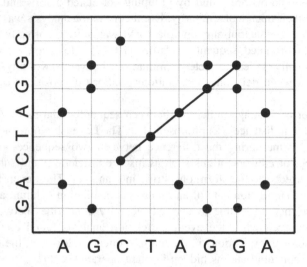

Fig. 2. Dot matrix comparison of two DNA sequences

3   Method for Identifying Sequential Alarms

The plant operation data recorded in DCS generally consist of the times alarms occurred and their tag names, as listed in Table 1. The proposed method first converts the plant operation data into a single alarm sequence by putting them in order by alarm occurrence time. Then, the similar regions in the alarm sequences are identified by comparing the alarm alignment with the sequence. Figure 3 shows an example of dot matrix analysis of plant operation data. Finally, the identified similar regions, which are assumed to be sequential alarms, are classified into sets of similar sequential alarms in accordance with the similarities between them.

Table 1. Example of plant operation data

Date/Time	Tag name of alarm
2013/01/01 00:08:53	A_1
2013/01/01 00:09:36	A_4
2013/01/01 00:11:42	A_2
2013/01/01 00:25:52	A_3
:	:

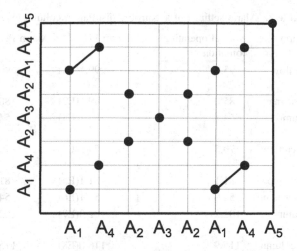

Fig. 3. Example of dot matrix analysis of plant operation data

4   Case Study

The method was applied to the simulation data of the azeotropic distillation column in Fig. 4 [11]. There were a total of 18 alarms in the DCS, which are denoted by E1–E18 in Table 2. Three types of malfunctions (Table 3), low flow rate coolant, low steam pressure, and valve stiction, were randomly caused in the process simulation, which was run using Aspen HYSYS 2.3 (AspenTech, Inc.). A defined operation for each malfunction was carried out after each malfunction occurred, as shown in Table 3. During a process simulation of 15 days, 18 types of alarm and 234 alarm occurrences were recorded in the plant operation data, as shown in Fig. 5.

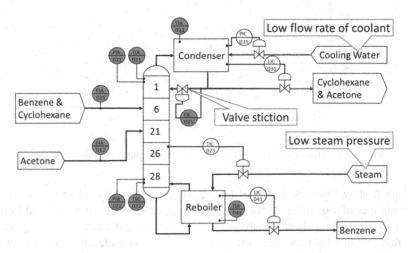

Fig. 4. Process flow diagram of azeotropic distillation column [11]

Table 2. Alarm settings of azeotropic distillation column [11]

Tag	Description	Normal operating condition	Alarm PH	Alarm PL	Unit
FIA012	Acetone flow rate	95.0	99.1(E1)	90.9(E10)	kg/h
FIA011	Feed flow rate	85.0	89.1(E2)	80.8(E11)	kg/h
TIA021	Top column temp	54.1	54.1(E3)	54.0(E12)	°C
TIA022	Bottom column temp	79.5	79.5(E4)	79.4(E13)	°C
TIA041	Reboiler temp	81.1	81.1(E5)	81.1(E14)	°C
TIA031	Condenser temp	54.0	54.1(E6)	54.0(E15)	°C
PIA021	Top column press	102.2	102.3(E7)	102.1(E16)	kPa
PIA031	Bottom column press	115.9	116.0(E8)	115.8(E17)	kPa
FIC025	Reflux flow rate	2830	2831(E9)	2829(E18)	kg/h

Table 3. Operations corresponding to assumed malfunctions [11]

Assumed malfunctions	Corresponding operations
Low coolant flow rate	Open reflux valve
Low steam pressure	Open steam valve
Valve stiction	Open reflux valve

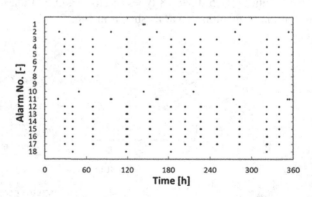

Fig. 5. Simulated plant operation data of azeotropic distillation column

Figure 6 shows the result of the dot matrix analysis of the plant operation data. A large number of sequential alarms in the plant operation data can be inferred from the multiple diagonal lines. It is possible to identify sequential alarms from Fig. 6. The results revealed that the proposed method is able to correctly identify similar sequential alarms in plant operation data.

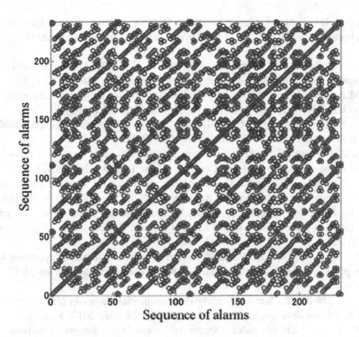

Fig. 6. Results of dot matrix analysis

5 Conclusion

Dot matrix analysis was applied to the simulated plant operation data of an azeotropic distillation column. The results revealed that the method is able to correctly identify similar sequential alarms in plant operation data. Classifying them into small numbers of groups with this method effectively identifies the sequential alarms at industrial chemical plants.

Acknowledgments. This work was supported by JSPS Kakenhi Grant Number 24560942.

References

1. The Engineering Equipment and Material Users' Association (EEMUA): Alarm Systems A Guide to Design, Management and Procurement Publication No. 191 Edition 2. EEMUA, London (2007)
2. International Society of Automation (ISA): Management of Alarm Systems for the Process Industries, ANSI/ISA-18.2-2009. ISA, North Carolina (2009)
3. International Electrotechnical Commission (IEC): IEC 62682 Management of Alarm Systems for the Process Industries. IEC, Geneva (2014)
4. Hollifield, B.R., Habibi, E.: Alarm Management: Seven Effective Methods for Optimum Performance. ISA, Research Triangle Park (2007)

5. Rothenberg, D.H.: Alarm Management for Process Control A Best-Practice Guide of Design, Implementation, and Use of Industrial Alarm Systems. Momentum Press, New York (2009)
6. Kondaveeti, S.R., Izadi, I., Shah, S.L., Balck, T., Chen, T.: Graphical tools for routine assessment of industrial alarm systems. Comput. Chem. Eng. **46**, 39–47 (2012)
7. Lesot, M.J., Rifqi, M., Benhadda, H.: Similarity measures for binary and numerical data: a survey. Int. J. Knowl. Eng. Soft Data Paradigms **1**, 63–84 (2009)
8. Yang, F., Shah, S.L., Xiao, D., Chen, T.: Improved correlation analysis and visualization of industrial alarm data. ISA Trans. **51**(4), 499–506 (2012)
9. Nishiguchi, J., Takai, T.: IPL2&3 performance improvement method for process safety using the event correlation analysis. Comput. Chem. Eng. **34**, 2007–2013 (2010)
10. Higuchi, F., Noda, M., Nishitani, H.: Alarm reduction of ethylene plant using event correlation analysis. Kagaku Kogaku Ronbunshu 36(6), 576–581 (2010) (in Japanese)
11. Kurata, K., Noda, M., Kikuchi, Y., Hirao, M.: Extension of event correlation analysis for rationalization of plant alarm systems. Kagaku Kogaku Ronbunshu 37, 338–343 (2011) (in Japanese)
12. Takai, T., Noda, M., Higuchi, F.: Identification of nuisance alarms in operation log data of ethylene plant by event correlation analysis. Kagaku Kogaku Ronbunshu 38 (2), 110–116 (2012) (in Japanese)
13. Akatsuka, S., Noda, M.: Similarity analysis of sequential alarms in plant operation data by using Levenshtein distance. In: Proceedings of the PSE Asia 2013, Kuala Lumpur (2013)
14. Levenshtein, V.I.: Binary codes capable of correcting deletions. Insertions Reversals Cybern. Control Theory **10**(8), 707–710 (1966)
15. Yujian, L., Bo, L.: A normalized Levenshtein distance metric. IEEE Trans. Pattern Anal. Mach. Intell. **29**(6), 1091–1095 (2007)
16. Gibbs, A.J., McIntyre, G.A.: The diagram method for comparing sequences. Its use with amino acid and nucleotide sequences. Eur. J. Biochem. **16**, 1–11 (1970)
17. Mount, D.W.: Bioinformatics Sequence and Genome Analysis, 2nd edn. Cold Spring Harbor Laboratory Press, New York (2004)

An Analysis of the Synergistic Effect in the Advertisement

Between the Television Commercials and the Internet Commercials

Tadahiro Yamada[1(✉)], Yumi Asahi[2], and Katsuhiko Yuura[1]

[1] Graduate School of Informatics, Shizuoka University,
3-5-1 Johoku, Naka-ku, Hamamatsu-Shi, Shizuoka 432-8011, Japan
gs14046@s.inf.shizuoka.ac.jp,
yuura@inf.shizuoka.ac.jp
[2] Department of Systems Engineering, Shizuoka University,
3-5-1 Johoku, Naka-ku, Hamamatsu-Shi, Shizuoka 432-8561, Japan
asahi@sys.eng.shizuoka.ac.jp

Abstract. In recent years, in the advertising market in Japan, the Internet commercials have expanded to the second media following the television commercials. The consumers came to refer to more information when they take the purchasing action. It is said that the Internet commercials have the synergistic effect by combining with the mass media such as the television commercials. The authors analyze the effect of the advertisement and the promotion including the synergistic effect between the Internet commercials and the mass media such as the television commercials by using the single source data. For example, the percentage that the consumers who watched the television commercials are led to the Internet commercials is analyzed. As a result of the analysis, it becomes possible to clarify the effect that the contact to the advertisement gives to the purchasing process. And it will become a key of planning the marketing strategy in the companies.

Keywords: Synergistic effect · Advertisement · Promotion · Single source data · Purchasing process · Marketing strategy

1 Introduction

The authors analyze the effect of the advertisement and the promotion including the synergistic effect between the Internet commercials and the mass media such as the television commercials to clarify the effect that the contact to the advertisement gives to the purchasing process.

1.1 The Advertisement and the Companies

The advertisement is a part of the marketing activities in the companies.

© Springer International Publishing Switzerland 2015
S. Yamamoto (Ed.): HIMI 2015, Part II, LNCS 9173, pp. 159–170, 2015.
DOI: 10.1007/978-3-319-20618-9_16

The commercial message is the short advertisement that is shown in the middle of the television program and the radio program. The companies show the commercial message to appeal the product to the consumers.

However, if the companies show the commercial message, it is not always possible appeal the product to the consumers. It is necessary for the companies to plan the marketing strategy by analyzing the effect of the advertisement and the promotion. For example, it is necessary for the companies to consider in the target customers or what kind of time zone the companies should show the commercial message.

1.2   The Situation in the Advertising Market in Japan in Recent Years

In recent years, in the advertising market in Japan, the Internet commercials that continue growing up have expanded to the second media following the television commercials. The decrease of the four mass media (the television commercials, the newspaper commercials, the magazine commercials, and the radio commercials) has continued.

The following figure shows the composition ratio of the sales of the advertising company in Japan. According to the composition ratio of the sales of the advertising company in Japan, the television time commercials occupy 20.1 %, and the television spot commercials occupy 26.1 % in the period on March 2014 [1] (Fig. 1).

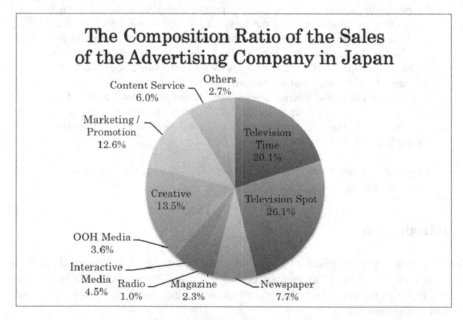

Fig. 1. The composition ratio of the sales of the advertising company in Japan [1]

If the television time commercials and the television spot commercials are totaled, only on the television commercials occupy 46.2 %. It is understood that the television commercials occupy about the half of the sales of the advertising company in Japan.

In other words, the center of the advertising market in Japan is still the television commercials.

In recent years, the Internet has spread by the innovation of the information technology. The companies came to do the advertising activities by using the websites of the Internet commercials for the marketing. The consumers came to be able to obtain great information from the Internet commercials.

In addition, CGM (Consumer Generated Media) in the Internet commercials has been attracted attention in recent years. CGM is the media that the consumers generate the contents by using the Internet [2]. The marketing activities using CGM have the advantage that can be done with little cost. The companies have especially taken the advertisement that uses SNSs (Social Networking Services) in CGM. SNSs are the websites of the community type that promote and support the connection of the person and the person [3]. The consumers came to be able to exchange the information with each other.

In this way, the consumers came to refer to more information when they take the purchasing action [4]. However, as the present condition, the companies can't use the Internet commercials well. In the future, it will become a point how the companies tell the effect of commercial message by using the Internet commercials in addition to the mass media such as the television commercials.

1.3 The Synergistic Effect in the Advertisement

By the spread of the Internet, the companies will need the method not to depend on only the mass advertisement such as the television commercials.

In the business of the advertisement, the technique of the cross media using two or more media centering on the Internet commercials has been attracting attention in recent years. The cross media is defined as aiming at the interaction by using two or more media. The means of combining two or more media are also used the media mix. The media mix means the combination of the media to maximize the reach to the consumers. The cross media is often used in the meaning of increasing the synergistic effect of promoting the purchasing action of the consumers by combining two or more media [5].

In the media mix that has been planned since before, the marketing strategy is planned based on the index of the audience rating of the television commercials or the number of subscriptions of the magazine commercials because the purposes of the media mix is the reach to the consumers. On the other hand, in the cross media that has been attracted attention in recent years, it is important to clarify the effect that the synergistic effect made between the media and the media gives to the purchasing process of the consumers.

Therefore, the authors decided to analyze the synergistic effect in the advertisement to clarify the effect that the cross media gives to the purchasing process of the consumers.

2 The Single Source Data

The authors analyze the synergistic effect in the advertisement by using the single source data offered from Nomura Research Institute, Ltd [6].

2.1   The Advantage of Analyzing by Using the Single Source Data

The single source data is the data that collected the multifaceted information such as the contact to the advertisement, the purchasing process, and the lifestyle from the same target person [7]. The single source data has the advantage that the relation between the contact to the advertisement and the purchasing process can be analyzed with a personal base.

In this way, in the single source data, the method of collecting the survey data from the same target person is used. By the method, the process of the marketing activities such as the advertisement and the promotion by the companies, and the purchasing process of the consumers can be understood. The purchase intention and the purchase situation for the specific products can be understood in the situation before and after the contact to the media. If the companies carry out two or more marketing strategies, the companies are not able to understand each effect. By using the concept of the single source data, the effect of the cross media is analyzed. For example, the percentage that the consumers who watched the television commercials are led to the Internet commercials is analyzed. In addition, it is also possible to compare it with the effect of the competitive products.

As a result of the analysis by using the single source data, it becomes possible to clarify the effect that the contact to the advertisement gives to the purchasing process.

2.2   The Single Source Data Used for the Analysis

The single source data that can be used for the analysis was offered from Nomura Research Institute. The single source data that can be used for the analysis is by the questionnaire survey. The subjects of the survey are about 3,000 people who live in the Kanto area in Japan. The period of the survey is about two months from May 14, 2011 to July 9, 2011.

The number of the respondents of the questionnaire survey is shown in the following table. The respondents of the questionnaire survey are 3,000 people in total. The respondents of the questionnaire survey can be distinguished each by sample ID. In addition, the demographic attributes of the sex, and the age are understood (Table 1).

The single source data are comprised of three of the media contact situation, the advertising situation, and the purchasing process situation.

Table 1. The number of the respondents of the questionnaire survey

Sex/Age	20 s	30 s	40 s	50 s	Total
Male	367	442	347	389	1,545
Female	336	412	323	384	1,455
Total	703	854	670	773	3,000

(Unit: people)

- In the media contact situation, there are the television program watching data, the magazine reading data, the newspaper reading data, the website watching data, and the retail channel using data.

- In the advertising situation, there are the magazine commercials advertising situation, the newspaper commercials advertising situation, and the television commercials contact frequency.
- In the purchasing process situation, there are the purchasing processes of the drinks, the foods, and the services, etc. (the 200 items in total)

In addition, the website watching data indicates the access number of days to the website. And, the television commercials contact frequency indicates the television commercials frequency of the items that each sample contacted from the start of the questionnaire survey date (May 14, 2011) until the second survey date.

In the purchasing process situation, the purchase intention and the purchase situation for the specific products (the 200 items in total) can be understood in the situation before and after the contact to the media.

The authors analyze by using the single source data that mentioned above.

3   A Consideration of the Target Customers

Before analyzing the synergistic effect in the advertisement, the authors consider the target customers for planning the marketing strategy.

3.1   The New Customers and the Repeat Customers

At first, the target customers can be classified in the new customers and the repeat customers. If the authors analyze by using the single source data that mentioned above, the authors can understand the purchase intention and the purchase situation for the specific products in the situation before and after the contact to the media. In other words, it can be understood whether the customers have bought the specific products before the contact to the advertisement.

Then, the authors define the new customers and the repeat customers as follows.

- The new customers are the target customers who have not bought the specific products before the contact to the advertisement.
- The repeat customers are the target customers who have bought the specific products before the contact to the advertisement.

By classifying the target customers in the new customers and the repeat customers, the authors analyze the effect of the promotion to each target customers.

3.2   The Use Situation of the Internet

In recent years, the companies came to do the advertising activities by using the websites of the Internet commercials for the marketing. In the future, it will become a point how the companies tell the effect of commercial message by using the Internet commercials.

Then, The authors analyzed the use intention of the Internet by the distinction of the sex and the age. Specifically, The authors understand whether the customers want to watch the general websites by using the personal computer. The result is shown in the following figure. This indicates the percentage of the respondents who answered that they want to watch the general websites by using the personal computer.

It is understood that the use intention of the Internet in 40 s is highest compared with other ages. And, the use intention of the Internet in 30 s is the second highest (Fig. 2).

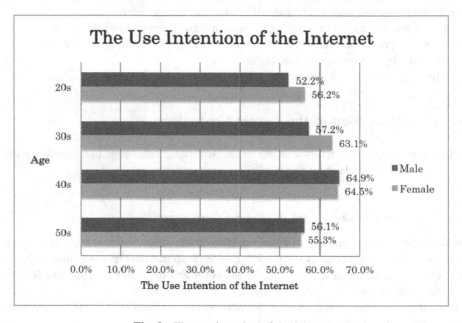

Fig. 2. The use intention of the internet

The use intention of the Internet becomes a reference in the following analysis. For example, because the use intention of the Internet in 40 s is highest compared with other ages, in the case of the target customers are the 40 s, it will be the most effective to use mainly the Internet commercials.

4   An Analysis of the Synergistic Effect Between the Television Commercials and the Internet Commercials

The authors analyze the synergistic effect between the television commercials and the Internet commercials. In this analysis, as the target items, the authors select the "Asahi Super Dry" and the "Iyemon".

The "Asahi Super Dry" is the beer sold in Japan. And, the "Iyemon" is the green tea sold in Japan. By using the 2 items with different category, the authors analyze each effect.

4.1   In the Case of the "Asahi Super Dry"

At first, in the case of the "Asahi Super Dry", the authors analyze the synergistic effect between the television commercial and the Internet commercial.

The following figure shows the purchasing process and the contact situation to the television commercial and the Internet commercial. The purchase intention and the purchase rate are shown separately for the new customers and the repeat customers. For the contact situation to the television commercial and the Internet commercial, the contact to the television commercial in the period of the survey is 3 times or more considers there is the contact to the television commercial. The contact to the Internet commercial in the period of the survey is once or more considers there is the contact to the Internet commercial (Fig. 3).

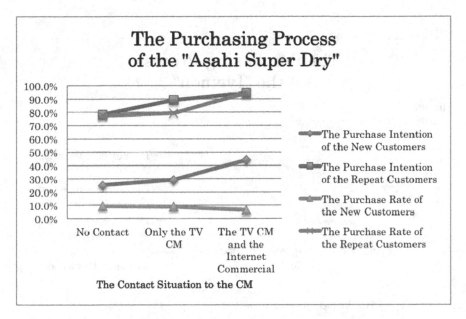

Fig. 3. The purchasing process of the "Asahi Super Dry"

For the new customers, even if there is the contact with both of the television commercial and the Internet commercial, the purchase rate is not rising. This does not mean that there is the synergistic effect. However, for the purchase intention of the new customers and the repeat customers, and the purchase rate of the repeat customers, there is the synergistic effect between the television commercial and the Internet commercial. For example, for the purchase intention of the new customers, it is 28.9 % in contact to only for the television commercial. However, it becomes 43.8 % in contact to both of the television commercial and the Internet commercial.

T. Yamada et al.

4.2 In the Case of the "Iyemon"

Next, in the case of the "Iyemon", as in the previous analysis, the authors analyze the synergistic effect between the television commercials and the Internet commercials. The "Iyemon" is a popular item competing for the top in the green tea sold in Japan.

The following figure shows the purchasing process and the contact situation to the television commercial and the Internet commercial. The purchase intention and the purchase rate are shown separately for the new customers and the repeat customers. For the contact situation to the television commercial and the Internet commercial, the contact to the television commercial in the period of the survey is 3 times or more considers there is the contact to the television commercial. The contact to the Internet commercial in the period of the survey is once or more considers there is the contact to the Internet commercial (Fig. 4).

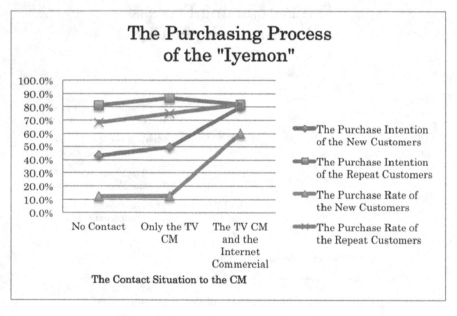

Fig. 4. The purchasing process of the "Iyemon"

For only the purchase intention of the repeat customers, even if there is the contact to both of the television commercial and the Internet commercial, it is not rising than the contact to the television commercial. However, as the figure shows, there is the synergistic effect except for it.

In the case of the "Iyemon", it is a point for the acquisition of the new customers that the contact to both of the television commercial and the Internet commercial.

5 An Analysis of the Percentage that the Consumers Who Watched the Television Commercials are Led to the Internet Commercials

The authors analyze the percentage that the consumers who watched the television commercials are led to the Internet commercials.

5.1 The Watching Rate of the Website

At first, the authors analyze the watching rate of the website. In this analysis, as the target item, the authors select the "Asahi Super Dry". The "Asahi Super Dry" is the beer sold in Japan.

The following figure shows the watching rate of the website of each age. The watching rate of the website are shown separately for the contact to the television commercial is 5 times or more, or less than 5 times (Fig. 5).

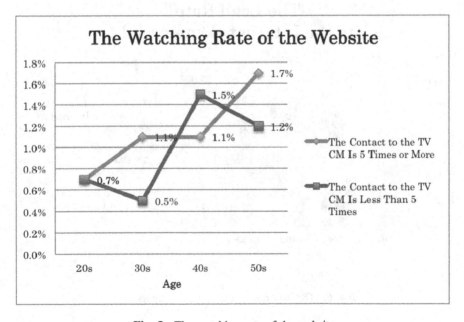

Fig. 5. The watching rate of the website

For the 30 s and the 50 s, the watching rate of the website is higher when the contact to the television commercial is 5 times or more than less than 5 times. For the 20 s, the watching rate of the website is 0.7 % for both of the contact to the television commercial is 5 times or more, and less than 5 times. For the 40 s that the use intention of the Internet is highest compared with other ages, the watching rate of the website is 1.5 % even if the contact to the television commercial is less than 5 times.

5.2   The Lead Rate to the Internet Commercial

Next, the authors analyze the lead rate from the television commercial to the Internet commercial. In this analysis, as the target item, the authors select the "VIERA". The "VIERA" is the television of Panasonic Corporation sold in Japan.

The following figure shows the percentage that the consumers who watched the television commercial watch the Internet commercial, the contact rate to only the television commercial, and the contact rate to both of the television commercial and the Internet commercial of each age. If the contact rate to only the television commercial, and the contact rate to both of the television commercial and the Internet commercial are totaled, it is the contact rate to the television commercial. For example, for 50 s in the age, the contact rate to only the television commercial is 89.0 %, the contact rate to both of the television commercial and the Internet commercial is 7.2 %, the contact rate to the television commercial is 96.2 %, and the percentage the consumers who watched the television commercial watch the Internet commercial is 7.5 % (Fig. 6).

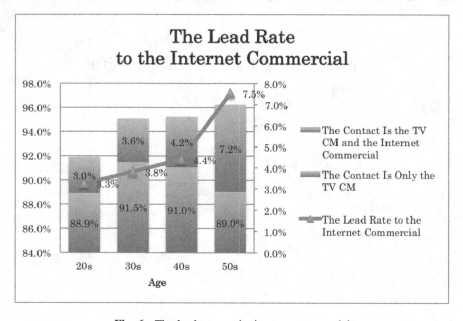

Fig. 6. The lead rate to the internet commercial

For the 50 s, the contact rate to the television commercial, and the percentage that the consumers who watched the television commercial watch the Internet commercial are highest compared with other ages. On the contrary, for the 20 s, these values are lowest compared with other ages. In addition, for the 30 s and the 40 s, although the contact rate to the television commercial is high, the lead rate from the television commercial to the Internet commercial is not so high. At more advanced ages, the contact rate to the television commercial, and the lead rate to the Internet commercial is higher.

6 Conclusion

6.1 Conclusion

The authors analyzed the effect of the advertisement and the promotion including the synergistic effect between the Internet commercials and the mass media such as the television commercials by using the single source data. The purpose of the analysis was to clarify the effect that the contact to the advertisement gives to the purchasing process.

As a result of the analysis, it was clarified that comparatively in many cases, the purchase intention and the purchase rate were higher when the contact to both of the television commercials and the Internet commercials, than the contact to only the television commercials. In other words, as an example of this paper, there is a certain degree of the synergistic effect between the television commercials and the Internet commercials.

In addition, the authors analyze the percentage that the consumers who watched the television commercials are led to the Internet commercials. As a result of the analysis, it was clarified that there was a difference in the watching rate of the website and the lead rate from the television commercials to the Internet commercials in each age.

6.2 Further Research

In this paper, the authors selected the "Asahi Super Dry", the "Iyemon", and the "VIERA" as the target items. However, the authors are not able to refer to the special quality of the target items. For example, the effect will be different at the time of the new items are released or the time of the items are renewed. It is necessary for the authors to analyze the effect in consideration of the category and the penetrance of the items.

Next, it is for the target customers. In this paper, the authors classified the target customers in the new customers and the repeat customers. In addition, the authors analyzed the effect separately for each age. However, it is not able to refer to the annual income and the lifestyle of the target customers. In addition to these, the various classification methods of the target customers can be considered. In this way, it is necessary for the authors to devise the classification methods of the target customers in the future.

Finally, it is for the target media. In this paper, as the target media, the authors selected the television commercials, and the websites of the Internet commercials. In the single source data that could be used for the analysis, the contact situation to the newspaper commercials and the magazine commercials also could be understood, however the authors did not include them in the target media. Moreover, the use situation of CGM in the companies could not be understood. In the future, it is necessary for the authors to consider including the situation of these media in the target media. In addition, for the website watching data, more detailed analysis will become possible if not only the number of accesses to the websites but the watching time at the time of the access to the websites and the number of watching of each pages can be understood.

References

1. Annual Report, Dentsu. http://www.dentsu.co.jp/ir/data/annual.html. Accessed 8 February 2015
2. CGM, E-Words. http://e-words.jp/w/CGM.html. Accessed 8 February 2015
3. SNS, E-Words. http://e-words.jp/w/SNS.html. Accessed 8 February 2015
4. Gilbride, T.J., Allenby, G.M.: Estimating heterogeneous EBA and economic screening rule choice models. Mark. Sci. **25**(5), 494–509 (2006)
5. Cross Media, Weblio. http://www.weblio.jp/content/cross-media. Accessed 8 February 2015
6. Insight signal, Nomura Research Institute. http://www.is.nri.co.jp/data/index.html. Accessed 8 February 2015
7. Single Source Data, Weblio. http://www.weblio.jp/content/single-source-data. Accessed 8 February 2015

Information and Interaction
for Driving

Development of a New Low Cost Driving Simulation for Assessing Multidimensional Task Loads Caused by Mobile ICT at Drivers' Workplaces. – *Objective-Fidelity Beats Equipment-Fidelity?*

Michael Bretschneider-Hagemes[✉]

Institute for Occupational Safety and Health of the DGUV (IFA),
Alte Heerstrasse 111, 53757 St. Augustin, Germany
michael.bretschneider@dguv.de

Abstract. Digitization of the world of work has led to drivers' workplaces frequently being equipped with information and communications technology (ICT) [1]. These workplaces often involve the use of several such digital systems. Owing to these systems' potential to distract the driver, they must be integrated into users' workplaces with appropriate attention to ergonomics, and tested by risk-free methods under laboratory conditions. A driving simulator designed and constructed for this purpose at the IFA forms the subject of this paper. Particular aspects of this simulator are its design, which is low-cost and assumed to deliver low fidelity, but which enables good overall simulation quality results to be achieved owing to a special software environment. Third parties are expressly invited to copy the simulator and pool their experiences.

Keywords: Driving simulation · Measurement of distraction · Mobile information and communications technology

1 Problem

The diverse uses of mobile information and communications technology at drivers' workplaces give rise to an increasing risk of distraction. This applies both to the vehicle manufacturers' factory-fitted systems and to aftermarket systems. The particular issue however concerns the combining of multiple aftermarket systems – often without careful consideration – that have never been tested by a (vehicle) manufacturer with regard to the task load associated with them. The systems in question are used for example for job assignment, scheduling and navigation, and for access to information on the move. Equipment typically includes tablet PCs, satellite navigation devices, laptops integrated into the driver's workplace for use in mobile technical services, telematics applications in logistics, etc. Whether the design of a workplace employing mobile IT is free of hazards must also be determined at company level by way of a risk assessment. Awareness of the problem is however fairly limited within companies. A driving simulator was to be created that can be used flexibly and under mobile conditions to test the

© Springer International Publishing Switzerland 2015
S. Yamamoto (Ed.): HIMI 2015, Part II, LNCS 9173, pp. 173–179, 2015.
DOI: 10.1007/978-3-319-20618-9_17

applications that are actually encountered in company operations. The purpose was to improve awareness of the issue and to permit objective study of it.

The IFA's driving simulator was developed for the purpose of analyzing the impact upon drivers' performance of multidimensional task loads in actual practical application scenarios, and for illustrating to users the hazards posed by distraction.

2   Design

The base frame was designed such that a driver's and a passenger's seat can be fitted to it. A passenger's seat is relevant because the equipment used for the secondary tasks to be tested is frequently secured to the seat or seat mounting rail (for example by means of a laptop console). A Logitech G27 steering wheel (with haptic force-feedback characteristic) and an H-pattern manual gearshift gate were located on a hight-adjustable base. A pedal mounting surface was provided on the floor frame (see Fig. 1).

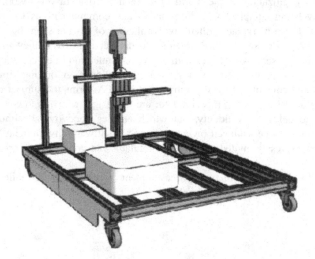

Fig. 1. Design sketch of the mobile IFA simulator, constructed from aluminum profiled sections

The frame was manufactured from standard aluminum profiled sections.

The items of equipment were selected with the aim of achieving the greatest possible realism. The force-feedback feature and the facility for simulation to be controlled by means of a conventional H-pattern manual gearshift gate and standard pedals (gas, brake, clutch) was intended to minimize the reactivity of the test arrangement, i.e. the confounding influence of unrealistic laboratory conditions upon the study result.

The compact dimensions and low weight of the simulator enable it to be used without difficulty at different locations for demonstration purposes. It can be used during company events such as safety training courses for the purposes of education and prevention (Fig. 2).

Fig. 2. The simulator in action at the World Congress for Safety and Health at Work 2014 in Frankfurt

3 Software Environment

The powerful but low-cost rFactor software application was used as the simulation environment. rFactor has its origins in the sim racing scene. This project enabled it to be used for the first time in a research application. For this purpose, a custom plugin was developed for the export of log files containing the essential performance parameters (see Fig. 3). Attainment of a high level of overall *simulator fidelity* is therefore claimed, despite relatively low *equipment fidelity* – for example, the driving simulator does not include a replica vehicle body. (In simple terms, the overall simulator fidelity refers to the overall realism attained by the simulation, together with the scope for extrapolation of the results to reality.) The *objective fidelity* (such as realistic dynamic vehicle behavior) and the *perceptual fidelity* (the degree to which the test subject perceives simulation to be realistic, following acclimatization) were attained to an extent often not reached by conventional simulation environments in the research sphere; for fidelity aspects, refer to [2]. A further benefit is the facility for the unrestricted creation of custom routes, together with a Google Maps interface, and the networking capability of the software used.

3.1 rFactor and IFA Plugin

The simulation environment enables any conceivable vehicle type to be used. This in turn enables the simulator to be adapted realistically to specific test subject collectives (such as use of the vehicle type in the company fleet, up to and including detailed design of the instrumentation – see Fig. 3).

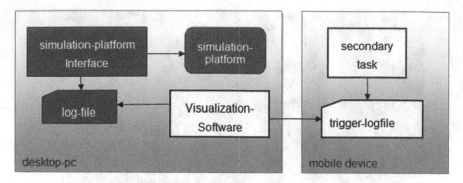

Fig. 3. Logical structure of the software components

The realism of the driving characteristics can be varied. Test runs showed that transfer of existing driving skills was better when the test subject was presented with the driving task in simplified form in the first instance (automatic transmission, steering assist, etc.).

The courses to be completed can be selected from a library of existing layouts, or created by users themselves (see Sect. 3.2). Preference was given to a user-generated layout in the interests of standardized driving tasks.

A plugin created by the IFA enables a number of driving parameters to be accessed. These are essentially the speed, the frequency of lane departures, and the braking behavior.

3.2   Bob's Track Builder

Bob's Track Builder is an add-on application by which courses can be designed freely and thereby adapted ideally to the objectives of the study. An interface to Google Maps enables real-life courses to be imported. The road surface and the landscape can also be adapted without difficulty.

4   Method

The usual test scenario provides each test subject with an acclimatization phase (unstructured driving practice) of adequate length. This is supplemented by standard-ized test runs. The test proper consists of a baseline run (driving over a standardized course without distraction) and a test run (driving with distraction/secondary task; the distraction task can be a 1:1 simulation of the actual applications within company operations). If applicable, a further run is performed in which a standardized reference task is used as the distraction. The form taken by the test scenario is determined by the specific objective of the study.

Statistical analysis of the data obtained with test subject collectives of adequate size enables the global task load of a secondary task to be determined in relative terms. Variants of the tasks can be retested and developed further as needed.

Fig. 4. View of the instruments in the r-Factor simulation

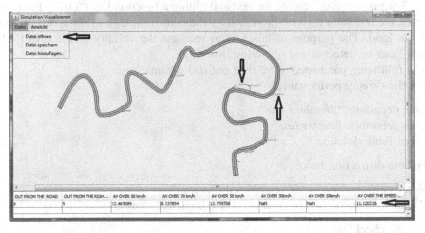

Fig. 5. Visual analysis of the course followed and the incidence of distractions (marked by arrows)

This purely quantitative approach can be supplemented by a qualitative analysis. The USB link between the tablet PC on which the distraction task is presented and the simulation PC enables the respective log files to be merged and processed for presentation in visual form (see Fig. 4). An analysis tool was programmed for this purpose. The exact driving line of a baseline run and that of a test run can be presented in a graph together with the point in time of the distraction. This provides the test subject with very rapid and informative feedback on his or her driving performance (Fig. 5).

For further extension of application and for reference purposes, existing, established standard simulations and test methods such as the Lane Change Task (LCT) in accordance with ISO 26022 [3] can easily be performed by means of the simulator in its current form. The hardware is fully compatible for this purpose.

5   First Impressions and Results

Visitors passing a trade-fair stand were spontaneously invited to take a test drive. 50 test subjects were recruited in this way; 44 of them were documented in full.

The test subjects were provided with verbal instructions on use of the simulator and on the subsequent procedure. Performance of a test drive, which under laboratory conditions would be indispensable, was unfortunately not possible under the given conditions. As a result, the unfiltered adaptation effect limited the suitability of the results for exploitation.

Each test subject completed one baseline run and one test run with distraction tasks on a standard course. Each run involved driving on a twisty country road for approximately three minutes. Oncoming traffic was not presented. The course was divided into five speed zones (30–70 km/h), marked by standard traffic signs.

Each test subject was instructed *to keep to the right-hand carriageway at the speed indicated by the signs*.

Following the baseline run, the distraction task was explained. This consisted of a scheduling message in the context of company operations, and was presented on a laptop. The task entailed reading the text and hitting a function key ("*OK*"). For part of the tasks, the test subjects were prompted by the text of the task to say a certain signal word out loud. The purpose of this was to increase the validity of the data ("*blind clicking*" can be detected and filtered in this way).

The following parameters were read out and documented.

For the driving performance:

- Lane departure: "*shoulder line*"
- Lane departure: "*center line*"
- Speed limit violation

For the distraction tasks:

- *Motor performance* of task completed: "yes/no"
- *Cognitive/acoustic performance* of task completed: "yes/no"

For the checklist:

- Duration of completion of the task

A constant deterioration in driving performance from the baseline run to the test run is evident for all sub-groups.

Lane departures are more frequent. Both the center line and the shoulder line were crossed inadvertently an average of once more often per run. Highway curve entry points were repeatedly missed owing to aversion of the gaze.

Speed limit violations were also more frequent. The average speed limit violation over the entire course was 0.5 km/h higher in the test runs than in the baseline runs.

- Observation 1: Speed limit signs were often missed.
- Observation 2: The test subject first eased off the gas, then attempted to "*make up*" time after completing the task (distraction).

Analysis of the data set filtered following successful completion of the task (distraction) yielded somewhat surprising results. It revealed no significant deviation in driving performance between the sub-groups (filtered for successful/unsuccessful completion of the distraction task). Based upon the observations, the conclusion at this stage is as follows:

- An individual who is already fully occupied does not even address the task, or ignores it and simply drives on.
- The test subject conducts "*information management*", i.e. he or she waits until a straight stretch of highway before addressing the distraction task.

Hardly any test subjects managed to address all the "*speaking tasks*" during the distraction task. 18 out of 44 test subjects completed at least 1 out of 3 "*speaking tasks*". Only 2 persons completed all *speaking tasks*, and these individuals indicated that they had a background in this area of research and had considerable experience with simulators.

6   Discussion

The driving simulator method outlined here is still at an early stage of development. The test runs described nevertheless demonstrated that the method discriminates, at least coarsely, despite the adaptation effects. This must be examined further under adequate laboratory conditions. The validity of the method is to be tested in the future by means of crossover trials employing established methods.

The advantage of this method, which is already evident, lies in the high simulation quality of the driving characteristics. The driving task is highly realistic. The suitability of the driving task and also of the distraction tasks for adaptation leads to a high level of acceptance at company level and thus contributes to the raising of awareness among the target group.

The facility for data to be analyzed qualitatively and presented visually is particularly useful for applications in prevention activity. Test subjects are frequently not aware of how negatively a distraction task has impacted upon their driving performance. Statistical analysis has proved to be of little benefit for prevention activity, the purposes of which are primarily educational. By contrast, visual analysis provides the test subjects with a quick and simple impression of the effect of distraction.

References

1. Bretschneider-Hagemes, M., Stamm, R., Kohn, M.: BGI/GUV-I 8696: Information – Einsatz von bordeigenen Kommunikations- und Informationssystemen mit Bildschirmen an Fahrerarbeitsplätzen. DGUV, Berlin (2009)
2. Regan, A.M., Lee, J.D., Young, L.K.: Driver Distraction: Theory, Effects, and Mitigation, p. 89. CRC Press/Taylor and Francis Group, Boca Raton (2009)
3. ISO 26022: Road vehicles. Ergonomic aspects of transport information and control systems. Simulated lane change test to assess in-vehicle secondary task demand (2010)

Differences in Driver Distractibility Between Monolingual and Bilingual Drivers

Isis Chong[(⊠)] and Thomas Z. Strybel

Center for Human Factors in Advanced Aeronautics Technologies,
Department of Psychology, California State University Long Beach,
1250 N Bellflower Blvd, Long Beach, CA 90840, USA
Isis.Chong@student.csulb.edu,
Thomas.Strybel@csulb.edu

Abstract. The present research sought to bridge the gap between research on driver distraction and the bilingual advantage by testing monolingual and bilinguals in a driving simulation similar to those encountered by drivers on a daily basis. The Lane Change Test (LCT) was used to test driving performance in the presence of a delayed digit recall task (2-back task) and three types of peripheral detection tasks (PDTs). Although performance came to be degraded as the complexity of tasks increased, the overall performance of the bilinguals was more negatively affected than their monolingual counterparts across the LCT, PDT, and 2-back task. Implications and limitations are discussed.

Keywords: Attention · Bilingual advantage · Driving · n-back task · Peripheral detection task

1 Introduction

Driver distraction and inattention has become an important factor in road safety, due to the proliferation of electronic devices and technology in modern automobiles. Consequently, drivers are presented with increasing amounts of information that can be relevant or irrelevant to the driving task. This information requires that drivers perceive, process, and select appropriate actions for all of the stimuli they encounter. From yielding to pedestrians crossing the street to monitoring traffic signals, drivers must remain alert and vigilant of their surroundings for safe and effective driving. Often, however, drivers face sources of distraction that divert their attention from the driving task, which may compromise safety. It is not surprising, therefore, that interest and research on driver distractibility is increasing. Research has shown that distractions such as talking on a cellular device can produce slower reactions to traffic [1] and increased difficulty processing new information [2]. Another focus of research on distractibility is how the characteristics of the driver him or herself influences distractibility. Factors such as driver experience, age and gender have been shown to affect driving [3, 4], although the results are not straightforward. In the present investigation, we examined another driver characteristic, bilingualism, on driver distractibility, because previous research has shown differences between bilinguals and monolinguals on several cognitive tasks.

© Springer International Publishing Switzerland 2015
S. Yamamoto (Ed.): HIMI 2015, Part II, LNCS 9173, pp. 180–189, 2015.
DOI: 10.1007/978-3-319-20618-9_18

Bilingualism is the ability to read, write, speak, and understand two or more languages [5]. Research suggests that cognitive differences exist between bilinguals and their monolingual counterparts [6]. For example, when compared to monolinguals, bilinguals have shown an increased ability to process verbal and perceptual information [7]. They are also more efficient at adjusting their attention to fit changes in the demands of a task [8–11]. This research has led some to suggest that the ability to fluently speak multiple languages creates a bilingual "advantage" in terms of better allocation of one's attentional resources. It is theorized that this advantage stems from a bilinguals' need to inhibit one language when using another language [7, 12].

In the preset study, we examined whether the bilingual advantage would affect driver distractibility, given the various cognitive demands made on drivers and the previously-noted cognitive advantages of bilinguals. Driving performance was measured with a standard Lane Change Test (LCT) and a modified Peripheral Detection Task (PDT). Typically, the PDT presents a single visual stimulus and the participant must detect its presence. We varied the PDT tasks to determine whether more ecologically-valid stimuli would show effects of distractibility on performance. Participants responded to either the left-right location of the stimulus or its movement. Dual task driving performance was assessed with a working memory task performed simultaneously with driving.

2 Method

2.1 Participants

Fifteen college students (8 monolingual) ranging from 21 to 31 years of age ($M = 24$) participated in this study. Nine females and six males participated in this study. Participants had normal or corrected-to-normal vision, and reported having no known hearing deficits. All participants were right-handed, had a California Class C non-commercial driver's license for three or more years prior to the experiment, and had, on average, 7 years of driving experience. All participants spoke fluent English; secondary languages amongst bilingual participants included Spanish, Cantonese, and French.

2.2 Measures

Bilingualism Measure. Participants were asked to complete a demographics questionnaire that included items that pertained to both driving and language. Language questions were obtained from previous language questionnaires [13, 14] and asked participants to rate their skill level for their reading, writing, speaking and listening ability. The rating scale ranged from "Very Poor" (1) to "Native-Like" (7). Bilingual participants were selected only if their reported secondary language ability ranged from "Functional" (4) to "Native-Like" (7).

Lane Change Test. The LCT was used to assess driving performance. The LCT is a driving simulation that is easy to implement and has been evaluated for reliability, validity, and sensitivity [15, 16]. The LCT features a 3-kilometer straight-lane track that presents lane change signs roughly every 150 m. Participants were instructed to drive at 60 km/hour for the length of the track and to make a total of 18 lane changes indicated by a lane change sign as quickly and efficiently as possible (Fig. 1). Participants used a G27 Logitech Force-Feedback Racing Wheel and pedal system to drive in the simulation. Three tracks (3 min each) were completed for every experimental condition. Participants were instructed to give priority to the driving task when completing additional secondary tasks. Given the response nature of the secondary tasks, all driving was completed with the left hand.

Fig. 1. LCT instructing a change to the center lane

Peripheral Detection Tasks (PDTs). Participants were instructed to make the appropriate button presses on an Ergodex keyboard with their right thumb and index finger when they identified a visual stimulus. The PDT stimuli were white circles that were projected onto the LCT image along the horizon line through the duration of each track. Participants were asked to complete three different PDTs in which stimuli were either (1) all stationary, (2) all moving, or (3) combined stationary and moving. For the two former conditions, participants were asked to determine the left-right location of the stimuli, and for the latter condition, whether the stimuli were stationary or moving (see Fig. 2). The white circles were randomly presented on either side at either 13" or 19" to the right or left of the center of the road and were 500 ms in duration.

2-Back Task. Participants were asked to recall prerecorded auditory items presented from a speaker to the right of the driver. The 2-back task featured 10-item sets that began with the word "next" and were followed by a random presentation of numbers (digits 0-9) every two-seconds. Every 10-item set lasted roughly 25 s and six sets (60 numbers) were played through the duration of a three-minute LCT track. Participants were instructed to recall the number, or item, they heard two items previously, as shown in Table 1. Thus, in each condition (three tracks) in which the 2-Back Task was used, participants were presented with a total of 180 numbers. This working memory

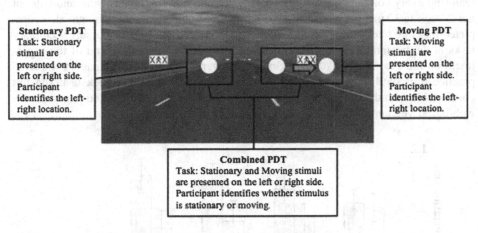

Fig. 2. PDT types. Stimuli are not to scale

Table 1. Visual representation of auditory 2-back task

Stimulus:	4	7	0	1	3	...
Response:	(no response)	(no response)	"4"	"7"	"0"	"1"

task resembles a conversation where pieces of information have to be temporarily stored and saved for a later point in the conversation.

NASA-TLX. Subjective workload was assessed using the NASA-TLX [17] a measure that asks participants to rate their perceptions of different items related to workload after completing a task. The levels measured include mental demand, physical demand, temporal demand, performance, effort, and frustration. A web version was used to collect responses [18].

2.3   Simulation Environment

All participants were run in a sound attenuated room where they faced a screen with a projected image. The projected image measured 46" × 61 ¾" and was used to display the LCT and the PDTs.

2.4   Testing Procedure

Each participant completed two 1.5-hour sessions on separate days. Following their written approval to participate in the study, and completion of the demographics questionnaire, participants were seated in front of a table with the steering wheel and pedals facing the projection screen. All participants ran in counterbalanced conditions featuring every combination of PDT (static, moving, and combined), with and without the 2-back task, making a total of six treatment combinations. Participants also completed baseline tracks in which they performed the driving task without any secondary tasks at the beginning of the experiment on the first day and at the end of the experiment on the second day. At the beginning of every condition, participants completed practice runs until they reached an 80 % accuracy rate for the 2-back task and felt comfortable with the PDT. After every condition, participants were asked to complete a web-based version of the NASA-TLX workload instrument (Fig. 3).

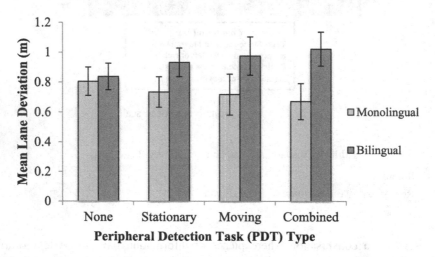

Fig. 3. Mean lane deviation in the driving task as a function of language proficiency and PDT type. Error bars represent ± 1standard error.

3 Results

3.1 LCT Lane Deviations

A 2 (language fluency: monolingual or bilingual) × 2 (2-back task: no 2-back or 2-back) × 4 (PDT type: none, static, moving, or combined) mixed factorial ANOVA was run to assess driving performance. For the LCT, higher lane deviations indicate poorer performance.

A main effect of 2-back task type was found, $F(1, 13) = 7.83$, $p = .02$, $\eta^2 = .38$. When completing the 2-back task, drivers had greater lane deviations, or poorer performance, ($M = .89$ mm, $SE = .07$ m) than when they did not complete the 2-back task ($M = .78$ m, $SE = .08$ m).

Additionally, although no main effect was found for PDT type or language fluency, a significant interaction was found between these two variables, $F(3, 39) = 4.15$, $p = .01$, $\eta^2 = .24$. Follow up analyses revealed that the nature of this interaction stems from differing performance between monolinguals and bilinguals for the combination PDT, $t(13) = -2.12$, $p = .05$, $d = -.49$. Specifically, bilinguals had greater lane deviations, or poorer performance, ($M = 1.02$ m, $SE = .14$ m) than their monolingual counterparts ($M = .67$ m, $SE = .08$ m) when driving and reported whether peripheral stimuli were stationary or moving.

3.2   2-Back Task

A 2 (language fluency: monolingual or bilingual) × 4 (PDT type: none, static, moving, or combined) mixed factorial ANOVA was run to assess differences in 2-back performance. A marginally significant main effect was found for language fluency, $F(1, 11) = 4.26$, $p = .06$, $\eta^2 = .28$, where bilinguals made a greater number of mistakes ($M = 16.93$, $SE = 3.94$) than monolinguals ($M = 4.96$, $SE = 4.26$). There was no significant main effect found for PDT type or interaction found between language fluency and PDT type (Fig. 4).

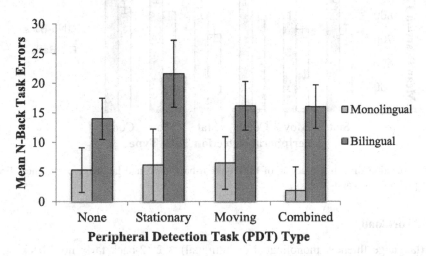

Fig. 4. N-back task errors as a function of PDT type and language proficiency. Error bars represent ± 1 standard error.

3.3   Peripheral Detection Tasks

A 2 (language fluency: monolingual or bilingual) × 2 (no 2-back or 2-back) × 2 (driver side: left or right) × 2 (eccentricity: near or far) × 3 (PDT type: none, static, moving, or combined) mixed factorial ANOVA was run on PDT reaction time.

A main effect of 2-back task was found for PDT reaction time, $F(1, 13) = 15.03$, $p = .002$, $\eta^2 = .54$. Participants were slower in responding to the PDTs when they complete the 2-back task ($M = 885.02$ ms, $SE = 64.89$ ms) than when they completed no 2-back task ($M = 771.16$ ms, $SE = 47.75$ ms).

A marginal main effect for PDT type was also found, $F(2, 26) = 3.07$, $p = .06$, $\eta^2 = .19$. Specifically, participants were slower in responding to the combination PDT ($M = 874.93$ ms, $SE = 47.44$ ms) than the stationary PDT ($M = 800.24$ ms, $SE = 66.93$ ms; $p = .05$) and moving PDT ($M = 809.11$ ms, $SE = 58.66$ ms; $p = .06$). No significant differences were found between the stationary and moving PDTs.

Finally, a significant interaction was found between language fluency, PDT type, and 2-back task, $F(2, 26) = 5.43$, $p = .01$, $\eta^2 = .30$. The effects of the 2-back task on PDT response latencies differed between monolinguals and bilinguals. Although monolinguals performed similarly for all three types of PDT, bilingual response times were longest for the combination PDT compared with response times in the stationary and moving PDT. In the combination PDT, bilingual response latencies were significantly longer for the 2-back task, compared with no 2-back task (Fig. 5).

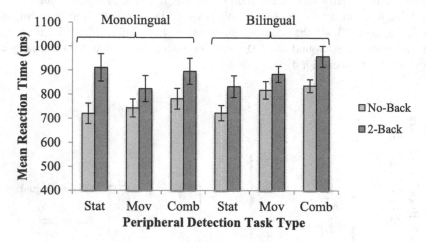

Fig. 5. Reaction time as a function of PDT type, n-back task, and language proficiency. Error bars represent ± 1 standard error.

3.4 Workload

A 2 (language fluency: monolingual or bilingual) × 2 (2-back task: no 2-back or 2-back) × 4 (PDT type: none, static, moving, or combined) mixed factorial ANOVA was run to determine differences in perceived workload assessed through the NASA-TLX. Greenhouse-Geisser corrections were used to address any sphericity violations.

A main effect of PDT was found, $F(1.89, 24.58) = 6.50$, $p = .006$, $\eta^2 = .33$. Conditions with no PDT ($M = 32.28$, $SE = 4.10$) were reported to be less demanding than the stationary ($M = 41.53$, $SE = 4.38$), moving ($M = 40.51$, $SE = 3.90$), and combined PDT conditions ($M = 41.17$, $SE = 4.26$). No significant differences were found between these three latter conditions.

A main effect of 2-back task was also found, $F(1, 13) = 30.50$, $p < .001$, $\eta^2 = .70$. Participants reported higher levels of workload for driving and performing the 2-back task ($M = 52.34$, $SE = 5.08$) than when no 2-back task was completed ($M = 25.40$, $SE = 4.03$).

A main effect of language fluency was found, $F(1, 13) = 5.21$, $p = .04$, $\eta^2 = .29$. Across all tasks, bilinguals reported higher levels of workload ($M = 47.74$, $SE = 5.31$) than monolinguals ($M = 30.01$, $SE = 5.67$).

Finally, there were no interactions found between PDT, 2-back task, or language proficiency for perceived workload (Fig. 6).

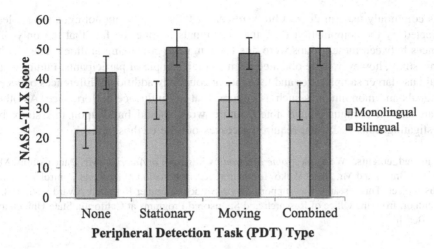

Fig. 6. Subjective workload as a function of PDT type and language proficiency. Error bars represent ± 1 standard error.

4 Discussion

The purpose of this study was to determine whether the previously reported bilingual advantage on standard tests of cognitive processing would apply to distracted driving. We were surprised to learn that bilinguals in our experiment were more affected by the distraction tasks than monolinguals. Although bilinguals and monolinguals performed equivalently on the LCT when performed alone, bilinguals performed worse on the LCT when the PDT and 2-back tasks were timeshared. Moreover, bilinguals had longer response latencies in some PDT conditions, committed more errors on 2-Back tasks and reported higher subjective workload across all task conditions. In summary, although bilingual processing advantages have been shown in many standard laboratory tasks, we showed a bilingual *disadvantage* for the LCT driving task when it was timeshared with the PDT and a working memory task.

The difficulties faced by bilinguals in completing the combinations of the afore-mentioned tasks can be seen in the results of the NASA-TLX workload measure, in which bilinguals reported experiencing greater workload than monolinguals. This suggests that the ability to handle inter-lingual conflict may only generalize to indi-vidual tasks and not to complex timesharing tasks. It should be noted, however, that the results of this study do not suggest the bilinguals are inherently poor drivers. Differ-ences in driving performance were only present when participants had to complete the additional secondary tasks. As such, further work should attempt to use varying levels of task complexity to investigate the point at which monolingual and bilingual dual task performance truly begins to differ.

Although the PDT tasks used here are not commonly used in investigations of LCT, they are more relevant to the driving task: drivers must not only detect stimuli in their environment, but also assess the threat of these stimuli, either to the vehicle or the stimulus itself. Our PDT tasks required more spatial processing than simple detection tasks commonly used in distractibility research. Interestingly, monolinguals were less distracted by the combination PDT than bilinguals despite the fact that the only differences between these groups were due the language processing abilities. The results of this study, however, were obtained from a small sample of participants. Future work should use larger sample sizes and take into account any additional differences between bilinguals and monolinguals such as culture, that my influence performance. As other researchers on bilinguals have noted, future work should build upon this study by investigating other tasks that require processes outside of those used here.

Acknowledgements. We thank *Alpine Electronics Research of America* (Mr. Dane Collins, Mr. Hirofumi Onishi and Mr. Hicks Wako) for their generous donation of the Lane Control Test used in this project. This research was supported by a Student Summer Research Award made to the first author, from the Office of Research and Sponsored Programs at California State University, Long Beach.

References

1. Stavrinos, D., Jones, J.L., Garner, A.A., Griffin, R., Franklin, C.A., Ball, D., Sisiopiku, V.P., Fine, P.R.: Impact of distracted driving on safety and traffic flow. Accid. Anal. Prev. **61**, 63–70 (2013)
2. Patten, C.J., Kircher, A., Östlund, J., Nilsson, L.: Using mobile telephones: cognitive workload and attention resource allocation. Accid. Anal. Prev. **36**, 341–350 (2014)
3. Rodrick, D., Bhise, V., Jothi, V.: Effects of driver and secondary task characteristics on lane change test performance. Hum. Factor Ergon. Manuf. Serv. Ind. **23**, 560–572 (2013)
4. White, C.B., Caird, J.K.: The blind date: the effects of change blindness, passenger conversation and gender on looked-but-failed-to-see (LBFTS) errors. Accid. Anal. Prev. **42**, 1822–1830 (2010)
5. Mio, J., Trimble, J., Arredondo, P., Cheatham, H., Sue, D. (eds.): Keywords in Multicultural Interventions: A Dictionary. Greenwood, Westport (1999)
6. Hilchey, M.D., Klein, R.M.: Are there bilingual advantages on nonlinguistic interference tasks? Implications for the plasticity of executive control processes. Psychon. Bull. Rev. **18**, 625–658 (2011)
7. Ben-Zeev, S.: The influence of bilingualism on cognitive strategy and cognitive development. Child Dev. **48**, 1009–1018 (1977)
8. Bialystok, E., Craik, F.I., Klein, R., Viswanathan, M.: Bilingualism, aging, and cognitive control: evidence from the Simon task. Psychol. Aging **19**, 290–303 (2004)
9. Hernández, M., Costa, A., Humphreys, G.W.: Escaping capture: bilingualism modulates distraction from working memory. Cognition **122**, 37–50 (2012)
10. Prior, A., Gollan, T.H.: Good language-switchers are good task-switchers: evidence from Spanish-English and Mandarin-English bilinguals. J. Int. Neuropsychol. Soc. **17**, 682–691 (2011)
11. Prior, A., MacWhinney, B.: A bilingual advantage in task switching. Bilingualism Lang. Cogn. **13**, 253–262 (2010)
12. Green, D.W.: Mental control of the bilingual lexico-semantic system. Bilingualism Lang. Cogn. **1**, 67–81 (1998)
13. Li, P., Sepanski, S., Zhao, X.: Language history questionnaire: a web-based interface for bilingual research. Behav. Res. Methods **38**, 202–210 (2006)

14. Carroll, R., Luna, D.: The other meaning of fluency. J. Advertising **40**, 73–84 (2011)
15. Mattes, S., Hallén, A.: Surrogate distraction measurement techniques: the lane change test. In: Regan, M.A., Lee, J.D., Young, K.L. (eds.) Driver Distraction: Theory Effects and Mitigation. CRC Press, Boca Raton (2009)
16. Rodrick, D., Bhise, V., Jothi, V.: Effects of driver and secondary task characteristics on lane change test performance. Hum. Factors Ergon. Manuf. Serv. Ind. **23**(6), 560–572 (2013)
17. Hart, S.G., Staveland, L.E.: Development of NASA-TLX (Task Load Index): results of empirical and theoretical research. Adv. Psychol. **52**, 139–183 (1988)
18. Sharek, D.: NASA-TLX Online Tool (Version 0.6) [Internet Application]. Raleigh, NC (2009). http://www.nasatlx.com

Urban Driving: Where to Present What Types of Information – Comparison of Head-Down and Head-Up Displays

Martin Götze[✉] and Klaus Bengler

Institute of Ergonomics, Technische Universität München,
Boltzmannstraße 15, 85747 Garching, Germany
goetze@lfe.mw.tum.de, bengler@tum.de

Abstract. In this paper, a comparison is made of different categorizations of the content of information given with a warning presented, either on a head-up or head-down display, in the context of urban driving. The study shows a significant advantage of the head-up display in terms of workload. No significant difference for three warning scenarios was found in a driving simulator experiment where the reaction times and the standard deviation of the distance to lane center were compared. The results will help build a generic and integrative HMI concept in the future.

Keywords: HMI · HCI · Urban · Driving · Cockpit · Hud · Hdd · Head-up · Display · Head-down · Instrument · Cluster · Warnings · Adas · Assistance systems · Driver

1 Introduction

1.1 Motivation

In the near future, additional use cases for advanced driving assistance systems (ADAS) in urban area driving scenarios will be needed. This need is brought on because of several reasons like higher complexity of the driving situation (Schröder, 2012), obstructions of road signs or other cars (Schartner, 2013). Urban driving is characterized by multiple road users like busses, motorcycles and trains, as well as weaker road users (ex. Pedestrians or cyclists). This may require the communication of additional information and warnings. New technologies such as the head-up display (HUD) and a programmable head-down display (HDD) will change how information and warnings are currently presented. Additionally, it is necessary to avoid overloading the driver caused by multiple displays and, as a consequence, more saccades, gaze shifts, and visual scanning (Recarte & Nunes, 2003). For this reason, the information presented in the HUD and HDD needs to be limited and presented carefully on the right display for the different types of information in order to avoid further increasing the already demanding scenarios of urban driving (Gevatter, 2006). While the HUD is suitable for warnings in particular (Reif, 2010), the HDD can present more detailed information without excessively distracting the driver (Petermann-Stock & Rhede, 2013).

© Springer International Publishing Switzerland 2015
S. Yamamoto (Ed.): HIMI 2015, Part II, LNCS 9173, pp. 190–200, 2015.
DOI: 10.1007/978-3-319-20618-9_19

1.2   Project UR:BAN

This paper reports the first step in a new generic and integrative HMI concept, part of a collaborative research project: UR:BAN (Urbaner Raum: Benutzergerechte Assistenzsysteme und Netzmanagement – Urban Space: User-oriented assistance systems and network management). UR:BAN is a 4 year project that started in 2012 and will be completed in 2016 (UR:BAN, 2013). Several industry and academic partners have joined in this project with the goal of revising current ADAS and traffic management systems for urban areas. The current study was carried out as part of UR:BAN, focusing on the human element in all aspects of mobility and traffic.

2   Method

2.1   Head-Up Display

One of the first to research Head-Up Displays in an automotive context can be attributed to Bubb (1978). The most crucial characteristic of this Human-Machine-Interface (HMI) is a virtual image in the line of sight of the driver. This image is the result of a reflection in the windshield and appears approx. 2.20 m in front of the eye (Schneid, 2008) with a viewing angle of 4° below the viewing direction of the driver. Reading information from the HUD maintains 40-50 % of the visual acuity for the driving scene since it is still in the parafoveal field of view while the visual acuity for the HDD drops down to approx. 10 % (Schmidtke, 1993). Figure 1 shows a comparison of the different angles and distances for the HUD and HDD.

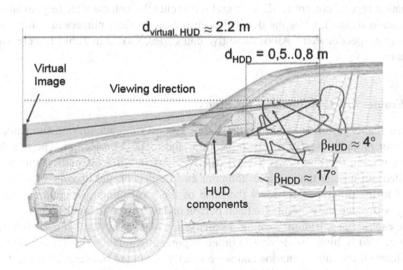

Fig. 1. Comparison of the different angles and display distances (HUD & HDD) (Miličić, 2010)

2.2   Head-Down Display

Head-Down Displays designate all in-vehicle displays where the driver has to move his head down to read the given information. The instrument cluster (IC) is one of those HDD and the display dealt with in this paper. The IC is one of the first components to transmit driving related information to the driver with an in-vehicle display. All types of information acquired by advanced driver assistance systems and in-vehicle information systems (IVIS) are presented on this primary human-machine-interface (Bengler et al., 2015). It usually consists of an analogue speedometer and a rev counter (Reif, 2010) with an additional small digital display; this allows for the possibility to display text and dynamic content (Winner et al., 2012). Many qualitative and quantitative requirements for the IC were published earlier (Götze, 2014).

2.3   Information Categories

In a previous study (Götze, 2014), five different information categories were defined: Action directives/request, situational information, attention control, conditional information, and detailed information. Each of the categories is defined by a different range and complexity of the shown information. The aim of all types is to trigger a different driver reaction. The first three categories are used for warnings. While action directives/ requests aim to concretely present the required driver action (e.g. demand to brake), the situational information indicates the specific type or location of the scenario (e.g. lane change warning), and attention control gives a general warning without specific information to increase the drivers attention to a risky situation (e.g. red warning sign). The last two categories are used to display non-critical information. The conditional information reports current HDD state and represents the vehicle state (e.g. availability or indication signals), while the detailed information displays numerical values or text content (e.g. speedometer). All of these five categories, shown in Table 1, were used in this study.

2.4   Framework Conditions of the Study

The participants performed an urban driving task in a 180° static driving simulator with side mirror projections, rear mirror projection, and a HUD projection. The simulation software used in this study was SILAB (SILAB, 2015). After the participants arrived, they filled out a demographic questionnaire and trained on the driving simulator and adapted to the different light level (because of the projections). All participants voluntarily performed the experiment. Each person had to drive two blocks (approximately 20 min. each) after a 10 min. training session. Each block was divided into 80 % urban driving and 20 % highway driving in order to prevent simulator sickness. Both blocks had different tracks and scenarios and were strictly permuted between all subjects. The participants operated either a HUD or HDD. Warnings, information, and navigation instructions were presented at the same position in both displays for all participants. Figure 2 shows the top middle position for the instrument cluster (HDD) and the middle position of the display over the current speed in the HUD. This procedure made

Table 1. Categorization of the content of information given with a warning/information (Götze et al., 2014).

Category	Description
Action directives/request	Concrete presentation of the required reaction e.g. demand to brake, navigation instructions
Situational information	Specific warning with indication of the type or location e.g. lane change warning
Attention control	General increase of attention or non-specific reference to risky situations e.g. warning tone
Conditional information	Representation of the vehicle state e.g. display of availability or indication
Detailed information	Numerical values or text content e.g. speedometer

Fig. 2. Position of the warnings and information shown in both displays

sure to expect all information at the same position over the trials to allow a low visual effort in finding the presented information.

The three warning categories (shown in Table 1) were used for three different risky scenarios: A parking vehicle, a pedestrian crossing the road and a fire truck taking the right of way. The two information categories were used to display either navigation information and the current speed, or status symbols. After each block, participants answered a questionnaire, rating the display type experiences in the last block. Additionally, the standardized NASA-TLX (Hart & Staveland, 1988) questionnaire was used to rate subjective workload. Furthermore, objective data was also recorded. After the experiment, all participants answered a final questionnaire comparing both display configurations.

2.5 Warning Scenarios

Warning Type: Action Request. This warning scenario of the type "action request" took place at a crossing with traffic lights. The participants saw the lights switching to the green signal quite early with no need to lower the speed or expect a traffic light change to red in the immediate future. After crossing the crossroad, an emergency vehicle took the right of way coming from the left side (see Fig. 3; scenario (a)). Without applying the brakes (or taking evasive action), an accident would have happened. The warning symbol with the additional text "BREMSEN" (brake) was shown in either display.

Warning Type: Situational Information. The "situational information" scenario (Fig. 3, scenario (b)) had a pedestrian crossing the road unexpectedly, hidden behind a van parking at the right side of the road. The speed allowed in this area was lowered to 30 km/h to give the participants a chance to avoid the accident. The warning symbol showed the parties involved in a potential accident (pedestrian) and the location of the threat (right side) as per definition in Götze et al. (2014).

Warning Type: Attention Control. The final warning scenario included the warning type for "attention control" where attention to a non-specific situation is communicated to the driver. The scenario involved a car pulling out of a parking spot (Fig. 3; scenario (c)). This car indicated leaving the parking spot quite late and simply pulled out just in front of the participant. The warning sign used in this scenario was a simple and generic warning triangle with no additional text.

2.6 Subjective and Objective Variables

In this study, different subjective and objective variables were examined. Different reaction times (RT) to the visual stimuli given on a display in the specific warning scenario and the SD of the distance to the lane center averaged over the whole track (Godthelp et al., 1984) were recorded. Stress and workload were also measured with the NASA-TLX to evaluate the different levels of visual load on different display positions. Lastly, participants graded the disturbance of status and indication symbols on a specific display.

NASA-TLX. For measuring the workload with the two different displays, the National Aeronautics and Space Administration Task Load Index (NASA-TLX) was used. The questionnaire measures on a 7-point scale. With increments of high, medium and low estimates for each point, it results in 21 gradations on the scales, where each complies for a score of 5 resulting in an overall score between 0-100. The topics addressed are the mental and physical demand, temporal demand, performance, effort, and frustration. A higher score on the scale corresponds to a higher workload.

Fig. 3. The three different scenarios with either warning symbols. Scenario (a) action request, scenario (b) situational information, and scenario (c) attention control.

3   Results

3.1   Participants

Thirty-two healthy volunteers participated in this simulator study with an average age of 26 years (SD = 3). Two participants had to be excluded because of simulator sickness. Twenty-five male and seven female participants were considered for the analysis. All of them had at least five years of driving experience and none of them suffered any visual impairments (visual acuity or color vision). For eleven volunteers, it was the first driving experience in a driving simulator, while the other twenty-one had driven at least once in a static driving simulator.

3.2   Objective Data

Statistical t-tests were performed to examine differences in the reaction time of the three warning categories and the standard deviation of the distance to the lane center.

Reaction Times. For the reaction time analysis, hits shorter than 200 ms and longer than 2000 ms were excluded as outliners. Additionally, for each participant, the mean reaction time was calculated and trials in a range M ± 2.5 SD were excluded.

The mean global reaction time for the two display types across all participants was calculated. With these results, a paired-sampled t-test was executed to examine any difference in global reaction time between the HUD and HDD. There was no significant difference found between the head-up (M = 1022.6 ms, SD = 296.9) and head-down (M = 1072.1 ms, SD = 408.4) display; t(29) = -1597, p = .121.

To examine the effect of the display position for the three different warning types ((a) action request, (b) situational information, (c) attention control) a paired-sampled t-test was executed for all three scenarios. There was no significant difference found for the RT in scenario (a) between the HUD (M_{HUD_a} = 1108.2 ms, SD_{HUD_a} = 232.5) and HDD (M_{HDD_a} = 1219.4 ms, SD_{HDD_a} = 479.4); $t_a(14)$ = -808, p_a = .432., neither in scenario (b) between the HUD (M_{HUD_b} = 1177.1 ms, SD_{HUD_b} = 231.5) and HDD (M_{HDD_b} = 1199.4 ms, SD_{HDD_b} = 323.1); $t_b(23)$ = -342, p_b = .735, nor in scenario (c) between the HUD (M_{HUD_c} = 830.5 ms, SD_{HUD_c} = 283.7) and HDD (M_{HDD_c} = 869.6 ms, SD_{HDD_c} = 361.9); $t_c(25)$ = 540, p_c = .594, see Fig. 4.

Distance to Lane Center. To examine the effect of the displays on lane keeping consistency, a paired-sampled t-test was executed for the standard deviation of the distance to lane center (DTL). For the DTL as well, no significant difference was found between head-up (M_{HUD} = .3388 m, SD_{HUD} = .0426) and head-down (M_{HDD} = .3462 m, SD_{HDD} = .0437) displays, see Fig. 5.

3.3   Subjective Data

NASA-TLX. The raw values without weighting were used to execute a paired-sampled t-test. For the global task load index, a significant difference was found between the head-up (M_{HUD} = 28.844, SD_{HUD} = 11.217) and the head-down (M_{HDD} = 34.188, SD_{HDD} = 14.579) display, t(31) = 2.873, p = .007, see Fig. 6.

Additionally, the NASA-TLX score for each of the six categories was used to execute another t-test to compare both display types. No significant difference between the displays was found for the mental demand (M_{HUD_MD} = 40.47, SD_{HUD_MD} = 22.01; M_{HDD_MD} = 46.41, SD_{HDD_MD} = 20.57), the effort (M_{HUD_EF} = 37.34, SD_{HUD_EF} = 21.99; M_{HDD_EF} = 42.81, SD_{HDD_EF} = 20.28), and the temporal demand (M_{HUD_TD} = 22.81, SD_{HUD_TD} = 20.79; M_{HDD_TD} = 25.00, SD_{HDD_TD} = 18.92). A significant difference was found for the physical demand (M_{HUD_PD} = 17.97, SD_{HUD_PD} = 17.09; M_{HDD_PD} = 22.50, SD_{HDD_PD} = 14.02); $t(31)\_PD$ = 2.159, p_PD = .039, the frustration (M_{HUD_FR} = 23.13, SD_{HUD_FR} = 19.76; M_{HDD_FR} = 31.25, SD_{HDD_FR} = 17.26); $t(31)\_FR$ = 2.707, p_FR = .011, and the performance (M_{HUD_PE} = 30.63, SD_{HUD_PE} = 19.45; M_{HDD_PE} = 36.72, SD_{HDD_PE} = 14.35); $t(31)\_PE$ = 2.365, p_PE = .024, see Fig. 7.

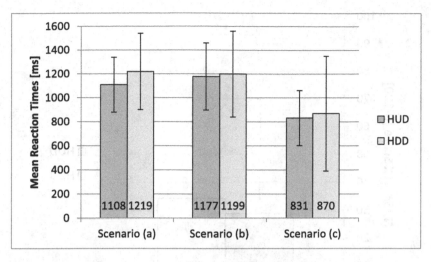

Fig. 4. Mean reaction times in [ms] for the three different scenarios with either HUD or HDD

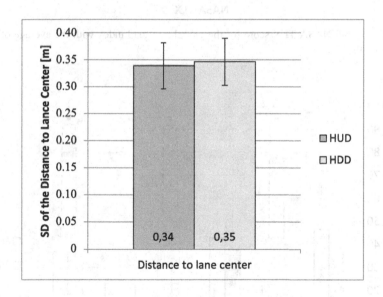

Fig. 5. The diagram shows the mean SD of the distance to lane center in [m] (with SD)

Additional Questionnaire. The last questionnaire after the participant finished both tracks grades both display on a 5-point likert scale and examined a significant difference for the HUD (M_{HUD} = 4.5, SD_{HUD} = 0.6) over the HDD (M_{HDD} = 2.3, SD_{HDD} = 1.4) regarding the subjective level of disturbance of status and indication symbols; $t(31)$ = 9.827, $p < .001$.

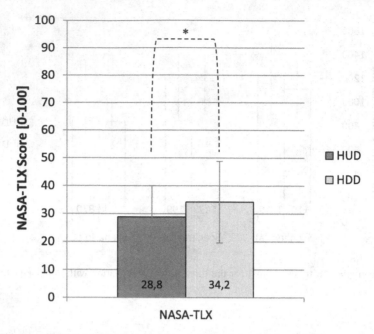

Fig. 6. The overall NASA-TLX score for the global task load index with the average of all six categories (with SD).

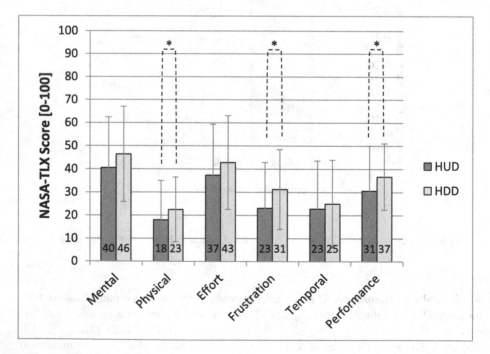

Fig. 7. The NASA-TLX score for the global task load index for each category (with SD)

4 Discussion

The aims of this study were to compare different types of information presented in a head-up or head-down display in an urban setting. The subjective analysis showed a significant preference for the head-up display presenting time critical warnings, dynamic information as the navigation or current speed, and driving related content (e.g. traffic sign recognition). Nevertheless, no objective difference was found for the reaction time in warning situations or lane keeping. One reason could be the scenario design of the warning scenarios, where some participants reacted to the potential risk earlier than the function could present the warning symbols. Status and indication symbols were significantly more disturbing in the HUD and should stay in the HDD since it brings no relevant advantage to have them in the driver's line of sight all the time. Only updates with those symbols (on/off/active) could possibly be presented in the HUD for a specific time interval.

The next steps will be to develop a first version of a generic and integrative HMI concept using the aforementioned components with an additional third component of a different modality (e.g. Acceleration Force Feedback Pedal for haptic stimuli or warning sounds for auditory stimuli), and evaluate it in a driving simulator. More ADAS could be integrated into this overall concept.

In conclusion, this paper shows the favored display (objective and subjective) for various types of presented information in the car while driving in an urban setting.

References

Bengler, K., Götze, M., Pfannmüller, L., Zaindl, A.: To see or not to see – innovative display technologies as enablers for ergonomic cockpit concepts. In: Electronic Displays Conference (2015) (in press)

Bubb, H.: Einrichtung zur optischen Anzeige eines veränderlichen Sicherheitsabstandes eines Fahrzeuges, DE 2633067 C2 (1978)

Gevatter, H.-J.: Handbuch der Mess- und Automatisierungstechnik in der Produktion, 2nd edn. Springer, Berlin (2006)

Godthelp, H., Milgram, P., Blaauw, J.: The development of a time-related measure to describe driving strategy. Hum. Factors 26(3), 257–268 (1984)

Götze, M., Bißbort, F., Petermann-Stock, I., Bengler, K.: A careful driver is one who looks in both directions when he passes a red light – increased demands in urban traffic. In: Yamamoto, S. (ed.) HCI 2014, Part II. LNCS, vol. 8522, pp. 229–240. Springer, Heidelberg (2014)

Hart, S.G., Staveland, L.: Development of NASA-TLX (Task Load Index): results of empirical and theoretical research. In: Hancock, P.A., Meshkati, N. (eds.) Human Mental Workload, pp. 139–183. Elsevier, Amsterdam (1988)

Miličić, N.: Sichere und ergonomische Nutzung von Head-Up Displays im Fahrzeug. Dissertation. Technische Universität München, München (2010)

Petermann-Stock, I., Rhede, J.: Intelligente Strategien für nutzerzentrierte MMI Konzepte im urbanen Raum. In: VDI Gesellschaft Fahrzeug- und Verkehrstechnik (Hrsg.), Der Fahrer im 21. Jahrhundert (VDI-Berichte, Nr. 2205, pp. 263–286) (2013)

Recarte, M.A., Nunes, L.M.: Mental workload while driving: effects on visual search, discrimination, and decision making. J. Exp. Psychol. Appl. **9**, 119–137 (2003)

Reif, K.: Fahrstabilisierungssysteme und Fahrerassistenzsysteme. Vie-weg + Teubner Verlag / GWV Fachverlage, Wiesbaden (2010)

Schartner, A.: Evaluation von MMI-Anzeige-Konzepten für Fahrerassistenzsysteme in urbanen Verkehrssituationen. Semesterarbeit, TU München, München (2013)

Schmidtke, H.: Ergonomie, 3rd edn. Carl Hanser Verlag, München (1993)

Schneid, M.: Entwicklung und Erprobung eines kontaktanalogen Head-Up-Displays im Fahrzeug. Dissertation. Technische Universität München, München (2008)

Schröder, T.: Analytische Betrachtung der Auswirkungen komplexer Verkehrssituationen. Diplomarbeit, TU München (2012)

SILAB : Driving Simulation and SILAB. Wivw.de (2015). http://www.wivw.de/en/silab/ Accessed on 30 January 2015

UR:BAN : UR:BAN - Benutzergerechte Assistenzsysteme und Netzmanagement. urban-online. org (2013). http://urban-online.org/en/urban.html Accessed on 28 January 2014

Winner, H., Hakuli, S., Wolf, G.: Handbuch Fahrerassistenzsysteme, 2nd edn. Springer, Dordrecht (2012)

Information Sharing System
Based on Situation Comprehensions
of Intelligent Vehicles to Improve Drivers'
Acceptability for Proactive ADAS

Takuma Ito[✉], Tatsuya Shino, and Minoru Kamata

The University of Tokyo, Bunkyō, Japan
ito@iog.u-tokyo.ac.jp

Abstract. This research focuses on improving elderly drivers' acceptability for proactive collision avoidance systems by passive information sharing with drivers. In this paper, visual contents by concentric circles for informing risky areas and ones by dot line for informing predicted path of surrounding traffic participants were proposed as the prototypes for sharing situation comprehensions of the intelligent vehicle. The evaluation experiment with a driving simulator revealed the effectiveness of the proposed visual contents for improving acceptability and the further challenges relating to the mental models of functions of intelligent vehicles.

Keywords: Automobile · Intelligent vehicle · Visual HMI · Acceptability

1 Introduction

In Japan, recent traffic accidents caused by elderly drivers are one of big issues. Since elderly drivers' physical and cognitive abilities are declined by aging, their risk of causing traffic accidents and their mortality rate are higher than those of young drivers. Thus, advanced safety technologies focusing on their features are required. For these problems, our collaborators [1] proposed vehicle control algorithms for driving assistance systems including partially automated driving. Distinguishing characteristic of the systems is a proactive intervention that intelligent vehicles intervene drivers' operations more early and softly than existing ones. Although such proactive systems could compensate decreased abilities of elderly drivers, they have potential problems to make drivers to feel anxieties because of the proactive characteristics. Indeed, our previous research [2] revealed problems of not being accepted and pointed out the necessities of HMIs for sharing information. For these problems, this research aimed to develop information sharing systems based on situation comprehensions of intelligent vehicles.

© Springer International Publishing Switzerland 2015
S. Yamamoto (Ed.): HIMI 2015, Part II, LNCS 9173, pp. 201–212, 2015.
DOI: 10.1007/978-3-319-20618-9_20

2 Design of Information Sharing System Based on Situation Comprehensions of Intelligent Vehicles

2.1 System Concept

Figure 1 shows the conceptual schematic of driving intervention by intelligent vehicles. This system assumes drivers' operations in usual safe situations and intelligent vehicle's interventions during approach to the risky situations. Examples of the target situations are as follows.

- Longitudinal control: Deceleration before passing through the blind spots due to parked cars, narrow alleys and so on.
- Lateral control: Avoidance of the parked car without approaching closely.

In these situations, elderly drivers sometimes can not conduct defensive driving appropriately and fall into more dangerous situations. Although existing emergent intervention systems have the possibilities of avoiding collisions, such emergent systems have risks of resulting in damages to the weak body of the elderly due to the large deceleration. Therefore, early and soft interventions by the intelligent vehicles are necessary. For realizing soft intervention, this research focuses on the proactive avoidance: based on the comprehensions of the surrounding traffic environments, the vehicle's intelligence starts the interventions to the driving with keeping enough proximities to avoiding targets earlier than existing ones.

As shown in the schematic of driving intervention, drivers' operations are not reflected to the vehicle control during interventions. In this situation, since drivers' basic functions from perception to operation do not always harmonize with parallel functions of the vehicle's intelligence from sensing to actuator control, acceptability for such systems sometimes decreases due to various conflicts [2]. For these problems, our research group proposed information sharing systems [3, 4]. Figure 2 shows the conceptual schematic of them. Since this research assumes Head-Up-Displays as the HMI device for information provision, the systems provide various kinds of visual contents based on the data of each function of the intelligent vehicle in order to prevent conflicts between the human driver and the intelligence of the automated vehicle. Although existing collision avoidance systems provide some kinds of information, the purpose of information provision and the characteristics of provision style are different from information sharing systems proposed in this research. Figure 3 shows the conceptual schematic of time series chart of existing collision avoidance systems while Fig. 4 shows that of information sharing systems. Compared to existing ones, information

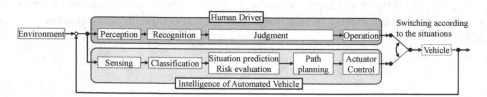

Fig. 1. Conceptual schematic of driving intervention by intelligent vehicle

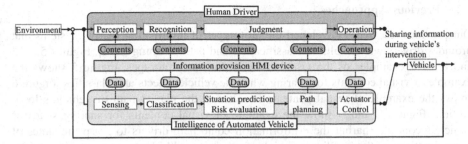

Fig. 2. Conceptual schematic of information sharing between human driver and vehicle's intelligence. Vehicle's intelligence sends data of each function to the HMI device for information provision. The HMI device provides the human driver with visual contents. Since provided contents are obtained not by the processes of recognition, judgment and operation but by the process of perception, vertical arrow dot-lines represent not the routes of information process but the targets of provided information.

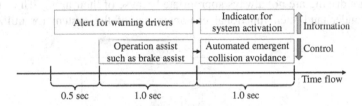

Fig. 3. Conceptual schematic of time series chart of existing systems for emergent collision avoidances. At first, the system activates the alert for warning drivers. Then, the system starts to assist driver's operation. When the situations become critical, the system starts to avoid collision automatically with indicating the system activation.

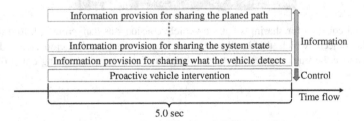

Fig. 4. Conceptual schematic of time series chart of proactive vehicle intervention system with information sharing. Before the situations become critical, the system starts to intervene the driver's operations. At the same time, HMIs start to provide various kinds of information for sharing states of various functions of the intelligent vehicle.

sharing systems start to provide simultaneously various kinds of information at the early phase of system's intervention. In addition, although existing ones provide alerts for the purpose of promoting the appropriate actions of the drivers, information sharing systems provide various kinds of information not for promoting driver's appropriate actions but for helping the driver to grasp the states of the intelligent vehicle.

2.2   Previous Approaches

Our previous researches developed the prototypes of information sharing systems that provides drivers with results of classification and path planning [3, 4]. Figures 5, 6, 7 and 8 show examples of the visual contents for our prototypes. Figure 5 shows the example of visual contents for sharing what the vehicle detects and classifies. Figure 6 shows the example of visual contents for sharing the planed path of vehicle's loco-motion. Figures 7 and 8 show the example of visual contents for sharing states of vehicle's control. Sharing these information could help drivers to grasp the states of some functions of the intelligent vehicle; further, it could improve acceptability of the drivers. As a result of evaluation experiments with a driving simulator, the effectiveness of information sharing for improving acceptability were verified. However, although the information could tell the targets of avoidance and plans of locomotion, it could not perfectly tell the reason why the system started the intervention so early and kept enough proximities. In other words, elderly drivers felt annoyed for excessively safe interventions from the subjective viewpoints of them. However, their subjective feel-ings to a safe driving are not always appropriate because of their aging. Thus, they are needed to understand such functional characteristics of the system for utilizing the

Fig. 5. Visual contents for sharing what the vehicle considers as dangerous [3]. Red rectangles indicates the objects which the intelligent vehicle considers as dangerous. A red sign of pedestrians above the truck indicates potential dangers of pedestrian's running out (Color figure online).

Fig. 6. Visual contents for sharing the planed path of vehicle's locomotion [4]

Fig. 7. Visual contents for sharing the state of automated deceleration [3]. A red inverse triangle indicates the deceleration sign in Japan. Red bars beside the inverse triangle indicate the remaining time of deceleration and shorten according to the time (Color figure online).

Fig. 8. Visual contents for sharing the state of automated avoidance [4]. Yellow signs on the bottom right corner indicate the activation of automated steering. Red bars beside the yellow sings indicate the remaining time of deceleration and shorten according to the time (Color figure online).

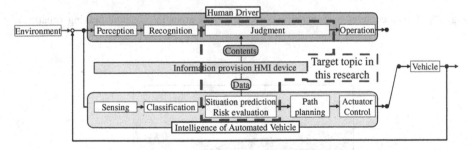

Fig. 9. Target topic in this research

proactive safety systems. Since handling this unsolved problem would have the possibility of improving acceptability much more, this research focused on the information sharing of the remaining functions: situation comprehensions as shown in Fig. 9.

2.3   Visual Contents for Sharing Situation Comprehensions

Although vehicle's intelligence understands surrounding situations by various cues, proactive vehicle controls use two kinds of important information: risk evaluation of surrounding situations and locomotion predictions of surrounding traffic participants. Thus, by using metaphors of such information, this research developed visual contents for sharing information as the prototypes implemented in the driving simulator. Figures 10 and 11 show the examples of visual contents for informing risky areas on each situation. Since some of proactive control algorithms [1] use mathematical potential calculations, these contents expresses concentric circles as risky areas by following the metaphor of mathematical potential. On the contrary, Figs. 12 and 13 show the examples for informing predicted paths of surrounding traffic participants on each situation. For both provision styles, visual contents were colored yellow and blinked slowly in order to prevent false recognition of the drivers.

3   Evaluation Experiment

Following protocols were approved by the School of Engineering the University of Tokyo IRB for human studies.

Fig. 10. Visual contents by concentric circles for risky areas in proactive braking situations

Fig. 11. Visual contents by concentric circles for risky areas in proactive steering situations

Fig. 12. Visual contents by dot line for predicted path in proactive braking situations

Fig. 13. Visual contents by dot line for predicted path in proactive steering situations

3.1 Experimental Methods

In this experiment, information sharing during activation of the proactive intervention was reproduced by a driving simulator. Experimental participants were 12 elderly drivers (65 to 75-years-old, M = 70, SD = 3) who were healthy and driving a car usually. Figure 14 shows the appearance of the driving simulator. This simulator has following equipments.

- Three front screens of which Field-Of-View is approximately 120° from the position of driver's seat.
- Stewart platform which reproduces motion cues. The scale factor of motion cue was set to 0.1 for the purpose of reproducing the initial feeling of the motion.
- Steering wheel with a servo motor which reproduces the reactive torque.

3.2 Experimental Scenarios

Figure 15 shows the schematic of the evaluation scenario for proactive braking. In this scenario, the intelligent vehicle detects the blind spot due to the parked car and predicts the possibility of pedestrian's running out. Based on the prediction, the intelligent vehicle starts to decelerate when Time-To-Collision becomes 5.0 s or less. The initial velocity on this situation was 40 km/h and the rate of deceleration was approximately 1.0 m/s^2.

Fig. 14. Driving simulator

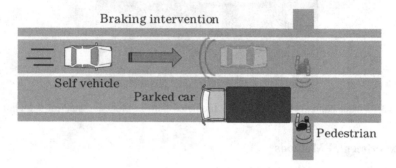

Fig. 15. Schematic of evaluation scenario for proactive braking

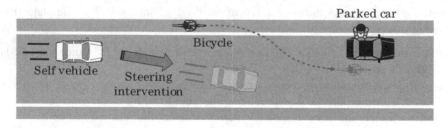

Fig. 16. Schematic of evaluation scenario for proactive steering

Figure 16 shows the schematic of evaluation scenario for proactive steering. In this scenario, the intelligent vehicle detects a parked car and a cyclist, and predicts the cyclist's lane change. Based on the prediction, the intelligent vehicle starts to steer when Time-To-Collision becomes 5.0 s or less. The initial velocity on this situation was 30 km/h.

Every single trip consisted of four times of above-mentioned situations. No visual contents were provided during the 1st and 3rd situations while visual contents were provided during 2nd and 4th situations. In addition, only one kind of visual contents was provided on every trip. For all situations in every single trip, same vehicle controls were reproduced regardless of information provision. These sequences aimed to make participants conscious about the basic state without information sharing and to decrease the order effects.

3.3 Investigation Methods

Experimental participants evaluated each visual content after they experienced. Focused points of evaluation were how much they accepted the system and what kinds of functions they subjectively considered that the system had. For the 1st point, they were asked by 9-grades questionnaires and the sentences of the questionnaires were as follows.

- Questionnaire for proactive intervention system without information provision: "How much do you want to adopt this system to your car?"
- Questionnaire for proactive intervention system with information provision: "On the condition that this system always provides information, how much do you want to adopt this system to your car?"

On the answer sheet, Japanese sentences equivalent to following ones were noted alongside some of grade points for the reference.

- Grade 9: I want to adopt it very much
- Grade 7: I want to adopt it a little.
- Grade 5: No opinion.
- Grade 3: I do not want to adopt it so much.
- Grade 1: I do not want to adopt it at all.

On the other hand, for the 2nd point, they were asked by multiple selection questionnaires. The questionnaire sentences were as follows.

A. Automated functions of avoiding objects and pedestrians.
B. Functions of detecting potentially collision objects.
C. Automated driving functions instead of the driver.
D. Safety functions for preventing traffic accidents.
E. Alert functions for dangers on the road.
F. Prediction functions of future situations based on surrounding traffic environment.
G. Alert functions for dangerous driving of the driver.
H. Safety functions for preventing the vehicle from approaching risky situations.
I. Advisory functions of the desired style of driving to the driver.
J. Support functions of driving without feeling tiredness.

Participants checked each questionnaire if they felt that the system had the function described by a questionnaire. Although some of above-mentioned sentences are true for the proposed system, main focuses in this research were whether the visual contents as shown in Figs. 10, 11, 12 and 13 could tell the existence and meaning of functions described in sentences F and H. These functions are the distinguish characteristics of proactive safety systems that intervenes earlier that existing ones.

3.4   Results

Figure 17 shows the evaluation results of acceptability for proactive braking on each condition of information provision. On the other hand, Fig. 18 shows the evaluation results for proactive steering. For both results, larger values indicates better evaluations. Although worst evaluation result goes worse a little on the condition of information provision about locomotion prediction for proactive braking, 2nd quartile values of acceptability are generally improved due to provision of information.

Table 1 shows the number of the answers for multiple selection questionnaires. Although main purpose of visual contents in this research were telling the existence and meaning of functions relating to questionnaires F and H, the numbers of "yes" for these questionnaires are relatively small. On the contrary, the numbers of "yes" for

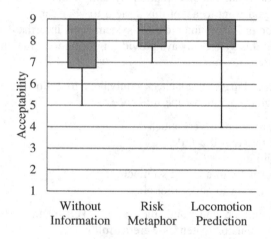

Fig. 17. Evaluation results of acceptability for proactive braking

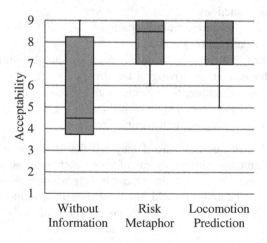

Fig. 18. Evaluation results of acceptability for proactive steering

Table 1. Number of the answer "Yes" for each questionnaire

Questionnaire		A	B	C	D	E	F	G	H	I	J
Proactive braking	Risk metaphor	7	7	4	7	7	3	2	4	3	1
	Predicted path	10	7	3	5	9	5	2	2	2	0
Proactive steering	Risk metaphor	11	7	4	4	9	7	2	1	3	1
	Predicted path	11	4	4	4	12	3	1	1	2	2

questionnaires A, B and E are relatively large. These results indicates that even visual contents proposed in this research could not perfectly tell the characteristics of the proactive controls similarly to our previous researches [3, 4].

3.5 Discussions

Although the information provisions by the visual contents were effective for improving acceptability for the proactive intervention systems, they could not perfectly tell the characteristics of the proactive systems that the system intervenes earlier than existing ones for the purpose of not approaching to the risky situations. Instead, they considered received information as something for alert systems and indicators of activating automated interventions. This seems to be caused by lacks of mental models for intelligent vehicles and their functions. If so, educations for the concept of the proactive systems have the possibilities of improvement on the understanding of the characteristics of the proactive intervention systems: further; it has the possibilities of improving the acceptability much more.

4 Conclusions

This research focused on the elderly drivers' acceptability for automated driving assistance systems; further, this research designed visual contents of HMIs for sharing information of intelligent vehicle's comprehensions. Based on the system architecture of the vehicle's intelligence, this research proposed two kinds of prototypes of visual contents: visual contents by concentric circles for informing risky areas and ones by dot line for informing predicted path of surrounding traffic participants. Then, this research conducted evaluation experiment by using driving simulators. The results were as follows.

- Proposed visual contents could improve the acceptability of the elderly drivers for the proactive intervention systems.
- Proposed visual contents could not perfectly tell the proactive characteristics.

Further improvement of the acceptability due to the enhancement of mental models which will be formed by the education for the proactive intervention systems, are the next step of this research.

Acknowledgement. This research has been conducted as a part of the research project "Autonomous Driving System to Enhance Safe and Secured Traffic Society for Elderly Drivers" granted by Japan Science and Technology Agency(JST), Strategic Innovation Creation Promotion Program.

References

1. Hasegawa, T., Raksincharoensak, P., Nagai, M.: Risk-potential based motion planning and control of proactive driving intelligence system for enhancing active safety. In: Proceedings of AVEC (2014)
2. Shino, T., Ito, T., Kamata, M.: Acceptability of proactive collision avoidance for elderly drivers. In: Proceedings of AVEC (2014)
3. Ito, T., Shino, T., Kamata, M.: Effectiveness of passive information sharing for elderly drivers from the viewpoint of acceptability for proactive braking assistance. In: Proceedings of JSAE Annual Congress 2014 Autumn (2014) (in Japanese)
4. Shino, T., Ito, T., Kamata, M.: Effectiveness of passive information sharing for elderly drivers from the viewpoint of acceptability for proactive steering assistance. In: Proceedings of JSAE Annual Congress 2014 Autumn (2014) (in Japanese)

An Analysis of Ear Plethysmogram
for Evaluation of Driver's
Mental Workload Level

Ahmad Khushairy Makhtar[1(✉)] and Makoto Itoh[2]

[1] Department of Risk Engineering, University of Tsukuba, Ibaraki, Japan
khushairy@css.risk.tsukuba.ac.jp
[2] Faculty of Engineering, Information and Systems,
University of Tsukuba, Ibaraki, Japan
itoh.makoto.ge@u.tsukuba.ac.jp

Abstract. Distracted driving has emerged as a factor of road accidents. Usage of cellular phones or car navigation systems has aggravated the problem. Therefore, the detection increase of drivers' mental workload has been a vital issue for establishing safety support systems. Studies on the estimation of driver's mental workload have been performed using a various devices. However, an applicable and a sensitive device is still vague. The purpose of this study is to develop a method to estimate driver's mental workload level through blood pulse wave analysis. In order to find a standard value that indicates high mental workload, two ways of analyzing pulse wave data have been studied: (1) Average Maximum Lyapunov exponent and (2) Normalized Maximum Lyapunov exponent. The result shows that, the analysis of average a Maximum Lyapunov exponent shows a significant different between the days with a secondary task and the days without the task.

Keywords: Mental workload · Plethysmogram · Safety · Driver assistance

1 Introduction

A comprehensive accident data in Japan recorded the number of road traffic crashes for the year 2013 reported a decrease of 5.4 % compared to in 2012 [1]. When looking for causes of the crashes, distracted driving, which includes 'looking elsewhere' and 'thinking of something', was 24.8 % of traffic crashes in 2013 [1]. It shows that distracted driving is an important issue to be solved in order to reduce the number of road accident fatalities. Aggravating the problem, various devices, such as mobile phones and car navigation systems used in vehicles, have become a trend nowadays. In addition, there are several studies concluded that the negative effects of using a phone may not result from operating the telephone, but mainly from make a conversation on the phone itself which can relate to 'mental workload' [2, 3].

Currently, the detection of mental workload level has increasingly important especially to develop a caution or warning system. In recent years, researches on state estimation of mental workload have been investigated with various devices. For instance, the study that employed physiological indices such as Electroencephalogram

© Springer International Publishing Switzerland 2015
S. Yamamoto (Ed.): HIMI 2015, Part II, LNCS 9173, pp. 213–224, 2015.
DOI: 10.1007/978-3-319-20618-9_21

(EEG) and Electrocardiogram (ECG) [4–6] can be given. However, it is quite hard to use such indices in an actual driving condition. Consequently a device which can estimate driver's mental workload without giving a driver a sense of restriction is required. Acknowledging the importance to develop a method to detect the driver's mental workload state, plethysmogram which is a device that records blood pulse wave is a promising candidate because it is non-interfere to the driving maneuvers.

There is research that concluded the possibility of using a plethysmogram to quantify the degree of fatigue that results from sitting for extended periods on a driving seats [7]. The usage of a plethysmogram has been expended in driving situation to monitor driver's blood pulse. This device which been located at steering of vehicle were design to predict heart attack while driving [8]. Thus, using plethysmogram is a promising way to monitor driver's condition.

In spite of that, there is still a problem in determining a standard threshold to determine high mental workload state [9]. Hence the goal of this paper is to find a standard threshold of high mental workload which applicable to many drivers.

2 Mental Workload and Its Measurement

2.1 Model of Mental Workload

The basic concept known about human mental workload is when opposing more mental workload, performance will deteriorate. A model developed by Meister [10] can explain the correlation between mental workload level and task performance. Later, De Waard [11] has further divided the model from three regions into six regions as shown in Fig. 1. As presented in the model, optimum performance is in Region A2. The operator can easily meet the needs of the task demands and achieve a satisfactory level of performance. Whereas the performance in region A1 and the A3 remains unaffected but the operator has undertaken efforts to maintain performance levels. In B region, operators are unlikely to maintain and performance begins to deteriorate. The degradation of performance in B region could be interpreted as the workload is high. While in C region, operator is interpreted as overload and performance at a minimum, while in D region, state of operator is affected [11].

As it is worth to estimate the state before the performance start to deteriorate, this research is particularly interested in the region B, i.e., to find the situation where the mental workload is high and performance start to deteriorate. Ideally when we able to estimate the mental workload region especially on Region B, we can design a support system such as warning system before the performance start to deteriorate.

In driving tasks, the source of driver's workload can be found both inside and outside the vehicle. Model in Fig. 2 could explain the relationship between both inside and outside source driver's mental workload. Both sources could effects driver's performance on the primary task which is safely control on vehicle. The higher demand of the sources to the driver's information processing resource, the effect on the performance of the primary task will be larger.

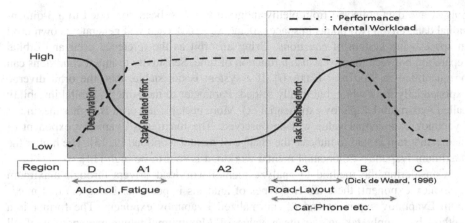

Fig. 1. Workload and performance in 6 regions [11]

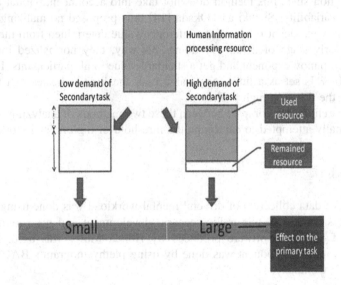

Fig. 2. Correlation between primary and secondary task

2.2 Measurement of Mental Workload

Measuring mental workload is challenging part of this research. According to O'Donnell & Eggemeier [12] cognitive distraction measurement could be divided into three measurement groups: (1) Physiological measures (2) Subjective measures, (3) Performance measures and. As mentioned previously, this research will focus on physiological measurement as main measurement and compared with other measurement groups. Specifically measuring blood pulse wave of drivers by using a Plethysmogram. Plethysmogram is a device to measure changes in volume of blood or air it contains within an organ or whole body. One of the method to analyse blood pulse wave from plethysmogram is by using maximum Lyapunov exponent. A time series of pulse wave data collected from plethysmogram was first been converted to a 3-dimensional data. Given two points in space, x0 and x0 +Δx0, each will generate its own orbit in space using system of equations. Using an orbit as the reference orbit and orbital separation between the two is also a function of time. Sensitivity to initial conditions can be quantified as $\|\Delta x(t)\| \approx e\lambda t\|\Delta x0\|$. If a system is not stable, then the orbit diverge exponentially for a while, but finally settled. Parameter to measure the orbital instability called maximum Lyapunov exponential (λ). More unstable the orbit is higher maximum Lyapunov exponential value will be observed. The maximum Lyapunov exponent of plethysmogram is said to indicate the change of mental workload [9, 13]. The higher the maximum lyapunov exponential mental workload is said to be high [14].

Considering the method to analyze mental workload drivers through maximum Lyapunov exponent, there are two types of analysis is possible. Using (1) raw maximum Lyapunov exponent and (2) normalized Lyapunov exponent. The former is a method by simply taking the mean value of Maximum Lyapunov exponent of all participants in a period of time. This is simple, but there is a concern about the accuracy of the evaluation since this method does not take into account individual differences and internal variability. Suzuki and Okada [14] thus proposed normalizing the maximum Lyapunov exponent based on the reference value determined from the measured data at the early stage of a run. By doing this way, they normalized the value of maximum Lyapunov exponent and get a standard value to all participants. Finally, the value of 120 % is set as a limit. Any value over the limit indicates that the mental workload of the driver is high [14].

This research tried to compare between these two methods of analyzing blood pulse wave and finally attempted to determine the threshold of high mental workload.

3   Method

The process of data collection of drivers' mental workload was done using the fixed-base driving simulator. While traffic scenario development and measurement of the movement of vehicles, software produced by Honda Motor was used. Measuring maximum Lyapunov Exponent was done by using plethysmogram's BACS Detector II's from CCI Company.

3.1   Participants

There were four males and four females with a mean age of 23.75 and Standard deviation of 5.44 have participated in the data collection process. Every participant holds a valid driver's license and drives almost daily.

3.2   Experimental Design

The main task was to drive safely in the left lane. Every participant had two types of traffic conditions, (a) None Hazardous Conditions (NHC) and (b) Hazardous Condition (HC). Under both conditions, participants were also asked to follow a lead vehicle (LV).

Figure 3 describes how the driving task were given to each participant in NHC. A Following Vehicle (FV) was located behind the HV to help participants maintain a following distance. In this traffic condition, FV drove with 65 km/h (constant speed) throughout 7 min trial. Some vehicles also exist in the right lane.

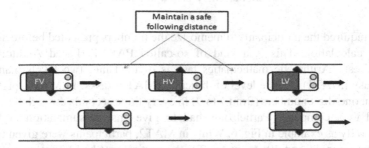

Fig. 3. Non hazardous condition (NHC)

While under HC participants were asked to maintain distance between LV and FV. At this time, both LV and FV cruised between speed of 65 km/h and 85 km/h. Intentionally LV and FV will make a sudden brake of 0.35 g and also a quick acceleration. The time to make a sudden brakes and quick acceleration has been set at random (approximately twice the speed changes for each 500 m run). Participants were told to keep a safe following distance and to be alert to sudden changes in the speed of both vehicles (Fig. 4). If they met with a crash during a trial, participants had to start a new trial all over again. This way, participants were tried their best for not involving with a crash.

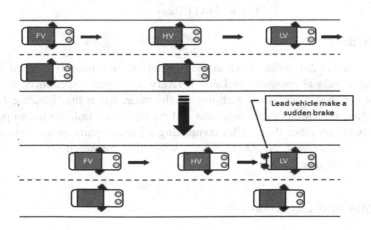

Fig. 4. Hazardous condition (HC)

For the secondary task participants were requested to carry out a two-minute Mathematical Arithmetic Task (MAT) in a 7-min run, 3 min after the start and 2 min before the trial is completed (Fig. 5).

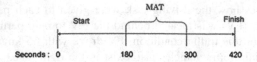

Fig. 5. MAT period in a trial

MAT required the participants to memorize the numbers presented before as well as solve the calculation. This is a kind of so-called PASAT (Paced Auditory Serial Addition Test). Arithmetic mathematics task is divided into two levels, namely the level of easy (MAT1) and the level of difficulty (MAT2) tasks. In MAT1, participants were given one-digit numbers (from 1 to 9) in every three seconds through the speakers connected to a computer. Participants had to give answer summation of last two numbers orally as example in Fig. 6. While in MAT2, participants were given two-digit numbers between 11 and 49. As in MAT1, the participants had to answer total of the last two numbers orally.

In each trial, the number of correct answer was calculated and the result was notified to participants after the end of a trial.

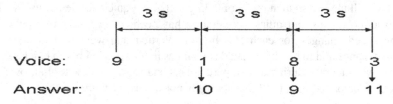

Fig. 6. MAT1 (Easy Level)

3.3   Procedure

In order to cancel any order effect, all participants were randomly divided into two groups respectively as presented in Table 1. Every participant experienced six days of experiments with six sets of run each day. In the table, BD is the 'Baseline Driving', there was Non Hazardous traffic condition and no secondary task has been opposed to the participants on those days. After completing all trials, participants were asked to answer the questionnaire NASA-TLX as a subjective measurement to estimate the workload in each task.

4   Results and Discussion

4.1   Raw Maximum Lyapunov Exponent

While performing a mathematical task, we were assumed that demand of mathematical task was remain unchanged during 2 min task. To know the mental workload of participants during the task period, the mean value of maximum Lyapunov exponent for that period has been calculated.

Table 1. Experimental procedure

Group 1		Day	Group 2	
Task	Traffic Condition		Task	Traffic Condition
BD		**One**	BD	
MAT1	NHC	**Two**	MAT2	HC
MAT1	HC	**Three**	MAT2	NHC
MAT2	NHC	**Four**	MAT1	HC
MAT2	HC	**Five**	MAT1	NHC
BD		**Six**	BD	

Figure 7 shows an example of raw maximum Lyapunov exponent data of a single run from one of participants. The dotted line is a time between 180 s and 300 s where a period which participants were carrying out Mathematical Arithmetic Task. It should be noted here that, in a single day without secondary task (BD), the mean value of raw maximum Lyapunov exponent has also counted from this time period. After calculating the average maximum Lyapunov exponent for that duration, an average of maximum Lyapunov exponent for the whole day (6 runs overall) has also been calculated.

Fig. 7. Example of time series maximum Lyapunov exponent data in a trial

Figure 8 shows the mean and standard deviation for maximum Lyapunov exponent between eight participants for each day. The graph shows that the average maximum Lyapunov exponent for the day with secondary task is higher than the days without a secondary task. In fact, according to ANOVA on this data, the main effect of the day is statistically significant ($F_{(5, 35)} = 4.27$, $p < 0.01$). The highest value of average maximum Lyapunov exponent is in the day when participants performed MAT2 under HC. Further Tukey's HSD test indicates that, there is a significant difference when compared MAT2HC with the first day (BD) ($p < 0.01$). This finding is interesting as this correlation is related to the participants performed a difficult level of mathematical arithmetic task (MAT2) while driving in difficult driving condition (HC). A significant difference was also been observed between the first day and MAT2NHC ($p < 0.05$). During this MAT2NHC, the participants had to perform a difficult level of MAT while the driving condition was at an easy level. There was also significant difference between the 1st day and MAT1HC. There was no significant difference between 1st day and MAT1NHC and between the first day and the last day of the experiment.

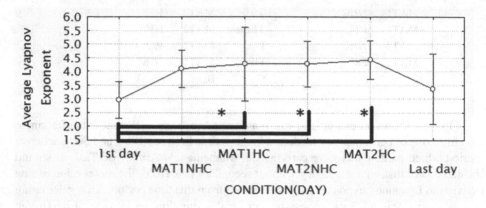

Fig. 8. Raw maximum Lyapunov exponent

One of the more significant findings to emerge from this result is that using raw maximum Lyapunov exponent may be acceptable to detect a very high mental workload. However, it would be difficult to distinguish a slightly high mental workload from low mental workload.

4.2   Normalized Maximum Lyapunov Exponent

As stated in previous chapter, we also tried to analyze maximum Lyapunov exponent by normalizing it. In this approach, it is necessary to select the "base interval" which is the time period that can be regarded as a mental-workload in low conditions.

Figure 9 shows how to determine the reference in a trial of a participant. The X-axis of the graph is time of a trial in seconds and the Y-axis is the normalized maximum Lyapunov exponent in percentage. The maximum Lyapunov exponent value along the 'base interval' was averaged and was set as 100 %. The maximum Lyapunov exponent is said to be higher than the base interval when the value is higher than 100 %.

Uniqueness of this study exists in the fact that considering that maximum Lyapunov exponent will increase according to the road alignments [9], we select two kinds of time period as a base interval. One is between 45 to 90 s of one trial and another one is between 60 to 180 s. The former base interval is period of run in a straight pathway and no elements that can be considered as the elements of the increasing value of maximum Lyapunov exponent. We set the time period between 60 to 180 s as an alternative of base interval. This interval was selected simply based on the length time is the same with the MAT interval (2 min).

The results of normalized Lyapunov exponent for aforementioned two base intervals were shown in Figs. 10 and 11. Statistical analysis was performed and there was

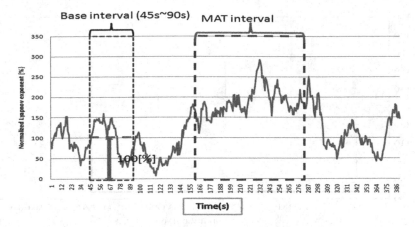

Fig. 9. Normalized maximum Lyapunov exponent data for one trial

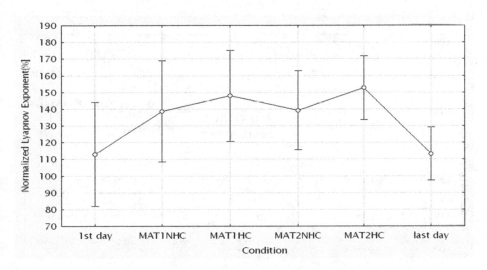

Fig. 10. Normalized maximum Lyapunov exponent (45 s-90 s)

no significant difference between these two base intervals. We can infer that further studies are necessary to investigate whether the selection of base interval is really needed or not.

4.3 Relationship Between the Subjective Measurement and Maximum Lyapunov Exponent

Figure 12 illustrates relationship between normalized maximum Lyapunov exponents and the subjective measurement of mental workload rated from NASA-TLX. The graph shows that the value of normalized Lyapunov Exponent was high when the task

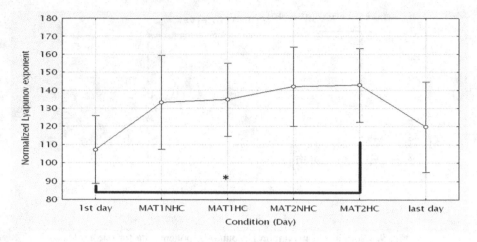

Fig. 11. Normalized maximum Lyapunov exponent (60 s-180 s)

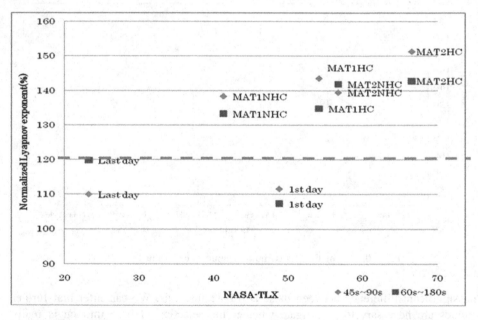

Fig. 12. Normalized Maximum Lyapunov exponent and subjective measurement

becoming more difficult. Hence, based on results of our experiment, the value of normalized Lyapunov exponent for normal driving (Baseline driving) is lower than 120 %. The result is in the lines of earlier literature [14] that found value of above 120 % indicates that the driver's mental workload is not in normal driving state in fact in high mental workload.

5 Conclusions

The present study was designed to investigate drivers' mental workload by focusing on physiological measurement. An experiment was conducted to gather data regarding driver's mental workload. The main conclusions of this research were as follows:

(1) From raw maximum Lyapunov exponent analysis, using raw maximum Lyapunov exponent may be acceptable to detect a very high mental workload.
(2) Two base interval has been implemented for normalized Maximum Lyapunov exponents. There was no significant difference of selecting the base interval according to the road conditions.
(3) When the value of normalized maximum Lyapunov exponent is 120 % or above, mental workload of drivers is not in ordinary driving state and might be high because of driving task or mental distraction.

6 Future Research

This research has thrown up many questions in need of further investigation as follows:

1. Future research on base interval selection may be required.
2. The studies on comparison between the effect of traffic conditions and mathematical arithmetic task on mental workload.
3. Further research on the possibility to distinguish between levels of mental workload.

Acknowledgement. We would like to thank all that gives us the possibility to complete this paper. Thanks are also given to the Universiti Teknologi MARA, specifically Faculty of Mechanical Engineering, to give financial support to the author to complete this study.

References

1. Japan National Police Agency, Statistics of road Accidents in Japan 2013 (2014)
2. Patten, C.J.D., Kircher, A., Ostlund, J., Nilsson, L.: Using mobile telephones: cognitive workload and attention resource allocation. Accid. Anal. Prev. 36(3), 341–350 (2004)
3. Patten, C.J.D., Kircher, A., Ostlund, J., Nilsson, L., Svenson, O.: Driver experience and cognitive workload in different traffic environments. Accid. Anal. Prev. 38(5), 887–894 (2006)
4. Ling, C., Goins, H., Ntuen, A., Li, R.: EEG signal analysis for human workload classification. In: Proceedings. IEEE SoutheastCon 2001 (Cat. No.01CH37208), pp. 123–130 (2001)
5. Sonnleitner, A., Treder, M.S., Simon, M., Willmann, S., Ewald, A., Buchner, A., Schrauf, M.: EEG alpha spindles and prolonged brake reaction times during auditory distraction in an on-road driving study. Accid. Anal. Prev. 62C, 110–118 (2013)

6. Borghini, G., Astolfi, L., Vecchiato, G., Mattia, D., Babiloni, F.: Measuring neurophysiological signals in aircraft pilots and car drivers for the assessment of mental workload, fatigue and drowsiness. Neurosci. Biobehav. Rev. **44**, 58–75 (2014)
7. Ochiai, N., Yasuda, E., Murata, K., Ueno, Y.: Development of simplified appraisal method of fatigue on sitting for extended periods by the data of finger plethysmogram. Japanese J. Ergon. **40**(5), 254–263 (2004). (In Japanese)
8. Web, T.: Electrocardiogram Check By Car Handle That Predict Heart Attack. Tokyo Shinbun, Tokyo (2013). (In Japanese)
9. Shimizu, T., Miao, T., Shimoyama, O.: Evaluation of Driver's status by Chaotic analysis of finger photoplethysmography, in Technical Report of The Institute of Electronics Information and Communications Engineers, pp. 35–38 (2004) (In Japanese)
10. Meister, D.: Behavioral Analysis and Measurement Methods. Wiley, New York (1985)
11. De Waard, D.: The Measurement of Drivers' Mental Workload. PhD Dissertation (1996)
12. O'Donnel, R.D., Eggemeier, F.T.: Workload assessment methodology. In: Handbook of Perception and Human Performance, Cognitive Processes and Performance, vol II. Wiley, New York (1986)
13. Enokida, S., Kotani, K., Suzuki, S., Asao, T., Ishikawa, T., Ishida, K.: Assessing mental workload of in-vehicle information systems by using physiological metrics. In: Yamamoto, S. (ed.) HCI 2013, Part I. LNCS, vol. 8016, pp. 584–593. Springer, Heidelberg (2013)
14. Suzuki, K., Okada, Y.: Evaluation of driver's mental workload in terms of the fluctuation of finger pulse. Trans. JSME **74**(743), 85–94 (2008). (In Japanese)

Education Method for Safe Bicycle Riding to Evaluate Actual Cycling Behaviors When Entering an Intersection

Hiroaki Kosaka[1]([✉]) and Masaru Noda[2]

[1] Department of Electrical Engineering, National Institute of Technology,
Nara College, 22 Yatacho, Yamatokoriyama, Nara 639-1080, Japan
kosaka@elec.nara-k.ac.jp
[2] Department of Chemical Engineering, Faculty of Engineering,
Fukuoka University, 8-19-1 Nanakuma,
Jonan-ku, Fukuoka 814-0180, Japan
mnoda@fukuoka-u.ac.jp

Abstract. In this study, we conducted a new educational method for safe bicycle riding to improve the riding manners of bicyclists riding manners to increase adherence to traffic rules. First, we conducted an experiment in which participants rode a bicycle and passed through an intersection to collect such data as bicycle speed and the rider's direction of glance. Next, we did a simulation in which a bicycle passed through an intersection to evaluate riding behaviors. Finally, an experimenter explained to the participants how they could improve their safe bicycle riding awareness using the data collected in the experiment and the simulation results. The participants learned that safety can be confirmed by looking right and left to decrease the risks of accidents.

Keywords: Educational method · Safe bicycle riding · Cycling behavior · Crossing collision

1 Introduction

Bicycles are a convenient vehicles, especially because bicyclists do not need a license. Such convenience and simplicity may increase a bicyclist's lack of safe bicycle riding habits. The numbers of crossing collisions between bicycles and pedestrians at intersections in Japan are increasing [1]. The dangerous riding behavior of bicyclists is a social problem in Japan. Crossing collisions account for around 50 % of all bicycle accidents [1]. Takemoto proposed a new educational method for car drivers using a driver model based on the analysis of driver behaviors when passing through intersections and a simulation that evaluated driving behaviors [2]. We tentatively applied the teaching methods proposed in the previous study [2] to a new method for bicyclists to improve their riding behaviors [5]. We also found that our teaching method was effective to raise safe bicycle riding awareness [5]. In this paper, we report our experiments with a new educational method for safe bicycle riding.

© Springer International Publishing Switzerland 2015
S. Yamamoto (Ed.): HIMI 2015, Part II, LNCS 9173, pp. 225–232, 2015.
DOI: 10.1007/978-3-319-20618-9_22

2 Experiment

2.1 Participants and Experimental Course

We conducted experiments to collect data while the participants passed an intersection. The participants in this study were nine college students 19–20 years old who volunteered for this experiment. Four of the nine participants passed through the intersection when they went to school and the remaining participant passed through the intersection around three times a week or few times a year. Figure 1 shows an intersection selected for collecting data in the experiment. We defined that the position where a participant just entered the intersection was zero and that the position of a participant before entering the intersection was minus and the position after entering the intersection was plus.

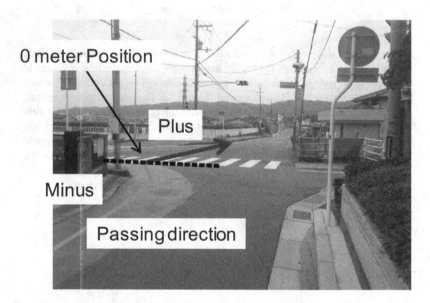

Fig. 1. Intersection for experiment

2.2 Apparatus

The experimenter used an Eye Mark Recorder EMR-9 (NAC) to record an image of the front view of the rider and the direction of glance. A laser displacement meter LD90-3300 (RIEGL) was used to record speed of the bicycle while passing through the intersection.

2.3 Procedure

The participants rode the bicycle and passed through the intersection shown in Fig. 1. We collected the speed of the bicycle and the participant's direction of glance while passing through the intersection. The traffic light turned green and no objects such as cars, bicycles or pedestrians obstructed the passing of the participants through the intersection. The experimenter recorded the participant's speed and direction of glance when passing through the intersection.

3 Experimental Results

We discuss the experiment results of eight participants because we failed to collect the data of one participant during the experiment.

Figure 2 shows the bicycle speed and the direction of glance while participant A passed through the intersection. Figure 2(a) shows that he rode at a speed almost between 10 and 15 km/h before entering the intersection. Figure 2(b) shows that he glanced left six times before entering it.

We calculated the average speed and the number of confirmations made by looking left for each participant to analyze the collected data. Figure 3 shows the average speed and the number of confirmations of each participant. The participants confirmed by looking left fewer times while passing through the intersection because they passed at a faster speed.

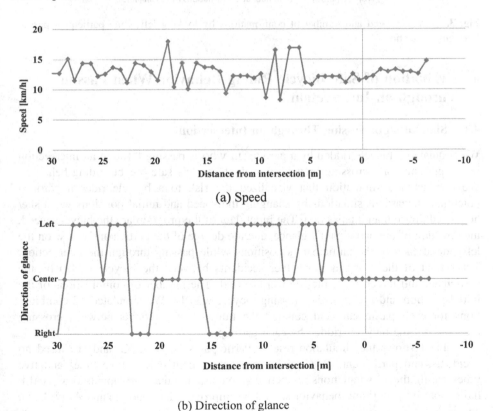

(a) Speed

(b) Direction of glance

Fig. 2. Speed of bicycle and direction of glance while participant A passed through intersection

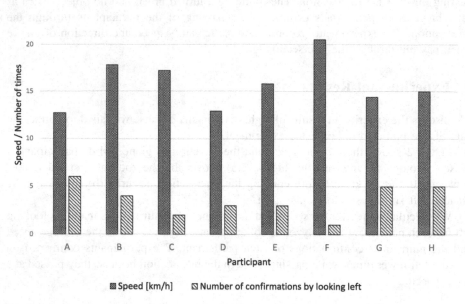

Fig. 3. Average speed and number of confirmations by looking left while participant passed through intersection.

4 Evaluation of Safe Bicycle Riding Behavior When Passing Through an Intersection

4.1 Simulation of Passing Through an Intersection

We simulated a bicycle ridden by a participant who is passing through an intersection in the presence of a crossing bicycle to evaluate her/his safe bicycle riding behavior. We conducted a simulation that visualized the risk to a bicycle rider in various potentially hazardous situations by changing the speed and initial positions when she/he passed through an intersection. The input data of the program are the bicycle speed, the direction of the participant's glance, and the degree of the participant's view on the left side at each of the participant's positions while passing through the intersection. The output of the program is whether accidents between the bicycle ridden by the participant and the crossing bicycle were caused. The number of combinations of the initial position and speed of the crossing bicycle was 12. We simulated 12 combinations for each participant and counted the number of accidents between crossing bicycles and the bicycles ridden by each participant.

Table 1 shows the simulation results. Participants A, D, E, G, and H caused no accidents, and participants B, C, and F caused accident twice, three times and five times during the 12 simulations respectively. We assume that participants B, C, and F have more bicycle riding behavior should be improved than participants A, D, E, G, and H.

Table 1. Accident rate

Participant	A	B	C	D	E	F	G	H
Accident rate [%]	0	17	25	0	0	42	0	0

4.2 Relation Between Bicycle Speed and Number of Confirmations by Looking Left and Accident Rate

Figure 4 shows the relation between bicycle speed and number of confirmations by looking left. The average speed of the participants who caused accidents in the simulation exceeded the speed of the participants who never caused accidents. This figure also suggests that the average bicycle speed was faster, and the number of confirmations by looking left was fewer. We assume that this is because participants must decrease the bicycle speed to make enough confirmations by looking left when passing through an intersection.

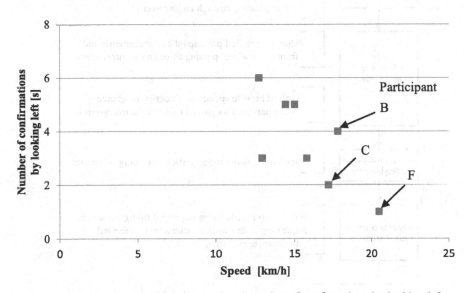

Fig. 4. Relation between bicycle speed and number of confirmations by looking left

5 Safe Bicycle Riding Education

5.1 Education Procedure

We educated the participants to improve their bicycle riding behavior and raise their awareness. Figure 5 shows our education procedure.

First, the experimenter questioned the participants about such items as knowledge of traffic rules for riding a bicycle. Next, the participants watched a video of their eye movements and front view while they passed through the intersection. They also saw graphs of bicycle speed and the direction of glance. The experimenter showed them their own simulation images and results. The experimenter also showed participants B, C, and F the results of the simulation in the case where they improved their bicycle riding behaviors. The experimenter explained that improving confirmations of safety by looking left decreased the risk of accidents to all the participants. Finally, participants drove on a driving simulator and encountered at a blind spot that a bicycle suddenly crossed the path of their car. After this, the experimenter explained to them that this was a case where it is difficult for drivers to see a bicycle while driving, and the driver caused an accident.

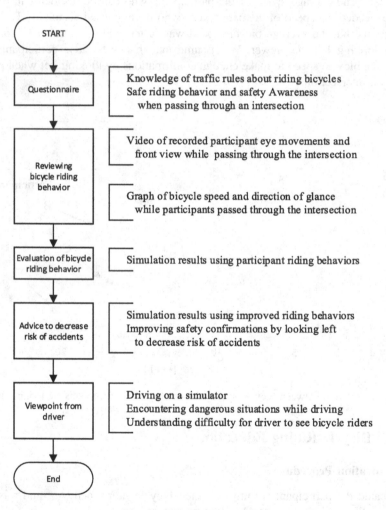

Fig. 5. Education procedure

5.2   Results

We conducted a questionnaire about the knowledge of traffic rules held by our participants about riding a bicycle, safe riding behaviors, and their awareness of safety when passing through an intersection. Table 2 shows the answers to one of the questionnaire questions: "How do you look left and right to confirm safety when entering an intersection?" An appropriate answer is: "I confirm safety by looking right and left many times when entering an intersection to see the far end of an intersection to avoid crashing into a crossing object at the intersection." No participants gave the appropriate answer. Participants C and F, who caused accidents in the simulation in Sect. 4.1, answered that they confirmed safety by sufficiently looking left and right when entering an intersection to prevent accidents. On the other hand, participants C and F glanced left only once or twice before entering the intersection based on their experimental results and their riding behaviors when entering the intersection were inadequate to prevent accidents.

After such education, all participants answered that they did not know that improving their safety confirmations by looking right and left decreases the risk of accidents, but they understood this after studying the simulation results using their own riding behavior data.

Table 2. Answers: how do you look left and right to confirm safety when entering an intersection?

Participant	Answer
A	No answer
B	I decide based on the situation and circumstances.
C	My own way of confirming safety by looking left and right when entering an intersection is enough to prevent accidents.
D	I am not sure.
E	I am not sure.
F	My own way of confirming safety by looking left and right when entering an intersection is enough to prevent accidents.
G	It is enough that I confirm safety by looking left, right, and left when entering an intersection.
H	I decide based on the situation and circumstances.
I	I am not sure.

6   Conclusion

In this study, we conducted experiments that focused on an educational method for safe bicycle riding. First, we experimentally collected participant riding behaviors while passing through an intersection. We evaluated their safe riding behaviors using the collected riding behavior data and the simulation data of bicycles ridden by participants who were passing through an intersection in the presence of a crossing bicycle under various conditions. Our evaluation results suggest that bicycle riders have to decrease their bicycle speed to confirm the safety by looking right and left and that riders have made enough confirmations by looking right and left only after they decrease bicycle speed when passing through an intersection.

Finally, we conducted safe bicycle riding education to raise the participants' bicycle riding awareness. The participants learned that safety can be confirmed by decreasing bicycle speed and looking right and left to decrease the risk of accidents.

Future research will verify the effectiveness of our education method.

Acknowledgements. This work was supported by JSPS KAKENHI 23500833.

References

1. Traffic Bureau, National Police Agency: Traffic accidents situation in 2013. http://www.e-stat.
   go.jp/SG1/estat/Pdfdl.do?sinfid=000023626210 (in Japanese)
2. Takemoto, M., Kosaka, H., Nishitani, H.: A study on the relationships between unsafe driving
   behaviors and driver's inner factors when entering a non-signalized intersection. J. Comput. **3**
   (9), 39–49 (2008)
3. Takemoto, M., Kosaka, H., Nishitani, H., et al.: Safe driving education through simulations
   based on actual driving data when entering a non-signalized intersection. In: FISITA World
   Automotive Congress 2008, F2008-02-029 (2008)
4. Kosaka, H.: Development of educational method for safe bicycle riding to evaluate actual
   cycling behaviors. In: Proceedings of 4th International Conference on Applied Human Factors
   and Ergonomics (AHFE), pp. 8941–8947 (2012)
5. Kosaka, H., Noda, M.: Pilot experiments in education for safe bicycle riding to evaluate actual
   cycling behaviors when entering an intersection. In: Yamamoto, S. (ed.) HCI 2013, Part II.
   LNCS, vol. 8017, pp. 515–523. Springer, Heidelberg (2013)

Self-perception of Assister Driver Responsibility and Contribution in Mutual Assistance System

Sui Kurihashi$^{(\boxtimes)}$, Yutaka Matsuno, and Kenji Tanaka

Graduate School of Information Systems,
The University of Electro-Communications,
1-5-1 Chofugaoka, Chofu, Tokyo 182-8585, Japan
kurihashi@tanaka.is.uec.ac.jp,
{matsuno, tanaka}@is.uec.ac.jp

Abstract. Noting the current deep interest in advanced driver assistance systems (ADAS), this study focuses on the "mutual assistance" paradigm, by which drivers mutually assist each other to promote a safer automobile culture. In our previous study, we examined the effectiveness of mutual assistance systems from both the recipient and assister sides using a driving simulator. In this paper, assister attitude changes, especially those related to their responsibility and contribution to an incident/accident, are compared for manual, semi-automatic and automatic warning scenarios. The results indicate that more positive attitude changes will result if "participants felt that he/she had some responsibility related to accident". Additionally, it was determined that semi-automatic warnings were most likely to engender feelings of responsibility in an assister. These experimental results indicate that semi-automatic mutual assistance system is the most effective examined technique for reducing the target level of risk.

Keywords: Mutual assistance · Warning system · Safety · Target level of risk · Attitude change

1 Introduction

Recently, a number of safety assistance systems for automobiles have been proposed and several advanced driver assistance systems (ADAS), such as adaptive cruise control (ACC) systems, are now being used to improve safety for individual drivers. However, in order to maximize the effectiveness of these technologies, it is necessary to decrease the driver's target level of risk by increasing his or her intrinsic motivation level. A target level of risk is the risk that a driver is willing to accept while still considering other relevant goals (such as destination arrival time).

Zink and Ritter [1] and Trimpop [2] advocated the use of participative methods such as safety circles to increase intrinsic motivation levels. Additionally, Trimpop [3] argued that "self-determination, participation, and responsibility can alter people's target level of risk". If the driver's target level of risk is not decreased, there is a greater potential for risk-taking behavior while driving. Wilde explains these phenomena in

© Springer International Publishing Switzerland 2015
S. Yamamoto (Ed.): HIMI 2015, Part II, LNCS 9173, pp. 233–242, 2015.
DOI: 10.1007/978-3-319-20618-9_23

terms of risk homeostasis [4, 5]. Thus, it can be said that the key to receiving the maximum level of benefits from ADAS technology is reducing the target level of risk. Since the authors consider the provision of assistance to be important decreasing a driver's target level of risk, self-determination should be an integral part of any system designed to stimulate driver responsibility.

In our previous work, Kurihashi *et al.* [6], we noted that assistance can be subdivided into three types, "individual assistance", "mutual assistance", and "public assistance". Figure 1 shows the relationship among these three assistance types. We further proposed reducing the target level of risk via the use of a "mutual assistance", which is a phrase that is often used in the disaster management field in Japan that means that "everyone helps each other" [7].

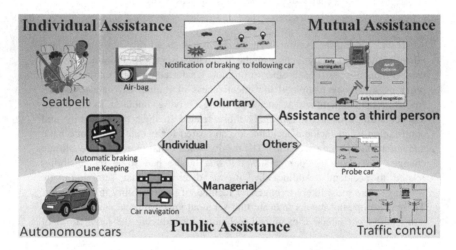

Fig. 1. Definition of three assistance types provided by driver safety systems [6]

In recent ADAS studies, a number of safety systems have been proposed such as Eyesight [8], NaviView [9], and others. However, such systems have not been classified in relation to mutual assistance even though the authors consider mutual assistance systems to be as crucial to enhancing the safety of automobile systems as they are in the disaster management field.

The authors also believe that mutual assistance systems have the potential to fulfill the higher needs of Maslow's hierarchy of needs [10], which hierarchically constructed in terms of "physiological", "safety", "love/belonging", "esteem" and "self-actualization" needs in an ascending order. Deficiencies, or needs, are said to motivate people when they are unmet. However, when these are satisfied, new needs emerge and the process continues.

When we consider that many existing ADAS technologies can fulfill needs related to "safety", we can then hypothesize that drivers look for opportunities to fill higher needs when the lower needs are met. However, it is also important to understand that the achievement of a safer automobile society may not be automatically selected. Instead, more immediate desires such as "reducing travel time" and "showing driving skill" may take precedence. Nevertheless, mutual assistance has the potential to fill such higher needs, and thus facilitate a safer automobile society, shown as in Fig. 2. This can be thought of in terms of "consciousness of helping each other" and "receiving gratitude from someone."

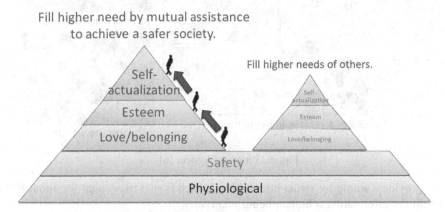

Fig. 2. Improved version of Maslow's hierarchy of needs

In this paper, we attempt to shed light on the driver attitude changes that occur when using a mutual assistance system, especially those related to responsibility consciousness or contribution.

2   Assumed Mutual Assistance System

In the case of Fig. 3, the right turning vehicle's driver (recipient) cannot see the oncoming vehicle (potential victim) since it is blocked by another vehicle (assister). For the sake of preventing such potential accidents, Kurihashi et al. [6] proposed a mutual assistance system that would allow an assister to provide a warning alert to the recipient regarding the existence of a car in his blind spot.

This system presupposes the use of charge-coupled device (CCD) cameras (or millimeter-wave radar) that have been installed on the side-view mirrors of the assister's vehicle in order to register the presence of automobiles and motorcycles in the vehicle's blind spot area. Additionally, the authors assume that as a warning presentation method, the body color of the assister vehicle changes unambiguously from its original color. Automobile body color changes can be achieved using technologies such as Fun-vii [11]. The envisioned merits of this system are as follows:

- To enable a driver to participate in a safety-related activity by producing a warning as an assister. This is expected to decrease the target level of risk for assister.
- To provide mutual assistance independently of road-to-vehicle or vehicle-to-vehicle communication. This can eliminate the threat of malevolent hacking via wireless communication technology.

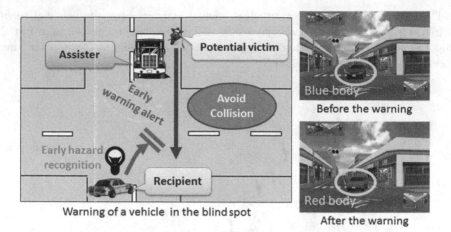

Fig. 3. Proposed system [6]

- To provide warning by visual information, which is said to account for about 80 % of all the information a human being receives.
- To strongly promote the view that we can help each other via visual information.
- To note the direction of an impending risk by using real-world information. This can eliminate various problems associated with heads-up displays, and also allows the system to show warnings on navigation system displays.

The system proposed in this paper is designed for experiments using a driving simulator, which can be easily developed by prototyping. For practical use in more realistic situations, alternative mutual assistance systems will need to be considered. This is left as future work.

3 Experimentation Environment

The experiments were undertaken by using a stationary driving simulator that uses complex computer graphics to provide a highly realistic driving environment. This simulated driving environment is projected on a 120-inch screen in front of the driver's seat and a 100-inch screen for the right-hand side view. The simulated horizontal forward field of view is 90° and the vertical field of view is 36° (Fig. 4).

In these experiments, test participants droved the assister side vehicle. Each scenario was an urban street route approximately 15 min in duration and included "*manual*", "*semi-automatic*", and "*automatic warning*" scenarios. If an assister activates his/her turn-signal lever, he/she can provide a warning to a recipient.

Manual Warning: Assisters can voluntarily provide a warning for a recipient and its timing is decided manually.

Semi-automatic Warning: Assisters can voluntarily provide a warning to a recipient and its timing is decided semi-automatically. If the assister activates the turn-signal lever up until 2.0 s before the collision, the warning is provided at exactly 2.0 s before.

Position of the two screens and the driver's seat   Photograph of experiment environment

Fig. 4. Experiment environment [6]

Automatic Warning: The system provides a warning automatically for a recipient and its timing is decided automatically.

All participants are given 5 min practice driving time to familiarize themselves with the simulator. During the practice drive, the participants were given an opportunity to experience driving on the warning recipient side. In the case of a successful warning, the recipient sends a return message by using the car horn with a probability of 50 %.

A total of 15 participants [one of which was a student (7 women and 8 men)] participated in this experiment. Their ages ranged between 21 and 26, and their driving experience ranged between 1 and 7 years. Informed consent was received from all test participants. Each was paid one 1,000 Japanese yen book coupon per hour.

4   Experimental Set-Up

4.1   Objectives

The objectives of this experiment was to determine the following:

1. What level of responsibility does the participant feel for the accident?
2. What level of contribution to avoiding an accident does the participant feel?
3. What kind of relationship exists between feelings of responsibility or contribution and attitude change?

4.2   Measurement

Responsibility or contributions to driver attitude change are measured by multiple and single answers. When choosing multiple answers, participants were asked to select all related items that fit the situation. When choosing a single answer, he/she was asked to select the single most relevant item from the provided list. Responsibility means that the participants felt that they knew "who was responsible" when accident occurred. Contribution means participants felt they knew "who contributed" to avoiding the accident. The authors designated the available choices as "assister", "system", "recipient", "potential victim", and "other".

Attitude change was measured using a simple five-point rating scale, where level 1 indicated that the assister felt a negative effect related to his/her task, and level 5 indicated that the assister felt a positive effect related to his/her task. Scores were collected for the following questions:

How much of...

- *your satisfaction is based on using the system properly?*
- *your satisfaction is due to assisting another person?*
- *your feeling of safety is based on your driving performance?*
- *your feeling of safety is based on sensing a risk factor?*
- *your frustration is based on the workload required to use the system?*
- *frustration is due to the system's actions?*
- *an effect does the system have on the cognition side of your driving?*
- *an effect does the system have on the operational side of your driving?*

4.3   Hypotheses

The working hypotheses in this experiment are as follows:

(A) An assister will feel the highest level of responsibility in a *manual warning* situation. In contrast, in an *automatic warning* situation, an assister will assume others are responsible.

(B) An assister will feel the highest level of contribution in a *manual warning* situation. In contrast, in an *automatic warning* situation, he/she only feels a slight sense of contribution.

(C) When an assister feels responsibility and contribution strongly, a positive attitude change will be strongly forthcoming.

5   Result and Discussion

5.1   Responsibility

Figure 5 shows the results for responsibility. The figure on the left shows the results for multiple answers while the one on the right shows results for the single answer. For multiple answers, all participants chose the recipient. In situations focusing on the assister, *semi-automatic warning* showed the highest level of responsibility. In *automatic warning* scenarios, some participants shifted blame onto the system. No participant chose "other" from the range of choices.

These results show that a *semi-automatic warning* system is the most efficient for engaging the assister, while an *automatic warning* system is unlikely to trigger an assister's sense of responsibility. In *semi-automatic warning* situations, the assister felt more responsibility than during *manual warning* situations, primarily because they felt that *manual warning* situations were too difficult to realistically permit success, so participants did not feel responsible. However, one participant said, "If I can't provide an alert in a *semi-automatic warning* situation, I will feel some responsibility because

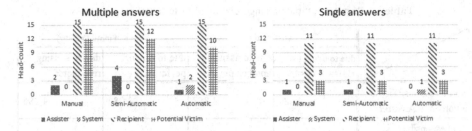

Fig. 5. Result for responsibility

even though that the usability of *semi-automatic* systems much improved than that of *manual* system". On the other hand, some participants shifted blame onto the system in the *automatic warning* situation. Overall, these results indicate that hypothesis A is partially correct.

5.2 Contribution

Figure 6 shows the results for contribution. The figure on the left shows the result of multiple answers, while the figure on the right shows the results for the single answer. For multiple answers, all participants chose assister in the *manual* and *semi-automatic warning* scenarios. In contrast, only one third of the participants chose assister for the *automatic warning* scenario. In addition, for their single answer, most participants chose the system in the *automatic warning* scenario. No participant chose assister or other from the range of choices.

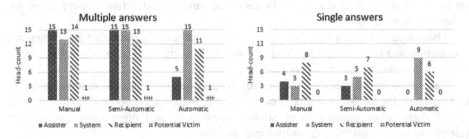

Fig. 6. Results for contribution

From these results, it is difficult to feel a mutual assistance contribution from the *automatic warning* system. Thus, it can be said that Hypothesis B is correct, but there is very little difference between *manual* and *semi-automatic warning*.

5.3 Attitude Change

Table 1 shows the average of the attitude change rating (p is p-value and significant level were set at 0.05). For multiple answers, the authors compared cases where "assister feels some responsibility is involved" (hereinafter referred to as some responsibility) and other cases (hereinafter referred to as no responsibility).

Table 1. Result of attitude change classified in terms of responsibility

	Satisfaction		Peace of mind (Safety)	
	due to using the system properly	due to assisting another person	due to driving performance	due to sensing risk factor
Some responsibility is involved to Assister	4.429	4.857	3.286	4.286
No responsibility is involved to Assister	3.526	3.500	3.263	3.816
p-Value	p = 0.118	p = 0.015	p = 0.954	p = 0.142

	Frustration		Effect on driving	
	by workload due to using system	due to system actions	for cognition side	for operation side
Some responsibility is involved to Assister	2.857	1.714	4.143	3.143
No responsibility is involved to Assister	2.763	1.816	3.105	3.053
p-Value	p = 0.886	p = 0.807	p = 0.011	p = 0.754

As a trend, some responsibility shows a higher rating than no responsibility for all items. The result of an analysis of variance (ANOVA), in particular, shows that there are significant differences on "satisfaction due to assisting another person" and "Effect on the cognition side of driving". On the other hand, few differences were noted for either "frustration" question.

These results suggest that the feeling of responsibility is important for enhancing satisfaction and has an effect on driving. That, in turn, means Trimpop's theory can be adapted to a mutual assistance system.

Table 2 shows another data analysis for the average of the attitude change rating. In this analysis, the authors compared cases of "the assister feels some contribution was made" (hereinafter referred to as some contribution) and other cases (hereinafter referred to as no contribution) in multiple answers.

As a trend, some contribution is higher rating than no contribution in all items, just as was noted for responsibility. In particular, the ANOVA shows significant differences on both "satisfaction" and "peace of mind (Safety) due to risk factor sensing", and "frustration based on the workload required to use the system".

This result suggests that it is important to feel a contribution is being made to enhancing satisfaction and peace of mind (safety). However, it is accompanied by a significant amount of frustration. In other words, the level of task frustration relates to how participants feel about their contribution to accident avoidance. Thus, from these results, it can be said that hypothesis C is correct.

Table 2. Result of attitude change classified in terms of contribution

	Satisfaction		Peace of mind (Safety)	
	due to using the system properly	due to assisting another person	due to driving performance	due to sensing risk factor
Some contribution is involved to Assister	4.057	4.143	3.343	4.114
No contribution is involved to Assister	2.300	2.200	3.000	3.100
p-Value	$p < 0.001$	$p < 0.001$	$p = 0.314$	$p < 0.001$

	Frustration		Effect on driving	
	by workload due to using system	due to system actions	for cognition side	for operation side
Some contribution is involved to Assister	3.257	1.971	3.314	3.086
No contribution is involved to Assister	1.100	1.200	3.100	3.000
p-Value	$p < 0.001$	$p = 0.028$	$p = 0.560$	$p = 0.732$

6 Conclusion

From the results of these experiments, the authors deduce that *semi-automatic warn-ings* are the most effective method of mutual assistance because the positive attitude changes engendered by this warning type have high potential to influence both responsibility and contribution levels. In particular, the significant increase of "satis-faction due to assisting another person" expressed by the participants meets the higher needs of Maslow's hierarchy, and the significant increase of "peace of mind (Safety)" and "effect on driving for cognition side" indicates participants' desire to achieve a safer automobile society.

Additionally, *semi-automatic warnings* are sufficiently effective from the recipient side [6]. As one participant noted, "*Automatic warnings* are good if you want to keep workloads low, but *semi-automatic warning* is another good option because con-sciousness is most enhanced in *semi-automatic warning* situations."

Thus to take advantage of these benefits, mutual assistance systems must include some voluntary activities, but not fully manual: The system should help the assister in some degree. The authors conclude that *semi-automatic warnings* might be the most appropriate.

Acknowledgement. The authors would like to thank researchers from the Japan Automobile Research Institute for their advice on this paper. They would also like to thank the participants in the experiments using the driving simulator for their cooperation. The authors thank anonymous reviewers for their constructive suggestions.

References

1. Zink, K.J., Ritter, A.: Mit Qualittszirkeln zu mehr Arbeitssicherheit: Praxisbeipiele f r die erfolgreiche pfung von Humanisierung und Wirtschaftlichkeit. Universum-Verl.-Anst, Wiesbaden (1992)
2. Trimpop, R.M.: Motivation zur arbeitssicherheit. Der Sicherheitsingenieur 4(5), 28–46 (1994)
3. Trimpop, R.M.: The Psychology of Risk Taking Behaviour. Elsevier, North Holland (1994)
4. Wilde, G.J.S.: Target Risk 2: A New Psychology of Safety and Health, 2nd edn. PDE Publications, New York (2001)
5. Wilde, G.J.S.: The theory of risk homeostasis implications for safety and health. Risk Anal. 2(4), 209–225 (1982)
6. Kurihashi, S., Matsuno, Y., Tanaka, K.: Evaluation of a mutual assistance system from both the recipient and assister sides. In: Proceedings of SICE Annual Conference 2014, pp. 1702–1707 (2014)
7. Cabinet Office Government of Japan: White Paper on Disaster Management *2013* (2013), (in Japanese)
8. Katahira, S., Shibata, E., Monji, T.: Development of an advanced stereo camera system. In: Proceedings of 14th Asia Pacific Automotive Conference, SAE Technical Paper 2007-01-3591 (2007)
9. Taya, F., Kameda, Y., Ohta, Y.: NaviView: virtual slope visualization of a blind area at an intersection. In: Proceedings of 12th World Congress on ITS, pp. 1–8 (2005)
10. Maslow, A.H.: A theory of human motivation. Psychol. Rev. 50, 370–396 (1943)
11. Fun Vii Concept Car. http://www.toyota.com/letsgoplaces/fun-vii-concept-car

Map Matching to Correct Location Error in an Electric Wheel Chair

Yuta Noriduki, Hirotoshi Shibata, Shigenori Ioroi,
and Hiroshi Tanaka$^{(\boxtimes)}$

Kanagawa Institute of Technology,
1030 Shimo-ogino, Atsugi-shi, Kanagawa, Japan
{s1485012, s1121081}@cce.kanagawa-it.ac.jp,
{ioroi, h_tanaka}@ic.kanagawa-it.ac.jp

Abstract. This paper presents a method of map matching that is a scheme for accurate guidance of an electric wheel chair. Indoor navigation seems to require more accurate guidance than outdoor areas, the location estimation by the rotary encoders embedded in the wheel chair cannot be satisfy the accuracy requirement, because estimation error is accumulated as the wheel chair travels. The authors propose the map matching that uses the building structure in order to compensate for accumulated position error. The corner detection and its position information are used for replacement as a correct position. The methods of the corner detection and the calculation model for the correct position are shown, and the validity of the proposed methods are confirmed by the experiment using a laser range finder.

Keywords: Electric wheelchair · Automatic traveling · Indoor positioning · Map matching · Laser range finder

1 Introduction

Many schemes have been proposed for the operation of an electric wheelchair for aged or physically disabled persons [1, 2]. The authors are now investigating automatic guidance for such a wheelchair that will allow its operation in an extensive indoor area. Spacious shopping malls, large hospitals and the like are complicated, making it challenging to reach a particular goal even for the physically healthy. Relevant studies of automated traveling technology have been pursued in recent years [3], including attempts to create a driverless car. Indoor navigation seems to require more precise guidance than outdoor areas, because corridors are narrower, and rooms are smaller than road. The room plates are used for landmarks to recognize a mobile robot location [4]. This scheme requires high accurate image recognition in any illumination environment. This paper presents a scheme for the accurate guidance of an electric wheel chair as it travels within an extensive indoor area. Map matching has been proposed to compensate for accumulated position error, using corner detection in corridors. This scheme does not require any addition of landmarks, and it is desirable from aspect of aesthetic purposes and workload of setting landmarks. This technique's effectiveness

S. Yamamoto (Ed.): HIMI 2015, Part II, LNCS 9173, pp. 243–252, 2015.
DOI: 10.1007/978-3-319-20618-9_24

has been verified by experiment, with an automatically controlled wheelchair traversing a corridor, including a corner.

2 Sequence to Target Position and Necessity of Error Correction

Figure 1 shows the sequence of events as an automatic wheelchair follows a route to the target spot. We assumed that the route to the target spot was composed of straight travel and 90°turns, which is normal in most buildings. The main actions to reach at target spot include straight travel, turns, and map matching to correct accumulated position error.

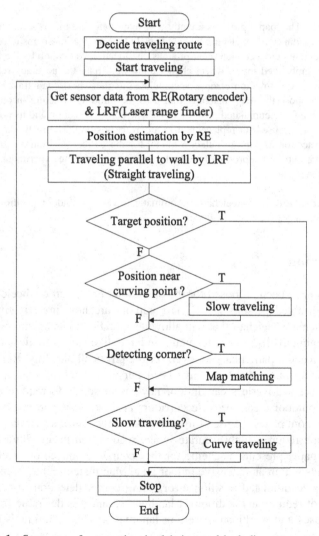

Fig. 1. Sequence of automatic wheelchair travel including map matching

Fig. 2. Electric wheelchair with LRF installed

The route is determined in advance by designating the start and target spot using the Dijkstra method and map information. We require arrival accuracy at the final target spot of better than about 10 in, which is based on the width of a door.

An electric wheelchair itself generally has two rotary encoders, and these sensors are used for automatic travel and position estimation. One encoder is installed in the left motor and one in the right motor, to detect each motor's rotation speed. The other sensor, a laser range finder (LRF), is used to detect the distance to nearby obstacles such as wall. The rotary encoder is also used for curved path travel, in which the right and left wheel rotation must adjust to the radius of curvature, and the LRF is used for straight travel detecting the distance to left- and right-and walls, and keeping the ratio of the distance constant. Figure 2 shows the electric wheelchair with its LRF installed on a pole to maintain a height sufficient to avoid obstacles such as a pedestrian in the corridor. The main specification of the LRF used in this investigation is summarized in Table 1.

Table 1. LRF Specification

Manufacturer	HOKUYO AUTOMATIC CO.,LTD
Type	UTM-30LX
Detection range	10mm ~ 30000mm
Accuracy	± 30 mm
Angle range	270 deg
Angular resolution	0.25 deg

The position of the electric wheelchair can be estimated by integration of the angular velocity of the two motors. However, this method is not precise, because of variables such as wheel slippage on the floor and pressure differences in the tires. This makes it necessary to compensate for position-estimate error to arrive precisely at the target spot.

3   Error Correction by Map Matching for Precise Travel

The authors propose error correction by map matching. Map matching itself is not a new technology [5]. It is widely used, especially for driving navigation to replace a car's road position when GPS yields an improbable position. Some markers are proposed for map matching that indicate the position in an indoor area. However, this method requires the installation of place markers, which becomes a burden and can be unsightly. We propose to use the structure of the building for reference points, specifically its corners, so that no markers need to be installed. The position estimated by the encoders is updated based on the position of a nearby corner. We propose this method for position estimation error correction.

3.1   Basic Principle of Corner Detection

To begin with, detecting the corner is required in order to use the proposed method. The LRF is used for corner detection. Figure 3 indicates the criteria for detecting at corner in the corridor. The distance detection limit of the LRF used in this investigation is 5.8 m. Therefore, anytime that at wall cannot be detected within 5.8 m is taken to indicate a corner, as shown in Fig. 3. The four possible patterns are indicated in this figure: no corner (straight corridor), L-shaped corner, T-shaped corner and Cross-shaped corner.

The angle range for corner detection depends on the structure of the corridor, as shown in Fig. 3, especially on the width of the corridor and the position of the LRF on the wheelchair. The wheelchair is assumed to travel along the center of the corridor in this investigation, and the angle ranges are examined in advance by using the LRF on the wheel chair. The range for the corridor (no-wall detection range) is set from 14.3° to 38.1°. The type of corner is determined from the characteristics of this no-wall region as shown in Fig. 3, from these choices: no region = L-shaped corner, one = no corner (straight corridor), two = T- shaped corner, three = Cross-shaped corner.

3.2   Evaluation of Detection Capability

Tests of corner detection were carried out in the area shown in Fig. 4. This area had The L-, T- and cross-shaped corners. Figure 5 shows one example of angle range variation of the no wall-region in a T-shaped corner, in which the travel direction of the

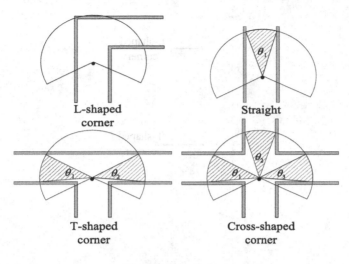

L-shaped
corner

Straight

T-shaped
corner

Cross-shaped
corner

θ_i :No wall detection range
$14.3° \leq \theta_i \leq 38.1°$

Fig. 3. Criteria for corner detection

wheelchair is shown in Fig. 4. The x axis indicates the travel time and y axis is the no-wall angle range. This no-wall region depends on the LRF measurement distance limit. Although only one no-wall region was found at the beginning, two no-wall regions appeared as the wheelchair traveled. The T-shaped corner was recognized at the moment of detected change, that is, from the one no-wall to the two no-wall condition. The first position satisfies the conditions for a no-wall region, i.e. from 14.3° to 38.1°, is regarded as the finding of the corner in this investigation. We call this point the node.

The evaluation test for corner detection was carried out in the area shown in Fig. 4. Sun illumination produces obstacle detection in the no-wall region, so a blind was used on the window so as to exclude direct sun-light in this experiment. The test result is shown in Table 2. Quite high detection performance was demonstrated for that corner in the usual room light environment.

3.3 Node Setting for Accumulated Error Correction

It is necessary to determine the position where corner detection occurs, and we call that point the node. Its position replaces the estimated position obtained by the rotary encoders, because the estimated position contains accumulated error. The geometrical model for determining the node position is shown in Fig. 6. The no wall detection range can be calculated from the building's corridor structure and the position of the LRF by geometry. When is between 14.3° to 38.1°, the wheelchair is at the corner. In this investigation, at the instant when the above condition is satisfied for the wheelchair, map matching is carried out, i.e. replacement of the estimated position by the node position. The meaning of the terms is shown in the figure.

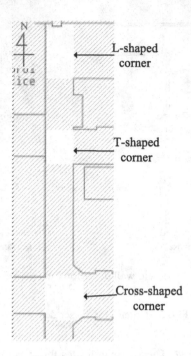

Fig. 4. Experimental area

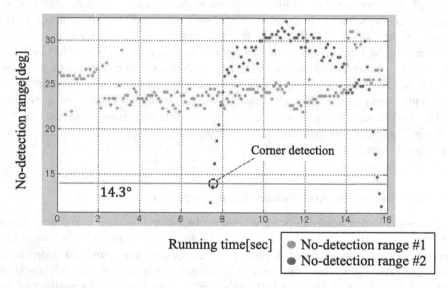

Fig. 5. Example of no-wall detection range transition and corner detection

Table 2. Evaluation test result for corner detection

Corner	L-shaped	T-shaped		Cross-shaped	
Travelling route	Curve	Curve	Straight	Curve	Straight
Success ratio	10/10	10/10	10/10	10/10	10/10

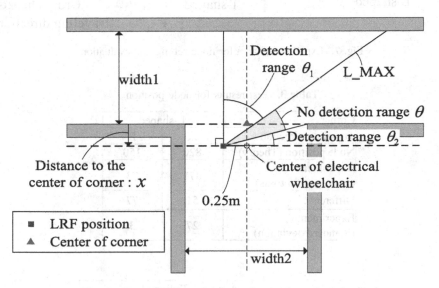

Fig. 6. Geometrical model for node position calculation

$$\theta = 90 - \theta_1 - \theta_2 \tag{1}$$

where,

$$\theta_1 = \cos^{-1} \frac{(width1 + x)}{L\_MAX}$$

$$\theta_2 = \tan^{-1} \frac{x}{(\frac{width2}{2} + 0.25)}$$

The position of nodes calculated by this proposed method is stored in the database. When at corner is detected by the traveling wheelchair, the estimated position is replaced by this node position to eliminate the accumulated position error. The scheme can be regarded as map matching in the widest sense of the term.

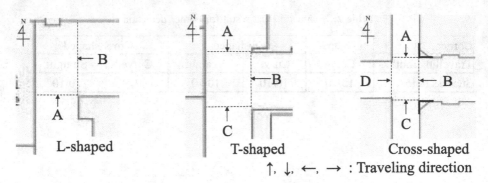

↑, ↓, ←, → : Traveling direction

Fig. 7. Experimental area for node setting and evaluation

Table 3. Test results for node position

Corner	L-shaped	
Traveling direction	A	B
Node position (Theory)	820	150
Experiment (Average of 5 trials)	871	73
Difference	51	77
Experiment (Standard deviation)	27	3

Corner	T-shaped		
Traveling direction	A	B	C
Node position (Theory)	10	80	30
Experiment (Average of 5 trials)	-55	36	-45
Difference	65	44	75
Experiment (Standard deviation)	5	8	9

Corner	Cross-shaped			
Traveling direction	A	B	C	D
Node position (Theory)	190	160	400	130
Experiment (Average of 5 trials)	200	135	394	80
Difference	10	25	6	50
Experiment (Standard deviation)	8	8	4	4

3.4   Evaluation Test for Node Detection Point

In the proposed method, the node position decision is quite important, because it governs the accuracy of the wheelchair's position by map matching. An experiment to evaluate the node position was carried out to confirm the validity of the proposed method and its accuracy. The experiment was carried out with the wheelchair traveling in the center of the corridor. The area is that shown in Fig. 3, and the traveling directions are shown in Fig. 7. Table 3 shows the experimental results and the theoretical values of the node position. The average and standard deviation for the experimental results are also shown. The maximum difference between experimental and theoretical values is 77 mm. The validity of the node determination was confirmed, and this result seems to establish that the position error of the wheelchair is less than tens of centimeters.

4   Automatic Travel Experiment and Position Estimation by Map Matching

An automatic travel experiment was carried out using the proposed scheme. The result is shown in Fig. 8. The black dots indicate the results with map matching. The grey dots are the results without map matching. The discontinuous points indicate map

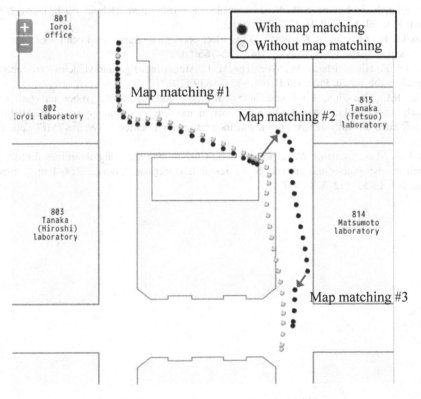

Fig. 8. Experimental results of map matching

matching locations. Map matching was carried out three times at each corner. The positioning of the wheel chair is not at the center of the corridor because it records the location of the LRF where it is attached to the wheelchair. It was verified that position correction by map matching was carried out correctly, and at the same time, the wheel chair traveled parallel to the wall and turned appropriately.

5 Conclusion

This paper presents a map matching method that uses the detection of corners in a corridor. This method enables high accuracy travel for a wheelchair in an extensive indoor area without adding and landmarks. Methods were proposed for corner detection and the calculation of the node points at the corners to enable map matching, and their validity was experimentally verified. Position evaluation for travel to specific places, and investigation of a travel method that includes the use of an elevator remain for further studies.

References

1. Simpson, R.C., Levine, S.P.: Voice control of a powered wheelchair. IEEE Trans. Neural Syst. Rehabil. Eng. **10**(2), 122–125 (2002)
2. Tanaka, K., Matsunaga, K., Wang, H.O.: Electroencephalogram-based control of an electric wheelchair. IEEE Trans. Robot. **21**(4), 762–766 (2005)
3. Luettel, T., Himmelsbach, M., Wuensche, H.-J.: Autonomous ground vehicles - concepts and a path to the future. Proc. IEEE **100**, 1831–1839 (2012)
4. Luo, R.C., Yu-Chih, L., Ching-Chung, K.: Autonomous mobile robot navigation and localization based on floor plan map information and sensory fusion approach. In: 2010 IEEE Conference on Multi sensor Fusion and Integration for Intelligent Systems (MFI), pp. 121–126 (2010)
5. Quddus, M.A., Ochieng, W.Y., Noland, R.B.: Current map-matching algorithms for transport applications: state-of-the art and future research directions. Transp. Res. Part C Emerg. Technol. **15**(5), 312–328 (2007)

Driving Evaluation of Mild Unilateral Spatial Neglect Patients–Three High-Risk Cases Undetected by BIT After Recovery

Tasuku Sotokawa[1,2(✉)], Takuya Murayama[2], Junko Noguchi[2], Yoko Sakimura[2], and Makoto Itoh[3]

[1] Occupational Therapy, Niigata University of Health and Welfare, Niigata, Japan
sotokawa@nuhw.ac.jp
[2] Niigata Rehabilitation Hospital, Niigata, Japan
[3] Faculty of Engineering, Information and Systems, University of Tsukuba, Ibaraki, Japan

Abstract. The respective driving abilities of three patients having a right hemisphere infarct and mild unilateral spatial neglect (USN) were examined. Neuropsychological examinations included the Behavioral Inattention Test Japanese version (BIT-J) and the Japanese version of the Wechsler Adults Intelligence Scale – Third edition. Their driving ability was assessed with a driving simulator test and on-road evaluation. Patients had no neglect based on the BIT-J, but showed some slight signs of USN on a driving simulator test and on-road evaluation. This study assessed risks of mild USN patient driving and explored possibilities of improving it using Advanced Driving Assistance Systems.

Keywords: Driving ability · Driving simulator · Stroke · Visual neglect · Neuropsychological test

1 Introduction

For many people, driving is an important activity of daily living. Previous reports have described that 30 %–66 % of stroke patients resume driving [1, 2]. Resuming car driving is an important concern for many stroke survivors and their families. Nevertheless, driving a car, a complex task, requires the integration of visual-perceptual stimuli, good judgment, decision making, and appropriate motor responses. These functional abilities might be affected by stroke, traumatic brain injury and other brain disorders. Above all, the unilateral spatial neglect (USN) is an extraordinary clinical phenomenon whereby patients appear to be unable to respond to objects and people located on the contralateral side to a cerebral lesion. It is one of many manifestations that can occur in people in the aftermath of a stroke. The incidence of USN has been reported to be as high as 82 % in right hemispheric stroke patients when assessed in the acute stage [3]. Although USN can be associated with damage to left or right hemispheres of the brain, it occurs more frequently and with greater severity following damage to the right hemisphere. The USN

© Springer International Publishing Switzerland 2015
S. Yamamoto (Ed.): HIMI 2015, Part II, LNCS 9173, pp. 253–261, 2015.
DOI: 10.1007/978-3-319-20618-9_25

USN patients Ignore on one side.
Clinically, most USN appear to leftside.

Amimoto K[4]

Fig. 1. Clinical case of unilateral spatial neglect

severity can vary from mild to severe. Mild USN has been assessed in several earlier studies.

Clinically, moderate or severe USN is regarded as severely affecting activities of daily living (ADL; Fig. 1, e.g., they frequently collide into surroundings during walking or wheelchair driving, ignore food on one side of the plate, and attend to only one side of the body). Therefore, moderate or severe USN is likely to pose a daunting obstacle to driving. However, the evaluation of driving ability in patients with mild USN is a multi-faceted matter that clinicians often encounter in their work. This report presents assessed driving ability and considers the possibility of advanced driver-assistance systems facilitating patients' resumption of safe driving.

2   Patients and Methods

Three patients were selected from a larger group of recovering stroke patients who had been referred for specialized driving ability evaluation. All were patients affected by visual neglect without hemianopia in the acute phase because of a right hemisphere infarction. In all three cases, the acute neurological diagnosis was supported by computerized tomography of the brain. None had any prior neurological disorder. All the patients possessed a valid driving license immediately before their stroke. Then they were active, non-professional drivers.

3   Methods

Some neuropsychological examination and the Driving-simulator test were performed for each patient before the on-road driving assessment. Detailed results are reported for the Behavioral Inattention Test Japanese version (BIT-J; Fig. 2) and the Japanese version of the Wechsler Adults Intelligence Scale third edition (JWAIS-3rd; Fig. 3). These tests are used widely in Japan.

BIT-J is a representative screening battery of tests used to assess the presence of USN. BIT is divided into two subtests. The Conventional subtest consists of six items.

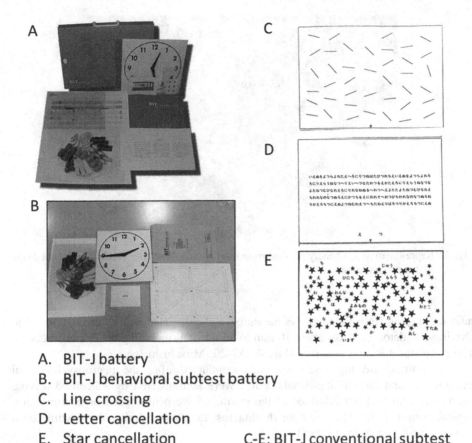

A. BIT-J battery
B. BIT-J behavioral subtest battery
C. Line crossing
D. Letter cancellation
E. Star cancellation   C-E: BIT-J conventional subtest

Fig. 2. Representative test battery of unilateral spatial neglect

Its Cut-Off score is 131. The Behavioral Subtest consists of nine items. Its Cut-Off score is 68. The Conventional subtest is paper-and-pencil based. If the patient's BIT-J score is less than the Cut-Off Score, then it is regarded as indicating the presence of USN. The inclusion criterion of this study was normal performance (score >131) on the BIT at the time of Driving evaluation, which indicated the recovery of USN. Actually, BIT takes about 40 min to administer, including the test instructions.

Clinically, JWAIS-3rd is a useful test for measuring intelligence in adults and older adolescents. It provided scores for Verbal IQ, Performance IQ, and Full Scale IQ, along with four secondary indices (Verbal comprehension, Working memory, Perceptual organization, and Processing speed). Particularly according to previous studies, Processing Speed (PS) is lower for elderly drivers who have had accidents. JWAIS-3rd takes about 3 h to administer, including the test instructions.

In the Driving-simulator test, the subject's task is Lane Tracking. Subjects must maintain the course continuously during driving on a road with random curves. The

Fig. 3. Representative test battery of measuring intelligence. Wechsler Adult Intelligence Scale 3rd edition Japanese version.

ratio of straying from the course is measured and calculated as the "error ratio." The Driving-simulator test takes about 10 min to administer, including the test instructions. The simulator has high precision (Fig. 4, DS-20; Mitsubishi Inc.).

The on-road driving assessment was conducted after the neuropsychological examination and the Driving-simulator test were administered by a licensed driving instructor, who was not informed of the results of the neurological or neuropsychological examinations. The one-hour driving test took place during the daytime on a closed course at a driving school.

The main domains assessed in the driving instructor's evaluation in the on-road driving test are presented in connection with the case descriptions.

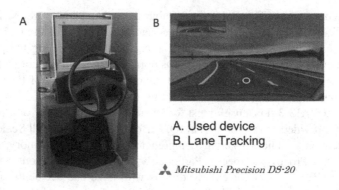

A. Used device
B. Lane Tracking

▲ *Mitsubishi Precision DS-20*

Fig. 4. Driving simulator

4 Results

Three patients possessed a valid driving license immediately before experiencing a stroke. All the patients had a statutory duty to undergo the Extraordinary Aptitude Test after recovering from the stroke.

4.1 Case 1

The patient was a right-handed man in his 30s who had undergone right putamen hemorrhage (Fig. 5-A). In the acute phase, the man had severe hemiparesis and moderate USN. Two and a half months after onset, he had no hemiparesis. No sign of neglect was detected by the BIT-J (Conventional subtest 145/146, Behavioral subtest 79/81).

His ADL and gait were independent: without assistance. Nevertheless, the man had hit obstacles in the left hemispace and showed low processing speed (PS of 86 by WAIS-3rd). In the Driving simulator test, his "error ratio" was biased strongly toward the left side (Fig. 6-A).

In the Driving evaluation, during a closed course test, the man showed left-sided visual inattention and poor lane position (e.g., the man's car was stopped too close to traffic while overtaking stopped traffic. The man's car was spaced too widely on the left side. He scraped the right rear while parking left and rearward.) (Fig. 7-A). The man's comments showed poor self-awareness of his driving performance (e.g., "It was not too bad."). From these results, we inferred that the man would have difficulty resuming safe driving. At a later re-evaluation (7 months later), the man's PS and self-awareness had improved (e.g., His PS was 102 by WAIS-3rd. He commented "I must drive carefully because I was terrible at driving."). He was conscious that his vehicle was too close to stopped traffic. He resumed car driving because he had become capable of safe driving. Subsequently, this man has had no accident for two years.

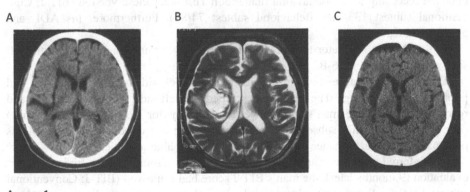

A: case1
B: case2
C: case3

Fig. 5. Computed tomography and magnetic resonance of three cases

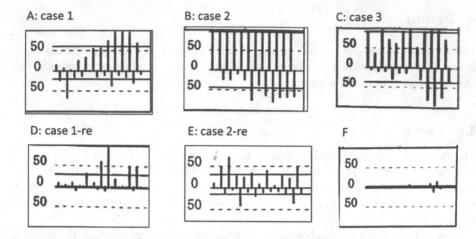

A: case 1   B: case 2   C: case 3

D: case 1-re   E: case 2-re   F

A-C: Results of first evaluation in each case
D,E: Results of re-evaluation in case1 and 2
F: Result of healthy subject

0(zero)-line is center line. If histogram's height exceed 50-line, the car is straying
from course. Upside is left, lower side is right.

Fig. 6. Error ratio of straying from the simulator course

4.2 Case 2

The patient was a right-handed man in his 50s with right putamen hemorrhage (Fig. 5-B).
In the early recovery phase, the man hit obstacles on his left side when using his
wheelchair. However, in the chronic recovery phase, no sign of neglect was
detected according to the Behavioral Inattention Test – Japanese version (BIT-J: Conventional subtest 133/146, Behavioral subtest 74/81). Furthermore, his ADL and
gait were independent.

In the Driving simulator test, his "error ratio" was strongly biased toward the left
side, as in Case 1 (Fig. 6-B).

During the Driving evaluation, the man showed left-sided visual inattention and
poor lane position (e.g., The man's car scraped the left side while parking left and
rearward. Overall, the man's car showed a tendency for exceeding speed limits.)
(Fig. 7-B). The man's subsequent comments demonstrated poor awareness of his
personal driving performance (e.g., "It was nice to be able to drive.").

We inferred that the man would have difficulty resuming safe driving. At re-
evaluation (9 months later), the man's BIT-J score had improved (BIT-J: Conventional
subtest 141/146, Behavioral subtest 81/81). In a closed course test, he was unable to
continue modifying his own behavior after he was cautioned. His comments still

showed poor self-awareness ("How slowly this car is moving!!"). We inferred that the man would have difficulty resuming safe driving because he was not able to reflect upon and modify his own driving performance. He has not resumed car driving following our recommendation to stop driving.

4.3   Case 3

The patient was a right-handed woman in her 50s with right putamen hemorrhage (Fig. 5-C). In the recovery phase, the woman hit obstacles on her left side when using a wheelchair. Furthermore, in the chronic phase, she hit obstacles on her left side during walking. However, no sign of neglect was detected according to BIT-J (Conventional subtest 142/146, Behavioral subtest 78/81).

In the Driving simulator test, her "error ratio" was biased strongly toward the left side, similarly to Cases 1 and 2 (Fig. 6-C).

In Driving evaluation, the woman showed left-sided visual inattention and poor lane position (e.g., The woman's car ran off to the left side while running an S-curve course. The woman's car ran the wrong way on right lane in left-hand traffic following running on an L-curve course.) (Fig. 7-C). Overall, the speed was too slow. The woman's comments included reports of poor self-awareness of her driving performance (e.g., "I feel quite safe when driving slowly."). We inferred that the woman would have difficulty resuming safe driving. She has not resumed car driving.

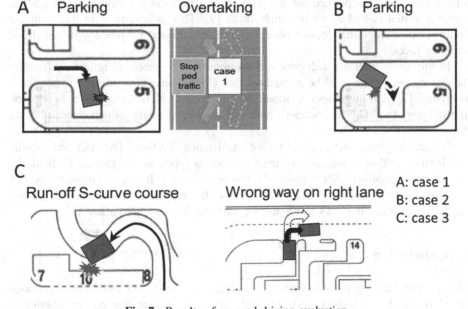

Fig. 7. Results of on road driving evaluation

5 Discussion

This study presented three patients who were affected of mild USN on driving. All patients had USN between acute phase and recovery phase. At the time of neuropsychological test, the patients had no signs of USN according to the BIT-J. However, they showed signs of USN in the Driving simulator test and Driving evaluation. In fact, mild USN might impair safe driving by causing difficulties in maintaining driving lines and optimum speed, or by narrowing and slowing the perception of the whole environment.

One interesting finding was that of a non-detectable type of USN using BIT-J, as mild USN. According to several previous studies, BIT-J were shown to be reliable and valid in patients with moderate or severe USN [5, 6]. Conversely, BIT-J has insufficient reliability and validity for patients with mild USN. For example, mild USN patients might learn to compensate by voluntarily directing their attention to the contralateral side of the lesion. Furthermore, mild USN patients might compensate by looking carefully again because BIT-J is a paper–pencil based test.

In addition, some reports of previous studies have described subtypes of USN [7, 8]. Regarding specific details, they might include personal neglect (inability to attend to either side of the person's body), peripersonal neglect (inability to attend to either side of the space within reaching distance), extrapersonal neglect (inability to attend to either side of the space beyond reaching distance). From a cognitive perspective, BIT-J corresponds to peripersonal neglect test because BIT-J is a desk test. Problems of peripersonal and extrapersonal space might be related to car driving.

Moreover, in this study, a non-detectable type of USN using BIT-J might be obvious only under certain circumstances as On Road Driving and using Driving Simulator. Taylor has pointed out that mild USN patients might show signs of USN in complex visual tasks but not in simple tasks [9]. This indication is in line with our findings that mild visual neglect patients might be affected by processing speed and complex tasks.

In this study, patients with poor self-awareness were unable to reflect and modify the driving performance. Ishiai pointed out that USN is linked inextricably to poor self-awareness [7]. Self-awareness is virtually synonymous with metacognition. In addition to problems of mild USN, a patient's poor self-awareness might influence resuming car driving.

In recent years, Advanced Driving Assistance Systems (ADAS) are rapidly developing: field and assistance systems of various types are developed. Particularly, ADAS might improve USN patients' driving performance. In this instantiation, ADAS (e.g., lane-keeping assist system, collision avoidance system, parking assist system) might decrease driving risks and assist the safe driving of USN patients.

6 Conclusion

USN patients' driving performance might reveal problems of one sided visual attention and show a lack of self-awareness of their driving performance. For their resumption of safe driving in addition to providing rehabilitation training, it is necessary to compensate for their deficits using ADAS.

References

1. Fisk, G.D., Owsley, C., Pulley, L.V.: Driving after stroke: driving exposure, advice, and evaluations. Arch. Phys. Med. Rehabil. **78**, 1338–1345 (1997)
2. Heikkilä, V.M., Korpelainen, J., Turkka, J., Kallanranta, T., Summala, H.: Clinical evaluation of the driving ability in stroke patients. Acta Neurol. Scand. **99**, 349–355 (1999)
3. Stone, S.P., Halligan, P.W., Greenwood, R.J.: The incidence of neglect phenomena and related disorders in patients with an acute right or left hemisphere stroke. Age Ageing **22**, 46–52 (1993)
4. Labo-Information, Tokyo Metropolitan University Liaison Office. http://www.tokyo-sangaku.jp/labo/%E7%B6%B2%E6%9C%AC-%E5%92%8C/
5. Halligan, P.W., Cockburn, J., Wilson, B.A.: The behavioural assessment of visual neglect. Neuropsychol. Rehabil. **1**, 5–32 (1991)
6. Hannaford, S., Gower, G., Potter, J.M., Guest, R.M., Fairhurst, M.C.: Assessing visual inattention: study of interrater reliability. Brit. J. Ther. Rehabil. **10**, 72–75 (2003)
7. Ishiai, S.: Behavioral Inattention Test Japanese Version. Sinko Igaku Syuppan, Japan (1999)
8. Mizuno, K.: Rehabilitation of unilateral spatial neglect. Medical Rehabilitation. MB Med Rehab, ZEN·NIHONBYOUIN·SYUPPANKAI, vol. 129 (2011)
9. Taylor, D.: Measuring mild visual neglect: do complex visual tests activate rightward attentional bias? N. Z. J. Physiotherapy **31**, 67–72 (2003)

Effect of Adaptive Caution on Driver's Lane-Change Behavior under Cognitively Distracted Condition

Huiping Zhou[1(✉)] and Makoto Itoh[2]

[1] Faculty of Engineering, Information and Systems, Tsukuba, Japan
zhouhp@css.risk.tsukuba.ac.jp
[2] University of Tsukuba, 1-1-1 Tennodai, Tsukuba, Ibaraki 305-8573, Japan
itoh.makoto.ge@u.tsukuba.ac.jp

Abstract. This paper investigates caution type message that is given to a driver in two ways. One refers to driver's characteristic of intentional eye movement for changing lanes, and the other is adaptive to driver state as well as the characteristic. Experimental results imply the two ways' effectiveness of improving the intentional checking behavior that might be degraded by a cognitively distracted secondary task. Meanwhile, this study also indicates that the later way is more effective for improving a maneuver of changing lanes. It is suggested that it would be more acceptable to consider driver state into a support system.

Keywords: Adaptive caution information · Driving safety · Cognitive distraction · Lane changes

1 Introduction

This study defines "driver distraction" as a diversion of a driver's attention away from activities critical for safe driving towards a competing activity [1]. The US National Highway and Safety Administration (NHTSA) reported that distraction-related crashes were responsible for 3,092 fatalities (9 % of all traffic-related fatalities) in 2012 [2]. Traditional crash studies based on eyewitness accounts or driver recall assigned responsibility for 10-12 % of all car-crashes to driver distraction [3–6]. Driver distraction was also reported as the most important contributing factor to the collision of lane changes. Many previous investigations showed that more than 60 % of accident of lane changes involved driver distraction [7–10]. In the United States, more than 60,000 people were injured each year due to in lane-change related accidents, and lane change crashes accounted for between 5-15 % of all motor vehicle fatalities [11]. Furthermore, research revealed that most drivers involved in lane-change accidents were not attempting to perform avoidance maneuvers when the mishap occurred because they did not see, or did not recognize, the presence of a collision hazard [12–14].

For enhancing driver recognizing some potential dangerous car, some support systems [15] have been made introduced into practical vehicles for recognizing a possible collision in a near future, e.g., caution-type support such as Volvo Blind Spot

© Springer International Publishing Switzerland 2015
S. Yamamoto (Ed.): HIMI 2015, Part II, LNCS 9173, pp. 262–271, 2015.
DOI: 10.1007/978-3-319-20618-9_26

Information System (BLIS®) and Mazda Rear Vehicle Monitoring System (RVM). Meanwhile, the type of protection functions, i.e., soft protection and hard protection, are developed for avoiding a collision when a driver tends to initiate a lane change [16]. Though those systems were shown to be effective to avoiding the possible collisions, drivers might feel noisy in cases of the frequent caution message because drivers might also be surprised by sudden protections when they initiate the maneuver of changing lanes.

Therefore, in order to improve driver acceptance and avoid driver's surprise on system's performance, some issues become important to be discussed before system operating a sudden protection: inferring driver intention, detecting driver state, and adaptive caution message. Resolving such issues is aimed to improve driver's intentional checking behavior and to prevent a risk of a collision in a near future maneuver of changing lanes.

Zhou et al. [17] investigated driver's eye movements before changing lanes and proposed a method to infer driver intentions effectively. Furthermore, Zhou et al. [18] showed that driver distractions affected driver's intentional eye movements for changing lanes even when a driver had the definite intention.

This study investigates caution type message that is given to a driver in two ways: one refers to driver's characteristic of intentional eye movement for changing lanes, and the other is adaptive to driver state as well as the characteristic.

2 Driver Model of Checking Behavior & Adaptive Caution Support System

2.1 Driver Model of Checking Behaviors

The study constructs an individual driver model by using eye movement of looking at the side-view mirror. Driver's eye movement is characterized by a change of a frequency of intentional eye movements ($f_{eye.}$), i.e., the number of checking behavior of looking at the side-view mirror over a 12-s period based on the study by Zhou et al. [5].

Checking behaviors for constructing individual driver model is constructed from a time point (t_o) at which a host vehicle begins to get close to a slow forward vehicle until a time point ($t_{init.}$) at which the host vehicle's body firstly touches the center line (See Fig. 1). Time points are recorded when $f_{eye.}$ transits from 0 to 1, 1 to 2, 2 to 3 and 3 to 4. Time length from t_o to each of the time points is defined as $T_{f=1}$, $T_{f=2}$, $T_{f=3}$, and $T_{f=4}$ respectively. Note that $T_{f=2}$ and $T_{f=3}$ are used for developing caution support systems.

2.2 Adaptive Caution Support System

When a driver intends to change lanes in a near future, four-phase support message (See Fig. 1) is served for cautioning a slower lead vehicle and closed behind vehicles:

- Arousing attention information (INFO1) for a slower lead vehicle at T_{100m} when the lead vehicle is closing to the host less than 100 m.

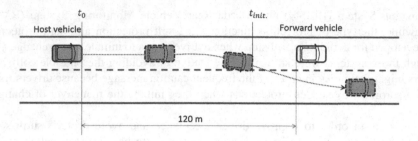

Fig. 1. Preparing phase of changing lanes

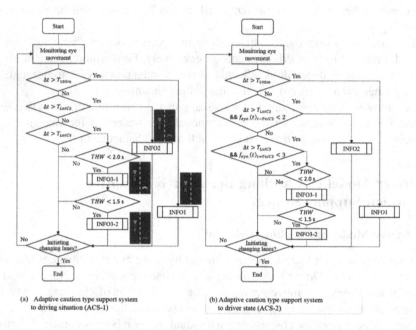

Fig. 2. Two types of adaptive caution systems

- Arousing information (INFO2) for an emergency of an approaching next-following car in cases of THW (the time headway) < 2 s after $T_{f=2}$ at which $f_{eye.}$ transited from 1 to 2 based on the individual model of checking behavior.
- Cautioning information (INFO3-1) for being approached by the next-following car in cases of $1.5s \le$ THW $< 2.0s$ after $T_{f=3}$ at which $f_{eye.}$ transited from 2 to 3.
- Cautioning information (INFO3-2) for being approached by the next-following car in cases of THW $< 1.5s$ after $T_{f=3}$.

This study proposes two ways of system supplying the four-phase caution message to a driver. One refers to driver's characteristic of intentional eye movement for changing lanes specified by driver's model (Adaptive caution system (ACS-1)) (See Fig. 1(a)). The other is adaptive to driver state as well as the characteristic (ACS-2) (See Fig. 1(b)).

Note that the four-phase support message is proposed for cautioning situation awareness, so that a collision risk would be not explained to participants when these messages
are supplied to them.

3   Method

3.1   Apparatus

A fixed-base driving simulator is used in data collection for constructing driver model
and a cognitive engineering experiment. It can simulate driving on an expressway with
two lanes (See Fig. 1). A speed governor is set up for preventing a host vehicle from
exceeding 90 km/h. One camera is equipped on the position of side-view mirror for
monitoring driver's eye movement. Note here that vehicles drive on the left-hand side
in Japan (Fig. 3).

Fig. 3. A fixed-base driving simulator

3.2   Participants

Five females and thirteen males, ranging from 19 to 23 years old (Mean = 20.4,
SD = 1.1), participate in the data collection and the experiment. Each participant holds
a valid driver's license. After receiving an explanation of the data collection and
experiment, all of them signed in information consent of participating the data collection and experiment.

3.3   Driving Scenario and Task

One trial consists of two scenarios, in each of which one lane change is possible. In
each scenario, all participants are instructed to drive at the maximum speed of 90 km/h
on the cruising lane. Each of them is allowed for changing lanes from a time point t_0 at

which the forward vehicle begins to decelerate from 90 km/h to 80 km/h (See Fig. 2). The lane change is initiated at a time point $t_{init.}$ at which the body of the host vehicle firstly touched the center line.

3.4 Secondary Task

A secondary task is conducted into the cognitive engineering experiment to simulate a distracting cognitive activity. In the secondary task, each participant is instructed to remember a route before a trial. He/she would be asked to choose the correct one from five choices during driving and to give the answer directly after finishing the trial.

3.5 Experimental Design

The experiment employs a 3 (support system: no caution support system (NCS), adaptive caution support system to driving situation (ACS-1), adaptive caution support system to and driver state (ACS-2)) × 2 (secondary task: no secondary task (NST) and a secondary task (ST)) design within participants. A two-factor analysis (ANOVA) is performed for all variables. A significant level of p = .05 is used.

3.6 Dependent Variables

This study investigates an effect of the secondary task on driver's intentional checking behavior of looking at the side-view mirror. Values of $f_{eye.}$ are collected at four phases:

- PreINFO1 from t_0 to T_{100m},
- INFO1to2 from T_{100m} to $T_{f=2}$,
- INFO2to3 from $T_{f=2}$ to $T_{f=3}$, and
- PostINFO3 after $T_{f=3}$.

In order to indicate effectiveness of the two types of support systems on driver's checking behavior. Averaged values of $f_{eye.}$ are analyzed at a phase after $T_{f=2}$, i.e. PostINFO2.

The time headways (THW) are recorded at $T_{f=1}$, $T_{f=2}$, $T_{f=3}$, $T_{f=4}$ and $t_{init.}$ for revealing effect of systems on driving behavior.

3.7 Procedure

On the first day, each participant is given an explanation of the data collection, including of apparatus and driving task. Then, he or she does approximately 5-minitue exercise for being familiar with the driving simulator. After 10-minitue rest, he or she is instructed to drive three trials and experience six lane changes for collecting his or he checking behaviors in order to construct individual driver model of checking behavior.

On the secondary day, each participant participate into the experiment. Firstly, after an explanation of driving task as same as that in the data collection, the two types of adaptive caution support system and the secondary task, the experimenter gives a training of familiarizing the two types of caution support system and the secondary task. All participants are asked to complete six blocks under 2×3 driving conditions. The 2×3 blocks' order is counterbalanced across participants. Each of which contains three trials.

4   Results

4.1   Driver Model of Checking Behavior

Figure 4 shows individual driver models for all participants and the mean value of f_{eye}. as a function of time. Mean values of $T_{f=2}$ and $T_{f=3}$ are 17.1 s $\pm$ 7.6 s and 29.1 s $\pm$ 7.4 s.

Values of $T_{f=2}$ and $T_{f=3}$ are used for the two types of adaptive caution support systems.

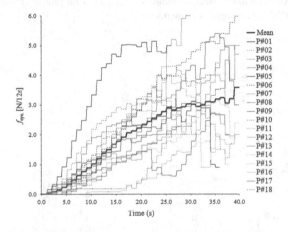

Fig. 4. Individual driver model of intentional checking behaviors

4.2   Effect of Adaptive Caution Message on Checking Behavior

Figure 5 shows averaged frequencies of intentional checking behaviors (f_{eye}.) at four phases of PreINFO1, INFO1to2, INFO2to3 and PostINFO3. An analysis of variance (ANOVA) was performed on averaged values of f_{eye}.. No interaction of driving condition $\times$ system type was shown (($F_{(2, 34)} = .99$, p $= .38$), and a main effect of driving condition was significant (($F_{(1, 17)} = 13.52$, p $< .01$). Furthermore, ANOVA was also operated at each of four phases. No interaction was shown at any phase of PreINFO1 ($F_{(2, 28)} = .98$, p $= .39$), INFO1to2 ($F_{(2, 28)} = 1.19$, p $= .32$), INFO2to3 ($F_{(2, 28)} = 1.28$, p $= .88$), and PostINFO3 ($F_{(2, 28)} = 0.38$, p $= .55$).

Figure 6 depicts averaged frequencies of intentional checking behaviors (f_{eye}.) at PostINFO2. An ANOVA showed no interaction of driving condition $\times$ system type

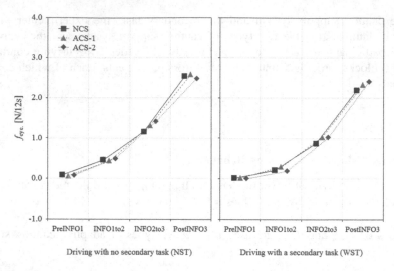

Fig. 5. Frequency of intentional checking behaviors ($f_{eye.}$) at four phases (PreINFO1, INFO1to2, INFO2to3 and PostINFO3). (Mean is shown.).

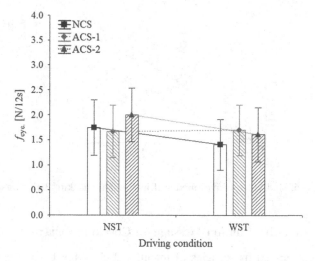

Fig. 6. Frequency of intentional checking behaviors ($f_{eye.}$) at a phase of PostINFO2. (Mean and standard errors are shown). NST = Driving with no secondary task, WST = Driving with a secondary task.

(($F_{(2, 34)}$ = 2.14, p = .13) and no effect of system type (($F_{(1, 17)}$ = .71, p = .50), but a main effect of driving condition was significant (($F_{(1, 17)}$ = 8.58, p < .01).

4.3 Effect of Adaptive Caution Message on Driving Behavior

Figure 7 depicts averaged THW at as a function of time points of $T_{f=1}$, $T_{f=2}$, $T_{f=3}$ and $T_{f=4}$. An ANOVA showed an interaction of driving condition × system type ((F (2, 114) = 5.66, p < .01). Tukey's test revealed the significant difference (p < .01) between any pair of ACS-1 v.s. NCS and ACS-2 v.s. NCS under each of driving conditions. Furthermore, the significant different between ACS-1 and ACS-2 was shown under WST driving condition (p < .05).

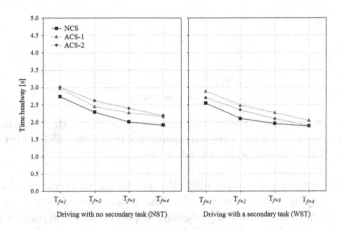

Fig. 7. The time headway (THW) as a function of time points of $T_{f=1}$, $T_{f=2}$, $T_{f=3}$ and $T_{f=4}$ under 2 driving conditions × 3 types of support systems. (Mean is shown.).

THW at the time point $t_{init.}$ at which changing lanes was initiated was shown in Fig. 8. An ANOVA showed no interaction of driving condition × system type (F (1, 17) = .15, p = .70) and no effect of driving condition (F (2, 34) = .06, p = .94). Main effect of system type was significant ((F (2, 34) = 5.72, p < .01). Tukey's test indicated that between any pair of ACS-2 v.s. NCS under each of driving conditions as shown in Fig. 8.

5   Discussion and Conclusion

Performing a cognitive activity affected driver's intentional checking behavior significantly, which agreed with Zhou et al. [18]. This study's results also indicated that a driver increased intentional checking to traffic environment through being given caution type message when he or she was distracted from driving task (See Fig. 5).

The four-phase caution message was supplied by two ways (ACS-1 and ACS-2). Results implied that both of the two ways were effective on improving driving behavior during the whole preparing phase for lane changes (See Fig. 7). More concretely, ACS-2 seemed more effective in cases of NST, ACS-1 seemed more effective in cases of WST.

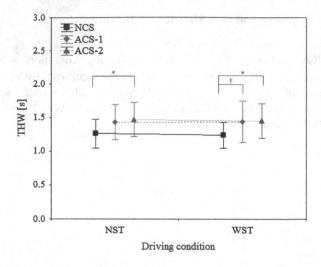

Fig. 8. Time headway (THW) at initiation of changing lanes ($t_{init.}$). (Mean and standard errors are shown.) Asterisk (*) indicates statistical significance ($p < 0.05$). NST = Driving with no secondary task, WST = Driving with a secondary task.

The caution information was not only effective during the preparing phase but also at initiating changing lanes (See Fig. 8). The result showed that a maneuver of changing lanes under ACS-2 was significantly improved with comparison to NST.

In this study, ACS-2 was adaptive to driver's state as well as driving situation. That is, a message would be given to a driver if the system did not think that he or she was distracted. Therefore, the investigation in this study implied that ACS-2 could decrease extra-message from support systems because ACS-2 was also shown effectively for improving driving safety.

Therefore, future work will try to investigate following issues:

- whether an adaptive caution information system can prevent a potential collision in near future lane changes,
- whether adaptive caution message could help driver to comprehend a sudden protection,
- what kind of information is essential at each of different phases.

References

1. Regan, M.A., Lee, J.D., Young, K.L. (eds.): Driver Distraction: Theory, Effects and Mitigation. CRC Press, Florida (2009)
2. National Highway Traffic Safety Administration: traffic safety facts: distracted driving 2010. Washington, DC: U.S. Department of Transportation (2012)
3. Eby, D.W., Kostyniuk, L.P.: Distracted-driving scenarios: a synthesis of literature. 2001 Crashworthiness Data System (CDS) Data, and Expert Feedback. Ann Arbor: University of Michigan Transportation Research Institute (2004)

4. Gugerty, L.J.: Situation awareness during driving: explicit and implicit knowledge in dynamic spatial memory. J. Exp. Psychol. Appl. **3**(1), 42–66 (1997)
5. Gugerty, L.J.: Evidence from a partial report task for forgetting in dynamic spatial memory. Hum. Factors **40**(3), 498–508 (1998)
6. McCarley, J.S., Vais, M.J., Pringle, H., Kramer, A.F., Irwin, D.E., Strayer, D.L.: Conversation disrupts change detection in complex traffic scenes. Hum. Factors **46**(3), 424–436 (2004)
7. Knipling, R.R.: IVHS technologies applied to collision avoidance: perspectives on six target crash types and countermeasures. In: Proceedings of the 1993 Annual Meeting of IVHS America: Surface Transportation: Mobility, Technology, and Society, pp. 249-259 (1993)
8. Wang, J., Knipling, R., Goodman, M.: The role of driver inattention in crashes: new stat was tics from the 1995 crashworthiness data system. In: Fortieth Annual Proceedings of the Association for the Advancement of Automotive Medicine, pp. 377-392 (1996)
9. Eby, D.W., Kostyniuk, L.P.: Driver distraction & crashes: an assessment of crash databases & review of the literature. Report UMTRI-2003-12. The University of Michigan, Transportation Research Institute (2003)
10. Lee, Y.C., Lee, J.D., Boyle, L.N., Ng Boyle, L.: Visual attention in driving: the effects of cognitive load and visual disruption. Hum. Factors **49**(4), 721–733 (2007)
11. Wang, J., Knipling, J.R.M.: Lane Change/Merge Crashes: Problem Size Assessment and Statistical Description. Technical report. Final Report, DOT HS 808075, National Highway Traffic Safety Administration (1994)
12. Chovan, J.D., Tijerina, L., Alexander, G., Hendricks, D.L.: Examination of lane change crashes and potential IVHS countermeasures. DOT HS 808 071. Washington, DC: National Highway Traffic Safety Administration (1994)
13. Eberhard, C.D., Luebkemann, K.M., Moffa, P.J., Young, S.K. Allen, R.W., Harwin, E.A., Keating, J., Mason, R.: Development of performance specifications for collision avoidance systems for lane change, merging and backing. Task 1 interim report: crash problem analysis. DOT HS 808 431. Washington, DC: National Highway Traffic Safety Administration (1994)
14. Tijerina, L.: Operational and behavioral issues in the comprehensive evaluation of lane change crash avoidance systems. J. Transp. Hum. Factors **1**(2), 159–176 (1999)
15. Itoh, M., Inagaki, T.: Design and evaluation of steering protection for avoiding collisions during a lane-change. Ergonomics **57**(3), 361–373 (2014)
16. Alonso, J.D., Vidal, E.R., Rotter, A., Mühlenberg, M.: Kostyniuk: lane-change decision aid system based on motion-driven vehicle tracking. IEEE Trans. Veh. Technol. **57**(5), 2736–2746 (2008)
17. Zhou, H., Itoh, M., Inagaki, T.: Eye movement-based inference of truck driver's intent of changing lanes. SICE J. Control, Meas. Syst. Integr. **2**(5), 291–298 (2009)
18. Zhou, H., Itoh, M., Inagaki, T.: Toward inference of driver's lane-change intent under cognitive distraction. Proc. SICE Annu. Conf. **2010**, 916–920 (2010)

Information and Interaction
for Learning and Education

Hand-Raising Robot for Promoting Active Participation in Classrooms

Saizo Aoyagi, Ryuji Kawabe, Michiya Yamamoto[✉],
and Tomio Watanabe

Kwansei Gakuin University, 2-1 Gakuen Sanda, Hyogo 669-1337, Japan
michiya.yamamoto@kwansei.ac.jp

Abstract. In Japanese school classrooms, it is important to promote hand-raising, because this motion reflects active participation in the classroom. In this study, a hand-raising robot is proposed. A prototype of the robot was developed based on typical hand-raising motions, which were measured in a separate experiment. In addition, experiments were conducted and the results suggest that fast, straight, and high hand-raising is the most favorable, and that the robot with the hand-raising is effective for promoting active participation in classrooms and enhancing student enjoyment when answering questions.

Keywords: Embodied interaction · Hand-raising · Motion analysis · Classroom

1 Introduction

In typical Japanese school classrooms, the teacher will lecture by standing at front of a room. Students listen while sitting at their desks. Hand-raising is a kind of arm motion, which is used by a student as a way to communicate intent to teachers or other students in such classrooms.

Hand-raising is very important [1, 2] because the motion reflects active participation in classrooms [3], and bodily motions are essential for interactional elements in communication [4]. Nevertheless, some students hesitate to raise their hands [5], and there are very few studies suggesting methods to help encourage students to raise their hands. In this study, a robot that imitates human hand-raising to promote active classroom participation was developed and evaluated through experiments.

2 Concept of the Hand-Raising Robot

The hand-raising robot's structure and appearance is designed to simulate a human arm and hand. It rests on students' desks, and can raise its "hand" in the same way a human does [6]. Figure 1 shows the concept behind promoting active student participation in the classroom. The robot raises its hand when students activate it.

Using the hand-raising agent makes it easy for hesitant students to indicate their intention in class. In addition, the robot provides a good example to students of the

© Springer International Publishing Switzerland 2015
S. Yamamoto (Ed.): HIMI 2015, Part II, LNCS 9173, pp. 275–284, 2015.
DOI: 10.1007/978-3-319-20618-9_27

Fig. 1. Concept for promoting active participation in the classroom

proper way to raise one's hand and for how to actively participate in classroom activities.

3   Measuring Student Hand-Raising

3.1   Purpose and Method of the Measurement

To determine the robot's motion, the authors attempted to simulate the motion of real students. Nevertheless, studies with such measurements could not be found. Therefore, the authors conducted an experiment to measure this motion.

The experimental environment was a room that imitates a classroom, with a large screen at the front. Figure 2 shows an example of the measurement scene. A mock classroom was visible to participants on the screen, along with some general-knowledge questions. Participants were asked to sit and answer questions after raising their hand. The participants were university students between 18 and 25 years old (16 males and 16 females). The experiment was recorded by a video camera (SONY HVR-A1 J) and a motion-capture system (VICON MX) at 100 Hz.

3.2   Cluster Analysis of the Hand-Raising Motion

Some patterns of the motion were found in the results of the measurement. A ward-method cluster analysis was conducted in order to classify the motions. From observing the participants raise their hands, three values were chosen as parameters, as seen in Fig. 3. The speed was estimated by moving the distance of the fingertip marker in ten frames. The angle represents the maximum angle of the elbow, and it was estimated by the position of the upper-arm marker and the lower arm marker. The height refers to the ratio of the height of the fingertip marker in each trial to the highest point for each participant.

Six clusters were extracted. A dendrogram and examples of the motion are shown in Fig. 4. Table 1 shows the parameter samples for each cluster. Cluster A is

Fig. 2. An example of measuring hand-raising

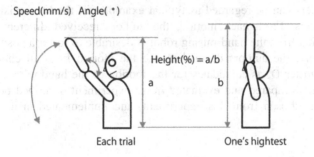

Fig. 3. Parameters for analyzing hand-raising motions

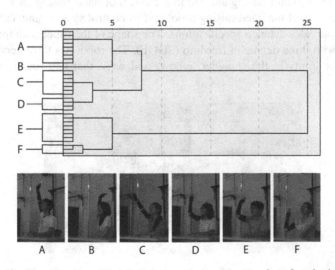

Fig. 4. Classification of hand-raising motions and examples of each cluster

Table 1. Parameter examples of each cluster

Cluster	Height (%)	Speed (mm/s)	Angle (°)
A	90.6	2796.0	174.3
B	92.3	4710.9	162.5
C	79.2	2347.3	171.1
D	75.0	1776.0	114.4
E	70.0	2234.9	110.0
F	47.3	2452.2	51.6

comparatively high, with the second-fastest hand-raising. The angle of the elbow in this cluster is straight. Cluster B is the highest and fastest hand-raising. The angle of the elbow in this cluster is also straight. Cluster C has straight elbows, and medium speed and height. Clusters E and F are flexed hand-raising. Cluster D contains diverse motions, making this cluster difficult to interpret.

These clusters can be regarded as typical examples of the hand-raising motion of Japanese students. From each motion, the authors received different impressions. Authentic motion from the hand-raising robot is desirable to foster a positive image for others. Therefore, the authors decided to use the motion from all clusters with the exception of cluster D, as candidates for the motion of the hand-raising robot. These candidates were compared and evaluated in an experiment described below. Finally, the motion was chosen from this experiment, and implemented in the hand-raising robot.

4   Development of the Hand-Raising Robot

A prototype for the hand-raising robot was developed. The robot was implemented with the concept of hand-raising and the five clusters of hand-raising motion. Figure 5 shows an overview of the hand-raising robot and its control system, and Table 2 shows the size, and provides detailed specifications. The shape of the robot is an imitation of a human arm, with three degree of freedom (3DOF). The robot has three servomotors as drive parts for joints in the shoulder, elbow, and wrist that can rotate in a vertical

Fig. 5. Overview of hand-raising robot prototype and its control system

Table 2. Size and elements of the hand-raising robot

Size	Width65 × height 122 × depth 280(mm)
Servo motor	VS-S092×J
Control board	Arduino UNO SMD R3
Power	DC 5 V
PC	panasonic CF = S10

direction. The actual size of the robot is approximately half that of an adult human arm. It was designed to be smaller in order to set it on top of a desk in a classroom. In addition, Arduino is used to control the robot's motion, and servomotors can be operated with software or with a physical button connected to the robot.

5 Impression Comparison Experiment for the Robot's Hand-Raising Motion

5.1 Purpose and Method of Comparison

An experiment was conducted to determine what type of motion is most impressive and suitable for the hand-raising robot.

Five arm motions were implemented in the robot, based on Clusters A, B, C, E, and F, extracted from the results of the measurements described above. Figure 6 shows an example of the robotic motion. The elbow angle, speed, and the positions of the fingertips were adjusted to correspond with human motion.

In addition to that, a 2DOF-version and a 1DOF-version of the motion were also implemented in the robot, if an equivalent impression is made with fewer degrees of freedom, it would be better to develop a more simplified robot. Figure 7 shows the 2DOF-version of the motion, using only the elbow and shoulder joint, and a 1DOF-version, with only the shoulder. Frontal views of the alternate versions were adjusted to coincide with the 3DOF version.

Finally, 15 motions were implemented in the robot, and these were evaluated by the participants in the experiment using a paired-comparison method. There were 10 participants (8 males and 2 females), and they were 21-25 years old. Each pair of motions with the same DOF were shown to the participants, and they were asked to choose the more impressive motion.

5.2 Comparison of Impressions with the Same DOF

The results of the paired comparison were analyzed, and summarized using the Bradly-Terry model, which represents the "preference" of each motion in a paired comparison based on the number of wins [7]. Figure 8 shows the Bradley-Terry model scores for the motions. The greater its score, the more impressive the motion was. Regardless of the DOF, a straight hand-raising motion (A, B, and C) made a better impression than flexed motions (E and F). In particular, the most impressive motion was from Cluster B

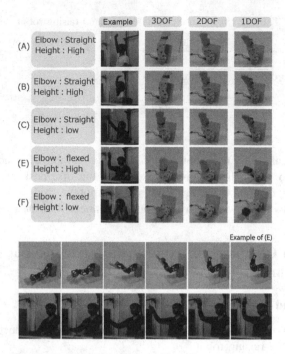

Fig. 6. Hand-raising motions from the pattern clusters

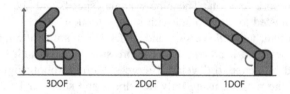

Fig. 7. Examples of motions with 3DOF, 2DOF, and 1DOF

in all DOFs. These results suggest that raising the hand high and quickly, and with a straightened elbow, is the most favorable.

In addition, the impressions of hand-raising were compared between different DOF in a separate experiment. The most impressive motion was always Cluster B, regardless of the DOF. More details for this experiment will be described in the presentation owing to limitations in space.

6   Evaluating the Hand-Raising Robot

6.1   Purpose and Method of Evaluation

An evaluation of the hand-raising robot was conducted. The purpose of the experiment was to confirm that the robot can, in fact, make it easier for students to raise their hands.

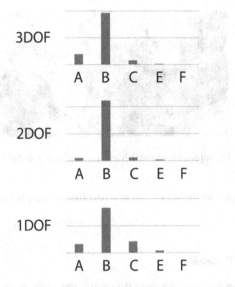

Fig. 8. Bradley-Terry model score for each motion

A situation where participants raised their own hand was compared with and one where they used the robot. 20 participants (10 males and 10 females) took part in the experiment; they were 18-23 years old.

Figure 9 shows the experimental environment and configuration. In the experiment, a participant sits at a desk upon which the robot is set. The robot was ultimately designed with the 3DOF version and motion implemented from Cluster B, because this was the most impressive motion in all DOFs. The robot was set to the right of the participant. An experimental scene is shown in Fig. 10.

The classroom scene and general-knowledge questions were displayed on the screen at the front. Participants answered questions after raising their hand, either manually or with the robot. Participants then answered a seven-scale questionnaire to evaluate hand-raising, after answering six general-knowledge questions. After answering the questions, they answered a six-item questionnaire concerning their

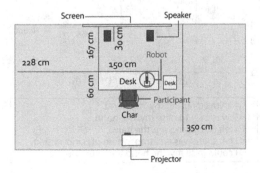

Fig. 9. Experimental environment

Fig. 10. Examples of manual hand-raising and robotic hand-raising

impressions with regard to the robot. Moreover, free descriptions of their thoughts were also gathered.

6.2 Results and Discussion

The results from the seven-scale questionnaire are shown in Fig. 11. A Wilcoxon signed-rank test was conducted in order to reveal differences between manual hand-raising and hand-raising using the robot, and these results are also shown in Fig. 11. Item 2 ("It was easy to raise my/the hand.") and Item 4 ("I felt there was an atmosphere of hand-raising.") show considerable differences at a significance level of 1 %. Item 3 ("I felt like raising my/the hand.") is even more different, at a significance level of 5 %. The hand-raising robot performed better for each item, with the exception of Item 1. These results indicate that the robot encourages hand-raising, and promotes active question answering.

The results from the six-item questionnaire about the participant's impressions of the robot are shown in Table 3. Approximately 80 % of the participants answered "yes" to Items 2, 3, and 6. This reveals that they felt positively toward the robot. In particular,

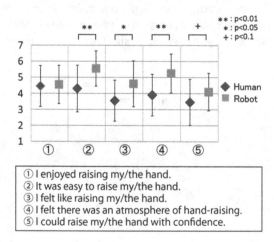

Fig. 11. Results of a seven-scale questionnaire to evaluate manual and robotic hand-raising

Table 3. Results of six-item questionnaire about impression of the robot

Item	Yes	No
1. I was happy that the robot was set on my desk	12	8
2. I enjoyed the classroom lecture	15	4
3. I enjoyed the answering questions	14	6
4. I felt that the robot was another me	6	14
5. I wanted to raise my hand alongside the robot	4	16
6. I felt affection toward the robot	16	4

Item 3 suggests that the robot enhanced their enjoyment in answering questions. This effect was supported by some of the responses provided in the free description.

However, approximately 80 % of the participants answered "no" to Items 4 and 5. Thus, the hand-raising robot was not regarded as an extension of the self. This is believed to be because the robot is a non-autonomous system that responds only to the user's operation. Consequently, it was regarded as a tool, rather than a robot.

7 Conclusion

In this study, a hand-raising robot was proposed, and a prototype of the robot was developed based on typical hand-raising motions that were measured in an experiment. According to the experiment, hand-raising that is fast, straight, and high is the most favorable, and this was used in designing the robot's motion. The consequences of this finding should not be limited to this prototype. It can be applied to any robot with arms.

In addition, an evaluation revealed that the robot is effective in promoting active participation in classrooms, while enhancing students' enjoyment in answering questions. Hand-raising was studied observationally. Therefore, this study is especially significant to the promotion of hand-raising in an academic setting.

This study revealed the effect of a single robot used by only one person. However, a classroom is a complex communicative environment, with several students and teachers. Thus, in future research, the authors plan to investigate the effectiveness of the hand-raising robot in an environment with many users.

References

1. Fuju, H.: A study on the relationships between kyosyu (hand raising), self-efficacy, outcome-expectancy and outcome-value (in japanese). Jpn. J. Educ. Psychol. **29**(1), 92–101 (1991)
2. Kawabe, R., Shigeno, Y., Yamamoto, M., et al.: Measurement of raise hands actions to support active participation in classes for learners (in Japanese). Correspondences Hum. Interface **15**, 157–160 (2013)
3. Fuse, M., Kodaira, H., Ando, F.: Positive class participation by elementary school pupils : motivation and differences in grade and gender (in Japanese). Jpn. J. Educ. Psychol. **54**(4), 534–545 (2006)

4. Watanabe, T.: Support for the creation of digital media art by embodied media (< Special Features > Art with Science, Science with Art) (in Japanese). IPSJ Magazine **48**(12), 1327–1334 (2007)
5. Hirata, M., Chibana, Y.: A study on pupils' self expression in through their active participation in an element classroom -developing a recognition scale of self expression- (in Japanese). Bulletin of Faculty of Education University of the Ryukyus **83**, 67–99 (2013)
6. Aoyagi, S., Kawabe, R., Sawa, N.: Development and evaluation of a hand raising robot for supporting active participation in class (in Japanese). In: IEICE Technical report 114(67), 237–242. (2014)
7. Hirotsu, C.: A goodness of fit test for the Bradley-Terry model by a multiple comparisons approach (in japanese). Qual. Jpn. Soc. Qual. Control **13**(2), 141–149 (1983)

Development of a Learning Support System for Class Structure Mapping Based on Viewpoint

Tatsuya Arai[1]([⊠]), Takahito Tomoto[2], and Takako Akakura[2]

[1] Graduate School of Engineering, Tokyo University of Science,
1-3 Kagurazaka, Shinjuku-Ku, Tokyo 162-8601, Japan
arai_tatsuya@ms.kagu.tus.ac.jp
[2] Faculty of Engineering, Tokyo University of Science, 1-3 Kagurazaka,
Shinjuku-Ku, Tokyo 162-8601, Japan
{tomoto,akakura}@ms.kagu.tus.ac.jp

Abstract. To be able to use knowledge, learners must arrange the relationships between information as a knowledge structure. A class structure is a typical knowledge structure. The skills required to build class structures are (1) identifying the attributes of the target instance, (2) selecting attributes of the target instance on the basis of several viewpoints, and (3) describing relationships between instances hierarchically. As a first step, learners need to understand "discrimination and inheritance" in a class structure; therefore, we have previously proposed a method for learning class structure construction. To facilitate the acquisition of skills for learners to build class structures, however, they should be supported in setting a viewpoint and selecting attributes of instances on the basis on that viewpoint. In this study, we propose a learning support system for selecting several attributes of each instance in the construction of a class structure based on several viewpoints.

Keywords: Systematization of knowledge · Learning class structure construction · Article structure

1 Introduction

To understand some fields, learners must arrange the relationships between information in the field as a knowledge structure. Let us start by looking at an example. Suppose a learner reads articles A and B in order to understand educational pedagogy. Article A describes the "analysis of learning effects" and "teaching methods," and article B describes "learning support systems" and "teaching methods." In this example, the learner needs to understand that the feature that the articles have in common is "teaching methods," whereas they have the different features of "analysis of learning effects" and "learning support systems." It is important for learners to understand aspects common to and different between several pieces of knowledge, and to organize as the knowledge structures by themselves.

© Springer International Publishing Switzerland 2015
S. Yamamoto (Ed.): HIMI 2015, Part II, LNCS 9173, pp. 285–293, 2015.
DOI: 10.1007/978-3-319-20618-9_28

A class structure is a typical knowledge structure. A class structure is composed of abstract concepts (classes) and instances (individuals). Instances are located at the bottom of the hierarchical structure. Attributes are used to characterize instances and classes. A class is generated by grouping instances that have an attribute in common. In this paper, we focus on the construction of a class structure based on viewpoint as a learning method for learners. We have developed a learning support system for the selection of attributes with instances.

2   Process of Class Structure Construction

In this section, we start by explaining the learning method for the conventional construction of class structure. Then, we describe the polysemy of class structures by viewpoint and proposed a support method for class structure construction.

2.1   Previous Research

Tomoto et al. [1, 2] and Arai et al. [3] developed a learning system for class structure construction by learners. In those studies a learning support system was developed that promotes the understanding of discrimination and inheritance relationships in a class structure. Tomoto et al. [1, 2] developed a learning support environment for concept map building with the aim of promoting an understanding of inheritance relationships, attributes of discrimination, and relationships between higher and lower classes. In addition, Arai et al. [3] developed a support system for class structure construction to help with errors in the inheritance relationships of a class structure. Results of the evaluation experiments in those studies showed that the systems promote construction of class structures by learners in consideration of the discrimination of attributes and inheritance.

These learning method for class structure construction require learners to build class structures when all attributes of the class structure are given. However, when people build a class structure, they select their own viewpoints. Therefore, the learner must be able to select attributes of an instance based a proper viewpoint.

2.2   Polysemy of Class Structures by Viewpoint

When learners build a class structure, it is changed by their viewpoint. Viewpoint provides the guidelines by which learners construct a class structure [4, 5]. They can get a better understanding of a target by re-organizing knowledge of the target based on their viewpoints [6].

Figure 1 shows a class structure of articles that is changed according to viewpoint. In the left panel, the attributes of article 1 "algorithm learning" and "programming education" are selected based on the viewpoint of "Target area of support." In the right panel, however, different attributes are selected such as "for beginners" and "for the learner." The structure is based on the viewpoint of "target users of support."

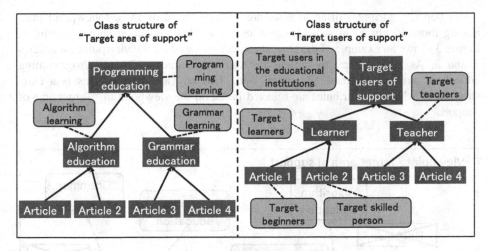

Fig. 1. Class structure based on different viewpoints for four articles

2.3   Class Structure Construction Tasks

In this section, we describe tasks required in building a class structure based on viewpoint and the errors that can occur when building the structure. Class structure construction can be divided in the following three steps:

(1) Identify the attributes of the target instance.
(2) Select attributes of the target instance on the basis of several viewpoints.
(3) Describe relationships between instances hierarchically.

Step (1) entails identifying multiple attributes of the target instances. In Fig. 2, the attributes of an article (article 1) are given as an example. This is the model displayed in step (1). The structure is displayed such that the learner does not consider the attributes required in the class structure construction but rather considers only whether article 1 has certain attributes.

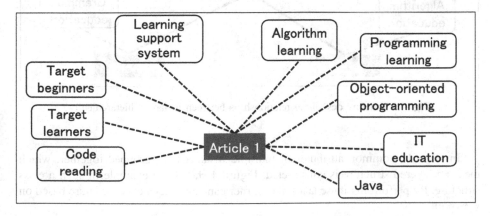

Fig. 2. Identifying the attributes of article 1

In step (2), attributes of an instance are selected based on the set viewpoint from among those identified in step (1), such as the attribute selection shown in Fig. 1. Figure 3 shows an example of the attribute selection based on the viewpoint for articles 1 and 3. As shown here, for article 1 "Algorithm education" and "Programming education" are selected and "Beginner" and "Learner" are deleted. This is a class structure in which the attributes are selected based on the viewpoint of "Target area of support."

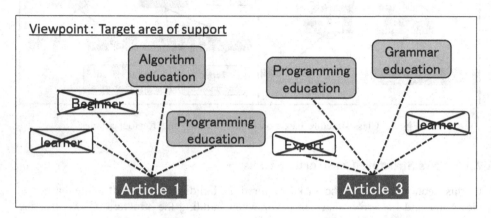

Fig. 3. Selection of attributes of two articles based on the viewpoint of "Target area of support"

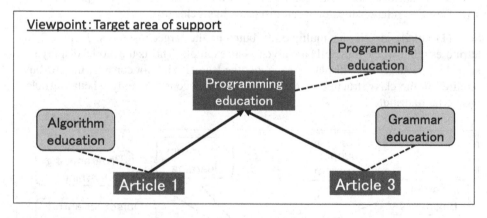

Fig. 4. Structure describing relationships between instances hierarchically

In step (3), common attributes of multiple instances are grouped together, which means a layered structure is constructed. Figure 4 shows the example of such a class structure. By performing these tasks, the learner can construct a class structure based on viewpoint.

2.4   Error by Learners

In this section, we describe the errors that occur when learners perform step (2) in Sect. 2.3. Our ultimate aim is to support all three steps, (1) to (3), but in this basic study toward this aim, we focus on the step (2). In this step, selection of too few attributes and selection of too many attributes are assumed as errors by learners. Figure 5 shows an example of the error of selecting too many attributes. Here we see the selection of attributes of article 1 based on the viewpoint of "Target area of support." The left panel shows the correct selection of attributes; the right panel shows the section of too many. In particular, the learner has incorrectly selected an attribute unrelated to the "Target area of support." If the attribute "Algorithm education" were left out, then the error would be selection of too few attributes. We believe that these errors in particular should be noted in the learning of class structure construction based on viewpoint. Accordingly, our support system helps students become aware of these errors.

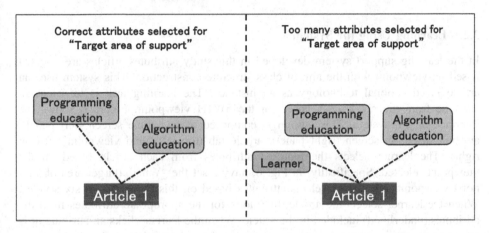

Fig. 5. Example of expected learner of error

3   Proposed Learning Method and Support System

Here, we propose support for the selection of attributes based on the viewpoint adopted in the construction of a class structure. As noted in Sect. 2.3, it is necessary to set a viewpoint when the learner builds a class structure. Setting an incorrect viewpoint will subsequently prevent correct selection of attributes. So, the system (teaching side) should control how the viewpoint is set. Therefore, in this study, we have developed a learning support system for selecting attributes based on a viewpoint that is formulated.

3.1   Formulate the Viewpoint

As a method for organizing articles, we apply the article organization method using the 5W1H (Who, What, When, Where, Why, How) format by Aoki et al. [7]. A research question by arranging characteristics of several articles based on viewpoint of the 5W1H. In this study, we used the three viewpoints "What," "Why," and "How." (Table 1).

Table 1. Viewpoint of 5W1H in science and technology articles

	Meaning
Who	Person to be assited
What	Target area of support
When	Support limiting
Where	Place where support is given
Why	Why support is needed
How	Means of providing support

3.2   Learning Using the System

In the learning support system developed in this study attributes articles are selected based on viewpoint with the aim of class structure construction. This system uses an article in educational technology as an instance. The learning task is to select an attribute from the six articles based on the 5W1H viewpoint. Figure 6 shows the interface of the system. This system is composed of an article screen (left panel), attribute selection screen (right panel), article tab (top left), and viewpoint tab (top right). The learner selects the required attributes from each article based on the viewpoint selected. Specifically, in Fig. 6, having set the "What" (target area of support) viewpoint, the learner selects attributes based on this viewpoint in six articles. When the learner selects the article, they look for the appropriate attributes from the attributes (underlined) included in the article. When the learner clicks an attribute, it is added to the attribute selection screen shown in the right portion of Fig. 6.

3.3   Feedback

Next, we describe the feedback method of the system. In Feedback is given in response to incorrect selection or omission of attributes. The reason for this is to remind learners of the errors of selecting too many or too few attributes. An example of the feedback is shown in Fig. 7, which presents the learner's answer and the correct answer for articles 1 and 2 under the "What" viewpoint. The learner's answer is lacking the attribute "mechanics." When the learner clicks the answer button, the system displays the following message as the first round of feedback: "The viewpoint of the missing attribute is *What*" Having received this feedback, the learner focuses on the "What" viewpoint and compares the selected attributes with the remaining attributes in the article. Thus, the learner is made aware of his or her error and will try to select another attribute. When the learner has submitted an incorrect modification, the system displays the following message as the second round of feedback: "The missing attribute from the *What* viewpoint is in article 2." From this feedback, the learner's focused is directed to

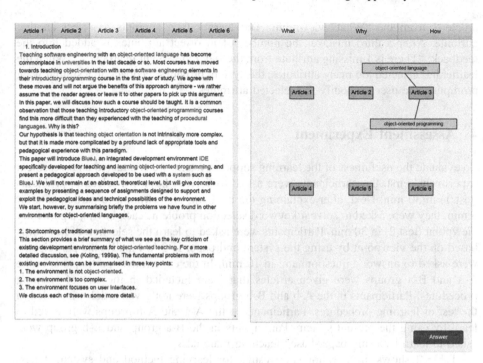

Fig. 6. Interface of the system

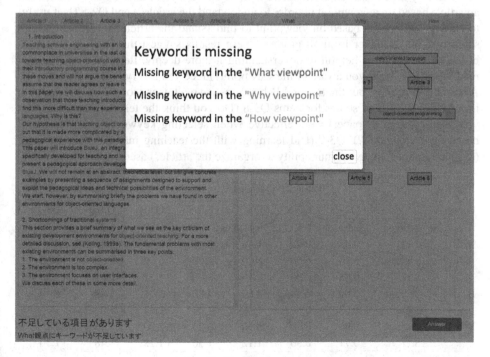

Fig. 7. Feedback screen

article 2 from the "What" viewpoint. The learner then attempts to select another attribute. After a third mistake, the number of incorrect attributes is added into the feedback: "There is 1 missing attribute from the *What* viewpoint in article 2." When the learner has selected too many attributes, the system provides feedback in a similar way, prompting the user to modify the selected attributes.

4 Assessment Experiment

To evaluate the usefulness of the learning support system, we conducted an assessment experiment. First, the participants were asked to solve 4 keyword selection problems (test 1) in 30 min. Next, after explaining the meaning of viewpoint to participants for 5 min, they were asked to solve 4 keyword selection problems each having a particular viewpoint (test 2) in 30 min. Participants were asked to learn the selection of keywords based on the viewpoint by using the system and paper in 3 h. Finally, the participants were asked to answer a questionnaire in 10 min. In the experiment, participants in the A-a and B-a groups were given articles that were included in the test of learning procedures. Participants in the A-b and B-b groups were not given articles included in the test of learning procedures. Participants in the A-a and A-b groups were asked to learn by using the present system. Participants in the B-a group and B-b group were asked to learn by using paper-based teaching materials.

Table 2 shows the questionnaire results for learning method and system. Questionnaire items were scored on a seven-point scale (1 = "I don't think so at all", 7 = "I think so very much"). The questionnaire items Q2-7 (Do you think it's effective to read an article based on a viewpoint in order to understand the article?) and Q2-8 (Is it useful to classify a keyword based on viewpoint to understand the article?)" received a high score of 6.00 or higher from all groups. These results suggest that reading an article based on viewpoint is helpful in understanding it more deeply. Item Q3-3 (When you read the article, were you aware of the viewpoint?) received a very high score from the A-a and A-b groups, but the B-a and B-b groups gave a lower score. The A-a and A-b groups also gave high scores for items Q3-8 (Do you think the teaching materials that you used (system or paper) were effective when selecting keywords from an article based on a viewpoint?), Q3-9 (Did learning with the teaching material that you used (system or paper) improve your ability to organize the article, based on the viewpoint?),

Table 2. Questionnaire results

Group		Q2-7	Q2-8	Q3-3	Q3-8	Q3-9	Q3-10	Q3-11
A-a	average	6.33	6.33	6.17	6.33	6.50	6.17	5.83
	S.D	0.47	0.47	1.46	0.47	0.50	0.69	0.90
A-b	average	6.25	6.50	6.00	7.00	6.00	6.25	6.00
	S.D	0.83	0.50	0.71	0.00	1.22	0.83	1.00
B-a	average	6.00	6.40	4.60	4.80	5.00	5.20	4.40
	S.D	0.63	0.80	1.36	1.47	1.67	1.00	1.36
B-b	average	6.00	6.50	5.50	5.25	5.00	5.25	4.25
	S.D	0.71	0.50	1.12	1.30	1.22	1.48	1.30

Q3-10 (Do you think the teaching materials that you used (system or paper) were effective for understanding the article?), and Q3-11 (Do you think that you got a better understanding of the target area by learning with the teaching material that you used (system or paper)?). These results suggest that the system can support learners in reading articles based on viewpoint and that it possibly helps learners understand articles more deeply.

5 Conclusions and Future Work

In this study, we have proposed a learning method and system for selecting the attributes based on viewpoint so that learners can construct a class structure. In the developed system the learner selects attributes of articles based on three viewpoints. In the future, the learning support system should be evaluated in more detail. Also, we plan to develop a learning support system for building class structures that integrates the attribute selection learning and hierarchical learning.

Acknowledgments. This research was supported by the Research Institute of Science and Technology for Society (RISTEX) and KAKENHI Grant Number 25750089.

References

1. Tomoto, T., Imai, I., Horiguchi, T., Hirashima, T.: A support environment for learning of class structure by concept mapping using error-visualization. J. Inf. Sys. Educ. **30**(1), 42–53 (2013)
2. Tomoto, T., Imai, I., Horiguchi, T., Hirashima, T.: error-based simulation for learning of meaning of class structure by concept mapping. In: Proceedings of ICCE2012 (11 poster acceptance in 23 submissions; acceptance rate 48%), Singapore (2012)
3. Arai, T., Tomoto, T., Akakura, T.: Development of error-visualization system for learning of inheritance in class structure. IEICE Trans. Inf. Syst. (Japanese Edition) **98**(1), 42–53 (2013)
4. Kiyotaka Miyazaki, Naoki Ueno.: Collection 3 Metaphor and Understanding. University of Tokyo Press, Tokyo(2007)
5. Yamanashi, M.: Collection 5 Metaphor and Understanding. University of Tokyo Press, Tokyo (2007)
6. Suzuki, H.: Similar and thinking. Kyouritsushuppan, Tokyo (1998)
7. Aoki, M., Hayashi, Y., Kojiri, T., Watanabe, Ts: Paper Classification for Supporting Creative Research. IEICE Technical report, **111**(85), 15-20 (2011)

A Ubiquitous Lecture Archive Learning Platform with Note-Centered Approach

Shinobu Hasegawa[1]([⊠]) and Jiangning Dai[2]

[1] Center for Graduate Education Initiative, Japan Advanced Institute
of Science and Technology, 1-1, Asahidai, Nomi, Ishikawa 923-1292, Japan
hasegawa@jaist.ac.jp
[2] School of Information Science, Japan Advanced Institute
of Science and Technology, 1-1, Asahidai, Nomi, Ishikawa 923-1292, Japan
daijiangning@jaist.ac.jp

Abstract. The main topic of this paper is to develop a cloud-based ubiquitous video on demand learning (u-VOD learning) platform for the lecture archives. The key ideas of the platform are note-centered and responsive function approaches with universal access. Learning style in only watching the archives tends to be passive. The note-centered approach enables the learners to improve such passive learning by means of note taking corresponding to a timeline of the archives. In addition, there are diverse variables in size, shape, performance, and input function for the ubiquitous/smart devices. The responsive function supports ubiquitous device dependency by HTML 5. The universal access would help operation and text input by application of existing speech recognition technique. Based on a proposed u-VOD learning model, we have developed the prototype platform which follows 3-tier architecture to implement it in a scalable way. We have also conducted a small case study to evaluate effectiveness of the platform. The results did not show significant effect compared with "without-note" condition. But, most of the subjects seemed to accept the proposed functions as the part of the u-VOD learning platform.

Keywords: U-VOD learning · Lecture archive · Note-centered approach · Responsive function · Universal access

1 Introduction

In recent years, advancements of wireless network and appearance of innovative smart devices realize a ubiquitous society where people can communicate with anybody, anytime, and anywhere [3]. On the other hand, diverse educational institutes provide open learning resources as open courseware (OCW) and/or massive open online courses (MOOCs). We are also delivering lecture archives, which record more than 1,000 face-to-face lectures per year in the form of video-on-demand (VOD) from April, 2006 in order to provide a supplemental learning environment in School of Information Science, JAIST [2]. Every learner in the world might be able to access such resources by means of spread of the ubiquitous society. In addition, universal access is required in the field of education to accept international students, disability students, and adult

S. Yamamoto (Ed.): HIMI 2015, Part II, LNCS 9173, pp. 294–303, 2015.
DOI: 10.1007/978-3-319-20618-9_29

students. Under these surroundings, ubiquitous learning (u-learning), which realizes a learning environment suited to each learner's situation at anytime and anywhere, has attracted attention from a number of researchers [6]. However, there are a couple of issues to use traditional e-learning contents, especially lecture archives, in u-learning as follows: (1) learning style in only watching the archives tends to be passive, (2) there are diverse variables such as size, shape, performance, and input function for the ubiquitous devices, and (3) universal access is not always supported.

The challenge of this research is to develop a cloud-based ubiquitous VOD learning (u-VOD learning) platform. The key ideas of the platform are note-centered and responsive function approaches with universal access. (i) The note-centered approach enables the learners to learn more actively by means of a note-taking function in which they not only take a note to the timeline of the archive but also ask a question and discuss with others. (ii) The responsive function approach provides suitable interfaces which respond to diverse constraint of the ubiquitous devices, and combines learning experience caused by the multiple devices. (iii) The universal access function supports operation and text input by application of existing speech recognition technique.

This paper first describes a process model of u-VOD learning for the lecture archives and then proposes a prototype u-VOD learning platform with 3-tier architecture to implement it in a scalable way. We have also conducted a small case study to evaluate effectiveness of the platform, especially for the note-centered approach. Unfortunately, the results did not show significant difference compared with "without-note" condition. But, most of the subjects seemed to accept the proposed functions as the part of the u-VOD learning platform.

2 Learning Process Model in U-VOD Learning

The advantages of u-VOD learning are that the learners would face few restrictions for time and space and learn at their own paces. In addition, Yunus et al. showed VOD has similar educational effect to traditional face-to-face lecture [8]. On the other hand, learning style with VOD is often passive and then difficult to reconstruct learning contents due to absence of interactivity [9]. In recent years, furthermore, the technique of responsive design becomes widely accepted to deal with diverse devices or screen sizes, which optimizes the design and layout of a Web application. But, it does not provide suitable functions for each device, but just controls showing or hiding the functions [1].

In order to resolve these issues for u-VOD learning, we first propose a u-VOD Learning process model which utilizes open lecture archives on the Web as learning materials, and enables the learners to share their learning outcomes with a learning community through the note-taking function as shown in Fig. 1. The model includes the following four phases repeatedly: watching, annotation, reflection, and collaboration.

Watching: The learners would watch an archive in diverse types of the ubiquitous device each of which has constraints such as size, shape, performance, and input function.
Annotation: They could take a note relevant to the contents of the archive as closed memos or opened comments.

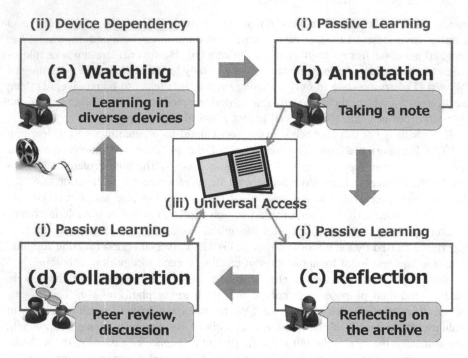

Fig. 1. Learning process model in U-VOD learning

Reflection: They could reflect on their learning process based on the note and the archive in order to memorize the contents.

Collaboration: They might communicate with others to share the knowledge learnt by the previous process. There are diverse effectiveness of collaboration such as learning by teaching, learning by observation, and learning by discussion.

This model regards u-VOD learning as the learning activity that the learners take, refer, and reconstruct the note depending on the learning phases and devices. We call it the note-centered approach. By designing the learning platform based on the model, they can expect to learn actively and self-directly with the interaction among the contents, the learning community, and themselves. It also enables them to centralize all learning experience conducted by different learning phases and devices into the note.

3   Prototype Development

3.1   System Architecture

In developing the prototype platform, we have adopted 3-tier architecture as shown in Fig. 2. A user interface tier provides an interactive web user interface by using the video element of HTML5, JavaScript, and CSS to fit the screen size limitation and input functions of the target device on the client side. A business logic tier offers server side functions such as user management, archive play control, and diverse types of note

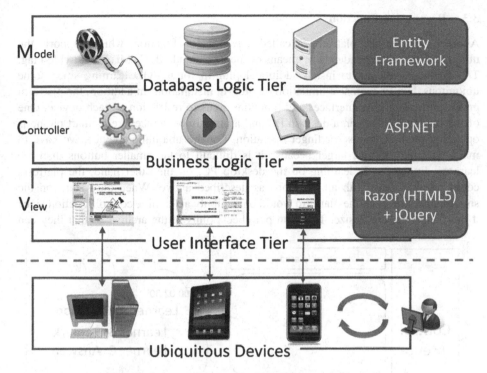

Fig. 2. 3-tier architecture for U-VOD learning platform

representation. A database logic tier uses Microsoft Windows server to host SQL server, the archive files and related tools. It enables us to implement a scalable cloud platform with secure and high performance. As a development environment, we have used ASP.NET MVC 3 which enables us to develop web applications in a similar way to develop Windows applications [4].

3.2 Archive Note Function

In order to improve passive style in u-VOD learning, we have developed a note function called "Archive Note". This function facilitates learning activity in the annotation phase by taking opened comments and closed memos regarding to the timeline of the archive. It then enables the learners to access a specific time of the archive easily in the reflection phase and to add text information to the archive as searchable keywords. If a learning community exists, moreover, they can share the note as a VOD forum like [5]. It is expected to refine their learning outcomes by collaboration. Figure 3 shows an example for usage of the function. If learner A posts a comment on 00:02:30 in an archive, other learners can start discussion by providing hints and making peer review.

3.3   Responsive Function

Another point of the platform is called a responsive function, which supports the ubiquitous device dependency by means of the new standard, HTML 5 with video tag. The learners need not to install additional plug-in for u-VOD learning since some ubiquitous devices impose a limitation on plug-in installation. In addition, the platform provides suitable user interfaces and functions so as to restriction of each device. One of the difference between a desktop PC and a ubiquitous device like a smart phone is operation method, mouse or finger operation. For the ubiquitous device, we have to make clickable buttons larger because it is difficult to tap smaller buttons than the learners' fingertips. In learning on the desktop PC, on the other hand, the platform could provide them with all functions as described above. When they learn on the smartphone, however, the platform would only supply an archive control function since it has a smaller screen size. They can put checkpoints to the archive so that they can

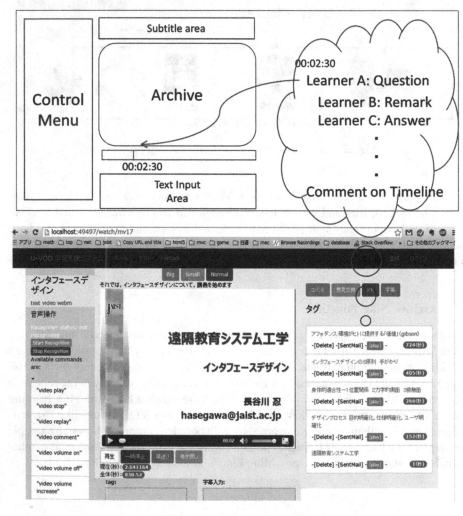

Fig. 3. Interface of archive note

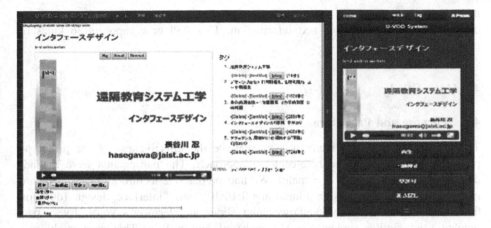

Fig. 4. Interface for iPad and iPhone with responsive function

play back the archive afterward. These learning activities are recorded on the server. Therefore, they can continue their learning from previous point, even with the different device use. The bottom of Fig. 3 is an example interface for the desktop PC and Fig. 4 shows example interfaces for iPad (left side) and iPhone (right side).

3.4 Universal Access Function

In order to provide universal access to the platform, we have also applied existing Web Speech API [7] to support the operation and text input of the application. Once the learners press a "start recognition" button and speak a type of operation, the function operates the system based on the results of the speech recognition. As shown in Fig. 5,

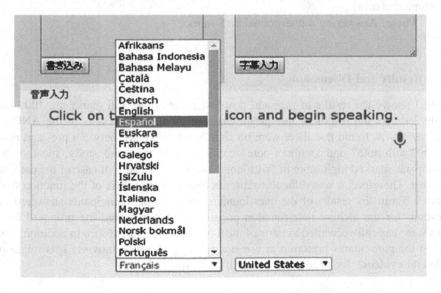

Fig. 5. Interface for universal access function

this function also provides them with the text input because some of the ubiquitous devices are difficult to input text information. This API now supports 36 kinds of language.

4 Case Study

4.1 Purpose and Procedure

The purpose of this case study was to evaluate the effectiveness of the prototype platform, especially for the note-centered approach. The participants were 8 graduate students (4 = female, 4 = male). We had prepared 2 lecture archives in regard to "system evaluation design (duration 00:16:10) and "interface design (duration 00:13:58), which had recorded PowerPoint slides and lecturer's voice. Every participant used similar screen size (11 inch) of laptop PCs. This case study was conducted as within-participants design. In the experimental condition (with-note condition), they were requested to learn the archive using the prototype platform. In the control condition (without-note condition), on the other hand, they used the prototype platform without the note-taking function. The procedure of the case study as follows:

1. Taking a pre-test regarding to the archive topic (5 min).
2. Learning the archive by using prototype platform (20 min).

   - With-note: They could post comments while watching the archive and read others comments with the archive note function.
   - Without-note: They could not use the archive note function.

3. Taking a post-test regarding to the archive topic (5 min).
4. 1st Phase: Taking a rest (15 min) and starting 2nd phase (with considering counterbalance).
   2nd Phase: Answering a questionnaire (5 min).

4.2 Results and Discussions

Table 1 shows the results of pre- and post-test scores (both full marks are 100), and Table 2 shows the results of the questionnaire. Based on the results of the ANOVA analysis, it was found that there were no significant difference between pre- and post-test in "with-note" and "without-note" conditions. In this case study, most of the participants marked high score in "with-note" condition because of ease of the pre- and post-test. Therefore, it was difficult to discuss about effectiveness of the function from Table 1. From the results of the questionnaire, most of the participants answered the questions for the archive note function positively. This indicated the proposed functions were basically accepted as parts of the u-VOD learning platform. In addition, over half of the participants preferred to use smartphones to watch movies. This might be collateral evidence for need of this kind of platform.

Table 1. Results for Pre- and Post-tests

Participants	With-note		Without-note	
	Pre-test	Post-test	Pre-test	Post-test
A	100	80	100	100
B	95	70	80	80
C	100	100	60	80
D	70	100	80	60
E	100	100	80	60
F	85	100	70	20
G	85	100	50	50
H	95	100	70	20
Mean	91.25	93.75	73.75	61.25
SD	112.5	141.1	226.8	869.6
F	0.1489		1.923	
Significance	n.s.		n.s.	

Table 2. Results of questionaire

Q1. Frequency of use for watching movie	
PC is high: 2	PC is slightly high: 0
Smartphone is slightly high: 1	Smartphone is high: 5
Q2. Effectiveness of others comments	
Agree: 2	Slightly agree: 6
Slightly disagree: 0	Disagree: 0
Q3. Effectiveness of your own comments	
Agree: 4	Slightly agree: 4
Slightly disagree: 0	Disagree: 0
Q4. Usefulness of proposed "archive note" function	
Others comments were useful: 2	Own comments were useful: 2
Both were useful: 4	Both were not useful: 0
Q5. Usefulness of voice operation	
Agree: 3	Slightly agree: 5
Slightly disagree: 0	Disagree: 0

5   Conclusion

This paper has proposed the u-VOD learning platform where the learners are able to not only take a note regarding to the timeline of the lecture archive, but also to use suitable interface demanding on constraint of each ubiquitous device. Moreover, the proposed platform supports universal access with voice operation and input. We believe this research might open the possibility for improving new type of u-VOD learning such as flipped learning.

We have also conducted the small case study to evaluate effectiveness of the platform, especially for the note-centered approach. Unfortunately, the results did not show significant effect compared with "without-note" condition. But, most of the subjects seemed to accept the proposed functions as the u-VOD learning platform.

In the near future, we will first develop a subtitle function as a part of the universal access function by using existing speech recognition technique. In addition, it would be necessary to add some functions such as mathematical and visual expression for note taking. After finishing these developments, a large volume of evaluation will be conducted to make sure firstly whether the learning effectiveness can be improved through learning with note-centered approach, and secondly whether the responsive functions are useful in diverse types of ubiquitous devices.

Acknowledgement. This work is supported in part by Grant-in-Aid for Scientific Research (B) (No. 26282047), from the Ministry of Education, Science, and Culture of Japan.

References

1. Ghiani, G., Manca, M., Paternò, F., Porta, C.: Beyond responsive design: context-dependent multimodal augmentation of web applications. In: Awan, I., Younas, M., Franch, X., Quer, C. (eds.) MobiWIS 2014. LNCS, vol. 8640, pp. 71–85. Springer, Heidelberg (2014)
2. Hasegawa, S., Tajima, Y., Matou, M., Futatsudera, M., Ando, T.: Case studies for self-directed learning environment using lecture archives. In: Proceedings of the Sixth IASTED International Conference on Web-based Education (WBE 2007), pp. 299–304 (2007)
3. Lyytinen, K., Yoo, Y.: Issues and challenges in ubiquitous computing. Commun. ACM **45**(12), 63–65 (2002)
4. Microsoft: Learn About ASP.NET MVC. http://www.asp.net/mvc (Accessed 19 February 2015)
5. Nakanishi, T., Shimada, S., Kojima, A., Fukuhara, Y.: Lecture video and scene-related knowledge sharing common platform design and its prototyping - a practical example of learner-centric open video content service. In: Proceedings of the 18th International Conference on Computers in Education, pp. 270–274 (2010)
6. Ogata, H., Yano, Y.: Context-aware support for computer-supported ubiquitous learning. In: Proceedings of The 2nd IEEE International Workshop on Wireless and Mobile Technologies in Education, pp. 27–34 (2004)
7. W3C: Web Speech API Specification. https://dvcs.w3.org/hg/speech-api/raw-file/tip/speechapi.html (Accessed at 19 February 2015)

8. Yunus, A.S.M., Kasa, Z., Asmuni, A., Samah, B.A., Napis, S., Yusoff, M.Z.M., Khanafie, M.R., Wahab, H.A.: Use of webcasting technology in teaching higher education. Int. Educ. J. **7**(7), 916–923 (2006)
9. Zhang, D., Zhou, L., Briggs, R.O., Nunamaker Jr., J.F.: Instructional video in e-learning: Assessing the impact of interactive video on learning effectiveness. Inf. Manag. **43**(1), 15–27 (2006)

Analysis of the Relationship Between Metacognitive Ability and Learning Activity with Kit-Build Concept Map

Yusuke Hayashi[✉] and Tsukasa Hirashima

The Department of Information, Hiroshima University, Hiroshima, Japan
hayashi@lel.hiroshima-u.ac.jp

Abstract. Metacognitive ability is one of important ability in learning. If learners can monitor their own cognition and know strategies to control it, they can make their thinking better and get better performance. Concept mapping gathers attention as a tool to facilitate metacognition. This study investigates the relationship between metacognitive ability and learning activity with Kit-build concept map (KB map). In KB map method concept maps cannot be built freely. A teacher forms what he/she wants to teach as a concept map. This is called goal map. And then, this is decomposed into separated nodes and likes. These parts are provides to learners and they make a concept map with the parts to represent their understanding. Like this, the method doesn't allow freedom to build concept maps. Instead, a teacher can grade maps of learners with consistency as the degree of the same parts as the gal map. The degree can be an important indicator of understanding of learners. Metacognitive ability can be decomposed into three sub abilities: metacognitive monitoring, control and knowledge. This study investigates correlation between these sub abilities and score of map. The correlation presents, in learning with KB map, which sub ability affect map score, that is, understanding of learner. The result shows there is the correlation between metacognitive control and map scores. From this result, it can be considered that Kb map helps learners to monitoring their cognition.

1 Introduction

Metacognition has received considerable attention in the research area of learning. Flavell 3 and Brown 2 have popularized the concept in the area of and cognitive psychology and educational psychology. Although the definition of it is not necessarily fixed in these fields metacognition is defined in terms of metacognitive knowledge and metacognitive skills. Many studies show the relation between metacognition and learning.

Concept maps are described as a metacognitive tool 4. Concept maps are graphic representations of a semantic structure of propositions based on the relationships among two or more concepts. There are many reports on the effects of concept maps on learners. As a method of concept map building there is Kit-build concept map 510. Although general concept map building allows learners to make nodes and links freely, this method provides learners with nodes and links (kit). Learners only use the kit to build concept map.

S. Yamamoto (Ed.): HIMI 2015, Part II, LNCS 9173, pp. 304–312, 2015.
DOI: 10.1007/978-3-319-20618-9_30

This study investigates the relation between meta-cognition and KB map. In the next section, the framework and the characteristic of KB map. Section 3 explains the experiments conducted in this study. Section 4 show the results of the experiments and give consideration to the result. Finally Sect. 5 concludes this paper.

2   Kit-Build Concept Map

Kit-build concept map is based on that the task to make concept maps is divided into two sub-tasks: segmentation task and structuring task 4. In the segmentation task parts of a concept map are extracted from learning resources. In the structuring task the parts are integrated into a concept map. One of the characteristics of KB map is that learners are given a set of parts for a concept map and then re-build the concept map from the parts. In this process, segmentation task is replaced with recognition task of the given parts. Parts are made from a concept map prepared by teacher. Such a concept map is called *goal map*. Parts are made by decomposing a goal map.

Figure 1 illustrates an example of a goal map. Teachers make goal maps as a representation of the structure of what they want learners to learn. Figure 2 illustrates an example of parts. It is call as *kit*. Although, in general concept map building, learners are required to extract parts from learning resources, in KB map building learners just recognize the parts.

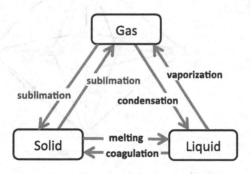

Fig. 1. An example of goal map

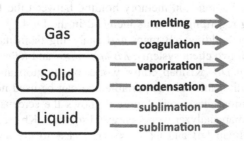

Fig. 2. An example of kit

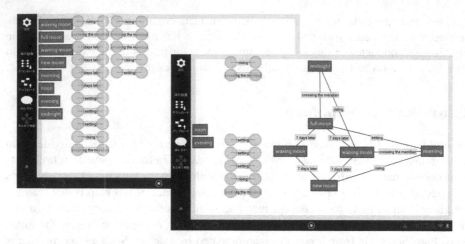

Fig. 3. The screenshot of KBeditor on tablet computers

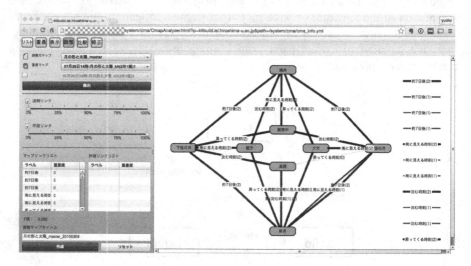

Fig. 4. A screenshot of KBanalyzer

In KB map building sub-task is different from general concept map building. However, there is no difference in memory holding between the KBmap and general concept map building regarding contents included in the kit 4.

KBmap system for building KB maps and analyzing them has developed 9. The system is composed of two client systems: *KBmap editor* and *KBmap analyzer*, and the server system *KBmap DB*. KBmap editor works on desktop and tablet computers. Especially, KBmap editor for tablet is portable and can be used not only in computer rooms but also in normal classroom. Figure 3 shows the screenshot of KBeditor on tablet computers. KBmap analyzer works on web browsers. Kb maps made by students are collected into KBmap DB and teachers can access to the data to analyze it on. Figure 4 shows a screenshot of KBanalyzer.

KBmap system is actually used in the classroom in an elementary school and junior high school. The practical uses show the advantages of KB maps on learning effect 9, formative evaluation for improvement of lesson 11 and collaborative learning support 6.

3 Experiments

This study conducts two experiments to investigate the relationship between kit-build concept maps and meta-cognition. In each experiment subjects are measured their metacognitive ability with a metacognition scale and make a concept map with kit-build approach.

3.1 Measurement of Meta-cognition

This study uses the adults' metacognition scale constructed by Abe and Ida. This is constructed based on Metacognitive Awareness Inventory that is composed as measure Metacognition 8. Abe and Ida translated this inventory into Japanese and modified it for adults 1. This modified inventory includes 28 items to measure meta-cognitive knowledge, monitoring and control. Eight items are related to meta-cognitive knowledge, nine items are related to meta-cognitive monitoring and eleven items are related to meta-cognitive control.

3.2 Experiment 1

This experiment uses kit-build concept maps about animals and plants. Figures 5 and 6 show these kit-build concept maps. Subjects are 23 university students and construct these kit-build concept maps with their knowledge.

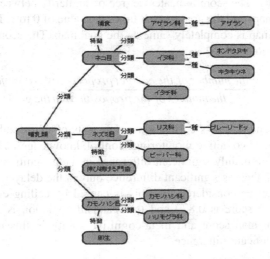

Fig. 5. Goal map used in experiment 1 (animals)

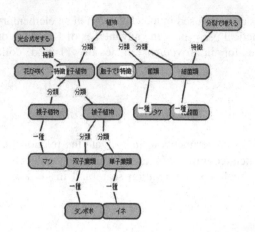

Fig. 6. Goal map used in experiment 1 (plants)

3.3 Experiment 2

This experiment uses a kit-build concept map about climate. Figure 7 shows the kit-build concept map. Subjects are 25 graduate school students. The characteristic of this experiment is that subjects build the concept map while reading a document about the topic. Firstly the subjects have practice to build concept map with another kit-build concept map within five minutes and then they build a concept map within 40 min. In addition to that, they build the same kit-build concept map one week later.

4 Results and Discussion

Figures 8, 9, 10 and 11 illustrate correlation coefficients between maps score and metacognitive ability. The score indicates degree of similarity between a map made by a subject (subject map) and the goal map. It takes the value of 0 to 1. If the score is 1, it means the subject map is completely same as the goal map. The score is calculated by the following equation:

$$mapscore = \frac{the\ number\ of\ the\ correct\ propositions\ in\ a\ subject\ map}{the\ number\ of\ the\ propositions\ in\ the\ goal\ map}$$

Tables 1, 2, 3 and 4 shows correlation coefficients of maps and factors of meta-cognitive ability: meta-cognitive monitoring, control, knowledge and total. As shown in the table, there are mainly significant difference in metacognitive control.

In Experiment 2 there is significant difference only in the delayed kit-build concept map building. It can be considered that this is caused by ceiling effect. In this map building the average score is 0.879 and the standard deviation is 0.137. If there is correlation between map score and meta-cognitive ability in this map, it would be difficult to find significant difference.

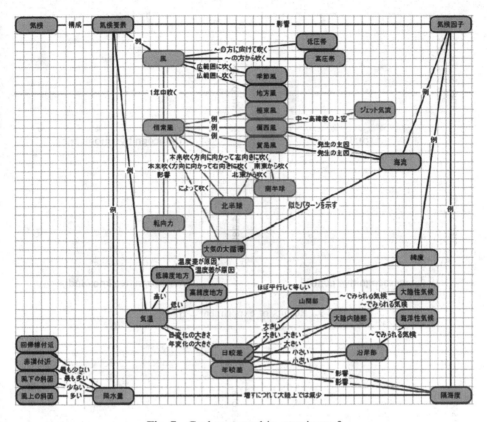

Fig. 7. Goal map used in experiment 3

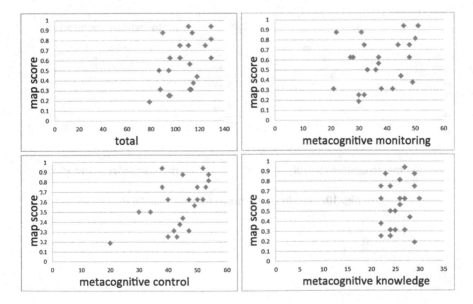

Fig. 8. Results of experiment 1(animals)

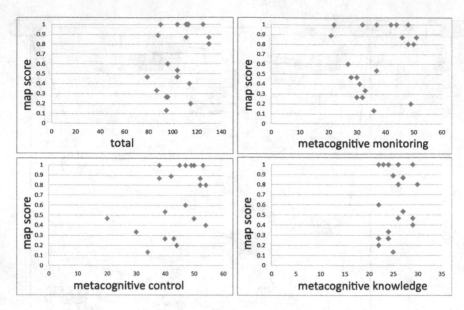

Fig. 9. Results of experiment 1 (plants)

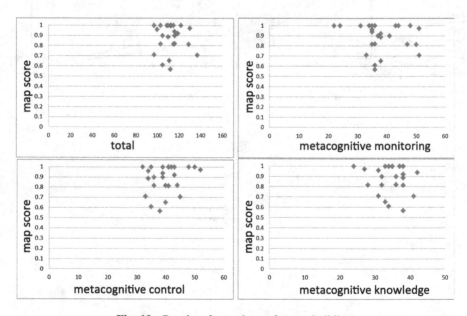

Fig. 10. Results of experiment 2 (map building)

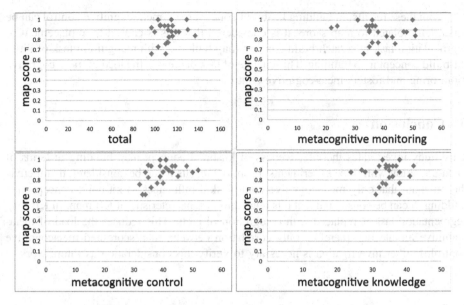

Fig. 11. Results of experiment 2 (delayed map building)

Table 1. Results of experiment 1 (animals)

	Monitoring	Control	Knowledge	Total
Correlation coefficient	0.276	0.464**	0.176	0.468**
p-value	0.203	0.026	0.421	0.024

$r_{0.05} = 0.396$

Table 2. Results of experiment 1 (plants)

	Monitoring	Control	Knowledge	Total
Correlation coefficient	0.201	0.399**	0.138	0.381
p-value	0.359	0.059	0.531	0.073

$r_{0.05} = 0.396$

Table 3. Results of experiment 2 (map building)

	Monitoring	Control	Knowledge	Total
Correlation coefficient	-0.142	0.242	-0.142	-0.040
p-value	0.347	0.105	0.345	0.791

$r_{0.05} = 0.380$

Table 4. Results of experiment 2 (delayed map building)

	Monitoring	Control	Knowledge	Total
Correlation coefficient	-0.088	0.443**	0.089	0.206
p-value	0.562	0.002	0.555	0.169

$r_{0.05} = 0.380$

From these results, in building kit-build concept map, meta-cognitive control can be potentially related to map score. It is considered that this is caused by replacement of segmentation task in scratch-build concept map building with recognition task of kit in kit-build concept map building. This change of task decreases the load of meta-cognitive monitoring and fosters meta-cognitive control.

5   Conclusion

This study investigates the effectiveness of kit-build concept map building in terms of meta-cognition with three experiments. From the results it can be considered that there is the potential that only meta-cognitive control skill influences to kit-build concept map building. It can be considered that it is related to the characteristic of KB map. In KB map segmentation task is replaced with recognition of parts. This reduces the load of meta-cognitive monitoring, therefore only correlation between map score and metacognitive control. Further investigation is necessary to verify this consideration as future work.

References

1. Abe, M., Ida, M.: An attempt to construct the adults' metacognition scale: based on metacognitive awareness inventory. J. Psychol. Rissho Univ. **1**, 23–34 (2010). (in Japanese)
2. Brown, A.L.: Knowing when, where, and how to remember: a problem of metacognition. In: Glaser, R. (ed.) Advances in instructional psychology, vol. I. Erlbaum, New Jersey (1978)
3. Flavell, J.H.: Metacognitive aspects of problem solving. In: Resnick, L.B. (ed.) The Nature of Intelligence, pp. 231–235. LEA, Hillsdale (1976)
4. Funaoi, H., Ishida, K., Hirashima, T.: Comparison of kit-build and scratch-build concept mapping methods on memory retention. In: Proceedings of ICCE 2011, pp. 539–546 (2011)
5. Hirashima, T., Yamasaki, K., Fukuda, H., Funaoi, H.: Framework of Kit-Build Concept Map for Automatic Diagnosis and Its Preliminary Use, RPTEL(Research and Practice in Technology Enhanced Learning), 1 (2015) (accepted)
6. Nomura, T., Hayashi, Y., Suzuki, T., Hirashima, T.: Knowledge propagation in practical use of kit-build concept map system in classroom group work for knowledge sharing. In: ICCE 2014 Workshop Proceedings, pp. 463–472 (2014)
7. Novak, J.D., Gowin, D.B.: Learning how to learn. Cambridge University Press, New York (1984)
8. Schraw, G., Dennison, R.S.: Assessing metacognitive awareness. Contemp. Educ. Psychol. **19**, 460–475 (1994)
9. Sugihara, K., Nino, Y., Moriyama, S., Moriyama, R., Ishida, K., Osada, T., Mizuta, Y., Hirahima, T., Funaoi, H.: Interactive use of kit-build concept map with media tablets. In: IEEE Seventh International Conference on Wireless, Mobile and Ubiquitous Technology in Education, pp. 325–327 (2012)
10. Yamasaki, K., Fukuda, H., Hirashima, T., Funaoi, H.: Kit-build concept map and its preliminary evaluation. In: Proceedings of ICCE 2010, pp. 290–294 (2010)
11. Yoshida, K., Sugihara, K., Nino, Y., Shida, M., Hirashima, T.: Practical use of kit-build comcept map system for formative assessment of learners' comprehension in a lecture. In: Proceedings of ICCE 2013, pp. 892–901 (2013)

The Effect of Problem Sequence on Students' Conceptual Understanding in Physics

Tomoya Horiguchi[1(⊠)], Takahito Tomoto[2], and Tsukasa Hirashima[3]

[1] Graduate School of Maritime Sciences, Kobe University, Kobe, Japan
horiguti@maritime.kobe-u.ac.jp
[2] Faculty of Engineering Division II, Tokyo University of Science, Tokyo, Japan
tomoto@ms.kagu.tus.ac.jp
[3] Department of Information Engineering, Hiroshima University,
Hiroshima, Japan
tsukasa@lel.hiroshima-u.ac.jp

Abstract. The effect of problem sequence on students' understanding in elementary mechanics is empirically examined. We used two types of problem sequences: and surface-blocked sequence. In the former, problems of which superficial feature is different but solution is the same are adjacent, while in the latter, problems of which superficial feature is similar but solutions are different are adjacent. Our hypotheses were: (1) Students who learned with structure-blocked sequence show better performance in solving simple problems because it would train students how to apply a solution in various situations. (2) Students who learned with surface-blocked sequence show better performance in solving complex problems because it would give students an exercise in choosing appropriate solution depending on the situation. (3) The effect of surface-blocked sequence appears more clearly when students are aware of the structure of problems. The results of experiment suggested our hypotheses are true.

Keywords: Science education · Effect of problem sequence · Conceptual understanding · Semantics of constraints · Mechanics

1 Introduction

In science education, it is an important goal for students to acquire the ability to make an appropriate model for a given task. They need to identify the intrinsic features of the system and its behavior they are considering, and formulate the relations of the features. We call such ability 'conceptual understanding.'

However, conventional problem practice hardly helps students reach such an understanding. Students often superficially read the solution of a problem and apply it wrongly to others without understanding the model [1, 2]. This is mainly because students tend to represent a problem based on its superficial features (called surface structure) rather than its structural features (called physical structure) [3]. For example, after a student solved 'a block on a slope' problem with 'Newton's 2nd law,' she/he

S. Yamamoto (Ed.): HIMI 2015, Part II, LNCS 9173, pp. 313–322, 2015.
DOI: 10.1007/978-3-319-20618-9_31

often tries to solve another 'a block on a slope' problem with the same law even if it should be solved with 'conservation of energy.'

In order to reach conceptual understanding, students should learn to infer the physical structure of problems from the surface structure, to which physical laws are applicable. Usually, students must do so by induction with a huge number of various problems because most of such expertise is implicit knowledge and hard to be taught explicitly [2]. This is not an easy task for students.

Therefore, it is very important to design a set of problems and sequence them appropriately so as to promote students' inductive learning [4]. For this purpose, we previously proposed a framework for indexing physical problems, with which one can design and sequence a set of problems systematically [5]. Its key technology is called 'Semantics of Constraints (SOC)' which is the conceptualization of experts' model-making process in physics. By using SOC, the physical meaning of constraints in a model and the assumptions behind them can be explicitly represented. That is, the surface/physical structure of a problem becomes explicit. Therefore, the difference of surface/physical structure between problems can be clearly described, which helps in sequencing a set of problems systematically. The question here is: What kind of sequences are effective?

In this paper, we report the result of the preliminary experiment in which how the problem sequences generated by using our framework effect on students' conceptual understanding in physics was examined. We used two types of problem sequences: structure-blocked sequence and surface-blocked sequence [6]. In the former, the problems which have different surface structures but the same/similar physical structures are adjacent (for example, two problems both of which are solved with 'Newton's 2nd law' are adjacent even if one is 'a block on a slope' problem and the other is 'a block connected to a spring on a floor' problem). In the latter, the problems which have the same/similar surface structures but different physical structures are adjacent (for example, two 'a block on a slope' problems are adjacent even if one is solved with 'Newton's 2nd law' and the other is solved with 'the law of conservation of energy'). We have two hypotheses: (1) Students who learned with structure-blocked sequence show better performance in solving simple problems (in which applying a physical law is sufficient) than those who learned with surface-blocked sequence. This is because the formers continue to apply a solution in various superficially different problems and fix how to apply it. (2) Students who learned with surface-blocked sequence show better performance in solving complex problems (in which combining multiple physical laws is necessary) than those who learned with structure-blocked sequence. This is because the formers encounter superficially similar problems and have to choose appropriate solution depending on the situation. Additionally, since the latter learning is more difficult, the effectiveness of surface-blocked sequence appears more clearly as to students who are aware of the structure of problems. We conducted an experiment to verify our hypotheses, and the result suggested they are true. The result would be the basis of sequencing physical problems adaptively to individual student in computer-based learning.

2 Hypotheses

2.1 Related Work

The effect of sequence of problems has been studied mainly from the viewpoint of transfer by analogy [7]. When a student tries to solve a new problem (target), she/he retrieves a problem she/he previously solved (base), and maps the elements of the base onto the target to generate a solution of the target. In this process, it is important to retrieve a base problem which is structurally similar to the target problem. If the similarity is only superficial, mapping of the elements fails to generate a solution. Therefore, how a set of problems are sequenced which are structurally and/or super-ficially similar to each other would greatly influence learning.

On this issue, Scheiter and Gerjets presented two hypotheses: Transfer hypothesis and near-miss hypothesis [6]. According to the former, learning with structure-blocked sequence (see Sect. 1) is more effective because surface-blocked sequence (also see Sect. 1) makes a student retrieve an inappropriate previous problem as the base. A superficially similar problem is easily retrieved but its solution isn't necessarily applicable to the target. According to the latter, learning with surface-blocked sequence is more effective because a small difference of superficial features would focus the intrinsic difference of structural features. Additionally, it was predicted that for students who were aware of the structure of problems, structure-blocked sequence is more effective because they can easily activate the structurally same solution as the current problem in such sequence, and that surface-blocked sequence is less effective because the solution of previous problems which is inappropriate for the current problem confuses them. These hypotheses were verified through experiments.

2.2 Our Hypotheses

In this paper, aiming at physics domain (mainly elementary mechanics), we examine which of surface-block or structure-block sequence is more effective for which of students who are or aren't aware of the structure of problems.

The domain of Scheiter and Gerjets [6] was word problem of arithmetic. The 'superficial feature' of problems was the 'cover story' which was the situation such as 'two electricians repair a lamp' and 'two people travels a distance toward each other.' The 'structural feature' of problems was the solution procedure with which problems were solved, such as 'work' (calculating the amount of work) and 'motion' (calculating the amount of motion). Problems were categorized by solution and each category had a typical cover story. Some problems' cover story corresponds to their solution (it is typical in their category), while some problems' cover story doesn't (it isn't typical in their category). Students had to identify the solution of problems without being con-fused by their cover story.

In physics, on the other hand, the matter is different. The superficial feature in mechanics problems is the components of the system in consideration and their spatial configuration. Unlike word problem, a small difference of situation doesn't necessarily cause a large difference of solution (e.g., a smooth floor is changed to be rough).

What causes large change of solution is the 'query' which is typically the amount to be calculated (e.g., as for the same system, Newton's second law is necessary for the value of an acceleration, while the law of conservation of energy is necessary for that of a velocity). Therefore, it is predicted that the similarity of superficial feature in mechanics problems less influences students than that in word problems (additionally, according to our experiment, not a few students can get aware of the difference of queries). Rather, surface-blocked sequence might give students an exercise in choosing appropriate solution depending on the situation, of which effect would appear in solving complex problems (in which multiple physical laws had to be combined). On the other hand, structure-blocked sequence might train students how to apply a solution in various situations. In spite of the superficial difference of problems, they could focus on the queries and less confused. This effect would appear in solving simple problems (in which applying a physical law is sufficient). Of course, since it is difficult to learn how to choose appropriate solutions in various situations (in our term, it is 'conceptual understanding'), the effect of surface-blocked sequence appear more clearly when students are aware of the structure of problems.

Therefore, our hypotheses are as follows: (1) Students who learned with structure-blocked sequence show better performance in solving simple problems (in which applying a physical law is sufficient) than those who learned with surface-blocked sequence. (2) Students who learned with surface-blocked sequence show better performance in solving complex problems (in which combining multiple physical laws is necessary) than those who learned with structure-blocked sequence. (3) The effect of surface-blocked sequence appears more clearly as to students who are aware of the structure of problems.

We conducted an experiment to verify our hypotheses. We designed both sequences of problems based on SOC framework (which means the learning effect revealed in this experiment can be computationally controlled in intelligent educational systems). Additionally, for making students aware of the structure of problems, we used SOC-based explanation [5]. It is the explanation about solutions of physical problems in which how to make the model necessary for solving a problem is shown focusing on why physical laws can applied in the situation (modeling assumptions are explicitly explained), and about relations between solutions in which how and why model/solution changes when the situation/assumptions is/are changed. We previously verified that SOC-based explanation facilitates students' awareness of the structure of problems and conceptual understanding [5]. The design, results and implication of the experiment are presented in the next section.

3   Experiment

3.1   Design

We conducted an experiment to verify our hypotheses. The purpose was to examine which sequence of problems promotes students' conceptual understanding more effectively under what conditions.

Subjects: Twenty-six undergraduates whose majors are engineering participated in.

Instruments: (1) Two sets of problems in elementary mechanics: They were called 'problem set 1 (PS-1)' and 'problem set 2 (PS-2).' Each set included fifteen problems of various surface/physical structures. Problems might have similar situations but different solutions, or have different situations but similar solutions. The sets had no common problem. (2) Usual explanation about the solutions of eleven problems in PS-1: The calculation of the required physical amount from the given ones was mainly explained. (3) SOC-based explanation about the solutions of the same problems as usual explanation. In addition to the solution of each problem, the differences between problems were explained about eight pairs of problems which had similar surface/physical structures. (4) A set of three worked-examples (called 'basic problems') which could be solved by applying 'Newton's second law', 'conservation of energy' and 'balance of forces' respectively. (5) Two sequences of problems which were called 'surface-blocked sequence' and 'structure-blocked sequence.' Each sequence included nine problems which were divided into three blocks. In surface-blocked sequence, each block included three problems which were superficially similar but had to be solved by applying different solution. In structure-blocked sequence, each block also included three problems which were superficially different but could be solved by applying the same solution. All problems could be solved by applying one of the three laws used in basic problems. (6) A set of three problems (called 'complex problems') each of which had to be solved by applying two of the three laws used in basic problems.

Procedure: In the first week, subjects were given PS-1 and asked to group the problems into some categories based on some kind of 'similarity' they suppose (any number/size of categories were allowed), then asked to label each category they made (called 'categorization task 1'). After that, they were asked to solve eight problems in PS-1 (called 'pre-test'). After a week, the subjects were divided into four groups: A1, A2, B1 and B2. A1 and A2 included six subjects respectively, and the average scores of both groups in pre-test were made equivalent. The subjects of these groups were given SOC-based explanation and asked to learn it (in order to make them aware of the structure of problems). B1 and B2 included seven subjects respectively, and the average scores of both groups in pre-test were made equivalent. The subjects of these groups were given usual explanation and asked to learn it (they wouldn't get aware of the structure of problems). Then the subjects of all groups were given basic problems and asked to learn them. After that, the subjects of A1 and B1 were given surface-blocked sequence while those of A2 and B2 were given structure-blocked sequence, and asked to solve the problems in the given order (called 'sequence-exercise'). In the third week, all subjects were given complex problems and asked to solve them (called 'complex-test'). After that, by using PS-2, 'categorization task 2' was conducted for all subjects in the same way as above. Finally, they were asked to solve eight problems in PS-2 (called 'post-test').

Measure: The awareness of the structure of problems was measured with the result of categorization tasks. The categories, their 'frequencies' (number of problems accounted for) and the time required were examined. The conceptual understanding was measured with the scores of tests and exercise. The ability to apply a simple solution (applying a physical law is sufficient) was measured with the scores of pre-/post-tests and sequence-exercise. The ability to apply a complex solution (applying two physical law is necessary) was measured with the scores of complex-test. The effect of sequence of problems was measured with the difference of the scores of tests and exercise between A1 and A2, and between B1 and B2.

3.2   Results

The result of categorization task 1 is shown in Table 1 (for B1 and B2) and Table 2 (for A1 and A2). Most of the subjects categorized problems based on the similarity of their superficial features, such as the components of the system (e.g., inclined plane, spring), the figures of motion (e.g., circular motion, free fall). Additionally, all subjects finished the task within thirteen minutes. The result of categorization task 2 is shown in Table 3 (for B1 and B2) and Table 4 (for A1 and A2). Many subjects who learned with usual explanation still categorized problems based on the similarity of their superficial features, while many subjects who learned with SOC-based explanation became to categorize problems based on the similarity of their structural features, that is, the dominant laws of problems (e.g., Newton's second law, balance of forces, conservation of energy). Additionally, all subjects of B1 and B2 finished the task within thirteen minutes again, while the subjects of A1 and A2 required from nine to thirty-five minutes. These results indicate that the subjects of B1 and B2 weren't aware of the structure of problems throughout the experiment, while those of A1 and A2 got aware of the structure of problems before sequence-exercise (the increase of the time

Table 1.   Categories in task 1 (B1 and B2)

	Number of subjects using category labels (N_1=14)	Average size of category (N_2=15)	Number of problems accounted for ($N=N_1 \times N_2$=210)	Number of problems wrongly accounted for (N^*=210)	Number of problems correctly accounted for ($N^C=N-N^*$)
Free fall	11	4.1	45	1	44
Inclined planes	9	3.3	30	1	29
Springs	10	2.6	26	1	25
Circular motion	10	1.9	19	0	19
String/tension	7	2.1	15	0	15
Collision	7	1.6	11	0	11
Accelerated motion	2	5.5	11	2	9
Linear motion	1	3	3	0	3
Second law	1	2	2	0	2
Pulleys	1	2	2	0	2
Friction	1	2	2	0	2
Balance of forces	1	3	3	2	1
Impulse	1	2	2	2	0
Others	13	4.4	57	0	57

Table 2. Categories in task 1 (A1 and A2)

	Number of subjects using category labels (N_1=12)	Average size of category (N_2=15)	Number of problems accounted for ($N=N_1 \times N_2$=180)	Number of problems wrongly accounted for (N^*=180)	Number of problems correctly accounted for ($N^C=N-N^*$)
Free fall	7	4	28	0	28
Springs	6	2.3	14	0	14
Inclined planes	3	3.7	11	0	11
Gravity	1	11	11	0	11
Circular motion	5	1.8	9	1	8
Balance of forces	4	4.8	19	11	8
Accelerated motion	2	3.5	7	0	7
Linear motion	2	3.5	7	0	7
Conservation of energy	4	2	8	2	6
Collision	2	2	4	0	4
Second law	3	2.7	8	4	4
Pulleys	2	1.5	3	0	3
Momentum	1	2	2	0	2
Centripetal/centrifugal force	1	2	2	1	1
Others	5	9.4	47	0	47

Table 3. Categories in task 2 (B1 and B2)

	Number of subjects using category labels (N_1=14)	Average size of category (N_2=15)	Number of problems accounted for ($N=N_1 \times N_2$=210)	Number of problems wrongly accounted for (N^*=210)	Number of problems correctly accounted for ($N^C=N-N^*$)
Springs	9	3.7	33	0	33
Inclined planes	6	5	30	1	29
Second law	7	3.6	25	3	22
Pendulum	8	2.5	20	4	16
Pulleys	4	3.8	15	0	15
Balance of forces	2	7	14	1	13
String/tension	6	2.5	15	3	12
Circular motion	7	1.6	11	2	9
Friction	5	1.4	7	0	7
Conservation of energy	2	4.5	9	3	6
period	3	1	3	0	3
Linear motion	1	2	2	0	2
Collision & momentum	1	1	1	0	1
Free fall	1	3	3	3	0
Others	7	5.1	36	0	36

Table 4. Categories in task 2 (A1 and A2)

	Number of subjects using category labels ($N_1=12$)	Average size of category ($N_2=15$)	Number of problems accounted for ($N=N_1 \times N_2=180$)	Number of problems wrongly accounted for ($N^*=180$)	Number of problems correctly accounted for ($N^C=N-N^*$)
Second law	10	4.4	44	5	39
Conservation of energy	7	4.3	30	4	26
Balance of forces	6	3.7	22	2	20
Springs	**4**	**4**	**16**	**0**	**16**
Inclined planes	2	3.5	7	0	7
Pulleys	2	3.5	7	0	7
Circular motion	4	1.3	5	0	5
Accelerated motion	1	4	4	1	3
Linear motion	1	3	3	0	3
Conservation of momentum	4	2	8	5	3
Simple harmonic/ periodic motion	3	1	3	0	3
Inertial force	2	1.5	3	0	3
Pendulum	2	1.5	3	0	3
Collision	2	1	2	0	2
String/tension	1	2	2	0	2
Friction	1	1	1	0	1
Impulse	1	1	1	1	0
Others	3	4.3	13	0	13

required suggests the subjects of A1 and A2 inferred the physical structure from surface structure).

The average scores in pre-/post-tests, complex-test and sequence-exercise are shown in Table 5. In pre-test, there was significant difference of average scores neither between A1 and A2 nor between B1 and B2 (t-test $p > .10$). In post-test, the average score of A1 was higher than that of A2, and the average score of B1 was higher than that of B2 though there was no significant difference (t-test $p > .10$). In sequence-exercise, the result was the same. In complex-test, on the other hand, the average score

Table 5. Average scores of tests and exercise

Average score (full mark)		Pre-test (55)	Sequence-exercise (60)	Complex-test (30)	Post-test (55)
Aware of structure	A-1: structure-blocked (N = 6)	33.3	56.7	13.3	49.5
	A-2: surface-blocked (N = 6)	29.7	55.7	21.3	40.0
Not aware of structure	B-1: structure-blocked (N = 7)	23.6	43.3	6.7	29.7
	B-2: surface-blocked (N = 7)	23.6	38.0	9.1	27.7

of A2 was higher than that of A1, and the average score of B2 was higher than that of B1. Additionally, there was significant difference between the average score between A1 and A2 (t-test $p < .05$).

The implication of these results is as follows. The subjects who learned with structure-blocked sequence showed better performance in sequence-exercise and post-test than those who learned with surface-blocked sequence whether they were aware of the structure of problems or not. On the other hand, the subjects who learned with surface-blocked sequence showed better performance in complex-test than those who learned with structure-blocked sequence whether they were aware of the structure of problems or not. The difference was more clear when students were aware of the structure of problems. These facts suggest our hypotheses are true: In physics, structure-blocked sequence is more effective in fixing how to apply a solution, so students show better performance in solving simple problems (in which applying a physical law is sufficient). On the other hand, surface-blocked sequence is more effective in learning to apply different solutions depending on the situation, so students show better performance in solving more complex problems (in which combining multiple physical laws is necessary). Since the latter learning is more difficult, the effectiveness of surface-blocked sequence appears clearer as to students who are aware of the structure of problems. Of course, the above implication is only suggested because in most cases there was no significant difference. It is necessary to confirm the validity of our hypotheses in additional experiment with more number of subjects.

4   Concluding Remarks

In this paper, we examined the effect of the sequence of problems in acquiring conceptual understanding in physics. Based on the idea that the relation between superficial and structural features in physics problems is different from that in word problems, we set two hypotheses. Through an experiment, our hypotheses were suggested to be true. It is our important future work to conduct additional experiment with more number of subjects to confirm our hypotheses.

As another approach to improve conceptual understanding of physics, we have investigated the functions to diagnose and generate feedback for correction of misconception [8, 9]. Influence of the sequence of problems to the misconceptions, effectiveness to correct them, and the way to combine these methods are also important research issues.

References

1. VanLehn, K.: Analogy events: how examples are used during problem solving. Cogn. Sci. **22** (3), 347–388 (1998)
2. VanLehn, K., van de Sande, B.: Acquiring conceptual expertise from modeling: the case of elementary physics. In: Ericsson, K.A. (ed.) The Development of Professional Performance: Toward Measurement of Expert Performance and Design of Optimal Learning Environments, pp. 356–378. Cambridge University Press, Cambridge (2009)

3. Chi, M.T.H., Feltovich, P.J., Glaser, R.: Categorization and representation of physics problems by experts and novices. Cogn. Sci. **5**, 121–152 (1981)
4. Hirashima, T., Niitsu, T., Hirose, K., Kashihara, A., Toyoda, J.: An indexing framework for adaptive arrangement of mechanics problems for ITS. IEICE Trans. Inf. Syst. **E77-D**(1), 9–26 (1994)
5. Horiguchi, T., Tomoto, T., Hirashima, T.: A Framework of Generating Explanation for Conceptual Understanding based on 'Semantics of Constraints,' Research and Practice in Technology Enhanced Learning (2015, to be appeared)
6. Scheiter, K., Gerjets, P.: Sequence effects in solving knowledge-rich problems: the ambiguous role of surface similarities. In: Proceedings of the CogSci2003, pp. 1035–1040 (2003)
7. Scheiter, K., Gerjets, P.: The impact of problem order: sequencing problems as a strategy for improving one's performance. In: Proceedings of the CogSci2002 (2002)
8. Hirashima, T., Horiguchi, T., Kashihara, A., Toyoda, J.: Error-based simulation for error-visualization and its management. Int. J. Artif. Intell. Educ. **9**, 17–31 (1998)
9. Horiguchi, T., Imai, I., Toumoto, T., Hirashima, T.: Error-based simulation for error-awareness in learning mechanics: an evaluation. J. Educ. Technol. Soc. **17**(3), 1–13 (2014)

A Topic Model for Clustering Learners Based on Contents in Educational Counseling

Takatoshi Ishii[✉], Satoshi Mizoguchi, Koji Kimita,
and Yoshiki Shimomura

Department of System Design, Tokyo Metropolitan University, Asahigaoka 6-6,
Hino-Shi, Tokyo 191-0065, Japan
t_ishii@tmu.ac.jp

Abstract. For improving the quality of education, we need to analyze the interaction among the learners and teachers. For example, we empirically know that an agreement among the learner and teacher on the point of learning motivation makes good lecture. For this purpose, this paper aim to characterize the interactions based on the contents in the interactions. This paper employs a topic model for characterizing the interactions. Topic model is a method for estimating topic (theme or subject) in documents and clustering the documents based on estimated topics. By using topic model, this paper analyzes contents in actual educational counseling.

Keywords: Educational engineering · Service engineering · Natural language processing · LDA

1 Introduction

Recently, various senses of values are appearing in society. Accompanying this situation, in higher education, the diversity of learners is increasing. Hereafter, the institution of the higher education must adjust their education for the various learners in order to improving their international competitiveness. For example, the universities in japan have implemented new entrance examination for measuring the ability that cannot be measured in paper test, web based learning/examination system, and new course for adult students who participate part-time. In this manner, the institutions of the higher education are needed to improve their faculty.

In order to improve the faculty for new learners, we employ the framework from service engineering, because we regard education as a kind of service. In service engineering, "service" is defined as the "application of competences (knowledge and skills) for the benefit of another entity or the entity itself" (Lusch and Vargo, 2014). In education, the learners gain knowledge and skills from activities with the faculty. In addition, the faculty gains know-hows (e.g., how to talk for learners' understanding). In this situation, faculty competence and learners competence is applied to the activity in the institution. In addition, the activity in the institution contributes for learners and faculty. Therefore, we regard the education in universities as a kind of service.

Recently, in service engineering, the important philosophy named Service Dominant Logic (SDL) is proposed (Lusch and Vargo, 2014). SDL has a concept for value

© Springer International Publishing Switzerland 2015
S. Yamamoto (Ed.): HIMI 2015, Part II, LNCS 9173, pp. 323–331, 2015.
DOI: 10.1007/978-3-319-20618-9_32

(bene-fit) called as "value in use" or "value in context". In SDL, the value of the service (and products) is created in the uses of the service (and products). In addition, this value depends on the context of uses, where context is defined as a "set of unique actors with unique reciprocal links among them". The value of service has two following features: (1) the value is co-created by the actors, and (2) the value is mutually constitutive. For instance, in a lecture, the value for learners is getting knowledge, and the value for teachers is getting experience for how to make good lecture. In this situation, the learners and teachers get the value mutually and these values are created among the interaction among the learners and teachers. Thus, for improving the value of target service, it is needed to consider the context of service and the interaction among the actors.

Accordingly, in order to improve the value of faculty, it is needed to consider the new learners' context and interaction among learners and teachers. For this final goal, the purpose of this paper is to propose a method that senses the learners' context from the interaction among the learners and teachers. In many case on the education, this interaction is described in natural language. For example, discussion, descriptions on the blackboard, mini-tests, homework, and the response for the homework are described by natural language. However, qualitative analysis (e.g., conversation analysis) by hand requires huge cost. In addition, digital data of interactions on Learning Management System: LMS are increased by the progress of information technologies.

From this background, this paper attempts analysis of those interactions without human hand. To achieve this, this paper applies a natural language processing method for characterizing the interactions. To be more precise, this paper applies Latent Dirichlet Allocation (LDA) (Blei et al. 2003) that is a method for estimating the topic in the documents, and for clustering those documents based on estimated topic. By using LDA, this paper can characterize the interactions based on the estimated contents. In this paper, to demonstrate the usability of the method, we show an application to analyze a counseling data.

2   Latent Dirichlet Allocation (LDA) (Blei et al. 2003)

This paper employs Latent Dirichlet Allocation (LDA) (Blei et al. 2003) for analyzing contents in interaction. This chapter introduces Latent Dirichlet Allocation (LDA) that is one of topic model. There are some topic models: Latent Semantic Analysis (LSA) (Deerwester et al. 1990), Probabilistic LSA (pLSA) (Hofmann 1999), Latent Dirichlet Allocation (LDA) (Blei et al. 2003), and more. Topic model is a method for clustering documents based on the topics (subjects or contents) in the documents. From these topic models, this study employs LDA for analyzing the interaction. LDA assumes and models that the document includes some abstract "topics" that are subject or contents in the documents. LDA estimates the topic of each word from bias of word frequency in the documents. By aggregating the topics of words in the document, LDA estimates the topic allocation of each document.

For example, there is an example document: "I want to learn English. Because I'm interest in European football, so I want to go Spain for watching football games." In this example, the result of LDA indicates that the word: "English" and "learn" have a topic of "English learner", and the other word: "football" and "game" have a topic of "football". Thus, this document has two main topics: "English learner" and "football".

LDA assumes that each document has multiple topics. On the other hand, LSA and pLSA assume that the document consist of one abstract topic. Thus, the assumption of LDA is fitter actual document, and has better accuracy than LSA and pLSA.

In our study, we assume that free descriptions for interaction include some topics of contents. For example, a counselling log about learning motivation will include two types of contents "as an English learner" and "as a football fun". LDA is able to model such case that various topics are included in a document. Therefore, in this study, LDA is employed for estimating topics in interaction.

3   A Topic Model for Clustering Learners Based on Contents in the Educational Counseling

In this chapter, we introduce an application of topic model for analyzing interaction among learners and teachers. An overview of this application is shown in Fig. 1. The first, we obtained learning counseling data. The next, we analyzed those data with LDA.

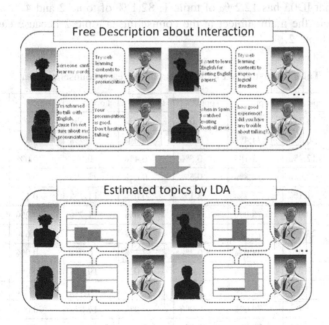

Fig. 1. Overview of the proposed method

3.1   Obtained Data

The first, we obtained the data of interaction. As this data, we employed educational counseling data for an English lecture for Japanese students. This lecture was given in 2014 for engineering students in Japan. The number of students is 23. The counseling is conducted for 17 learners in Japanese. We got the 17 voice data from 17 counseling, and then converted the voice data to 17 text data. Thus, we got 17 text data from 17 learners. This text data included speeches from learners and teachers. We used verbs and nouns for analysis. The statistics of the 17 text data is shown in Table 1.

Table 1. The statistics of the 17 text data

Number of words	139834
Number of vocabulary	7044
Average of # words	8225.5
Standard division of # words	2558.8

3.2   The Result of LDA for the Obtained Data

The next, we analyzed the obtained text data based on LDA. The results are shown in Tables 2 and 3.

Table 2 shows the estimated topic allocation (rate) for each data. In addition, the cells with Top 30 % values are painted red. For example, the column of ID03 in the table shows that ID03 has 12.2 % of topic 1, 82.1 % of topic 2 and 4.7 % of topic 7. From this result, the main subject in the counseling is topic 2 because each data has over 70 % of topic 2.

Table 2. Estimated topic allocation for each counseling data

ID	Topic1	Topic2	Topic3	Topic4	Topic5	Topic6	Topic7
ID01	13.4%	82.0%	1.0%	0.0%	3.6%	0.0%	0.0%
ID02	0.4%	74.4%	0.0%	0.0%	0.7%	24.5%	0.0%
ID03	12.2%	82.1%	0.5%	0.4%	0.0%	0.0%	4.7%
ID04	0.0%	72.8%	0.5%	0.0%	25.2%	0.0%	1.5%
ID05	1.1%	77.7%	2.1%	0.0%	11.2%	0.1%	7.7%
ID06	0.0%	78.0%	0.0%	0.0%	1.7%	20.2%	0.0%
ID07	23.1%	76.1%	0.0%	0.0%	0.2%	0.6%	0.0%
ID08	0.0%	62.6%	0.2%	37.1%	0.0%	0.0%	0.1%
ID09	0.0%	79.0%	1.4%	0.0%	19.6%	0.0%	0.0%
ID10	0.0%	75.4%	1.8%	0.0%	0.4%	0.0%	22.5%
ID11	0.7%	79.6%	0.0%	0.9%	17.8%	0.0%	0.9%
ID12	0.0%	80.5%	0.7%	0.0%	11.6%	7.1%	0.0%
ID13	0.1%	76.5%	0.0%	0.0%	0.0%	0.0%	23.3%
ID14	16.6%	77.3%	0.0%	0.0%	5.8%	0.0%	0.3%
ID15	1.9%	75.3%	0.0%	0.1%	1.0%	21.7%	0.0%
ID16	3.6%	72.9%	0.0%	0.0%	22.0%	1.5%	0.0%
ID17	0.0%	64.9%	35.1%	0.0%	0.0%	0.0%	0.0%

Table 3. The representative 5 words of 5 topics

Topic1	Topic2	Topic3	Topic4	Topic5	Topic6	Topic7
Research	English	United kingdom	United kingdom	Review	United kingdom	Aerospace
Graduate school	Talk	Friends	Motivation	Unit	Football	Technical term
Society	Understand	Dormitory	Speech	Quality	World cup	Presentation
Infrastructure	Pronunciation	Company	Sing	Studio session	Challenge	Paper
Museum	Question	English conversation	Golf	Click	Game	Oral

Table 3 shows the representative 5 words for each topic from LDA analysis. From this table, we can understand what word appears with high probability in each topic. For example, in the topic 7, the words "Aerospace" and "technical term" appeared. Therefore, we can understand the topic 7 is about the research of aerospace engineering.

4 Consideration

4.1 Meaning of Each Topic

The first, we need to consider the meaning of each topic. The most frequent topic was topic 2, and this topic was regarded as "talking about English lecture". The words "talk" and "pronunciation" are subjects of talking in English, and the words "understand" and "question" have relations to instructional activity. Therefore, topic 2 was regarded to "talking about English lecture". Of course, all of the counseling has topic 2 with high rate, because this is the main theme in the counseling. In the same manner, topic 1 was as "talking about academic", topic 3 was as "talking about studying in abroad", topic 4 was as "talking about learning motivation for English", topic 5 was as "talking about learning contents", topic 6 was as "talking about European football", and topic 7 was as "talking about the research of aerospace engineering"

4.2 Clustering the Counseling Data

Moreover, we can cluster the 17 counseling data based on contents similarity. This clustering did not require human hand. (Only the meaning for clusters requires human power.) We regarded topic rate as feature vector, and calculate similarity (i.e., cosine similarity, and J-S divergence as distance).

In this result, 17 counseling data were clearly divided to 6 clusters. The counseling data were divided by including - excepting topic 2. For example, the biggest cluster is the set of ID04, ID05, ID09, ID11, ID12, and ID16. Each data in the cluster includes topic 5. In short, these learners talked about web-learning contents in the counseling. Therefore, summarizing these results, LDA characterized each counseling data based on contents of counseling.

4.3 Application for Improving Faculty

From these result and consideration, we could understand what contents were talked about in each data. For example, 6 learners (ID04, ID05, ID09, ID11, ID12, and ID16) talked about web learning contents, and they probably interest in learning on the web contents. Other 4 learners (ID01, ID02, ID07, and ID14) and 2 learners (ID10 and ID13) talked about their research on graduate school. In addition, the former group (ID01, ID02, ID07, and ID14) talked about infrastructure, and the latter group (ID10 and ID13) talked about aerospace. These were probably their majors. This analysis found out a part of learners context. This result is expected to be utilized for improving faculty.

The last, we checked the relationship among this clustering result and other statistics those are expected to characterize learning activity. To be more precise, we checked the interrelation among the clustering result, performance measured by an examination, personality, interest for web contents, and the ability for self-regulated learning. Table 4 shows all learners' performance, personality, interest, the ability for self-regulated learning, and results of the clustering result by LDA application.

Table 4. The clustering based on counseling contents, performance, personality, interest, and the ability for self-regulated learning for each learners.

ID	Performance	Personality	Self-regulated	Interest	LDA
ID01	2	A	A	B	B
ID02	-	D	C	B	C
ID03	1	A	C	A	B
ID04	2	B	A	A	A
ID05	0	B	A	C	A
ID06	1	A	D	B	C
ID07	0	A	D	C	B
ID08	1	C	A	B	F
ID09	0	D	B	A	A
ID10	0	C	B	D	D
ID11	1	-	-	-	A
ID12	4	A	B	-	A
ID13	0	A	B	B	D
ID14	0	B	D	A	B
ID15	1	D	C	D	C
ID16	0	A	A	C	A
ID17	0	C	D	A	E

The "performance" is indicated the deference of before and after test grade. The learners took the OPIc examination (The American Council on the Teaching of Foreign Languages) twice: before and after the counseling. The "personality" indicates clustering result of personality. The learners were characterized using big 5 personality test (Murakami and Murakami, 2001). We divided learners to 4 cluster based on features of big 5 test. The "self-regulated" indicates the ability of self-regulated learning. We employed the item set and the scoring in (Gouda et al. 2012), and we clustered learners to 4 cluster based on the scores. The "interest" indicates the clustering of interest for web learning contents. We employ ARCS model (Keller 2010) for characterizing the interest for web contents. For detecting interrelation, we removed three data: ID02, ID11 and ID12 that included missing values.

Figure 2 shows scatter plots and Spearman's rank correlation coefficient for each pair among the values. This result was output by R (The R Project for Statistical Computing). Unfortunately, we could not find out the pair having strong correlation. This result possibly bring out this analysis do not have utilize for characterize educational activity. (The number of data may be insufficient to draw conclusions. From this data, we could not find out strong interrelation among other 4 statistics either.) Therefore, the future work includes following two tasks: (1) to find the educational activity (or statistics) related with this clustering result, and (2) to validate those relation by obtains sufficient data.

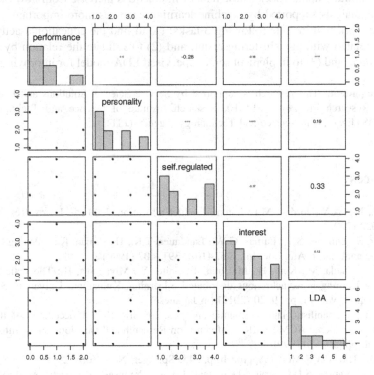

Fig. 2. The result of scatter plots and Spearman's rank correlation coefficient for each pair of values in Table 4.

Moreover, the future work includes finding the interaction contents that have strong interrelation for the educational activity. There are variations of LDA processing the documents with tags. For example, there is a Labeled-LDA model (Ramage 2009). In These models, the model estimate topics from not only words frequency but also tags.

In addition, we can indicate topic meaning by tagging documents. (These models are called as "semi-supervised model"). Those models is expected to characterize contents in interaction based on target statistics. For example, if the documents are tagged on the point of performance ("up", "stay", and "down"), these models will provide what contents (or words) are included in each performance group. Therefore, the future work includes (3) to implement semi-supervised LDA model for improving utility.

5 Conclusion

In this paper, for analyzing actual educational counseling, we applied LDA that is a natural language processing method. This application provided the result of clustering based on contents in the counseling. For this clustering, this application did not require human's hand. Thus, this application is a way to reduce cost of qualitative analysis for the counseling. LDA can apply other various data (e.g., discussion on lecture or LMS, and/or a submitted homework). These data of interactions increase from now on. Thus, qualitative analysis supported by machine learning becomes more important.

Future work will include following 3 tasks: (1) to find the educational activity (or statistics) related with this clustering result, and (2) to validate the relation by obtains sufficient data, and (3) to implement semi-supervised LDA model for improving utility.

Acknowledgement. This research is supported by Service Science, Solutions and Foundation Integrated Research Program (S3FIRE), Research Institute of Science and Technology for Society (RISTEX), Japan Science and Technology Agency (JST).

References

Blei, D.M., Ng, A.Y., Jordan, M.I.: Latent dirichlet allocation. J. Mach. Learn. Res. 3(2003), 993–1022 (2003)

Deerwester, S., Dumais, S.T., Furnas, G.W., Landauer, T.K., Harshman, R.: Indexing by latent semantic analysis. J. Am. Soc. Inf. Sci. 41(6), 391–407 (1990)

Gouda, Y., Yamada, M., Kato, H., Matsuda, T., Saito, Y., Miyagawa, H.: The scale for self-adjusting learning in asynchronous distributed e-learning. Kumamoto University education annual report, vol. 15, pp. 9–20 (2012) (in Japanese)

Hofmann, T.: Probabilistic latent semantic analysis. In: SIR 1999 Proceedings of the 22nd Annual International ACM SIGIR Conference on Research and Development in Information Retrieval, pp. 50–57 (1999)

Keller, J.M.: The ARCS Model Approach, p. 345. Springer, New York (2010)

Lusch, R.F., Vargo, S.L.: Service-Dominant Logic: Premises, Perspectives, Possibilities. Cambridge University Press, Cambridge (2014)

Murakami, Y., Murakami, C.: Handbook of Big Five Personality Test. Gakugeitosho, Tokyo (2001). (in Japanese)

Ramage, D., Hall, D., Nallapati, R., Manning, C.D.: Labeled LDA: a supervised topic model for credit attribution in multi-labeled corpora. In: EMNLP 2009 Proceedings of the 2009 Conference on Empirical Methods in Natural Language Processing, vol. 1 (2009)

The American Council on the Teaching of Foreign Languages (n.d.). Oral Proficiency Assessments (including OPI & OPIc). http://www.actfl.org/professional-development/assessments-the-actfl-testing-office/oral-proficiency-assessments-including-opi-opic. Accessed March 2015

The R Project for Statistical Computing (n.d.). http://www.r-project.org/. Accessed March 2015

Method to Generate an Operation Learning Support System by Shortcut Key Differences in Similar Software

Hajime Iwata[(⊠)]

Kanagawa Institute of Technology,
1030 Shimo-ogino, Atsugi, Kanagawa 243-0292, Japan
hajimei@nw.kanagawa-it.ac.jp

Abstract. Some software packages have the same purpose, but different operation methods. Users typically choose software that they find easier to operate. However, this is not always the case, and users may be confused by software operations in similar software packages. This study focuses on software shortcut keys. End users can operate software efficiently when they learn shortcut keys because they are independent of GUIs. Herein a learning operation support system is proposed to illustrate the difference in shortcut key functions between software packages. This system analyzes software manuals and source codes to extract shortcut key combinations and functions, and the results are color-coded displays of shortcut key combinations that carry out the same function by software package.

Keywords: Software operation learning support system · Operation consistency · Shortcut keys · Usability

1 Introduction

Different companies and groups have developed software for the same purpose. For example, web browsers (Internet Explorer, Google Chrome, Firefox, Safari, etc.) are designed to read web pages. Each platform (Windows, Android, Max OS X) has its own default, but users tend to employ software that they are familiar with and find easy to use. However, the security policy of a company or group may prohibit users from installing software freely. Additionally, there are situations when users must use existing software (e.g., a computer kiosk at a hotel). Therefore, users may not always use their preferred software.

Operation method varies by software package. Even software packages for the same purpose have different operation methods. If users have experience with similar software, they may accept software operations of different package. However, this behavior may depend on the software as end users may be confused about software operations. If the operation method differs from other software, end users have to learn to operate new software. Although it is desirable for software packages have consistency between them, this may not be a priority for software developers.

© Springer International Publishing Switzerland 2015
S. Yamamoto (Ed.): HIMI 2015, Part II, LNCS 9173, pp. 332–340, 2015.
DOI: 10.1007/978-3-319-20618-9_33

In addition, the mainstream method to operate software is a GUI (Graphical User Interface) using pointing devices (hereafter referred to as a mouse). Using a mouse, end users can operate software intuitively. However, the design of GUIs greatly varies not only by software package but also by software version. Therefore, this study focuses on software shortcut keys, which are an assigned combination of keyboard strokes that correspond to a specific function. Even if the software's version is changed, the shortcut keys maintain consistency for basic operations, allowing end users to operate the software efficiently and intuitively without depending on the GUIs once the shortcut keys are learned.

This paper proposes a learning support system to operate software by illustrating the differences in shortcut keys for specific functions in software packages by analyzing software manuals as well as source codes to extract shortcut key combinations and functions. The generated system displays shortcut key combinations to carry out the same function in different software by color.

This paper is organized as follows. Section 2 describes the operation method of the software and operation learning support system. Section 3 details the consistency of software operations. Section 4 discusses the architecture of the proposed system. Section 5 evaluates this system. Finally, Sect. 6 concludes this paper.

2 Learning Support for the Software Operation

2.1 Learning Software Operations

Easy-to-learn is one characteristic of software usability as learning software operations allows users to competently operate software [1]. When end users obtain new software, the first task is to learn the operations. Software often has multiple operation methods (e.g., choosing from a menu, starting from an icon, etc.). Learning all the operations is not easy, but because most users deploy the software immediately, they learn as part of the interface. Initially users learn operation methods to conduct necessary functions, and later improve their competency by learning effective operations. Because not all users have positive experiences with a specific operation method, it is important that software has multiple operation methods.

2.2 Software Operation Methods

Current software generally employs the GUI system. In a GUI, the input is mainly through a mouse. End users can select functions using a GUI and by watching the screen. Consequently, software operations are performed intuitively. In addition, devices (e.g., tablet or smartphone) are adopting touch panels. Therefore, end users are able to choose a function of the software even if they are inexperienced.

However, input via a mouse is time consuming because the mouse pointer must be moved, especially if input content is large. Additionally, operations of the touch panel can be difficult as users must tap the desired screen location precisely. Some software also supports gesture operations, which call functions in accordance to the specific trace when drawn with a mouse, but a gesture operation can be misrecognized or end users may not recognize the function. Therefore, using only GUIs does not provide a high input efficiency.

A keyboard is commonly used by PC users. Another method to carry out software functions is to use shortcut keys. A shortcut key, which is designed to increase work efficiency, is an assigned combination of keys corresponding to a specific function. This allows end users to operate software without depending on GUIs.

Support and assignment for shortcut keys vary by software package. As a result, a shortcut key combination may not be assigned a function or may be assigned different function depending on the software package. End users who employ shortcut keys of other software unconsciously may have to exert much effort to learn new shortcut key operations.

2.3 Related Works

Means for users to learn software operations include the operation manual, help system, and tutorial system. However, these means are burdensome on software developers, and methods have been proposed to assist in operation learning of end users. We have proposed a method to generate a tutorial system by UML diagrams [2] and based on end users' operation logs and source programs [3]. Our tutorial system, which is executed as the software is actually used, simulates the software running so that end users can learn to operate it.

Chi et al. have proposed a method to generate a mixed media tutorial systems [4]. This method approach is mixed two types of tutorials, static tutorials and video tutorials. This method generates screen capture video by into steps using software logs. Generated tutorial shows static information, and highlights interactions through mouse pointer by end users, this tutorial played video tutorial. This method is only supported for mouse operation. When end users have to learn keyboard operation, this approach is not enough for user support.

Li et al. have proposed a gamified interactive tutorial system [5]. Gamification is as using elements of video games enhance to user experience. This method approach expresses the progress model of the user by event driven state machine. The tutorial system provide real-time feedback and recognize success and fail. This system provides real-time audio visual feedback to end users for gamification. End users concentrate this method for a long time and they can learn complicated operation. However, the target of this system is operation complicated to some extent to satisfy a factor of gamification. When end users want to learn only efficient operation about software with the use experience, it is unsuitable.

3 Consistency of Software Operations

Consistency of a design allows users to perform an operation easily and intuitively. If end users know that the same command and movement always produce the same result, they can use a system with confidence. Because consistency makes software easier to learn, the efforts of end users are also reduced. Commonly, consistency of assembly

Table 1. Function of select shortcut keys by web browser

Shortcut key	IE	Firefox	Chrome
F1	Show help pages	-	Show help pages
F7	Cursor browse	Cursor browse	-
Ctrl + K	Duplicate tub	Focus on find text field	Focus on find text field
Ctrl + Shift + N	-	Redisplay a closed window	Open a secret window
Shift + ESC	-	-	Display task manager

operations, including shortcut keys, is maintained in a software package, but tends to vary between software packages.

On the other hand, shortcut keys are typically determined by the operating system (OS) [6]. Instead of choosing a function in a menu with a mouse, the keyboard is used. An example is overwrite preservation (save) in the Windows OS, which can be invoked by simultaneously depressing the Ctrl key and s key. The application side can also use this function. Thus, the shortcut key in the software should match that of the OS.

However, the meaning in the user interface, placement, and the operation of the keyboard may vary according to the OS. Because the operation method may also vary according to the hardware, software developers must maintain consistency between software and different OSs.

Shortcut keys also depend on the software setting. Most shortcut keys are assigned a common functionality. However, the correspondence of shortcut keys may vary according to the intention of the developer or an environmental difference. In addition, a function may not have an equivalent shortcut key.

Herein I surveyed the difference in shortcut keys in software with the same purpose (e.g., web browsers). As web browsers are mainly used in Windows, the shortcut keys in Internet Explorer (IE), Firefox, and Google Chrome were investigated. Table 1 shows a partial list of shortcut keys.

In common software, the allotment of shortcuts may differ, and developers may not maintain operation consistency with the OS. Therefore, a system to automatically generate the difference in shortcut key operations would be beneficial. The proposed system allows end users to easily learn software operations.

4   Proposed System Architecture

Figure 1 shows an example of the generated operation learning support system. This generated system displays shortcut key combinations by function name. The color-coded system helps users learn the proper combination. Red denotes the commonly used key, blue is the usage to be learned, and purple denotes the same key. This operation learning support system allows end users to comprehend the shortcut key operations visually.

Figure 2 depicts the system's architecture, which involves five steps.

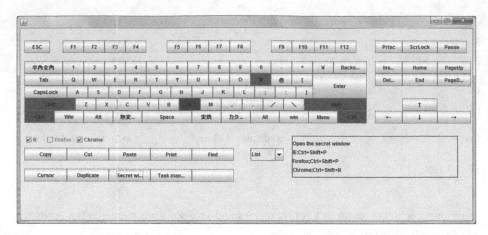

Fig. 1. Example of the generated operation learning support system

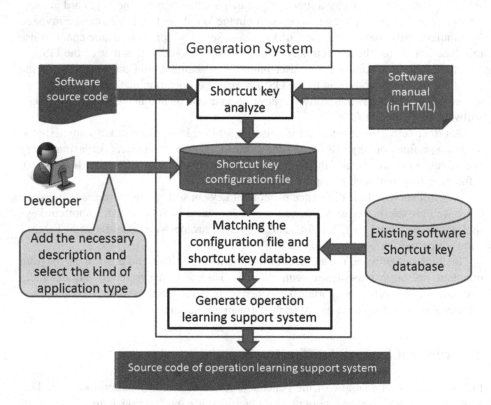

Fig. 2. System architecture

1. Analyze a shortcut key combination and the support method from the software manual and source code.
2. Generate the configuration file based on the analysis results.
3. Add the necessary description to a configuration file (such as the function name of the shortcut key, explanation of the function, operation of the shortcut key) and select the software type.
4. Extract a shortcut key database based on the configuration files.
5. Generate the source code of the shortcut key learning software corresponding to the software.

4.1   Analyzing Shortcut Key Combinations

This system analyzes the software source codes and software manuals. Currently, this system supports software source code written in Java and manuals written in HTML. The source code for shortcut keys written in Java is implemented by the "setAccelerator" method, while manuals in HTML often use a table format to describe shortcut keys. The proposed system parses the HTML files using jsoup library [7], check Table tag (<TR> and <TD>). Shortcut keys' descriptions are often including "+" character and modifier key name, such as Ctrl (Control), Shift, Meta. For example, a save overwrite function shortcut key is described [Ctrl + S] in manuals. Other independent shortcut keys are Function keys (F1 to F12), Home key, End key and Back Space key. When these character string are included, this text is the explanation of the shortcut key. Therefore, the proposed system checks the text in the table.

4.2   Generating the Configuration File Based on Analysis Results and Adding Necessary Descriptions

The system generates a setting file from the analysis in Sect. 4.1. The configuration file contains shortcut key combinations, function names, and the explanations of the function. However, this analyzed data is insufficient to generate the shortcut key learning support system because a software update may alter the shortcut key allotment.

Therefore, the software developer must add necessary data to this setting file. The configuration file data is generated in the CSV format. The content in the setting file is as follows:

- Name of the software
- The developer inputs the software name. The name of this item is displayed as software target for the learning support.
- Type of application
- The developer selects the type of application, which is purpose of the software and the type of learning support. This system uses information to match the representative existing software in the purpose of use.

- Shortcut key description
- The software developer inputs function names, shortcut key combinations, and explanations of the function to show buttons and a combo box. The functions are often inputted sequentially from the top.

4.3   Comparing the Configuration File to the Existing Software Shortcut Key Database

The proposed system compares the configuration file described in Sect. 4.2 to the existing software shortcut key database, which is created beforehand. This database compiles frequently used shortcut keys and is in the same format as the configuration file.

This system is composed of the type of software described in the configuration file and the purpose of the shortcut key settings of the same software from an existing software shortcut key database.

4.4   Generating a Shortcut Key Learning System

This system generates the source code of the learning system based on the configuration file and an existing software shortcut key database. The generated learning system displays the buttons of the frequently used functions. Currently the learning system is limited to the top ten functions. If there are more than ten, the remaining functions are displayed in a combo box. The learning system is generated in Java source code.

5   Evaluation

To evaluate the proposed system, the number of automatically extracted shortcut keys in the target software was examined. Target software packages have source code written in Java and a manual written in HTML. Each software package was evaluated separately. The items evaluated in the Java source code were the shortcut key combinations and variable names substituted for function names. The items evaluated in the HTML manual were shortcut key combinations and the explanation of the function. Tables 2 and 3 show the results.

As a result of source code analysis of the Java software, proposed system was able to extract the all shortcut key combinations in three software. In addition, proposed system was able to extract the variable name of the part of GUI which supported. However, about the UML diagram tool, proposed system was not able to extract the combination of shortcut keys. This is because this tool implemented an original class and a method to add shortcut key.

As a result of analysis of the HTML manual, proposed system was able to extract a combination and the explanation of all shortcut key combinations in the Web browser. However, image drawing software has the shortcut key combinations that the combination without the modifier keys. Proposed system was not able to extract these

Table 2. Evaluation of automatically extracted data from Java source codes

Software Type	Extracted shortcut key combinations	Extracted shortcut key variable names	Number of all shortcut keys
Text editor	7	7	7
FTP software	16	16	16
Image drawing tool	27	27	27
UML diagram tool	5	5	65

Table 3. Evaluation of automatically extracted data from HTML format manuals

Software	Extracted shortcut key combinations	Extracted explanation of the function	Number of all shortcut keys
Web browser	164	164	164
Image drawing Software	70	70	78
Mail client software	129	129	159

shortcut keys. In addition, proposed system extracted shortcut keys combination to each OS because the mail client was multi-platform. In the case of a HTML manual made assuming the plural OS's, proposed system should extract shortcut key combinations to the current OS.

6 Conclusion

In this paper, I propose a learning support system for shortcut key combinations. Even if end users are inexperienced with a software package, this system allows them to easily learn and deploy shortcut key combinations. Consequently, this method can assist end users, especially in unfamiliar environments such as a street kiosk.

In the future, I intend to:

- Increase the analysis precision of the shortcut keys.
- As functions within an application increase, so does the burden on developers. To resolve this, I intend to improve the analysis precision of shortcut key data.
- Develop an automatic updating system for the existing software shortcut key database
- The existing software shortcut key database was created manually. In the future, I would like to devise a method that automatically updates the database by referring to web pages.

References

1. Nielsen, J.: Usability Engineering. Morgan Kaufmann, San Francisco (1994)
2. Iwata, H., Shirogane, J., Fukazawa, Y.: Automatic generation of tutorial systems from development specification. In: Baresi, L., Heckel, R. (eds.) FASE 2006. LNCS, vol. 3922, pp. 79–92. Springer, Heidelberg (2006)

3. Iwata, H., Shirogane, J., Fukazawa, Y.: Generation of an operation learning support system by log analysis. In: Proceedings of 2nd International Conference on Software Engineering and Data Mining (SEDM) (2010)
4. Chi, P., Ahn, S., Ren, A., Dontcheva, M., Li, W., Hartmann, B.: MixT: automatic generation of step-by-step mixed media tutorials. In: Proceedings of the 25th Annual ACM Symposium on User Interface Software and Technology (UIST) (2012)
5. Li, W., Grossman, T., Fitzmaurice, G.: GamiCAD: a gamified tutorial system for first time autocad users. In: Proceedings of the 25th Annual ACM Symposium on User Interface Software and Technology (UIST) (2012)
6. Microsoft Windows Develop Center - Desktop Guidelines section. http://msdn.microsoft.com/en-us/library/windows/desktop/aa511440.aspx
7. jsoup: Java HTML Parser. http://jsoup.org/

Learning State Model for Value Co-Creative Education Services

Koji Kimita[(✉)], Keita Muto, Satoshi Mizoguchi, Yutaro Nemoto,
Takatoshi Ishi, and Yoshiki Shimomura

Department of System Design, Tokyo Metropolitan University, Tokyo, Japan
{kimita, t_ishii}@tmu.ac.jp, {muto-keita,
mizoguchi-satoshi, nemoto-yutaro}@ed.tmu.ac.jp,
yoshiki-shimomura@center.tmu.ac.jp

Abstract. Achieving learning objectives is considered as a value in use for higher education service. To achieve learning objectives, a teacher needs to grasp a learning state at each time point and then determine a target state that should be achieved by the next time point. With regard to the target state, the teacher also needs to achieve consensus with the learner. This study aims to support teachers in grasping the learning state and achieving consensus with the learner. To that end, we propose a model to represent changes in the learning state and the relationship between learning state and learning and instructional events.

Keywords: Service engineering · Value co-creation · Consensus building

1 Introduction

Recent aging trends in society, coupled with a falling birth rate, have caused the market to shrink. As a result, many service companies have found it necessary to seek out potential customers who are not their traditional targets. Higher education institutions have faced the same problem; because of the declining population of 18-year-olds, higher education institutions are targeting new types of learner, such as adult learners with full-time jobs. However, these institutions do not necessarily provide the kind of education that satisfies these new types of learner; in fact, they provide them with the same learning environment and tools as are offered to traditional students. To attract new types of learner, higher education institutions must therefore provide education that takes account of learners' perspectives.

From the viewpoint of services, learners in higher education institutions can be regarded as customers. The value of a service is always perceived and determined by the customer on the basis of value in use [1]. In this sense, the value of an education also need to be determined by learners. In addition, to create value in use, learners need to work as co-producers [1]. Therefore, for the creation of value in education, teachers must provide effective contents, and learners must develop adequate learning behaviors. However, it is difficult for learners to recognize educational value prior to receiving the lecture. Generally, value can be specified in terms of interactions between teacher and learner. For value creation in education, this study aims to support teachers to provide effective contents, and learners to perform adequate learning behaviors.

S. Yamamoto (Ed.): HIMI 2015, Part II, LNCS 9173, pp. 341–349, 2015.
DOI: 10.1007/978-3-319-20618-9_34

To do so, this study focuses on consensus building between teacher and learner and develops a model to represent a process of consensus building. In addition, we propose a method to determine a strategy for realizing both effective content provision and adequate learning behaviors.

The paper consists of the following sections. Section 2 introduces the approach taken in this study, first by introducing a definition of a service and then by elaborating a process of educational service. Section 3 explains the proposed method for consensus building. Section 4 reports the results of an application of the proposed method to a lecture. Section 5 discusses the results, and Sect. 6 presents our conclusions.

2   Approach of This Study

2.1   Definition of a Service

Service Engineering is a new engineering discipline whose objective is to provide a fundamental understanding of services, as well as concrete engineering methodologies to design and evaluate services. In Service Engineering, "service" is defined as an activity between a service provider and a service receiver to change the state of the receiver [2–4]. Note that the term "service" is used in a broad sense, and so the design target includes both intangible human activities and tangible products.

According to the definition, a receiver is satisfied when their state changes to a new desirable state. Since the value of a service is determined by the receiver, service design should be based on the state change of the receiver. For design purposes, it is necessary to find a method to express state changes of the receiver. In service design, the target receiver's state is represented as a set of parameters called "receiver state parameters" (RSPs) [2–4]. As shown in Fig. 1, RSPs are changed by "service contents" and "service channels." Service contents are material, energy, or information that directly changes the receiver's state. Service channels transfer, amplify, and control the service contents.

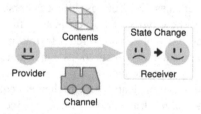

Fig. 1. Definition of a service [2–4]

2.2   Proposed Educational Process

From the services viewpoint, learners in higher education institutions can be regarded as customers, and the value of an education is therefore determined by learners. In addition, learners work as co-producers in value creation; in other words, while teachers must provide effective contents, learners must perform adequate learning behaviors. In order to realize such an educational service, this study proposes to employ the education process shown in Fig. 2. First, a teacher (corresponding to a contents designer) develops an assumption about value in use for learners. In this study, service is defined as an activity between a service provider and a service receiver that changes the state of the receiver [2–4]. According to this definition, value is represented as state change that is desirable for the receiver. In this step, then, the teacher identifies what constitutes the valuable state for learners, that is, the state in which the value of the education is achieved. On this basis, the teacher designs educational contents and suggests them to the learners. Here, the teacher needs to build a consensus with learners about the educational contents and the value being offered. After building this consensus, the teacher then provides the educational contents and conducts a formative evaluation in order to improve them. Finally, an overall evaluation is conducted.

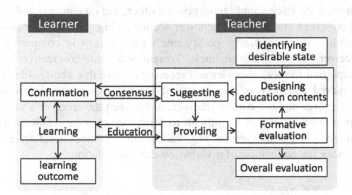

Fig. 2. Overview of the proposed education process

3 A Method for Consensus Building by Using a Learning State Model

3.1 Overview

In order to realize the educational service outlined above, a teacher and a learner need to build a consensus about learning state at each learning stage. Subsequently, the teacher defines learning goals and then determines the instructional and learning behaviors that are required to achieve the learning goals. To this end, the present study focuses on consensus building between teacher and learners, developing a model to represent a process of consensus building. In this model, the process of consensus building is represented as a transition between learning states. This model enables teacher and learner to share an ideal state transition for the learner through agreement of instructional and learning behaviors. In addition, a method is proposed for formulating a strategy for achieving learning goals.

As a perspective on building consensus, this study adopts a model of service value co-creation [5]. The rest of this section introduces the detail of this model. Section 3.2

then explains the proposed learning state model, and Sect. 3.3 proposes a method for formulating a strategy for building consensus about instructional and learning behaviors.

A Model for Service Value Co-creation. Figure 3 illustrates the proposed service model, which includes the co-growth of provider and receiver, along with its driver. A provider proposes a value to a receiver through contents and channels. The receiver perceives the proposed value in a specific context. In response to the perceived value, the receiver modifies his/her actions, and the provider also modifies their actions to improve the service. In this model, value is co-created by such modifications of providing and receiving action in use of the service. Here, reflectiveness is regarded as the ability to appropriately modify one's own actions. The original meaning of "reflect" is to modify one's own actions by comparing one's own ideal model with the current state. However, the value of a service is co-created by mutual interactions between provider and receiver. Each should reflect on the other, and on contents and channels as well as on themselves. As shown in the lower section of Fig. 3, reflectiveness is defined here as an ability to appropriately modify one's own actions in comparing the ideal provider, receiver, contents, and channels. To realize a value co-creative service, it is extremely important for both provider and receiver to have this ability. Idealizing each other is a required condition of the service; if there is a large gap between the provider's ideal receiver and the current receiver, or between the receiver's ideal provider and the current provider, it will be difficult to form a co-creative relationship between provider and receiver. For that reason, negotiation and consensus building around these gaps is necessary for realization of a viable co-creative relationship.

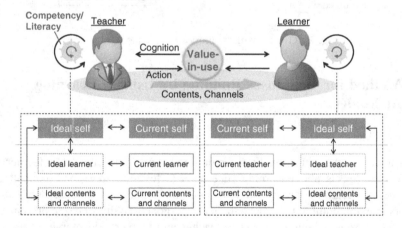

Fig. 3. A model for service value co-creation [5]

3.2   Learning State Model

Figure 4 presents an overview of the proposed learning state model, which consists of two elements: learning states and instructional/learning events. These learning states are described from the viewpoint of the service value co-creation model, in terms of

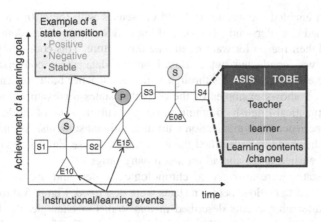

Fig. 4. Overview of the learning state model

a teacher (provider), learner (receiver), and learning contents and channels. In addition, each viewpoint includes a current state (ASIS) as well as an ideal sate (TOBE). Instructional/learning events, on the other hand, are described in terms of learning and instructional theory. For example, instructional events include instructional behavior, such as recommendation of learning contents; learning events include learning behavior, such as review of learning contents. This model represents a process of consensus building.

3.3 Method for Analyzing the Consensus-Building Process

This method begins from an identification of states in which the teacher achieves consensus with the learner on the basis of lecture data. One example of such data might include a questionnaire and conversation between teacher and learner. The relevant states are identified as current state (ASIS) or ideal state (TOBE), as seen from the viewpoints of teacher, learner, and learning contents/channels.

Next, the states are arranged in chronological order, and instructional/learning events that realize transition between states are then described. Finally, the teacher determines a strategy for consensus building that will achieve the learning goals. To determine this strategy, the teacher analyzes the state transition of a learner who has achieved those learning goals, specifying the states that are required to obtain consensus, a sequence for obtaining consensus, and instructional/learning events for obtaining consensus.

4 Application

For determination of a strategy for consensus building, the proposed method was applied here to an English lecture for a graduate and an undergraduate student in the engineering department. In this case, we first extracted those states through which the teacher built consensus with the student. In this lecture, each student received counseling that enabled the teacher to build consensus with them. In this counseling, the teacher aimed to understand what kind of learning contents the student had worked on to date, and their reason for wanting to take this lecture. This counseling took about one hour and was conducted twice. Based on the data about conversation during counseling, we extracted the states through which the teacher built consensus with the student. Figure 5 shows examples of the extracted states-for example, we identified experience of practical English communication as a current state of the learner, as this student had experienced communication with international students. As an ideal learner state, on the other hand, we identified the opportunity to use English after graduation, as this student wished to go abroad on a company program.

Next, the states were arranged in chronological order, and instructional/learning events that realized transitions between states were described. Figure 5 shows examples of instructional/learning events described in this step. For example, the teacher conducted an instructional event on "hearing about opportunities for using English after graduation", building consensus about an ideal state of the learner, who hoped to go abroad with the company. In addition, by conducting an instructional event on "suggesting target abilities of English", they reached agreement about increasing speaking volume.

Finally, we determined a strategy for consensus building that achieved learning goals. This lecture aimed to help students to understand how learning English can be used as a communication tool, providing an opportunity to communicate with students at a university abroad. To determine the strategy, the teacher must analyze the state transition of a learner in achieving learning goals, specifying states that are required to obtain consensus, a sequence for obtaining consensus, and instructional/learning events for obtaining consensus. This application therefore adopted the OPIC (Oral Proficiency Interview-computer) test [6], which evaluates English communication ability. The test was conducted before the first counseling session and again after the second. Next, from among students who achieved a target learning goal, we selected students who achieved a level on the OPIC that had been agreed between teacher and student. By analyzing the state transitions of these students, we were able to specify a strategy for consensus building. In particular, we specified states required to obtain consensus, a sequence for obtaining consensus, and instructional/learning events for obtaining consensus. Figure 6 shows the strategy specified on the basis of these results, which first acknowledged future opportunities for the student to use English and then reached agreement about the level of English ability required to avail of this opportunity. On that basis, the teacher suggested a target OPIC level and the e-learning contents required to achieve that level.

5   Discussion

The reported study analyzed the data from counseling between teacher and learner, specifying the strategy for consensus building that achieved the target learning goal. We conducted a follow-up survey with the student who achieved the target learning goal, which revealed that the student had completed 11 of the 13 e-learning contents recommended by the teacher. As progress on these e-learning contents was not

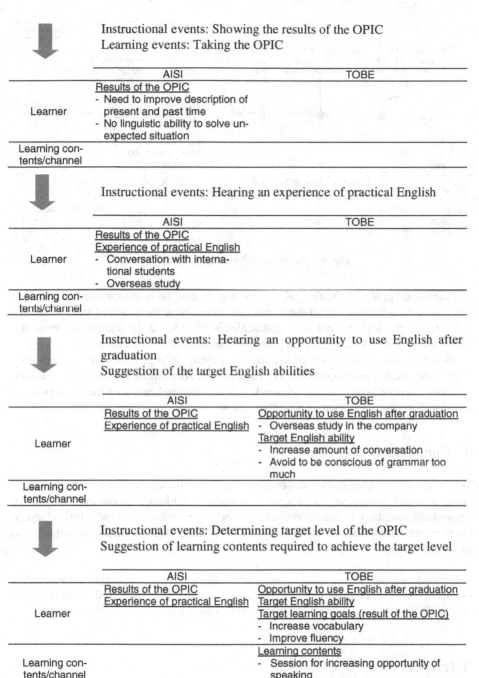

Fig. 5. A process of consensus building in the English lecture

348   K. Kimita et al.

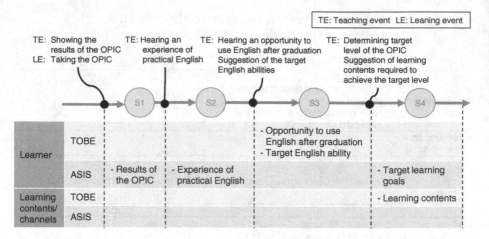

Fig. 6. The strategy for consensus building

considered in grade evaluation of the lecture, it can be assumed that the student recognized the effectiveness of these contents in reaching the required level of ability and selected the learning behavior that achieved this. Since the student achieved the level agreed with the teacher, these contents can be considered effective.

Based on this result, it is expected that identifying an appropriate strategy not only enables the teacher to suggest effective contents but also supports students in selecting adequate learning behaviors. Future work will include application of the strategy in an actual lecture and validation of its effectiveness.

6 Conclusion

This study focuses on consensus building between the teacher and learners, developing a model to represent a process of consensus building. In the application, we determined a strategy to realize providing effective contents and conducting adequate learning behaviors. Future works include the application of the identified strategy to an actual lecture.

Acknowledgements. This research is supported by Service Science, Solutions and Foundation Integrated Research Program (S3FIRE), Research Institute of Science and Technology for Society (RISTEX), Japan Science and Technology Agency (JST).

References

1. Vargo, S.L., Lusch, R.F.: Evolving to a new dominant logic for marketing. J. Mark. **68**(1), 1–17 (2004)
2. Shimomura, Y., Hara, T., Arai, T.: A service evaluation method using mathematical methodologies. Ann. CIRP **57**(1), 437–440 (2008)

3. Shimomura, Y., Tomiyama, T.: Service modeling for service engineering. IFIP Int. Fed. Inf. Process. **167**, 31–38 (2005)
4. Shimomura, Y., Arai, T.: Service engineering - methods and tools for effective PSS development. In: Sakao, T., Lindahl, M. (eds.) Introduction to Product/Service-System Design, Chapter 6, pp. 113–135. Springer, Heidelberg (2010)
5. Nemoto, Y., Uei, K., Kimita, K., Ishii, T., Shimomura, Y.: A conceptual model of co-growth of provider and receiver towards value co-creative service. In: Proceedings of the 2nd International Conference on Serviceology – ICServe 2014, pp. 124–126 (2014)
6. ACTFL. http://www.languagetesting.com/oral-proficiency-interview-by-computer-opic

Development of a Seminar Management System

Yusuke Kometani$^{(\boxtimes)}$ and Keizo Nagaoka

School of Human Sciences, Waseda University,
2-579-15 Mikajima, Tokorozawa, Saitama 359-1192, Japan
kometani@aoni.waseda.jp, k.nagaoka@waseda.jp

Abstract. The role of universities in imparting of knowledge is declining as e-learning and massive open online courses become widespread, and eventually only seminar activity will remain on university campuses. It is important to make seminars the central component of university education, and to think of them as a "university within a university". Within this educational philosophy, each seminar should compete as an attractive educational experience that students want to participate in, and should aim to achieve high quality. In this paper, we report the development of an integrated seminar management system to support seminar activities.

Keywords: Seminar activity · University within a university · Seminar educational philosophy · Seminar management system

1 Seminar Activity for a "University Within a University"

In most advanced nations, the rate of matriculation to higher education now far exceeds 50 %, and according to the American education scholar Martin Trow, higher education is nearly universally available in these countries. Different methods of providing universal access through distance education, such as the OpenCourseWare program and massive open online courses (MOOCs), have rapidly gained prominence since the beginning of this century, and universities around the world have been pressed to change with the times. Although it seems that most lecture-type classes are likely to be offered through distance education to off-campus locations in the near future, discussion- and participatory-type lessons are still performed mainly at university campuses and require in-person attendance at the school. One type of educational model is centered on seminar activities. In particular, each seminar activity offered by a university instructor should fill a role in a larger framework, which defines the curriculum, and these seminar activities should support the particular educational philosophy established for a "university within a university." In this paper, we report the development of an integrated seminar management system (SMS) to support seminar activities. We propose a function for supporting undergraduate research as one aspect of SMS.

The proposed system is based around an electronic portfolio (e-portfolio). A key concept is that students can discover their strengths and weaknesses through reflection on evidence provided by their studies. In line with this, it is expected that introducing an

© Springer International Publishing Switzerland 2015
S. Yamamoto (Ed.): HIMI 2015, Part II, LNCS 9173, pp. 350–361, 2015.
DOI: 10.1007/978-3-319-20618-9_35

e-portfolio into seminar activities will result in improved student motivation and attitude toward the seminar activities. The twin purposes of this research are to develop an e-portfolio system that is appropriate for studying evidence gained through seminar activities and to verify that the e-portfolio supports seminar activities. In this paper, we focus on the specific research activity of "creating the research topic" (CRT). We examine the utility of using an e-portfolio for CRT support by analyzing study evidence and the results of a questionnaire.

2 Investigation of Student Attitudes Toward Seminar Activities

To clarify the guidelines for developing the SMS, student attitudes toward seminar activities are investigated. Seminar activities have rarely been compared across different seminars. The policy of active seminar support is clear from collecting, comparing, and considering the viewpoints of students who use seminars.

2.1 Methodology

A questionnaire survey and interview were performed with 30 fourth-year students [1] who attend a seminar in the School of Human Sciences, Waseda University. Questions belonged to categories such as "reason for seminar choice", "comparison of seminars and lectures", "usual seminar activity", "extracurricular activities besides seminar activity", and "ideal seminar".

2.2 Results and Discussion

In the questionnaire, 13 of the 30 students mentioned that an "ideal seminar" is a seminar in which a "good relationship between students and teachers" is forged. Students do not regard seminars as a place for advanced research; rather, they think of it as a community for building interpersonal relationships. Here, the definitions of "good" and "ideal" depend on personal values, and they should be similar for the student and the teacher involved in the seminar.

Ten of the 30 students mentioned that seminars managed by students on their own initiative are ideal. This suggests that it is desirable to change the role of teacher to that of a mentor, and that supporting students so that they can act on their own initiative would improve their motivation in seminars.

3 Development of SMS

3.1 Objective of SMS

According to the results in Sect. 2, the objective of SMS is to promote the development of students and teachers as a community. Introducing mentoring should also help support the learning community [2]. Teachers can also learn as they teach [2], contributing to the growth of a community. So we place the teacher in the seminar activity as the primary mentor and supporting mentoring as a main policy for SMS.

Based on the results in Sect. 2, it is also important for the development of individuals and the community that students feel that seminars are relevant. For effective course advice [3], it is useful to accumulate student information, so that new students can compare themselves with other students, and discover their aptitude for courses. Thus, we think it is also important to use e-portfolios in a seminar, and to make it possible to offer guidance when students choose suitable seminars. Therefore, e-portfolios are fundamental to SMS. Initially, we construct the overall design of the e-portfolio for accumulating the learning evidence from the seminar activity.

3.2   Seminar Activities

In designing an integrated e-portfolio for seminar activities, the seminar activities in the authors' laboratory were used as a prototype model. The content of the seminar activities was organized, and each activity was classified into one of three activity categories (Table 1).

"Research activities" constitute the core seminar activities. "Interaction inside the laboratory" aims at removing obstacles in the path of seminar students, enhancing knowledge through discussion, and improving motivation to learn through things such as job search assistance and class reunions that include alumni. "Interaction between laboratories" aims at promoting intellectual exchange with new people and other activities that cannot be done through ordinary seminar interactions.

3.3   Design of an e-Portfolio

To promote reflection by students through use of an e-portfolio, it is important to accumulate the content for the e-portfolio in a way that addresses each educational objective [4] and to use different kinds of portfolio structures [5]. In this paper, the design of the e-portfolio for seminar activities is based on the framework proposed by Ueno and Uto [5]. A development portfolio is a portfolio that provides structure for portfolios having various purposes, and using a variety of portfolios provides more support to students than a single portfolio alone can provide. Liqin and Chunhui [4] classified portfolios into four types, with lower types forming a subset of higher types. The relation among the four kinds of portfolios is as follows:

career portfolio ∋ course portfolio ∋ topic portfolio ∋ content portfolio.

Here, "career portfolio ∋ course portfolio" indicates that a course portfolio is one part of a career portfolio, and so on. A career portfolio is built over a long period of time and includes activities from across one's entire time at university and life after graduation. Below this, a course portfolio is created for a subject course, a topic portfolio is created for each topic within the course, and a content portfolio is created for each unit within a topic and contains the student's output on that unit. An overview of an integrated portfolio for seminar activities is shown in Table 1. The hierarchical

Table 1. Overview of design of an integrated e-portfolio for seminar activities

Career portfolio	Course portfolio
Research activity	- Creating research topic
	- Plan and practice
	- Analyze and evaluate
	- Write and present
Interaction inside the laboratory	- Mentoring
	- Adlib speech
	- Project-based learning activities
	- Training camps
	- Job searches
	- Alumni association activities
Interaction between laboratories	- Interactions with invited lecturers
	- Interactions with members of other seminars at the same university
	- Interactions with other domestic universities
	- Interactions with overseas universities

structure of the career portfolio and course portfolio can be seen here. Based on the e-portfolio in Table 1, a design is required to accommodate the extra in-depth data and the support function for which data was used.

4 Support Function for Creating Research Topic

We describe the CRT support function, developed as a function of SMS, based on the portfolio design in Table 1 in this chapter. It is important for students to read articles to suggest research topics. Understanding and explaining research articles allows students to identify gaps in previous research and generate new ideas. However, it is time consuming and difficult for seminar teachers to check how students read articles, and provide individual guidance on literature research. In this chapter, we develop a support system to help students learn how to read articles as a part of seminar activity.

4.1 Learning Method

It is important for students to summarize each article and explain the relationship of the article to the literature as a whole as learning method. We define the learning method as follows.

(a) Students make a summary of each article.
(b) Students make a "mixed summary", which explains the relationship between the articles.

4.2 Support Method

This method offers students useful indexes to help them evaluate and improve their summaries. We define suitable indexes calculated according from the sentences. A good mixed summary should have at least two of the following properties in the sentences of the summary:

1. The main points of each article are reflected.
2. The mixed summary discusses the relationship between the articles, rather than simply summarizing them one after the other.

We define two indexes, "similarity" and "mixing degree" to help students create mixed summaries that satisfy criteria (1) and (2).

Similarity

We assume that the words in an article summary and a mixed summary are related. Then, we define similarity Sim_i of article i to mixed summary U by the following Eq. (1).

$$Sim_i = \frac{|W_i \cap W_U|}{|W_i|} \tag{1}$$

Here,
W_i: Set of nouns in article i
W_U: Set of nouns in summary U

This index will provide feedback to students on how they can improve their summaries, for example, "There are no words in the mixed summary from each article" and "Are you using the correct phraseology?" This can motivate students to modify the mixed summary and their individual article summaries.

Mixing degree

The similarity cannot show whether a student is explaining the relationship between articles. So we introduce the "mixing degree" to measure how well the article information is combined and explained. The indexes, M_{inter} and M_{intra}, are introduced. M_{inter} is the mixing degree of the whole mixed summary and M_{intra} is the mixing degree of each sentence.

To calculate M_{inter}, the order in which nouns appear in the sentences in the mixed summary $(1, 2, ..., n)$ is obtained. M_{inter} is defined in Eq. (2).

$$M_{inter} = \frac{\sum_{i=1}^{n-1} c_{i\{i+1\}}}{n-1} \tag{2}$$

Here,
n: The number of the noun in mixed summary U

$$c_{ij} = \begin{cases} 0 \begin{pmatrix} the\ i\ th\ noun\ and\ the\ j\ th\ noun\ included\ in\ U \\ are\ included\ in\ only\ the\ same\ articles \end{pmatrix} \\ 1(Other) \end{cases}$$

If the content of articles are not mixed and are only combined, M_{inter} will be small. To increase M_{inter}, students must relate words from different articles to create a mixed summary.

M_{intra} is defined by Eq. (3).

$$M_{intra} = \frac{\sum_{i=0}^{|S|} D_i}{|S|} \tag{3}$$

Here,

$$D_i = \begin{cases} 0 \left(\begin{array}{c} \textit{All nouns included in sentence i of mixed summary U} \\ \textit{are included in only the same articles} \end{array} \right) \\ 1 (\textit{Other}) \end{cases}$$

S: The set of the sentence in mixed summary U

To calculate M_{intra}, we examine each sentence included in the mixed summary. When the words used in a sentence are taken from several articles, M_{intra} is large. To increase M_{intra}, students must relate words from different articles, which may encourage students to identify a new links between articles. Feedback from these three indexes may help students to understand each article better and find more links between articles.

4.3 System Development

We developed a learning support system that can calculate three indexes for the summaries made by students and feed back the numerical value of the indexes to students. Figure 1 shows the user interface of the learning support system.

A student reads articles and inputs the summary of each article into the entry field on the left side of the screen. Next, the student refers to the content of each summary and relates the content of two or more individual articles in the mixed summary entry field on the right side of system screen. The student presses a diagnosis button, the system compares each summary with the mixed summary and calculates the similarity and mixing degree. The calculated indexes are shown in a fixed location on the screen. The student corrects the article summaries and the mixed summary with reference to these indexes. The student can amend inaccurate expressions and relationships in the mixed summary and in each article summary. This will help students notice important expressions and key words that they may have missed.

4.4 Practice

4.4.1 Method

A study was conducted to evaluate the proposed indexes and the system. The participants were eight third year students in our department. The study was conducted from January 8 to January 22, 2015. The students were assigned to a seminar when they

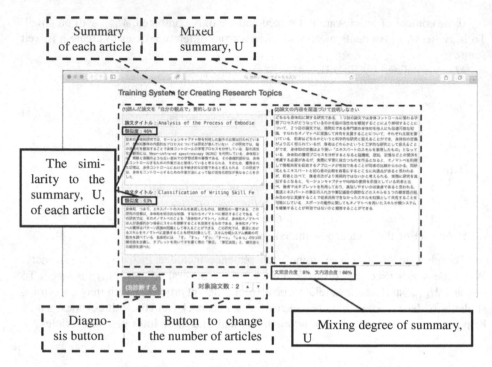

Fig. 1. User interface of the learning support system

entered the third year. They continued to study in the same seminar in the fourth year and proceeded to graduate study. The third year students read articles, made presentations, and participated in discussions to prepare for fourth year. The participants were students who read articles repeatedly from April 2014.

Two tasks were given to the students: reading two articles or reading three articles, and then writing a mixed summary. For the two-article task, students chose two articles from those that they had already read during their usual seminar activity, and made individual article summaries and a mixed summary. For the three-article task, they chose one new article in addition to two articles they had already read, and made individual article summaries and a mixed summary. The results were shared with the students on January 15, 2015 (two-article task) and January 22, 2015 (three-article task).

A questionnaire survey was conducted after the tasks. We expected that the indexes and the system would have the following effects.

- The content of articles would be understood better.
- Participants would be more aware of correct phraseology.
- Participants would be more aware of the relationship among different articles.
- The indexes and systems would be useful for selecting what participants should read next.

Based on these expected effects, the (1) similarity, (2) mixing degree, and (3) learning using the system were evaluated by the students. Questions were prepared about each area, and the participants give answers on a five-point Likert scale ("1. I don't think so" to "5. I think so") and through free description.

4.4.2   Results and Discussion

Table 2 shows the number of times each participant received feedback. Participants A, B, and D received more than twice the amount of feedback for each task compared with the other participants. This suggests that the participants modify their summaries after feedback and receive repeated diagnoses. Participants F, G, and H only completed the two-article task.

Tables 3 and 4 show the changes in the indexes when participants A and B modified their summaries. The results for the two- and three-article tasks are placed in one table because two cases are ongoing.

Initially, we found that the mixing degree in both participants was always 100 %. This shows that the students use words from different articles in the same sentence. Therefore, that M_{intra} is useful for helping students become more deeply aware of the relationships among articles. The results for participant A in Table 3 show no big changes in similarity, but that there is a clear change in M_{inter} in the 3rd and 4th diagnosis. Every time a check is repeated, the similarity tends to increase, and we can also confirm the M_{inter} for participant B in Table 4 gradually increases.

The improvement in the mixing degree in a sentence was used to confirm the results for participant A. We compared the 3rd and 4th diagnoses for participant A. Table 5 shows a comparison of the sentences in a mixed summary by participant A. One of the sentences in the 4th diagnosis is not seen in the 3rd diagnosis, "because students esteem activity in time", which participant A indicates as a reason. This shows that the mixing degree provides useful information for students to consider where they can add an expression or keyword in sentences (Table 5).

Next, we check the change in the similarity. Table 6 shows a comparison of sentences in the summary of article 1 by participant B. In the 6th diagnosis, the type of MOOC participant in the study is discussed. However, in the 7th diagnosis this description is removed, and only a specific instance is mentioned by participant B as "Even if learning goals are achieved, some person who doesn't accomplish the learning activity is included in the number of finish". Thus, the type of MOOC participant is not essential information in this summary. Therefore, participant B tried to eliminate expressions that are not important. The similarity is useful for students to identify which expression or words are important.

Table 7 shows the results of questionnaire survey. They show that many students have a positive impression of each indexes and the system. Participant E gave a negative evaluation for Q1-2 and Q3-4. "Q 1-2: Correct phraseology" was poorly rated because Participant E did not modify summaries after feedback. This result suggests that it is important to include a mechanism to motivate students to improve the summary repeatedly, for example, through peer assessment.

Table 2. Number of diagnoses

Task	Participants							
	A	B	C	D	E	F	G	H
Two articles	2	7	1	4	1	2	1	2
Three articles	3	2	1	3	1	-	-	-

Table 3. Feedback for participant A

Diagnosis number	Similarity of article 1	Similarity of article 2	Similarity of article 3	M_{inter}	M_{intra} (%)
1	13	21	-	20	100
2	19	23	-	16	100
3	19	23	46	20	100
4	15	23	46	30	100
5	18	23	46	30	100

Table 4. Feedback for participant B

Diagnosis number	Similarity of article 1	Similarity of article 2	Similarity of article 3	M_{inter}	M_{intra} (%)
1	15	5	-	12	100
2	26	16	-	15	100
3	26	16	-	12	100
4	36	36	-	16	100
5	50	54	-	15	100
6	42	60	-	27	100
7	53	60	-	26	100
8	53	60	11	26	100
9	53	60	60	32	100

Participant E gave the reason for negative evaluation of "Q 3-4: When the system became available from the first term in the third year, did you want to try it?" as "It is difficult. There was not enough experience in reading articles at the start of third year." Participant C gave the opinion "Experience in reading articles is important for appreciating the usefulness of the system." Therefore, it is important to consider the timing of the introduction of the system to students. However, positive opinions were obtained, such as "I wanted to gather many articles to read", "The system should be

Table 5. Mixed summary by participant A

Diagnosis number	Sentences of mixed summary
3	... Therefore, a teacher is concerned with factors that make the interaction between the group members competitive between the students by a teacher communicates with a teacher aggressively also working, and the group study which will be in the lesson time later aggressively, and when making activity enrich, learning motivation may also improve in seminar activity.
4	... Therefore, a teacher is concerned with factors that make the interaction between the group members competitive between the students by a teacher communicates with a teacher aggressively also working, and the group study which will be in the lesson time later aggressively, and when making activity enrich, learning motivation may also improve in seminar activity **because students esteem activity in time**.

Table 6. Summary of article 1 by participant B

Diagnosis number	Sentences from the summary of article 1
6	... The viewpoint of the educational effect analysis based on participant data is shown for so becoming reference of evaluation based on the result of analysis of the former lecture. **There are four types of MOOC participant: a wait-and-see learner, a knowledge acquisition learner, a learning activity accomplishment learner, and a knowledge confirming learner. Even if learning goals are achieved, anyone who is a learning activity accomplishment learner is not included in the number of people who finish.** All lesson movies were viewed, although there were many people who did not take the test. Without considering the purpose of attendance, it is not possible to consider the learning outcome. ...
7	... The viewpoint of the educational effect analysis based on participant data is shown for so becoming reference of evaluation based on the result of analysis of the former lecture.
	Even if learning goals are achieved, people who do not accomplish the learning activity are included in the number of people who finish. All lesson movies were viewed, although there were many people who did not take the test. Without considering the purpose of attendance, it is not possible to consider the learning outcome. ...

used in the long run, and I would like to check the outcome", "It seems useful for deciding which areas of research to investigate", "I think more directionality on its graduation theme was decided early." This shows that the system should be introduced as early as possible after students start to read articles.

Table 7. Questionnaire results

#	Question	Participant	A v.	S .D.
Q 1-1	Writing a summary with the similarity index in mind helped me understand the content of the articles better		4 .6	0 .7
Q 1-2	To increase the similarity, I started paying attention to correct phraseology		4 .3	1 .0
Q 1-3	Writing a summary with the similarity index in mind was useful for me to decide what I read next		4 .5	0 .8
Q 2-1	Writing a summary with the mixing degree in mind helped me understand the content of the articles better		4 .3	0 .9
Q 2-2	Writing a summary with the mixing degree in mind helped me identify links between articles		4 .1	0 .6
Q 2-3	Writing a summary with the mixing degree in mind helped me to decide what to read next		4 .4	0 .9
Q 3-1	Writing a summary using this system helped me to decide what to read next		4 .4	0 .7
Q 3-2	Writing a summary using this system helped me identify a research topic		4 .3	0 .7
Q 3-3	The system was useful		3 .8	0 .9
Q 3-4	When the system became available from the first term in the third year, did you want to try it?		4 .0	1 .1

5   Conclusion

In this work, we developed an SMS to support seminar activity. Support through CRT was proposed as a function of SMS. The study results showed that the system helped students learn effectively.

In future work, we intend to design a system for accumulating detailed data and analyzing support functions based on the e-Portfolio design in this research. We also intend to improve the CRT function. For example, introducing a peer assessment process may be a good way to motivate students.

Acknowledgements. This research was partially supported by a Grant-in-Aid for Scientific Research (No. 26350288) from the Japanese Ministry of Education, Culture, Sports, Science and Technology.

References

1. Nakatani, N.: Undergraduate Student Attitudes for seminar activity, Graduation thesis in Faculty of Human Sciences, Waseda University (2015) (in Japanese)
2. Porter, L.R.: Mentoring in online learning communities. In: Proceedings of the International Conference on Computers in Education (ICCE2002), pp. 1444–1445 (2002)
3. Taha, K.: Automatic academic advisor. In: 8th International Conference on Collaborative Computing: Networking, Applications and Worksharing (Collaboratecom 2012), pp. 262–268 (2012)
4. Liqin, Z., Chunhui, W.: The construction of teachers' professional growth e-portfolio on the basis of moodle platform. In: The 9th International Conference on Computer Science and Education (ICCSE 2014), pp. 894–897 (2014)
5. Ueno, M., Uto, M.: ePortfolio which facilitates learning from others. Jpn. J. Educ. Technol. **35** (3), 169–182 (2011). (in Japanese)

Analysis of Multiple-Choice Tests Through Erroneous Choices Using a Technique of Automatic Problem Generation

Noriyuki Matsuda[1($\boxtimes$)], Hisashi Ogawa[2], Tsukasa Hirashima[3],
and Hirokazu Taki[1]

[1] Faculty of Systems Engineering, Wakayama University, Wakayama, Japan
{matsuda, taki}@sys.wakayama-u.ac.jp
[2] The Joint Graduate School in Science of School Education, Hyogo University
of Teacher Education, Hyogo, Japan
ogawa@hyogo-u.ac.jp
[3] Department of Information Engineering, Hiroshima University, Hiroshima,
Japan
tsukasa@lel.hiroshima-u.ac.jp

Abstract. In multiple-choice problems, incorrect choices that hide correct answer do not play the only significant function. A more significant function is to capture learner errors and provide learners with the opportunity to amend those errors. In this sense, explanation texts for incorrect choices might be important in allowing learners to amend their own errors correctly. In this paper, we term this "meaningful erroneous choice." We confirm the existence of meaningful erroneous choice through actual problems used in an examination. We then compare choices using a technique of automatic problem generation. The result indicates that the difference between correctness knowledge and incorrectness knowledge plays an important role in problem posing.

Keywords: Multiple-choice problems · Automatic problem generation · E-learning · Prolog

1 Introduction

Erroneous answers in multiple-choice problems not only make the correct answer more difficult to determine, but also indicate why the correct choice is suitable and the erroneous one unsuitable when compared to the correct answer. Munby [10] asserts that erroneous answers should prompt learners to make careful considerations before making their selection; in this scenario, learner instruction is affected by the selected choice, and texts explaining the erroneous answers. We distinguish between "meaningless erroneous distracters" (MDs) and "meaningful erroneous choices" (MCs). The latter (MCs) stimulate learning through a ripple effect. For instance, MCs can explain why an answer is incorrect, but MDs do not provide such an explanation, stating only "because it differs in appearance from the correct answer."

This paper attempts to explain the role of MCs as compared to MDs. Our approach followed two steps. Firstly, we have surveyed and analyzed multiple-choice tests from

© Springer International Publishing Switzerland 2015
S. Yamamoto (Ed.): HIMI 2015, Part II, LNCS 9173, pp. 362–369, 2015.
DOI: 10.1007/978-3-319-20618-9_36

actual learning material and examinations. Secondly, we have attempted to generate the erroneous choices surveyed using a technique to generate multiple-choice tests. This technique is one of Simulation of Erroneous Solutions (SES), which generates erroneous choices with explanations of the error through problem solving knowledge written in Prolog. We have tried to confirm the differences in generating techniques between meaningful and meaningless choices.

Through surveying erroneous choices in 80 multiple-choice tests, a university teacher and a high school teacher have estimated the design intention of the tests and analyzed the process of problem construction.

Our SES is a method of generating a solution from incorrect knowledge to incorrect answer, through a perturbation from problem-solving knowledge to knowledge of incorrect answer derivation. The perturbation is projected onto the design intention of the teacher who creates the problem, and expresses the difference between the erroneous solution and the correct solution. For instance, a 48-question and 128-explanation text was automatically generated from 17 Prolog clauses regarding knowledge about SES. The SES has the potential to generate relevant choices and erroneous solutions. In this paper, we are concerned with the difference in perturbation that generates meaningful and meaningless choices. Meaningful perturbation changes slightly correct solutions written in Prolog and the latter perturbation randomly changes solutions. We also discuss the differences between the explanation texts that were generated automatically by SES.

2 Analysis of Erroneous Choices

We analyzed actual problems randomly collected from an information technology engineers' examination in Japan. Two teachers, a university teacher and high school teacher who create problems professionally, read all problems and discussed whether incorrect choices should be categorized as MDs or MCs. They then selected MD or MC for each choice. Incorrect choices were classified into the following five categories (A to E).

- A. Problems that require selection of concepts to satisfy any given conditions (16 problems and 48 choices)
  All erroneous choices satisfy some part of the given conditions in a problem. For example, Problem 1 below consists of three erroneous choices that satisfy the given condition "protocol used on TCP/IP network."

(Problem 1) Which of the following is a TCP/IP protocol that provides a bidirectional interactive text-oriented communication facility using a virtual terminal connection?

(a) FTP
(b) HTTP
(c) SMTP
(d) TELNET

Therefore, all incorrect choices are recognized as MCs that can be generated by perturbation; such as changing some part of the knowledge. For example, incorrect choice (a) FTP can be generated by changing "text-oriented communication facility" into "computer file transfer facility."

- B. Problems that can be solved using procedural knowledge (32 problems and 96 choices)
  An answer is obtained using a procedural solution, such as a calculated problem.

(Problem 2) When the manipulations shown below are executed for the empty stack, which of the following are the appropriate remaining data in the stack?
```
push 1 -> push 2 -> pop -> push 3 -> push 4 -> pop ->
push 5 -> pop
```

(a) 1 and 3
(b) 2 and 5
(c) 1 and 5
(d) 4 and 5

Twenty-four incorrect choices are recognized as MDs because it is impossible to find an adequate reason for error. Seventy-two incorrect choices are recognized as MCs. For example, meaningful erroneous choice (d) in Problem 2 is obtained by replacing "stack" with "queue."

- C. Problems that require selection of an explanation
  (42 problems and 126 choices)
  Problems provide explanatory choices for a word given.

(Problem 3) Which of the following is the most appropriate explanation of DHCP?

(e) A protocol that automatically provides an IP address and networking parameters
(f) A protocol used in order to access a directory service
(g) A protocol that sends emails
(h) A protocol that converts a private address to a global address

All incorrect choices were recognized as MCs. Seventy-two incorrect choices explained another concept that could be distinguished with a correct answer. Twenty-four incorrect choices partially switched in explanation of another concept. Twenty-four incorrect choices partially switched in the opposite meaning word. Six incorrect choices partially switched in an explanation of similar concepts.

- D. Problems that require selection of a correct combination
  (Eight problems and 24 solutions)
  Problems provide a combination of relationships, such as causal relationship and correlations.

(Problem 4) Which of the following is the appropriate combination of a threat and countermeasure of information security? (The upper row shows a threat and the lower row shows a countermeasure.)

(a) Logical data destruction by misoperation
     Disk array
(b) Earthquake and fire
     Data duplication in a machine using a virtual machine

(c) Unauthorized access to data during transmission
     CRC by HDLC
(d) Alteration of message
     Digital signature by public key encryption

All incorrect choices are recognized as MCs. They are generated by switching in another related concept or simply other concept which has no relation.

- E. Problem that requires selection of a correct order
  (Two problems and six choices)
  Problems provide the relationship of the order or position as choices.

(Problem 5) Which of the following is an appropriate order to establish ISMS of JIS Q 27001:2006?

1. Create an application declaration
2. Select management objectives for risk operation and control measures
3. Analysis and assessment of risk

(a) 1 -> 2 -> 3
(b) 1 -> 3 -> 2
(c) 2 -> 3 -> 1
(d) 3 -> 2 -> 1

All incorrect choices are recognized as MDs. The correct answer for Problem 5 is choice (d). However, a reasonable cause of error cannot be found.

   We have confirmed the existence of MCs in actual problems. Next, we consider the difference between MDs and MCs in problem posing.

3   Simulation of Erroneous Solution

To consider the differences between MDs and MCs, we use a technique of automatic problem generation. We have already proposed a technique to generate problems and explanation of incorrect choices, called Simulation of Erroneous Solution (SES) [7, 11]. Currently, much research exists, for example, in an e-Learning context. Automatic generation techniques that use text processing and statistical analysis [3, 6, 9], a corpus thesaurus of general knowledge within a particular field [2, 5, 13], and domain ontology [1, 4, 8, 12] have been suggested. While these techniques can automatically generate large numbers of problems at a single time, SES can generate multiple-choice problems and explanation texts for incorrect choices (see Fig. 1). Before this, SES used correctness knowledge to solve the problem. This knowledge is written in Prolog, so we can obtain the correct answer by running the Prolog code. To express learner errors, we defined perturbation, which slightly changes the correctness knowledge to simulate learners' incorrect solutions. This perturbation is also written in Prolog clauses. In this way, we can obtain the incorrect answer and its explanation text, which is constructed of clauses in the resolution process in Prolog with a template of explanation.

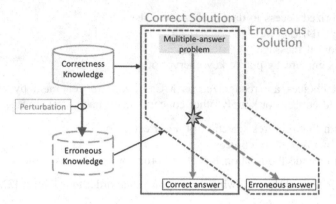

Fig. 1. Outline of SES provides erroneous choices and explanations for the errors with perturbation of correctness knowledge. Perturbation that slightly changes correctness knowledge expresses learners' erroneous solutions.

Here, we start to prepare SES to generate Problem 2. Correctness knowledge is shown in Fig. 2. It includes rules for stack and queue. The "Push" operation is the same and the "Pop" operation is different.

```
% Knowledge
%    For Stack
push(A, stack)  :- retract(stack(B)),     asserta(stack([A|B])).
pop(stack)      :- retract(stack([_|B])), assert(stack(B)).
%    For Queue
push(A, queue)  :- retract(queue(B)), asserta(queue([A|B])).
pop(queue)      :- retract(queue(A)), shift(A, B), asserta(queue(B)).

% Private Procedure
shift([_], []).
shift([A|B], [A|C]) :- shift(B, C).
```

Fig. 2. Correctness knowledge for Problem 3

The given condition in the problem is shown in Fig. 3. There, stack and the procedure of push and pop are empty.

```
stack([]).
procedure-stack :- push(1, stack), push(2, stack), pop(stack), push(3, stack),

                   push(4, stack), pop(stack), push(5, stack), pop(stack).
```

Fig. 3. Given conditions in Problem 3. When we execute this Prolog code with correctness knowledge in Fig. 2, the correct answer and explanation text for the correct solution are generated.

Next, we write down the perturbation for the learner's error, such as misunderstanding of stack and queue (see Fig. 4). When perturbation is added on top of correctness knowledge, the MC (d) and explanation text are generated.

```
pop(stack) :- retract(stack(A)), shift(A, B), asserta(stack(B)).
```

Fig. 4. Perturbation of Problem 3. It shows a misunderstanding of stack and queue. When this perturbation is added on top of correctness knowledge in Fig. 2, meaningful erroneous choice (d) is obtained.

On the other hand, MD is randomly generated from a combination of list [1–3] except for the correct answer [1, 3].

Thus, perturbation of correctness knowledge has a significant function for MCs. Perturbation might be considered to capture learner errors in order to give the learner important learning opportunities. In addition, perturbation might be considered to express a teacher's educational intention. Therefore, the teacher who created the problem naturally writes down an explanation of the incorrect choice to lead a learner to the correct solution.

Another example is shown below. A problem asks an adequate bio-indicator in river (see Fig. 5). A perturbation shows learner's typical misunderstanding about the relation between electrical conductivity (EC) and dissolved matter in the river. Correct knowledge is that EC is proportional to the amount of dissolved matter. Typical incorrect

---

Problem: When the river's EC is low, flow volume is also low, and upstream land is not used as forest. What is the bio-indicator?

Correct answer	Plecoptera
Erroneous answer	Corixidae
Erroneous answer	Chironomidae
Erroneous answer	Luciola

Text explaining the erroneous answer

Corixidae: Incorrect. If EC is low and flow volume is low, you should assume that a small amount of dissolved matter is present. Did you mistakenly think there would be a large amount of dissolved matter?

The correct understanding is that because EC and flow volume are low, a small amount of dissolved matter will be present. Since a small amount of dissolved matter is present and the upstream land is not used for forest, the water quality will be clean. As the water quality will be clean, the bio-indicator will be Plecoptera. Therefore, the correct answer is Plecoptera.

Fig. 5. An example problem which asks bio-indicator. A learner needs to know the relations that the amount of dissolved matter is determined by upstream land use, flow volume, and electrical conductivity (EC), and also that the bio-indicators are determined by water quality.

knowledge is that EC is inversely proportional to the amount of dissolved matter. Therefore perturbation is to change from direct proportion to inverse proportion. Such perturbation can generate MCs which can have some explanation to fix typical misunderstanding about the relationship between EC and dissolved matter. On the other hand, random selection for bio-indicator or living things in river can generate MDs. MDs cannot have no explanation about the error.

4 Conclusions

We have confirmed the existence of MCs through actual problems in an examination. In addition, we have compared MCs and MDs with regard to perturbation of SES. We believe that incorrect choices are not only distracters but also capture learners' errors. In future work, through automatic problem generation, perturbations for MCs should be analyzed into categories and formulated.

References

1. Alsubait, T., Parsia, B., Sattler, U.: Mining ontologies for analogy questions: a similarity-based approach. In: Klinov, P., Horridge, M. (eds.) OWLED, CEUR Workshop Proceedings, vol. 849 (2012)
2. Brown, J.C., Frishkoff, G.A., Eskenazi, M.: Automatic question generation for vocabulary assessment. In: Proceedings of HLT/EMNLP 2005, pp. 819–826 (2005)
3. Correia, R., Baptista, J., Mamede, N., Trancoso, I., Eskenazi, M.: Automatic generation of cloze question distractors. In: Proceedings of the Interspeech 2010 Satellite Workshop on Second Language Studies: Acquisition, Learning, Education and Technology (2010)
4. Holohan, E., Melia, M., McMullen, D., Pahl, C.: Adaptive e-learning content generation based on semantic web technology. In: International Workshop on Applications of Semantic Web Technologies for E-Learning (SW-EL 2005) – at the 12th International Conference on Artificial Intelligence in Education AIED 2005, pp. 29–36 (2005)
5. Sumita, E., Sugaya, F., Yamamoto, S.: Measuring non-native speakers' proficiency of English by using a test with automatically-generated fill-in-the-blank questions. In: Proceedings of ACL 2005 Workshop: Building Educational Applications Using Natural Language Processing, pp. 61–68 (2005)
6. Gotoh, T., Kojiri, T., Watanabe, T., Iwata, T., Yamada, T.: Automatic generation system of multiple-choice cloze questions and its evaluation. Knowl. Manag. E-Learn. Int. J. 2(3), 210–224 (2010)
7. Matsuda, N., Ogawa, H., Hirashima, T., Taki, H.: A Generating Technique and Knowledge Representation of Multiple-Answer Problems for Learning with Solving Knowledge, Research and Practice in Technology Enhanced Learning (2015)
8. Mitkov, R., Ha, L., Karamanis, N.: A computer-aided environment for generating multiple-choice test items. Nat. Lang. Eng. 12(2), 177–194 (2006)
9. Moser, J.R., Gütl, C., Liu, W.: Refined distractor generation with LSA and stylometry for automated multiple choice question generation. In: Thielscher, M., Zhang, D. (eds.) AI 2012. LNCS, vol. 7691, pp. 95–106. Springer, Heidelberg (2012)
10. Munby, J.: Read and Think. Longman, Harlow (1968)

11. Ogawa, H., Kobayashi, H., Matsuda, N., Hirashima, T., Taki, H.: Knowledge externalization based on differences of solutions for automatic generation of multiple-choice question. In: Proceedings of the 19th International Conference on Computers in Education, pp. 271–278 (2011)
12. Papasalourosa, A., Kotisb, K., Kanarisb, K.: Automatic generation of tests from domain and multimedia ontologies. Interact. Learn. Environ. **19**(1), 5–23 (2011)
13. Lin, Y.C., Sung, L.C., Chen, M.C.: An automatic multiple-choice question generation scheme for English adjective understanding. In: Workshop on Modeling, Management and Generation of Problems/Questions in eLearning, the 15th International Conference on Computers in Education, Hiroshima, Japan, pp. 137–142, November 2007

Proposal of an Instructional Design Support System Based on Consensus Among Academic Staff and Students

Shuya Nakamura[1(✉)], Takahito Tomoto[2], and Takako Akakura[3]

[1] Graduate School of Engineering, Tokyo University of Science,
1-3 Kagurazaka, Shinjuku-Ku, Tokyo 162-8601, Japan
nakamura_shuya@ms.kagu.tus.ac.jp
[2] Graduate School of Engineering, Tokyo Polytechnic University,
1583 iiyama, Atsugi-Shi, Kanagawa 243-0297, Japan
t.tomoto@cs.t-kougei.ac.jp
[3] Graduate School of Engineering, Tokyo University of Science,
1-3 Kagurazaka, Shinjuku-Ku, Tokyo 162-8601, Japan
akakura@ms.kagu.tus.ac.jp

Abstract. In this paper, we propose an instructional design-based method for supporting academic staff and students in value co-creation within the university setting. The term co-creation adopted in this study comes from the field of service engineering and is defined as the mutual creation of value by service providers and service beneficiaries. Co-creation is realized by consensus among them. Within the university setting, the service providers are the academic staff and the beneficiaries are students. Here, we propose a model of co-creation in universities and then present a support method based on a syllabus and learning motivation for co-creation. Finally, we discuss the co-creation support system.

Keywords: Instructional design · Co-creation · Service engineering

1 Introduction

In this paper, we discuss a model of co-creation and a co-creation support system within the university setting on the basis of instructional design. In recent years, Japanese universities have been required to improve education according to the social background of students. The declining birthrate has led to the coining of the phrase *daigaku zen'nyū jidai* (era of open university admissions). With declining enrollment, it is becoming difficult to manage universities. However, making entrance examinations easier to attract more students lowers the quality of higher education institutions. Therefore, universities need a way to respond to the needs of society while maintaining the quality of education. To do so, instructional design based on the needs of the students is useful, but this approach can be difficult because the academic staff at universities is often composed of researchers rather than professional educators. In this study, we apply the concept of co-creation from service engineering and propose a model of co-creation within the university setting. Then, a support method is designed to share the needs of students and academic staff. We conclude with a discussion of the support system for implementing instructional design considering the quality of education.

© Springer International Publishing Switzerland 2015
S. Yamamoto (Ed.): HIMI 2015, Part II, LNCS 9173, pp. 370–377, 2015.
DOI: 10.1007/978-3-319-20618-9_37

2 Co-creation

Co-creation is an important concept in service engineering. It is possible to measure the productivity improvement and efficiency of services to be provided. Our aim is to improve the service quality of university instruction. Toward this end, it is important to have not only the efforts of service providers but also the cooperation of service beneficiaries. Co-creation is realized through the actions of both providers and beneficiaries, facilitated by the perceived value of service. The perception of value requires self-reflection. Perception of the value of service and mutual efforts to create the value leads to ideal providers, ideal beneficiaries, and ideal services (see Fig. 1) [1].

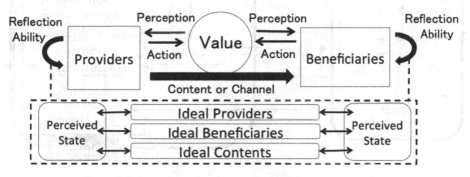

Fig. 1. Co-creation

Here, we treat university education as a service. We regard academic staff as service providers and students as service beneficiaries. The academic staff now must provide instruction in increasingly specialized subjects to satisfy the requirement of maintaining the value of education. In other words, academic staff and students must respond to the needs of society. To maintain the value of education, academic staff and students needs to act perceiving the ideal academic staff, ideal students and ideal education. In this paper, we define the ability of students for understanding the needs of society as "literacy," and the ability of academic staff for meeting the need of society and students as "competency". We consider that education with high value is made possible by the academic staff's competency and the student's literacy. One purpose of the proposed system is to clarify the mechanism of service provision in education using the concepts of competency and literacy.

3 Proposed Method

In this section, we describe the proposed method of instructional design support. To realize courses where co-creation can be performed, academic staff must suggest an educational plan for students. We consider it necessary for students to confirm and understand the plan before they join the course. We define such confirmation as *consensus*. Academic staff and students form the consensus, and then they join the course and together assess whether they can achieve the goal of the course. In the next lesson, academic staff determines the educational approach utilizing the assessment results. Then the assessment is performed again. The model is shown in Fig. 2. We describe the instructional design support method based on this model.

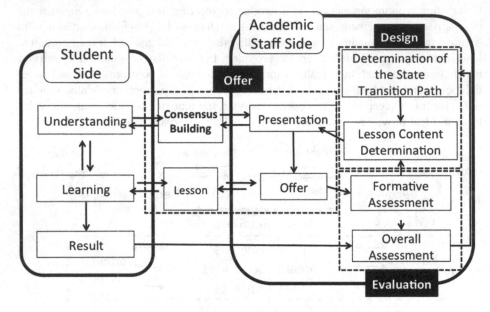

Fig. 2. Model of consensus among student and academic staff

3.1   Syllabus

A *syllabus* is often used for instructional design at universities. It is a useful tool for giving an overview of a course and indicating its purpose. The syllabus plays a significant role in teaching. Many universities publish syllabuses on the Internet. There are several studies to arrange for crossing search [2]. Syllabuses provide students with useful information and help them make a comparison of a subject between universities.

The contents of a syllabus are as follows [3]: course name, academic staff name, undergraduate department, grade level, number of units, time, place, textbooks, reference books, teaching goals, lesson plans, and evaluation methods. At many universities, the rules and form of syllabuses are assessed for ease of understanding. Students can obtain an overview of the course and understand its flow. However, the syllabus is currently made by only academic staff. Therefore, it could be insufficient for meeting the needs of students.

We suggest the syllabus as a material for sharing educational goals among teachers and students. For co-creation, it is most important to share the value of the course. Yet the value is usually invisible. We consider the syllabus to serve as a visible material for sharing co-created value. Academic staff should systematically conduct courses. Then, they can reflect on one lesson and make improvements for the next. To improve a course systematically, academic staff needs to recognize the relation between the purpose of the course and its content. For this, it is necessary to gradually divide the purpose into several sub-goals. The relation between concrete sub-goals and contents is clear. Therefore, it is easy to share consensus among academic staff and students. In the next subsection, we explain the method for dividing the course's purpose into sub-goals based on Hayashi et al. [5].

3.2 Details of the Lesson Plan

The syllabus is a written education plan. And typically covers a total of 15 lessons for a university course. The educational goals of a course can be achieved by achieving the teaching objectives in each of the course's lessons. To achieve a lesson goal, students must acquire the targeted knowledge and abilities. Giving students a means of checking the acquisition of the required knowledge and abilities in the lesson will facilitate consensus building among academic staff and students in the course. Figure 3 shows an example of a detailed syllabus. Here, the course is composed of 15 lessons. In each lesson, learning contents are described, as are the methods for acquiring knowledge and abilities. Providing the descriptions from the syllabus after each lesson is effective because it is an adequate method for assessing the status of the previous lesson. However, it is difficult for academic staff to construct a dynamic syllabus. Hayashi and Mizoguchi [5] propose a methodology for constructing an adequate pedagogy based on ontology. We use the methodology for co-creation. After a lesson, academic staff and students create the syllabus together. By this action, they understand and share the value of contents.

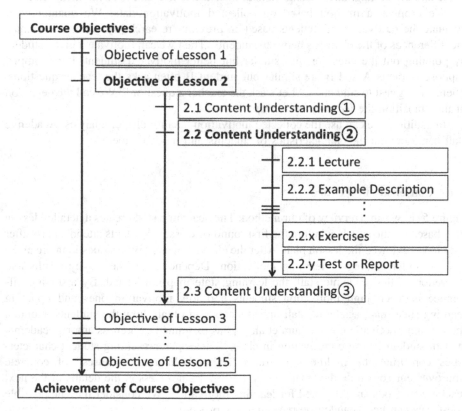

Fig. 3. Details of the syllabus

3.3   Method for Learning Motivation

Even if the relation between sub-goal and contents is made clear, it has no value without the motivation of students. For co-creation, action by students is necessary. In this subsection, we propose a method for improving the motivation of students. In a typical class, there are some students with low motivation students and others with high motivation. Therefore, academic staff must be able to identify the students with low motivation and increase their motivation. There are two way to determine a student's motivation. One is assessment by a questionnaire. Another is observation of the student's behavior during class. In co-creation, gaps in perception between academic staff and students are an issue. For example, if a teacher assesses a student as having low motivation even though the student studies hard, then it could lead to a drop in motivation. Therefore, we investigated whether there is a gap in the assessment of motivation between academic staff and students [4]. Figure 4 shows the results of assessment by academic staff for motivation (scored as high or low). Six factors were associated with an assessment of high motivation (Class participation without prompting, Course content pointed out, Reaction, Performance, Active communication, Seat position). Two factors were associated with an assessment of low motivation (Nonparticipation, Use of electronic devices). These eight factors were composed of several elements. From this cause-and-effect diagram, students can see how academic staff assesses their behavior.

We propose a method based on collected motivation data. We quantitatively evaluate the motivation of students based on previous research [4]. Also, we evaluate the differences of the elements between students. Then we can motivate a given student by pointing out the behavior of a similar but better motivated student. For example, suppose students A and B are similar but student B often asks the teacher questions. Then, we suggest to student A, "Let's ask the teacher a question!" We call the depiction of this transition the *learning state map*.

In addition, we can use the collected motivation data for cluster analysis. Academic staff can ascertain the characteristics of students and motivate them.

3.4   Consensus Procedure

Figure 5 shows an overview of our method. The academic staff creates a detailed lesson plan based on the syllabus before the first round of classes. Students attend a class after they have reviewed the lesson plan. After the class, they are given a questionnaire and a test for understanding of learning motivation. Depending on the survey results and discretion of the academic staff, the learning state map is updated. By assessing difference between high motivation students and low motivation ones and updating learning state map, academic staff and students can obtain how the students maintain the learning motivation. Nakamura et al. [4] has examined awareness among academic staff of student learning motivation in class. "Factors" representing student characteristics constitute the middle bone of a fishbone diagram. "Causes" of concrete improvement constitute the small bones. Before the next lesson the details of the next teaching methods are presented for learning motivation. We consider that the possible consensus can be expanded by repeating this process.

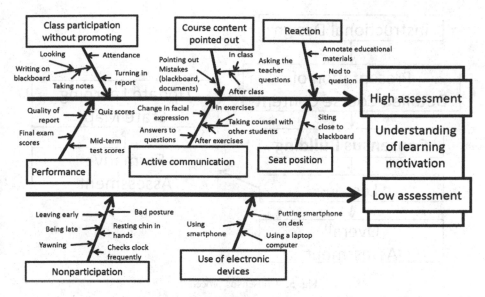

Fig. 4. Factors considered by academic staff regarding student motivation in the class model

4 Support System

In this section, we describe the design of a support system for the proposed method. The system requires the following five functions.

1. Support for refining the syllabus and to design lesson plan.
2. Support for inputting item about learning motivation.
3. Automatic updating of the learning state map of each student and each group categorized by cluster analysis.
4. Generating transitions in the learning state map for each student, each group and academic staff.
5. Sharing of and referral to various types of collected data.

The first function is implemented based on previous research [5]. The second function is realized by inputting data. Students report their motivation in questionnaires. Academic staff assesses student motivation by observation. By third function, the system derives the learning state based on collected motivation data according to previous research [4] and displays the learning state map about individual learner and specified group by cluster analysis. In the fourth function, the system provides information to students and academic staff for improving student motivation. Academic staff and students can see data on changes in learning motivation on the server. Also, students can feel the value of the class and of their own growth. These functions create consensus and support co-creation (Figs. 5 and 6).

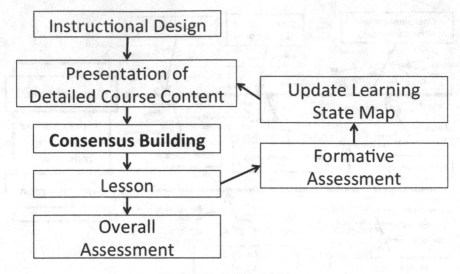

Fig. 5. Consensus procedure

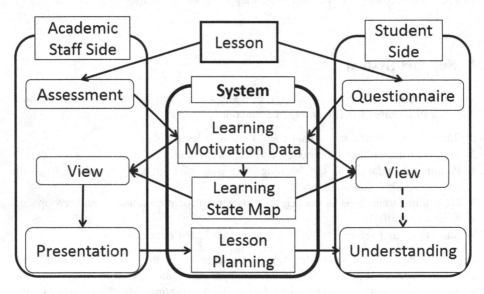

Fig. 6. Consensus procedure

5   Conclusions and Future Work

In this paper, we proposed a model, a method, and a support system for co-creation within the university setting. Consensus is most important concept for co-creation, but it is invisible and difficult to share. We consider the syllabus to be useful tool for the sharing of learning content and a means for acquisition of required knowledge and abilities. In addition, we suggested a learning state map based on a cause-and-effect diagram from previous research. This map enables sharing of students' learning motivation and means of improve. We also designed the support system based on the proposed method. Here we considered only lesson content and student motivation. In the future work, we should discuss knowledge and abilities of students. The production is important for sharing the value of a course. Then, we plan to implement the support system and evaluate it.

Acknowledgements. This research was supported by the Service Science, Solutions and Foundation Integrated Research Program (S3FIRE) of the Research Institute of Science and Technology for Society (RISTEX).

References

1. Shimomura. H.: Development of implementation of co-creation value by improving the higher education and providers of competency that target beneficiaries literacy. Service Science. Solutions and Foundation Integrated Research Program. http://www.ristex.jp/servicescience/project/2013/03/
2. Kawaba, T., Tsuchiya, T., Koyanagi, K.: Development of universal web syllabus system. Jpn. J Educ. Technol. **35**, 61–64 (2011)
3. Ministry of Education, Culture, Sports, Science and Technology.: For reform situation such as educational content in University (Overview). Office for University Reform. http://www.mext.go.jp/a_menu/koutou/daigaku/04052801/__icsFiles/afieldfile/2014/11/18/1353488_1.pdf
4. Nakamura, S., Tomoto, T., Akakura, T.: Consciousness of academic staff about motivation of students in class. In: IEICE General Conference 2015, p. 210 (2015)
5. Hayashi, Y., Mizoguchi, R.: Lesson planning by reuse of practical expertise in teaching strategies. In: Proceedings of the Annual Conference of JSAI 28, pp. 1–4 (2014)

Development of a Speech-Driven Embodied Entrainment Character System with Pupil Response

Yoshihiro Sejima[1]([⊠]), Yoichiro Sato[1], Tomio Watanabe[1],
and Mitsuru Jindai[2]

[1] Faculty of Computer Science and System Engineering, Okayama Prefectural
University, 111 Kuboki, Soja-Shi, Okayama, Japan
sejima@ss.oka-pu.ac.jp
[2] Graduate School of Science and Engineering, University of Toyama, 3190
Gofuku, Toyama-Shi, Toyama, Japan

Abstract. We have developed a speech-driven embodied entrainment character called "InterActor" that had functions of both speaker and listener for supporting human interaction and communication. This character would generate communicative actions and movements such as nodding, body movements, and eyeball movements by using only speech input. In this paper, we analyze the pupil response during the face-to-face communication and non-face-to-face communication with the typical users of the character system. On the basis of the analysis results, we enhance the functionalities of the character and develop an advanced speech-driven embodied entrainment character system for expressing the pupil response.

Keywords: Human interaction · Nonverbal communication · Avatar-Mediated communication · Line-of-Sight · Pupil response

1 Introduction

In human face-to-face communication, not only verbal messages but also nonverbal behavior such as nodding, body movement, line-of-sight and facial expression are rhythmically related and mutually synchronized between talkers [1]. This synchrony of embodied rhythms in communication is called entrainment, and it enhances the sharing of embodiment and empathy unconsciously in human interaction [2].

In our previous work, focusing on the line-of-sight of embodied interaction, we analyzed the eyeball movement using line-of-sight measurement device and proposed an eyeball movement model [3]. In addition, we earlier developed a speech-driven embodied entrainment character called "InterActor" that has functions of both speaker and listener for supporting human interaction and communication. This character would generate not only communicative movements and actions such as nodding, body movements, and blinking that are coherently related to voice input, but also line-of-sight actions such as eye contact and glancing aside on the basis of the proposed model. The effectiveness of the proposed eyeball movement model and the developed

S. Yamamoto (Ed.): HIMI 2015, Part II, LNCS 9173, pp. 378–386, 2015.
DOI: 10.1007/978-3-319-20618-9_38

character was demonstrated by the sensory evaluation methodology adopted in a communication experiment [4].

On the other hand, it is confirmed that the pupil response of human is enlarged or reduced in order to adjust the amount of light in eyeball [5]. In addition, the pupil response has a function which relates human emotions such as human-interest and degree of stress [6, 7]. Moreover, during recent years, newer measurement methods that evaluate the level of human-interest based on the pupil response were proposed and a line-of-sight measurement system was developed without calibration [8, 9]. These previous researches were targeted at the interaction between human and artifact device such as display, picture, and poster. However, an approach that focuses on the pupil response during human interaction has not been designed thus far. Therefore, it is essential and imperative to develop an embodied communication system that enhances the empathy in human interaction on the basis of analyzing the pupil response unconsciously.

In this paper, focusing around the pupil response in human face-to-face communication, we perform an analysis of the pupil response for human interaction using an embodied communication system with a line-of-sight measurement device. On the basis of the analysis results, we enhance our existing character and develop an advanced speech-driven embodied entrainment character system for supporting human interaction and communication. The system uses only speech input to generate a character's pupil response as well as nodding and body movements.

2   Analysis of Pupil Response

In order to analyze the pupil response in human interaction and communication, a communication experiment was carried out using the embodied communication system with line-of-sight measurement device.

2.1   Experimental System

In this experiment, an embodied communication system was developed to measure the line-of-sight and analyze the typical pupil response of talkers during human interaction and communication. The experimental setup is shown in Fig. 1. This system consists of a Windows 7 workstation (CPU: Corei7 2.93 GHz, Memory: 8 GB, Graphics: NVIDIA Geforce GTS250), magnetic sensors (Polhemus FASTRAK), a headset (Logicool H330), and a line-of-sight measurement device. In this system, two talkers were seated face-to-face across tables. The distance between the talkers was 1200 mm based on a personal space. In addition, in order to compare the communication style, non-face-to-face communication scene was generated by inserting a partition between the talkers. The size of partition was 1820 x 910 mm. The talker's line-of-sight was measured by the developed line-of-sight measurement device [3]. Figure 2 shows the outline of the device. The dichroic mirror in the device has a function that transmits visible rays, and reflects infrared rays. The reflected image of a talker's eyeball was input to a PC through an A/D converter. The pupil movement was measured according to the following procedure. First, the binary image was generated using the reflected image on

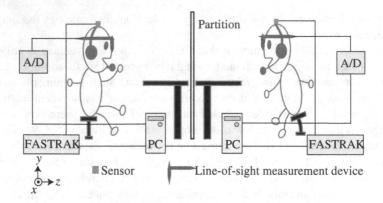

Fig. 1. Setup of the experimental system

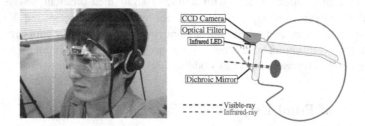

Fig. 2. Line-of-sight measurement device

the basis of the prepared threshold by brightness. Next, the position and size of the talker's pupil were calculated using the ellipse fitting function in Open Source Computer Vision Library (OpenCV). Here, the sample rate was 30 fps. The positions and angles of talker's head movement were measured by magnetic sensors placed on the top of talker's head at 30 Hz. The voice was sampled using 16 bits at 11 kHz with a headset. The measured data was recorded on an HDD in real-time.

2.2   Experimental Method

The experiment was performed under the conditions that the talkers interchangeably played the roles of a speaker and a listener called "Role play experiment," and was later engaged in a free conversation called "Free conversation experiment". In Role play experiment, children's stories were introduced as conversational topics. In Free conversation experiment, conversational topics were not specified. In these experiments, the following two modes were compared: in one mode (a), there was no partition between talkers and in the other (b), there was a partition between the talkers. The subjects were 10 pairs of talkers (10 males and 10 females). Each pair was presented with the two modes in a random order.

The experimental procedure adopted was as follows:

- First, the subjects selected two well-known children's stories and confirmed their summaries.
- Next, the devices for the pupil measurement were calibrated and the subjects used the system for around 2 min freely for familiarization.
- Then, they were asked to talk on conversational topics for 3 min in separate roles (speaker and listener) in each mode.
- Then, the roles of the speaker and listener were interchanged, and the subjects communicated in each mode for 3 min in the abovementioned manner.
- Lastly, the subjects engaged free conversation for 3 min in each mode.

2.3   Analysis of Pupil Response

Focusing on the amount of the pupil response change, talker's pupillary area was analyzed in the each experiment. Here, three subjects were removed from analysis, because the calibration data collected was not accurate. The pupillary area was calculated by the estimated ellipse size. Figure 3 shows the example of time changes of pupillary area. On the basis of this figure, we defined a "unit." The unit is the period between an eye-blink and the next eye-blink. We calculated the average of pupillary area in units. The evaluation of pupillary area was done by the ratio using the calibration data as the standard. Figure 4 shows the result of ratio of pupillary area. In this

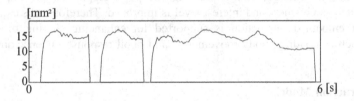

Fig. 3. Example of changes of pupillary area with time

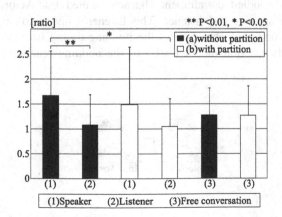

Fig. 4. Result of average of pupillary area

figure, it is showed that the speaker's pupillary area was enlarged about 1.5 times in both two modes. It is considered that the stress of task as "lecture" was prevalent with the speaker. In addition, from the results of the t-test, in the Role play experiment, the significance level between the speaker and the listener is 1% in mode (a). However, mode (b) which does not visualize the body of the talkers (owing to the partition between the speakers) has no significance level between the speaker and the listener. This result shows that recognizing the partner enhances the effectiveness of the conversation. In Free conversation experiment, there was no significance level, even though the role play of speaker and listener was interchanged between the subjects.

Thus, these results demonstrated that the pupil response has relations with the speaker's speech in human interaction and communication.

3 Development of a Speech-Driven Embodied Entrainment Character System with Pupil Response

3.1 Concept

The core concept of this research is shown in Fig. 5. In this research, an advanced speech-driven embodied entrainment character called "InterActor" is developed to express the pupil response unconsciously on the basis of speech input. InterActor is an interactive avatar that represents the talker's nonverbal behaviors. The talkers can realize embodied communication with or through the InterActors during which the pupil of character enlarged. By expressing the pupil responses, the impression of character such as vividness and interest level is improved. Therefore, it is expected that the human embodied interaction is supported for enhancing sharing of embodied rhythms such as nodding, body movements, and pupil response unconsciously.

3.2 Interaction Model

In order to support human interaction and communication, we have already developed a speech-driven embodied entrainment character called InterActor, which has the functions of both speaker and listener. The listener's interaction model includes a nodding reaction model which estimates the nodding timing from a speech ON–OFF pattern and a body reaction model linked to the nodding reaction model [10]. The

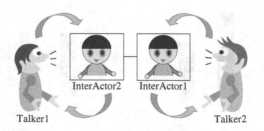

Fig. 5. Concept

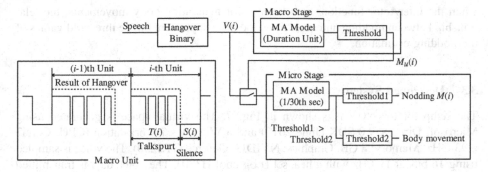

Fig. 6. Interaction model

timing of nodding is predicted using a hierarchy model consisting of two stages - macro and micro (Fig. 6). The macro stage identifies a nodding response, if any, in a duration unit which consists of a talkspurt episode $T(i)$ and the following silence episode $S(i)$ with a hangover value of 4/30 s. The estimator $M_u(i)$ is a moving-average (MA) model, expressed as the weighted sum of unit speech activity $R(i)$ in Eqs. (1) and (2). When $M_u(i)$ exceeds a threshold value, nodding $M(i)$ is also an MA model, estimated as the weighted sum of the binary speech signal $V(i)$ in Eq. (3).

$$M_u(i) = \sum_{j=1}^{J} a(j)R(i-j) + u(i) \tag{1}$$

$$R(i) = \frac{T(i)}{T(i) + S(i)} \tag{2}$$

$a(j)$: linear prediction coefficient
$T(i)$: talkspurt duration in the i th duration unit
$S(i)$: silence duration in the i th duration unit
$u(i)$: noise

$$M(i) = \sum_{j=1}^{K} b(j)V(i-j) + w(i) \tag{3}$$

$b(j)$: linear prediction coefficient
$V(i)$: voice
$w(i)$: noise

The body movements are related to the speech input in that the neck and one of the wrists, elbows, arms, or waist are operated when the body threshold is exceeded. The threshold is set lower than that of the nodding prediction of the MA model, which is expressed as the weighted sum of the binary speech signal to nodding. In other words, when the InterActor functions as a listener for generating body movements, the relationship between nodding and other movements is dependent on the threshold values of the nodding estimation.

3.3 Developed System

The setup for this system is shown in Fig. 7. The virtual space is generated using Microsoft DirectX 9.0 SDK (June 2010) and a Windows 7 workstation (CPU: Corei7 2.93 GHz, Memory: 8 GB, Graphics: NVIDIA Geforce GTS250). The voice is sampled using 16 bits at 11 kHz with a headset (Logicool H330). The voice data is transmitted through the Ethernet in each system. The frame rate to represent CG characters is 30 frames per second.

In this system, the character was developed for expressing the pupil responses. Figure 8 shows the developed characters. The eyeball of this character was the focus of the experiment. The enhanced eyeball is shown in Fig. 9. The eyeball consists of the white of the eye, iris, and pupil by 3D model. It is developed with a sense of depth of iris by forcing the surface into the core of eyeball. The smooth pupil response is realized by generating the forward and back movement of the black 3D model (pupil) on the Z-axis at 0.05 *pixel/frame*. The size of enlarged pupil is a half as large as normal size on the basis of the experimental results (Fig. 10).

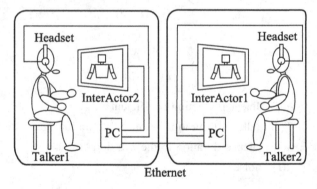

Fig. 7. Set up of the developed system

Fig. 8. Developed characters

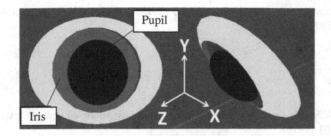

Fig. 9. 3D model of eyeball

Fig. 10. Example of pupil response

With the developed eyeball, when talker1 speaks to InterActor2, InterActor2 responds to talker1's utterance with appropriate timing through its entire body motions, including nodding, blinking, and actions, in a manner similar to the body motions of a listener. The nodding movement of the developed character is the falling-rising motion of the head in the front-back direction at 0.1 rad/frame. The blinking movement is the same as the nodding movement at 0.5 rad/frame with an exponential distribution [11]. The body movement is defined as the backward and forward motion of the body at a speed of 0.025 rad/frame. In addition, InterActor1 generates pupil response based on the talker1's utterance. In this manner, two remote talkers can enjoy a conversation via InterActors within a communication environment in which the sense of unity is shared by embodied entrainment and empathy unconsciously, like typical human conversations.

4   Conclusion

In this paper, we analyzed the pupil response in the face-to-face and non-face-to-face communication. The results of the analysis are summarized as follows. Under the condition that the roles of speaker and listener are fixed, the speaker's pupil is enlarged about 1.5 times in face-to-face communication specially. The results demonstrated that the pupil response is related to speech in human embodied interaction and communication. On the basis of the analysis, we developed an advanced speech-driven embodied entrainment character system for expressing the pupil response. The system uses only speech input to generate a character's pupil response, but produces the outcome of typical human conversations.

Acknowledgments. This work was supported by JSPS KAKENHI Grant Number 26750223, 26280077, 25330239.

References

1. Condon, W.S., Sander, L.W.: Neonate movement is synchronized with adult speech. Science **183**, 99–101 (1974)
2. Watanabe, T.: Human-entrained embodied interaction and communication technology for advanced media society. In: Proceedings of 16th IEEE International Symposium on Robot and Human Interactive Communication (RO-MAN2007), pp. 31–36 (2007)
3. Sejima, Y., Watanabe, T., Jindai, M.: An embodied communication system using speech-driven embodied entrainment characters with an eyeball movement model. Trans. Jan. Soc. Mech. Eng. Ser. C **76**(762), 340–350 (2010). (in Japanese)
4. Sejima, Y., Watanabe, T., Jindai, M.: An avatar-mediated speech-driven embodied communication system with an eyeball movement model. In: Proceedings of IADIS International Conference e-Society 2013, pp. 291–298 (2013)
5. Matthew, L.: Area and brightness of stimulus related to the pupillary light reflex. J. Opt. Soc. Am. **24**(5), 130 (1934)
6. Hess, E.H.: Attitude and pupil size. Sci. Am. **212**(4), 46–54 (1965)
7. Iijima, A., Kosugi, T., Kiryu, T., Matsuki, K., Hasegawa, I., Bando, T.: Evaluation of stressed condition using pupillary responses. Trans. Japn Soc. Med. Biol. Eng. **49**(6), 946–951 (2011). (in Japanese)
8. Nagamatsu, T., Kamahara, J., Tanaka, N.: User-Calibration-Free Gaze Estimation Method Using Both Eyes Model. Industrial Publishing co. ltd., Japan, vol. 23, no. 6, pp. 29–34. (2012) (in Japanese)
9. Kikuchi, K., Takahira, H., Ishikawa, R.: Development of a device to measure movement of gaze and hand. IEICE Trans. Fundam. Electron. Commun. Comput. Sci. **97**(2), 534–537 (2014)
10. Watanabe, T., Okubo, M., Nakashige, M., Danbara, R.: Interactor: speech-driven embodied interactive actor. Int. J. Hum. Comput. Interact. **17**, 43–60 (2004)
11. Watanabe, T., Yuuki, N.: A voice reaction system with a visualized response equivalent to nodding. Adv. Hum. Factors/Ergon. **12A**, 396–403 (1989)

Development of a Learning Support System for Reading Source Code by Stepwise Abstraction

Keisuke Watanabe(✉), Takahito Tomoto, and Takako Akakura

Faculty of Engineering, Tokyo University of Science, 1-3 Kagurazaka,
Shinjuku-Ku, Katsushika, Tokyo 162-8601, Japan
{watanabe_keisuke,tomoto,akakura}@ms.kagu.tus.ac.jp

Abstract. We describes the development of a support system that facilitates the process of meaning deduction by stepwise abstraction in two steps: unifying processing and specifying the meaning of the unified processing. We developed a tool that supports stepwise abstraction with a function that points out learners' mistakes and makes them aware of their errors. We conducted experiments using the learning support tool and found that the system and process are possibly effective.

Keywords: Programming learning · Learning support system · Stepwise learning · Meaning deduction

1 Introduction

In recent years, the importance of information technologies in the general advancement of society has been recognized with the spread of mobile terminals such as personal computers and mobile phones. Along with this, education on information processing has been offered to a wide range of students at institutions of higher education such as universities. Programming education is part of such efforts and increasingly support is needed for fostering learners' problem-solving ability.

In lectures on programming, problem solving is taught by having the learner consider an algorithm or source code to achieve a particular goal. However, in addition to writing code to meet requirements, it is also necessary that programmers be able to read an algorithm or source code and to extract its requirements.

It is important to think in stages in order to understand the overall mechanism by grasping the meaning of individual elements and their function in combination. We also consider a stepwise approach to be important in the above programming process. Here, we focus on the process of reading source code. We define step-by-step thinking in this process as "stepwise abstraction" and support the learner in reading source code.

© Springer International Publishing Switzerland 2015
S. Yamamoto (Ed.): HIMI 2015, Part II, LNCS 9173, pp. 387–394, 2015.
DOI: 10.1007/978-3-319-20618-9_39

2   The Programming Process

2.1   Support for Learning to Read Source Code

In previous research, the process of reading source code has been broken down into two steps: reading comprehension and meaning deduction (see Fig. 1). In reading comprehension, leaners convert source code to an abstract representation such as a flowchart [1]. In this way, they can recognize source code as a representation that is independent of the programming language. In meaning deduction, learners see the abstract expression and consider what it is doing. Kanamori et al. developed a support method for meaning deduction where flowcharts are shown, prompting the learner to consider their meaning [2, 3].

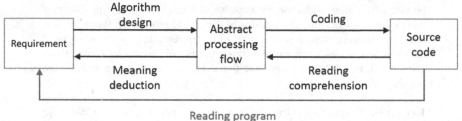

Fig. 1.   The process of programming

2.2   Stepwise Refinement

Shinkai and Sumitani [4] focused on "Algorithm design" shown in Fig. 1 and support this process by stepwise refinement. This involves refining the problem requirements in a top-down manner. In other words, the requirements for the stated problem are divided into sub-goals. This refinement is done repeatedly, further dividing sub-goals into unit equivalent to flowchart symbols that satisfy part of the problem requirements. A benefit to learners is that the processing that satisfies the requirements of the problem becomes easier to understand by step-by-step detailing.

3   Stepwise Abstraction

3.1   Description of Stepwise Abstraction

Shinkai and Sumitani [4] studied support for algorithm design by stepwise refinement, but we also consider it important to apply step-by-step thinking in meaning deduction, which is a reverse process of algorithm design. Here, we propose the support method for the process of meaning deduction and call it "stepwise abstraction". Meaning deduction is performed after the stage of reading comprehension. In this process, learners are required to deduce the meaning of the program which is expressed by abstract processing flow such as flowcharts. The learners are required to consider the meaning of the processing flow. However, if they are novices and cannot consider enough, they cannot conduct this process. In this research, we support this process by stepwise abstraction.

Figure 2 shows the example of the stepwise abstraction. The stepwise abstraction step consists of two steps: (1) unify processing and (2) specify the meaning of the unified processing. First, learners look source code and consider the meaning of each line. Second, they unify several related lines as processing. In the case of Fig. 2, "i = b", "b = a" and "a = i" are unified. This step is unify processing. Next, learners consider and specify the function of the unified processing. In the case of Fig. 2, they may specify this function composed of 3 lines as a function which replace "a" and "b". This step is specify the meaning of the unified processing. Once this is done, learners have completed one abstraction step. Learners are required to repeat this step for understanding requirement gradually. In other words, stepwise abstraction involves abstracting the meaning of each source code line in a bottom-up manner. We believe that the proposed abstraction process is beneficial to learners because it allows them to easily understand the requirements.

3.2   Support Method for Stepwise Abstraction

Here, we propose a support method to facilitate understanding in meaning deduction by stepwise abstraction process for learners who cannot arrive at the requirements through the abstraction process. There are possible mistakes that learners can make in the steps of unifying processing and specifying the meaning of the unified processing.

On possible error in unifying processing is that the learner could make an incorrect unification. In addition, there is a possibility that overly abstract unifications are made. Strictly speaking, overly abstract unifications are not incorrect. Overly abstract unification, however, make difficulties in specifying the meaning step because learners must consider complex processing. So support is needed to ensure the stepwise abstraction is done in appropriately sized steps. To address these issues, we prompt learners to modify their answers by providing them with hints as feedback.

4   Learning Support System

4.1   Interface

Figure 3 shows the learning screen of the learning support system that we developed. Learners learn according to the model described in Sect. 3. The translation of the source code is shown in the right corner and source code in the left corner. First, learners unify processing by selecting checkboxes corresponding to the translations and clicking the "Unify processing" button (see Fig. 4). If this is done correctly, the unified processing appear in selection list of the learner's correct answers. Several alternatives are available in the selection list. Figure 5 shows a screen in the middle of the process.

After the learner has repeated these operations, the panel in which the user selects the requirement is shown. If the learner can correctly derive the "requirement", the

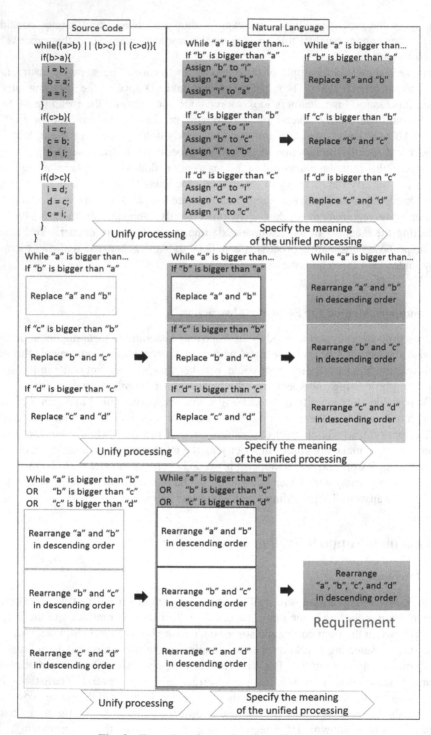

Fig. 2. Examples of stepwise abstraction process

Pr. 1 ▾	Let's unify processing

while((a>b)||(b>c)||(c>d)){
  if(b>a){
    i=b;
    b=a;
    a=i;
  }
  if(c>b){
    i=c;
  ...
	☐ While "a" is bigger than "b" or ....
	☐ If "b" is bigger than "a"
	☐ Assign "b" to "i"
	☐ Assign "a" to "b"
	☐ Assign "i" to "a"
	
	☐ If "c" bigger than "b"
	☐ Assign "c" to "i"
	...

Unify processing	Check unified processing Check specifying the meaning of the unified processing

Fig. 3. Initial screen of the system

☐	While "a" bigger than "b" OR ...
☐ Decleard integer type a,b,c,d,i	If "b" bigger than "a"
☐ While "a" bigger than "b" OR ...	
☐ If "b" bigger than "a"	
☑ Assign "b" to "i"	
☑ Assign "a" to "b"	
☑ Assign "i" to "b"	

Fig. 4. Screen for unifying processing

While "a" is bigger than "b" OR ...	While "a" is bigger than "b" OR ... ▾	
If "b" is bigger than "a"	If "b" is bigger than "a" ▾	
Assign "b" to "i" Assign "a" to "b" Assign "i" to "a"	"a" and "b" ▾	▾
		Assigning
If "c" is bigger than "b"	If "c" is bigger than..	Switch
		Plus

Fig. 5. Screen for naming unified meanings

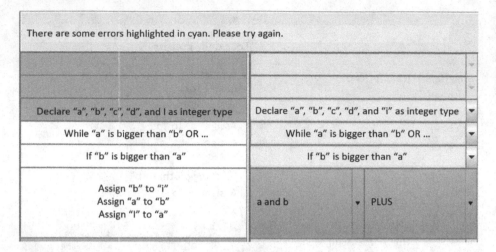

Fig. 6. Example of the hint feedback against naming error

message panel displays "Great! You gave the correct answer!". If the learner gives the wrong answer, the system displays a hint as feedback.

4.2   Hints for Feedback

Stepwise abstraction is a process within meaning deduction. It is necessary that all operations be done correctly. In addition, if learners cannot do a step correctly, they cannot proceed to the next step. So the system returns hints as feedback for each of two tasks: "Unify processing" and "Specify the meaning of the unified processing". We described two types of mistakes that are made when unifying processing. The system returns the messages "There are some errors in the highlighted parts" for simple errors and "You can make a few more small groups of unified processing (see the highlighted parts)" for the error of overly abstract unifications. In the step of specifying the meaning of the unified processing, the system highlights the incorrect part and returns a message such as "Please try again". Figure 6 shows the example of the hint feedback against naming error.

5   Experiment

We conducted an experiment to evaluate the effectiveness of the stepwise abstraction process and our system.

5.1   Experimental Methods

We conducted an evaluation experiment with 6 university students who had experience with programming lectures. First, we conducted a 20 min pretest and divided the students into a control group and experimental group so that there was no difference in average pretest score between the groups. Then, we gave a lectures on programming and assigned exercises on reading source code. The experimental group used the proposed system, and control group did the exercises on paper; the content of the exercises was the same in both groups. It should be noted that we described stepwise abstraction step and use of the system to the experimental group, but we did not describe these to the control group. After the exercises, we conducted a 20 min posttest. The test and exercise problems were in format where we gave the meaning of each source code line and the learner was asked to give a set of unified processing. We used the same six problems in pretest and posttest. The learner was given 1 point for correctly deriving the requirement.

5.2 Experimental Results

Table 1 shows the results of the experiment. The average pretest score was 1.67 in both the experimental group and the control group. In the posttest, on the other hand, the average score in the experimental group was 3.67 versus 2.67 in the control group. The number of participants in this experiment was small, so we cannot say the system is effective. However, participant C in the experimental group was scored 2 points in posttest despite scoring 0 points in the pretest. At this time, we can say only that it is possible for some learners to understand and capture the meaning of source code through step-by-step abstraction.

Table 1. Experimental results

	Experimental group			Control group		
	A	B	C	D	E	F
Pretest	3	2	0	4	1	0
Posttest	5	4	2	5	3	0

In addition, participants B and C successfully completed the tasks of unifying processing and specifying the meaning of the unified processing, though they were unable to do so in the pretest. Therefore, we may say that our system provide an opportunity for learners to consider step-by-step abstraction.

6   Conclusions and Future Work

In this study, we defined stepwise abstraction as a new process of meaning deduction as a part of learning to read source code. Further, we developed a system based on the new process. As a result, we found the possibility that the process and system might be effective. In future work, it is necessary to conduct further experiment with more participants and to conduct a questionnaire to evaluate the proposed system and process. Also, we anticipate that learners will be able to better understand algorithms through the interaction of stepwise refinement and stepwise abstraction.

Acknowledgements. This research was supported by the Research Institute of Science and Technology for Society (RISTEX).

References

1. Arai, T., Kanamori, H., Tomoto, T., Kometani, Y., Akakura, T.: Development of a learning support system for source code reading comprehension. In: Yamamoto, S. (ed.) HCI 2014, Part II. LNCS, vol. 8522, pp. 12–19. Springer, Heidelberg (2014)
2. Kanamori, H., Tomoto, T., Akakura, T.: A proposal of learning by reading in computer programming and development learning support system for meaning deduction. IEICE Trans. Inf. Syst. **J97-D**(12), 1843–1846 (2014) (Japanese Edition)
3. Kanamori, H., Tomoto, T., Akakura, T.: Development of a computer programming learning support system based on reading computer program. In: Yamamoto, S. (ed.) HCI 2013, Part III. LNCS, vol. 8018, pp. 63–69. Springer, Heidelberg (2013)
4. Shinkai, J., Sumitani, S.: Development of programming learning support system emphasizing process. JSET Mag. **31**(Suppl), 45–48 (2007)
5. Nakano, A., Hirashima, T., Taukeuchi, A.: An Intelligent learning environment for leraning by problem posing. IEICE Trans. Inf. Syst. **J83-DI**(6), 539–549 (2000) (Japanese Edition)
6. Sugiura, M., Matsuzawa, Y., Okada, K.: Introductory education for algorithim construction: understanding concepts of algorithm through unplugged work and its effects. IPSJ Mag. **49**(1), 3409–3427 (2008)

Information and Interaction
for Culture and Art

Virtual Jizai-Ryu: Hi-Fidelity Interactive Virtual Exhibit with Digital Display Case

Yuki Ban$^{(\boxtimes)}$, Takashi Kajinami, Takuji Narumi, Tomohiro Tanikawa, and Michitaka Hirose

Graduate School of Information Science and Technology,
The University of Tokyo, Tokyo, Japan
{ban,kaji,narumi,tani,hirose}@cyber.t.u-tokyo.ac.jp

Abstract. This paper proposes a high-definition digital display case for manipulating a virtual exhibit that has linking mechanisms. This technique enhances the understanding of dynamic exhibits. It is difficult to construct interactive contents of dynamic virtual exhibits, because measuring the mechanism invokes the risk of an exhibit's deterioration, and it takes tremendous efforts to create a fine spun computer graphics (CG) model for mechanisms. Therefore, we propose an image-based interaction method that uses image-based rendering to construct interactive contents for dynamic virtual exhibits using the interpolation between exhibit pictures with a number of deformational conditions and viewpoints. Using this method, we construct a high-definition digital showcase and exhibit the interactive content at a museum to evaluate the availability of our system.

Keywords: Digital display case · Image-based interaction · Digital museum · Virtual reality

1 Introduction

Recently, museums have been very interested in the introduction of digital technologies such as virtual reality (VR) and mixed reality (MR) into their exhibitions. Using these technologies, they aim to effectively show background information about their exhibits. However, most of these digital technologies are not suitable for designing an exhibit that a museum requires, and it is difficult to use these technologies as an effective approach for current exhibits' designs. To solve this problem, Kajinami et al. [7] focused on display cases, which have been used for exhibits at some museums. They constructed a prototype of the Digital Display Case, which demonstrated an exhibit using VR technologies. This system enabled users to interact with the virtual exhibition and provided them with the information about exhibits.

On the other hand, content creation is one of the problems for creating such interactive exhibition. To create a traditional interactive VR content, it was popular to use a physical simulation. However, to authentically reproduce the exhibit's behavior, it was required to precisely create a model in a computer and

© Springer International Publishing Switzerland 2015
S. Yamamoto (Ed.): HIMI 2015, Part II, LNCS 9173, pp. 397–408, 2015.
DOI: 10.1007/978-3-319-20618-9_40

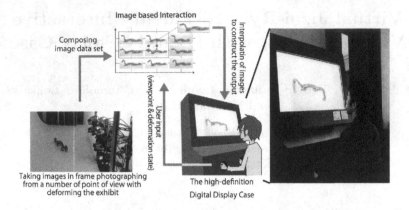

Fig. 1. High-Definition Digital Display Case

hence risk the deterioration of exhibits while measuring their features. Therefore, in this paper, we propose a high-definition digital display case that can
convey the dynamic behavior of exhibits such as structures (Fig. 1). To create
the interactive contents of dynamic virtual exhibits, we propose an image-based
interaction method that uses image-based rendering. This method allows us to
construct high quality realistic contents without the risk of an exhibit's deterioration such as disintegration of its structures.

2   Related Works

2.1   Digital Technologies for Museums

Although some digital devices like information kiosk or videos about exhibits
are already introduced into museums, most of them are placed outside of the
exhibition rooms. This is because curators in museums, who design exhibitions,
do not know how to use it effectively, while they know much about conventional
exhibition devices. We have to consider this know-how that museums used for
exhibits, to introduce digital technologies into museums.

Digital technologies which are used for exhibitions in museums can be categorized in two types. One is the consequential type which display the information
for exhibitions incrementally, and the other is the straightforward type which
convey the exhibitions' information as the devise of exhibition.

As the former, a theater system is already introduced. Several studies have
been conducted on the gallery talk in the theater [20]. These systems can present
the highly realistic images or models about the theme of the exhibition. However
it is difficult to introduce the system into the exhibition rooms, and this type
of system have to hold visitors for a long time to exhibit. There are also more
researches that use digital technology at a gallery talk in an exhibition room.
A gallery talk is a conventional way for museums to convey exhibit's background
information to their visitor. However, it is difficult to have frequently or individually because of the problem of lack of sufficient help. Gallery talk robot [10] is

one solution for this problem, which realize gallery talk from a remote person. Mobile devices are also used to convey the information about exhibits [6].

As the latter, the technologies for straightforward exhibits, some researches constructed the system that superimposes the information on actual exhibitions using MR display system. To superimpose an exhibit's information, the Head Mounted Display (HMD) was usually used [9], however a wearable system like HMD have a difficulty of management when we introduce them into permanent exhibition. On the other hand, there are some works which use half mirrors to superimpose the information on actual exhibitions [3], and a method which use a projector which dis- play the information depending on the measured user's point of view [8,14].

2.2 Interactive Exhibit Using Digital Technology

On the other hand, some exhibit system which enable users to touch the virtual exhibitions have been studied. Nara University Museum held an exhibit where visitors could experience to read Japanese traditional scrolls by rolling a bar device using the digital data of the scroll. Wakita et al. constructed a system which enable users to touch the digital archived fabric, by displaying haptic feedback with a SPIDAR device based on data of the fabric taken with the laser range scanner [21].

These systems realize experiences in which users touch virtual exhibition, and convey the exhibition's information about weight, texture and so on. However, these systems display physically static exhibitions, so they do not enable users to operate dynamic virtual exhibitions. Therefore in this paper, we aim to construct the exhibit system which can convey the exhibition's information about the dynamic characteristics like mechanism. To convey these information, realizing the experience in which users manipulate exhibitions is considered most effective. Therefore, we constructed the Digital Display Cases where users can touch and manipulate the virtual exhibition.

2.3 Technology for Creating VR Contents

There are some methods that can be used for constructing the dynamic contents in our proposed high-definition Digital Display Case. One of these methods is the way of 3D models and bones. However, if the contents have the complex dynamic structure, it is difficult to reproduce the model with precise mechanism. Therefore in this paper, we focused on the image-based rendering(IBR) method which composes the photo taken by the camera with the virtual position, using photos taken from various viewpoints. IBR uses Image-based modeling(IBM) method which is the geometry estimation using a number of photos, and View Morphing method which interpolates the difference between photos.

IBM methods rely on a set of two-dimensional images of a scene to generate a three-dimensional model and then render some novel views of this scene. IBM focused on detecting, grouping, and extracting features like edges, faces, and so on, present in a given photo and then trying to interpret them as three-dimensional clues. The main IBM methods include the reconstitution of rough three-dimensional geometry [4], the method with the stereo matching with cameras whose positions and parameters are known [11], and the method with the Structure from Motion(SfM) which refers to the process of estimating three-dimensional structures from two-dimensional image sequences which may be coupled with local motion signals [18].

On the one hand, Seitz et al. [16] proposed View Morphing method which composes the image taken from the virtual point of view using the Image Morphing method [22], not using the estimation of the three-dimensional geometry. Image Morphing method is a technique to compose the natural interpolated image depending on the movement and distant of corresponding feature points or segments [2,17]. This method is often used to interpolate between images taken from different angles, but some researches try to interpolate a movement in scenes using the morphing technique. The method Manning et al. proposed is able to compose an interpolated image like a movie from images that show an object with the linear uniform motion [13].

Applying these methods, it can be considered that we are able to construct the realistic dynamic contents by deforming the exhibition's image with the estimation of the structure from the matching of feature points between images, not by creating the precise mechanical model.

3   Image-Based Interaction

From these findings, we constructed the Digital Display Case which enables users to interact with the dynamic virtual exhibits with the deformation mechanics. In the previous paper [7], we constructed a prototype of Digital Display Case which enables users to handle the virtual exhibits and to look round them. On the one hand, in this paper, we realize the display system which enables users to feel the structure of the exhibitions by manipulating the virtual exhibits with their hands, and aim to help users understand for the dynamic characteristics of the exhibitions.

To realize interactive contents for VR/MR system, it is a usual method to construct the model with the shape and the behavior, and to construct the contents in real time on the basis of the model's simulation outcome to input. However, to reproduce the exhibit's behavior truly by the simulation, it is important to analyze the exhibit's structure precisely, and to elaborate model from the result of the analysis. To analyze the exhibit's mechanism, it may be needed to deconstruct it, however in that case, it is necessary to ensure restoring to original state. Therefore, before we deconstruct the exhibit, the precise affirmation and inspection of the inner structure using pertinent materials and X-ray. Besides, if we detect the exhibit's structure, it requires huge effort to calculate the physical characteristics like spring and damper modulus precisely for reproducing the structure.

To solve these problems, we propose image-based interaction based on image-based rendering, as the method to construct high-definition interactive contents

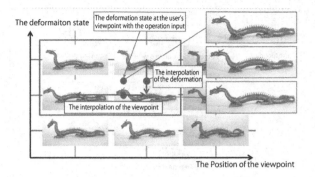

The deformaiton state

The deformation state at the user's viewpoint with the operation input

The interpolation of the deformation

The interpolation of the viewpoint

The Position of the viewpoint

Fig. 2. Interpolation of viewpoint and transformation by Image-based Interaction

easily. This method constructs a realistic content with freedom degrees for the deformation state of the exhibition and the position of the point of view from given images, depending on the manipulated input and the viewpoint. This method is able to reduce the risk of the exhibit's degradation attached to the analysis of the structure, and has an advantage to avoid the necessity of elaborating CG models (Fig. 2). In particular, the system composes the exhibit's image corresponding to the interaction, by interpolating images which we captured frame by frame with degree of freedom for the deformation state and the point of view (Fig. 1).

To increase the construction speed, the system interpolates images by segmenting them into small meshes and deforming them. The system deforms the image using the Rigid MLS method [15] and uses the corresponding points detected by the following process as the control points. This method determines the deformation amount of a mesh (Δm) based on the position of the control points $q = (q_0, q_1, ..., q_{n-1})$ using the MLS method. Using this method, the deformation amount of a mesh is presented as $\Delta m = D(q)$. First, we interpolate between three images using the two-dimensional parameters of the deformation state or the viewpoint position (Fig. 4). The deformation that is constructed using the interpolated images is the combination of interpolations for both degrees of freedom as presented in the following equation: $\Delta m(t_0, t_1) = D_{0 \to 1}(t_0) + D_{0 \to 2}(t_1)$. For cxamplc, if point group q_0 in Imagc 0 corresponds to point group q_1 in Image 1, the deformation amount is calculated using $D_{0 \to 1}(t_0) = D((1 - t_0)q_0 + t_0 q_1)$. An image with more similar deformation states is used as the base image. Therefore, when $t < 0.5$ Image 0 is used; otherwise, Image 1 is used. For the interpolation, the system uses control points that are related to the content's motion. To detect motion, the SIFT feature values [12] are calculated for both images, and corresponding points are detected using these feature values in the images (Fig. 3). For these corresponding points, the system uses RANSAC algorithm [5]. The collection of corresponding points that resemble motion are identified as one part. Then, outliers that do not belong to this part are removed. An interpolated image (see Fig. 4) is composed when this process is expanded to two dimensions and is applied to three images with different deformation states.

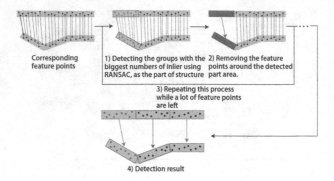

Fig. 3. Process of Parts Estimation

Then, we adapt this method to change both the viewpoint position and deformation state (Fig. 2). The interpolated image is controlled using four parameters: the viewpoint position coordinates ($v = (v_0, v_1)$) and the deformation states
($p = (p_0, p_1)$). Finally, the deformation amount of the image is the combination of
the interpolation effect caused by the viewpoint (D_v) and the interpolation effect
caused by the deformation state (D_p) as follows: $\Delta m(v, p) = D_v(v) + D_p(p)$.
These two effects can be estimated as the following equation regarding the
mutual effect. In these equations, $D_{v(p_0,p_1)}$ represents the two-dimensional interpolation for the deformation state v at $p = (p_0, p_1)$, and $D_{p(v_0,v_1)}$ represents the
two-dimensional interpolation for the position of viewpoint p at $v = (v_0, v_1)$.

$$D_v(v) = (1 - p_0 - p_1)D_{v(0,0)}(v) + p_0 D_{v(1,0)}(v) + p_1 D_{v(0,1)}(v)$$
$$D_p(p) = (1 - v_0 - v_1)D_{p(0,0)}(p) + v_0 D_{p(1,0)}(p) + v_1 D_{p(0,1)}(p)$$

Using these methods, the system can compose the interpolated image, which
can adapt to the changes in the viewpoint position and the deformation state
of an exhibit. Figure 4 shows the deformation state of the exhibit that is constructed using the interpolation of images with three different deformation states.
The comparison with the actual image shows that the interpolation works as
designed. Because this method composes the interpolated image based on an
image with the most similar state to the desired one, it is difficult to adapt to
the change in occlusions. Therefore, when a considerable shift appears in self-
occlusion due to changes in the viewpoint position or the deformation state,
there is a risk for an image gap occurrence at the scene where the base image
is switched. To solve these problems by an efficient data acquisition, we should
quantify the conditions in which the interpolations for the viewpoint or the
deformation state are broken and set the index for the camera's position and the
exhibit's movement when images are taken.

Because this method composes an interpolated image based on an image
with the most similar state to the desired one, it is difficult to adapt to changes
in occlusions. Therefore if the huge shift of self-occlusion comes up when the
position of viewpoint or the deformation state change, it invokes the risk of

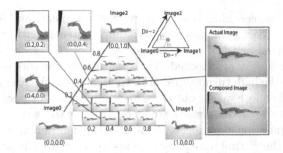

Fig. 4. Interpolation among three images

occurring the gap of images at the scene where the based image is switched. Besides, if the parts of structure are so small and the difference of the motion between each part is so huge, the system is not able to detect a sufficient amount of corresponding feature points on parts in the parts estimation, and fails to construct an applicable interpolated image.

To solve these problems by efficient data acquisition, we should quantify the conditions where the interpolations for the viewpoint or the deformation are broken, and set the index for either the cameras' positions and the exhibit's movement when taking images.

4   Composition of Virtual Jizai-Ryu

We integrated the image-based interaction method into the system that detects user's manipulation and constructed a high-definition digital display case that enables a user to manipulate a virtual exhibit (Fig. 1). We used a "Jizai-Ryu" which is a free-motion ornament of dragon as the dynamic exhibit. It is a cultural asset developed in Japan.

It is a kind of figure model which can change its posture with the accurate movable structure. Since it is a national treasure, almost no one is permitted to touch it. Therefore, it is very difficult to know its structure. The curators in the museum want their visitor to manipulate this ornament to feel how it works, but that's not possible because it is a national treasure. Also they can not to deconstruct it for the analysis of its structure because there is a risk to deteriorate this exhibit.

Therefore we realize the exhibition which is able to convey the potential of this ornament's movement to visitors effectively, although normally this ornament is displayed in the fixed state.

To generate a content of the exhibition, we used the image composed by the image-based interaction based on images photographed in frame photographing by a camera array while manipulating the free-motion ornament. In this paper, we focused on the movement of the head and tail of the dragon, and took images in frame photographing while manipulating these two parts in the range in which the dragon's body did not move. Finally, the system composed the interpolated image from these fifteen images for each part's movement, and joined the head side and the tail side to compose the dynamic contents, with which users can manipulate the head and tail of the dragon at once.

Furthermore, it was anticipated that hundreds of visitors experienced this system in day, so the high turnover rate of experience and the ease of maintenance were required. Therefore we cut out the three-dimensional display function which needed visitors to wear 3D glasses, and constructed the device which realized the virtual manipulation experience. Regarding the maintenance, we constructed the interface for the virtual manipulation experience using the simple method in which users handled the bar to get a weight, not using complex haptic devices.

The user grips the green bar as shown in Fig. 5 and put his/her hands into the system's designated space. The system detects the operation input and calculates an output using the image-based interaction method. Using this output, the system shows the user's hands as if s/he manipulates the virtual exhibit. In this process, we can manipulate the dragon's head and tail by handling the bars inside the designated space.

Figure 5 shows the process of how an exhibit is manipulated using bars inside the system's designated space. Web cameras are placed in these spaces to detect the condition of bars and user's hand using the HSV color space. First, the system detects the movable area of the operating parts such as the head and tail. Then, it calculates the area that contains all operating parts. The system also detects the area in which the center of a manipulating bar moves beforehand and represents a hand image on the movement trajectory of the operating parts based on the relative correspondence of these two areas (Fig. 6). For the deformation state, which is determined by the positions of the head and tail, the system constructs an interpolated image of the head and tail sides of the dragon using the image-based interaction method. Then, the system blends both images in the center of the trunk. Finally, the system superimposes the extracted hand image to give users a sense manipulating the Jizai-Ryu with their actual hands. In the previous work, we confirmed that if we show the captured an image of the hand which the movement is distorted, users feel that they move their hands as the movement of the hand's image on the monitor. It is confirmed that this illusion modifies the perception of shapes that users touch [1], and it can be considered that the similar effect occurs in this time, and the sensation that users manipulate the exhibition with their own hand can be enhanced.

5   Validation of Virtual Jizai-Ryu

We made the high-definition Digital Display Case available to the public, by exhibiting it at the Tokyo National Museum's 140 Year Anniversary Special Exhibition: "Flying Dragon" from Jan. 2nd, 2012 to Jan. 29th, 2012. Over the duration of the exhibition, we exhibited two type of displays, one was the high-definition Digital Display Case which enabled users to experience manipulating the exhibit with their own hands with the method of detecting the manipulation input (referred to as Experience type) (Fig. 1), and the other was the exhibition

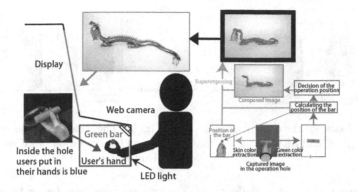

Fig. 5. Process for creating interaction

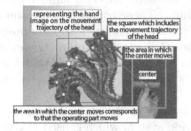

Fig. 6. Position for interaction.

Fig. 7. Operation with the touch panel

which enabled users to manipulate the exhibit with touch panel as the compared condition (referred to as Touch panel type) (Fig. 7). We exhibited Experience type for 12 days, and exhibited Touch panel type for 13 days.

With Touch panel type display, users could manipulate the movements of the head and tail, by switching 30 images taken in frame photographing while manipulating the exhibition little by little.

5.1 Questionnaire for Visitors

We had questionnaires to the part of visitors who experienced our system during this exhibition, and got answers from 301 visitors who experienced Experience type and 267 visitors who experienced Touch panel type.

Figure 8 shows the evaluation of the composed image (5 = totally good, 1 = totally bad). The answers for the deformation of the exhibit's image indicate that the deformation of Experience type got the equal evaluation of the deformation of Touch panel type. In this case, the image of Touch panel type contents are constructed based on more than twice the number of images than the number of images that compose the image of Experience type. Therefore this result indicates that our interpolation method is able to construct the dynamic contents with fewer images without a reduction in quality. On the one hand, the evaluation

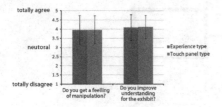
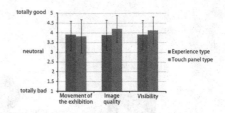

Fig. 8. Feedback for the content of exhibition (Ave. and SE)

Fig. 9. The answer to questions about manipulation and mechanism(Ave. and SE)

of the composed image's visibility of Experience type was lower than that of Touch panel type. It is considered that the disturbance in a captured hand's image and the obscuring the exhibition with the superimposed hand reduced the evaluation of the composed image's visibility. These comment were shown in the open question. Therefore we should enhance the quality of superimposing hands, and examine the way of hand's superposition which counteracts viewing of the virtual contents. Besides, it can be seen in the open question that there is a great demand of dynamic virtual contents with highly free-dimension and users want more various dynamic distortion.

Figure 9 shows that the answer of the evaluation of the manipulating sense with users' own hands indicates the manipulation system which is used in Experience type was evaluated equal to that in Touch panel type (Fig. 9). Visitors who experienced our system contained a lot of elderly adults who looked unaccustomed to the digital device. However, these visitors' evaluation of Experience type was equal to that of Touch panel type which is typically considered as the intuitive operation. Therefore, it can be said that the operation system which detects gripping manipulation used for Experience type was intuitive enough to display the interactive contents for various visitors.

5.2   Review from Curators

20 Curators who worked in Tokyo National Museum experienced this system, and we got reviews from them. First, most of them said that it was very interesting experience that the ornament of the dragon deformed as a function of the user's manipulation, and the quality of the photo-based contents were appropriate to the exhibit in the museum. Some curators said that the superimposed hands' image enhanced the feeling that they manipulated the exhibition with their own hands, and felt moving their hands as displayed on the monitor. Besides, how the user manipulated the dynamic virtual exhibition can be seen around the system, so visitors around the system were easy interested in the exhibition. These comments indicated that high-definition Digital Display Case using the image-based interaction method was useful for the exhibit in the museum.

On the other hand, some were confused about how to move their hands in the holes. It is considered that the reason of this confusion was the difference of freedom degree between the contents deformation and the movement of users' hands. To solve this problem, we should expand the freedom degree of the image deformation, or show the visual guide as the cue of the hand's movement.

Other curators mentioned that they want to convey their visitors exhibitions' haptic sensation. This system made users handle the bar to convey the weight, regarding of the experience turnover and the maintenance, however using the similar weight or quality of material for the gripping parts or displaying them with the cross-modal effect like the visuo-haptic interaction [19] is possible to help realizing the realistic haptic experience.

6 Conclusion and Future Works

In this paper, we proposed the high-definition Digital Display Case which can convey visitors the dynamic characteristics of the exhibition like the structure. As the method to construct the interactive contents of dynamic virtual exhibits, we proposed the image-based interaction method based on image-based rendering. With this method, we can avoid the risk of the exhibit's deterioration with the measuring of mechanism. This method interpolates pictures of an exhibit with a number of deformational conditions and viewpoints

Using this method, the high-definition digital display case which enable users to interact with the virtual dynamic exhibit. This system detects the position where the user handles the object from the web camera to get the operation input. We constructed the exhibit which displayed the "Free-Motion Ornament of Dragon" in the Tokyo National Museum. In this exhibit, we got feedbacks from visitors and curators of this Digital Display Case.

To derive more detailed specifications for the system, we should expand the freedom degree of the contents deformation. Currently, this system can display two-dimensional deformation, so we aim to expand this method to three-dimensional deformation using the interpolating method with the three-sided pyramid, not with the triangle like in this paper. Furthermore we will try to display the exhibits' shape, weight, quality of material in ease using the cross-modal effect like the visuo-haptic interaction [19]. With these improving technique and a great deal of consideration, we aim to realize the goal high-definition Digital Display Case.

Acknowledgements. This research is partly supported by "Mixed Realty Digital Museum" project of MEXT of Japan. The authors would like to thank all the members of our project. Especially Makoto Ando and Takafumi Watanabe from Toppan printing.

References

1. Ban, Y., et al.: Modifying an identified curved surface shape using pseudo-haptic effect. In: *HAPTICS 2012 IEEE*, pp. 211–216 (2012)
2. Beier, T., Neely, S.: Feature-based image metamorphosis. In: SIGGRAPH 1992 papers, pp. 35–42 (1992)

3. Bimber, O., Encarnação, L.M., Schmalstieg, D.: The virtual showcase as a new platform for augmented reality digital storytelling. In: Proceedings of the Workshop on Virtual Environments, pp. 87–95 (2003)
4. Debevec, P.E., Taylor, C.J., Malik, J.: Modeling and rendering architecture from photographs: a hybrid geometry-and image-based approach. In: Proceedings of the 23rd Annual Conference on Computer Graphics and Interactive Techniques, pp. 11–20 (1996)
5. Fischler, M.A., Bolles, R.C.: Random sample consensus: a paradigm for model fitting with applications to image analysis and automated cartography. Commun. ACM **24**(6), 381–395 (1981)
6. Hiyama, A., et al.: A real world role-playing game as an application of the guide system in a museum. In: Proceedings of the 14th ICAT, pp. 29–34 (2004)
7. Kajinami, T., et al.: Digital display case: museum exhibition system to convey background information about exhibits. In: VSMM **2010**, pp. 230–233 (2010)
8. Kim, H., Nagao, S., Maekawa, S., Naemura, T.: Mrsioncase: a glasses-free mixed reality showcase for surrounding multiple viewers. In: SIGGRAPH Asia 2012 Technical Briefs, p. 10 (2012)
9. Kondo, T., Manabe, M., Arita-Kikutani, H., Mishima, Y.: Practical uses of mixed reality exhibition at the national museum of nature and science in tokyo. In: Poster Program, p. **27** (2009)
10. Kuzuoka, H., Yamazaki, K., Yamazaki, A., Kosaka, J., Suga, Y., Heath, C.: Dual ecologies of robot as communication media: thoughts on coordinating orientations and projectability. In: Proceedings of the SIGCHI Conference on Human Factors in Computing Systems, pp. 183–190 (2004)
11. Labatut, P., Pons, J.-P., Keriven, R.: Efficient multi-view reconstruction of large-scale scenes using interest points, delaunay triangulation and graph cuts. In: Computer Vision. ICCV 2007, pp. 1–8 (2007)
12. Lowe, D.G.: Distinctive image features from scale-invariant keypoints. Int. J. Comput. Vision **60**, 91–110 (2004)
13. Manning, R.A., Dyer, C.R.: Interpolating view and scene motion by dynamic view morphing. In: 2013 IEEE Conference on Computer Vision and Pattern Recognition, vol. 1, pp. 1388–1388 (1999)
14. Nakashima, T., Wada, T., Naemura, T.: Exfloasion: multi-layered floating vision system for mixed reality exhibition. In: VSMM 2010, pp. 95–98, October 2010
15. Schaefer, S., McPhail, T., Warren, J.: Image deformation using moving least squares. ACM Trans. Graph. **25**, 533–540 (2006)
16. Seitz, S.M., Dyer, C.R.: View morphing. In: ACM SIGGRAPH 1996 Papers, pp. 21–30 (1996)
17. Smythe, D.B.: A two-pass mesh warping algorithm for object transformation and image interpolation. Rapp. Tech. **1030**, 31 (1990)
18. Snavely, N., Seitz, S.M., Szeliski, R.: Photo tourism: exploring photo collections in 3d. ACM Trans. Graph. **25**(3), 835–846 (2006)
19. Taima, Y., et al.: Controlling fatigue while lifting objects using pseudo-haptics in a mixed reality space. In: HAPTICS 2014 IEEE, pp. 175–180 (2014)
20. TNM&TOPPAN. http://www.toppan-vr.jp/mt/
21. Wakita, W., Akahane, K., Isshiki, M., Tanaka, H.T.: A texture-based direct-touch interaction system for 3d woven cultural property exhibition. In: Computer Vision-ACCV 2010 Workshop, pp. 324–333 (2011)
22. Wolberg, G.: Image morphing: a survey. Vis. Comput. **14**(8), 360–372 (1998)

Next Step of Cultural and Creative Products - Embracing Users Creativity

Chia-Ling Chang[1] and Ming-Hsuan Hsieh[2(✉)]

[1] Department of Creative Product Design and Management,
Far East University, Tainan City, Taiwan, ROC
idit007@gmail.com
[2] Department of Computer-Aided Industrial Design,
Overseas Chinese University, Taichung City, Taiwan, ROC
mhhsieh@ocu.edu.tw

Abstract. The use of cultural design products can improve products unique-ness and strengthen emotional consumer experience. In recent years, the concept of "open innovation" has initiated the age of "individual creativity", more and more users are showing a higher interest in expressing their design idea and being concerned in creative products which express themselves.

In this study, the creative users demand as the starting, propose "Cultural and creative user-based product Innovation Pattern". The steps of pattern are described below: (1) Prepare cultural themes and collect elements, (2) Extract cultural elements, (3) Transform cultural elements of product components, (4) Develop product interface, (5) Design creativity-friendly interface, (6) Proto-type, and (7) Inspect the features of products. Since ancient times, the bat was used as a mascot in decorative arts as a symbol of good fortune and happiness as a characteristic of Chinese culture. We toke the bats as a cultural theme to practice the "Cultural and creative user-based product Innovation Pattern". This study escaped the existing cultural and creative product design methods by importing the users creativity into cultural products, refining the relationship between classic archives and users, and successfully developing "users per-missible creativity development" into cultural and creative products. This study also was able to break the traditional cultural products usage intentions by not only allowing users to freely change the shape of the products, but also to meet the functional needs based on different needs. In this study, users' creativity-based, classical culture collections for reference, the development of the key of cultural elements proposed by "Cultural and creative user-based product Inno-vation Pattern" have lead cultural and creative designers to new strategies of thinking and designing. The archives will be more variable, interesting, and creative while logically maintaining Chinese cultural and conservative feel for daily life in the modern world. When the users practice their creativity based on transitional culture, they help maintain the cultural continuity, applicability, and value.

Keywords: Users creativity · Cultural and creative product · Open innovation · Innovation pattern

© Springer International Publishing Switzerland 2015
S. Yamamoto (Ed.): HIMI 2015, Part II, LNCS 9173, pp. 409–419, 2015.
DOI: 10.1007/978-3-319-20618-9_41

1 Background

Chinese culture profoundly contains many precious treasures. In recent years, Chinese culture has caught worldwide attention, and gradually moved towards the world stage. No matter whether it was in the heritage art auction market, or in the drawn films, it is gradually catching people's eye. From a *product design* view within the global competition market, the use of cultural features design application, not only improve uniqueness of products, but also better provides an emotional consumer experience. It is evident in developed countries of the importance of highlighting the cultural and creative design innovations for a competitive advantage. In terms of cultural and creative industries mixed with the consumer process in modern culture, functional product development will gradually focus more on spiritual values (Chen, 2009).

In recent years, the concept of "Open Innovation" (Chesbrough, 2003), made it possible for enterprises to realize the importance of users' creativity in their products. With each new generation, there is a stream of creativity that flows in this era of "individual creativity". More producers are asking users to get involved in areas such as: product components, tools or methods to the users. The products must meet the "user's creativity". Increasing numbers of users are showing a keener interest on design, and concern the products which can express themselves.

However, the current cultural product design still stays in *static state* product design. This study suggests that the cultural product design has become a focus of concern. It is suggested that the designers should focus more on products cultural components, narrative and artistic value, as well as the users' ability to appreciate or "re-create" an action. This means the products in addition to the requirements of basic functions must also be expected to be individual through one's own unique design ideas in the same way *Self-Realization* indicates in the first level of Maslow's Hierarchy of Needs. For designers, design is not only to meet consumer demands, but also more importantly through design transformation create products to meet cultural legacy and cultural creativity.

2 Literature Review

2.1 Users' Creativity

In the past, the mass production and manufacturing was about the concept of "Modularization." However, recently the importance of consumer awareness has been raised. Over time, standard products sales have declined due to not meeting consumer demands of creativity. Consumers live with a lot of creative ideas in their daily lives and try to play the role of the designer. Consumers attempt to change the shape or function to meet their own unique creative goals individually (Moreau and Dahl, 2005).

Observe the history of the development of industrial products, more products are willing to open creativity towards end user, such as: product components, tools or methods of the user, to meet the users' desire of their own design of the final product appearance or function (von Hippel E. & Katz R., 2002; Chan & Lee, 2004). In the past, research topics focused more on product patterns forming the final decision.

Moreover, the Design experience patterns were considered before the final decision without consideration to the level of the users. Users basically just own a *choose rights* and nothing more than practically *design rights*. In the role of postmodernism, consumer-oriented product development has been replaced by post-design (Luh, Lin, and Chang, 2005), with respect to post-modernism. In modernist terms, it was the emotion and gain that consumers expected and did not buy, but the experience gained through the purchase.

Users' creative concept proposes that designers open part of the designing rights to consumers. It will satisfy consumer demand in the creative product diversification. Even if they own limited abilities, they still can be creative to design, transform and other ways participate in part of the product design (Luh and Chang, 2007).

2.2 The Cultural Product Design

The rise of cultural and creative industries has increased the importance to aesthetics. This increase on economic power has become a major competitive key to countries' enterprises. More people have proposed "aesthetic design force" as another indicator of strength. By re-interpretation of the deep meaning of the intangible culture, cultural creativity feeds into operational design techniques in order to give concrete expression to the different carriers. The growth of aesthetic economy, cultural style and highlights of the lifestyle design, is becoming more favored by consumers.

Cultural assets cover a wide scope. It can be summarized into two areas: tangible cultural and intangible cultural. The first part includes historic buildings, natural landscape, cultural landscape, floral, fauna, regional life objects, etc. The second part includes things such as Tang poetry, Sung lyrics, classical literature, religions, customs, festivals, ritual, and behaviors. Lee (1996) considers culture as referring to "products of human activities, including tools, social life used to maintain the laws and institutions that depend on spiritual life all the art products, but also includes many the human activity history in the creation process." Highlighting the presence of the cultural characteristics, from the design side, the elements of national culture, such as symbols, lines, stories, shapes, and colors help to explore the product design and give information. Therefore, the consumers, in addition to the actual use of its functionality, can sense the designer through the commodity characteristics through desired shapes conveying the culture, to create a moving and common of emotional interaction.

To strengthen the product depth, scholars recently have proposed the cultural product design as the base. Yeh, Lin, and Hsu Yeh, Lin and Hsu (2011) employed a technique used in classical Poetry Literary Spirit as the starting point on how to master the background of the traditional "poetry" by capturing the key implications for analysis of morphology and content. Through the body and spirit, they were able to convert the essence of "poetry" to actual cases of "poetry" of product design, and put it into "God-shaped poetry conversion". Yang, Ho, and Luh (2011) utilized the three great classics: "Weave Dream of Red Mansions (織夢紅樓)", "Four Beauties (四大美人)", "Jin Yong Woman (金庸女俠)" to create actual metalworking creations. A construction of "Creative Tree" from the concept of base text, context, and gestalt, and from the proposed" hierarchy of Gestalt-oriented authoring mode shape ", he proposed six procedures. These include: (1) Topic definition and data collection, (2) Excerpt and arrangement creative members, (3) Development and expansion of Gestalt level, (4) Screening the best level of Gestalt, (5) Story line definition and specific preparation, and (6) Creative practice and transition. Wang and Hong (2011) had proposed the metaphor of cultural and creative goods design patterns, using the similar relationship to build up the relevant context of people, events, and substance. Using a characteristic angle for dismantling and reassembling, one could design metaphorically and innovatively.

This study suggests that the cultural product design has become the focus of social concern. Designers should focus on such products not only to cultural elements, story ideas and artistic value, but also can not ignore the users' ability of rich interpretation of "resign" and "re-creation" acts. Currently, consumers rich diverse ideas and products can expect to show a unique and interactive style. Therefore, this study attempts to integrate the traditional culture of creative users, breaking the established range of cultural products and forms. It can be changed with the users' own creative appearance and features of products that makes the products escape the static artistic and cultural norms to achieve a new meaning and purpose of interaction.

3   The Cultural Product Innovation Patterns

This study analyses products based on users' creativity, attributed to common characteristics. Continued importance on cultural property towards historical and cultural objects for the design of application objects have been made "based on the user's creative product innovation model" to develop and meet the new cultural and creative products. By utilizing the user's creativity, one will strengthen the change and richness of cultural and creative goods.

3.1   Users' Based Creative Product Features

Such products are found mostly in single elements presented as non-integrity products. Essentially, users obtain a self-realization from a product creation process and become participants in the design of the products after purchase. From product suppliers, one can effectively reduce the cost and process time. Due to space restrictions, a outline of common features for these products are as follows:

3.2   Reassembled Components

Product components could be optionally replaced by users, components could be provided by manufacturer or easily obtained by users themselves. Some elements of the product may be reassembled by users to change the product mix, or replaced with renovation elements, to alter, amplify the product's use, or external morphology and function with variability.

4   Creative Friendly Interface

Interface-based takes on important interaction between the media and users' of the products. Human factors engineering scholars have proposed "friendly interface" to consider users' physiological, psychological state, to assist users more easily in operating the product, which is designed to reach a preset functions and objectives of the product (Fisk, 1999 & Mueller, et al., 1998). "Users Successive Design (USD)" aims to assist users to easily use their own product ideas, rather than the default preset. Clearly highlighting the differences between the two, USD products interface refers to "creative-friendly interface". Users of USD products meet highly creative and friendly interface exchange and they can effectively reduce the user's ability to achieve the threshold of creation.

5   Freely Design Authorities

Which means that the product can be re-designed or provided the possibility of further innovation. Product is preset design freedom, based on individual creative will, creative needs and design capabilities of users. Users can continuously design and development of the use of the different stages of the product shape, function, and even the original product categories.

6   Toleration

In the designer angle of view, "design is a purpose to solve a problem and will solve the problem correctly." Which means that designers have already offered one or more preset correct solutions for users. Others designers have not included this deeming it to be a "mistake" or "non" solution. "Toleration" that is a correct target system default, allows the users to reach the target when making a user mistake (Wu, 2004). However USD Product encourages users to conduct a variety of re-creations, allowing the user to change the original goals set. Then after the users design is derived from a variety of forms, the product can be regarded as reasonable and more creative and meaningful in its results. It's not only the result of a simple expansion or extension of the product, which can accept the "right" spirit which is greater than the allowable "wrong" sense. It has been called "toleration" here. Under this context, USD products will be considered as the integration platform for designers and users to show creativity.

6.1   The Users' Based Cultural and Creative Product Innovation Patterns

In this study, the creative users demand as the starting, construct creative user-based innovation patterns of cultural products. The steps are described below:

Step 1: Prepare Cultural Themes and Collect Elements.
Historically, when each parties has a unique culture, customs, atmosphere, and breeds diverse and rich cultural objects, one needs to avoid misunderstanding. Innovative design must develop a cultural theme first and create deeper understanding of the cultural context and spiritual meaning. Cultural themes drawn two methods: one is according to who、what、when、where、what, sometimes historical people, events, dynasties, regions, and other characteristics of the cultural heritage as the theme. The other is on emotional and personal preference or market-orientation to define the main topic to select what is most in line with market expectations or potential. According to the theme of collecting the relevant elements, one can do this in order to facilitate subsequent design thinking. Currently, Taiwan has build a number of national Digital Collection libraries, such as: Taiwan E-learning and Digital Archive Program (典藏臺灣)" http://digitalarchives.tw/. It collects over 3.2 million collections with content integrity, and by professionals who confirm the correctness of cultural materials in order to avoid cultural misinterpretation.

Step 2: Extract Cultural Elements.
To reduce cultural cognition error by designers and users, you maybe focus on interviews, questionnaires, product analysis, ethnography to define the users' awareness of cultural elements. The collection of cultural elements, can be categorized according to appearance, usage behavior, or ideology as a basic classification. Appearance then can follow by sizes, scale, colors, textures, shapes, surfaces, ornamentation, lines, details of the deal. The usage of behavior is in accordance with the functionality, interoperability, ease of use, safety, or structure. Ideology is in accordance with a special meaning, story, emotions and other abstract symbols and other projects proposed which may represent a key element to the design theme of cultural goods component of the transformation.

Step 3: Transform Cultural Elements of Product Components.
Product is composed by components, and each component carries and develops product capabilities. When units can carry most of the functionality of products, one can develop a single component, known as "primary components". Conversely, if the component is attached to the main demand components, in order to show the special features, it can possess, a particular feature, called "secondary components." To use "shape appearance", the "usage behavior", "ideology" of cultural elements to convert primary and secondary components into products, create complete product functionality.

Step 4: Develop Product Interface.
Product interface can be divided into specific "physical interface" is responsible for connecting between each components; and psychological "cognitive interface" is responsible for the interaction between product and consumer. Therefore, in the physical interface, designers must develop ways of engaging primary and secondary components, such as the common bonding method: mortise, snap, hook clasp, rings, bonding, plug, stapling, stitching, etc. according to the material properties of the components to develop a reasonable product interface.

Step 5: Design Creativity-friendly Interface.
To encourage users to conduct a variety of product re-design, re-creating behavior, cognitive friendliness of the interface that need to be reached, one could allow the users to be able to use both the knowledge and ability to design, create, as far as possible without additional study. In addition, an engaging way should come with an "undo feature" to allow the creation of a user to easily reply or reset. Designers may use product design techniques, such as product semantic interface to guide the users' creative friendliness.

Step 6: Prototype.
Primary and secondary components and interfaces can be founded by a common computer graphics, 3D printing, product sketch and functional models. The product components can be molded to test functional and creative diversity.

Step 7: Inspect Features of Products.
To confirm the product meets with users' needs based on cultural and creative products, it needs to be inspected by four features based on "users creativity" as mentioned. If one of them does not reach the requirements, you need to return to Step three.

7   Practice

In this study, the demand for creative users is the beginning point. According to the proposed "users' orientation of the cultural and creative product design patterns" and procedures are to target historical and cultural objects as the design of the application object, to develop creative innovations for users and to strengthen the cultural and creative goods to enrich design. The following example of steps can be taken.

Step 1: Prepare Cultural Themes and Collect Elements.
Since ancient times, the bat because the word sounds like blessing, rich,prosperity, the bat was used as a mascot in decorative arts as a symbol of good fortune and happiness as a characteristic of Chinese culture. Therefore, the shape of bats often appears in many traditional patterns, as seen on some of the old buildings, furniture and objects. Presenting bats as a cultural theme, from the website of " Taiwan E-learning and Digital Archive Program (典藏臺灣) http://digitalarchives.tw/ can collect bat culturally relevant artifacts and then chart a bat cultural artifacts profile (Table 1).

Step 2: Extract Cultural Elements.
Using the chart one can find connections between specific elements or searches. For example, if one wanted to know the connection between all the imagery of a bat and focus on the shape as a symbol, such as the overall shape being wide and flat, with symmetrical and rounded wings and the color that was used will most likely be the color of objects itself. Next sort by the bat's symbolic references, the function of the tread patterns which are mostly found in clothing accessories. Next, the connections of these six bat relevant artifacts to 30 survey respondents whose average age is 20.2 years old to yield the results of "Bat Lock (蝙蝠花旗鎖)" is the easiest understandably object to recognize. So this selection of Bat lock (ancient Chinese lock) (see Table 1) is a key

Table 1. Bat cultural artifacts profile

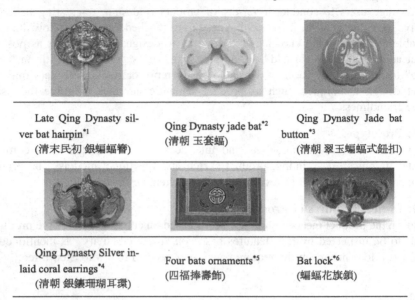

Late Qing Dynasty silver bat hairpin[*1] (清末民初 銀蝙蝠簪)	Qing Dynasty jade bat[*2] (清朝 玉套蝠)	Qing Dynasty Jade bat button[*3] (清朝 翠玉蝙蝠式鈕扣)
Qing Dynasty Silver inlaid coral earrings[*4] (清朝 銀鑲珊瑚耳環)	Four bats ornaments[*5] (四福捧壽飾)	Bat lock[*6] (蝙蝠花旗鎖)

element in this sample or the product component conversion design. According to its context and morphological characteristics, the deduction related design elements, structural proportions, and simplified the shape would be suggested.

Step 3: Transform Cultural Elements of Product Components.

To make the product in line with modern style and processing costs, designers use "flaky unit" concepts to simplify the shape of the bat lock. While retaining the outside contour, removing cloud-shaped patterns with texture details and central wing lettering, one can adjust wing spacing, develop the main components according to the context (Fig. 1). In addition, if the main component composition space gap is too large, one can develop a smaller size of the secondary compartments. The material of components may be made of a toughness and elasticity of PP (polypropylene), in order to meet users creative development from space limitations.

Step 4: Develop Product Interface.

According to the principle of bonding, the die assembly by two points are composed on a planar shape. Three points or more can be assembled to complete the 3D shape, for greater product features by taking three assembly points for the primary and secondary components linking the interface. Between the head and wings of the three main components will create a round pits design. Three rounded bumps are designed on the top of the tail and wings for every two components to be snapped together.

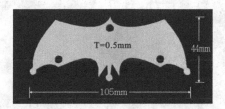

Fig. 1. The simplified process of Bats locks

Fig. 2. The mode with bat image

Step 5: Design Creativity-friendly Interface.
Using rounded pits and bumps to connect all components together, simply snap together without additional cognitive learning. A process similar to the Lego System, may allow the user repeat for a variety of three-dimensional stitching or removal of the creative interface easily.

Step 6: Prototype.
Using Autodesk to draw die, CNC machining cutting mode, complete the image of the product components several bat pieces of bats (Fig. 2), then create a creative puzzle design.

Step 7: Inspect the Features of Products.
Brainstorming with multiple users focusing on user's personal and creative needs of functional requirements of the product, one can combine memorable variability to the product. Figure 3 shows the results of the combination, including: a large flower pendant, a round-fu plate, a compartment tray. There are over three uses and aspects by four features based on users creativity (Table 2).

The work with the users can choose the number of units in different pieces freely such as: combined into large flower pendant, small nightlights, birdlike reflections, beautiful lighting forms and enjoyable thelights that are genuinely interesting. Different sizes of combination can be used for different purposes, both in practical and modern fashion, for blessings, for prosperity or for peace. Both are practical as gifts or for personal use. It contains both cultural meaning and practical value drawing one closer to culture within one's daily life.

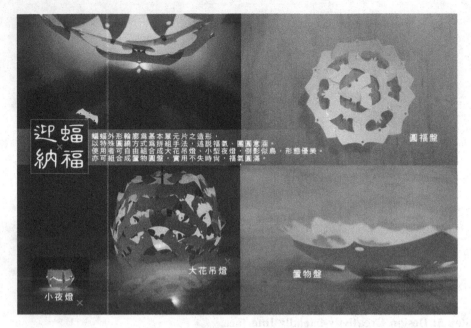

Fig. 3. The outcome of design

Table 2. Description of feature inspection

Feature	Result	Description
(1) Reassembled components	Y	All the components are reassembled
(2) Creative friendly interface	Y	Users do not need extra learning, fastening components intuitively
(3) Freely design authorities	Y	Creative achievement seen by the users, the product shape diversity, across containers, lamps of different functional categories.
(4) Toleration	Y	The creative process, the users can change the ideas any time all results can be regarded as a reasonable result.

8   Conclusion

In response to rapid information exchange and trends of creative development being diversified, the rise in consumers who are into unique, emotional consumption is increasing. They don't just buy a simple object. They are concerned with their inter-action with products. (Friesen, 2001). In this study, users' creativity-based, classical culture collections for reference, the development of the key of cultural elements proposed by "Cultural and creative user-based product Innovation Pattern" have lead cultural and creative designers to new strategies of thinking and designing. On the other hand, it makes the product a deep part of cultural literacy. For the consumers, historical artifacts are no longer unfamiliar and distant. The development of user-creative products will be satisfied. Cultural artifacts will be more changeable, interesting, creative, and logical while upholding Chinese cultural conservation in modern daily life.

Acknowledgement. This study was supported by the Ministry of Science and Technology of the Republic of China (MOST 103-2221-E-240-004).

References

Wang, H.H., Hung, J.L.: A metaphorical method for product design in cultural and creative industry. J. Des. **16**(4), 35–55 (2011)

Lee, Y.Y.: Culture and Accomplishment. Youth culture, Taipei (1996)

Luh, D.B., Lin, N., Chang, C.L.: Successive design. In: The proceeding of 2005 World Chinese Industrial Design Conference, pp. 305–308 (2005)

Luh, D.B., Chang, C.L.: User successive design: concept and design process. J. Des. **12**(2), 1–13 (2007)

Chen, H.Y.: . A Study on the Information Design of Cultural Product. Department Of Product Design, Ming Chuan University. Master thesis (2009)

Yang, T.L., Ho, M.C., Luh, D.B.: Gestalt-oriented approach to form creation. J. Des. **16**(4), 19–34 (2011)

Yeh, M.L., Lin, P.H., Hsu, C.H.: Applying poetic techniques of shape-spirit transformation in cultural creative design. J. Des. **16**(4), 91–105 (2011)

Fisk, A.D.: Human factors and the older adult. Ergon. Des. **7**(1), 8–13 (1999)

Friesen, G.B.: Co-creation: when 1 and 1 make 11. Consult. Manage. **12**(1), 28–31 (2001)

von Hippel, E., Katz, R.: Shifting innovation to users via toolkits. Manage. Sci. **48**(7), 821–833 (2002)

Chesbrough, H.: Open innovation: how companies actually do it. Harvard Bus. Rev. **81**(7), 12–14 (2003)

Chan, T.Y., Lee, J.F.: A comparative study of online user communities involvement in product innovation and development. In: Proceedings of 13th international conference on management of technology, Washington D.C (2004)

Wu, N.E.: Coverage in fault-tolerant control. Automatica **40**(4), 537–548 (2004)

Moreau, C.P., Dahl, D.W.: Designing the solution: the impact of constraints on consumers' creativity. J. Consum. Res. **32**(1), 13–22 (2005)

Association of National Dimensions of Culture with Perceived Public Sector Corruption

Denis A. Coelho[✉]

Human Technology Group, Department of Electromechanical Engineering,
Universidade da Beira Interior, 6201-001 Covilhã, Portugal
denis@ubi.pt, denis.a.coelho@gmail.com

Abstract. Corruption, and in particular, public sector corruption, is currently one of the most talked about problems in the world. Following on previous work on the association of national measures of dimensions of culture proposed by Gert Hofstede (1983) with manufacturing strategies (in countries across continents) and road fatalities (in countries within the European Union), this contribution focuses on association with perceived public sector corruption. This is based on the 2014 Corruption Perception Index - CPI (a Transparency International index), measuring the perceived levels of public sector corruption in 175 countries and territories. Power distance is positively associated with corruption, while individuality is negatively associated with perceived corruption (number of countries and territories included from across five continents: 69).

Keywords: Power distance · Individualism · Corruption perception index · Correlation analysis

1 Introduction

In the current paper, an association approach (Barata and Coelho 2014; Coelho 2014; Coelho et al. 2013; Coelho 2011) is used to identify cultural predispositions based on national cultural dimensions (Hoefstede 1980; Smith-Jackson and Essuman-Johnson 2014) for behaviors leading to a tendency for more perceived public sector corruption. Capturing perceptions of corruption of those in a position to offer assessments of public sector corruption is considered the most reliable method of comparing relative corruption levels across countries (Transparency International 2015). Corruption generally comprises illegal activities, which are deliberately hidden and only come to light through scandals, investigations or prosecutions, but there is no meaningful way to assess absolute levels of corruption in countries or territories on the basis of hard empirical data. Despite a few possible attempts to do so, such as by comparing bribes reported, the number of prosecutions brought or studying court cases directly linked to corruption, these cannot be taken as definitive indicators of corruption levels (instead, they show how effective prosecutors, the courts or the media are in investigating and exposing corruption) (Transparency International 2015).

© Springer International Publishing Switzerland 2015
S. Yamamoto (Ed.): HIMI 2015, Part II, LNCS 9173, pp. 420–427, 2015.
DOI: 10.1007/978-3-319-20618-9_42

2 National Dimensions of Culture

The argument according to which culture exerts a profound influence on the innovative capacity of a society has been largely supported by empirical research. Barnett (1953) postulated a positive correlation between the individualism of a society and its innovative potential: the greater the freedom of the individual to explore and express opinions, the greater the likelihood of new ideas coming into being. Hofstede (1980) indicated that societies that score high on individualism and low on power distance tend to display higher growth and innovation rates. Shane (1993) found that individualistic societies that accept uncertainty and exhibit a low level of power distance are those who attain better innovation performance. Hussler (2004) introduced a culture-based taxonomy of innovation performance. Societies that succeed by innovating on their own are those that possess a "culture of endogenous innovation". Vice versa, those countries with high uncertainty avoidance and high power distance can be defined as "cultures of imitation".

The six measures of national cultures, initially identified by Hofstede (1980, 1983, 2001), are summarized as follows:

1. Power Distance Index (pdi) - Power distance is the extent to which less powerful members of organizations expect power to be equally distributed (Hofstede 1980). In low power distance countries there is limited dependence of subordinates on their bosses. Power is very decentralized as well as decision-making. In contrast, in high power distance countries, hierarchy is the fundamental principle on which all relationships are based. Power is centralized as well as decision-making, leading to more emphasis on formal methods for gathering and analyzing external information (Flynn and Saladin 2006).
2. Individualism versus Collectivism (idv) - Individualism is the degree to which people are oriented towards acting as individuals as opposed to acting as a group (Hofstede 1980). In individualist countries people tend to value individual success and achievement. Members of individualist countries are autonomous and confident, tending to rely primarily on their own ideas (Snell and Hui 2000). In collectivist countries, people are bound in groups such as the extended family or the village and are more likely to rely on information provided by others in formulating their opinions (Snell and Hui 2000).
3. Masculinity versus Femininity (mas) - Masculinity is the extent to which success and aggressiveness are valued (Hofstede 1980). In high masculinity countries, high earnings, advancement through opportunities and challenging work are mostly emphasized. The use of information to support decision-making is dependent on its expected effectiveness in gaining advantage over competitors (Flynn and Saladin 2006). In contrast, in high femininity countries, relationships, concern for the others, inclusiveness and society's best interest are valued. Cooperation is often a visible feature. The use of information to support decision-making is very typical of a feminine national culture (Wacker and Sprague 1998).
4. Uncertainty Avoidance Index (uai) - Uncertainty avoidance is the degree to which people feel confident about the future (Hofstede 2001). National cultures that score

high in uncertainty avoidance have an emotional need for rules. Vice versa, national cultures that score low in uncertainty avoidance dislike formal rules, setting them only when it is necessary (Flynn and Saladin 2006).

5. Long Term Orientation versus Short Term Normative Orientation (ltowvs) - Long term orientation stands for the fostering of virtues oriented towards future rewards, in particular perseverance and thrift. It's opposite pole, short term orientation, stands for the fostering of virtues related to the past and present, in particular, respect for tradition, preservation of 'face' and fulfilling social obligations.

6. Indulgence versus Restraint (ivr) - Indulgence stands for a society that allows relatively free gratification of basic and natural human drives related to enjoying life and having fun. Restraint stands for a society that suppresses gratification of needs and regulates it by means of strict social norms.

Geert Hofstede conducted one of the most comprehensive studies of how values in the workplace are influenced by culture. He analysed a large database of employee value scores collected within IBM between 1967 and 1973. The data covered more than 70 countries, from which Hofstede first used the 40 countries with the largest groups of respondents and afterwards extended the analysis to 50 countries and 3 regions. Subsequent studies validating the earlier results include such respondent groups as commercial airline pilots and students in 23 countries, civil service managers in 14 counties, 'up-market' consumers in 15 countries and 'elites' in 19 countries. In the 2010 edition of the book Cultures and Organizations: Software of the Mind, scores on the dimensions are listed for 76 countries, partly based on replications and extensions of the IBM study on different international populations and by different scholars.

In what concerns the current validity of Hofstede's cultural measures, criticisms addressed to the construct of national culture as a suitable variable for differentiation, apply directly to all four measures (Coelho 2011). Different corporate, organizational, industrial and/or sector specific cultures may co-exist within the same firm and might as well conflict and counterbalance the national one (Vecchi and Brennan 2009). Furthermore, in many countries, different ethnic or national cultures co-exist (Au 2000), as result of people mobility around the globe. Within the same country, different sub-cultures might persist, standing apart on religious, language or ethnicity grounds. As a consequence, the four measures of national cultures could be far from being reliable proxies for cultural homogeneity for a given national culture (Vecchi and Brennan 2009).

The data extracted from Hofstede's measures of national culture, that was used in the correlation analyses is presented in Table 1. The data has been cross-validated in an empirical study by van Oudenhoven (2001) for Belgium, Denmark, Germany, United Kingdom, Greece, Spain and the Netherlands. The country scores on the dimensions are relative - societies are compared to other societies. It is thought that these relative scores have been proven to be quite stable over decades. The forces that cause cultures to shift tend to be global or continent-wide - they affect many countries at the same time, so that if their cultures shift, they shift together, and their relative positions tend to remain the same.

Table 1. Hofstede's national dimensions of culture for the 69 countries included in the analysis (source: http://www.geerthofstede.com/research—vsm, accessed February 2015), joined with the Corruption Perception Index 2014 – perceived level of public sector corruption (Transparency International, URL: http://www.transparecncy.org) (legend of headings given in main text).

Country	pdi	idv	mas	uai	ltowvs	ivr	CPI 2014
Argentina	49	46	56	86	20	62	34
Australia	36	90	61	51	21	71	80
Austria	11	55	79	70	60	63	72
Bangladesh	80	20	55	60	47	20	25
Belgium	65	75	54	94	82	57	76
Brazil	69	38	49	76	44	59	43
Bulgaria	70	30	40	85	69	16	43
Canada	39	80	52	48	36	68	81
Chile	63	23	28	86	31	68	73
China	80	20	66	30	87	24	36
Colombia	67	13	64	80	13	83	37
Costa Rica	35	15	21	86	-	-	54
Croatia	73	33	40	80	58	33	48
Czech Rep	57	58	57	74	70	29	51
Denmark	18	74	16	23	35	70	92
Ecuador	78	8	63	67	-	-	33
El Salvador	66	19	40	94	20	89	39
Estonia	40	60	30	60	82	16	69
Finland	33	63	26	59	38	57	89
France	68	71	43	86	63	48	69
Germany	35	67	66	65	83	40	79
Great Britain	35	89	66	35	51	69	78
Greece	60	35	57	112	45	50	43
Guatemala	95	6	37	101	-	-	32
Hong Kong	68	25	57	29	61	17	74
Hungary	46	80	88	82	58	31	54
India	77	48	56	40	51	26	38
Indonesia	78	14	46	48	62	38	34
Iran	58	41	43	59	14	40	27
Ireland	28	70	68	35	24	65	74
Israel	13	54	47	81	38	-	60
Italy	50	76	70	75	61	30	43
Jamaica	45	39	68	13	-	-	38
Japan	54	46	95	92	88	42	76
Korea South	60	18	39	85	100	29	55
Latvia	44	70	9	63	69	13	55
Lithuania	42	60	19	65	82	16	58

| Luxembourg | 40 | 60 | 50 | 70 | 64 | 56 | 82 |
Country	pdi	idv	mas	uai	ltowvs	ivr	CPI 2014
Malaysia	104	26	50	36	41	57	52
Malta	56	59	47	96	47	66	55
Mexico	81	30	69	82	24	97	35
Morocco	70	46	53	68	14	25	39
Netherlands	38	80	14	53	67	68	83
New Zealand	22	79	58	49	33	75	91
Norway	31	69	8	50	35	55	86
Pakistan	55	14	50	70	50	0	29
Panama	95	11	44	86	-	-	37
Peru	64	16	42	87	25	46	38
Philippines	94	32	64	44	27	42	38
Poland	68	60	64	93	38	29	61
Portugal	63	27	31	104	28	33	63
Romania	90	30	42	90	52	20	43
Russia	93	39	36	95	81	20	27
Serbia	86	25	43	92	52	28	41
Singapore	74	20	48	8	72	46	84
Slovak Rep	104	52	110	51	77	28	50
Slovenia	71	27	19	88	49	48	58
Spain	57	51	42	86	48	44	60
Suriname	85	47	37	92	-	-	36
Sweden	31	71	5	29	53	78	87
Switzerland	34	68	70	58	74	66	86
Taiwan	58	17	45	69	93	49	61
Thailand	64	20	34	64	32	45	38
Trinidad & T.	47	16	58	55	13	80	38
Turkey	66	37	45	85	46	49	45
U.S.A.	40	91	62	46	26	68	74
Uruguay	61	36	38	100	26	53	73
Venezuela	81	12	73	76	16	100	19
Vietnam	70	20	40	30	57	35	31

3 Corruption Perceptions Index

In the early 1990s, there was no global convention aimed at curbing corruption, no way to measure corruption at the global scale and corruption was a taboo topic. Many companies regularly wrote off bribes as business expenses in their tax filings, the graft of some longstanding heads of state was legendary, and many international agencies were resigned to the fact that corruption would sap funding from many development projects around the world (Transparency International 2015). Having seen corruption's impact during his work in East Africa, retired World Bank official Peter Eigen, together

424   D.A. Coelho

with nine allies, set up a small organisation to take on the taboo: Transparency International was established in 1993 (Transparency International 2015).

The 2014 Corruption Perceptions Index by Transparency International ranks more than 100 countries and territories based on how corrupt their public sector is perceived to be. It is a composite index – a combination of polls – drawing on corruption-related data collected by a variety of reputable institutions (African Development Bank Governance Ratings 2013, Bertelsmann Foundation Sustainable Governance Indicators 2014, Bertelsmann Foundation Transformation Index 2014, Economist Intelligence Unit Country Risk Ratings 2014, Freedom House Nations in Transit 2013, Global Insight Country Risk Ratings 2014, IMD World Competitiveness Yearbook 2014, Political and Economic Risk Consultancy Asian Intelligence 2014, Political Risk Services International Country Risk Guide 2014, World Bank - Country Policy and Institutional Assessment 2013, World Economic Forum Executive Opinion Survey (EOS) 2014, World Justice Project Rule of Law Index 2014). The index reflects the views of observers from around the world, including experts living and working in the countries and territories evaluated.

The CPI is an indicator of perceptions of public sector corruption, i.e. administrative and political corruption. It is not a verdict on the levels of corruption of entire nations or societies, or of their policies, or the activities of their private sector. As such, citizens of countries or territories that score at the lower end of the CPI often show the same concern about and condemnation of corruption as the public in countries that perform strongly. The Corruption Perceptions Index ranks countries between 0 (highly corrupt) to 100 (very clean). In 2014, Denmark occupied the top spot as the world's least corrupt nation while Somalia and North Korea were tied for the most corrupt countries, according to the CPI 2014 by Transparency international (2015).

Moreover, the CPI is limited in scope, capturing perceptions of the extent of corruption in the public sector, from the perspective of business people and country experts. The CPI is also accompanied by a Confidence Interval that reflects some of the uncertainty associated with a country's CPI score. It is calculated by looking at the range of scores given by all the data used to calculate that country's score, such that a wider interval reflects a wider variation in the data for that country (files.transparency.org/content/download/1900/12610/file/CPI2014_ResultsSpreadsheet.xlsx).

Countries with a high value of CPI have lower levels of perceived public sector corruption than countries with a lower CPI score, e.g. Portugal with a 2014 CPI score of 63, has more perceived public sector corruption than the United States boasting a 2014 CPI score of 74. The CPI scores are shown in the last column of Table 1, which also shows the dimensions of national culture for each of the 69 countries included.

4   Analysis of Association (Pearson Correlation)

Statistical analysis was performed oin the data shown in Table 1, with the assistance of STATA software. The Pearson correlation factor was calculated for association between the Corruption Perception index scores and the national measures of culture. Only two significant and strong correlations were found as a result of this statistical analysis.

The power distance index was found to be negatively associated with the Corruption Perceptions Index 2014 in the sample considered (n = 69) with a correlation factor of −0.6503 (p-value = 0.00). This result suggests that higher power distance cultures (with highly centralized power and decision-making) tend to have lower CPI scores, which indicates more perceived public sector corruption. On the other hand, countries with lower power ditance (with decentralized power and decision-making) tend to have higher CPI scores, which indicates lower levels of perceived public sector corruption.

The individualism versus collectivism measure of culture was found to be positively associated with the Corruption Perceptions Index 2014 in the sample considered (n = 69) with a correlation factor of +0.6651 (p-value = 0.00). This result indicates that cultures that score high in individualism (where individuals are autonomous and confident) also tend to score high on the CPI, which indicates lower levels of perceived public sector corruption. On the contrary, highly collectivist societies (where people are more likely to rely on information provided by others in formulating their opinions) tend to show lower scores on the Corruption Perceptions Index, which translates into higher levels of perceived public sector corruption.

It is generally known that power distance, for example, is correlated with income inequality, and individualism is correlated with national wealth (Hofstede Centre 2015). Hence, income inequality and national wealth would logically associate with the CPI. This has been shown for national wealth in a recent clustering study by Michal Paulus and Ladislav Kristoufek at Charles University in Prague, Czech Republic, that has circulated on social media showed association between national wealth and the CPI 2014 scores (less corrupt countries are also richer), a result that corroborates the present study's finding suggesting that individualistic societies are less corrupt.

Interestingly, total traffic fatalities per European Union country in the period from 2010 to 2012 had been found to be very much associated with two dimensions of national culture: power distance and uncertainty avoidance (Barata and Coelho 2014). From the current analysis, power distance is again one of the national measures of cultures that is most strongly associated to the object of interest in the current paper (perception of corruption in the public sector).

References

Au, K.Y.: Intra-cultural variation as another construct of international management: a study based on secondary data of 42 countries. J. Int. Manage. **6**, 217–238 (2000)

Barnett, H.G.: Innovation: The Basis of Cultural Change. Mc Graw Hill, New York (1953)

Barata, I.G., Coelho, D.A.: Traffic fatalities traffic fatalities and serious injuries in europe – a study of association with cultural, demographic and income variables. In: Proceedings of Applied human Factors and Ergonomics international Conference – AHFE 2014, Krakow, Poland, July 2014

Coelho, Denis A.: Association of CCR and BCC efficiencies to market variables in a retrospective two stage data envelope analysis. In: Yamamoto, Sakae (ed.) HCI 2014, Part II. LNCS, vol. 8522, pp. 151–159. Springer, Heidelberg (2014)

Coelho, D.A.: A study on the relation between manufacturing strategy, company size, country culture and product and process innovation in Europe. Int. J. Bus. Glob. **7**(2), 152–165 (2011)

Coelho, D.A., Harris-Adamson, C., Lima, T.M., Janowitz, I., Rempel, D.M.: Correlation between different hand force assessment methods from an epidemiological study. Hum. Factors Ergon. Ind. **23**(2), 128–139 (2013)

Flynn, B.B., Saladin, B.: Relevance of Baldridge constructs in an international context: a study of national culture. J. Oper. Manage. **2006**(24), 583–603 (2006)

Hofstede Centre (2015). Strategy – Culture – Change. URL: geert-hofstede.com. Accessed February 2015

Hofstede, G.: Culture's Consequences: Comparing Values, Behaviour, Institutions and Organizations Across Countries. Sage Publications, Thousand Oaks (2001)

Hofstede, G.: National cultures in four dimensions: a research-based theory of cultural differences among nations. Int. Stud. Manage. Organ. **13**(1/2), 46–74 (1983)

Hofstede, G.: Culture's Consequences: International Differences in Work-related Values. Sage Publications, London (1980)

Hussler, C.: Culture and knowledge spillovers in Europe: new perspectives for innovation and convergence policies? Econ. Innov. New Technol. **13**(6), 523–541 (2004)

Shane, S.: Cultural influences on national rates of innovation. J. Bus. Ventur. **8**, 59–73 (1993)

Smith-Jackson, T., Essuman-Johnson, A.: Cultural ergonomics.- overview and methodologies. In: Smith-Jackson, T.L., Resnick, M.L., Johnson, K.T. (eds.) Cultural Ergonomics – Theory, Methods and Applications. CRC Press, Boca Raton (2014)

Snell, R.S., Hui, S.K.K.: Towards the Hong Kong learning organization: an exploratory case study. J. Appl. Manage. Stud. **9**(2), 150–175 (2000)

Transparency International (2015). Transparency international – The Global Coallition against Corruption. www.transparency.org. Accessed February 2015

Van Oudenhoven, J.P.: Do organizations reflect national cultures? a 10-nation study. Int. Intercult. Relat. **25**, 89–107 (2001)

Vecchi, A., Brennan, L.: A cultural perspective on innovation in international manufacturing. Res. Int. Bus. Finance **23**, 181–192 (2009)

Wacker, J.G., Sprague, L.G.: Forecasting accuracy: comparing the relative effectiveness of practices between seven developed countries. J. Oper. Manage. **16**(2), 271–290 (1998)

K-Culture Time Machine: Development of Creation and Provision Technology for Time-Space-Connected Cultural Contents

Taejin Ha[1], Younsung Kim[1], Eunseok Kim[1], Kihong Kim[1],
Sangmin Lim[2], Seungmo Hong[2], Jeain Kim[3], Sunhyuck Kim[3],
Junghwa Kim[3], and Woontack Woo[3(✉)]

[1] KAIST CTRI, 305-701 Daejeon, South Korea
{taejinha,mbovary,scbgm,kihongkim}@kaist.ac.kr
[2] PoSTmedia Inc., 135-502 Seoul, South Korea
{ssmlimm,hsm}@postmedia.co.kr
[3] KAIST GSCT, 305-701 Daejeon, South Korea
{jeainkim86,kshl015,jungwhakim,wwoo}@kaist.ac.kr

Abstract. The "K-Culture Time Machine" project develops technologies to structure diverse cultural content from associated organizations and projects, including the "Cultural Heritage hub-bank," and construct new cultural content connected to time and space, then develop a technique that provides the structured content to industries (culture, tourism, IT) and the public. To integrate heterogeneous dataset, designing a new data model is a vital process for our project. As Europeana designed data model which aims to integrate and link several data set across cultural institutions of Europe, we also invented a new data model that encompasses a wide range of metadata for cultural institution in Korea. This approach and data model aim to provide a possibility of semantic link between heterogeneous dataset. This project also provides services with various visualization techniques (virtual reality, augmented reality, etc.) for cultural heritage by traveling through a variety of historical periods in its contents. Last, the project develops image-based time-space content configuration techniques and a software framework that enables visualization with various devices. We perform a validation and feedback process of research and development on the implemented prototype service "Journey of a Korean world cultural heritage".

Keywords: Context-of-interest · Augmented reality · Spatial co-presence · Semantic data model · Linked open data

1 Introduction

Recently, cultural heritage-related policies around the world have been converted from a paradigm of preservation of cultural heritage to one of services application. In the case of the European Union, through the "Europeana" project [1], it has built a web portal that can provide easy access to digital resources of European museums, libraries,

© Springer International Publishing Switzerland 2015
S. Yamamoto (Ed.): HIMI 2015, Part II, LNCS 9173, pp. 428–435, 2015.
DOI: 10.1007/978-3-319-20618-9_43

archives, and audiovisual collections. This lets normal users find, share, use, and be inspired by the rich cultural and academic heritage of Europe.

On the domestic side, several agencies have tried to utilize a wide range of heritage-related content educationally, productively, and conservatively, with the goal of openness of cultural heritage and openness to users. Also, affiliated and related organizations such as the Cultural Heritage Administration [2] are promoting the "cultural heritage hub-bank" project [3] to digitize information of cultural heritage, as well as the Culture and Information Integration project.

The "K-Culture Time Machine" project uses a variety of cultural technologies to structure diverse cultural content from associated organizations and projects, including the "Cultural Heritage hub-bank," and construct new cultural content connected to time and space, then develop a technique that provides the structured content to industries (culture, tourism, IT) and the public. To integrate heterogeneous dataset including aforementioned "Cultural Heritage hub-bank", designing a new data model is a vital process for our project. As Europeana designed data model which aims to integrate and link several data set across cultural institutions of Europe, we also invented a new data model that encompasses a wide range of metadata for cultural institution in Korea. This approach and data model aim to provide a possibility of semantic link between heterogeneous dataset.

The project is developing an open smart platform that exploits the semantic context of cultural heritage contents over the level of raw data to provide customized services to users. This project also provides services with various visualization techniques (virtual reality, augmented reality, etc.) for cultural heritage by traveling through a variety of historical periods in its contents. Last, the project is developing image-based time-space content configuration techniques and a software framework that enables visualization with various devices (Fig. 1).

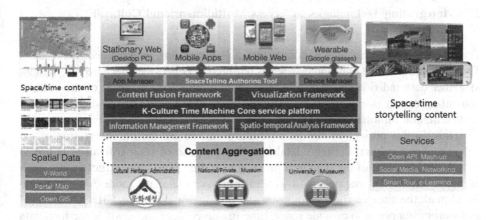

Fig. 1. Overall procedure of the K-culture time machine project.

We perform a validation and feedback process of research and development on the implemented prototype service "Journey of a Korean world cultural heritage".

Fig. 2. Possible examples of the implemented prototype service.

The target service is a major cultural heritage that effectively couples tangible and intangible cultural heritage by considering the verification of content fusion techniques and the accuracy of the time-division layer of virtual space-time traveling (Fig. 2).

2 Enabling Technology

We aim to provide new content that could interest the younger generation accustomed to smart devices by utilizing time-spatial data and visualization techniques (AR, VR, etc.). For this purpose, we research development information management framework, spatio-temporal analysis framework, content fusion framework, visualization framework, and context-aware framework. For developing these frameworks, integrated data model and metadata standard for various cultural institutions are core element. Then we develop authoring tools, mobile SDK, and a mesh-up service that allows space-telling service (Fig. 3).

2.1 Integrating Technologies to Access Multidimensional Cultural Content

Technology for generating a data structure and integrating heterogeneous metadata: The cooperation of the relevant agencies is required to collect data because it is difficult to gather data individually. Also, because of the variety of metadata of the cultural content agency, it is difficult to maintain the consistency of the linked data model for spatiotemporal information integration.

Thus, in this project we design a standard data model for the integration of the heterogeneous cultural heritage database. The purpose of standardization is not to switch the structure of the data to a metadata holding individual structure but each metadata are to be mapped to a general-purpose metadata model. We need to benchmark the site of a similar domestic and international service, CIDOC-CRM [4] and Europeana portal to provide space-time fusion content and analyze the metadata for the content that institutions hold. We also examine cases suitable for the content acquisition system and obtain advice on designing the metadata from domain experts.

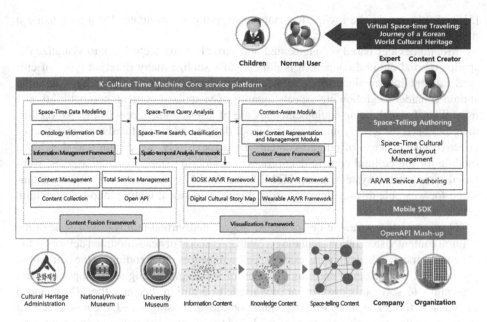

Fig. 3. Block diagram of the K-culture time machine project.

Research on technology for extracting causal relationships and correlations for time, space, subject, and field of content: If the content data model is not proper, the correlation/causality extraction techniques cannot produce a good result. Therefore, by performing the data model design and verification step repeatedly, we can determine a suitable design direction. To do this, we benchmark the existing algorithms to extract cause/correlation and design a data model that can easily extract correlation.

Studying a technique for creating a new space-time relationship in accordance with the relevance of the content: For some improper results of the space-time relationship generated by the algorithm, the user action of the service level is required. In this case, administrators can view and edit the results using the editing tools. They are able to edit the generated space-time relationship and also create a new space-time relation-ship. The editing tools are designed to allow for future scalability.

2.2 AR/VR-Based Visualization Technique of Space-Time Cultural Content

Automated 3D image feature map generation technique using image capture and a wearable display of mobile equipment: Operation processing speed can be lowered to the level of the mobile and wearable devices. By adopting the sensor information of the mobile device to the computer vision and image processing algorithms, the algorithm can be optimized and faster. We develop image capturing, 3D point reconstruction, and matching feature points. The technique of generating a feature descriptor and matching

[5] it should run in the low-performance computing environment for a user using a mobile or wearable device.

Mobile devices based on augmented and virtual reality techniques to visualize the spatiotemporal cultural content: It is difficult to visualize many different types of cultural content information in a single rendering layer. Thus, visualization technique should consider the following aspects: quality of visualized content, compatibility and reliability of visualization equipment, and ease of information access [6]. Based on this, there is a need for a study on automatic layout design and a structured representation of effective visualization of culture content. To achieve this, we design and develop a module for the cultural content data process considering static/dynamic aspects, web-based visualization systems using HTML5 standard [7], user gaze information acquisition for wearable display devices, and a three-dimensional feature-map-based culture content layout method.

Head-mounted wearable-device-based augmented/virtual-reality-based space-time cultural content visualization technology: With expansion of head-mounted devices in the PC environment, calculation processing speed will be lower depending on the computing power level. Optimization and simplification of image processing and computer vision algorithms to solve this problem are required. In addition, because the 3D enhanced graphics performance also varies depending on the processing speed, there is a need for polygon rendering optimization studies. In addition, an animated and interactive K-culture time machine is an important part of the user's understanding of a historical fact.

2.3   Participation/Share-Enabled Open Cultural Content Platform

Multidimensional query processing techniques for combined time and space content: Content search performance may be degraded due to the ambiguity of the multidimensional query, and the processing time may also be delayed by a large amount of data. To address this, rather than a simple keyword-based search, a semantic-based search technique is necessary to improve search performance. While taking advantage of an open-source search engine for multi-level data access, it is necessary to reduce the processing time through the optimized search algorithm research and development so that users (viewers) can experience content related to the cultural heritage of the various forms they wish to see in the heritage (video, sound, 3D augmented reality content).

Open service platform technology supports heterogeneous cultural content and links, convergence: A participation-sharing platform must be able to guarantee personal security. In order to solve this problem, personal information requests should be minimized and basic personal information should be stored encrypted.

With reference to public data API, we design Open API and user-specific service scenarios and develop an appropriate participation/sharing platform for each scenario. An authoring tool for linking and convergence of heterogeneous cultural content is essential to its development, and corresponding common UI components increase its reusability. This also aims to develop user-participatory service models to enable a wide range of users, including cultural commentators, who are free to develop augmented-reality-based story-telling [8] and share the content of the story rather than consuming one-way content from a content delivery service provider [9].

2.4 Prototype Service to Spread the Space and Temporal Culture Content

2D/3D map-based cultural content and spatial information fusion: It is not a simple process to access POI information in an open map. The development of multi-layer rendering techniques will be integrated. In addition, there is a need for a variety of representations in accordance with the story (map). Development of the open map-based UI may define various types of representation, such as moveable story-maps, depending on the time, distributed-space-based story, meaning-based visualization, etc.

Mobile and web-based AR/VR pilot service development: Compatibility with mobile OSs and devices is addressed using a function that is not dependent on the hardware (standard method). A problem may occur when processing data that are not appropriate for the standard time division precision supported by the services provided, which can be designed in consideration of the UI to choose the precision according to the data. Technically, the mobile app is developed as a hybrid method to avoid overlapping between platforms. Web development uses a standardized approach that does not depend on the particular browser.

Technology to create a space-time combined culture content creation and distribution package: The content and distribution package generated could have difficulty performing the actual service. Content should be generated by taking into account the type of service and distribution package (web-based, mobile-system-based, and wearable-system-based). Also, content-creation and package-generation functions should be built into the editing tool. In addition, the metadata format of the space-temporal content can also be standardized, as can the data format (visualization) for loading the information needed for visualization.

3 Prototype Development

We developed a prototype application of the K-Culture Time Machine, an in-situated authoring and viewing system, for augmented reality-based tour guidance that helps a user to easily create and experience an augmented reality scene of a cultural heritage. In the authoring step, a user takes a picture of the object of interest and searches digital content related to the cultural heritage on the semantic web. These kinds of authorized augmented reality scenes are saved into a virtual map based on the GPS based position. In the future, many other users can also modify or complement the authorized augmented scene based on the virtual map. In the viewing step, visitors can trigger the augmented scene if they follow and close their viewing device on the observation viewpoint, which was previously generated by authors in the authoring step. Then, visitors can experience the augmented scene of the cultural heritage by downloading authorized content with ARML (Augmented Reality Markup Language) format [10]. The application is possible through three-dimensional computer vision technology, and its precision is very high compared to the approximate location based information visualization utilizing existing GPS sensor (Fig. 4).

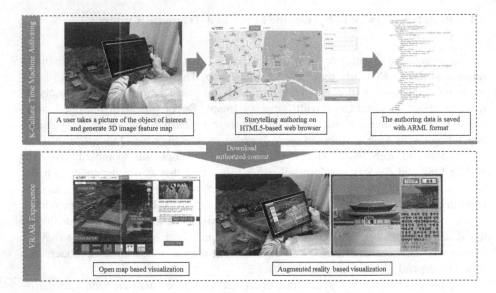

Fig. 4. Authoring and experience of the K-culture time machine.

4   Conclusion

This study presents a basis for providing a space-time-associated possibility of inte-grated heritage. The material of the different parts of cultural heritage has the potential to be utilized in a variety of ways, including digital visualization. Beyond the tradi-tional closed and administrative cultural heritage information architecture, an integrated and organically managed heritage information structure will contribute to the activation of cultural heritage.

The user-context-aware framework is designed on the basis of the standard protocol to provide the appropriate service by identifying the individual service user's physical, environmental, and resource context. These features are expected to recommend meaningful content from much unconstructed content, provide guidance, and enable personalized space-telling.

Acknowledgments. This research was supported by Ministry of Culture, Sports and Tourism (MCST) and Korea Creative Content Agency (KOCCA) in the Culture Technology (CT) Research & Development Program 2014.

We would like to thank Nohyoung Park, Jeonghun Jo, Hyun Yang, Kyungwon Gil, Hayun Kim, Juhee Suh, and Jaeyeon Ahn for collaboration in this research.

References

1. Europeana. www.europeana.eu
2. Cultural heritage administration. www.cha.go.kr

3. Cultural heritage digital hub-bank. http://hub.cha.go.kr
4. ICOM: Definition of the CIDOC conceptual reference model (2013)
5. Ha, T., Lee, H., Woo, W.: DigiLog Space: Real-time dual space registration and dynamic information visualization for 4D+ augmented reality. In: International Symposium on Ubiquitous Virtual Reality (ISUVR), pp. 22–25 (2012)
6. Goodhue, D.L., Thompson, R.L.: Task-technology fit and individual performance. MIS Q. **19**(2), 213–236 (1995)
7. HTML5. http://www.w3.org/TR/html5
8. Ha, T., Kim, K., Park, N., Seo, S., Woo, W.: Miniature alive: augmented reality-based interactive digilog experience in miniature exhibition. In: CHI 2012 Extended Abstracts on Human Factors in Computing Systems, pp. 1067–1070 (2012)
9. Ha, T., Woo, W.: design considerations for implementing an interactive Digilog Book. In: Ioannides, M., Magnenat-Thalmann, N., Fink, E., Žarnić, R., Yen, A.-Y., Quak, E. (eds.) EuroMed 2014. LNCS, vol. 8740, pp. 732–739. Springer, Heidelberg (2014)
10. Augmented Reality Markup Language (ARML). http://www.opengeospatial.org/projects/groups/arml2.0swg

Experience Simulator for the Digital Museum

Yasushi Ikei[1]([✉]), Seiya Shimabukuro[1], Shunki Kato[1], Kohei Komase[1],
Koichi Hirota[2], Tomohiro Amemiya[3], and Michiteru Kitazaki[4]

[1] Tokyo Metropolitan University, Hachioji, Tokyo 191-0065, Japan
ikei@computer.org
[2] The University of Tokyo, Bunkyo, Tokyo 113-8656, Japan
uhirota@mail.ecc.u-tokyo.ac.jp
[3] NTT Communication Science Laboratories, Atsugi, Kanagawa 243-0198, Japan
amemiya.tomohiro@lab.ntt.co.jp
[4] Toyohashi University of Technology, Toyohashi, Aichi 441-8580, Japan
mich@tut.jp

Abstract. This paper describes a design philosophy and an implementation example of a simulator of bodily experience as a potential exhibit style of a future digital museum. An experience transfer method is discussed first to introduce a physical reliving of the past person's body motion itself. The new bodily reliving experience is such that the follower person replicates the motion of the other person. A working hypothesis is proposed in which the body of the reliving user is a part of the display media of the multisensory VR system that projects a virtual body backward from the real body. A specificity of the bodily experience in voluntariness is also discussed. The sensation of walking as both for the self body and others' body were rated under some visual and vestibular display conditions. The result showed that the vestibular stimulation markedly enhanced the sensation of walking, and that the self body with a first person view produced the highest rating.

Keywords: Bodily media · Backward projection · Multisensory display

1 Introduction

Methodology of a museum in which we hand real objects on to the next generation has progressed markedly by the virtual reality (VR) technology. A new method of an interactive exhibit [1,2] in addition to a static exhibit has been explored at the museum by incorporating digital technology [3,4]. A change from only seeing objects to experiencing them is gradually introduced to the field.

One of objectives of a museum is to organize and transfer mostly historical 'object' from the culture, fine art, science, industry, and life, to the mass of people. As a method to serve for this purpose, valuable objects were accumulated and preserved to show them to the public in a way that has been referred to as a museum format. A basic form is to transfer objects to people in the future, and to transfer something implied by those objects. This is an only way to transfer

© Springer International Publishing Switzerland 2015
S. Yamamoto (Ed.): HIMI 2015, Part II, LNCS 9173, pp. 436–446, 2015.
DOI: 10.1007/978-3-319-20618-9_44

complete value of the authentic entity to the public. No other way may out-weigh the method. The typical form is the exhibition of an original real thing (the primary source material) which can only be seen at the specific museum in the word, which is a symbolic style of the museum. The genuine object is an absolutely important and primary existence, and that is an untouchable for preservation. The authentic objects which can not be installed in the museum (e.g. an architecture or what already lost) have been embodied by physical mod-els and transferred to following generations. The physical embodiment allows people a comprehensive use of multisensory perceptions, which introduces an extremely effective impact as an actual object (if succeeded). These are the most effective methods to transfer an object that has a three dimensional struc-ture. They can transfer information not handled by an indirect representation of literal or visual media (the secondary material). The VR technology among digital technology allows humans to perceive the three dimensional structure of the real space as it is, so that it can best contribute to the transfer of object as discussed above. In addition, the interaction between objects and humans can be replicated by the VR technology. Since objects are usually artifacts that existed with humans, the interaction with humans has been essential for their existence. Interaction with objects is an *experience* for humans, and the objects are natu-rally exists for an experience. The real situation how objects are used, the type of interaction, the context of use, the sensations on phases, and overall impression produce the experience. To transfer such an experience is the essential inher-itance of the cultural property of objects. Until now, objects themselves have been transferred in a museum since such an experience discussed above could not be handed on. The VR technology has enabled the museum to transfer the experience of objects.

2   Experience Transfer

There are two methods to transfer and replay the past experience. The first one is to build the environment of the past to experience the situation. If the same environment where the past user immersed is reproduced as similar as possible, almost the same experience is possible as the past users performed by using reproduced special environment. The traditional method for this direction was to build a real park in which original buildings are brought and repaired, or replicated to provide the past environment to the people in the present. The replication of a world by the VR technology drastically changed the methodology. It enabled to provide a space and an object that are flexibly reconstructed, and allowed people to experience the world.

The production of a space allows the pseudo experience of a specific archi-tecture, a vehicle and a tool that are similar to original ones. The participant experiences the world by oneself in the space that is equivalent to that the past people encountered. Although the experience is similar to that the past people obtained, it is not the experience of the action taken by one's own choice in the specific context in a particular background of the day. Even though the environ-ment was the same, the experience is not the same one which the past people performed and obtained. The experience is not just what the past people really obtained.

The second way is to prepare the experience of the past itself for transfer in that a traditional reliving experience is involved. Although a reliving experience is to capture the experience of others vividly as if he/she oneself performed the experience, a traditional reliving experience was based on reception of information through a book or a movie audio-visually. This is just looking into the world the other person experienced during the presentation of a particular story. This activity is basically understanding the experience of others. It is an experience of observation as a bystander, although nominally toled as if he/she experienced by oneself. Of course, it is one form of experience transfer in a sense. However, a bodily sensation that can not be transferred exists inevitably in this type of reliving experience since the experience is inherently obtained through a body motion.

The reliving experience of an architecture or a tool may be truly obtained by doing completely the same physical motion as the past person did using the body to move around or manipulate in the same way. Thus, to transfer the past experience as it was is to reproduce the spatial motion of the person, specifically the past bodily motion, on to the other person's body. Of course, sensory information of the environmental space is recorded and replicated as accurately as possible for the other person. This requires the same body motion of the past person in the space to be replicated completely, however it is usually impossible and inefficient to make the same body motion of the person who relives the past experience. Then, the problem is whether if the VR presentation of bodily movement is possible. A procedure for this presentation is first to record actual experience and then to reproduce it. The recording method has been discussed and developed in the context of lifelog.

A valuable experience for the museum may involve a special body motion skill such as an Olympic level athletic skill, and the body motion of a person with a particular skill which is recognized to be preserved to the next generation. More generally, a walk experience of world tourist sites or adventure activities in the frontier will be accepted as valuable experiences for many people. Since the diversity of bodily activities of humans is huge, to share such rich experiences produces a new unprecedented value.

3 Bodily Reliving Experience

We consider the transfer of experience that involves the body movement. The objective of the study is to make the past spatial activity of other persons the experience of the follower who traced the activity. We call this replication of the body motion the bodily reliving experience.

Since the experience is performed by the body, the body of the follower needs to be restricted to the motion of the precedent, and subject to it. Reliving is to become another person at the time, which means clearly that the follower person will not have a free experience. The experience itself already exists and the follower traces the experience, as the movie observer does not choose the behavior of the actor. The bodily sensation is also provided in the form of recorded motion in the past. The experience obtained is what the other person performed in the past real space. The reliving experience of this is a replication of a reality as what is created in the VR technology. The feature of the reliving experience is that the reality is filtered by the precedent person.

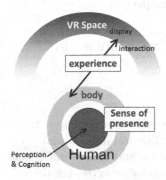 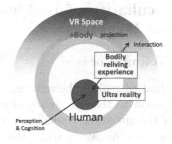

Fig. 1. VR experience   **Fig. 2.** Bodily reliving experience

Traditionally, the reliving media was based on a replication by a literal book or a movie. This paper proposes that the fusion of the body of an experiential follower itself and an advanced sensory display device makes a new presentation media for the reliving experience. We hypothesize that the own body is a part of the media. Figures 1 and 2 indicate models of a usual VR experience and the bodily reliving experience. A center circle indicates the human CNS (central nervous system) for the perception and cognition, and the ring means the body of the human. A half ring indicates the artificial VR space.

In Fig. 1 the VR space means a space of experience created by multisensory display. The experience is established by the interaction between the human (the CNS and the body) and the space. The experience will have an equivalent value of the real experience when the user feels the sense of presence to the space.

Figure 2 shows that the body of an experiential follower represented by a ring is fused with the VR space. This means that the body of the follower is a part of the presentation media that is a VR space by multisensory displays. This is a structure to transform the other person's experience on to the own body experience by moving the body on the media side separating the body from the control of the CNS; the body receives stimulus for presenting the virtual body motion. Now that the CNS, the subject of cognition, obtains the bodily reliving experience rendered by the space and the body. The sense of presence in this setting is different from that of usual situation. In this sense, we call this the ultra reality. The approach to form the bodily reliving experience is largely different from the usual case of the virtual reality where the past environment is rebuilt for a new experience.

The reproduction of the environment of the virtual reality focuses an objective space replication, then the replicated space is conceptually independent from the person who receives the experience. The reality by the virtual reality is an objective reality, while the world created for the bodily reliving experience is a subjective reality of a predecessor. The latter reality has been given a meaning by anyone else; the reality was constructed by other people. The reality to experience is already established as in watching a movie. The difference is that the world is always rendered from the first person perspective.

4   Peculiarity of Bodily Reliving Experience and Hypothesis

4.1   Voluntariness

A method to realize the reliving experience is based on providing a variety of information to the five senses in addition to traditional audio visual presentation of the situation. Specifically the proprioception and tactile information of the body are displayed while the real body is totally reserved for them if the whole body is used as the media to present a physical experience. Although we have obtained an empirical knowledge through the TV or a movie in an ordinary reliving experience, in the bodily reliving experience, the bodily action of the other person needs to be reproduced through the body of the experiential follower. The body of the follower is a device within the presentation media to produce sensations. The reliving experience has a peculiarity in which the bodily experience is the first-person experience, and at the same time it is regulated heteronomously by a predecessor as discussed above. An ordinary experience is created and obtained solely due to the active physical motion selected by oneself in facing the space of the real world. In this sense, the reliving experience based on the existence of other person's experience conflicts the nature of the active experience of the self. The reliving experience may not be recognized as an experience in that meaning. The point is a voluntariness of the experience. An experiential follower can not have voluntariness since the reliving experience is to trace the experience of others. If the essence of the reliving experience is to have the scenario of the other person, it may contradict the voluntariness essential for an ordinary experience. It is an interesting argument indeed; this inconsistency stemmed from the prerequisite we placed above where the self body is not one's own.

4.2   Creation of Virtual Body

The first problem to install the bodily reliving experience is to what extent the body of the experiential follower should be identical to the predecessor's body. The body of the follower is driven by the VR display device externally, which imparts the sensation of motion perceived and attended. A trivial method to make the sensation identical to the bodily sensation of the predecessor may be that the follower should move as the same amount as the predecessor. However, it is not an efficient solution, since it is not actually possible to force the body motion of the follower to be identical to the predecessor's motion completely. The degrees of freedom of the human body motion is not small and the speed of the motion is fast. In addition, what is essential here is not the replication of the body motion itself, but the creation of the *sensation* of body motion. The point of the bodily reliving experience is to avoid the complete copy of motion by an efficient stimulation method to multisensory sensation related to the body motion.

The bodily reliving experience we pursue is essentially the projection image of the self body. It is the sensation of oneself who experience the objective space, and also the sensation of the self body. The self body is evident existence in the real world generally. The existence is definite, however it is only evident through the sensory system which has ultimate importance. However, this confidence is disrupted if the sensory system is fooled. Botvinick [5] demonstrated the illusion in which the user loses the body image by repeated false input to the sensory system. This phenomenon to recognize a rubber hand as ones own suggests that the body image is able to be projected to the other object.

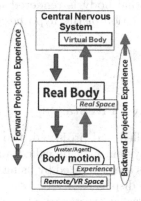

Fig. 3. Virtual body by backward projection (revised from [6])

The rubber hand illusion is an incredible fact since the hand is the key part of a human body to interact with the world. The fact that the body image is not firmly defined is usable for the creation of bodily reliving experience. The self projection by which the self body is visible in a virtual space is one of the VR features [7]. It is important in the sense that it enables interaction with the environment, and positions oneself in the space to introduce the sense of presence. In addition, it provides visibility from other people. The projected self is usually called a virtual body.

An avatar is also the body image of the player in the net game/space. The both represent the self body image, and they are the media of interaction with the space and other avatars. This type of projection represents the image of self body in the other space based on the intention of the user. This is a forward projection of the self control to the other space. On the other hand, the bodily reliving experience is a reverse (backward) projection where the past experience of the predecessor is projected to the current self body in the real world. Figure 3 indicates the relation.

The usual forward projection is used to drive body motion in the real space by a command from the CNS holding a self will. The real motion is projected again to the avatar motion in the other space. The avatar is the self body of the other space. The experience in the other space is created through the avatar. On the other hand in the backward projection, the experience in the past other space is projected to the current self body. The self body control is dominated by the external device and set under the passive state. The hypothesis of the bodily reliving experience states that the body image[1] created by the self body motion should be that of the precedent body. The body image stored in the CNS is virtually replaced by projection of the other person's body.

If the mapping of the body image from various personalities to the follower is ideally performed, the body image may be regarded as virtualized to accept nominal diversity. In Fig. 3, the virtual body in the CNS indicates the projected body image. A hypothesis may be presented that a great number of experiences would be obtained if the virtual body is rendered in any forms using the self body as a medium. The validation of the hypothesis has been performed in a small step.

5   Experience Simulator

5.1   Multisensory Display—FiveStar [8]

If the virtual body is controlled and projected, the system is able to create a variety of experiences. The system may be called an experience simulator in a sense where many experiences are generated by using the self body and its senses stimulated by a multisensory display.

Figure 4 indicates the direct-contact part of the multisensory display. The vestibular stimulation is produced by the seat motion. The proprioception of the lower limb is stimulated by the pedal and slider. The vibratory stimulation is added to the user at the skin of the back, thigh, and the sole of the feet. The visual display of 85-in 3-D (passive) LCD monitor (KD-84X9000, Sony) is placed about 120 cm in front of the user. In addition, a wind display of four circulators and a 5.1-ch audio system are installed around the seat. The user sits on the seat wearing polarized glasses, headphones, and shinbone stimulators to receive multisensory information. The visual angle is about 76° in the horizontal direction.

Figure 4 shows the motion seat and the user. The seat provides three dimensional motion (lift translation, roll, and pitch rotational motion) to the participant with three electric actuators (PWAM6H010MR-A, Oriental Motor, Inc.).

---

[1] This implies the both of body image and body schema [9] here.

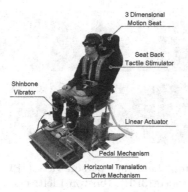

Fig. 4. FiveStar Devices

The translational motion of the actuator is up to 200 mm/s with a maximum amplitude of 100 mm (position resolution: 0.01 mm) within a load of 600 N. The rotational speed is up to 1.25 rad/s with the maximum rotational angle of 0.3 rad. This three-dof motion creates motion stimulation of the head of a sitting user to impart controlled vestibular sensation in accordance with the rotation at the joint angle of the lower limbs of the real body to project a virtual body.

5.2 Bodily Reliving Experience—Diversity of Expression

Experiences replicated by the FiveStar system should be diverse specifically in the museum. To examine representation capability to provide bodily diversity created by the system, six conditions for presenting walking sensation were compared. Figure 5 shows the views that the participants watched. Eleven participants recruited in the university performed the experiment.

The objective of the experiment was to evaluate the sensation of walking body of six different body types: the self body, a slim body type, a fat body type, an adult (CG) body type, a child (CG) body type, and a sumo wrestler (CG) body type. Since each participant has a different body, the seat motion needed to be differently adjusted to present the sensation of walking in the six body types. We asked the participant to adjust the seat motion first to best imitate the walking in those bodies. Note that only the seat motion was used in this experiment to clarify the effect of vestibular stimulation. (The lower limb stimulator of proprioception and the tactile stimulators were not used.) The number of target bodies to represent was six, and the number of media conditions was five, then thirty settings in total to rate the sensation of walking were introduced in the experiment. The motion of the seat was regulated to the trajectory that each participant adjusted. The participant was instructed to get into (be immersed in) the target body and to walk as if he/she were in the body.

After the adjustment of the seat motion for all conditions, the participant was asked to rate the walking sensation on a visual analogue scale from 'no walking sensation (not in the walking state)' to 'the real walking sensation (in the walking state)'. The ends of the line segment were marked 0 and 100.

Fig. 5. Walking movies. (top) Left: first person view (1PP), center: male live video (3PP), right: fat man live video (3PP), (bottom) left: male adult CG (3PP), center: child CG (3PP), right: sumo wrestler CG (3PP)

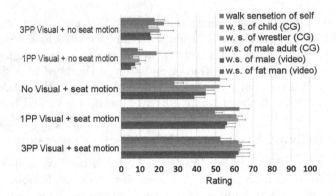

Fig. 6. Walking sensation produced by different stimulations in visual and seat (vestibular) presentation.

Figure 6 shows the result of the rating on the sensation of walking as the person shown in the view (with the visual mode) or designated by the experimenter (in the first person view mode). The result clearly indicates that the seat motion contributed markedly on the sensation of walking. Of course, a visual presentation has a certain effect on the sensation of walking as shown in the rating of the no-visual/with seat motion that was lower than the visual/with seat motion, however the seat motion had a very large effect. If the seat motion is not provided, the third person perspective was better in imparting the sensation of walking.

The rating varied differently between a self walking sensation and the other's walking sensation. For the self-body walking sensation, the first person view (1PP) with seat motion condition produced the highest rating of a walking sensation. It was a natural view for the participant. As for the other's body walking sensation, the sumo wrestler 3PP view with seat motion was the highest rating. This may be due to ease of qualitative understanding the bodily feature and motion based on the visual image by which the motion sensation of other's was collected. Actually, the visual presentation provides most part of information on the walking of the others. It is suggested that the first person perspective is appropriate for replication of the self body walking, while the third person perspective is suited for the others where the feature of the bodies are easily understood.

6 Conclusion

The digital museum is a new direction of object exhibition, and its flexibility and interactivity of information presentation using ICT and/or VR technology will introduce unprecedented development of the museum exhibit. Visitor's bodily experience is an essential direction for the purpose of the original museum objective. The present paper provides part of fundamental knowledge for sharing the experiences of action in the world. The motion of a seat could effectively enhanced the sensation of walking that may be applicable to the experience of seeing a large object such as architectures in the word heritage. As a preliminary result, the first person view of the participant with the seat motion created the highest sensation of walking that would introduce a vivid virtual tour of the world.

The next goal of the bodily reliving experience is to build a museum of body by projecting any body with body virtualization. It is to involve, as an objectives of VR, the conquest of the body in addition to that of the space and time. The body of the follower is made transparent and replaced by the other person's body to obey the action of others. It has special characteristics in that the voluntariness of the body motion is lost although it is the experience of the self. It is related to cognitive property of the body ownership to define what is the self body, and the agency to define voluntariness. To provide an explanation between these issues and the bodily reliving experience is one of the important future works of the study.

Acknowledgments. The author wish to thank Professor Michitaka Hirose at the University of Tokyo for his invaluable advice for the research. This research was supported in part by the Strategic Information and Communications R&D Promotion Programme (SCOPE) of MIC, and by grant-in-aid scientific research (A) of MEXT, Japan.

References

1. Exploratorium. http://www.exploratorium.edu/
2. Imura, J., Kasada, K., Narumi, T., Tanikawa, T., Hirose, M.: Reliving past scene experience system by inducing a video-camera operator's motion with overlaying a video-sequence onto real environment. ITE Trans. MTA **2**(3), 225–235 (2014)
3. Barry, A., Trout, J., Debenham, P., Thomas, G.: Augmented reality in a public space: the Natural History Museum, London. Computer **45**(7), 42–47 (2012)
4. Li, Y.-chang, Liew, A.W.-chung, Su, W.-poh, The Digital Museum : Challenges and Solution. In: IDCTA2012: 8th International Conference on Digital Content, Multimedia Technology and its Applications, pp. 646–649 (2012)

5. Botvinick, M., Cohen, J.: Rubber hands 'feel' touch that eyes see. Nature **391**, 756 (1998)
6. Ikei, Y., Okuya, Y., Shimabukuro, S., Abe, K., Amemiya, T., Hirota, K.: To relive a valuable experience of the world at the digital museum. In: Yamamoto, S. (ed.) HCI 2014, Part II. LNCS, vol. 8522, pp. 501–510. Springer, Heidelberg (2014)
7. Tachi, S., Hirose, M., Sato, M.: Virtual Reatlity. Corona Inc., Brooklyn (2010)
8. Ikei, Y., Abe, K., Hirota, K., Amemiya, T.: A multisensory VR system exploring the ultra-reality. In: Proceedings of VSMM 2012, pp. 71–78 (2012)
9. Berlucchi, G., Aglioti, S.M.: The body in the brain revisited. Exp. Brain Res. **200**, 25–35 (2010)

Virtual Aquarium: Mixed Reality Consisting of 3DCG Animation and Underwater Integral Photography

Nahomi Maki[✉] and Kazuhisa Yanaka

Kanagawa Institute of Technology,
1030 Shimo-ogino, Atsugi-Shi, Kanagawa 243-0292, Japan
{maki,yanaka}@ic.kanagawa-it.ac.jp

Abstract. Virtual aquariums have various advantages when compared with real aquariums. First, imaginary creatures and creatures that are difficult to maintain in real aquariums can be displayed. Second, virtual aquariums have similar soothing effects as an actual aquarium. Therefore, we developed a new virtual aquarium through integral photography (IP), wherein virtual fishes are created with 3DCG animation and real water. Stereoscopic view is possible from all directions above the water tank through the IP and without the need for special glasses. A fly's eye lens is sunk in the water resulting in larger focal length for the fly's eye lens and an increase in the amount of popping out. Therefore, a stronger stereoscopic effect is obtained. The displayed fishes appear to be alive and swimming in the water, an effect achieved through three-dimensional computer graphics animation. This system can also be appreciated as an artwork. This system can also be applied to exhibit already-extinct ancient creatures in aquariums or museums in the future.

Keywords: Integral photography · Three-dimensional computer graphics · Animation

1 Introduction

A large number of people keep fishes in their homes and/or offices because of its soothing effect. Recent progress in computer graphics technology has made it possible to create an aquarium using virtual reality. Virtual fish has many advantages compared to real fish. For instance, keeping virtual fishes remove limitations as to the type of fish kept in the tank. From fishes that live deep in the sea to fictional creatures, one's imagination would be the limit. Fishes that have perished can also be restored and brought back to life.

Figure 1 shows the concept of our system. Creatures created through three-dimensional computer graphics (3DCG) animation appear to be alive and swimming at the surface and beneath the water.

© Springer International Publishing Switzerland 2015
S. Yamamoto (Ed.): HIMI 2015, Part II, LNCS 9173, pp. 447–456, 2015.
DOI: 10.1007/978-3-319-20618-9_45

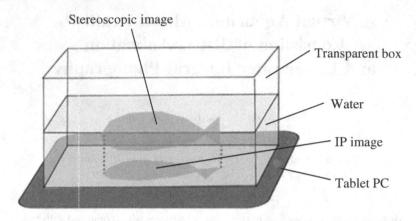

Fig. 1. Concept of our system

2 Related Work

Our virtual aquarium may share similar concepts with a virtual water tank where a display is arranged on one side of the water tank. In such cases however, displaying the creature in water can be difficult.

AquaTop Display: A True Immersive Water Display System [1]: a display that projects two-dimensional (2D) images on the surface of the water clouded with bath salts. In contrast, our study enables the display of a stereoscopic image as if it actually exists in the water and not only on the surface.

Three-dimensional (3D) crystal engraving or Bubblegram [2]: 3D designs are generated inside a solid block of glass or transparent plastic by irradiating a laser beam inside the material. The objects appear to exist inside the block. However, once it is created, changing the shape or moving the object becomes impossible. In comparison, our system enables animating the 3DCG image displayed inside the water.

3 Integral Photography

We adopted an integral photography (IP) in this system because IP is indisputably the most ideal system among various 3D display systems developed to date. IP, which was invented by Lippmann in 1908 and has been improved continuously, has an advantage in that it provides both horizontal and vertical parallax without the need to wear stereo glasses.

Currently, popular autostereoscopic systems such as the lenticular system and parallax barrier system provide a parallax only in the horizontal direction. Therefore, viewers can see 3D objects from any position only within a certain field of view. In this respect, IP is a technology that has nearly the same advantages as holography. Moreover, IP is considerably more feasible than holography because silver halide photography and laser technology are not required. Composed of a normal flat panel display (FPD), such as a liquid crystal display or an organic light-emitting diode, as well as a fly's eye lens, as illustrated in Fig. 2, IP is also electronically rewritable. Although color reproducibility depends on the FPD, the reproducibility is still generally excellent.

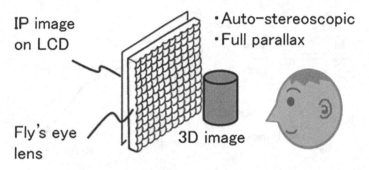

IP image on LCD

• Auto-stereoscopic
• Full parallax

Fly's eye lens

3D image

Fig. 2. Simple integral photography system

Nevertheless, IP has not been widely used until now. One possible reason is that the extremely high initial cost of fly's eye lens production when produced using a metal mold. Conventionally, because the lens pitch of the fly's eye lens is considered an integral multiple of the pixel pitch of FPD, the lens should be custom-made according to the pixel pitch of FPD. However, this step can be very costly.

The invention of the extended fractional view (EFV) method [3–5], which is a new method of synthesizing an IP image, drastically changed this situation. In the EFV method, both an integer and an arbitrary real number are allowed as ratio between the lens and pixel pitches. The physical difference between the pitches is processed by software. Therefore, the initial high cost of customizing a fly's eye lens is reduced because a comparatively inexpensive ready-made fly's eye lens can be used in combination with various FPDs.

IP is also effective in expressing the glittering effect of a material, such as gems, because the light emitted from each convex lens of a fly's eye lens depends on its direction [6–8].

4 System Configuration

In this paper, an IP was introduced and the creature can be seen in the water. The IP was laid flat to ensure that observation from the top is possible. Figure 3 shows the composition of our system, which consists of a tablet PC with retina display, a plastic box with water, and fly's eye lens sunk in the water. In this system, the use of water has two implications.

First, water is essential for imaginary underwater life. This system is a type of mixed reality in which real water and imaginary creatures exist in the same space. In common mixed reality systems, objects created with CG are synthesized with real space using transparent type head-mounted display (HMD). In this system however, IP is used instead of HMD.

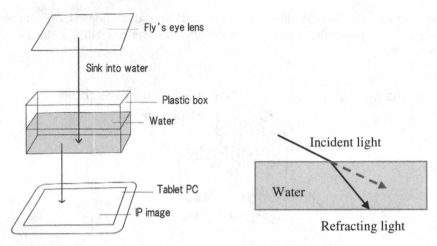

Fig. 3. System configuration.   **Fig. 4.** Refraction on the surface of the water

A higher reality is provided because the refraction of the light occurs on the surface of the water as shown in Fig. 3.

Second, an advantage is that the focal length of each convex lens of the fly's eye lens is enhanced when immersed in water [5]. The refractive index of the fly's eye lens is at 1.5, and its focal length is increased by about three times the original after being sunk in water. As a result, the amount of popping out of underwater objects is tripled, and a higher stereoscopic effect is obtained (Fig. 4).

5   Creating a 3DCG Scene

The 3DCG scene consists of two swimming creature models and water surface textures. The scene is created in Autodesk Maya.

5.1   3DCG Models

The imaginary fishes were modeled as shown in Fig. 5. The material for the surface had some transparency and was colored light blue. Bead-like materials of various colors were added to the surface to give the impression of a constellation, similar to the modeling for live fish. The addition of bead-like material was done to add mystery and differentiation with the real fishes. Incandescence was also applied to the surface causing it to emit a faint light that enhances the sense of transparency and existence.

Next, bones were set in the model fishes as shown in Fig. 6. One long backbone was applied to the model from the head to the tail. The backbone was formed with several small bones and then sectioned. By dividing the backbone into several sections, the fishes could bend from left to right, ensuring smooth movement.

Lights were also set in the scene. The final appearance of the rendered fish is shown in Fig. 7.

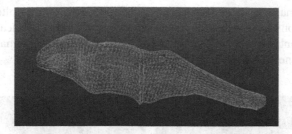

Fig. 5. Imaginary fish 3DCG model surface.

Fig. 6. Bones of imaginary fish 3DCG model.

Fig. 7. Rendered imaginary fish 3DCG model

In this scene, two fish models were created and made to appear to exist at different depths. A contrast in positions is necessary to evoke the sense of depth using IP.

5.2   Background

Two plane 2D images, which were painted the surface of the water, were placed in the scene as shown in Fig. 8. One image was placed in front of the fishes and the other placed at the back.. The back image emits a light reflected on the surface of the water, whereas the front image emits a waving light reflected on the bottom. The sense of depth was emphasized by adding the two layers of images to the fishes in the scene.

The design of the surface of the water was processed as one 2D image plane by using Adobe Photoshop as shown in Fig. 9. The design was created based on the white light reflected on real water. However, image blurring could occur when the synthesized IP image is viewed through the fly's eye lens (1 mm pitch). Therefore, when the color contrast is weak, the image becomes difficult to see clearly. Hence, the blue and white contrasts were strengthened to enable the white ripple mark to stand out. The rendered scene from the view of camera is shown in Fig. 10.

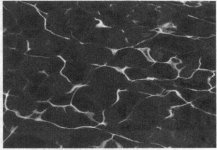

Fig. 8. Two layers of water surface.   **Fig. 9.** 2D image of water surface

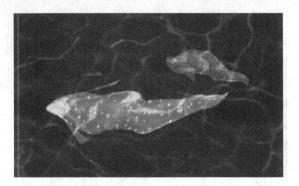

Fig. 10. Rendered scene

6   Animation

Animating to show movement is important in this case because it will make the fishes seem alive. This time, the creatures were designed based on real fishes. Swimming fishes repeat similar movements. Therefore their movements have a certain periodicity. This movement is similar to how humans walk, that is, they move mostly by repeating the same movement over and over. By focusing on this point, one cycle of the movements was created and then repeated. This repetition enabled us to save time in calculating for the rendering.

The speed of the animation should not be too fast because it takes time to integrate the views from the right and left eyes and to perceive stereoscopic views. When a movement is too fast, a possibility exists that the amount of popping out will decrease.

One fish was placed in the front and the other at the back in this work. The repetitive animation cycle of the swimming movement of the two fishes, which were depicted as shaking their bodies from left to right, was created and its one round period was set to eight frames. The two fishes shake their bodies from left to right in opposite directions. The eight frames of the movement are shown in Fig. 11. When the eighth frame is played, the loop begins once more from the first frame, and repeats this cycle continuously. These frames are displayed as GIF animation.

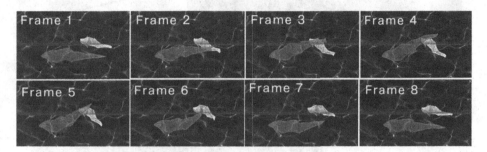

Fig. 11. Animation cycle of eight frames of fishes swimming

7 Synthesis of IP Image

Generating an IP image for each frame of the animation is necessary. Figure 12 shows all the motifs of each frame, which were rendered from 32 × 32 camera positions by using our MEL script. An IP image was synthesized from the 1,024 rendered images by using our technology, called the extended fractional view method [3–5].

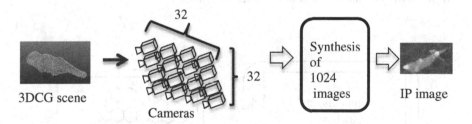

Fig. 12. Process of synthesizing IP images

Figure 13 show an IP image of one of the eight frames. The bottom right image is a magnified image of part of the upper left image. We created GIF animation by connecting the synthesized IP images.

Each IP image of the GIF animation is then shown on the retina display of the iPad and observed through the fly's eye lens, which was placed at the bottom of the plastic tank filled with water. Figure 14 shows the dimensions of the retina display of the iPad

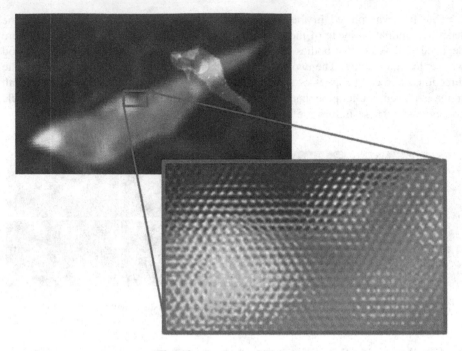

Fig. 13. Synthesized IP image

and the fly's eye lens. Users can view auto-stereoscopic creatures with horizontal and vertical parallax from anywhere above the water tank. The resolution of the displayed 3D objects is sufficiently high because of the iPad retina display and the extended focal length of the fly's eye lens placed in the water. The amount of pop-out from the bottom of the water is also sufficiently large.

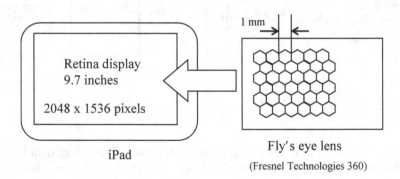

Fig. 14. Hardware setup

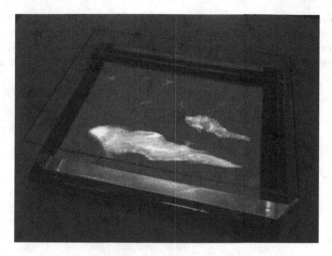

Fig. 15. Photo of the finished product

8 Conclusion

Figure 15 shows a new virtual aquarium that displays imaginary creatures created in 3DCG as if they were swimming under water. Strong stereoscopic view was possible due to the contrast effect, wherein the two fishes and the surface of the water were placed at different depths. Animation was added to give the impression that the fishes were swimming in the water. This system can be appreciated as an artwork because of its beauty, which is very apparent when viewed in a semi-dark room. The soothing effects of a real aquarium can be replicated by placing this system in homes, offices or public spaces. This system could also be utilized to display long-extinct and ancient creatures in aquariums or museums in the future.

References

1. Matoba, Y., Takahashi, Y., Tokui, T., Phuong, S., Yamano, S., Koike, H.: AquaTop Display: a True Immersive Water Display System, In: ACM SIGGRAPH 2013 Emerging Technologies (2013)
2. Wikipedia. http://en.wikipedia.org/wiki/Bubblegram
3. Yanaka, K.: Integral photography suitable for small-lot production using mutually perpendicular lenticular sheets and fractional view. In: Proceedings of SPIE 6490 Stereoscopic Displays and Applications XIV, vol. 649016, pp. 1–8. (2007)
4. Yanaka, K.: Integral photography using hexagonal fly's eye lens and fractional view. In: Proceedings of SPIE 6803 Stereoscopic Displays and Applications XIX, 68031 K, pp. 1–8. (2008)
5. Yoda, M., Momose, A., Yanaka, K.: Moving integral photography using a common digital photo frame and fly's eye lens. In: SIGGRAPH ASIA Posters (2009)

6. Maki, N., Yanaka, K.: Underwater integral photography. In: IEEE VR 2015 Demo (2015)
7. Maki, N., Yanaka, K.: 3D CG integral photography artwork using glittering effects in the post-processing of Multi-viewpoint Rendered Images. In: HCI International (2014)
8. Maki, N., Shirai, A., Yanaka, K.: 3DCG Art expression on a tablet device using integral photography. In: Laval Virtual 2014 VRIC (2014)

Enhancing Abstract Imaginations of Viewers of Abstract Paintings by a Gaze Based Music Generation System

Tatsuya Ogusu[1(✉)], Jun Ohya[1], Jun Kurumisawa[2],
and Shunichi Yonemura[3]

[1] Global Information and Telecommunication Institute, Waseda University,
Bldg. 29-7, 1-3-10 Nishi-Waseda, Shinjuku-Ku, Tokyo 169-0051, Japan
tatsuyaogusu@akane.waseda.jp
[2] Faculty of Policy Informatics, Chiba University of Commerce, Ichikawa, Japan
[3] Faculty of Engineering, Shibaura Institute of Technology, Tokyo, Japan

Abstract. The purpose of abstract painters is to let viewers get the various images and abstract images. However, viewers who do not have enough knowledge of art, cannot easily get abstract images. The authors have proposed a music generation system that utilizes viewers' gazes. It can be expected that the authors' music generation system can prompt the viewer of abstract paintings to imagine abstract images, which the painter intended to express. This paper explores whether the authors' music generation system can enhance abstract imaginations of persons who see abstract paintings, by subjective tests. Experiments using 19 subjects and eight abstract paintings were conducted for the two cases in which the subjects see the abstract paintings without hearing any music and while hearing the viewers' gaze based music generated by the authors' system. Experimental results imply that "hearing gaze based music" could enhance the viewers' abstract imagination.

Keywords: Paintings · Music · Gaze behavior · Imagination

1 Introduction

Kandinsky, who is a pioneer in the field of abstract painting, left many works that could aim at depicting music [1, 2]. Music is very abstract expression, but that can present various abstract images to listeners [3]. Kandinsky's purpose of depicting music using colors is considered not to let viewers see his works as abstract paintings, but to let viewers feel abstract images that can be felt on listening to music. However, if viewers do not have enough knowledge of art, they cannot easily get abstract images from abstract paintings [4].

To enhance abstract images of viewers of abstract paintings, the authors have proposed a music generation system that utilizes viewers' gazes [5, 6]. Using a gaze detection equipment, the system detects the gaze of a viewer who sees an abstract painting, where the viewer's gaze moves over the painting, and tends to stay at certain points. At each of the points at which the gaze stays, the color of that point is converted to sound so that as the gaze moves, music that consists of converted sounds in time series is generated. It can be expected that the authors' music generation system can

© Springer International Publishing Switzerland 2015
S. Yamamoto (Ed.): HIMI 2015, Part II, LNCS 9173, pp. 457–464, 2015.
DOI: 10.1007/978-3-319-20618-9_46

prompt the viewer of the abstract painting to imagine various abstract images that the painter intends to express.

Concerning music composition using still images such as drawings and/or paintings, Xenakis developed a system called UPIC [7, 8], which scans a still image so that lines and points in the image are converted to sounds using a computer. UPIC's algorithm assigns vertical coordinates of the image to pitch and horizontal coordinates to timeline. However, as the temporal change in the position in a still image, the horizontal scan might not be very reasonable. Another example of combining paintings and music is Iura's work entitled "Map" [9], in which the color pointed by the user's mouse, which is an alternative of the viewer's gaze, is converted to sound. However, to our knowledge, Iura has not explored the effectiveness of his proposed system.

This paper explores whether the authors' music generation system can enhance the viewer's abstract imaginations from abstract paintings such as Kandinsky's works, by subjective tests.

2 Gaze Based Music Generation System

The authors' music generation system detects the gaze of a person who views an abstract painting by a gaze detection equipment such as the Eye Tracker. The gaze tends to stay at certain points in the painting for certain durations. At each of such staying points, color information and shape information of figures, is obtained. The diagram in Fig. 1 illustrates the authors' gaze based music generation system.

1. The gaze of a person who views the abstract painting is detected by a gaze detection equipment such as the Eye-Tracker, and each gazed point is tracked in the abstract painting. The tracked points of the gaze are smoothed with a simple averaging that uses the gaze points in the 15 frames prior to the current frame. This could remove noise due to blinking and false recognition.
2. Gazed regions (objects or figures) are extracted from the painting using the gazed points. Specifically, as shown Fig. 2, the gazed region, which consists of multiple pixels, is obtained by finding a region with similar colors to that of the gazed point in the neighborhood of the gazed point. Here, the color similarity is obtained by computing the Euclidean distance D between the color P (R, G, B) of the gazed point and the color P' (R, G, B) of a pixel in the neighborhood. Note that the values of R, G, and B range between 0 and 255 and that if D is smaller than 30, the color of that pixel in the neighborhood is judged to be similar to the color of the gazed point.
3. Key, chord and melody are determined by the averaged color of the gazed region. This paper determines the key, chord and melody by using the authors' proposed method [5, 6], which converts color to sounds based on correspondence between tonality and the colors people with synesthesia feel. Music tempo is determined by the area of the gazed region. Sound position between left and right is determined by the centroid of that region.
4. The parameters determined in 3 are converted to MIDI (Musical Instrument Digital Interface), and are sent to the software synthesizer so that music (sound series) is generated.

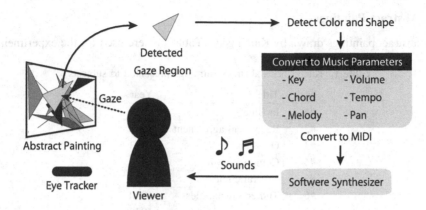

Fig. 1. Gaze based music generation system

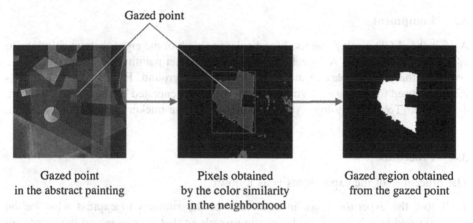

Fig. 2. Gazed region obtained by the gazed point in the abstract painting

3 Experiments

As described in Sect. 1, the authors' music generation system is expected to prompt the viewer of the abstract painting to imagine abstract images such as ones people feel from music. Experiments that explore whether the authors' proposed system can actually prompt the viewer's abstract images were conducted. The experiments compare the two cases in which the viewers see abstract paintings, while hearing the music generated by the authors' system and without hearing any music. Subjects are asked to utter what they feel during the experiments, and their utterances are recorded. The recorded utterances are analyzed by the Protocol analysis [10]. Details of the experiments are as follows.

3.1 Subjects

Nineteen (19) male and female students participated in the experiments. All of the subjects have normal eyesight and hearing.

3.2   Abstract Paintings

Eight abstract paintings drawn by Kandinsky (Table 1) were used for the experiments.

Table 1. Kandinsky's abstract paintings presented to subjects

No.	Title	Year
#1	In Blue	1925
#2	Reciprocal agreement	1942
#3	On white 2	1923
#4	Composition 8	1924
#5	Several circles	1926
#6	Thirteen rectangles	1930
#7	Yellow painting	1938
#8	Yellow-red-blue	1925

3.3   Equipment

A 15 inches LCD display was used for displaying each of the eight abstract paintings to each of the 19 subjects. A digital image of each abstract painting was displayed at the center of the LCD display in the black colored background. Headset (SONY MDR-Z30) was used for letting each subject hear the music generated by the authors' system. Tobii REX (Tobii Technology AB) was used for the eye-tracker in the authors' system.

3.4   Procedure

The procedure of the experiments is as follows.

1. Before the experiment, we instruct each of the subjects to express what he/she thinks and how he/she feels, by uttering words so that we can record the words he/she utters.
2. Four of the eight abstract paintings are presented to each subject without music. The other four paintings are presented to each subject while playing the music generated based on the detected gaze. The order of displaying the eight abstract paintings and whether "with" or "without" music are determined at random for each subject. Each painting is displayed for at least 30 s till the subject does the operation for terminating that display. The subject's utterances are recorded during the time the painting is displayed.
3. Unless the displayed painting is the final one, return to 2. after 5 s interval. If it is the final one, the experiment for that subject is over.

4   Results

4.1   Abstract Image and Concrete Idea

The recorded words uttered by the nineteen subjects are analyzed. This paper defines "abstract image" as "image without concreteness", which is different from associations of objective and/or realistic things. Namely, abstract images include subjective images such as impressions and remarks as well as vague imaginations that could correspond to nouns that represent intangible things. Therefore, we classify the subjects' utterances into the following two categories.

- **Category A "Concrete Idea":** Concrete, tangible things such as specific objects.
- **Category B "Abstract Image":** Abstract imaginations or intangible things such as adjectives and impressions.

Examples of uttered words classified into Categories A and B are listed in Table 2.

Table 2. Examples of words classified into the two categories (Category A: concrete idea; Category B: Abstract image).

Category A	Category B
watermelon	night
record disk	bright
crow	interesting
guitar	space
human	showy
pen	dirty
door	fantasy

4.2 Numbers of Uttered Words in Categories A and B

To explore whether the authors' music generation system can enhance the viewer's abstract imaginations, we compare the numbers of utterances classified into the category A and category B in case of "without music" and "with music".

The numbers of uttered words in each of the two categories in case of "with music" and "without music" are shown in Fig. 3. In Fig. 3, each number indicates the mean value of the total numbers of the words uttered by the 19 subjects for the eight abstract paintings. It turns out that in case of "without music" the number of utterances classified into category A is larger than category B, and that in case of "with music (hearing gaze based music)" category B is larger than category A. As a result of conducting t-test, p-value is less than 0.05 for the number differences between category A and category B in case of "without music" and "hearing gaze based music". These results support that the authors' music generation system can enhance viewers' abstract images more than "without music" situation.

4.3 Numbers of Uttered Words in Each Abstract Painting

The numbers of utterances classified into category A and category B for each of the eight abstract paintings are explored in case of "without music" and "with music (hearing gaze based music)". Figures 4 and 5 show the mean value of the total numbers of the words uttered by the 19 subjects for each of the eight abstract paintings in case of "without music" and "with music", respectively. As shown in Figs. 4 and 5, it turns out

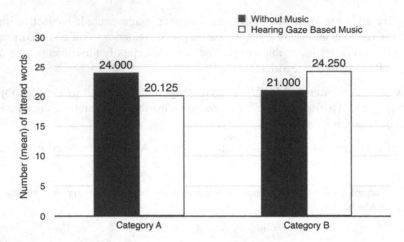

Fig. 3. Mean numbers of uttered words in each category in case of "without music" and "with music (hearing gaze based music)".

that except for #5, the mean numbers for category B in case of "with music (hearing gaze based music)" are larger than "without music". In addition, as shown in Fig. 5, it turns out that the mean numbers of utterances in category B for #5 and #6 in case of "without music" are larger than category A.

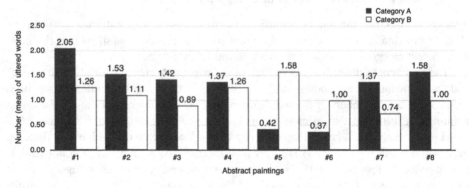

Fig. 4. "Without music":Mean numbers of uttered words for each abstract painting

5 Discussion

As described in Sect. 4.2, in case of "without music", the number of utterances classified into category A is larger than category B, and that in case of "with music (hearing gaze based music)" category B is larger than category A. This could mean the authors' gaze based music generation system can enhance viewer's abstract imaginations.

As described in Sect. 4.3, only in the abstract painting #5, the number of utterances in category B in case of "without music" is larger than "with music (hearing gaze based

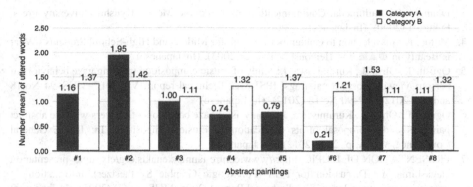

Fig. 5. "With music (hearing gaze based music)": Mean numbers of uttered words for each abstract painting.

music)", while in case of the other paintings, category B's utterances in case of "with music" are larger. On the other hand, in case of "without music", in only #5 and #6, the numbers of uttered words in category B are larger than category A. These phenomena could indicate that the contents and/or features of abstract painting influence on the effect of the authors' music generation system. In particular, in the abstract paintings #5 and #6, which enhance abstract imagination in case of "without music" more than "with music", only circles and rectangles are depicted, respectively, while various shapes are depicted in the other paintings. Compared with the other paintings, these two paintings use colors with lower brightness and saturation. This could mean that what are depicted in abstract painting affect viewers' abstract imaginations.

The above results could imply that we need to explore relationships between the contents of abstract paintings and music generated by the authors' system.

6 Conclusion

This paper has explored the effectiveness of prompting abstract paintings' viewers' abstract imaginations by the authors' gaze based music generation system. Experiments using 19 subjects and eight abstract paintings were conducted for the two cases in which the subjects see the abstract paintings without hearing any music and while hearing the viewers' gaze based music generated by the authors' system. The experimental results imply that "hearing gaze based music" could enhance the viewers' abstract imagination. Remaining issues include that we need to explore relationships between the contents of abstract paintings and music generated by the authors' music generation system.

References

1. Kandinsky, W.: Concerning the Spiritual In Art. Courier Corporation, Pittsburgh (1914)
2. Kandinsky, W.: Point and Line to Plane. Courier Corporation, Pittsburgh (1947)

3. Iwamiya, S.: Multimodal Communication of Music and Movie. Kyushu University Press, Fukuoka (2000). (In Japanese)
4. Motoe, K.: Introduction to Contemporary Arts, for Middle and High-School Students –What is Beauty in ●▲■ ? –. Heibonsha, Tokyo (2003). (In Japanese)
5. Ogusu, T., Ohya, J., Kurumisawa, J.: Study of music composition utilizing gaze behaviors of persons viewing abstract paintings. IPSJ SIG Technical report, Vol.2012–MUS–94 No.18 and Vol.2012–SLP–90 No.18 (2012). (In Japanese)
6. Ogusu, T., Ohya, J., Kurumisawa, J.: Analysis of gaze behaviors of viewers who see abstract paintings and   proposal of its application to music composition. In: IEICE General Conference, vol. A, p. 254, (2012). (In Japanese)
7. PRÉSENTATION DE L'UPIC. http://www.centre-iannis-xenakis.org/cix_upic_presentation
8. Nagashima, Y.: Discussion for PGS (Polyagogic Graphic Synthesizer), information processing society of Japan. SIG Technical Report, 2005–MUS–59 (7) (2005). (In Japanese)
9. Iura, T.: New creative for imagery and music in digital media - expressive effect through audio and visual interaction -. J. Kansai Univ. Fac. Inf. **34**, 1–20 (2011). (In Japanese).
10. Kaiho, H.: Introduction to Protocol Analysis. Shinyosha, Tokyo (1993)

Supporting Work and Collaboration

Possible Strategies for Facilitating the Exchange of Tacit Knowledge in a Team of Creative Professionals

Søren R. Frimodt-Møller$^{(\boxtimes)}$, Nanna Borum, Eva Petersson Brooks, and Yi Gao

Department of Architecture, Design and Media Technology, Aalborg University Esbjerg, Niels Bohrs Vej 8, 6700 Esbjerg, Denmark
{sfm,nb,ep,gao}@create.aau.dk

Abstract. This paper discusses strategies for improving how creative professionals embrace new digital tools into their workflow, in context of the EU-funded international research project IdeaGarden, which aims at developing tools and scenarios that facilitate creative collaboration. In previous research by the authors, a preference for analog tools over digital has been detected among creative professionals. In a new series of interviews done at the same workplace, it is shown that it is possible for a designer to build up *tacit knowledge* of the field in which he works, for use in a digital environment. Using examples from the interviews alongside examples from the literature on tacit knowledge, we try to describe a path for further inquiry into the challenge of facilitating the designer's shift from analog to digital tools via facilitating the exchange of tacit knowledge between co-workers, especially via making amendments to the physical arrangement of the workplace.

Keywords: Digital tools · Creative work practices · Tacit knowledge · Workplace design

1 Introduction

In this paper, we discuss different strategies for improving how creative professionals embrace new digital tools into their workflow. The discussion draws on studies done in context of the EU-funded international research project IdeaGarden, which aims at developing tools and scenarios that facilitate creative collaboration.

In previous research [1], the authors have collected evidence from qualitative interviews done at LEGO® Future Lab's office in Billund, Denmark, supporting the hypothesis that creative professionals, designers in particular, prefer to work with analog tools, both in the ideation process and in the development of actual designs. In a new series of studies done at the same workplace, an interesting anomaly has, however, presented itself: It is actually possible that a designer would work in a

© Springer International Publishing Switzerland 2015
S. Yamamoto (Ed.): HIMI 2015, Part II, LNCS 9173, pp. 467–475, 2015.
DOI: 10.1007/978-3-319-20618-9_47

digital medium as a starting point, if the person has sufficient expertise to translate in his mind between the more conceptual structure of the digital artifact and its physical counterpart. The level of knowledge possessed by such a person is typically tacit knowledge: Knowing, without testing in practice, what would fit together well in an actual, physical LEGO® model, is not necessarily something that can be verbalized in the form of a full manual, but seems to rely on a kind of pattern recognition that is trained through experience. There have, however, been studies of how tacit knowledge may be transferrable in informal, case-based encounters between co-workers, and it is precisely this possibility that motivates the research presented in this paper.

After a short discussion of the use of analog vs. digital tools in the creative workplace with LEGO® Future Lab as the main example, we discuss how tacit knowledge of analog work processes may help creative professionals embrace digital tools, and conclude with suggestions for how the creative work environment may be arranged to facilitate the possible exchange of tacit knowledge between co-workers. The latter aspect is addressed through examples formulated by other researchers within the IdeaGarden project who have been working with the workspace as a parameter for the successful creative collaboration.

2 Method

In the original study of work practices at LEGO® Future Lab [1], five semi-struc-tured, situated interview sessions [2] were conducted over a three-day period with a total of six participants (one interview had two interviewees). In the new series of studies, 5 more interviews were conducted, similarly semi-structured and situated, more specifically in LEGO® Future Lab's offices in Billund, Denmark. Each interview ran roughly 35 min, including short show-and-tell sessions with the in-terviewees at their individual work desks in the office. One interviewee also took part in the original interview sessions done by the authors, while the authors knew another of the interviewees from previous conversations at meetings in the Idea-Garden project. The interview sessions used an ethnographic approach [3], making an effort to observe and understand the participants' work practices in context of their working environment. The interviews were recorded in sound files and ana-lyzed according to three focal points: (1) the use of analog vs. digital tools, (2) the influence of the environment on the work process, and (3) the participant's relation to the IdeaGarden prototype installed in LEGO® Future Lab in the first half of 2014. The latter point of analysis is not addressed here in detail, only as a byproduct of the discussion of (1).

As the present study focuses on the designer's relation to analog and digital tools as well as the creative environment, the quotes chosen are taken from the three interviews done with designers, whereas the other two interviews done with project managers has mainly served as a reference for keeping track of the logistic details of LEGO® Future Lab's physical environment.

The names of the interviewees have been changed in the text to secure their anonymity.

3 Analog vs. Digital Tools in the Creative Workplace

The preference for analog tools in creative workplaces manifests itself in many ways. In LEGO® Future Lab, a front-line innovation department of LEGO® Group, the analog tools are, of course, often LEGO® bricks, but also include post-its, pen and paper and other materials used to create quick mock-ups of designs. In all except one interview, the tendency with respect to designers preferring analog over digital tools, made apparent in the previous studies documented in [1], repeats itself, as evidenced by the following quotes:

> "I practically never build digitally [...] In the phase we are in right now [of a specific project], it is the experience that is the driving force. We have to present the experience, and in that case it is just as convenient for us to just build something physically and then use that. We don't have to look at pricing issues, or if something is built 'correctly' – those things are further down the road. I think it's easier to just build things in one go and then you have that [as a reference]."
> Morten, designer

> "[...] I sketch something, and take a picture and then email to myself. [That way] I can paint it better in Photoshop. [...] I do a quick sketch and then I redo it in Photoshop like when you trace out an image. It's easier for me to get the scale right [that way]. Photoshop is a bit abstract. I know what an A4 piece of paper is when I see it. In Photoshop it is on the screen and I can zoom in and zoom out so it is a bit abstract what the sizes are actually [...] It is just easier with pen and paper." Sam, designer

Because embodiment triggers different thought processes, thereby possibly fueling a creative process that has otherwise come to a halt when a person is just sitting in front of a computer screen all the time (see e.g. [4]), the preference for analog tools among creative professionals is understandable. However, the two quotes above showcase other aspects of analog tools, which are particularly interesting in the scope of the present paper. The two designers are not simply emphasizing the preference for a more tactile or haptic mode of interaction with their surroundings, but argue for using physical artifacts rather than their digital counterparts, because the former gives them a better *understanding* of the latter. Interestingly, this understanding seems to be case-specific: When a designer works on a new case, a new understanding has to be gained through interaction with physical objects. As we will see shortly, there might, however, be possibilities for training more generalizable conceptual skills via the interaction with physical artifacts.

3.1 Embracing Digital Tools in an Analog Workflow – an Anomaly

One of the oldest members of LEGO® Future Lab, a model builder employed by LEGO® Group for more than 30 years, states in the interview the authors did with him, that as a starting point, he prefers to build models digitally, in the software LEGO® Digital Designer, rather than with real physical bricks:

> "I very often start building digitally. I build in LEGO® Digital Designer, so that's really where I often start [...] and then I just sit and play with the digital bricks and build something, because a lot of times it is really just something people need for a presentation – they don't really need the physical product [at first], so my 'playing' or building often starts digitally." Stig, model builder

When confronted with the fact that no one else of the designers the authors had spoken to in the past and present studies had stated a preference for the digital medium when working on models, he confided that

> "[…] Not a lot of people [build digitally], but I actually think it's fast and you can do a whole lot of sketches quickly [that way]. Then of course, I have the background and knowledge that enables me to see what is stable and what is instable."

Apparently, via his many years of building with LEGO® bricks, the model builder had simply trained the ability to see whether a design would have a solid construction or not, without having to hold it in his hands. Unlike other LEGO® Future Lab members, he had built up a general knowledge of how bricks fit together, something he could use in many different cases without having to necessarily refer to a physical model. (It should, however, be mentioned that the model builder of course also experimented with physical bricks once in a while and lots of small models on his desktop and shelves. He merely stated a preference for the digital medium when working on new models.)

The kind of knowledge the model builder has trained is, however, exactly something, which is trained. Although he would probably be able to explain on a case to case basis whether a particular model was stable or not, he would most likely not be able to fully transfer his knowledge in one big explanation, because the knowledge in question is a skill, rather than a fixed set of facts. In epistemological terms, the model builder has built up *tacit knowledge* of the field in which he works. In the following, previous research on tacit knowledge will be discussed in context of the present study.

4   Previous Studies of Tacit Knowledge

The concept of tacit knowledge is widely used in epistemology (and philosophy in general). As an example, Leonard and Sensiper [5] provide the case of how nurses often have a good intuition of what is wrong with a patient, but without being able to justify this 'knowledge' in the concrete, evidence-based terms that a physician would. Nurses learn to recognize patterns and little signs that lead them to a hypothesis of the patient's state, without having to take a lot of tests first. This so-called tacit knowledge is tacit because it is difficult to translate into concrete rules, instructions or other pieces of information that would help others reach the same insight.

It is however, possible, as is argued by Panahi et al. [6], that tacit knowledge can be mediated by informal encounters and case-based discussions between co-workers. While Panahi et al. provide support for social media as a way of helping co-workers share tacit knowledge among each other, another angle, which the IdeaGarden project also discusses [7] is to consider how to shape the environment of the creative collaboration, such as to facilitate informal and ad hoc communication between co-workers, e.g. quick interactions regarding a specific problem, examples given by one person to another of how to solve a specific problem via a demonstration etc. In the following, it will be considered whether such improvements on the physical environment of the creative workplace can facilitate a transfer of tacit knowledge.

5 Possible Strategies for Improving the Sharing of Tacit Knowledge in the Creative Workplace

As discussed in Sect. 3.1, the skills the older designer, who preferred constructing models digitally, had developed are most likely not directly transferrable to other team members. They are, however, drawn upon by other team members, in informal encounters:

> "[…] we all sit quite closely in here, so behind me there are two electronics people who are not part of the design team. So if I need to spar with some electronics guy, there's one right behind me. Otherwise, we are 6 people who are sitting here physically [at a cluster of tables] who can have a bit of back and forth across the table whenever. […] I use Philip a lot who sits right across from me, because he also builds stuff. The other designers are probably more 'concept' people, but they go to me with questions on elements, technique and such. It's like, if you're sitting with something you can just say 'what do you think about this'?" Stig, designer

The particular kind of informal encounters the designer, Stig, describes in this quote are of an intimate kind, in the sense that the interactions take place in a small-group environment. This particular kind of environment is something that LEGO® Future Lab seems to encourage:

> "We often try to move stuff around so people sit together with some of the people they work with, and that that makes our work more fluent. Like right now, all of us designers are sitting down in one corner, and then those you work together with are sitting like close to you." Morten, designer

Within the IdeaGarden project, a small team consisting of partners from Kiel University (CAU), the University of Applied Sciences Upper Austria (FHOOE) and the design company EOOS has been working on the challenge of designing spaces that can afford different levels of creative collaboration. One such level of collaboration is exactly the type of intimate interaction hinted at in the quotes above. In order to facilitate this type of interaction the so-called "Space" team within IdeaGarden has worked on suggestions for setting up "intimate spaces" (see [7], 42), which afford interaction in small groups, and in addition, integrate digital and analog working tools in a small environment. One suggestion for an intimate creative working space is the tabletop projection setup shown in Fig. 1.

Another issue is, however, encouraging co-workers who otherwise work 'solo' to engage in ad hoc interactions with each other. In a workspace like LEGO® Future Lab, these interactions happen outside of the individual's personal workspace, inspired by the specific surroundings:

> "Right next to where I am sitting there is this little U-shaped booth with a couple of tall tables, and on two sides there are shelves, and on the third, long side there is a whiteboard where we can write and put up post-its. That means that you get out of this 'sitting-at-your-computer' situation, and both of the work modes I have, where I sit at my computer and write [on the one hand] and when we build, put up things on the wall, do brainstorms and such – it's all connected now, because [the two kinds of situation] are physically close, and I think that makes a huge difference." Morten, designer

A specific space at LEGO® Future Lab that used to be separate from the main office, namely the building area where team members can build things in LEGO® bricks,

Fig. 1. Tabletop projection setup, where one side of the table (left) has a projection on it emitted from the projector in the middle, affording collaboration in a digital environment (e.g. on presentations), whereas the other side of the table is open for regular, analog work processes (i.e. writing and drawing on paper etc.).

either for project purposes or as a means of recreation, is now an actual part of the office. This has improved ad hoc communication a lot:

> "[Having the building area inside the office] is perfect. It's a lot more... It's better in terms of... There is [a higher] frequency of meeting other people in the building area now than before. More people work more time in the building area because it is so close to their desks. So [there are] more chances of meeting people. Earlier you had to have a task to go down and solve it and come back. Now it is like you can work in both spaces at the same time." Sam, designer

As a small digression, not everyone finds the building area equally useful when it comes to building itself:

> "[...] If you use these [he holds up a handful of LEGO® bricks], someone has to go over [to the main storage] and get more. So if you know you need a lot of something, it's easier to go over there [to the main storage] and bring a box with back. It's not like we are short of LEGO® bricks here! [The building area] is fine, if you have something specific to build, but if you really want to explore [possibilities], it is nice to have a large volume [of bricks], and it's easier pick over there [at the main storage], so you don't have to empty [the building are] completely. We have the selection here, just not the volume." Morten, designer

However, the building area still seems to be a typical example of what the IdeaGarden Space team has denoted a "non-hierarchic space" ([7], 45), more specifically, a space where people are encouraged to interact with the surroundings as equals, e.g. without having pre-established hierarchies influencing the interaction.

Where the building area is a stable space (disregarding the occasional moving around of the different office sections), the IdeaGarden Space team has also worked with ways of turning any area into a non-hierarchic space, i.e. a temporary space for interaction ([7], 43). The motivation for working with temporary spaces comes from

Fig. 2. Temporary space defined via a 'play carpet', a carpet-like desktop area, which affords both analog interaction (post-its, physical models etc.) and projections, i.e. use as a canvas.

the another test bed of the IdeaGarden project, namely the Muthesius Academy of Fine Arts and Design in Kiel, where students due to space issues often have to use whatever area is available for meetings, e.g. sometimes even hallways, corridors etc. An example of a possible set-up for defining a temporary space can be seen in Fig. 2.

Whether the above strategies with respect to defining areas for ad hoc interaction will actually result in case-based communication, aiding the transfer of tacit knowledge is a topic for further research. It is worth noting, however, that LEGO® Future Lab members recognize that the workplace needs to be arranged so as to better facilitate the informal modes of interaction mentioned above. Responding to a question regarding a recent rearrangement of LEGO® Future Lab's office, a designer confides that

> "Unfortunately it works the same. Even though we have changed [the] space we haven't changed the [working] style. We are looking into how we can change it. It's a bit hard for us, just because everyone is so used to do what they do, it is so hard to implement, but we would like a lot more creative spaces to brainstorm or gather… so a lot of white board spaces and shar [ing] of some models would help but we don't really have that as much now." Sam, designer

5.1 Accessibility

Another factor influencing the team members of LEGO® Future Lab in their acceptance of digital tools into their workflow is something as simple as immediate availability. The IdeaGarden digital whiteboard prototype developed by researchers at FHOOE has been placed within the office of LEGO® Future Lab in ways that do not necessarily afford everyday interaction with it. One installation is kept in the far back of the open office space behind dividing boards, whereas another installation of the board is in a separate room. All interviewees verify that the digital whiteboards are being used, but not to the degree to which it was intended:

"The problem [with the installation of the digital whiteboard in a separate room] is that if someone has booked the room, you cannot access it, and as you can see [on the board outside the room], the room is almost booked for the entire day because we frequently use it for meetings." Morten, designer

"I haven't really used [the digital whiteboard environments] very often, because it hasn't quite fitted into any of what we are sitting with, and we are [also] very used to working with post-it notes. When we are sitting at the tables and doing a quick brainstorm it's very convenient to just... yeah. [...] I am probably a person of habits [...] and for us who are sitting there together, we would have to move somewhere else to do that [if using the digital whiteboard]. It would maybe be different if we had a tablet on the table and could save, share and so on [on that]." Stig, designer

"I think the biggest issue that people mention is that we don't know how to start it up. Something as simple as [that] it is powered down. The effort of starting it up – sometimes it is just easier to use the [analog] white board and a marker, so the benefit of [getting] it started up – people haven't found that benefit yet. [...] We've tried to use it for ideation, yes. Because it is online it was cool to find examples using Google images mostly so that everyone could see the same. [...] That was cool" Sam, designer

Finding ways of integrating digital tools such as the digital whiteboard developed within the IdeaGarden project so as to make them natural part of the work environment, and thereby used, is another aspect of working with the office space, which is not directly related to tacit knowledge, although a swifter change between the analog tools and their digital counterparts on an accessible digital whiteboard could maybe aid the transfer of tacit knowledge of analog work processes to the digital counterpart of those processes.

6 Conclusions and Further Perspectives

Although one must not underestimate the role of embodiment in the strong preference for analog tools we have previously described (see Sect. 3), it is worth exploring if a better tacit knowledge-based understanding of the embodied know-how of analog work practices could help creative professionals embrace digital tools, and if the transfer of such tacit knowledge between more experienced co-workers and their younger colleagues could be facilitated by additions to or rearrangements of the workplace.

In connection with the discussion of the IdeaGarden whiteboard prototype in context of LEGO® Future Lab, the importance of making digital tools readily available and accessible to the users is also highlighted.

Another perspective, which has not been pursued in detail within the IdeaGarden project, is the possibility of using gamification strategies to draw in users of the digital environment. The initial versions of the IdeaGarden digital whiteboard environment had simple games like tic-tac-toe integrated in order to help users learn basic controls with the associated digital pens, but an actual strategy for how games or other fun activities could make creative professionals embrace the new digital tools, has not yet been explored.

References

1. Borum, N., Petersson, E., Frimodt-Møller, S.R.: The resilience of analog tools in creative work practices: a case study of LEGO future lab's team in billund. In: Kurosu, M. (ed.) HCI 2014, Part I. LNCS, vol. 8510, pp. 23–34. Springer, Heidelberg (2014)
2. Buur, J., Ylirisku, S.: Designing with Video: Focusing the User-Centred Design Process. Springer, London (2007)
3. Pink, S.: Doing Visual Ethnography, 2nd edn. Sage, Thousand Oaks (2007)
4. Rohde, M.: Analog Tools Foster Reflection, Creativity and Flow. Blog post at the website *Rohdesign*, 12 June 2006. http://rohdesign.com/weblog/2006/6/12/analog-tools-foster-reflection-creativity-and-flow.html. Accessed 7 November 2014
5. Leonard, D.A., Sensiper, S.: The role of tacit knowledge in group innovation. In: Leonard, D.A. (ed.) Managing Knowledge Assets, Creativity and Innovation, pp. 301–323. World Scientific Publishing Co., Singapore (2011)
6. Panahi, S., Watson, J., Partridge, H.: Social media and tacit knowledge sharing: developing a conceptual model. World Acad. Sci. Eng. Technol. **64**, 1095–1102 (2012)
7. Frimodt-Møller, S.R., Georgis, C., Doerr, K., Bekiari, C., Richter, C., Ruhl, E., Albrecht, J., Kristoferitsch, L., Grossauer, E.-M., Leong, J., Perteneder, F., Zimmerli, C., Nebeling, M., orrie, M.: IdeaGarden #318552. D 3.4 Design Specifications Document, version 2, public report, made as a deliverable within the research project IdeaGarden for the European Commission, Submitted 24 October 2014. Available on the IdeaGarden website, www.ideagarden.com

Innovation Compass: Integrated System to Support Creativity in Both Individuals and Groups

Yoshiharu Kato[1,2(✉)], Tomonori Hashiyama[2], and Shun'ichi Tano[2]

[1] Fujitsu Limited, Kawasaki, Japan
ykato@jp.fujitsu.com
[2] Graduate School of Information Systems,
The University of Electro-Communications, Tokyo, Japan
{hashiyama,tano}@is.uec.ac.jp

Abstract. This study intends to present the concept of a mechanism that will lead to generate active innovations that can change our society. We first analyze the general process of innovations and identify core elements that lead to innovations. We then analyze existing tools and systems that support the creation of innovations in relation to core elements. This analysis leads to the building of the innovation model. We propose an "innovation compass" based on the innovation model that is an integrative system that enhances human creativity to generate innovations. It supports both individual and group creativity. It not only supports rational aspects of innovation processes but also stimulates the motivation of innovators.

Keywords: Innovation · Creative support · Serendipity · Network · Motivation

1 Introduction

The ICT industry is evolving daily with a core focus on business and its use of the Internet. The ICT industry to date has used advanced technology to create high performance, high quality products, and we can expect it to solve various social problems while providing new products and services. However, we must be careful of how capabilities are applied to the market and environmental changes. In other words, companies must create new customer value with a continual understanding of market changes. Drucker asserted that, in "management", the objective of companies is "customer creation" [1]. He also said that in a constantly changing society, companies must continually create new customers. This requires innovation.

The essence of innovation does not simply mean technical innovation, but includes the idea of continuing to create innovative products and services that provide societal value. This is not accomplished through machines but through the creativity of human beings. There are demands for systems that will increase human creativity for people to be imaginative and produce new things. However, most support systems until now have not been distributed to the developers and engineers for whom they were designed. It is difficult to comprehensively and expansively support creativity. Thus, we propose a system to support human creativity that focuses on value creation in this study.

© Springer International Publishing Switzerland 2015
S. Yamamoto (Ed.): HIMI 2015, Part II, LNCS 9173, pp. 476–487, 2015.
DOI: 10.1007/978-3-319-20618-9_48

Section 2, analyzes the elements and processes necessary for creating new values, confirms how these elements and processes are attained in existing systems, and reviews their issues. Section 3, proposes an "innovation compass", which is a support system for human creativity. This is a system for comprehensively supporting both individual and group creativity. Section 4 concludes the paper.

2 Innovation Model

Innovation, as it is used in this paper, is defined as "creating new value and generating change that contributes to society". However, because the solving of immediate problems is the basis of innovation, we have not excluded activities for everyday improvements. Thus, we will first analyze the necessary elements and processes to achieve innovation by considering the creativity support system we propose.

2.1 Necessary Elements and Processes to Achieve Innovation

Many innovation models have been presented in the past, and the requisite elements and processes presented in them have been critical to achieve innovation. We will first analyze these elements and processes, and clarify the types of models we should build. In doing so, we will examine what have been identified as ten representative models [2–11] for generating innovation, thoughts, discoveries, and ideas.

The first involves the ten items required for discovery as noted by Nobel laureate (chemistry) Eiichi Negishi in "Hakken to ha Nanika" (What Is Discovery?) [2]. These ten items are desire, needs, planning, systematic exploration, knowledge, ideas, judgment, willpower, optimism, and serendipity. These indicate what is required for discovery, based on the things that have been deemed necessary over many years of individual research. Of note is that these items have aspects of emotion and behavior, and not simply intellect.

The second model is "Innovation: The Five Disciplines For Creating What Customers Want" [3]. This article is a compilation from the results of consultation conducted by Stanford Research Institute (SRI) International at various corporations. The five disciplines referred to in the title are important needs, value creation, innovation champions, innovation teams, and organizational alignment. Because this article was written within the context of corporate consulting, the focus is on organizations and teams, as well as the roles of leaders. In terms of value creation, it is characteristic in its assertion that success is accomplished through the use of tools.

The third model of innovation is proposed in "Where Good Ideas Come From" [4], which is a publication that considers innovation from an ecological standpoint. The seven laws noted therein are the adjacently possible, liquid networks, the slow hunch, serendipity, error, exaptation, and platforms. This article has a particular focus on the environment in which innovation occurs. In particular, it notes that making connections requires fluidity, noise, and mistakes, and that platforms are necessary for generating creativity.

The fourth model of innovation is "The Innovator's DNA" [5]. This article discusses the five skills of innovators, viz., associating, questioning, observing, networking, and experimenting. In particular, it emphasizes the importance of finding connections between things that appear to be unrelated, and the necessity for interacting with various types of people. In addition, it asserts the necessity for experimentation.

The fifth representative model comes from "Managing Flow: The dynamic theory of knowledge-based firm" [6], which suggests that companies creating knowledge use the socialization, externalization, combination, and internalization (SECI) process [7] to generate output. This output is comprised of following items: values, ba (it is a place for knowledge creation), dialogue, dynamic knowledge assets, and leadership. In particular, this article asserts that when one feels as if one is contributing to society through one's actions, that individual then demonstrates capabilities. In doing so, a dialog with one's companions, and understanding and accepting different ways of thinking become important.

A sixth model is the four-fold "SECI Model" [7]. Of these four, explicit knowledge and tacit knowledge work hand-in-hand in moving forward spirally, which causes new knowledge to be formed in both individuals and organizations.

A seventh model is found in "Theory U" [8], which states that focusing on people's interiority leads to an understanding of future prospects and actions. The five steps in this theory are co-initiating, co-sensing, presencing (connecting to the source of inspiration and will), co-creating, and co-evolving. The article suggests that inner wisdom is found through creating a common will, observing, and listening. This process leads to prototypes and the creation of new products.

The eighth model is the "Introduction to Design Thinking Process Guide" [9], published by The Hasso Plattner Institute of Design at Stanford. Five key steps are outlined: empathize, define, ideate, prototype, and test. According to this guide, understanding users and defining the essence of issues is critical to innovation. The guide also advocates user feedback is obtained on what has been created to further improve the product.

The ninth model is the "W-gata Mondai Kaiketsu Model" ("W-shaped problem-solving Methodology") [10] presented in Jiro Kawakita's "Hasso-Ho" ("Creative thinking method") in which exploration is equivalent to problem-solving, and thought levels and experience levels progress along a W-shaped curve. Determination is made as to whether problems can be solved by exploration, observation, generation of hypotheses, or adoption of hypotheses. The KJ-method suggested in this article is Kawakita Jiro's creative thinking method and most popular problem-solving methodology in Japan.

The tenth model is found in "A Technique for Producing Ideas" [11] by Young, which presents the process of individual idea creation. It states that "ideas are new combinations of old elements", and divides the process into five steps of gathering materials, masticating materials, an incubating stage, the birth of an idea, and shaping and development of the idea.

2.2   Analysis of Innovation Mode

Elements Necessary for Innovation. We reviewed elements and processes necessary to achieve innovation from the surveyed content above (Table 1). Of these items, the following five stand out as being common, i.e., "network", "motivation", "idea creation", "action and practice", and "needs".

Table 1. Necessary analysis of elements for innovation.

Item / Case	Network	Motivation	Idea Creation	Action and practice	Needs
1 Negishi Eiichi, The ten items required for discovery [2]	—	• Desire • Will power	• Serendipity, • Idea, • Knowledge, • Judgment • Systematic exploration	• Optimism • Plan	Needs
2 Innovation: The five disciplines for creating what customers want [3]	Innovation teams	Organizational alignment	Value creation	Innovation champions	Important needs
3 Where good ideas come from: The natural history of innovation [4]	• Exaptation • Liquid Networks • Platforms	—	• Serendipity, • Error, • The Slow Hunch • The Adjacent Possible	—	—
4 The Innovator's DNA: Mastering the five skills of disruptive innovators [5]	Networking	Questioning	• Associating • Observing	Experimenting	—
5 Flow Management: The dynamic theory of knowledge-based firm [6]	• Ba	• Dynamic knowledge assets	• Value • Dialogue	Leadership	—
6 The knowledge-creating company: How Japanese companies create the dynamics of innovation [7]	—	• Socialization • Internalization	Externalization	Combination	—
7 Theory U: Learning from the future as it emerges [8]	—	• Co-Initiating • Co-Sensing • Co-Evolving	Presencing	Co-creating	—
8 An introduction to design thinking process guide [9]	—	• Empathize • Define	Ideate	• Prototype • Test	—
9 Hasso-Ho (Creative thinking methods) [10]	—	—	• Exploration • Observation • Hypothesis generation • Inference	• Plan • Observation • Verification	—
10 A technique for producing ideas: Advertising age classics library [11]	—	—	• Gathering materials • Masticating materials • Incubating stage • Birth of idea	Shaping and development of idea	—

Of particular importance to fulfil market "needs" is "idea creation", which requires the interaction of various people who serve as a "network". Further, members must have a common "desire" in regard to their purpose, which is tied to social significance and a sense of mission, and is the source of everything. Generating results requires "motivation" and "action and practice", even though "motivation" is important for continuing to strive for success without giving up. In particular, motivation can be thought of as being both extrinsic and intrinsic. Intrinsic motivation involves relationships with others, leverages one's own capabilities, and develops according to one's own decisions. Conversely, extrinsic motivation is based on monetary or other forms of remuneration. It has been noted that intrinsic motivation is more important than extrinsic motivation for improving intellectually creative activities.

Innovation Processes. We next conducted process-oriented analysis. The corresponding processes are listed in 1 [2] and items 6 to 10 [7–11] in Table 1. Figure 1 compares these innovation processes. Of these processes, "sympathy", "creation", "practice", and "succession" stand out as being four common steps. As can be seen in Table 2, all individuals (1) have feelings that are "sympathetic" to other members and identify the "root of the problem", and in (2), creation occurs. After a prototype is created that is (3) "evaluated and tested", followed by "feedback" as part of "action and practice". The individuals then (4) "inherit" assets that have been created, and use them to solve the next issue. In step 2) of creation, the analysis of items 1, 9, and 10 result in further subdivisions of "problem institution", "gathering information", "serendipity", and "judgment/decision". These are all elements required for individual idea creation.

Innovation Model. Figure 2 outlines an innovation model that provides a comprehensive overview of these elements, and which is comprised of the four steps of "sympathy", "creation", "practice", and "succession". The step of "creation" is further subdivided into "problem institution", "information gathering", "serendipity", and "judgment/decision". Not included in this model from a process standpoint are "network" and "motivation", which are both collaborative in nature, and are thought to be necessary to the overall innovation process. A network is required to generate diverse ideas, through encounters between new people and information, followed by the sharing and exchange of information through connections with groups or other individuals. Motivation impacts will and behavior, as it is the driving force behind processes. Innovation can be enhanced and scaled even for very demanding problems by driving and expanding the process.

2.3   Prior Research and State of Systems

We analyzed required elements and processes in innovation in the previous subsection. On the basis of that analysis, we were able to present a model of innovation. Many systems and tools have been created to support human creativity. We surveyed the scope and coverage of innovation-related systems and tools for innovation using the innovation models presented in Fig. 2. Table 3 summarizes the results we obtained from our survey.

KJ-method [10] is a methodology for supporting ideation and has been used in many studies. Examples of these include a KJ-based study on systems to systems to support the idea gathering phase using radio-frequency identification (RFID) [12], and the Group KJ-method support system utilizing digital pens (GKJ) [13] groupware tool for supporting idea generation. Cheatstorm [14] researched the confluence of random information as a way of supporting new idea generation while brainstorming. Many studies have been done on system from the perspective of creating networks and a sense of place to support the introduction of social matching [15]. These systems have supported the introduction of people where creating networks has been difficult. Research has been done on the use of prototyping in the development of next-generation display interfaces [16], and this research has explained the impact of prototyping on the realization of ideas.

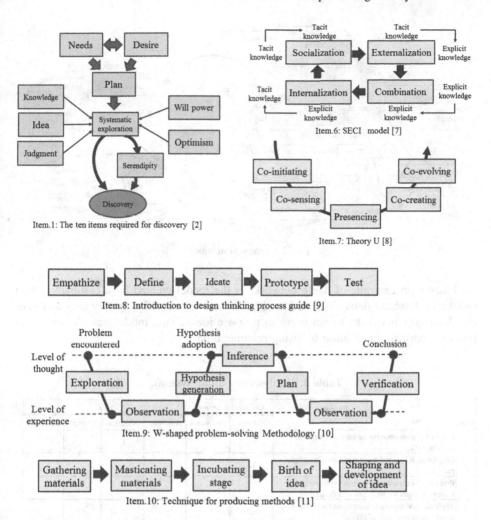

Item.1: The ten items required for discovery [2]

Item.6: SECI model [7]

Item.7: Theory U [8]

Item.8: Introduction to design thinking process guide [9]

Item.9: W-shaped problem-solving Methodology [10]

Item.10: Technique for producing methods [11]

Fig. 1. Comparison of processes in innovation

Table 2. Analysis of processes in innovation.

Process common element	1) Sympathy	2) Creation	3) Practice	4) Succession
Cooperative elements	Network / Motivation			
Content of process common elements	·Construction of common will ·User understanding ·Sharing of tacit knowledge	·Divergent thinking ·Ideas ·Serendipity ·Convergent thinking	·Prototype ·Practice ·Action ·Evaluation	Succession of experience

2) Elements of creation	Problem institution	Information gathering	Serendipity	Judgment/decision
Detailed content	Specifics of problem essence	·Daily collection of information ·Meeting people and obtaining information	·Flashing ·Awareness ·New combinations	Decisions on solutions in problem solving

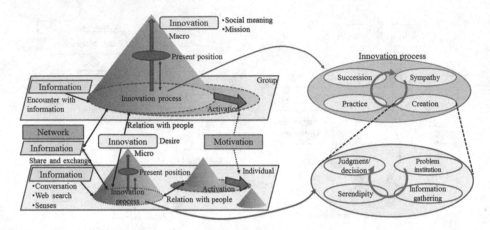

Fig. 2. Innovation model

Finally, an example of using networks is the model created by a company called Quirky [17], whose details can be found in Subsect. 2.4. Briefly, Quirky uses a system that harnesses networks to get users to propose ideas. This model has elements that improve extrinsic motivation by using remuneration.

Table 3. Analysis of existing systems.

Item	Element / Case	Cooperative elements		Process			
		Network	Motivation	Sympathy	Creation	Practice	Succession
1	Opinion exchange convergence support system using RFID tags [12]	✓			✓		
2	GKJ: Group KJ method support system utilizing digital pens [13]	✓			✓		
3	Brainstorm, chainstorm, cheatstorm, tweetstorm: New ideation strategies for distributed HCI design [14]				✓		
4	Application and analysis of interpersonal networks for a community support system [15]	✓					
5	Paperbox- A toolkit for exploring tangible interaction on interactive surfaces [16]					✓	
6	Process of quirky [17]	✓	✓				

2.4   Model for Generation Information Using Networks

Quirky [17] is a successful example of a company with a process that leverages networks. Quirky is a New York startup that has been in business since 2009. The open processes used by Quirky have users proposing products they would like to have made. The company forms communities with users to jointly create products and market them. The specific process used by the company is outlined in Fig. 3. Individuals, who also happen to be users, submit their ideas to communities, and the values in commercializing these ideas are voted on within these communities, which therefor winnows down the proposed ideas. Quirky later decides whether to commercialize the ideas. If the company moves forward with commercialization, it solicits opinions from the community as to product designs and naming, and then shifts to production. The greatest characteristic of this system is its influence, or the level of contribution an individual makes to products being developed. Quirky allocates money to individuals according to their influence, as well as profits from product sales. These generating ideas, voting on ideas, creating designs, and naming products are all assessed as to their level of contribution. Product manuals publicize the names of those that made contributions and where they made them. These are all ways to increase extrinsic motivation.

The Quirky model was designed to produce new innovations through the use of social networks. Moreover, there is an underlying possibility that aggressively increasing the number of worthy participants in development will lead to something unimagined.

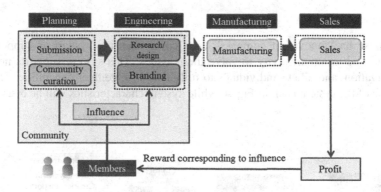

Fig. 3. Process in quirky

2.5 Issues with Existing Systems

We analyzed existing systems from the perspective of elements and processes required for innovation. The results obtained from this analysis ware the discovery that none of these systems was comprehensive and they limited their scope to only a portion of the innovation process. In particular, we could find no examples of connecting motivation with creativity.

Generating a large volume of ideas in projects requires individuals to propose good ideas. This in turn requires linking individuals to projects. The Quirky model is an example of leveraging a network to recruit ideas. Of course, that model has been successful as a means of gathering a broad range of ideas through communities. However, idea proposals have relied on individuals in Quirky, and their system does not support individual creativity. In addition, participation in projects and information gathering has also been left to individuals. This means that there have been limited encounters between people and information, which likely means little diversity. Thus, while there are examples of networks being used, information in these examples is only shared after the participants have been determined. Information gathering and exchanges must be done prior to the stage where participants have formed groups.

We can surmise from these analyses that there is insufficient support for both groups and individuals when it comes to creativity. There is also a need to support the linking of networks and motivation to produce creativity. We specifically identified three issues to be resolved.

- There is a lack of reinforcement for network activities in relation to gathering information that relies on individual actions or a meeting of people.
- The creation of ideas is entrusted to individuals, but support for individual creation is insufficient.
- Despite the fact that innovation is produced by people, there is a lack of motivational support for these people.

3 Proposed Creativity Support System

3.1 System Overview

We propose an "innovation compass" as a comprehensive system to support both individual and group creativity to solve these issues. This system supports networks and motivation, and allows individuals to fully demonstrate their capabilities. There is an outline of the system itself in Fig. 4, while system characteristics will be discussed in Subsect. 3.2.

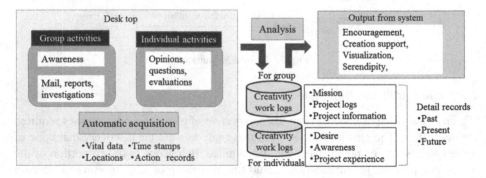

Fig. 4. Outline of creativity support system

We used a two-pronged approach to achieve such a system. First, there was separate support for both groups and mechanisms. Second, daily activity data ware gathered and analyzed for both individuals and projects in the form of creativity work logs (CWLs), as outlined in Fig. 4. The CWLs logged data for groups and individuals, and provided detailed records of the past, present, and future. Analyses of CWLs enabled systems to reach out to qualified people and projects. Moreover, CWL analysis served to strengthen interpersonal and individual-information interactions, ensured diversity, and enabled new insights. These analyses could also be used when offering support and making assessments.

3.2   System Characteristics

The Bridge Function (Bridging People, Information, and Invitations). Project registration occurs at the start of a new project. Likewise, individuals begin to participate in projects. The group CWL collects the status of project activities, and continually and automatically updates this information. For example, there are expectations not only toward voluntary participants in a project, but the system also proactively promotes the participation of qualified individuals, as can be seen in Fig. 5. For example, member A is informed of project X through the "bridge function", and by participating in the project a place is created to demonstrate A's capabilities. This satisfies the individual's sense of competency, increasing his/her intrinsic motivation. In addition, when B finds alignment between individual specialties and the issues in project X in Fig. 5, the bridge function provides answers to B from the system. The system assesses the effectiveness of the information in response to answers from B. The individual CWL of B is updated in doing so. For example, introducing personnel might be considered part of providing information, in which case B would be evaluated as a person whose specialty is making introductions using that individual's expansive network. Thus it becomes possible to reflect personal characteristics in an individual's CWL.

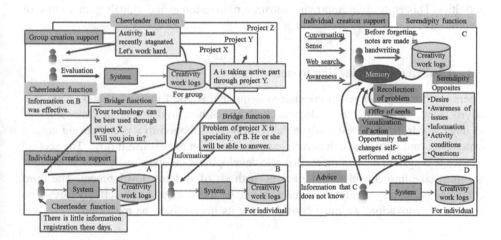

Fig. 5. Function of innovation system

Serendipity Function (Creativity Support, and Support of Insightfulness). When member C inputs information, the system presents content opposing the input information, automatically shuffles the accumulated information, and periodically provokes awareness of the issues as can be seen in Fig. 5. Individual awareness of issues becomes questionable over the passage of time, and the system can occasionally renew this awareness. In addition, the system can provide methods used to solve past issues to solve current issues. Furthermore, it provides one-stop management of all individual action records and emotion records: thus, allowing an individual to visualize their actions. This enables you to be aware of your creation and how your design is linked to actions and emotions, which become the springboard for reforming individual action. If member C presents information on personal issues, member C can obtain advice that would not have known from member D in Fig. 5.

In addition, all types of information can be input at any time and from anywhere, as can be seen in Fig. 5. For example, team members can use mobile terminals that identify handwriting to record data on the spot while they are riding on trains or taking walks. This is done because people have short memories, and such data must be recorded before it is forgotten.

Cheerleader Function (Emotional Support and Motivation). Project progress and energy must be managed from the systems side, as outlined in Fig. 5. For example, our system monitors project progress and team energy, and when few comments are being made, the system can automatically send messages of encouragement and support to team members. Where team members suffer from a lack of ideas, they themselves can lend each other encouragement. Such encouragement can also be given in response to individual activities. When member B is assessed as having provided effective information in Fig. 5, it becomes possible to visualize the contribution B has made to the project. This allows for accurate accounting of contributions made by both individuals and groups when projects conclude, and awards can be granted based on individual activities. This ends up in improving intrinsic motivation as individuals gain a sense of significance.

3.3   Challenges in Achieving Systems

There are three challenges in creating systems that support individual and group creativity. First, there is the technological challenge of how to differentiate statements, or in other words, how to best analyze the level of contribution to a project using tagged statements, and how to match accumulated information to best use it now. The second challenge is system development. Because development involves many diverse aspects, we must take into consideration efficient methods of systems development. The third challenge is creating standards for assessment. As it is difficult to objectively assess the success of innovation, we must consider how its impact is to be measured.

4   Conclusion

We proposed a system to support creativity undertaken by both individuals and groups. We believe that we have created an opportunity for individuals to use abilities that they have not been able to use before. In addition, this system can act as a platform for innovation.

This system can be greatly varied according to work styles. It can even be thought of as a proposal for a new style of work that is not merely an extension of current continuous workflows. It is undeniable that starting something new can be difficult. Even if individuals have ideas, they often have no way of bringing these to fruition. However, companies can take on new challenges by creating environments in which organizational barriers are eliminated and individuals' capabilities can be leveraged in group settings. People in the future will also need to conquer difficult issues, such as emerging environmental issues. To do so, it is necessary to accumulate individual knowledge and further increase problem-solving expertise as part of a group. We expect that this system will contribute to resolving numerous issues.

References

1. Drucker, P.F.: Management: Tasks, Responsibilities, Practices. HarperBusiness, New York (1993)
2. Negichi, E.: Watashi no Rirekisyo No.21(My personal history): Morning newspaper dated, 22 October 2012, Nikkei Inc. (in Japanese) (2012)
3. Carlson, C.R., Wilmot, W.W.: Innovation: The Five Disciplines for Creating What Customers Want. Crown Business, New York (2006)
4. Johnson, S.: Where Good Ideas Come from: The Natural History of Innovation. Riverhead Trade a member Penguin Group (USA) Inc, New York (2010)
5. Christensen, C.M., Dyer, J., Gregersen, H.: The Innovator's DNA: Mastering The Five Skills of Disruptive Innovators. Harvard Business Review Press, Boston (2011)
6. Nonaka, I., Toyama, R., Hirata, T.: Flow Management: The dynamic Theory of Knowledge-Based firm. Palgrave Macmillan, New York (2008)
7. Nonaka, I., Takeuchi, H.: The knowledge-Creating Company: How Japanese Companies Create The Dynamics of Innovation. Oxford University Press, Oxford (1995)
8. Otto Schamer, C.: Theory U: Learning from The Future as it Emerges. Berrett-Koehler Publishers, San Francisco (2009)
9. The Hasso Plattner Institute of Design at Stanford: An Introduction to Design Thinking Process Guide (2012)
10. Kawakita, J.: Hasso-Ho(Creative thinking method), Chuko Shinsyo, No.136, Chuokoron-Shinsya Inc. (in Japanese) (1996)
11. Young, J.W.: A Technique for Producing Ideas: Advertising Age Classics Library. McGraw-Hill, New York (2003)
12. Shimizu, Y., Sunayama, W.: Opinion exchange convergence support system using RFID tags. In: Bekki, D. (ed.) JSAI-isAI 2010. LNCS, vol. 6797, pp. 331–340. Springer, Heidelberg (2011)
13. Miura, M., Sugihara, T., Kunifuji, S.: GKJ: Group KJ Method Support System Utilizing Digital Pens. IEICE Transactions on Information and Systems E94.D(3), 456–464 (2011)
14. Faste, H., et al.: Brainstorm, Chainstorm, Cheatstorm, Tweetstorm: New Ideation Strategies for Distributed HCI Design, CHI 2013 Proceedings of the SIGCHI Conference on Human Factors in Computing Systems pp. 1343–1352. ACM, New York (2013)
15. Hamasaki, M., Takeda, H., Ohmukai, I., Ichise, R.: Application and analysis of interpersonal networks for a community support system. In: Sakurai, A., Hasida, K., Nitta, K. (eds.) JSAI 2003. LNCS (LNAI), vol. 3609, pp. 226–236. Springer, Heidelberg (2007)
16. Wiethoff, A., et al.: Paperbox: A toolkit for exploring tangible interaction on interactive surfaces, C&C 2013 Proceedings of the 9th ACM Conference on Creativity & Cognition pp. 64–73. ACM, New York (2013)
17. Quirky. https://www.quirky.com

Automatic Generation of Integrated Process Data Visualizations Using Human Knowledge

Felix Mayer[✉], Ulrich Bührer, Dorothea Pantförder, Denise Gramß,
and Birgit Vogel-Heuser

Faculty of Mechanical Engineering, Institute of Automation and Information
Systems, Technische Universität München, München, Germany
{mayer,buehrer,pantfoerder,gramss,
vogel-heuser}@ais.mw.tum.de

Abstract. The increasing complexity of industrial processes leads to complex process visualizations. Amongst other things, this is often due to the fact that a visualization engineer does not have deep knowledge of all physical and logical relations inside a plant. Additionally, different operators have to work with the same visualization despite the fact, that their personal preferences, abilities and needs differ. Having to work with unclear and confusing visualizations leads to an increased workload for plant operators and thus to higher error rates. Due to cost and time constraints, creating better or user-specific visualizations manually is not possible, especially because taking the operators' specific knowledge and experience into account is difficult.

This paper presents a concept to automatically generate process visualizations and support systems by the usage of a knowledge base and an influence model. This allows for operator-specific visualizations, considering preferences, abilities and needs. It also eases the visualization engineer's work by automatically choosing suitable diagrams and their properties. Additionally, by providing a system to acquire the operator's knowledge, complex relations inside a plant can be made accessible and utilized for optimizing the production process and visualization.

Keywords: Knowledge base · Visualization · 3D · Operator support

1 Introduction

Nowadays, visualizations of industrial processes need to display more and more data, as processes get more complex and devices offer more data. These visualizations are used by different personnel, e.g. technicians and process operators, for monitoring tasks. While working with such complex visualizations, the operator needs to closely monitor all relevant data, basing decisions on his observations, while performing additional tasks, such as administrative tasks. Consequently, the operator's workload and mental demand is increased. Operator's tasks are challenging and can only be

© Springer International Publishing Switzerland 2015
S. Yamamoto (Ed.): HIMI 2015, Part II, LNCS 9173, pp. 488–498, 2015.
DOI: 10.1007/978-3-319-20618-9_49

accomplished by skilled and trained personnel. An appropriate and elaborated mental model, which is developed through experience, is required to handle these complex tasks. This is the base for the operator's assessment of the current situation in process monitoring and leads to a selection of operator actions. Additionally, in case of critical situations, the operator's actions are often highly time-critical and errors while handling these situations may have extensive consequences, such as environmental pollution. Taking these points into account, the human-machine interface between the plant and the operator is therefore an important part for any industrial process that has to be designed thoroughly.

Designing visualization for a process is a complex task, done by engineers that preferably possess deep knowledge of the plant and process. Additionally, the visualization engineer needs deep knowledge of human-machine interaction and programming in general. While designing the visualization for a given industrial process, the engineer needs to decide on how and where the process and all relevant process values should be displayed within the visualization. In process industry, this is often solved by simply displaying an abstract 2D representation of the plant's geometry and by placing the process values close to the sensors that generate them. This often leads to cluttered and unclear visualizations that further increase the workload of the operator, who has to select and integrate the given information according to their mental model of the process.

However, the operators' mental models are not only based on monitoring of the process. Their knowledge of the process is often gathered throughout many years, enabling the operator to take appropriate actions in critical situations. This allows them to provide information beneficial to the production process, especially in recurring or critical situations. This is due to the fact, that operators possess great deals of experience and system knowledge of their plant, which has not been taken into account during the engineering of the plant and process. This experience may contain knowledge regarding parameters and their relations, detection of critical plant states, and general process optimizations. Hence, collecting this knowledge promises great potential to optimize the production process.

This paper introduces different interactive methods of knowledge acquisition and provides results of their first evaluation, according to their applicability to the production environment. These methods include text based approaches as well as visual approaches. Combining this collected information and big data from modern intelligent sensors, existing models of the plant can be optimized. These optimized plant models provide the foundation for further optimizations, which enhance the production process.

Additionally, this paper proposes a concept for the architecture of a knowledge-based approach for automatically choosing and configuring diagrams for process visualizations in order to help the visualization engineer. The provided algorithm, which supports choosing adequate diagrams and diagram configurations, can simplify the process of designing visualizations.

Both concepts can be brought together to form a comprehensive approach to improve the operator's integration into the production process and reduce the operator's workload. The concept also closes the knowledge-loop between visualization engineer, process and operator.

2 State of the Art

As stated above, operators of industrial processes combine information from different sources in order to understand the current process and the plant's state.

The assessment of the current process and plant state requires appropriate situation awareness. Situation awareness is a model of the dynamic environment, which is the activated part of the operator's mental model. It involves the perception of environmental elements, the comprehension of their meaning and the projection of future states [End95]. The operator's mental model is a prequisite for achieving situation awareness [Joh83]. The mental model of operators contains components, relations and functions of the monitored plant and process. The operator's goals determine which mental model is selected for the current situation and consequently, leads the perception of elements at a given point in time and thus selection for further processing. The mental model enables the interpretation and comprehension of the perceived element of the dynamic environment and allows the projection of future states.

Depending on the task, different visualizations are chosen [VDI3699], this includes the utilization of different colors and shapes. Multiple guidelines and norms for the design of visualizations exist, e.g. VDI 3850-1 [VDI3850], VDI 3699 and ISO 9241 [ISO9241], all of them deal with aspects of representing real-world systems. None of those guidelines and norms deal with aspects of integrated process visualizations that offer significant benefits according to Wickens' Proximity Compatibility Principle (PCP) [WiAn90]].

With the PCP, Wickens defined influences on the generation of mental models and the effort associated by doing so. According to Wickens, the operator's workload can be reduced by following the principles of mental and spatial proximity. The fewer information sources there are and the better they are mentally and spatially integrated, the lower the information access costs are. Highly integrated visualizations thus minimize the effort needed to create a comprehensive mental model. Creating high spatial proximity is comparatively easy, as values that should be considered coherently should also be displayed close to each other on the screen. Integrating multiple values into as few diagrams as possible maximizes the effect of spatial proximity, because relations are already clearly displayed and thus do not have to be created by the operator. Mental proximity means that all relevant data is displayed in such a way that an operator is relieved by the data prepared for easy access and understanding. This leads to less frustration and less workload.

The PCP states that integrative tasks, meaning the gathering of information by combining data, e.g. set different data in relation to each other, benefits from a 3D representation. Tasks requiring a high level of attention, e.g. reading a value over a longer period of time, benefit from a 2D representation. Wickens states that even the integration of undetailed information already produces better results.

According to John et al. [JCSO01], the advantage of a 3D visualization depends on the given task. In accordance to Wickens, they showed in several experiments that the identification of specific data is difficult in 3D. In contrast, if integration of various data is required for specific tasks, 3D facilitates performance and reduces cognitive demand.

For the task of human information processing using mental models, Rasmussen [Ras86], Hacker [Hac80], Wickens [WiHo00] and Card et al. [CMN86] created different sequential, capacitive and quantitative models in order to describe the complex process by using different views. Those findings, as well as findings concerning three-dimensional visualizations, have to be considered while generating process data visualizations. Depending on the complexity and integration of the data, a three-dimensional presentation could be beneficial to the operator's workload. Wickens et al. [WML94] defined tasks for three levels of information integration (low, medium, high) and the suitability of 3D representations for those three levels. The benefits of 3D visualizations were also shown by Tory et al. [TKAM06]. An example of integrated 3D process data visualization was given by Mayer et al. [MPVH13].

Optimizing operator workload while gathering knowledge at the same time is a difficult task to accomplish, as operators should not be distracted from their work, especially during the process control task in a plant. With post-tests, important information gets lost, as misperceptions can be forgotten. Therefore, data is less reliable as there is a tendency to overgeneralize and over rationalize [NiWi77]. Consequently, it is most promising to measure knowledge about causes, actions and relationships right after a problem is solved [SkAu99].

3 Goals /Requirements

Derived from to the description of the current processes for designing process visualizations as well as the state of the art, the overall goal for a new concept is to simplify the initial creation, and its successive adjustment and adaptation. During the lifetime of industrial plants – typically up to 30 years – the electrical equipment and especially the software are appended and changed on multiple occasions. The current, purely manual processes of (re-)designing and (re-)implementing a visualization can thus be improved and accelerated by automating them based on specialists' knowledge, e.g. of engineers and operators. This also includes considering all relevant legal requirements such as colors of buttons and font sizes as well as safety regulations. Additionally, evolving research findings, e.g. Wickens' PCP, have to be taken into account, in order to reduce the operators' workload, which in turn reduces failure rates.

In order to be able to also include the knowledge of stakeholders that do not have engineering knowledge, the new approach should not depend on any programming language but should instead be model-based to reach a greater number of users.

Regarding interactive operator knowledge acquisition, the main goal is to maximize production potentials by optimizing the existing models of the plant, based on existing operator knowledge on causes and relations of process components. In order to not distract the operator from controlling the plant, the knowledge collection has to be unobtrusive. To automate the collection, seamless integration into the existing modeling environment is required. Since human inputs might be erroneous or imprecise, the knowledge acquisition must be able to handle uncertainties and consist of an inherent validation process for error detection.

4 Concept

The proposed architecture consists of two systems: the visualization generator and the knowledge acquisition system, designed to help the operator as well as the engineer and technical personnel. Both systems can be viewed separately but unfold their true potential only in conjunction with each other and aim at significantly reducing the overall workload of all stakeholders.

In Fig. 1, the comprehensive approach of the visualization generator and the knowledge elicitation system are displayed. In short, both subsystems share a central knowledge base (1). The visualization generator thereof generates a customizable influence model (2) that is afterwards processed by an algorithm (3), taking into account the operator's profile (4) and generating the final visualization code (6) to be displayed (7) by using inherent criteria (5). The knowledge elicitation system, surrounded by the dotted line, extracts part of the operator's (8) mental model (9), checks for validity (11) and stores the information in the central knowledge base.

Based on this concept, plants are able to support all human operators, which are in turn able to provide beneficial knowledge about their plant. Both systems are described in detail in the following.

4.1 Acquisition of Operator Knowledge

Operators (8) often possess valuable knowledge and experience of 'their' machine or plant, which can be utilized to improve the quality of existing knowledge bases (1) and optimize production processes (12). Therefore, it is beneficial to collect existing operator knowledge (9) with the goal to gain knowledge about causes and relations between different process components as well as corrective information in specific

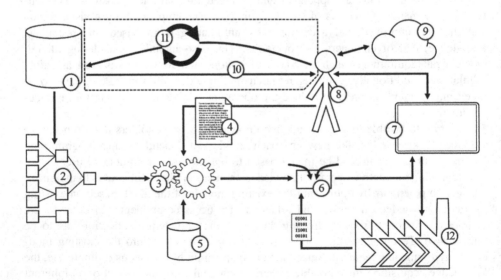

Fig. 1. Overview of the proposed architecture

situations in addition to the system model. In order to avoid unnecessary distractions from plant operation and to avoid operator's frustration, the knowledge collection must be unobtrusive and intuitive to use while also considering time efficiency.

For this purpose, different concepts for the acquisition of knowledge during plant operation are introduced in the following. In Fig. 2, an overview of the proposed concepts is given. Therein, problem trees, cause and effect graphs and input based on text blocks are illustrated exemplarily.

Problem Trees (PT) visualize causes and problem chains. Consequently, PTs aid the operator in detecting problem causes and, thereby, in performing maintenance tasks. To enable knowledge collection, the operator is able to enter additional problem causes within the existing problem tree, based on his experience and mental model of the plant.

Cause-Effect graphs (CEG) illustrate relations between different parameters of the production. Such a CEG is based on the existing knowledge base (1). In this context, the knowledge acquisition is enabled by allowing the operator to increase or decrease the influence one parameter has on another, thereby, the quality of the knowledge base is improved. In order to extend the existing knowledge base, the operator is also allowed to add additional parameters and further influences.

Text Blocks (TB), similarly to CEGs, depict dependencies between causes and effects. Furthermore, they also define the correlation between problems and their causes. For this purpose, text blocks of different characters are combined. The combination of a cause (e.g. Pump X clogged) with a specific value or intensity (e.g. high, low) with a problem (e.g. product viscosity) and its specific value through a correlation (e.g. causes, increases) enables a description of a problem and its cause. The combination of TBs regarding different parameters, their correlation and intensity, enables input and visualization of cause and effect correlations. As a result of the predefined TB-structure, the application of speech recognition technologies is

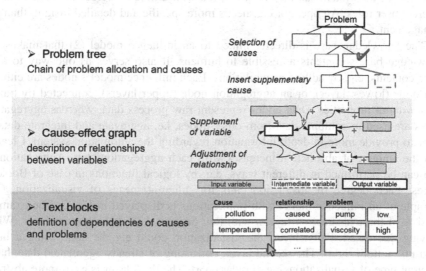

Fig. 2. Knowledge acquisition concepts

simplified and can be utilized to further reduce distractions for the operator during knowledge acquisition.

Since user interactions might be erroneous, the collected data must be verified and validated (11) before resulting process enhancements may be implemented into the production process. In order to allow verification of the collected knowledge and to continuously optimize the knowledge base and production processes, the individual operator interactions with the physical system are recorded and correlated to the collected knowledge. To avoid data privacy issues, the data collection is anonymized.

This approach to knowledge acquisition is aimed at closing the knowledge-support loop (cp. Fig. 1). Consequently, through adequate visualizations, plants are able to support human operators, which are in turn able to provide beneficial knowledge about their plant, further improving plant models and, thereby, recommended actions provided by the visualization. As plant safety is a major concern, the changes proposed by- and collected from human operators need to be verified for accuracy first, before comprehensive changes to the model of a plant or the production process can be propagated.

4.2   Visualization Generator

The visualization generator consists of different components, as displayed in Fig. 1. The overall state of a system, i.e. the current state of all actuators, sensors and products, can be extracted by combining different process values. This is normally done by the operator.

In this concept (Fig. 1), a knowledge base (1) is used to store all known interrelations between the technical system and its process, represented by process data of sensors and actuators. Thus, it can be used to deduce, which process values should be combined in order to extract additional information from a given set of process data. This state of the system can then be presented with different degrees of abstraction for different user roles. An operator e.g. needs more specific and detailed insight, than the management.

The knowledge base is directly linked to an influence model (2) that makes the knowledge base's contents accessible to humans. It also serves as one way to alter those contents, e.g. by adding new relations. Each influence model's nodes are either a data node (lowest layer), or an aggregation node (upper layers), connected by transitions without properties. Data nodes represent raw process data, whereas aggregation nodes are used to combine data from other nodes, i.e. aggregate and integrate data in order to provide more in depth information regarding the automation system. Clearly, also the amount of abstraction increases with each aggregation step. Aggregation of data can be performed in different ways, e.g. by logical functions in case of Boolean values. Each degree of abstraction calls for different means of visualization. One example of an influence model with implications is displayed in Fig. 3. The example consists of three abstraction layers, with raw process data at the bottom layer. When viewing this detailed first layer, the visualization could e.g. be done using a helix diagram (bottom right). The second layer, consisting of already aggregated data, has a different type of visualization, e.g. a radar chart. The third layer is even more abstract,

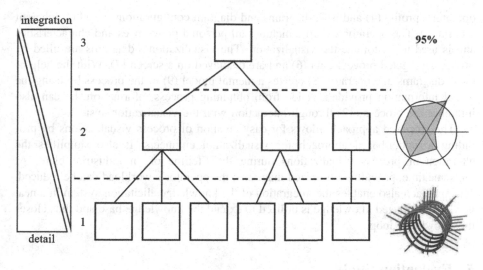

Fig. 3. The influence model

e.g. consisting solely of a simple number. That way different information for different roles is created and visualized.

The decision of what type of diagram is used to display certain nodes is not performed by the influence model, but an algorithm (3) that also considers the user's characteristics (4). The user's characteristics include its profile, e.g. color blindness, age, personal preferences, e.g. for specific diagrams and his role, e.g. operator or technical personnel. With the help of this information as well as the influence model, the algorithm chooses suitable visualization diagrams and their configuration, i.e. which colors to use, which axis to use for what value, etc. The algorithm uses a sets of rules (5) for this task, e.g. normally a temperature is displayed from blue (cold) to red (hot) in contrast to the green-to-red color gradient for other process data. Therefore, whenever a user starts using the visualization, the algorithm can create diagrams suitable for this user, as long as its characteristics are known. Afterwards it is possible to switch between the generated visualizations, based on the user.

The last step, before finally displaying the visualization on a screen (7), is to fill the diagrams with actual data from the industrial process (6). This last step differs from other visualization systems as it also applies the configured aggregations to the raw data.

Because visualizations for specific users can automatically be created after the initial model has been created, each user can thus have a customized visualization that fits its needs and preferences, thus lessening the workload.

In summary (cp. Fig. 1), all interrelations of a plant and its process are stored inside a knowledge base (1). Parts of the knowledge can automatically be elicitated and processed in order to form an influence model (2) between the process, the process values and the plant geometry. This influence model can be customized, e.g. by the visualization engineer, in order to be able to handle special situations and requirements. The influence model is processed by an algorithm (3) that chooses, in accordance to the operator's profile (4) and role, diagrams and diagram configurations based on inherent criteria (5). The operator's profile includes all personal preferences and characteristics and is used to customize the visualization. The visualization's diagrams are filled by raw or aggregated process data (6) and are displayed on a screen (7). With the help of these diagrams, the operator (8) creates a mental model (9) of the process by using the visual information provided. Aside from obtaining process information, he can also influence the process (12) through interaction with the visualization system.

The proposed approach allows for easy creation of process visualizations by providing a model-based approach for visualization engineers. It also simplifies the alteration of process visualizations during the lifetime of an industrial plant. At the same time, providing optimized diagrams, the operator's workload can be reduced. The approach also enables the integration of the knowledge elicitation system in a neat way. The extracted knowledge is utilized to extend the knowledge base and thus closes the knowledge loop.

5 Evaluation Study

As a first evaluation of the proposed concepts and their applicability to plant operation, a small study with experts from the manufacturing industry was carried out. Within this study, the application of PTs was seen critical, as the effort to enter new problems and their derived causes was seen as potentially tedious and, therefore, too distracting for the operative implementation. CEGs on the other hand, were seen as potentially applicable, due to their focus on point and click interactions. Regarding the input mechanisms, TBs were given the best rating, but their visualization was seen lacking. Therefore, a combination of the CEGs as a visualization tool and input mechanisms based on TBs were identified as the optimal knowledge collection tools. Therefore, the authors will focus future works on developing such a combined operator support system.

6 Benefits

By combining the two presented approaches, a closed knowledge loop is achieved. On the one hand, the knowledge gathered from the operator by the knowledge elicitation system is utilized to improve the diagrams and visualizations by altering the underlying influence model. Interrelations unknown at the time of engineering can be detected, acquired and implemented during the whole lifetime of a plant. Likewise, erroneous assumptions made during the engineering-phase can be corrected in later stages of a plant's life cycle.

On the other hand, the way in which information is presented by the visualization aids in extracting the operator's knowledge and storing it. This knowledge elicitation supports the identification of hidden plant interrelations, while minimizing interfering with the operator's work. The extracted knowledge of plant, process and product can e.g. be used to generate visualizations that show the required, relevant data, so that work is easier for new operators, which do not have comprehensive experience and knowledge. Providing optimized diagrams in respect to data integration and operator support reduces, according to Wickens PCP, the operator's workload and thus leads to fewer errors while operating a plant. Alternatively, operators are able to handle greater amounts of data while maintaining the same workload-level. Especially, regarding big-data aspects, the possibility to automatically aggregate and integrate data for visualization purposes, provides new possibilities.

All of these benefits can be achieved without having to write code, as the two approaches are model-based. This does not only influence the complexity to create an adapted visualization, but also the time required to do so.

7 Summary and Outlook

The work presented in this paper outlines the concept of an improved integration of the operator and the visualization engineer in day-to-day process control. By providing a system to automatically generate process visualizations from a knowledge base, containing physical and logical interrelations within an industrial plant, the individual needs and preferences of operators, e.g. concerning color-blindness, can be addressed. Likewise, physical and logical changes of the plant and new findings concerning the display of data can be taken into account, automatically adjusting the global knowledge base. In order to support plant evolution during its life cycle, the operator's knowledge about the process and the plant, which includes information about relations, and critical as well as recurring situations, is continuously acquired. Consequently, the plants models are constantly adapted, thereby optimizing the plant's models. This leads to an increased plant efficiency and improved operator support. To elicitate an operator's knowledge, multiple approaches were introduced.

Based on the first performed evaluation by industry experts, these concepts will be further evaluated in future work. Additionally, future work will consist of creating the individual modules of the presented approach and implementing the system as a whole. This also includes the evaluation of the presented approach against current and traditional approaches.

References

1. Card, S., Moran, T.P., Newell, A.: The Psychology of Human Computer Interaction. Lawrence Erlbaum Associates, Hillsdale (1986)
2. Endsley, M.R.: Toward a theory of situation awareness in dynamic systems. Hum. Factors J. Hum. Factors Ergon. Soc. **37**(1), 32–64 (1995)
3. DIN EN ISO 9241-110: Ergonomics of human-system interaction (2006)
4. Hacker, W.: Allgemeine Arbeits- und Ingenieurpsychologie: Psychische Struktur und Regulation von Arbeitstätigkeiten. Huver, Bern (1980)
5. John, M.S., Cowen, M.B., Smallman, H.S., Oonk, H.M.: The use of 2D and 3D display for shape-understanding versus relative-position tasks. Hum. Factors J. Hum. Factors Ergon. Soc. **42**(1), 79–98 (2001)

6. Johnson-Laird, P.N.: Mental Models: Towards a Cognitive Science of Language. Inference and Consciousness. Harvard University Press, Cambridge (1983)
7. Mayer, F., Pantförder, D., Vogel-Heuser, B.: Design and implementation of an integrated, platform independent 3D visualization of complex process data. In: 12th IFAC IFIP/IFORS/ IEA Symposium on Analysis, Design, and Evaluation of Human-Machine Systems (HMS 2013), Las Vegas (2013)
8. Nisbett, R.E., Wilson, T.D.: Telling more than we can know: Verbal reports on mental processes. Psychological Review (1977)
9. Rassmussen, J.: Information Processing and Human-Machine Interaction: An Approach To Cognitive Engineering. North-Holland, New York (1986)
10. Skourup, C., Aune, A.: Decision support in process plants: visualisation of experiences. In: International Conference on Human Interfaces in Control Rooms, Cockpits and Command Centres, Bath (1999)
11. Tory, M., Kirkpatrick, A.E., Atkins, M.S., Möller, T.: Visualization task performance with 2D, 3D and combination displays. IEEE Trans. Visual Comput. Graphics 12(1), 2–13 (2006)
12. VDI/VDE 3699 Blatt 2: Prozessführung mit Bildschirmen – Grundlagen (2005)
13. VDI/VDE 3850 Blatt 1: Gebrauchstaugliche Gestaltung von benutzerschnittstellen für technische Anlagen – Konzepte, Prinzipien und grundsätzliche Empfehlungen (2000)
14. Wickens, C.D., Merwin, D.H., Lin, E.L.: Implications of Graphics Enhancements for the Visualization of Scientific Data: Dimensional Integrality, Stereopsis, Motion and Mesh. Hum. Factors J. Hum. Factors Ergon. Soc. 36(1), 44–61 (1994)
15. Wickens, C.D., Andre, A.D.: Proximity Compatibiliy and Information Display: Effect of Color, Space and Objectness on Information Integration. Hum. Factors J. Hum. Factors Ergon. Soc. Santa Monica 32(1), 61–77 (1990)
16. Wickens, C.D., Hollands, J.G.: Engineering Psychology and Human Performance. Prentice Hall, New Jersey (2000)

A Head-up Display with Augmented Reality and Gamification for an E-Maintenance System: Using Interfaces and Gamification to Motivate Workers in Procedural Tasks

Allan Oliveira[1(✉)], Nahana Caetano[2], Leonardo Castro Botega[3],
and Regina Borges de Araújo[1]

[1] Federal University of São Carlos, São Carlos, São Paulo, Brazil
{allan_oliveira, regina}@dc.ufscar.br
[2] Coca Cola FEMSA, São Paulo, São Paulo, Brazil
nahana.caetano@kof.com.mx
[3] Univem, Marilia, Marilia, São Paulo, Brazil
botega@univem.edu.br

Abstract. A current challenge in industrial systems, such as E-maintenance, responsible for gathering all maintenance-related data in a single system, is how to display information to users. This same challenge is present when considering new devices for visualization, such as Head Mounted Displays -HDM (e.g. Google Glass). Advanced interfaces such as Augmented Reality (AR) and Head-Up Display (HUD) provide a means to display these information for users. However, there is still a lack of theoretical design studies (studies that do not consider current technologies limitations) of Augmented Reality and HUD. Another problem in industrial scenarios is motivation, especially considering repetitive procedural works. Therefore, this paper present and discuss a high fidelity theoretical prototype of an interface for maintenance, that uses Gamification techniques to motivate the user, and AR and HUD to display information in a HMD device.

Keywords: Augmented reality · HUD · Gamification · Maintenance

1 Introduction

A current challenge in the maintenance of industries is obtaining and using knowledge. E-Maintenance is a new field of Information and Communication Technology that unites maintenance engineering with software engineering, management and business administration [1]. It is defined as the union of two tendencies in industry [1]: the rising importance of maintenance and the accelerated development of Information and Communication Technologies.

Information in an E-Maintenance system must be used to extract rules to generate knowledge, which will be capitalized to create a corporative memory of the company. Nevertheless, visualization solutions for such knowledge are scarce, as studies show that 45 % of an operator shift is spend searching and reading procedures [2].

© Springer International Publishing Switzerland 2015
S. Yamamoto (Ed.): HIMI 2015, Part II, LNCS 9173, pp. 499–510, 2015.
DOI: 10.1007/978-3-319-20618-9_50

Bagemann et al. [3] reinforces the need for visualization solutions in project PROTEUS, by defining the delivery of data to operator actors in a strategic and tactical level as one of the three central functions.

Another E-maintence system, TELMA, also discusses the importance of using PDAs or Head Mounted Displays (HMD) for visualization, increasing the user understanding of the situation [4].

Consequently, several studies were conducted about industrial accidents, and the incorrect manipulation of the process by the operator was appointed as their major cause [5]. They prove that data visualization in maintenance, both in procedure and intelligence level, are crucial. In contrast, considering mobile user interface design (both PDAs and HMDs are mobile), Sá and Carriço demonstrated that studies of design or with a user centered perspective are lacking [6].

Augmented Reality (AR) is a potential technology for data visualization in E-Maintenance, because it can bring knowledge to the physical world, assisting operators to execute their tasks without stopping to consult manuals. There are already many solutions that use AR in maintenance, and some of them are analyzed in Oliveira et al. [7].

Furthermore, considering HMDs, another visualization technology to explore is a Head-Up Display (HUD), in which the User Interface (UI) is projected in the display. In this paper, the word HUD is used based on the Game Development domain, in which it is considered a way to present information to users, in other words, a user interface media (and not a device). Therefore a HUD interface refers to 2D information projected on the user display.

Combining both solutions, an interface with HUD and AR elements should:

- Display as little information as possible, while providing the necessary information in the correct time;
- Allow easy access to data and optimize the information presentation;

Besides visualization, another need in industries is motivation solutions. There is a direct influence between skill and motivation, because, although high skill indicates possible high productivity, motivation is the lever that controls the final result of efficiency. As studied by Kiassat [8], motivation and boredom are two of the main factor responsible for error in some industries.

A motivation strategy currently discussed in work environments is Gamification, in which game design techniques are applied to work problems [9]. Even in procedural tasks, classic game design motivation techniques can be applied to motivate users [10].

In this paper it is proposed and analyzed a high fidelity User Interface prototype for maintenance activities, which uses AR and HUD as visualization technologies, and Gamification as a motivational technique for the procedural tasks. This theoretical interface and the application underneath it are connected to an E-Maintenance System, to be able to obtain, in real time, data for the user. The focus of the paper is not on technological constraints and therefore any current limitation is ignored to provide an optimal User Interface.

This paper is divided in: (II) reward and motivation theory; (III) the procedure; (IV) the User Interface prototype; (V) discussion and conclusions.

2 Reward and Motivation

Umstot et al. [11] were among the firsts to suggest strategies to enrich the work and make it more interesting, challenging and significant. This could be done by adding dimensions such as abilities variety, task identity, task significance, autonomy and feedback. These factors, together with communication with other people, are essential to ensure motivation and satisfaction.

Procedural tasks can lack these dimensions. Therefore, workers that face routines that are too specialized or simplified, besides feeling unsatisfied with their activities, can also face negative physiological consequences, such as RSI (Repetitive Strain Injury). Examples are works in assembly lines, or those in which a machine forces the rhythm the worker has to follow.

Maintenance, which is the domain explored in this paper, is a strictly procedural work, although with some unpredictability. Beyond being repetitive, it usually leaves a low margin for high level and impactful decision making, reducing the satisfaction levels in this type of work.

Procedural tasks are also common in many games, one category being MMORPG (Massive Multiplayer Online RPG), due to the necessary repetition of actions to obtain better rewards (also called grinding in game development). The main difference of what generally makes an MMORPG "fun" and a procedural industrial task "boring", is the immediate reward and the expectancy of getting better rewards.

The Skinner Box theory [12] explains why conditioning players in MMORPGs is possible. This theory proves that it is possible to project a behavioral modification system based on the systematic reinforcement of the desired behavior, in other terms, give an immediate reward for a task. Therefore, by stimulating and satisfying their users with instant rewards, MMORPGs become engaging, while maintenance can be considered boring.

This theory is taken to extreme levels by some game developing companies, making games that are borderline gambling, causing compulsive addiction in users. Many studies were made to understand the nature of addiction in online gaming [13] or to identify if these games are passing the barrier of illegality [14].

One of the methods used currently to improve user satisfaction with work is Gamification, which is applying game elements and game design techniques to non-game related problems, such as business and social challenges. Gamification is applied to improve user experience and engagement in a task [15], usually through a simple reward system (therefore, it's a Skinner Box). As far the authors know, there are no applications of Gamification as a motivating force in maintenance.

Several Gamification strategies can be used to improve motivation/satisfaction and decrease boredom. For example, in the simpler level, interfaces could be graphically designed to look like games, just to give users the idea of being in a game. In a medium level, interfaces can be used to display the user reward (salary) for executing a task, both in regular salary (man-hour value) and in the annual bonus calculated based on performance. Finally, in a more advanced level, Gamification could be applied to dictate each user task, for instance, placing the work inside a real game.

The focus of this paper is on the medium level of Gamification, whereas the financial reward of the user for his task will be integrated in real time with the UI. Furthermore, key performance indicators established by companies will be used to increase even further the feeling of immediate reward. These indicators are indices used by enterprises to define and measure an employee performance, and usually an annual bonus is calculated based on these indicators.

In this paper, the four key performance indicators used are: assiduity, safety, mission and record. Assiduity is assessed by punctuality and absenteeism. Safety is evaluated by fulfilling norms and policies. Missions are evaluated by completing tasks, considering that each task demands a different level of effort and therefore they have different weight in the score. Finally, record is assessed by comparing the user performance with the mean performance of all collaborators, in other words, comparing how above the mean was the user for a task.

3   The Procedure

The task example showed in this paper uses dummy data and the step by step process and the values presented are merely illustrative:

- User arrives at work and logs in the system;
- Receive the task and accept it;
- Request information about the equipment, including reliability and sensor information;
- Equips the Personal Protective Equipment (PPE);
- Executes a preventive test in the airplane turbine;
- Opens the turbine and identifies a problem;
- Fix and replace a specific asset;
- Receives a score for the task.

4   The UI Prototype

E-maintenance technology has the goal to facilitate access to any maintenance-related data to users. However, few studies show how a User Interface for such a system would be. Therefore, in this section, a UI prototype is presented, with the goal to display data already available in E-Maintenance systems, but currently inaccessible in tasks of a technical nature.

The first set of UIs is an introduction to the system, routine and tasks, and can be seen in Fig. 1. Interface A is the first one showed to the user (after he logs in the system), and gives as options access to tasks, a calendar with the planning of the day, reports and news. The first step to Gamification is in there, because the user can also access a personal and team ranking. This ranking is created based on the result of each mission (showed to the user at the end of the task). The goal is to motivate users, allowing them to compare their performance in real time with their coworkers.

Fig. 1. (A) Initial system UI; (B) Daily routine UI; (C) Task initiation UI

Interface B of Fig. 1 is designed to introduce users in theirs daily schedule. This interface also introduces the first key performance indicator, assiduity, by ranking the user based on his/her punctuality and absenteeism.

Interface C is the start of a new task, showing the necessary procedures and the estimated time to complete each procedure.

The second interface, from Fig. 2, has the goal of presenting equipment detail to the user. In this figure, interface A shows the equipment and some related information. Interface B displays statistical data about the equipment, such as reliability (calculated

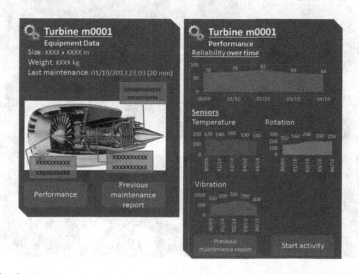

Fig. 2. User Interface for complex data and information about an equipment

over the lifetime of the equipment), and sensor data collected over the last operation (vibration, temperature, rotation).

Interface of Fig. 3 is a combination between Augmented Reality and HUD. In the upper left corner, there is a list of equipment the user should acquire, with markings to show which ones were already obtained. Additionally, a green light is projected on top of the next equipment to be acquired (in this case, the glasses), to guide users in choosing only the necessary and correct equipment. Furthermore, in the right corner of the screen, there are buttons representing additional features of the system. They allow users to film or take pictures in real time of the work, to start a VOIP conversation when in need of help, to access system documentation and help and to visualize a map of the place.

Interface from Fig. 4 is activated when a preventive test is executed in the equipment. During this test, a HUD element is showed with real time information, in the form of graphics, of the equipment sensors. Complementing the HUD, there are three information projected on top of the equipment, based on the sensors reading. Temperature is projected in the turbine through a colored heat map. Rotation is projected through a circular green arrow, to demonstrate rpm. Finally vibration is projected through the yellow arrows located around the turbine, and they move according to the current vibration.

Figure 5 shows an interface to warn users about possible risks identified in the equipment, by projecting messages on top of the parts that are the source of the risk. In this figure, UI was visually expanded to improve readability. Risks are also classified in category and danger level, and to avoid clutter it is possible to filter only by category or danger.

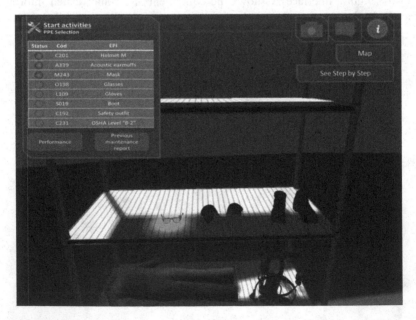

Fig. 3. Track assistant interface to help equip protective personal equipment

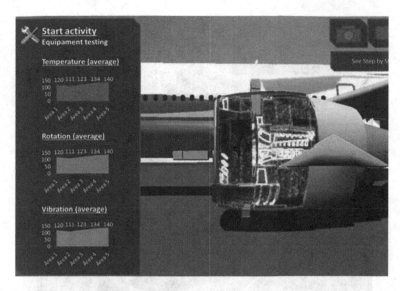

Fig. 4. Interface using AR by projecting sensor measured data (temperature, rotation and vibration) on top of the equipment.

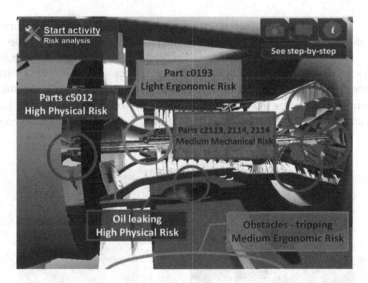

Fig. 5. Interface to improve risk awareness (information size in this figure is increased for better visualization in the paper).

Interface from Fig. 6 guides users through a procedure. In this UI, there is a HUD showing the amount of steps from this procedure, and the current one. There is also an AR interface showing what and where is the current step, highlighted and blue, and the next two steps, uncolored. A more produced AR assembly interface can be seen in Henderson and Feiner [16].

Fig. 6. Procedure guidance interface

In Fig. 7 there is an interface showing the result of the user task performance. Presented in interface A is the time spent on the procedure, and then the score received in assiduity, safety ("following policies and procedures"), mission ("change of turbine part") and record, although in this last the user didn't received any score. In interface B the user score is compared with other coworkers. Both interfaces have the goal to motivate our user by showing information about performance to give an immediate feedback, and the colleagues' performance to promote a healthy competitiveness in the work.

Fig. 7. User Interface with performance feedback based on key performance indicator

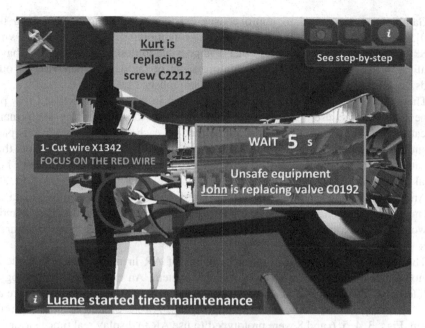

Fig. 8. Interface for teamwork awareness

Finally, interface from Fig. 8 was added to the paper, even though it is not part of the procedure, to illustrate a UI of teamwork awareness. In this interface, the WAIT sign was designed to capture the user attention and help in synchronizing steps of the user procedure with dependencies with other coworkers' procedures.

At the same time, the interface is also informing what two other coworkers are currently doing. Whenever a coworker is near the user, the interface displays their activities in the form of AR (projected on top of them), such as the warning "Kurt is replacing screw C2212". On the other hand, when the coworker is far, their activities are displayed as a HUD in the corner, such as "Luane started tires maintenance".

Finally, the user activity is displayed on top of where it should happen, with a picture of the necessary tool, description of the action and a warning of common mistakes ("Cut wire X1242. Focus on the red wire.").

5 Discussion and Conclusions

This paper proposes a high fidelity UI prototype for maintenance activities, which uses Augmented Reality and HUD in a Head Mounted Display as visualization technologies, and Gamification as a solution to the motivation problem in procedural tasks.

The proposed User Interface prototype has several goals. The first goal is to demonstrate how Gamification can be used in a maintenance context, both in input data and presentation output.

Gamification is applied to improve user experience and engagement in a task [9,10], normally through the theory of operant conditioning chamber (also known as the Skinner box) [12], which proves that it is possible to design a system of behavior modification based in the systematic reinforcement of the desired behavior, in other words, to give an immediate reward for the accomplished task.

There are several ways to explore Gamification in a work context, and this prototype explored the user performance indicator, also known as Key Performance Indicator (KPI) [17]. These indicators are defined by each company, and in this paper the indicators assumed are assiduity, safety, mission and records. Based on these indicators, many decisions could be made in the enterprise, such as vertical or horizontal promotions or an annual bonus.

Another goal is to explore a HUD-like interface for access to complex data and information in maintenance, considering the E-Maintenance system. In Figs. 1 and 2, UI would be voice controlled, therefore the possible interactions have be clear for users.

The third goal is to propose different forms of AR in maintenance, considering technologies aggregated by the E-Maintenance system. An example of technology is the Internet of Things (IoT), which will deploy sensors in objects of the work place and allow a reading of the environment through them. Aware of this richness of information, Figs. 3, 4, 5, 6 and 8 were prototyped to use AR to display real time sensor data to users.

The next goal is to explore procedure and risk awareness of the maintenance activities in a UI. Several AR interfaces for maintenance were proposed in literature [7], but always focusing on procedure, while the prototype in this paper also focus on awareness of risks during the task (Fig. 5).

The last goal is to explore a team awareness interface. The improvement of team situation awareness is an important research in industry [18], especially to avoid accidents, and the prototype from Fig. 8 is a step in this direction.

Finishing this discussion, a future option is to integrate the interface (and the application) in a higher level of Gamification (the advanced level). This would imply the connection of the application to a virtual world, in such a way that real world actions would (like the correct and efficient execution of a task) give virtual rewards to the worker. For instance, a day of work could result in an item or virtual coin in a virtual game (like a facebook game, or an MMORPG like World of Warcraft). This way, users would feel real life connect to the virtual world, and could be motivated by not only physical (material) rewards like money, but also virtual rewards, and thus be motivated through this virtual gratifications. According to Reeves and Read [15], this practice is unavoidable and will probably be applied to every work in the future, as a way to stimulate and motivate to obtain higher productivities.

Besides Gamification, there are other strategies that can be used to motivate workers and can be adopted in the future. Big data could be used to collect interesting information about the person life that can help motivate, such as the following messages demonstrates (they are presented to the user):

- Remember that today your *"favorite sport team"* is playing at 10 pm, and in days that you conclude more than 5 missions, your team has a 75 % win rate. Keep up the good work!
- This is the last mission today and the guiding system will follow you closer to assist finishing it faster, so you can go home. By the way, your son just posted that he arrived home.
- This mission will be long, with an average duration of 8 h. However, by the end of it, you will have fulfilled your goal for the month!

Concluding, in this paper it is explored a User Interface without technological limitations for maintenance activities, considering visualization and interface solutions, such as Heads-up Displays (HUD) and Augmented Reality (AR), and design proposals for enhancing the user motivation, such as Gamification. In future projects, this prototype will be evaluated with usability heuristics and user testing in a simulated virtual environment.

Acknowledgments. The authors wish to thank CNPq and FAPESP for the support to the INCT-SEC Project, processes 573963/2008-8 and 08/57870-9.

References

1. Holmberg, K.: Introduction E-Maintenance, pp. 1–3. Springer, London (2010)
2. Ott, J.: Maintenance executives seek greater efficiency. Aviation Week Space Technol. **142** (20), 43–44 (1995)
3. Bangemann, T., Rebeuf, X., Reboul, D., Schulze, A., Szymanski, J., Thomesse, J.-P., Thron, M., Zerhouni, N.: PROTEUS - Creating Distributed Maintenance Systems through an Itegration Platform. J. Comput. Ind. **57**(6), 539–551 (2006)
4. Levrat E., Iung B.: ―TELMA: A full E-Maintenance platform‖, in Centre de Recherche en Automatique de Nancy Université (2007)
5. Nazir, S., Colombo, S., Manca, D.: The role of Situation Awareness for the Operators of Process Industry‖. Chem. Eng. Trans. **26**, 303–308 (2012)
6. Sá M., Carriço L.: ―Lessons from early stages design of mobile applications‖, In: Proceedings of the 10th international conference on Human computer interactionwith mobile devices and services (MobileHCI 2008), pp. 127–136 ACM (2008)
7. Oliveira, A., Araujo, R., Jardine, A.: A Human Centered View on E-Maintenance. Chemical Engineeriing Transactions **33**, 385–390 (2013). ISBN 978-88-95608-24-2, ISSN 1974-9791
8. Kiassat A.: System Performance Analysis Considering Human-related Factors, Doctor of Philosophy thesis, University of Toronto (2013)
9. Deterding, S.: Gamification: Designing for motivation. Interact. **19**(4), 14–17 (2008)
10. Flatla D.R., Gutwin C., Nacke L.E., Bateman S., Mandryk R.L.: Calibration Games: Making Calibration Tasks Enjoyable by Adding Motivating Game Elements. In: Proceedings of the 24th annual ACM symposium on User interface software and technology (UIST '11), pp. 403–412 (2011)
11. Umstot, Denis D., Bell, Cecil H., Mitchell, Terence R.: Effects of job enrichment and task goals on satisfaction and productivity: Implications for job design. J. Appl. Psychol. **61**(4), 379–394 (1976)
12. Ferster, C.B.: BF Skinner. Copley Publishing Group, Schedules of reinforcement (1997)

13. Hsu, S.H., Wen, M.-H., Wu, M.-C.: Exploring user experiences as predictors of MMORPG addiction‖. Comput. Educ. **53**(3), 990–999 (2009)
14. Methenitis, M.: A Tale of Two Worlds: New US Gambling Laws and the MMORPG‖. Gaming Law Rev. **11**(4), 436–439 (2007)
15. Reeves B., Read J.: Total Engagement: Using Games and Virtual Worlds to Change the Way People Work and Businesses Compete. Harvard Business School Press, Boston (2009)
16. Henderson, S., Feiner, S.: Exploring the Benefits of Augmented Reality Documentation for Maintenance and Repair. IEEE Trans. Visual Comput. Graphics **16**(1), 4–16 (2010)
17. Weber A., Thomas R.: "Key Performance Indicators: Measuring and Managing the Maintenance Function, Ivara Corporation (2005)
18. Endsley, M., Robertson, M.: Situation Awareness in aircraft maintenance teams. Int. J. Ind. Ergon. **26**(2), 301–325 (2000)

Representation Model of Collaboration Mechanism with Channel Theory

Patchanee Patitad and Hidetsugu Suto[✉]

Muroran Institute of Technology, Hokkaido 050-8585, Japan
info@sdlabo.net
http://www.sdlabo.net

Abstract. In this paper, a mathematical model of collaboration mechanism is proposed. Channel theory is utilized to accomplish this goal. Collaboration between engineering course students and entertainment media course students was represented by using the proposed model. As the results, there are two infomorphisms were deduced from the classifications. It means the students could gain new knowledge from the collaboration process and we can say that the collaboration is effective. To verify the effect of the collaboration, a workshop was conducted. During the workshop, the participants were asked to answer the questionnaires to investigate how the knowledge of each member changed. The number of the keywords of the first questionnaire and the second questionnaire were compared. The number of keywords of entertainment media course grow 95 % on average. Meanwhile, the number of keywords of engineering course grow 150 % on average. As the results, the participants can enlarge their knowledge from the collaboration.

Keywords: Collaboration · Channel theory · Knowledge sharing

1 Introduction

Nowadays, knowledge has the powerful influence which leads business organization to survive in the competition among firms. Knowledge sharing stands for exchanging and transmitting knowledge among individuals, groups, and organizations for the purpose of improving organizational competitiveness [1]. Knowledge sharing is a fundamental means through which employees can contribute to knowledge creating, innovation, and ultimately the competitive advantage of the organization [2]. Many researches have shown that knowledge sharing and fusion are positively related to reductions in production costs, faster completion of new product development projects, team performance, firm innovation capabilities, and firm performance [3]. Due to the advantages of knowledge sharing, many organizations pay attention to knowledge management system to support knowledge sharing.

Collaboration is a promised method which provides benefits of knowledge sharing to us. Collaboration is a process in which two or more members from different area participate in knowledge transmitting process for achieving a common task or a goal [4]. During collaboration process, synergetic effects among

© Springer International Publishing Switzerland 2015
S. Yamamoto (Ed.): HIMI 2015, Part II, LNCS 9173, pp. 511–521, 2015.
DOI: 10.1007/978-3-319-20618-9_51

team members would contribute to generate novel knowledge. So, collaborations which derive powerful synergetic effects are required in teamwork. However, the way to produce effective collaboration is implicit because collaboration is a complex, multi-dimensional process which is characterized by constructs such as coordination, communication, meaning, relationships and trust [5]. Thus, this study aims to propose a mathematical model of collaboration mechanism in order to investigate the process.

Channel Theory [6] is utilized to achieve this goal, and Chu space [7] is adopted to account for knowledge in collaboration system. Chu space is a mathematical construction, which represents scheme of infomorphism. To verify the proposed model, an example of collaboration in an international design workshop is shown.

2   Literature Reviews

2.1   Related Works

There are many researches have found that a team which consists of different disciplines members succeeded to create new idea [8,9]. According to these researches, the combination of diverse backgrounds members played an important role to bring about the new idea. As these examples show, different perspective is an important factor to create effective collaboration.

During collaboration process, synergetic effects among team members contribute to generate novel knowledge. However, there are a few researches which focus on qualitative analysis in collaboration process. Thus, a representation model of collaboration mechanism is proposed in order to support the qualitative analysis. The model is built based on Channel Theory. Channel Theory provides a logical framework to discuss transition of meaning through a collaboration.

Channel theory has been used in various fields. For example, Suto et al. have proposed a representation model for communication medium with Channel Theory [10]. This model is used to describe semantic information flow, which is corresponding to a kind of medium. Kawakami et al. have proposed a framework of modeling that involves diversity and context dependencies base on Channel Theory [11]. It has the potential to describe diverse understanding based on the information flows. Schorlemmer [12] proposed a formalization of knowledge sharing scenarios by using diagram in the Chu category. Basic ideas of Channel Theory and Chu spaces are referred briefly in the following sections.

2.2   Channel Theory

Channel Theory provides a mathematical framework of qualitative theory of information. The basic concepts of Channel Theory consist of classification, local logic, infomorphism, and information channel.

A **classification:** $\langle A = tok(A), typ(A), \models_A \rangle$ consists of a set of objects to be classified; $tok(A)$, called the "tokens of A," a set of objects used to classify the tokens; $typ(A)$, called the "types of A," and a binary relation $\models_A$ between $tok(A)$ and $typ(A)$ indicating the types into which tokens are classified.

Given a classification A, a pair $\langle \Gamma, \triangle \rangle$ of subsets of $typ(A)$ is called a "sequent of A." A token $a \in tok(A)$ **satisfies** $\langle \Gamma, \triangle \rangle$ if a is of type α for $\forall_\alpha \in \Gamma$; then a is of type β for $\exists_\beta \in \triangle$. If every token $a \in A$ satisfies $\langle \Gamma, \triangle \rangle$; then $\langle \Gamma, \triangle \rangle$ is called a "constraint" supported by A, and denoted as $\Gamma \vdash_A \triangle$.

A **local logic:** $\mathcal{L} = A, \vdash_{\mathcal{L}}$, $N_{\mathcal{L}}$ consists of a classification A, a set $\vdash_{\mathcal{L}}$ of sequents of A called the constraints of $\mathcal{L}$, and a set $N_{\mathcal{L}} \subseteq tok(A)$ of tokens called the **normal tokens** of $\mathcal{L}$, which satisfy all the constraints of $\mathcal{L}$.

$\mathcal{L}$ is **sound** if $N_{\mathcal{L}} = tok(A)$. $\mathcal{L}$ is **complete** if $\vdash_{\mathcal{L}}$ includes all the constraints supported by A. Given a classification A, a sound and complete local logic, called $Log(A)$, is generated from A.

An **infomorphism** is important relationship between two classifications and provides a way of moving information back and forth between them. Infomorphism $\langle f^\vee, f^\wedge \rangle$ is a pair of functions, in which $f^\vee$ is a function from the types of one of these classifications to the types of the other, and $f^\wedge$ is a function from the tokens of one of these classifications to the tokens of the other. Given two classifications A and B, an infomorphism from A to B written as $A \rightleftharpoons B$ satisfies the following Fundamental Property of Infomorphisms:

$$f^\vee(b) \models_A \text{ iff } b \models_B f^\wedge(\alpha) \tag{1}$$

for each token $b \in tok(B)$ and each type $\alpha \in typ(A)$. Relationship between two classifications, A and B is shown in Fig. 1.

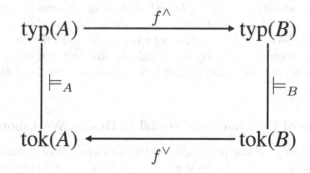

Fig. 1. Infomorphism of between classification A and classification B

An **information channel:** $C = f_i : A_i \rightleftharpoons C$, where $i \in I$, is an index family of infomorphisms with a common codomain C called the "core the channel." I is an index set.

2.3   Chu Spaces

Category theory (CT) has been provided a unified language for managing conceptual complexity in mathematics and computer science. Barr used Channel

Theory as models of linear logic. Subsequently, Pratts has applied Chu space on variety of mathematical objects [13].

A Chu space A over a set S is a triple (A, r, X), consists of a set A of *tokens*, a set of X of *types*, and a function $r : A \times X \to S$ gives a binary relation, and S is a set consists 0 and 1. In the Chu space context, tokens are usually called *points*, while types are called *states*. It becomes possible to represent a variety of structured objects.

Let $\mathbf{A} = (A, r, X)$ and $\mathbf{B} = (B, s, Y)$ be two Chu spaces. A *Chutransform* from $\mathbf{A}$ to $\mathbf{B}$ is a pair (f, g) consisting of functions $f : \mathbf{A} \to \mathbf{B}$ and $g : \mathbf{Y} \to \mathbf{X}$ such that $s(f(a), y) = r(a, g(y))$ for all a in $\mathbf{A}$ and y in $\mathbf{Y}$. It can be seen that the notion of classification is corresponding with the notion of Chu space and also an infomorphism is a kind of Chu transform.

3   A Model of Collaboration Mechanism

In order to clarify the way to produce an effective collaboration, the mathematical model of collaboration mechanism is proposed based on Channel Theory. The outline of proposed model is shown in Fig. 2. Assume a situation in which two members who have different academic backgrounds work jointly in a group. Each solid circle indicates a set of knowledge held by a member. Due to the different disciplines, each knowledge is different with another. That is why the two circles do not overlap entirely with each other. Due to synergetic effects in the collaboration, team performance cannot be calculated as a simple union of the abilities of each member $(A \cup B)$. Possible knowledge domain of the team can be indicated as grey area $(R - (A \cup B))$. This situation can be represented by using classification of Channel Theory as shown below the circles in the Fig. 2. Here, we can deduce the knowledge, which can be obtained from synergetic effects by using infomorphism. By using this scheme, we can evaluate an effect of a collaboration by representing what new knowledge can be gotten from the collaboration.

3.1   Example of Collaboration Model in Design Workshop

To verify the ability of the proposed model, an example of collaboration in a design workshop is used for a case study. The collaboration between engineering course students and entertainment media course students is discussed. Knowledge of engineering course students are performed as classification of engineering knowledge. Meanwhile, classification of entertainment media knowledge shows knowledge of entertainment media course students.

Classification of Engineering Knowledge (A). A classification of engineering knowledge can be described as a classification as following:

$$tok(A) = \{AR\ code, GPS, Voice\ commands\}$$
$$typ(A) = \{Information\ pull, Interaction, Information\ push\}$$

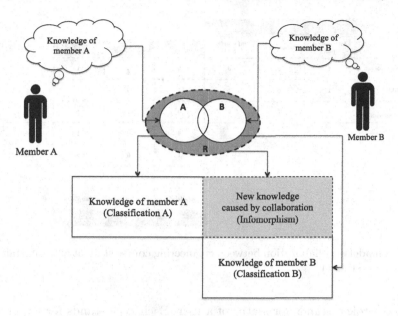

Fig. 2. A representation model of collaboration mechanism

$$AR\ code \models_A Information\ pull \qquad\qquad GPS \models_A Information\ pull$$
$$GPS \models_A Information\ push \quad Voice\ commands \models_A Information\ pull$$
$$Voice\ commands \models_A Interaction$$

Each token stands for an information technology such as AR (Augmented Reality) code, GPS (Global Positioning System) and Voice commands respectively. Each type stands for a property of the technology. Each type stands for a type of communication. Type of "Information pull" means information is provided when the user requested it. Type of "Interaction" means information is provided through interaction with the system. Type of "Information push" means the system give the user a notification when information is available. For instance, voice commands is suitable for interactive information pull system. The classification can be represented as a Chu map shown in Fig. 3 (A).

Classification of Entertainment Media Knowledge (B). Requirements of users are indicated as entertainment media knowledge. The classification of entertainment media knowledge is described as a classification as following:

$$tok(B) = \{Elder, Adult, Child\}$$
$$typ(B) = \{Readability, Entertainment, Simplicity\}$$

$$Elder \models_B Simplicity \qquad Adult \models_B Readability \quad Adult \models_B Simplicity$$
$$Child \models_B Entertainment \quad Child \models_B Simplicity$$

(A)			(I)			
Information pull	Interaction	Information push				
AR Code	1	0	0	0	0	1
GPS	1	0	1	1	0	1
Voice commands	1	1	0	0	1	1
				0	0	1	Elder
				1	0	1	Adult
				0	1	1	Child
				Readability	Entertainment	Simplicity
				(B)		

Fig. 3. A model of collaboration between engineering course student and entertainment media course student

Here, each token stands for status of a user. Each type stands for requirement of the users. For example, older declines visualization and they need simplicity design. The classification can be represented as a Chu map shown in Fig. 3 (B).

Infomorphisms from a to B (I). An infomorphism from A to B is derived as shown in Fig. 3 (I). Eventually, the collaboration between them can be represented as matrices shown in Fig. 3 by using the proposed method. The model consists of three classifications, i.e. A, B, and I. Each line in the matrix (I) means a combination between a token in classification A and a token in classification B. For example, "AR code" in (A) is combined with Older in (B) because the first line of (I) has the same element of the first line in (B). While, each column in the matrix (I) means a combination between a type in classification A and a type in classification B. For example, Gameness in (B) is combined with "Interaction" in (A) because the middle column of (I) and (A) have the same element. In this case, infomorphisms are established from "classification of engineering knowledge" to "classification of entertainment media knowledge." Two infomorphisms have been deduced as shown in Fig. 4.

Each situation explains new knowledge, which engineering course students and entertainment media course students can obtain in the collaboration process.

1	2
0 0 1	0 0 1
1 0 1	0 1 1
0 1 1	1 0 1

Fig. 4. Infomorphisms from engineering knowledge to entertainment media knowledge

It implies that there are two situations could occur when engineering student and entertainment media student collaborate in a workshop. First infomorphism shows that

$$f^\wedge(AR\ code) = Elder, \quad f^\wedge(GPS) = Adult, \quad f^\wedge(Voice\ commands) = Child$$

This infomorphism shows us that AR code is corresponding to elder, GPS is corresponding to adult and Voice commands technology is corresponding to child. These results provide us a new knowledge for selecting proper information technology device in accordance with the user's generation, i.e. we should provide AR code technology for elder, GPS for adult and Voice commands for child. Meanwhile, second infomorphism shows that

$$f^\wedge(AR\ code) = Elder, \quad f^\wedge(GPS) = Child, \quad f^\wedge(Voice\ commands) = Adult$$

From this infomorphism, AR code technology can be implied as same as infomorphism 1. But GPS is corresponding to child and Voice commands is corresponding to adult.

From the above discussion, we can say that the collaboration is effective because it can provide new knowledge to the members.

4 Case Study: International Design Workshop

To verify the discussion in the previous section, an international design workshop was held in Hokkaido, Japan from 25–28, October 2014. The participants were students from engineering courses of universities in Japan and students from an entertainment media course of an university in Thailand. The theme of this workshop is "Enhance tourism." The schedule of the workshop is described as follows:

Collecting Before Data. Before start collaboration process, a questionnaire was conducted in order to observe current knowledge of each member. Participants were asked to answer the questionnaire within 30 minuets. The questionnaire was open questions in which participants are asked to describe their ideas about how to enhance tourism in Hokkaido by describing as keywords, methods and expected results.

Survey. During the workshop, members were instructed to observe many famous sightseeing places in Hokkaido, Japan. The instructor assigned participants to take photographs of interesting things that they found by using Category cam application. Category cam application is an application which helps users to take photographs together with a short note. After a user took a photograph, he/she can select labels from Kansei (Emotion), Cultural, Physical and Other, that explain the photograph accurately. Then, the user can give a short note about the photograph. By using this application, a user can record their impression easily. Snapshots of screen of Category cam application are shown in Fig. 5.

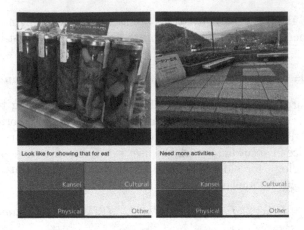

Fig. 5. Snapshots of screen of category cam application

Group Work and Presentation. After the survey step, members were divided into four groups. Each group was comprised students of engineering course and students of entertainment media course. Members made group discussions with own team members to propose a project to enhance tourism in Hokkaido. During the group discussions, KJ method [14] was conducted. KJ method is a fundamental tool to organize ideas and data through a brainstorming. During the process of KJ method, all members were sharing their observed information by using the photographs and short note, which were taken in the survey stage. Then, they worked together to create a project to develop tourism in Hokkaido, Japan. In the last day of the workshop, each group made a presentation about their proposal. Scenes of the workshop are shown in Fig. 6.

Fig. 6. Scenes of the international design workshop

Collecting After Data. After the presentation was finished, the participants were asked to answer the questionnaire again to investigate how the knowledge of each member changed. The questions in the second questionnaire was same as the first one. Examples of completed questionnaire sheets are shown in Fig. 7. Important keywords were picked up from the questionnaires. The number of the keywords of the first questionnaire and the second questionnaire were compared. The number of keywords of entertainment media course grow 95 % on average. Meanwhile, the number of keywords of engineering course grow 150 % on average. The results are shown in Fig. 8 as bar graphs. From the results, we can see that participants can enlarge their knowledge from the collaboration. Consequently, we can say that this workshop could make effective collaboration.

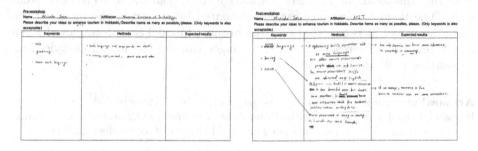

Fig. 7. An example of a set of questionnaire of a member

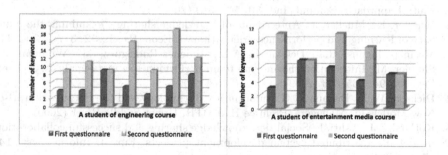

Fig. 8. The number of keywords which have gotten from participants by comparing between the first and second questionnaires

5 Conclusion

In this paper, the authors have represented a model of collaboration mechanism based on Channel Theory. Collaboration between engineering course students and entertainment media course students was represented by using the proposed model. In the example, classification A stands for knowledge of engineering student and classification B stands for knowledge of entertainment media student. As the results, there are two infomorphisms were deduced from the classifications. It means the students could gain new knowledge from the collaboration process and we can say that the collaboration is effective.

To verify the effect of the collaboration, a workshop was conducted. The participants were student from engineering courses of university in Japan and students from an entertainment media course of university in Thailand. During the workshop, the participants were asked to answer the questionnaires to investigate how the knowledge of each member changed. The results show that the participants can enlarge their knowledge from the collaboration.

The proposed model can represent new knowledge which members can obtain from the collaboration. This new knowledge could lead the team to novel solutions. The team performance can be estimated by analyzing the model of the team. Moreover, it is expected that the proposed model can be employed when a new team is organized. The team manager can use the model as a decision supporting tool for organizing a team.

Acknowledgement. This work was supported by Grants-in-Aid for Scientific Research from Japan Society for the Promotion of Science (NO.23611025) and Grants-in-Aid for research advancement from Muroran Institute of Technology (2014).

References

1. Cheng, T.: Knowledge sharing in virtual enterprises via an ontology-based access control approach. Comput. Ind. **59**, 502–519 (2008)
2. Matzler, K., Mueller, J.: Antecedents of knowledge sharing - examining the influence of learning and performance orientation. J. Econ. Psych. **32**, 317–329 (2011)
3. Mesmer-Magnus, R.J., DeChurch, A.L., Jimenez-Rodriguez, M., Wildman, J., Shuffler, M.: Information sharing and team performance: a meta-analysis. J. Appl. Psychol. **94**, 535–546 (2009)
4. Dickson, W.G., DeSanctis, G.: Information Technology and the Future Enterprise: New Models for Managers. Prentice Hall PTR, Upper Saddle River (2000)
5. Kotlarsky, J., Oshri, I.: Social ties, knowledge sharing and successful collaboration in globally distributed system development projects. Eur. J. Inform. Syst. **14**, 37–48 (2005)
6. Barwise, J., Seligman, J.: Information Flow: The Logic of Distributed Systems. Cambridge Univ. Press, Cambridge (1997)
7. Barr, M.: Autonomous Categories. Lect. Notes. Math., vol. 752. Springer, Heidelberg (1979)
8. James, W.Y.: Technique for Producing Ideas. McGraw-Hill Professional, New York (2003)
9. Brown, T., Wyatt, J.: Design thinking for social innovation. Stanford Soc. Innov. Rev. Winter **8**(1), 30–35 (2010)
10. Suto, H., Patitad, P., Kang, N.: A collaboration support tool for multi-cultural design team based on extended ADT model. In: Yamamoto, S. (ed.) HCI 2014, Part I. LNCS, vol. 8521, pp. 548–557. Springer, Heidelberg (2014)

11. Kawakami, H., Hattori, T., Shiose, T., Katai, O.: Modeling of system diversity based on qualitative information theory. Wseas. Trans. Syst. **10**, 2411–2417 (2006)
12. Schorlemmer, M.: Duality In Knowledge Sharing. The University of Edinburgh, UK (2002)
13. Pratt, V.: Chu space and their interpretation as concurrent objects. In: van Leeuwen, J. (ed.) Computer Science Today. LNCS, vol. 1000, pp. 392–405. Springer, Heidelberg (1995)
14. Kawakita, J.: The Original KJ Method (Revised Edition). Meguro, Tokyo (1991)

Using Wearable and Contextual Computing to Optimize Field Engineering Work Practices

Roberto S. Silva Filho[(✉)], Ching-Ling Huang, Anuj Tewari,
James Jobin, and Piyush Modi

GE Global Research, 2623 Camino Ramon, San Ramon, CA 94583, USA
{silva_filho, chingling.huang, anuj.tewari,
jobin, modi}@ge.com

Abstract. Industrial work, as performed in field engineering and manufacturing, is inherently different from traditional office work. Industrial work is highly mobile and physical, and involves continuous interaction between people and machines in settings such as factory floors, power plants, oil rigs, locomotive maintenance yards, etc. This domain has recently benefitted from a set of disruptive technologies such as the Internet of Things (IoT) [2], mobile and wearable computing, and contextual software applications. In particular, GE's Industrial Internet initiative [1] aims at researching new ways to connect people and machines, enabling communications between people and traditional software systems, between people at work, and between people and intelligent machines. When allied with wearable and mobile computing, the Industrial Internet enables new forms of contextual user experiences focusing on the delivery of the right information to the right user at the right time and place. Moreover, these new technologies have enabled experiences that better adapts to industrial workers' needs. For example, using virtual reality glasses and natural language interaction, workers can readily access information about their tasks at hand, the machines nearby, and people located at a distance. This is achieved with minimal distraction, in a proactive way, leveraging the knowledge about each person's tasks and surroundings. In this paper, we describe a general approach and architecture designed to support contextual and mobile applications in the industrial domain and the application of this architecture in the development of the MyWorld application, a contextual mobile applications that works as a single point of entry for a field engineer's needs.

Keywords: Mobility · Collaboration · Wearable computing · Field engineering · Smart manufacturing · Virtual reality · Workflow automation

1 Introduction

In industrial application domains such as service engineering and manufacturing, people, machines, and information must come together to achieve common goals. People utilize various tools and interact with multiple machines and devices to perform complex tasks. Those tasks usually must follow well-defined procedures and guidelines and are subject to continuous quality checks. Workers' expertise may vary according to the tasks they have to perform, and collaboration may emerge motivated by different

© Springer International Publishing Switzerland 2015
S. Yamamoto (Ed.): HIMI 2015, Part II, LNCS 9173, pp. 522–533, 2015.
DOI: 10.1007/978-3-319-20618-9_52

needs such as information, reporting, quality assurance, etc. Machines are becoming not only tools utilized in the production but also important sources of information that, when mined and analyzed, can be used to improve operational and maintenance efficiency. For example, machines can supply production quality information, energy consumption, and key performance parameters that can be used to diagnose problems, trigger maintenance procedures or adjust the production throughput. Moreover, industrial environments have different data, information and work dependencies among people. For example, workers in a factory have parts and supply dependencies on one another, and must perform their work under pre-defined quality guidelines that are usually assessed by other workers. Field engineers need to follow inspection and maintenance procedures during factory operation outages to recover the proper operation of machines while minimizing downtime and production delays. Railroad inspectors need to assess the safety of train cars, and must find the best ways to reposition those cars in order to load the next train.

In spite of these well-known requirements, today's service and manufacturing information systems are less than optimal. They are implemented for traditional desktop computing environments, and therefore, lack the mobility and contextual characteristics of industrial workspaces. Consequently, in many of today's industrial environments, traditional modes of interaction such as paper and radio communication are still commonplace. Workers rely on printed schematics, field notes, and radio links with experts. Very often, workers have to commute back and forth from field offices located far away from the workshop in order to search for documents, write reports, e-mail experts or interact with managers. In this context, the goal of our research is to address those and other industrial work inefficiencies, and provide the user with contextual information in a way that does not obstruct her work. We achieve this by combining contextual and communication services with mobile and wearable computing platforms, together with environmental sensing.

This paper is organized as follows. In the next section, we discuss the physical and information architecture utilized in our approach. We showcase the use of this architecture in the development of MyWorld as described in Sect. 3. We then conclude by discussing lessons learned from the use of the approach and some user feedback in Sect. 4, and discuss related work in Sect. 5.

2   General Approach and Architecture

To address the afore-mentioned characteristics of industrial work, automation systems should embrace the mobile and collaborative nature of industrial work by means of integrated hardware and software systems. From a hardware perspective, the system must be portable: wearable and/or mobile, and must cope with weak network connectivity and disconnected operation, which are common in industrial environments. Furthermore, it should be portable and compatible with the type of hands-on tasks performed by industrial users. From a software perspective, the system must support deep context harvesting from multiple corporate sources, continuous environment sensing, including surrounding environmental and wearable devices and machines, as well as indoor and outdoor positioning systems integration. Additionally, information should be properly formatted and delivered to users using naturalistic interfaces including head mounted displays, audio visual clues and tactile notifications (e.g. vibration).

Figure 1 illustrates the type of integration between the smart machines and tools, wearable devices, and corporate information systems we aim at supporting. Information from smart machines and devices are combined with corporate information systems data such as task models, schematics, documents, historical databases, and with indoor and outdoor location positioning systems. That information is used to anticipate and deliver information to users, and to guide users through complex procedures. By utilizing devices such as head mounted displays, wearable and mobile computers, users have unobtrusive access to information with minimal impact to the task at hand.

From a software architecture perspective (shown in Fig. 2), the system combines information mined from cloud-based information services with real-time environmental sensing. This information is processed locally and delivered to end-users via natural language and augmented reality interfaces. The main software components of our reference architecture include:

Corporate Cloud-Based Services: These services provide standardized access (mainly in the form of RESTful Web services [3]) to existing and legacy information systems including Customer Relationship Management (CRM) databases, Factory Management System (FMS), and Enterprise Resource Planning (ERP) systems. These systems are mined for relevant information including project-specific documents, user assigned tasks, preferences, and schedules. This information is abstracted and managed by the context fabric, which externalizes that information to client-side contextual services in each wearable and mobile client instance.

Collaboration Services: These are another important class of cloud-based services. They enable user location and communication with key personnel in the field, e.g., managers and experts in equipment and procedure. Video and document sharing is also supported allowing for communication between workers and experts.

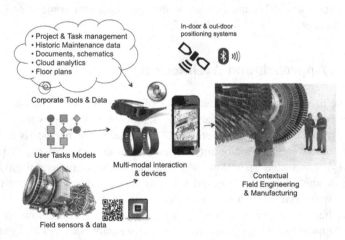

Fig. 1. Integrated contextual mobile services overview

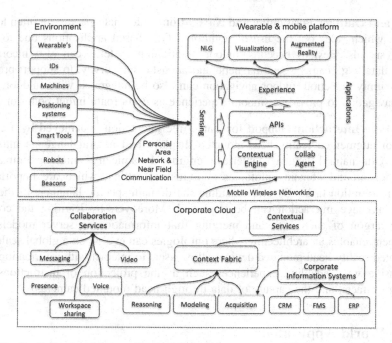

Fig. 2. General architecture for industrial internet contextual wearable computing

Wearable and Mobile Software Platform: Comprises a set of software services that combine data from cloud services with real-time information from the environment. They work closely with hardware devices such as head mounted displays and smart phones to support different types of experiences including gestures, natural language and touch, but provide a single point of access to user information. The multi-modal, multiple-device characteristic of the wearable platform allows users to select between different modes of interaction and information channels. For example, one can choose to display document data in the heads-up display or in the wearable device, to receive notifications as audio or as visual clues, and to interact with the system via touch or voice. Offline operation is another important characteristic of the software architecture. Both client-side agents for the context engine and collaboration services are supported. They provide caching, delayed updates, and prefetching of data in support of dis-connected operation.

Contextual Services: At the core of our wearable and mobile software platform there are contextual services responsible for gathering information from different sources, abstracting them into domain models, and supporting contextual queries relevant to each application. The context engine consists of cloud-based and mobile-based services. This separation allows disconnected operation and integration with user-specific surroundings information.

Environmental Sensing: Provides a set of protocols and interfaces to machines in the field, beacons, RFID tags, smart tools, as well as communication with other wearable devices.

Indoor and Outdoor Positioning and Navigation: Industrial systems are often located indoors, which rules out the use of traditional GPS-based applications due to weak satellite signals. Besides beacons, indoor positioning systems can also incorporate sensory data, e.g., camera, geo-magnetic and acoustic site survey, to support presence and proximity detection. Indoor navigation can also be integrated with outdoor, GPS-based navigation to provide a smooth experience as users roam in/out both domains.

Hands-Free Interaction: Support for hands-free interaction is achieved by a combination of augmented reality head-mounted displays and natural language interfaces (NLG). Our natural language interface engine dynamically builds grammar and knowledge around domain ontologies in industrial setting, which are important in speech recognition tasks. By understanding the domain-specific language of the user, natural language interaction can be improved. Moreover, by learning the context-specific jargon of each user, and merging that information in server models, this component enables an architecture where ontologies can evolve on a global scale. The augmented reality head mounted devices allow users to interact with information in an unobtrusive way, enabling experiences such as the projection of instructions over existing artifacts, and the capture of data through head mounted cameras.

3   MyWorld Application

In order to showcase the different components of our reference architecture, and the mobile and collaborative experiences it affords, we developed a contextual prototype application called MyWorld. This mobile application is a single point of access to information needs of field engineers. In doing so, it works as a tool for optimizing field workers performance in their daily activities. MyWorld combines indoors navigation, task guidance, access to maintenance documents, and communication channels to experts. From a hardware perspective, MyWords integrates capabilities from Google Glass (wearable computing), iPads (mobile device), iBeacons (BLE – Bluetooth Low Energy – presence beacons installed in the environment), and Augmented Reality applications for field maintenance operations.

In a typical site inspection scenario, a field manager walks through the factory or maintenance yard floor wearing a Google Glass. The MyWorld app running on this device utilizes image recognition software to identify nearby assets. It identifies individual milling machines, CNCs and other assets. Assets are complex machinery and heavy-duty equipment used in manufacturing, energy generation, transportation, among others. Once an asset is recognized, a query to cloud services is issued, looking for current status and historical operational and maintenance information of that asset. A health status of the machine in focus is then computed, and conveyed to the field manager through a hue (green, red, yellow), which is superposed around the asset image in the Google Glass. This allows the field manager to easily identify the health condition of the asset. If the machine requires any kind of maintenance, a red or yellow hue is shown around the asset with a brief description of the problem. The field manager is then given the option to dispatch a qualified field engineer (or FE) to fix or service the machine. In this process, the system locates the best field engineer based on past work orders, experience with the asset at hand, and his calendar availability from corporate cloud services.

Once an FE is assigned to the job and arrives at the site, he can use MyWorld application, executing on his iPad (shown in Fig. 3) to quickly locate tools and navigate to the faulty asset. The site is properly instrumented with iBeacons [4] used to tag machines and work cells. Through in-door location algorithms, those beacons provide the exact location of the user in the factory floor, together with a map with relevant assets.

Once the FE arrives at a work site, he utilizes this map to locate the asset, and to get directions to that machine from his current location. The application updates the user location in real time. With assets and field engineers positioned on the factory floor, indoor navigation can guide a field engineer with turn-by-turn instructions. This is useful in situations where field engineers are unfamiliar with a site they are assigned to work at. There have been instances where an FE had to spend 2 h finding the right tools for a 10-minute maintenance job simply because the factory floor had an unfamiliar layout and thus much time was spent on locating the tools.

One example screenshot of indoor navigation is shown in Fig. 4 where the FE is guided on the map to reach the Tool Depot via the Milling Station. In order to facilitate the asset location, a photo is shown at the top left corner of the app. The in-door map continuously updates the user location with respect to existing assets, and provides a suggested route for the maintenance task. In the example of Fig. 4, the user first gathers tools in depot, then returns to milling station for repair.

Once the FE retrieves the required tool and locates the asset needing his attention, an overview of the asset including past activities, sensor readings, and repair history are automatically displayed, as seen in Fig. 5. In Fig. 5, as one example, we see the historical data and detailed maintenance procedure for a milling Station. On the right-hand side of Fig. 5, the relevant events in this asset's history are listed as reference. Only events

Fig. 3. Screenshot of MyWorld application: with iBeacon technology, assets and the field engineer (blue circle) are positioned on the factory digital map (Color figure online).

Fig. 4. Screenshot of MyWorld application: Indoor turn-by-turn navigation enabled by iBeacons installed on site.

relevant to current tasks are shown in this asset lifeline for simplicity. On the left-hand side of Fig. 5, suggested tasks to maintain or fix this asset are listed for field engineer to perform. This combined presentation of status and procedures allows the field engineer to quickly understand what to do without go through pages of asset manual.

Figure 6 shows a detailed maintenance procedure available when the FE clicks on one of the tasks shown in Fig. 5. Note that the detailed instructions in the procedure are prepared by the contextual engine based on analysis of the machine data, identified

Fig. 5. Screenshot of MyWorld application: On the right-hand side, we see the relevant events in this asset's history. On the left-hand side, we see suggested maintenance tasks.

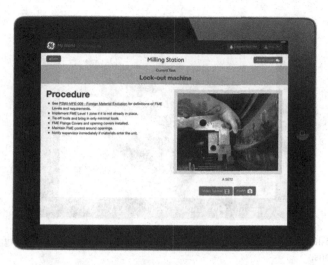

Fig. 6. Screenshot of MyWorld application: Each task in Fig. 5 is explained in details with video to play and augmented reality to help field engineer perform the task.

issue, and the known best practice to resolve the issue. If necessary, the FE can also play one or multiple video clips to demonstrate how to perform the task correctly. Again, this simple way of presenting a procedure allows FE to quickly understand what to do without going through pages of manual.

Additional help can be obtained by using Augmented Reality (or AR). By combining real-time video and 3D asset models, MyWorld provides superimposed step-by-step instructions indicating how to service complex assets. This interactive instruction user interface can greatly help the FE to understand the task at hand and the steps required for its execution. For example, in Fig. 7 we see a real-time view of an asset

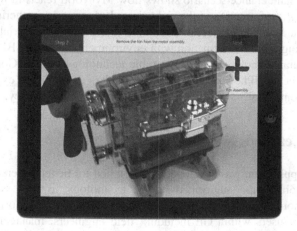

Fig. 7. Screenshot of MyWorld application: Augmented Reality is superimposed on real-time images to give the users step-by-step instructions how to remove the fan assembly.

Fig. 8. Screenshot of MyWorld application: Workflow is integrated with the augmented reality (AR) instructions.

(in this case an engine used for demo purposes) that needs to be serviced. The FE utilizes the iPad and its camera as AR lenses where animated 3D models are used to convey step-by-step instructions. As the FE moves the viewing angle, the superimposed AR will also adjust its rendering so that the AR component is always in the right position with respective to the asset.

MyWorld's user experience is highly contextual, and integrated with the user workflow. As shown in Fig. 8, once the machine is dissembled and problem has been identified (a low fluid level in this example), a menu with action options is provided. Using this menu, the FE can order the fluid and schedule downtime within the app itself. Using the information about the site, and the maintenance procedure itself, MyWorld will also automatically update the maintenance procedure status and notify the site manager when the FE has successfully repaired the asset.

This typical maintenance scenario shows how MyWorld reacts to the user context to provide the right information at the right time. It does so by gathering information form different data sources: project management tools, training material, and expertise databases, mashing up this information with environment data using BLE beacons and camera, and leverages the potential of wearable technology such as Google Glass and mobile devices such as iPhones and iPads. The result is an improved experience where FE can access contextual information to improve operation efficiency.

4 Lessons Learned

The MyWorld application was developed as a test bed for better understanding the use of wearable, mobile, and augmented reality technology in field engineering and manufacturing domains. To this extent, we have showcased MyWorld capability to different types of users within GE including field engineers, management and technology leaders, and have conducted workshops with potential users. This has enabled us to obtain valuable feedback.

These are some of the issues that have been raised as concerns include: the need for adequate ergonomics and usability of both hardware and software platform; the need to cope with unreliable connectivity; Adequate location and positioning in in-door locations; and adequate battery life for a typical work day shift.

Perhaps the most common feedback received with respect to wearable technology has been the need for ergonomics and user-driven ability to control the activation/ deactivation of the technology. For instance, in the words of one FE, "once it goes down, it stays down". Imagine a field worker is using a wearable device, and while performing a task in the field, he has to put it down on the ground or workbench for some reason (e.g., safety and regulation, obtrusion of his view sight or movement, etc.). When this happens, the chances are high that it will stay down and the worker will not put the wearable device back on later. The main lesson here is that any wearable device has to be comfortable and ergonomic enough that a worker does not need to put it down at any point during his daily routine. As a result, we have been porting MyWorld application to industrial-grade head-mounted computing devices that are closely integrated with FEs safety equipment, and that can be repositioned away when not needed while not removing it completely from the body. We are testing head mounted displays that can slide in and out of the user's view sight, and that can be mounted on existing hard hats and safety glasses.

Connectivity is also an important concern that was expressed during our interviews. While the use of mobile technology can significantly improve a worker's productivity, it can also become an impediment if resources become unavailable due to lack of connectivity. Imagine a worker relying on his mobile device for accessing documents and updating status and workflows, and for some reason, the connectivity to the cloud fails. This could mean that he is not able to complete his task, forcing him to wait for the connectivity to be restored or to fall back on low-tech methods such as pen and paper. Adoption of mobile technology will be hindered and workers may reject the technology altogether. As a consequence, we have been developing offline operation algorithms and technology to support disconnected operation.

The lack of reliability and the range of existing indoor location technology poses another set of challenges to using wearable technology. For example, the integration with existing devices such as Bluetooth beacons is not always seamless. Sometimes, it takes a few seconds to lock on to a beacon signal, which means that the worker has to wait until then, thereby delaying his work. We are currently working on technologies that improve the reliability and responsiveness of indoor location.

The battery life of wearable devices is another potential source of usability issues. Most of the devices currently available in the market are not capable of lasting an entire workday, especially if the work involves capturing any video. We have been researching several options as well as algorithms to improve the power efficiency of the applications.

5   Related Work

The experiences afforded by our integrated approach have benefited form research in both industry and academia. Our work combines some of these ideas in the construction of a context-aware software architecture that incorporate contextual information, multi-modal interfaces, virtual reality and mobility. This section discusses some related work in these fields.

Anticipation of workers' needs in industrial environments has been described in [5]. In particular, context information has been used in industrial applications as a way to optimize network bandwidth, power consumption and resource utilization of mobile devices. Context has also been applied to optimize processes in field work automation [6]. Our work exploits the use of context information for optimizing voice interactions and indoor location and task automation, anticipating end-users needs and optimizing user experiences.

A comprehensive survey of technologies for context-awareness in for the internet of things is available in [7]. Current technology is largely focused on the gathering and abstraction of information form sensors and equipment in the field. Our architecture leverage on the functionality provided by our own context engine that integrates not only data from the environment but also from corporate information sources.

Previous work on mobile applications for field service showed the benefits of mobility in these environments [8], and of the use of virtual reality as guiding mechanism in complex tasks [9, 10]. These approaches, however, have little focus on IoT integration and wearable computing. More recently, the work described in [11] presents many challenges faced in the development of industrial field service mobile applications, showing the need for further research in the areas of: indoor positioning systems, beacons, voice and mobile devices; while the work described in [12] showcases the application of IoT and mobility in industrial settings. Our work adds to this body of knowledge, by showcasing the benefits of context-aware mobile & wearable computing for service engineering.

Acknowledgements. The authors gratefully acknowledge the contributions and feedback received from our colleagues, Raju Venkataramana, Bo Yu, and Joe Bolinger. Their contributions to the MyWorld app described in this paper and their feedback have been immensely helpful in writing this paper.

References

1. Introducing the GE's Industrial Internet. http://www.ge.com/stories/industrial-internet
2. Mattern, F., Floerkemeier, C.: From the internet of computers to the internet of things. In: Sachs, K., Petrov, I., Guerrero, P. (eds.) Buchmann Festschrift. LNCS, vol. 6462, pp. 242–259. Springer, Heidelberg (2010)
3. Fielding, R.T., Taylor, R.N.: Principled Design of the Modern Web Architecture. In: Proceedings of the 22Nd International Conference on Software Engineering, pp. 407–416. ACM, New York, NY, USA (2000)
4. Nieminen, J., Gomez, C., Isomaki, M., Savolainen, T., Patil, B., Shelby, Z., Xi, M., Oller, J.: Networking solutions for connecting bluetooth low energy enabled machines to the internet of things. IEEE Netw. **28**, 83–90 (2014)
5. Aehnelt, M., Bader, S., Ruscher, G., Krüger, F., Urban, B., Kirste, T.: Situation aware interaction with multi-modal business applications in smart environments. In: Yamamoto, S. (ed.) HCI 2013, Part III. LNCS, vol. 8018, pp. 413–422. Springer, Heidelberg (2013)

6. Aleksy, M.: Context-sensitive and semantic-based mobile applications in industrial field service. In: 2011 9th IEEE International Conference on Industrial Informatics (INDIN), pp. 1–91 (2011)
7. Perera, C., Zaslavsky, A., Christen, P., Georgakopoulos, D.: Context aware computing for the internet of things: a survey. IEEE Commun. Surv. Tutor. **16**, 414–454 (2014)
8. Aleksy, M., Stieger, B., Vollmar, G.: Case study on utilizing mobile applications in industrial field service. In: IEEE Conf. on Commerce and Enterprise Computing, 2009. CEC 2009, pp. 333–336 (2009)
9. Tumler, J., Mecke, R., Schenk, M., Huckauf, A., Doil, F., Paul, G., Pfister, E.A., Bockelmann, I., Roggentin, A.: Mobile augmented reality in industrial applications: approaches for solution of user-related issues. In: 7th IEEE/ACM International Symposium on Mixed and Augmented Reality, ISMAR 2008, pp. 87–90 (2008)
10. Engelke, T., Keil, J., Rojtberg, P., Wientapper, F., Webel, S., Bockholt, U.: Content first - a concept for industrial augmented reality maintenance applications using mobile devices. In: 2013 IEEE International Symposium on Mixed and Augmented Reality (ISMAR), pp. 251–252 (2013)
11. Aleksy, M., Stieger, B.: Challenges in the Development of Mobile Applications in Industrial Field Service. In: 2009 International Conference on Network-Based Information Systems, NBIS 2009, pp. 586–591 (2009)
12. Tesfay, W.B., Aleksy, M., Andersson, K., Lehtola, M.: Mobile computing application for industrial field service engineering: a case for ABB service engineers. In: 2013 IEEE 38th Conference on Local Computer Networks Workshops (LCN Workshops), pp. 188–193 (2013)

Information and Interaction for Safety, Security and Reliability

SAW-Oriented User Interfaces for Emergency Dispatch Systems

Leonardo Castro Botega[1,2(✉)], Lucas César Ferreira[1],
Natália Pereira Oliveira[1], Allan Oliveira[2], Claudia Beatriz Berti[2],
Vânia Paula de Neris[2], and Regina Borges de Araújo[2]

[1] Computing and Information Systems Research Lab (COMPSI),
Marília Eurípides University (UNIVEM), Marília, São Paulo, Brazil
{lucascesarf, natalia}@univem.edu.br
[2] Wireless Networks and Distributed Interactive Simulations Lab (WINDIS),
Computer Science Department - Federal University of São Carlos (UFSCar),
São Carlos, São Paulo, Brazil
{leonardo_botega, allan_oliveira, claudia.berti,
vania, regina}@dc.ufscar.br

Abstract. Situational awareness (SAW) is a concept widely spread in application areas that require critical decision-making, such as in emergency dispatching systems. SAW is related to the level of consciousness that an individual or team has to a situation. SAW-oriented UI for critical systems require specialized user interfaces to provide operators a dynamic understanding of what is happening in an environment. The information to be managed by such interfaces affects the way operators in an emergency dispatch system acquire, maintain and recover SAW. A challenging issue on the design of SAW-oriented interfaces is how the human-system interaction process can be redesigned for the enhancement of SAW considering environments with potential large scale heterogeneous multi sensors data in complex, ever-changing situations. The problem is increased when such information is subject to uncertainty, which may compromise the acquisition of the situational awareness. Also, humans are expected to make decisions based on their own understanding of what is going on, which allied to experience and expertise can be valuable assets to be used to process refinement during the construction of an incremental knowledge. The goal of this paper is to introduce a conceptual framework to create specialized interfaces that support the participation of operators in the process of SAW acquisition. Such SAW-oriented interface presents a tight integration between the operator and the other phases of an assessment process, such as information quality assessment, information fusion and information visualization. A robbery event report, in an emergency dispatch system, is used as a case study to demonstrate practical and promising results of the applicability of our solution.

Keywords: Situational awareness · User interfaces · Information fusion · Situation assessment

© Springer International Publishing Switzerland 2015
S. Yamamoto (Ed.): HIMI 2015, Part II, LNCS 9173, pp. 537–548, 2015.
DOI: 10.1007/978-3-319-20618-9_53

1 Introduction

Situation Assessment processes, such as Data and Information Fusion, fed by multiple heterogeneous sources and computational intelligence are used to react to the environment changes and help humans providing them means for not only the development of the perception and understanding of what is going on at the environment, at a certain time and space dimension, but also the anticipation of events to come. This routine is known as Situation Awareness (SAW) [1].

A challenging issue on Situation Assessment community is to determine how the process can be redesigned for the enhancement of SAW, which can be severely degraded if low quality information is produced and propagated throughout the process, jeopardizing decision-making [2].

SAW-oriented systems in the support of decision-making rely on data and information quality to provide humans a better understanding of what is happening in the environment. Imperfect information provided by such systems affect the way users perceive cues of events or how they relate them in a meaningful situation, making users susceptible to SAW errors [3].

Both humans and systems may be overwhelmed by the challenges of information processing. Hence, operators and computers need to collaborate and share the responsibilities for the achievement of common goals and tasks the situation assessment may need [4].

When humans and systems interact towards the assessment of situations in an inference process, SAW can be better acquired, maintained and even restored. Many actual SAW-oriented interfaces describe the human role in a semi-automated fashion. Three main user centered views emerge to enrich the final picture with or without intermediate feedback: humans not only as consumers, but also producers of information and humans as actors on the information [5, 6]. Such interfaces seem to lack a deeper investigation on the implications and related issues of the human intervention to build and maintain SAW. The most recent approaches present opportunities for human interaction on each assessment level for enhancing SAW [7].

However, such interfaces, although including the human as actor in the situation assessment process, do not provide access to information across the process and from mono and multi sources.

Hence, this paper introduces a conceptual framework for SAW-Oriented User Interfaces to Emergency Dispatch Systems and also proposes a new interface to promote a tighter integration between situation assessment systems and humans to build and maintain SAW. The goal is to present an interface that can integrate spatial and temporal control of assets, information scoring, information filtering (by quality or domain-specific attributes), data and information modification, visualization cues adaptation and different level fusion-related services access.

Information from an urban robbery situation report is used to illustrate the features of our innovative interface. Such domain presents challenges that are better accommodate by a SAW-oriented interface, such as data acquisition from multiple heterogeneous sources (starting with a voice call from a victim of robbery), the monitoring of the assessment process and the refinement of assessment results.

2   Related Work

This section presents the state-of-the-art regarding SAW-oriented interfaces.. Existing solutions typically aim to empower the operator and the system by intensifying their relationship with information to build a more feasible representation of situations. Among the related work are interaction frameworks for SAW, specialized interfaces and general systems that relies on human-information discourse.

Nwiabu et al. [8] discussed UIs for command and control systems (C2) for the prediction of hydrate formation in pipelines and subsea pipelines. The interface is based on the results of a hierarchical task analysis which decomposes complex scenario objectives into small tasks. The UI is capable of automatic reconfiguration to adapt itself to the current situation and reduce the mental effort of the operator.

Yu et al. [9] presented a new visualization context through the UI, which has an interpretation engine for the operator's needs, defining which information must be presented. For the improvement of the operator's comprehension, a mechanism of fuzzy control was proposed to perform a diffuse search based on specific keywords of the application domain by operators' interactions.

Onal et al. [10] developed a UI based on methods for improving SAW and also for minimizing the mental effort of heavy mining machines. The layout of the UI is based on guided interaction, support panels, virtual maps and multiple screens. Such components are integrated to help operators to avoid accidents due to information overload in operational duties. A Goal-Driven Task Analysis (GDTA) was applied to identify requirements.

Chai and Du [11] developed a framework to support SAW acquisition in a command and control system (attacks in the battlefield). Such framework is based on the use of fused data and classification rules to help recognizing and explaining enemy assets and evolution, in a dynamic environment.

Gomez et al. [12] created an interface prototype to increase SAW of decision-makers while monitoring soccer games in real time. Their performance enables a timely allocation of rescuers to incidents responses. A wireless sensor network is responsible for capturing heterogeneous data and sending them to the operator's interface, which is entirely based on temporal context for representing the scenario. The visualizations include the location of rescuers and the location of the incident inside a stadium.

Feng et al. [13] developed a decision support system that incorporates shared SAW among agents that extract relevant information about entities and represent them to the operator. These agents have the following set of goals and strategies for each SAW level: missions, plans, actions and physical attributes. Then, they are responsible for generating recommendations about the scenario. The UI deals with the spatial-temporal aspects of the evolution of missions. A limited interaction with the recommendations is allowed.

Besides being efficient solutions for the specific application domains, such solutions are limited regarding the management of information being propagated throughout the cycle of situation assessment. Our approach innovates on promoting a full control of the information that is produced on each phase, using uncertainty representation and refinement methods as a resource to control the knowledge that is created, represented and used to assess situations.

3 A Conceptual Framework to Enhance Situational Awareness for Emergency Dispatch Systems

A conceptual framework to enhance Situational Awareness for Emergency Dispatch Systems and its main components that describe how the processes of information inference, assessment, visual representation and human-system information refinement can be exploited to support SAW mediated by a specialized UI are depicted in Fig. 1. Crucial components are highlighted (orange).

The framework was used to develop a SAW-oriented interface to a robbery event reporting, as part of an emergency dispatch system.

Before performing any information analysis, our framework receives the output of an acquisition phase. Such acquisition performs a Natural Language Processing (NLP) to identify objects, attributes and properties from audio calls reported to the Military Police of São Paulo State (PMESP) in Brazil. As an output, it is produced a set of interrelated objects and properties that we call *Situation*. Such Situation is then submitted to Information Quality Assessment.

At the Information Quality Assessment, the produced situation is submitted to an analysis of the following required quality dimensions: completeness related to the presence or absence of objects or attributes that describe them; currency (timeliness dimension), which helps to determine the "age" of the information and so take timely actions; and uncertainty, when operators hold only a partial knowledge about a

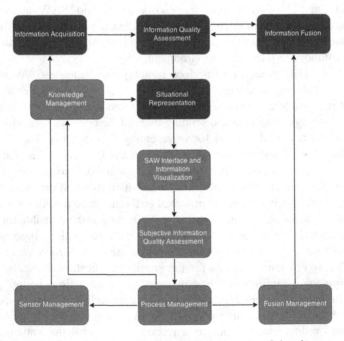

Fig. 1. Conceptual framework for describing the UI in the context of situation assessment (Color figure online)

Situation. In our domain we consider uncertainty as a generalization of the other dimensions. Situations are entities that evolve overtime and must have their information quality indexes updated every time new information arrives or is produced, and also their uncertainty value.

The product of acquisition and quality assessment is a situation knowledge that must be represented. In our complete situation assessment system, the ontology model was chosen to represent the semantics of the generated information, due to the flexibility on representing relations among objects. In this phase it is already known the objects, attributes and possible relations among them. In situation assessment systems, it is called Level 1 and Level 2 of assessment, also corresponding to the levels of Perception and Comprehension of a Situation Awareness [14]. It is this knowledge that must be encoded into visualizations and managed by the UI.

Acquisition process generates entities that will be codified in visualization. To complement it, information integration can be performed using the already produced objects as input. This integration, known as Information Fusion, is capable to produce in a lower dimensionality, new objects and new semantic relations that also must be represented graphically. The product of this phase, named Situation, is submitted to information quality assessment, which enriches the existent situation knowledge and is encoded into posterior visualizations.

The UI itself holds the information management of the whole process. Our interface is a collaboration workbench where both system and the operator provide and convey information as a partial knowledge that evolves overtime. Therefore, every time new information is provided by one of these main actors, the other one must process and rebuild it as a new knowledge.

In the emergency dispatch domain, the interface is present where a human operator observes, get oriented, decide what to do and then take some action, which can be either request information refinement or take a domain specific decision. In our approach, this is where the system share partial knowledge generated by the other phases and then listen to the operators' inputs in a cyclic fashion. The methods for refinement are discussed further in the paper.

Held by the UI, the visualizations convey the aggregated knowledge about situations. There are two graphical methods available for the analysis of the specialist: the map-based visualization and the hierarchical graph of relations.

The use of overlays in a geo-referenced map is a requirement for the emergency dispatch system operations, being dependent of location attributes, crucial to determine the attendance to an emergency event. Hence, the other objects that compose a situation complement the visualization with information about criminals, victims and stolen objects for instance, each one with their own description.

The adoption of a graph structure is justified by the need of hierarchical knowledge about how the information is built regarding situations and their objects. It is necessary that police operators know how each situation is composed, and with which objects and attributes. Such hierarchy was obtained through the requirement analysis with the PMESP. Situation is the central entity, composed by the relation among objects and their attributes and ramifications. Object can be identified and have no relations at all, hence, can be in independent hierarchies. In this case, even when not composing a situation, it must be represented. In our case study, a situation is a robbery event report and its objects are victims, criminal, location and robbery object, each one with a set of characteristics that we call attributes.

The next section introduces the development of our interface and practical results using information from the emergency management domain. Moreover, it is discussed how the principles of interface design from Endsley [14] were interpreted and employed in the development of our interface. Also, positive and negative aspects of each principle are presented (considering our robbery event case study).

4   The SAW-Oriented User Interface Development: Robbery Report

For the requirements elicitation of the development of our UI, two approaches were adopted: the Goal-Driven Task Analysis (GDTA) and the Guidelines for Designing for Situation Awareness, both introduced by Endsley [14]. The GDTA helps designers to list all needed information to stimulate each of the three SAW levels (Perception, Comprehension, Projection) and related tasks to help obtain them. To acquire such information, a questionnaire and an observation in site were applied to specialists. This approach also helped to define priorities and decisions that must be performed during the observation of information.

In this section it is presented the principles for the development of each component of our UI and the design choices based on the state-of-the-art. It is also highlighted the benefits and drawbacks of each design choice for our domain.

4.1   Organize Information According to the Goals

Organizing the information according to the goals, established in the GDTA analysis, is the confirmation of the crime and help operators to acquire SAW using the collected and processed information from the assessment system.

To obtain this result, the information was structured around goals, thus goal-driven and not data-driven. Hence, the interface was divided into three different but inter-connected views. Figure 2 presents the main view interface for the acquisition of SAW in emergency events.

The first view (bottom left) in the UI is an object's table for incoming events, containing: information source, objects found by acquisition and fusion, added time information and the information quality (overall uncertainty about object) assessed.

The second view is a map-based GIS-like window, with visualizations as overlays geo-located according to the location of the acquired data. Each object has its own overlay, e.g., criminal, stolen object, location of the event and victims. Each overlay is actionable by the user interaction to expose the attributes associated with the object. When a certain object is spotted in the map view, the correspondent object in the object's table is highlighted. The reverse process also highlights the overlay on the map.

The third view is a frame to support the already mentioned relational graph. Similar to the map-based overlays and the object's table, every node from the graph can be

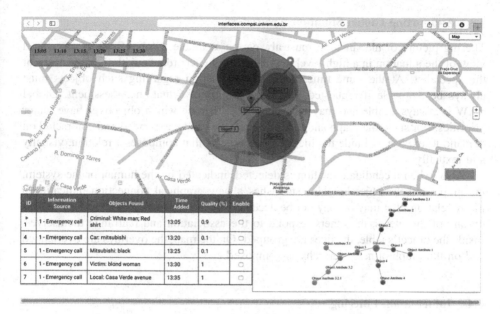

ID	Information Source	Objects Found	Time Added	Quality (%)	Enable
1	1 - Emergency call	Criminal: White man; Red shirt	13:05	0.9	○
4	1 - Emergency call	Car: mitsubishi	13:20	0.1	○
5	1 - Emergency call	Mitsubishi: black	13:25	0.1	○
6	1 - Emergency call	Victim: blond woman	13:30	1	○
7	1 - Emergency call	Local: Casa Verde avenue	13:35	1	○

Fig. 2. Main view interface for the acquisition of SAW in emergency events

selected to extract more information and link with the other view of the interface. The selected node is highlighted when the complementary information is highlighted on the map and object table. The graph can also be rearranged and have their hierarchy updated overtime, to be discussed further.

4.2 Presenting Level 2 of Awareness

The goal is to present the information needed by a second level of awareness directly to support the comprehension as a result of minimum processing, as a first hint of a situation that is probably happening. The idea is to present some values already calculated instead of relying on specialist calculation over Level 1 of SAW data.

Some situations (made by objects and attributes) can be calculated a priori to reduce the mental calculation of the specialist that operates the system. For instance, the automated part can make information fusion of several objects of type "location", identified in the acquired information. Hence, instead of presenting all input information separately, fused information with lower dimensionality and more significance can be adopted. Therefore all events with the same location, and other attributes such as a car or a kind of weapon, can be combined into single and meaningful information.

In case where no automatic fusion occurs, the operator can perform it him/herself in any of the three views by dragging one representation onto another. Such approach is known as interface fusion and is one of the refinement approaches to be detailed further. This approach helps to avoid cluttering in case of several simultaneous events but neglects a higher granularity in level of attributes.

4.3 Supporting Global Situation Awareness

The big picture of the situation must always be available. Global SAW is an overall view of the situation in a high-level language and in accordance with the objectives of the specialist. At the same time, detailed information regarding such objects must always be available if requested. In most systems of Situation Assessment, Global SAW is always visible and may be crucial to determine which objectives have major priorities. For such, the graph and the object's table can be expanded and contracted on demand to expose and hide the hierarchy of objects that composes a relation, visually and textually.

Also, when a candidate relation is detected, indicated by the human or the system, the graph and the object's table establishes a new graphical connection indicating a likely relation, that may or may not be accepted by the specialist. By new associations on any of the views, the others respond to the association and rearrange themselves. Inside the object's table, the lines are grouped. On the map, the overlays are overlapped and on the graph, a new hierarchy is composed.

4.4 Information Filtering

To avoid the overload, non-related SAW information must be filtered. The interface must present only the crucial information to reach the SAW objectives in each task by each moment. For such, it was developed an interactive filter. As the information is inferred by the acquisition phase, the existent information about any of the objects can be omitted or highlighted to a specific analysis.

Such filter is useful for reducing search space and determining fusion candidates through visual analysis. However, SAW does not occur instantly. Humans take a certain time to get oriented regarding situations and critical attributes. A bad filtering can compromise the visibility and the dynamic of the system that changes overtime. Also, global SAW can be depredated and prevents human being proactive.

4.5 Explicitly Identify Absence of Information

Humans deal with the absence of meta-information as something positive. If there are positive readings, they think a missing reading is also positive when actually it can be extremely conflicting and imprecise. Humans act differently when they know if there are probabilities of something going wrong. Abscess of information is dealt as correct and reliable. There are two variations of the problem: no hazards, when information was analyzed and there is no threat; and no hazards unknown, when there is some places that were not covered or with sensor limitations.

Also, stress and workload can cause people to not pay attention to missing information. Humans are dependent on visual. Others just know because of experience. In military applications, dashed lines are used to represent the unknown. As is the case of an unknown attribute, the overall quality index (uncertainty) is the adjusted color.

4.6   Support the Verification of Information Reliability

People consider sensor reliability to support and weigh their reviews of the information produced and presented. Thus, they can benefit if they know that certain information is not reliable.

Although the reliability of values can be numerically presented, authors state that use of luminance levels are advised (brighter for the most reliable).

Not only about the reliability in general, but factors that allow the reliability of a sensor can be evaluated/accessed (factors determining the reliability - sensor reading context). For such our interface shows uncertainty with the use of rings (auras) around objects representation. The closer to the green, the higher is the quality of the data. The closer to the red, the worse is the quality of the data.

Furthermore, by interacting with nodes on graph, overlays on map and information in the object's table, the composing information quality indexes are presented to illustrate how such uncertainty was inferred. Such approach allows specialists to verify local and global quality indexes on demand.

4.7   Representing Historical Events to Follow up Information Evolution

The UI presents graphic and interactive access to historical information by a timeline. To accomplish this, a time ruler with time intervals indicative of arrival information that was delivered to the system was implemented. In our approach of situation assessment system, a situation is something that evolves overtime. Past situations can be also restored and re-inferred.

Hence, specialists can access an event in history and view information objects, attributes and situations on demand. When selecting a historical event, the other views are set to show the information of the selected event.

Thus, there is a possibility of returning in the past and also to monitor events in real time, besides being able to advance directly to a specific time. As a negative side, there is a possible loss of focus on relevant current events and confusion about the actuality of events.

4.8   Support Access of Confidence and Uncertainty in Composite Information

The UI shows the quality scores of alternative forms. In this case, categorical information tends to be faster (high, medium, low) and the fewer categories, a little faster and tend to better accept the lowest rates. Numerical, analog and ranking tends to generate slower decisions.

For a complete understanding of the situation, multiple ways of representing the probability of information are used (integrated separated and geo-located).

The auras around representative icons have its color changed according to the quality attribute. In this case, the color scale follows a Likert scale of five colors according to the index. When information representing a combination of other information (fusion products) exists, the aura color is calculated in accordance with the combined attributes of the individual indices. These individual attributes can be accessed by interaction of the list of events in specific vision. All detailed information will follow the color scale and also have numerical values.

4.9   Support the Upgrade of Quality Levels for Users

As operators need to assess the quality of information readings, there must be a way for this to occur quickly and easily. The confirmation or contradiction/denial of relevant contextual information must be clearly shown.

If reliability is affected by some other value, the information must be displayed very close to the readings, to make a rapid assessment, by showing these specific values of a field situation rather than reliability. This allows the operator to know how much to trust particular pieces of data in the current instance or to adjust the system for more reliable data.

If the system infers information based on other data, they should be displayed in a way to allow rapid determination of what data is known and what is inferred.

The interface provides an option to enter a new quality index, so that the human can evaluate the information or individual event after the fusion. This interaction can occur in the list of individual events map or graph. A ruler is displayed so that the index is adjusted. As positive aspects, quality Scores are always updated (situation and objects/attributes). However, the dynamic scenario nature can prevent the constant updating.

4.10   Support Uncertainty Management by Information Refinement

When information is uncertain to the specialist, the UI must provide access to information refinement functions. In our approach, the specialist is able to perform refinements by three different process management functions: Sensor Management, Fusion Management and Knowledge Management.

By Sensor Management, the specialist is able to select information sources, request reading, set new operational parameters and also disprove acquired data. As our Acquisition also provide objects and attributes, this function can also trigger new mining and classification routines.

The Fusion Management was developed to allow specialists to manually determine the fusion parameters, instead of relying on the automatic process of integration right after the information acquisition, which combines every object and attributes found.

Finally, the Knowledge Management is about the manual contribution that specialists can make to the incremental knowledge that him and the system build overtime. Information can be corrected and semantically restructured. Hence, the associations between objects, made by other process can be redone. Certain nuances about the synergy of objects and the relationship among them in the scenario can only be inferred by humans.

5 Conclusions

This paper explores an UI for an emergency situation system and the efforts made to improve the Situation Awareness process through visualization and data fusion, represented in the UI.

These areas have been largely studied in literature, with several data fusion models and SAW-based interfaces to improve the Situation Awareness process. However, there is a lack of deeper investigation on the human intervention to build, maintain and recover Situation Awareness.

Therefore, the UI proposed aims at studying this collaboration between human and system to develop a better SAW. To demonstrate the effectiveness of this UI, several SAW UI design guidelines are analyzed and commented on their impact on how this UI was molded.

The conclusion is that empowering the specialist and the system, by intensifying their relationship to build a more feasible representation of situations, has a potential to improve SAW that has not yet been explored.

In future projects, this UI will be evaluated with user testing (usability) and a Situation Awareness evaluation, compared to UIs that do not allow human-system collaboration in the fusion process.

References

1. Endsley, M.R.: The challenge of the information age. In: Proceedings of the Second International Workshop on symbiosis of humans, artifacts and environment, Kyoto, Japan (2001)
2. Kokar, M.M., Endsley, M.R.: Situation Awareness and Cognitive Modeling. IEEE Intell. Syst. **27**(3), 91–96 (2012)
3. Llinas, J., Bowman, C., Rogova, G., Steinberg, A.: Revisiting the JDL data fusion model II. In: 7th International Conference on Information Fusion (2004)
4. White Jr., F.E.: Data fusion lexicon. In: Technical Panel for C3, Data Fusion Sub-Panel. Naval Ocean Systems Center. Joint Directors of Laboratories, San Diego (1987)
5. Rogova, G., Bosse, E.: Information quality in information fusion. In: 13th Information Fusion (2010)
6. Batini, C., Cappiello, C., Francalanci, C., Maurino, A.: Methodologies for data quality assessment and improvement. ACM Comput. Surv. **41**(3), 1–52 (2009)
7. Blasch, E.: High level information fusion (hlif): survey of models, issues, and grand challenges. IEEE A&E Syst. Mag. **27**, 4–20 (2012)
8. Nwiabu, N., Allison, I., Holt, P., Lowit, P., Oyeneyin, B.: User interface design for situation-aware decision support systems. In: 2012 IEEE International Multi- Disciplinary Conference Cognitive Methods Situation Awareness and Decision Support, pp. 332–339, March 2012
9. Yu, S., Deng, L., Zhang, Y.: Visualization user interface for decision support systems. In: 2009 Ninth International Conference on Hybrid Intelligent Systems, pp. 63–66 (2009)
10. Onal, E., Craddock, C., Endsley, M.R., Chapman, A.: From theory to practice: How designing for situation awareness can transform confusing, overloaded shovel operator interfaces, reduce costs, and increase safety. In: ISARC 2013, pp. 1517–1525 (2013)

11. Gous, E.: Utilizing cognitive work analysis for the design and evaluation of command and control user interfaces. In: 2013 International Conference Adaptive Science Technology, pp. 1–7, November 2013
12. Chai, H., Du, Y.: A framework of situation awareness based on event extraction and correlation for military decision support. 2012 IEEE International Conference Mechatronics Automation, vol. 1, pp. 192–196, August 2012
13. Feng, H., Teng, T.H., Tan, A.H.: Modelling situation awareness for context-aware decision support. Expert Syst. Appl. **36**(1), 455–463 (2009)
14. Endsley, M.R.: Designing for Situation Awareness, pp. 19–21. CRC Press, Boca Raton (2012). 365

A Method for Generation and Check of Alarm Configurations Using Cause-Effect Matrices for Plant Alarm System Design

Takashi Hamaguchi[1(⊠)], B. Mondori[1], Kazuhiro Takeda[2],
Naoki Kimura[3], and Masaru Noda[4]

[1] Graduate School of Engineering, Nagoya Institute of Technology,
Nagoya, Japan
hamachan@nitech.ac.jp
[2] Graduate School of Engineering, Shizuoka University, Shizuoka, Japan
tktaked@ipc.shizuoka.ac.jp
[3] Faculty of Engineering, Kyushu University, Fukuoka, Japan
nkimura@chem-eng.kyushu-u.ac.jp
[4] Department of Chemical Engineering, Fukuoka University, Fukuoka, Japan
mnoda@fukuoka-u.ac.jp

Abstract. An alarm system must provide useful information to operators as the third layer of an independent protection layer when a chemical plant is at abnormal situation. Therefore, a design method of a plant alarm system is important for plant safety. Because the plant is maintained in the plant lifecycle, the alarm system for the plant should be properly managed through the plant lifecycle. To manage changes, the design rationales of the alarm system should be explained explicitly. This paper investigates a logical and systematic alarm system design method that explicitly explains the design rationales from know-why information for proper management of changes through the plant lifecycle. In this paper, we propose a method for generation and check of alarm configurations using cause-effect matrices for plant alarm system design. The matrices are based on a cause-effect model and used for generation and check of alarm configurations.

Keywords: Plant alarm system design · Cause-effect matrices · Alarm management

1 Introduction

In most chemical plants, a distributed control system (DCS) is installed to keep the process variables stable. In these plants, the main role of the operators is to supervise plant operations by using process alarms, both normal and abnormal. The DCS is an effective means of decreasing the operator's load of normal operation, and the number of operators has recently decreased due to the introduction of advanced control systems. Although the frequency of accidents is very low, the load of an operator in an abnormal situation has become heavier. When critical alarms are generated, operators face difficult tasks including complex decision making for detection, diagnosis,

© Springer International Publishing Switzerland 2015
S. Yamamoto (Ed.): HIMI 2015, Part II, LNCS 9173, pp. 549–556, 2015.
DOI: 10.1007/978-3-319-20618-9_54

assessment of urgency, and countermeasure planning. In abnormal situations, the DCS is not effective because of its lack of diagnosis systems or decision-support systems to prevent accidents or disasters. Therefore, a plant alarm system is very important to support safe operation.

2 Alarm Management Lifecycle

To support the safety of plant operations, the Independent Protection Layers has been proposed (CCPS, 2001) [1]. When the plant is in an abnormal situation, an alarm system consisting of critical alarms must provide useful information to operators. Because plant modifications occur in the plant lifecycle, the plant alarm system needs to be properly managed throughout plant lifecycle. A framework and first alarm to manage the alarm system lifecycle had been proposed (ISA, 2009) [2] and the revised illustration has been proposed in IEC 62682 (IEC, 2014) [3]. The alarm management lifecycle in IEC 62682 with our focused area in this paper is shown in Fig. 1.

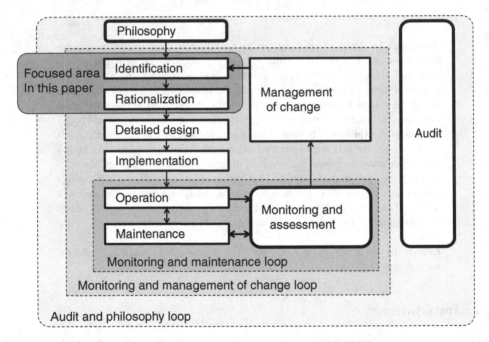

Fig. 1. Alarm management lifecycle in IEC 62682

3 Alarm System Design Using CE Matrices

3.1 CE Model

Operation modes of plant can be estimated, such as steady state, start up, shut-down, or abnormal situation operation. Cause-effect relationships between state variables such as process variables and manipulated variables in the operation modes can be represented by a cause-effect (CE) model constructed of nodes and arcs. A CE model of example plant is shown in Fig. 2.

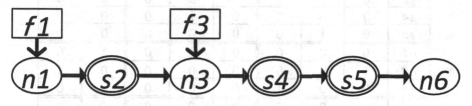

Fig. 2 CE model of example plant

The CE model is a diagram for the propagation of abnormalities that shows the propagation process for abnormalities after a fault has occurred. The CE model is based on the material and energy balances of the plant that could be constructed from the plant topology. The nodes in the model represent state variables in the plant. The arcs represent the directed influence between variables. Takeda et al. [4], Kato et al. [5], and Hamaguchi et al. [6] proposed some logical and systematic alarm system design based on CE model.

Let S be a set of all measured variables of state variables and s be the element of S. Double line nodes represent measured variables. Let N be a set of all unmeasured variables of state variables and n be the element of N. Single line nodes represent unmeasured variables. Let F be a set of all fault origins variable to be distinguished by alarm system and f be the element of F. Rectangle represent fault origins variables to be distinguished by alarm system.

3.2 CE Matrices

In this paper, we convert the CE model to CE matrices to generate the pairings between the fault origins variables F and measured variables S as alarm state triggers and check the qualitative adequacy as the alarm configurations by computer, automatically. The CE matrices have elements 0 or 1. Column variables and row variables correspond causes and effects, respectively. When the (i, j) element of the CE matrices are 1, the j-th column variable affects the i-th row variable.

3.3 CE Matrix G

A CE matrix G explains the plant model. The CE matrix G has rows and columns corresponding to the measured variables S, unmeasured variables N, and fault origins variables F.

The CE matrix G of the CE model in Fig. 2 is shown in Table 1. The "1" at the $(4, 7)$ element of Table 1 shows that the fault origins variable, $f1$, affects the unmeasured variable, $n1$.

Table 1. CE matrix G of the Plant

Causes	S: Measured variables			N:Unmeasured variables			F:Fault origins variables	
Effects G	$s2$	$s4$	$s5$	$n1$	$n3$	$n6$	$f1$	$f3$
$s2$	0	0	0	1	0	0	0	0
$s4$	0	0	0	0	1	0	0	0
$s5$	0	1	0	0	0	0	0	0
$n1$	0	0	0	0	0	0	1	0
$n3$	1	0	0	0	0	0	0	1
$n6$	0	0	1	0	0	0	0	0
$f1$	0	0	0	0	0	0	0	0
$f3$	0	0	0	0	0	0	0	0

The rows are grouped: S: ($s2$, $s4$, $s5$), N: ($n1$, $n3$, $n6$), F: ($f1$, $f3$).

3.4   CE Matrix A

An alarm configuration 1 is shown in Fig. 3. The fault origin variables $f1$ and $f3$ are paired $s2$ and $s4$, respectively.

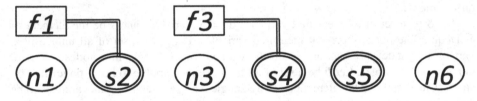

Fig. 3. Alarm configuration 1

A CE matrix A explains the alarm configurations. This CE matrix A can be generated automatically from unit matrix. Because each column variable of this CE matrix A always has only one "1". The CE matrix A can be generated easily to apply substitution of unit matrix.

The CE matrix A_1 of the alarm configuration 1 in Fig. 1 is shown in Table 2. The "1" at the (7, 1) element of Table 2 shows that the measured variable, s2, is used as an alarm sensor for the fault origins variable, $f1$.

3.5   CE Matrix GA

A CE model of the example plant with alarm configuration 1 is shown in Fig. 4. The propagations from alarm sensors, $s2$ and $s3$, are modified by alarm configuration1.

The alarm loop model GA_1, which explains the effect of the subset of C under the alarm configurations 1, is calculated by the Boolean multiplication of two matrices, G and A_1. The CE matrix GA_1 of the alarm loop model with alarm configuration 1 in Fig. 4 is shown in Table 3.

Table 2. CE matrix A_1 as alarm configuration 1

	Causes	S: Measured variables			N:Unmeasured variables			F:Fault origins variables	
Effects	A_1	s2	s4	s5	n1	n3	n6	f1	f3
S:	s2	0	0	0	0	0	0	0	0
	s4	0	0	0	0	0	0	0	0
	s5	0	0	1	0	0	0	0	0
N:	n1	0	0	0	1	0	0	0	0
	n3	0	0	0	0	1	0	0	0
	n6	0	0	0	0	0	1	0	0
F:	f1	1	0	0	0	0	0	1	0
	f3	0	1	0	0	0	0	0	1

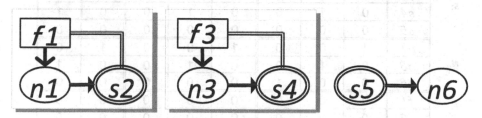

Fig. 4. CE model of an example plant with alarm configuration 1

Table 3. CE matrix GA_1 of the alarm loop model with alarm configuration A_1

	Causes	S: Measured variables			N:Unmeasured variables			F:Fault origins variables	
Effects	GA_1	s2	s4	s5	n1	n3	n6	f1	f3
S:	s2	0	0	0	1	0	0	0	0
	s4	0	0	0	0	1	0	0	0
	s5	0	0	0	0	0	0	0	0
N:	n1	1	0	0	0	0	0	1	0
	n3	0	1	0	0	0	0	0	1
	n6	0	0	1	0	0	0	0	0
F:	f1	0	0	0	0	0	0	0	0
	f3	0	0	0	0	0	0	0	0

3.6 CE Matrix R

A reachability matrix R is defined by using GA as followed

$$R = \sum_{k=1}^{\infty} (GA)^k$$

If dimension of GA is n, the reachabity matrix R is defined as followed.

$$R = \sum_{k=1}^{n-1} (GA)^k$$

Using this method, result of the reachability matrix R_1 by GA_1 indicate the effect between variables under alarm configuration 1. The effect of fault origin $f1$ arrives at the alarm variables $s2$ and the alarm loop can work. The effect of fault origin $f3$ arrives at the alarm variables $s4$ and the alarm loop can work, too. The reachability matrix R_1 is shown in Table 4.

Table 4. Reachability matrix R_1 by GA_1

Causes	S: Measured variables			N:Unmeasured variables			F:Fault origins variables	
Effects	R_1	$s2$	$s4$	$s5$	$n1$	$n3$	$n6$	$f1$	$f3$
S:	$s2$	1	0	0	1	0	0	1	0
	$s4$	0	1	0	0	1	0	0	1
	$s5$	0	0	0	0	0	0	0	0
N:	$n1$	1	0	0	1	0	0	1	0
	$n3$	0	1	0	0	1	0	0	1
	$n6$	0	0	1	0	0	0	0	0
F:	$f1$	0	0	0	0	0	0	0	0
	$f3$	0	0	0	0	0	0	0	0

3.7 Bad Alarm Configuration

Here, a bad alarm configuration 2 is explained. The alarm configuration 2 is shown in Fig. 5. The fault origin variables $f1$ and $f3$ are paired $s5$ and $s4$, respectively.

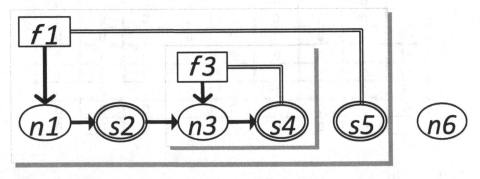

Fig. 5. A CE model of an example plant with alarm configuration 1

The CE matrix A_2 of the alarm configuration 2 in Fig. 5 is shown in Table 5. The CE matrix GA_2 of the alarm loop model with alarm configuration 2 is shown in Table 6.

Table 5. CE matrix A_2 as alarm configuration 2

Causes	S: Measured variables			N:Unmeasured variables			F:Fault origins variables	
Effects A_2	s2	s4	s5	n1	n3	n6	f1	f3
S: s2	1	0	0	0	0	0	0	0
s4	0	0	0	0	0	0	0	0
s5	0	0	0	0	0	0	0	0
N: n1	0	0	0	1	0	0	0	0
n3	0	0	0	0	1	0	0	0
n6	0	0	0	0	0	1	0	0
F: f1	0	0	1	0	0	0	1	0
f3	0	1	0	0	0	0	0	1

Table 6. CE matrix GA_2 of alarm loop model with alarm configuration A_2

Causes	S: Measured variables			N:Unmeasured variables			F:Fault origins variables	
Effects GA_2	s2	s4	s5	n1	n3	n6	f1	f3
S: s2	0	0	0	1	0	0	0	0
s4	0	0	0	0	1	0	0	0
s5	0	0	0	0	0	0	0	0
N: n1	0	0	1	0	0	0	1	0
n3	1	1	0	0	0	0	0	1
n6	0	0	0	0	0	0	0	0
F: f1	0	0	0	0	0	0	0	0
f3	0	0	0	0	0	0	0	0

The reachability matrix R_1 by GA_2 is shown in Table 7. The effect of fault origin $f3$ arrives at the alarm variables $s4$ and the alarm loop can work. But, the effect of fault origin $f1$ doesn't arrive at the alarm variables $s5$. Therefore, the alarm configuration 2 is judged to a bad configuration.

Table 7. Reachability matrix R_2 of the Plant GA_2

Causes	S: Measured variables			N:Unmeasured variables			F:Fault origins variables	
Effects R_2	s2	s4	s5	n1	n3	n6	f1	f3
S: s2	1	0	1	1	0	0	1	0
s4	1	1	1	1	1	0	1	1
s5	0	0	0	0	0	0	0	0
N: n1	0	0	1	0	0	0	1	0
n3	1	1	1	1	1	0	1	1
n6	0	0	0	0	0	0	0	0
F: f1	0	0	0	0	0	0	0	0
f3	0	0	0	0	0	0	0	0

4 Summary

In this paper, we propose a method for generation and check of alarm configurations using cause-effect matrices for plant alarm system design. The matrices are based on a CE model and used for generation and check of alarm configurations. The design algorithm can be the first step to bridge the discontinuity of plant alarm system design and alarm management.

Acknowledgement. This work was supported by JSPS KAKENHI Grant Number 24310119, 25282101 and has been conducted under the Japan Society of the Promotion of Science (JSPS) 143rd committee on Process Systems Engineering.

References

1. CCPS, Layer of Protection Analysis, New York, American Institute of Chemical Engineers, Center for Chemical Process Safety (2001)
2. ISA, Management of Alarm Systems for the Process Industries, North Carolina (2009)
3. IEC, 62682 ed.01: Management of Alarm Systems for the Process Industries (2014)
4. Takeda, K., Hamaguchi, T., Noda, M.: Plant alarm system design based on cause-effect model. Kagaku Kogaku Ronbunshu **36**(2), 136–142 (2010)
5. Kato, M., Takeda, K., Noda, M., Kikuchi, Y., Hirao, M.: Design Method of Alarm System for Identifying Possible Malfunctions in a Plant Based on Cause-Effect Model. In: 11th International Symposium on PSE (2011)
6. Hamaguchi, T., Takeda, K., Noda, M., Kimura, N.: A Method of Designing Plant Alarm Systems with Hierarchical Cause-Effect Model. In: 11th International Symposium on PSE (2011)

Parking Autonomous Skids

James Hing$^{(\boxtimes)}$, Ross Boczar, and Kyle Hart

Naval Air Warfare Center – Aircraft Division, Lakehurst, NJ, USA
{james.hing,ross.boczar,kyle.m.hart}@navy.mil

Abstract. Autonomous movement of materiel aboard an aircraft carrier can potentially be accomplished using robotic skids. This work proposes a simple human machine interface (HMI) and a control algorithm that would enable a sailor to control and park multiple robotic skids. This work specifically looks at an artificial potential field approach to parking multiple robotic skids (non-holonomic) within a user defined boundary. Optimal goal locations within the boundary for the skids are calculated through convex optimization techniques.

Keywords: Non-holonomic · Artificial potential fields · Autonomous parking

1 Introduction

To support naval aviation aboard aircraft carriers, aviation ordnance is transported from the magazines to the flight deck and loaded onto aircraft. This process, called "Strike Up", can take a significant amount of time as sailors push weapons skids through a circuitous route from the magazines to a staging area on the flight deck called the "Bomb Farm". The Strike-Up process is one of the major bottlenecks to increasing mission-capable sortie rate (deployment of aircraft).

Robotics weapons transporters have been touted as a way of improving sortie rate and optimizing manpower. A true advantage of an autonomous transport system would be for a single operator to control multiple systems ("swarm"). In previous works on swarm control, little focus has been on the action of autonomously parking multiple systems. Seen in Fig. 1 left, weapons skids spend much time parked in various locations along their routes such as on elevators or in portions of hangar decks. This work has developed a Human Machine Interface (HMI) and the appropriate control methods towards supervisory control for parking multiple skids in a cluttered and dynamic environment. This system will reduce the time it takes for a single operator or multiple operators to move the systems and setup in /exit from elevators or storage areas.

The HMI consists of 4 parts: (1) Automatically defining optimal parking locations for each weapon skid within a boundary, (2) the control method for moving multiple non-holonomic weapon skids, (3) a user interface and (4) extracting robot /obstacle pose.

The rest of this paper is organized as follows: Sect. 2 provides a brief overview of related work in this area. Section 3 describes the 4 parts of the HMI system. Section 4 presents some simulation and hardware test results and Sect. 5 concludes the paper with a discussion and future work.

© Springer International Publishing Switzerland 2015
S. Yamamoto (Ed.): HIMI 2015, Part II, LNCS 9173, pp. 557–568, 2015.
DOI: 10.1007/978-3-319-20618-9_55

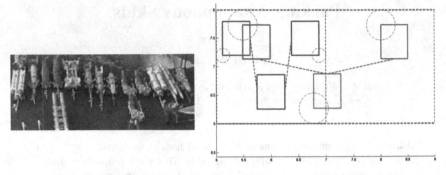

Fig. 1. (Left) Example of Skids parking on an elevator, (Right) Example of optimizing the spacing for three mechanized skids. (*Red/Light Grey*): solution in large contour. (*Blue/Dark Grey*): solution in smaller contour (Color figure online).

2 Related Works

Formation control of multiple robotic vehicles, also known as groups or swarms, has been a very active area of research. Robotic swarms have different advantages in different applications. In many cases, the behavior of the swarm can produce abilities that outweigh the abilities of a single member. An example would be a group of robots carrying an object of a weight heavier than the payload limit of a single robot alone. In other cases, the act of moving groups of vehicles all at once rather than individually increases performance and throughput such as in the transportation of material (which is the case study used in this work). Many different strategies have been developed for the control of these swarm formations under different kinds of scenarios such as movement of a formation in a corridor or amongst obstacles. A majority of these control strategies can be categorized as either leader-follower [1], behavior-based [2], or virtual structure approach [3].

While the works listed above present strategies for the movement of formations from point A to point B with obstacles along the way, they are not suitable for the task of parking formations of non-holonomic robotic vehicles. Less focus has been on the control of multiple non-holonomic robotic vehicles during parking tasks. Multiple works have focused on single mobile robotic platforms during parking [4] [5]. The example of weapons movement on a carrier demonstrates a Navy specific scenario where parking occurs multiple times during transport and there are multiple hetero-geneous sized skids.

This work focuses on the parking aspect of swarm formation control. Specifically the focus is on a behavior-based, potential field approach for parking multiple non-holonomic vehicles in dynamic environments (i.e. moving obstacles) within a defined contour (parking space /area). This is a desirable method for real-time path planning because the computation requirements for obtaining the potential factors are low.

Multiple works have utilized a potential field approach to maintain formation of a swarm of non-holonomic robots while moving to a target location [6–8]. Those works focused on maintaining a formation (aka shape) during movement or maintaining a formation on a predefined contour line. However, for parking tasks which require optimizing the space within the area enclosed by a contour, the above methods as presented are not suitable. To our knowledge, the only work related to this aspect of optimizing the space within an area enclosed by a contour is the work by Ekanayake and Pathirana [9]. In their work, they developed a scalable control algorithm to navigate a group of mobile robots into a predefined shape and spread them inside while avoiding inter-member collisions. However, each robot was treated as an omnidirectional point mass with each robot having the same mass and mobility. Lastly, their work did not consider dynamic obstacles within the environment.

In this work, we have greatly extended the work presented in [10] that used potential fields to maneuver a single non-holonomic rectangular robot through a static obstacle course to a goal location. While [10] only focused on a single robot and static obstacles, their practical method of local obstacle avoidance offered a good starting structure from which to extend the control and parking of multiple non-holonomic rectangular skids.

3 Autonomous Skids Parking System

3.1 Optimal Parking Locations

First we look at the problem of optimally filling a given shape with a swarm of rectangular robots. This is representative of defining the optimal parking locations of each robotic skid within an allocated parking area of the ship (e.g. elevator, hangar bay, etc.).

Formulation. Consider the problem of arranging N rectangular robots inside a given shape, with respective positions (x_i, y_i), lengths l_i, and widths w_i. We consider a swarm of planar robots in $\mathbb{R}^2$. We assume that the desired swarm formation includes consistent orientation across all robots, which we take without loss of generality to be $\theta_i = 0, \forall i$.

Floor Planning. Following the formulation set out in Chapter 8 of Boyd & Vandenberghe [11], we can pose this as floor planning problem: minimizing some objective while packing the rectangular robots into a given shape, with no overlap between robots. Using convex optimization for VLSI floor planning is common; see [12]. The objective being optimized can be the size of the shape itself or some other metric, such as intra-robot spacing. As stated, the no-overlap constraint can lead to a combinatorial optimization problem which is often computationally intractable. Thus, we need to impose some structure on the swarm configuration in order to pose a tractable convex optimization problem.

Relative Positioning. Inspired by 8.8.1 of [11], the problem of reducing the combinatoric constraints can be solved by the construction of two N-node directed acyclic graphs describing the relative positioning between the robots: $\mathcal{H}$ (horizontal) and $\mathcal{V}$ (vertical). A set of tractable relative positioning constraints is predicated on the existence of a directed path between each pair of robots (represented by nodes i and j) in either $\mathcal{H}$ or $\mathcal{V}$.

Though many different schemes can be used, our method attempts to use minimal edges, though we do not currently have any proof of minimality. Two possible schemes, based on square and diamond arrangements, are seen with N = 9 in Fig. 2.

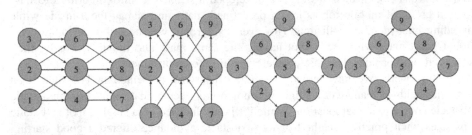

Fig. 2. (1) Square horizontal relative position graph $\mathcal{H}$, (2) Square vertical relative positioning graph $\mathcal{V}$, (3) Diamond horizontal relative positioning graph $\mathcal{H}$, (4) Diamond vertical relative positioning graph $\mathcal{V}$.

These graphs describe the relative horizontal and vertical positioning between nodes: for example, node 4 is to the right of and below node 2. With a directed edge denoted by (i,j), the positioning constraints are given by:

$$x_i + l_i \leq x_j, \forall (i,j) \in \mathcal{H}. \tag{1}$$

$$y_i + w_i \leq y_j, \forall (i,j) \in \mathcal{V}. \tag{2}$$

These inequalities are linear, and are therefore convex. For our particular graph structure, the number of constraints grows as $O(N)$.

Spacing Constraints. We can also impose minimum distance constraints (which could also be variables to be maximized) of the form:

$$\left\| p_i - p_j \right\|_2 \geq D_{ij}, \forall i \neq j, \quad i,j = 1,\ldots,N. \tag{3}$$

where $p_i = \left[\frac{x_i + l_i}{2}, \frac{y_i + h_i}{2} \right]^T$, x_i, y_i is the lower left corner, and p_i is the center. Though this leads to a non-convex problem, there are several convex relaxations, restrictions, or reformulations which can be employed.

(1) *Linear Approximation*: As seen in [11], we can replace the constraints (3) with ones of the form:

$$a_{ij}^T (p_i - p_j) \geq D_{ij}, i < j, i,j = 1,\ldots,N. \tag{4}$$

where $\|a_{ij}\|_2 = 1$. As an example, a simple heuristic for choosing a_{ij} is to first solve a feasibility program without constraints (4), with optimal solution $\hat{p}_i$, and to then set $a_{ij} = (\hat{p}_i - \hat{p}_j)/\|\hat{p}_i - \hat{p}_j\|_2$.

(2) *Relative Position Spacing*: We can also exploit the relative positioning constraints and change constraints (1) and (2) to:

$$x_i + l_i + \alpha_{ij} \le x_j, \forall (i,j) \in \mathcal{H}. \tag{5}$$

$$y_i + w_i + \beta_{ij} \le y_j, \forall (i,j) \in \mathcal{V}. \tag{6}$$

In this case, we could maximize some weighted combination of α_{ij}, β_{ij}, which represent horizontal and vertical spacing, in order to maximize some function of intra-graph spacing. Additionally, we can impose minimum distance constraints α_{min}, β_{min}.

(3) *SDP Relaxation*: If we consider the robots as point masses, maximizing the spacing becomes a variant of the well-known circle-packing problem. However, SDP relaxations of this problem are not known to work well in practice [13].

Bounding Shape Constraints and Spacing Maximization. For simplicity, we limit the desired shape to a convex polygon which can be expressed in the form $Az \le b$ where $A \in \mathbb{R}^{m \times 2}$, $z \in \mathbb{R}^2$, $b \in \mathbb{R}^2$. Feasibility constraints are then of the form $Ap_{ik} \le b$, where we denote p_{ik} as the position of the k th corner of the i th rectangular robot. These constraints can also be reduced using graphs $\mathcal{H}$ and $\mathcal{V}$. Section 8.5.1 of [11] formulates the problem of finding the largest Euclidean ball contained inside a polyhedron, given by $Az \le b$ as:

$$\max \quad R.$$
$$\text{subject to } a_i^T x + R \|a_i\|_2 \le b_i, i = 1, \ldots, m. \tag{7}$$
$$R \ge 0.$$

with variables x and R. Due to convexity of both the bounding shape and the rectangular robots, we can find the placement of robot j which maximizes the shortest distance between the robot and the bounding shape by solving the convex optimization problem:

$$\max R.$$
$$\text{subject to } a_i^T p_{jk} + R \|a_i\|_2 \le b_i, \forall i, k. \tag{8}$$
$$R \ge 0.$$

We can also impose a minimum Euclidean distance with the constraint $R \ge R_{min}$.

An example of a solution to this problem is seen in Fig. 3 left. Thus, for a multi-robot swarm, we can maximize some concave function of these distances, which we now represent as $R = [R_1, R_2, R_j, \ldots, R_N]$:

$$\max \phi(R).$$
$$\text{subject to } a_i^T p_{jk} + R_j \|a_i\|_* \le b_i, \forall i, j, k. \tag{9}$$
$$R \succeq 0.$$

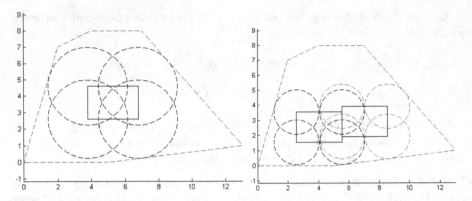

Fig. 3. Left) Optimized L^2 boundary spacing. Right) Optimized swarm-minimum L^2 boundary spacing.

Figure 3 right shows an example of a 2-robot swarm with no minimum spacing constraint, maximizing $\phi(R) = min_j\{R_j\}$. Assuming a constant shape, the number of constraints grows as $O(N)$.

Combined Boundary/inter-Robot Spacing. Using both boundary spacing and intra-robot spacing constraints, we can form a convex optimization problem. For this formulation, we use relative position spacing constraints, and assume no special weighting (though this can be easily added). Thus our problem is:

$$
\begin{aligned}
\max \quad & \psi(\alpha, \beta, R). \\
\text{Subject to } & x_i + l_i + \alpha_{ij} \le x_j, \forall (i,j) \in \mathcal{H}. \\
& y_i + w_i + \beta_{ij} \le y_j, \forall (i,j) \in \mathcal{V}. \\
& a_i^T p_{jk} + R_j \le b_i, \forall i,j,k.
\end{aligned}
\tag{10}
$$

$$
\left.
\begin{aligned}
p_{j1} &= \left[x_j, y_j\right]^T \\
p_{j2} &= \left[x_j + l_j, y_j\right]^T \\
p_{j3} &= \left[x_j + l_j, y_j + w_j\right]^T \\
p_{j4} &= \left[x_j, y_j + w_j\right]^T
\end{aligned}
\right\} \forall j.
$$

$$R \succ 0.$$

The function ψ is used to quantify sums, averages, or minimums of distances. However, the objective function must remain concave, so ψ will usually be some type of "maximin" function such as (11).

$$
\psi_1(\alpha, \beta, R) = \min_{(i,j)\in\mathcal{H},(i,k)\in\mathcal{V}}\{\alpha_{ij}, \beta_{ik}, R_i\}.
\tag{11}
$$

Once formalized, these optimization problems can be solved using the CVX software package [14].

Structured Optimization. Since many of these objective functions involve minimums of spacing variables, the optimization often finds an optimal solution at a "bottleneck" - a subset of robots are tightly packed across some cut of the contour, with relevant inequality spacing constraints being equality (known as *active constraints*). Thus, the placement of robots far away from the bottleneck may be closer than normal and appear suboptimal, as spacing them out further than the minimum does not improve the objective.

Thus a "structured optimization" approach may be used to iteratively improve the qualitative solution:

- $C = \emptyset, K = \{allconstraints\}$
- For $i = 1...N_{iter}$:
  - Solve the optimization problem with constraints $K\backslash C$, including removing C from the objective function and holding constraints C to their fixed values.
  - Determine which constraints are active (A), and set $C = C \cup A$. Store values of constraints in C achieved at the optimal point.

3.2 Non-holonomic Skid Control

Our approach extends the artificial potential field frame work in [10] to drive multiple non-holonomic vehicles. In [10], each platform has virtual action points applied to the front and rear of the vehicle that are used to apply both attractive and repulsive forces from the goal and obstacles respectively. The attractive goal force is the tangential vector at the front action point of the robot to the radius that comes in contact with the orientation of the goal front action point. Obstacle forces behind the vehicle's pivot point produce a repulsive force at the rear action point and obstacles in front of the pivot point produce a force at the front action point. All forces are proportional to the inverse of the cube distance between obstacle points and robot body. The resultant force F_R is a summation of the attractive force from the goal F_G and the forces from detected obstacles F_O. Forces acting on the rear action point are inverted and applied to the front action point during this summation. The equations for F_G and F_O can be found in [10] and are not presented here due to page limitations (Fig. 4).

The extensions to the algorithm we have implemented are as follows:

1. Reference [10] assumes that the front of the robot is always desired to be driven toward the goal orientation. Instead, implementing the same method for the front action point with the rear action point allows a decision to be made on which end of the vehicle to drive towards the goal. In many cases, driving the rear action point towards the goal location results in a shorter travel distance than using the front action point. This requires the calculation of the arc length for the front arc and the rear arc to determine which is the shorter path.
2. Multiple skids controlled at the same time. This is a relatively straight forward extension to [10] as each skid calculates its' own resultant force vector based

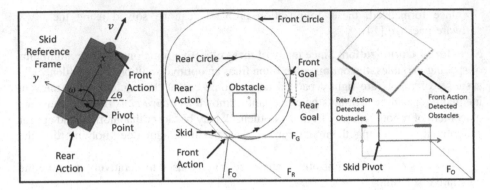

Fig. 4 Left) Reference frame for skid/robot, Middle) Top down view of the force vectors and trajectory options during travel to parked goal location. Right) Skid frame view of obstacle shown in image left.

on its commanded goal location, current position, and detected surrounding obstacles. Surrounding skids are simply treated as moving obstacles to each other during the force calculations however we have implemented a weighting coefficient that allows inter-skid forces to be tuned differently from other obstacle forces.

3. Addition of a weighting function to the goal force. In [10], the goal force is always given a magnitude of 1 as its importance is to define the tangential direction along the arc to the goal orientation. The addition of weighting function based on the distance to the goal has enabled the ability to move robots through formations as seen in the Results section.

The resulting command to the robot, based on the resultant force vector, is a forward or reverse speed and a rotation about the pivot point (in this particular case the pivot is the middle point of the axle between the two rear wheels):

$$\begin{bmatrix} v \\ \omega \end{bmatrix} = \begin{bmatrix} F_{Rx} \\ \frac{F_{Ry}}{x} \end{bmatrix}. \tag{12}$$

where v is the commanded forward or reverse speed in the skid frame, ω is the angular velocity commanded to the robot, F_{Rx} is the horizontal component of the resultant force vector F_R in the skid frame, and x is the distance (in the skid frame) to the action point (either front or rear) that the current force vector is acting on.

3.3   The User Interface

The user interface, shown in Fig. 5, is inspired by the notion of enabling a sailor to select assets (robotic skids) in one ship location and select the goal location of that asset in another location. In actual implementation it is expected that the sailor would not have an actual camera top down view but instead would have a map view

Fig. 5. Simple user interface for selecting robots, selecting the goal parking contour, and monitoring progress.

of the ship. The interface allows the user to select the desired robots and define a bounding box where the assets will park. During bounding box select, the user defines the general orientation that will be applied to all systems within the boundary. Optimal spacing of the robots is automatically calculated and goal locations are sent to the control algorithm to drive the robotic systems. At any moment during travel the user can select any of the moving assets and define a new goal location. Also, if during travel, an obstacle occludes part of the parking boundary drawn by the user, a smaller boundary that does not encompass the obstacle can be defined and new parking locations defined using the same optimization algorithm. An example is shown in Fig. 1 right. Otherwise, the obstacle is treated as normal and would cause a repulsive force against the skid whose parking spot is occluded or is close to the obstacle.

3.4   Robot & Obstacle Localization

For hardware tests, currently positions of the robots and obstacles are extracted from images obtained from a top down camera. A background subtraction method is used to extract the foreground objects (robots /obstacles) and a pattern matching algorithm is used to identify robot pose at each frame. Each robot has LIDAR sensor that scans 180° in front of the robot and a series of ultrasonic sensors that cover the back 180° of the robot. The top down camera also supplies the user with a view from which to select robots and define goal locations. At each frame the pose of the robots are extracted and input into the multi-robot control algorithm. In simulation, each skid knows its goal location, and world location and pose. Obstacle/other skid detection is based on a simulated LIDAR located at the pivot point of the robot with a range of 5 m and scan angle of 360° with a resolution of 0.36°.

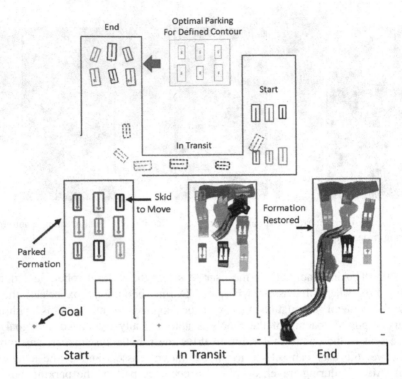

Fig. 6. (Top) Simulation of multiple non-holonomic heterogeneous skids moving to a parked formation (dotted lines represent the robot location at time step 200). (Bottom) Simulation of a single skid moving through an already parked formation. Positions at each frame are printed to give a visual of the actual trajectories of each skid.

4   Results and Discussion

The algorithms were tested in simulation with $N > 3$ simulated skids and hardware with $N \leq 3$ robots. For the hardware tests, shown in Fig. 5, a kinematic model of the weapons skid was derived and applied to constrain the motion of the robotic research platforms (through software). Many successful scenarios were tested with examples shown in Figs. 5 and 6. In particular, Fig. 6 bottom shows an example scenario where skids have all parked in a formation and one skid is desired to travel through the formation to a goal location. The nature of the artificial potential field approach allows for this behavior to occur rather naturally. As the skid moves through the formation, the formation itself expands out to let the desired skid through and then contracts back. This is achieved with each skid only knowing its goal location, its current position, and detected distances to surrounding obstacles/other skids. Each skid does not need to communicate directly with other skids to corroborate motion plans as would be needed if more advanced motion planning algorithms were used. This artificial potential field approach lessens the infrastructure needed on the robot for computation and network communication needs. However, a major bottleneck to this approach is the high probability of reaching local minimum, especially when the number of robots or obstacles increases. While many scenarios were successful in our tests, there were a number of scenarios where the final configuration was not achieved due to certain robots reaching local minimums. There are however, many algorithms developed such as the one presented in [15] to handle and escape from these situations.

5 Conclusions and Future Work

This work has presented a simple HMI and artificial potential field approach to parking multiple autonomous non-holonomic skids. The HMI allows the user to select desired robotic skids from a top down view and draw a boundary for which to park the robotic skids. Optimal parking locations within the boundary for each skid are automatically calculated using convex optimization approaches. Simulation and hardware tests have shown successful parking in optimal locations within a boundary as well as moving skids through an already parked formation. While we have not yet implemented the ability to handle local minimums, future work will investigate implementing one of the many escape methods published. We will also consider the use of a hybrid approach using RRT* to escape from the local minimum areas as well. We are also currently investigating the use of simultaneous localization and mapping (SLAM) results for each robot which will be shared amongst each robot and the user interface. This would negate the need for a top-down camera to generate the global position and pose information of the robots however it does increase the computational needs as well as the communication needs of each robot to share their maps of the world.

References

1. Cowan, N., Shakerina, O., Vidal, R., Sastry, S.: Vision-based follow-the-leader. In: IEEE/RJS International Conference on Intelligent Robots and Systems (2003)
2. Scharf, D.P., Hadaegh, F.Y., Ploen, S.R.: A survey of space formation flying guidance and control (part 2). In: American Control Conference, Boston (2004)
3. Ren, W., Beard, R.W.: A decentralized scheme for spacecraft formation flying via the virtual structure approach. In: American Control Conference, Denver (2003)
4. Kondak, K., Hommel, G.: Compuation of time optimal movements for autnomous parking of Non-holonomic mobile Platforms. In: International Conference on Robotics and Automation, Seoul (2001)
5. Masaki, H., Kangzhi, L.: Automatic parking benchmark problem: experimental comparison of Nonholonomic control Methods. In: Chinese Control Conference, Hunan (2007)
6. Lawton, J., Beard, R., Young, B.: A decentralized approach to formation maneuvers. IEEE Trans. Robot. Autom. 19(6), 933–941 (2003)
7. Liang, Y., Lee, H.-H.: Decentralized formation control and obstacle avoidance for multiple robots with Nonholonomic constraints In: American Control Conference, Minneopolis (2006)
8. Elkaim, G., Kelbley, R.: A Lightweight Formation Control Methodology for a Swarm of Nonholonomic Vehicles. In: IEEE Aerospace Conference, Big Sky (2006)

568   J. Hing et al.

9. Ekanayake, S., Pathirana, P.: Formations of robotic swarm: an artificial force based approach. Int. J. Adv. Rob. Syst. **7**(3), 173–190 (2010)
10. Seki, H., Shibayama, S., Kamiya, Y., Hikizu, M.: Practical obstacle avoidance using potential field for a nonholonomic mobile robot with rectangular body. In: IEEE International Conference on Emerging Technologies and Factory Automation (2008)
11. Boyd, S., Vandenberghe, L.: Convex Optimization. Cambridge University Press, Cambridge (2009)
12. Luo, C.: Novel Convex Optimization Approaches for VLSI Floorplanning. University of Waterloo, Waterloo (2008)
13. Maximizing minimum distances between points placed in a polygon [Online]. Accessed http://math.stackexchange.com/questions/718733/maximizing-minimum-distance-between-points-placed-in-a-polygon
14. Grant, M., Boyd, S., Ye, Y.: CVX: Matlab Software for Disciplined Convex Programming. Springer, Heidelberg (2008)
15. Kokosy, A., Defaux, F.-O., Perruquetti, W.: Autonomous navigation of a nonholonomic mobile robot in a environment. In: IEEE International Workshop on Safety, Security, and Rescue Robotics, Sendai (2008)

SAFT: Firefighting Environment Recognition Improvement for Firefighters

Jin Hyun Park[1(✉)], In Jin Baek[2], and Su Ji Han[2]

[1] Department of Visual Comm, Kaywon University of Art and Design,
Uiwang, Korea
tb6009@gmail.com
[2] Department of Interaction Design Graduate School of Techno Design,
Kookmin University, Seoul, Korea
{injin.baek, thingkingsparrow}@gmail.com

Abstract. This study is to develop a device that enables to protect life of firefighters and facilitate firefighting activities. In many cases, the existing studies focus on the development of firefighting suites with many sensors and entire network system. In contrast, there are not many studies related to simple device easily used for protecting one's life in fire firefighters is likely to encounter more frequently. As a result from the field research and focus group interview, it has been recognized that rapid concept prototype is possible to develop by using open source hardware. It has been also found that the device is required to combine with the existing equipment and it should be unit device with single function.

Keywords: Wearable · Firefighting system · Navigation · Space recognition

1 Introduction

Fires can cause great damage, both to human life and property. In terms of human life damages, victims could be firefighters as well as people to be rescued. According to the statistics regarding firefighters, the number of people to be taken care of by one firefighter in Korea is a several hundred more than that of other countries [6]. Compared to firefighters in Japan and Hong Kong, it is more than 60 %. Since the number of population taken care of by one firefighter is large in Korea, the number of firefighters' fatalities also tends to grow in last 10 years (2009−2012). The high number of population per one firefighter and the growth of the number of firefighting operations may cause the increase.

Major causes leading to firefighter's death are called 'six operational incidents' which accounts for 78.8 % of the total firefighters' fatalities [1]. Looking at the causes in a descending order of portions, traffic accident during fire operation accounts for 21 %, building collapse while suppressing fire 19 %, removal of respirator face piece and suffocation due to lack of oxygen 13 %, drowning accident by flowing water with strong current 11 %, falls during fire operation 6 % and suffocation in manhole 6 %. A half of the six causes are building collapse, suffocation and falls that occur while firefighters are in a fire (Table 1).

© Springer International Publishing Switzerland 2015
S. Yamamoto (Ed.): HIMI 2015, Part II, LNCS 9173, pp. 569–578, 2015.
DOI: 10.1007/978-3-319-20618-9_56

Table 1. Comparing firefighter's death in 3 countries (Source: 2013 statistics report)

	Number of firefighter ('06)	Number of firefighter's death ('02 ~ '06)	Rates of firefighter's death (per 10,000)	Severity rate of firefighter's death
Korea	30,199	6.4	2.12	0.21
USA	316,950	32.6	1.03	0.10
Japan	156,758	6.6	0.42	0.04

In this sense, it is necessary to design and develop equipment and system that enables to directly assist firefighters in their firefighting operation since their injuries and deaths could lead to an increase of victims in fire situation as well. According to results from the research, there are some studies to develop firefighting equipment combining with new technologies including Internet of Things in US and Europe [6]. Most of the studies focus on the development to reduce damage to human life in fire and protect firefighters against firefighting operations by taking advantage of new technology [10, 11]. However, reality is that there are not many outcomes that are practically used in fire situation due to limitation in their concepts or cost [9]. To overcome these problems, this study is based on UX design process in order to improve the firefighter's working environment. This point is what differentiates our study from the existing ones.

Since opinions and needs of firefighters participating in firefighting operation are crucial in determining the direction and the result of this study, scope of the study is limited to domestic field and target of user survey has been conducted for firefighters working with Uiwang fire station at Uiwang, Gyeonggi province.

A prototype was developed by results from researches and literature studies. The prototype was used as a tool to verify our ideas. The simulated fire experience was useful to test the prototype and to enhance our understanding what the fire situation looks like. To collect information on the operational system running in actual fire-fighting environment and fire ground, we conducted focus group interview (FGI). Additionally, in-depth interview was conducted to explore the actual and specific needs of firefighters.

1.1 SAFT System Overview

SAFT stands for "save from the backdraft". It is a project starting from the idea of saving firefighters against dangerous situation like backdraft. The objectives of the study are as follows:

1. The system has to meet the requirements of firefighters and usability in practical fire ground has highest priority.
2. The system can be developed with low cost by employing open source hardware.
3. The system should be upgraded consistently by means of communication with firefighters.

1.2   Related Work

Thinking about what is protecting firefighter's life and supporting their fire operation in fire situation, it could be things that can reduce risk factor, help them decide what to do next, allow them to see invisible objects, and facilitate communication with other crews. In this section, we will explore some of the existing studies conducted to support the fire operation and find out what makes our study different from others.

1.3   Characteristics of the Existing Works

ProeTEX is a project that develops smart wearables using electronics fibres. The smart textiles enable to continuously monitor life signs (biopotentials, breathing movement and cardiac sounds) and biosensors (sweat, dehydration, electrolytes, stress indicators, $O2$ and $CO2$). Power generated by energy transformed by textile abrasion, photovoltaic and thermoelectric energy can be stored and supplied to the embedded equipment enabling low-power short-range wireless communication [4]. WearIT@Work project is developing a wearable form of electronic system [5]. ProFiTex project is developing a protective system comprising electronic devices such as infrared cameras and localization sensors integrated into the firefighters clothing. This system provides 3D image of an indoor environment reconstructed with data obtained by the clothing. The image may be helpful for firefighters to set their walking direction. In particular, it will be significant useful for exploring the space where they lose their visibility in a smoke-filled room or blackout room [2].

The Fire Information and Rescue Equipment (FIRE) project is devising a device that can provide a variety of external information to the firefighter through HMD (Head-Mounted Display) [12]. NIST Smart Firefighting project conducts the study to combine the firefighting equipment and robot. This system is designed to provide data such as firefighter's location, vital sign and mental state in real time basis [7]. Wearable Advanced Sensor Platform (WASP) developed by US research consortium is a wearable product attaching a location tracking sensor and a physiological state-monitoring sensor. Globe Manufacturing company produces a shirt integrating with sensors, while Zephyr Technology manufactures a hockey-puck-shaped monitoring system to track heart rate and blood pressure etc. TRX Systems produces a location tracking device and a 3D tracking map system [3]. The product of Zephyr Technology is designed to monitor up to 60 people at a time, so it can be used to monitor the changes of physiological states of firefighters in different situations. Another is NEON® Mission Essential System of TRX Systems. The system is capable of tracking location of firefighter in 3D space on real time basis. The system can communicate wirelessly in two ways: (1) the traditional radio network and (2) new wireless communication network like WIFI and 3G/4G network via Android OS smartphone. Thus disaster managing head quarter can comprehensively recognize the firefighting operation progress. It is obvious that the systems have advantage in monitoring if firefighters attending in fire are in danger and rescuing them from risk situation. However, the downside of the systems is that they do not provide sufficient information that can allow the firefighters to cope with their immediate situation.

While there are a number of studies that are being actively conducted in firefighting field, the problem is that prototype has limitation in terms of safety. For this reason, there are not many practical examples that the prototypes are used in actual fire ground. In these studies, it is critically important to obtain data generated by using the prototype in an actual fire since it is hard to test a prototype in a simulated fire due to the difficulty of reproducing the fire situation [8].

Based on the discussion as above, the characteristics of the existing studies can be summarized as follows:

1. The system consists of heart rate sensor to understand physiological state of firefighter.
2. The system uses various sensors monitoring temperature and detecting toxic gas to understand a surrounding environment of firefighter.
3. The system is equipped with Bluetooth or 3G/4G mobile network to transmit data.
4. The related studies can be divided into two categories: (1) studies on wearable device attaching various sensors and (2) studies on network transmitting data.

The research results of SAFT indicates that there are not sufficient studies on a method to allow firefighters recognize their surrounding space and move swiftly while they fight against fire in a smoke-filled room.

According to the characteristics of the existing projects, we found a number of problems in those studies.

First, the existing projects tend to be conducted in a large scale. Their goal is to develop an integrated system extensively ranging from wearable device to tracking system. To develop such a large-scale system, huge amount of money is typically required. High cost was number one impediment to block progress of the studies. It is hard to continuously use high value equipment in fires that may happen very frequently.

Second, the existing projects sacrifice usage of the device due to offering too many functions. Typically it takes not much time when firefighters are dispatched to the fire ground and start their operation. In other words, immediate response is critical in the fire. Equipment with too many functions and required to learn how to use is practically useless in such an urgent situation. HUD is one of expensive equipment. However, HUD should be verified in terms of how much information is necessary to provide to firefighters in a firefighting operational environment from the perspective of interface.

Third problem is lack of priority among functionalities provided by the existing systems. The existing systems offer lots of functions without validating the priorities required by firefighters, which might only add unnecessary things. Therefore it is necessary to develop a device that actually assists firefighters with their operation by providing a top functionality with highest priority. While toxic gas concentration and temperature might be helpful for firefighters to realize their surrounding environment, offering heart rate data to firefighter needs to be reconsidered because it might not be big help for firefighting operation.

Based on these problems found in the process of research, SAFT project aims to actively reflect the opinions of firefighters attending to a fire with avoiding high cost technologies and complicated functions.

2 Defining Issues and Derivation of Sensors

We define the problems the firefighters are supposed to face with when entering a fire. In addition, sensors to be used are derived.

(1) Understanding space (visible)
- Sensors: ultrasonic, infra-red sensor, azimuth sensor and acceleration sensor

Smoke occurring in a fire is dangerous factor threatening the firefighters. Firefighters use smoke penetrate lantern when approaching a fire spot. Interview with firefighter indicates that they cannot see properly because of high density smoke and they cannot recognize 1 m ahead from them even if they are using smoke penetrate lantern that can make surroundings lighter but it is no use in heavy smoke. Consequently, they walk slowly by holding and touching the wall by hands. While they are walking, they are exposed to dangerous environment such as stairs, holes on ground, cliff. In many cases, the firefighters get damages or injured by falls while they retreat after suppressing a fire. Even though two or three member team carry a water hose together, sometimes a firefighter has to move by himself/herself rescuing people in large space. In this case, information to help them recognize their direction will be helpful for the firefighters [13]. In an urgent situation where the firefighter needs to return back, the information will be useful for the firefighter to decide the retreating path.

(2) Understanding Environment (invisible)
- Sensors: temperature sensor, atmospheric sensor, chemical detection sensor

Most of firefighters wear respiratory protective apparatus since toxic gas tends to be generated in a fire. If a fire takes place in a factory, chemicals stacked in the factory ignite many fires. Consequently, the fire could consistently generate toxic gas even after suppressing the fire. In this case, the firefighters should wear respiratory protective equipment all the time. It should be noted that a significant number of firefighters are dead due to breathing in toxic gas during post-fire period.

Temperature can be used as criteria to understand current status of environment. The firefighters can understand progressing direction and moving path of the fire. It will also be helpful to realize an urgent situation such as backdraft.

(3) Recognizing Physiological Status
- Sensors: Heart rate sensors, gyro sensors

Heart rate is a good indicator that allows the firefighter to recognize his/her physiological status. While physiological status monitoring data is critically important for understanding physical and psychological status of firefighter, the data is not necessary to provide to firefighters themselves. Instead of that, it will be better to use the data to monitor states of all the firefighters participating in firefighting operation from the commanding head quarter as done in WASP system.

(4) Communication (Recording, interaction among internal and external people)
- Devices and Technologies to be used: Mobile network and Cloud server

With use of IoT (Internet of Things) technology being actively conducted recently, it can be achieved to record an actual situation and condition. Data sent by sensors can be fundamental information to carry out a variety of studies on a fire. 3G/4G LTE enables to transmit data with very high speed so that people can understand the fire location in three dimensions.

3 Concept Prototype

The purpose of the first concept prototype is to test if the ideas suggested in our research practically worked or not. The first prototype was designed and produced in a form of full size helmet based on open source hardware, Arduino attaching various sensors. Testing if environment data collected from sensors can be effectively recognized carried out experiment. To do this, data sent by sensors attaching in helmet are transmitted to computer with graphical user interface (GUI).

3.1   Overall Architecture of Concept Prototype

The prototype consists of fire fighting helmet, PC, mobile device, and cloud server. Helmet consists of senor unit and helmet UI. Based on the sensors derived in the research, sensor unit is comprised of several sensors such as ultrasonic wave sensor and compass sensor, heart pulse sensor and four temperature sensors.

Helmet UI was implemented by applying a mechanism of Head-Up Display (HUD). Reflection panel attached on smartphone screen is placed at the position right above the firefighter's eyes. In this prototype, in order to improve intuitive understanding of sensed data, both of forward sight and screen UI are to be seen at the same time. To do this, GUI of smartphone (Nexus 5) is placed and black acrylic reflective panel is placed at the front of helmet. The black acrylic panel will reflect the smartphone screen to be seen by the person who wears the helmet (Figs. 1 and 2).

As for control unit, MacBook Pro was used. The control unit processes the sensed data using Flash and Netlab toolkit. GUI is constructed based on the sensed data as

Fig. 1. Prototype of fire fighting

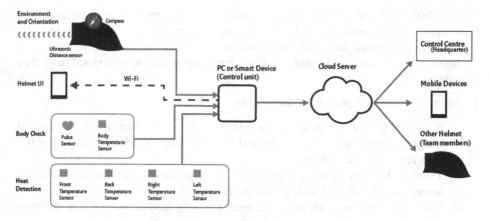

Fig. 2. Saft system overview

input using Flash. Once the control unit receives the sensed data by way of widget of Netlab toolkit, it transmits the data to UI and cloud server, xively.com.

Xivley server is in charge of collecting and recording all the sensor data sent by helmet. The data gathered at the server will be transmitted to control center or other firefighter as needed.

4 Simulation

To evaluate the usage of our prototype and validate our hypothesis established in this study, we conducted field test in a smoke evacuation simulation room at Uiwang fire station. Three-member-team enter the room without any protective equipment. Participants only can guess that there are some obstacles located at ceiling and on floor. After opening several doors, participants could escape from the room. Finally they could be evacuated through the exit, after experiencing a simulated backdraft. Completing the experience, a firefighter wears the prototype helmet and performs an experiment from entering the house to getting out of there through the exit [14]. The firefighters have an interview after they finish their test.

5 User Research

Based on the results from user survey and simulation process with prototype, we propose a new device to allow firefighters to enhance their visibility with no delay. Research problem to be specifically investigated in this user survey is as follows.

Research problem: A smart helmet attaching ultrasonic and azimuth sensors assist firefighters with recognizing a structure of an actual surrounding space.

The survey was conducted by means of focus group interview for six male and one female firefighter who have experience attending to fires over 500 times. Prior to in-depth interview, the participants were asked about personal information and their experience on firefighting in order to smoothly carry out the interview and get understanding of actual firefighting environment.

Interview questions are divided into three parts depending on behavioral pattern of firefighter.

1. Associated with the process of firefighting.

    - It is hard to distinguish the place where a fire starts even using the thermal imaging camera because the camera shows the image that looks like full of fire with red color everywhere.
    - There is difficulty in using equipment due to obstacles scattered around a fire scene, though we have various equipment.
    - Since a fire barrier is set up at the entrance, it is hard to use tools at the time entering an entrance.

2. Performance of firefighting in a fire scene.

    - We identify obstacles touching them by hands before entering the building because of the heavy smoke.
    - Many firefighters die of falls because they cannot see anything about floor because of the heavy smoke.
    - The information is likely to be helpful since we lose our sense of direction after all while we keep moving here and there.

3. The process of retreat after completing firefighting.

    - We retreat from the fire scene following the water hose we carried for extinguishing a fire.
    - Two-way radio transceiver is installed at inside of helmet. However, we cannot use it because it is tough to speak with firefighter mask.

The results from a verification experiment and user interview demonstrate that the prototype is developed suitable for the objectives of this study. Based on the insights found in this process, we derive a number of things necessary to improve. Next section lists up and explains the findings.

6 Findings

First, validation for four sensors has proved. Particularly, it has been demonstrated that ultrasonic sensor effectively assists firefighters with providing better understanding for the surrounding space even before checking obstacles and objects with touching by hands. Owing to ultrasonic sensor, firefighters enable to recognize where wall or objects are in the space even without losing their visibility. However, it is found that information on the floor is necessary for preventing risk from falls.

Second, quality of air filled in the space is also important information to be offered in order to prevent death from toxic gas. This can be achieved by sensing the concentration of carbon monoxide and carbon dioxide

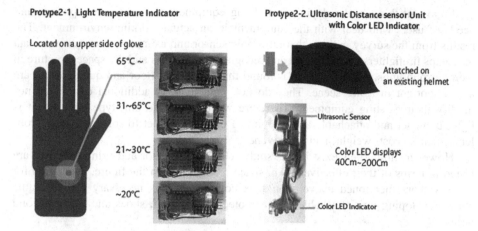

Fig. 3. Second concept of prototypes

Third, it is necessary to reduce complexity of user interface when showing the information sent by various sensors on Head Up Display (HUD). Furthermore it is found that acoustic output such as beeping sound and voice rather than visual output will be better because hearing effect is more intuitive.

Finally, they do not want to wear additional device since their existing helmet is already heavy. Moreover they do not want to make a hole or make any change to their helmet because they have concern that the change might affect helmet's durability. Combining the insights elicited so far, we reach the bottom line: (1) a device is required to be light-weight and compact unit type, and (2) a device is required to be short-range recognition device sensing and notifying the environment information by easily being attached and detached at any point of helmet.

We build second concept prototype with open source hardware based on our user research result. The new prototype is designed for the individual functions and places in the best position. Each sensor is separated as an individual unit. The ultrasonic sensor module changed the design from the built in module to attach on to the helmet. Temperature sensor unit placed on top of the glove. We use LED for the indications of the distance and temperature for the fast reading. Also it is easy to extend with Bluetooth module to transfer data through the mobile network (Fig. 3).

7 Conclusion

This study aims to propose a device that can protect firefighters from injury and fatality in a fire and assist them with their firefighting activities. The results from desk researches indicate that a number of studies related to development of firefighting equipment integrating with IT technology have been conducted around the world. However, there are few outcomes being practically used. We consider that this is because the studies focus too much on applying high-level technology rather than thinking about users' needs. For this reason, our study was carried out based on UX design process.

Important thing in developing firefighting equipment is to focus on opinions and needs of users who deal with the equipment in an actual working environment. The results from the survey indicate that ultrasonic sensor and azimuth sensor generate data that helps firefighters to understand and recognize the objects and the space structure in their surroundings. Additionally, it is found that data about floor and quality of air are also important in a fire scene. They do not want to wear additional equipment nor modify their existing equipment. Therefore we propose the unit type device that is light, compact and attachable at any point of existing helmet to solve practical problems such as cost, weight, and effectiveness.

However, limitations exist in this study. Ultrasonic sensor and azimuth sensor are tested in terms of their effectiveness in space recognition. In the future, evaluation for other sensors mentioned above should be conducted. It is necessary to extend the study-developing unit attachable to fire protective clothing, shoes and glove beyond helmet.

References

1. Yun, C.Y.: A Study on the Implementation of A Fire Detection and Rescue System based on Ubiquitous Sensor Network, vol. 34, pp. 325–329. Korean institute of Communications and Information Sciences, KICS Press, Seoul (2009)
2. Schönauer, C., et al.: 3D building reconstruction and thermal in fire brigade operations mapping. In: AH 2013, pp. 202–205 (2013)
3. Globe Manufacturing Company: Wearable advanced sensor platform. http://www.globeturnoutgear.com/innovations/was
4. Magenes, G. et al.: Fire fighters and rescuers monitoring through wearable sensors: the ProeTEX project. In: IEEE, 3594–3597 (2010)
5. Lawo, M.: wearIT@work Project. http://www.wearitawork.com
6. National Emergency Management Agency: Statistics report (2013). http://www.nfds.go.kr
7. Occupational Health & Safety: NIST sponsoring smart firefighting workshop. http://ohsonline.com/articles/2014/03/20/nist-sponsoring-smart-fire-fighting-workshop.aspx
8. Feese, S., et al.: CoenoFire: monitoring performance indicators of firefighters in real-world missions using smartphones. In: Ubicomp 2013, pp. 83–92 (2013)
9. Mun, S.J.: Fire Protection of the Basic Data for Practical Use, pp. 48–51 2010. Korean Institute of Fire Science & Engineering, KIFSE Press, Seoul (2010)
10. Jan, Y.G.: A Study on Pedestrian Dead Reckoning for Enhancing Indoor Positioning Accuracy of Fireman, pp. 1671–1672. Korean Society of Civil Engineers Press, Seoul (2014)
11. Cho, Y.H.: Implementation of android based intelligent prevention of disaster management application. In: Proceedings of 2011 KIIT Summer Conference, pp. 208–210 (2011)
12. Bretschneider, N., et al.: Head mounted displays for firefighters. In: IFAWC (2006)
13. Chmelar, P., et al.: The Fusion of Ultrasonic and Optical Measurement Devices for Autonomous Mapping, pp. 292–296. IEEE (2013)
14. Dyrks, T., et al.: Designing for firefighters—building empathy through live action role-playing. In: ISCRAM (2009)

Modelling of a Business Process for Alarm Management Lifecycle in Chemical Industries

Kazuhiro Takeda[1(✉)], Takashi Hamaguchi[2], Naoki Kimura[3], and Masaru Noda[4]

[1] Graduate School of Engineering, Shizuoka University, Shizuoka, Japan
tktaked@ipc.shizuoka.ac.jp
[2] Graduate School of Engineering, Nagoya Institute of Technology, Nagoya, Japan
hamachan@nitech.ac.jp
[3] Faculty of Engineering, Kyushu University, Fukuoka, Japan
nkimura@chem-eng.kyushu-u.ac.jp
[4] Department of Chemical Engineering, Fukuoka University, Fukuoka, Japan
mnoda@fukuoka-u.ac.jp

Abstract. A plant alarm system is one of important safety equipment. Instrument Society of America has proposed an alarm management lifecycle. Although the lifecycle shows guideline of alarm management, business process activities and information exchange between the activities concerned with alarm management are not represented. To perform the alarm management lifecycle, a business process model for alarm management is necessary. In this paper, we propose an alarm management business process model, called AMBPM here after. We have developed the AMBPM based on a business process model for a plant lifecycle engineering. The AMBPM represents business process activities concerned with an alarm management and information exchange between the activities. In a case study, a business flow of an alarm system design process was derived from the AMBPM. The business flow represents specific activities and information for the respective step, whereas the AMBPM represents whole information concerned with the activities.

Keywords: Alarm management lifecycle · Plant lifecycle engineering · Business process model · Business flow

1 Introduction

Chemical plants treat hazardous and/or toxic materials. Furthermore, the plants are operated at high pressure and/or at high temperature. When an accident occurs in the plant, the materials and/or huge energy may be released and environment is greatly damaged. Therefore, the plants must be at safe states. For the plant safety, independent protection layers (IPLs) (Fig. 1) [1] have been proposed. The protection is constructed with eight layers. A plant alarm system performs as the third layer. The plant alarm system alert operators the abnormal status of the plant and guide the countermeasures for each accidents. Their alarms are critical alarms for the plant safety and process alarms for the product quality. This paper treats with the critical alarms for the plant

© Springer International Publishing Switzerland 2015
S. Yamamoto (Ed.): HIMI 2015, Part II, LNCS 9173, pp. 579–587, 2015.
DOI: 10.1007/978-3-319-20618-9_57

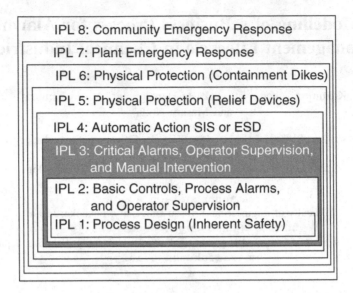

Fig. 1. Independent protection layers

safety. The plant alarm system should be properly managed through the plant lifecycle. To properly manage the plant alarm system, the activities concerned with the plant alarm system and information flows between the activities in the plant lifecycle should be explicitly expressed. Furthermore, constraints, available inputs and expected outputs of each activities should be explicitly expressed to develop supporting tools for the activities. To explicitly express activities and information flow, a business process model (BPM) have been proposed. This paper proposes an alarm management business process model (AMBPM) and the derived business process flows.

2 Alarm Management Lifecycle

To properly manage the plant alarm system, ISA (Instrument Society of America) has proposed an alarm management standard [2]. In the standard, an alarm management lifecycle (AMLC) has been proposed as shown in Fig. 2. The AMLC contains three loops; a monitoring and maintenance loop, a monitoring and management of change loop and an audit of philosophy loop.

3 BPM Approach for Plant Alarm System Management

To perform the activities in the AMLC, relationships among the activities and the other activities as the engineering in the plant lifecycle should be explicitly expressed. Namely, whole activities, contains them in the AMLC, in the plant lifecycle engineering should be explicitly expressed. To explicitly express activities and information flow, a BPM have been proposed.

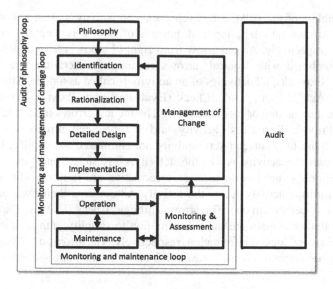

Fig. 2. Alarm management lifecycle

3.1 Template of BPM

PI STEP (Process Industries Standard for the Exchange of Product model data Consortium) standardized a plant structure. In the PI STEP, IDEF0 (Integrated Definition for Functional model standard, Type-zero) [3] is used as an activity modeling method and PIEBASE (Process Industry Executive for archiving Business Advantage using Standards for data Exchange) model [4] is used as a framework. Fuchino et al. (2010) [5] extended the PIEBASE model and proposed a PDCA + P.R. (plan, do, check and act + provide resources) template. Shimada et al. (2012) [6] proposed a BPM of Plant-LCE (Plant Life-Cycle Engineering) based on the template. Fuchino et al. (2010) [5] proposed an overview template to overview whole the BPM. In this paper, a AMBPM is based on the BPM of Plant-LCE, and an overview template of the BPM (Fig. 3) is based on the overview template proposed by Fuchino et al. (2010) [5].

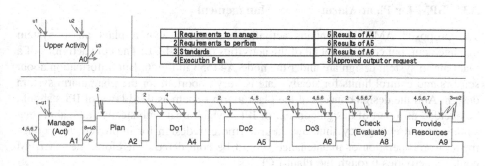

Fig. 3. Template of business process model

In the template of the BPM, a box represents an activity and an arrow represents information. Arrows into left, top and bottom of a box is 'input', 'control' and 'mechanism', respectively. An out arrow from right of a box is 'output'. 'Mechanism' arrows are combined with 'control' arrows to simplify. Activities are constructed hierarchically. Expanded all activities of an activity is called as a node. These activities are 'Manage (Act)', 'Plan', 'Do', 'Check (Evaluate)' and 'Provide Resources'. The 'Do' activities may be two or more activities. The request arrows from 'Manage (Act)' activity to 'Provide Resources' activity and the resource arrows from 'Provide Resources' activity to 'Manage (Act)' activity are eliminated to simplify. Each output information from the activity A1 to the activityA7 is stored and gave to the next activity. To simplify, the arrows to store information are omitted. The each output information from the activity A2 to the activity A8 contains their own output information and the upper stream one. The arrows through 'Check (Evaluate)' and 'Provide Resources' activities contain the same information to simplify, although these arrows contains checked and logged information, respectively. The arrows u1, u2 and u3 in the upper activity are respectively the arrows 1, 3 and 8 in the node.

3.2 BPM Approach

The plant alarm system should be managed and maintained through the plant lifecycle. To perform activities adequately, the activities concerned with the plant alarm system management in the plant lifecycle and information flows among the activities should be explicitly expressed as a BPM. Furthermore, constraints, available inputs and expected outputs of the activities are required to be explicitly expressed to select or develop supporting tools for the activities. This paper proposes an AMBPM in the plant lifecycle. Even if the developed AMBPM is incomplete, the AMBPM approach has following merits;

- The activities can be properly performed along with alarm management lifecycle.
- Whole activities are hierarchically expressed.
- Required information to perform each activities is obvious.
- Requirements for tools used by each activities are defined.

3.3 BPM for Plant Alarm System Management

The proposed AMBPM contains activities concerned with a plant alarm system management, but contains not all of the activities of Plant-LCE. The core activities of a plant alarm system design are under the node A44553 in Fig. 6. But, information about sensors and control limits for steady state is very important for the plant alarm system design. And the design concept of the plant alarm system as third layer of IPLs should be decided as a part of design concept of IPLs which treat with steady state, abnormal situations and emergency shutdown. Furthermore, redesign for improvement requirements from operation or maintenance should be considered. Therefore, the AMBPM contains activities through the Plant-LCE.

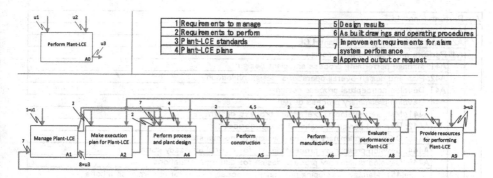

1 Requirements to manage	5 Design results
2 Requirements to perform	6 As built drawings and operating procedures
3 Plant-LCE standards	7 Improvement requirements for alarm system performance
4 Plant-LCE plans	8 Approved output or request

Fig. 4. Node A0 "Perform Plant-LCE" of AMBPM

In Fig. 4, green arrows represent information about requirement of change, and orange arrows represent the other information. As shown in Fig. 4, the activity A1 'Manage Plant-LCE' receives requirements 1 = u1 to manage and requires to perform the activities A2, A4, A5 and A6. The activity A2 'Make execution plan for Plant-LCE' receives the request and makes execution plans. The activity A4 'Perform process and plant design' receives the plan and performs the process and the plant design. The activity A5 'Perform construction' constructs the plant along with the design. The activity A6 'Perform manufacturing' manufactures by the constructed plant.

A part of an activity tree of the AMBPM concerned with plan alarm system design process is shown in Fig. 5, because the whole AMBPM is very large. A core node of plant alarm system design process of AMBPM is the node A44553 as shown in Fig. 6.

In the node A44553, the activity A445533 'Develop alarm source signals' selects or newly designs alarm source signals. The activity A445534 'Develop alarm limits' develops alarm limits for the alarm source signals. The activity A445535 'Develop alarm algorithms' develops alarm algorithms. This node contains main activities for the plant alarm system design process. To perform these activities, information about constraints, tools and standards for the activities are very important. The information should be available and easy to use. Furthermore, explicitly describing the structure of activities which generate the information using the AMBPM, design rationale for the plant alarm system can be specified. Therefore, the plant alarm system can be designed logically.

3.4 Business Flow for an Example Design Process

A business flow for an example design process is illustrated as a green arrow in Fig. 7. The flow passes through many activities. Some activities are activated at several times. Referred information for each activate time are not always the same. For these reasons, it is difficult to express the business flow directly on the AMBPM in a readable way. So, we transcribe the example business flow as shown in Fig. 8.

The requirements for a plant alarm system design are given to the activity A445531 "Manage developing detailed design for plant alarm system". The activity is activated

A0: Perform Plant–LCE					
	A1: Manage Plant–LCE				
	A2: Make execution plan for Plant–LCE				
	A4: Perform process and plant design				
		A41: Manage performing process and plant design			
		A42: Plan and design overall operational design philosophy			
		A43: Develop conceptual process design			
		A44: Develop preliminary process design			
			A441: Manage developing preliminary process design		
			A442: Plan and design operational design concept		
			A443: Develop preliminary process design for normal steady state		
			A444: Develop preliminary process design for normal unsteady state		
			A445: Develop preliminary process design for abnormal situations		
				A4451: Manage developing preliminary process design for abnormal situations	
				A4452: Plan and design preliminary process design concept for abnormal situations	
				A4453: Allocate abnormal situations to IPL	
				A4454: Develop backup process design for abnormal situations	
				A4455: Develop preliminary process design for IPL3	
					A44551: Manage developing preliminary process design for IPL3
					A44552: Plan and design preliminary process design concept for IPL3
					A44553: Develop detailed design for plant alarm system
					A445531: Manage developing detailed design for plant alarm system
					A445532: Plan and design detailed design concept for plant alarm system
					A445533: Develop alarm source signals
					A445534: Develop alarm limits
					A445535: Develop alarm algorithms
					A445536: Evaluate performance of developing detailed design for plant alarm system
					A445537: Provide resources for developing detailed design for plant alarm system
					A44554: Develop detailed design for fault diagnosis system
					A44555: Develop countermeasures corresponding to the plant alarm system
					A44556: Evaluate performance of developing preliminary process design for IPL3
					A44557: Provide resources for developing preliminary process design for IPL3
				A4456: Develop preliminary process design for IPL4	
				A4457: Evaluate performance of developing process design for abnormal situations	
				A4458: Provide resources for developing process design for abnormal situations	
			A446: Develop preliminary process design for emergency shutdown		
			A447: Evaluate performance of developing preliminary process design		
			A448: Provide resources for developing preliminary process design		
		A45: Develop preliminary plant design			
		A46: Develop final process design			
		A47: Develop final plant design			
		A48: Evaluate performance of process and plant design			
		A49: Provide resources for performing process and plant design			
	A5: Perform construction				
	A6: Perform manufacturing				
		A61: Manage manufacturing			
		A62: Make production plan			
		A63: Perform production			
		A64: Perform maintenance			
		A65: Evaluate performance of manufacturing			
		A66: Provide resources for manufacturing			
	A8: Evaluate performance of Plant–LCE				
	A9: Provide resources for performing Plant–LCE				

Fig. 5. A part of activities tree of AMBPM concerned with plant alarm system design process

as the activity A445531a "require plant alarm system design following the requirements". The activity gives the requirements to the activities A445532, A445533, A445534, and A445536.

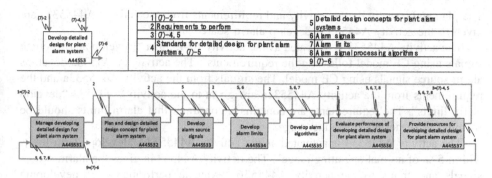

1	(7)-2	5	Detailed design concepts for plant alarm systems
2	Requirements to perform		
3	(7)-4, 5	6	Alarm signals
4	Standards for detailed design for plant alarm systems, (7)-5	7	Alarm limits
		8	Alarm signal processing algorithms
		9	(7)-6

Fig. 6. Core node of plant alarm system design process of AMBPM

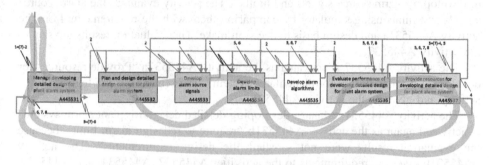

Fig. 7. Business flow of the example process of plant alarm system design

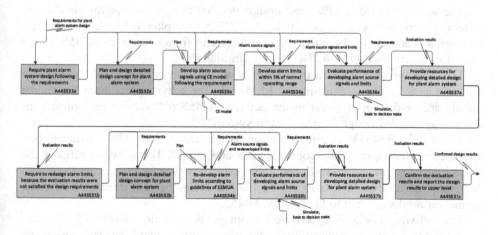

Fig. 8. Business flow of the example process of plant alarm system design

The activity A445532 "Plan and design detailed design concept for plant alarm system" is activated as the activity A445532a by requirements from the activity A445531a. The activity A445532a makes plan and design detailed design concept.

The plan and concept by the activity and requirements from the activity A445531a are given to the activity A445533 "develop alarm source signals".

The activity A445533 is activated as the activity A445533a "Develop alarm source signals using CE model following the requirements". The activity A445533a develops alarm source signals using CE model. The signals from the activity A445533a and the requirements from the activity A445531a are given to the activity A445534 "develop alarm limits". The requirements are contains a constraint that alarm limits should be within 5 % of normal operating range.

The activity A445534 is activated as the activity A445534a "develop alarm limits within 5 % of normal operating range". The activity A445534a gives the alarm source signals and limits to the activity A445536 "evaluate performance of developing detailed design for plant alarm system".

The activity A445536 is activated as the activity A445536a "Evaluate performance of developing alarm source signals and limits". The activity evaluates the alarm source signals and limits using simulator by comparing them with the requirements from the activity A445531a and design basis to decision make. The evaluation results are sent to the activity A445537.

The activity A445537 is activated as the activity A445537a "Provide resources for developing detailed design for plant alarm system". The sent results are logged by the activity and given to the activity A445531.

The activity A445531 "Manage developing detailed design for plant alarm system" is activated again as the activity A445531b "require to redesign alarm limits, because the evaluation results were not satisfied the design requirements". The activity A445531b gives the requirements to the activities A445532, A445534, and A445536. The constraint is changed from "within 5 % of normal operation range" to "according to guidelines of EEMUA".

The activity A445532 "Plan and design detailed design concept for plant alarm system" is activated again as the activity A445532b to re-plan and re-design concept. The plan and concept by the activity and requirements from the activity A445531b are given to the activity A445534 "Develop alarm limits".

The activity A445534 is activated again as the activity A445534b "re-develop alarm limits according to guidelines of EEMUA". The activity gives the alarm source signals and re-developed limits to the activity A445536 "evaluate performance of developing detailed design for plant alarm system".

The activity A445536 is activated again as the activity A445536b "Evaluate performance of developing alarm source signals and limits". The activity evaluates the alarm source signals and re-developed limits using simulator by comparing them with the requirements from the activity A445531b and design basis to decision make. The evaluation results are sent to the activity A445537.

The activity A445537 is activated again as the activity A445537b "Provide resources for developing detailed design for plant alarm system". The sent results are logged by the activity and given to the activity A445531, again.

The activity A445531 "Manage developing detailed design for plant alarm system" is activated again as the activity A445531c "confirm the evaluation results and report the design results to upper level". The activity A445531c gives the confirmed design results to upper level.

In the example business flow, the activities and information are specified at each activate time. Therefore, the activities and information exchange between the activities concerned with alarm management become clear.

4 Summary

In this paper, we tried to express an AMBPM to manage a plant alarm system. By referring the AMBPM, business process activities and information exchange between the activities concerned with alarm management become clear. The AMBPM has following merits.

- The activities can be properly performed along with alarm management lifecycle.
- Whole activities are hierarchically expressed.
- Required information to perform each activity is obvious.
- Requirements for tools used by each activity are defined.

In a case study, a business flow of an alarm system design process was derived from the AMBPM. The business flow represents specific activities and information for the respective step, whereas the AMBPM represents whole information concerned with the activity.

Acknowledgement. This research has been conducted under the Japan Society of the Promotion of Science (JSPS) 143rd committee on Process Systems Engineering.

References

1. CCPS, Layer of Protection Analysis, New York; American Institute of Chemical Engineers, Center for Chemical Process Safety (2001)
2. ISA, Management of Alarm Systems for the Process Industries, North Carolina (2009)
3. NIST, Integration Definition for Function Modelling, Federal Information Processing Standards Publication, 183, National Institution of Standards and Technology (1993). http://www.itl.nist.gov/fipspubs/idef02.doc
4. PIEBASE (Process Industries Executive for Achieving Business Advantage using Standards for Data Exchange) Activity Model Executive Summary (1998). http://www.posc.org/piebase/
5. Fuchino, T., Shimada, Y., Kitajima, T., Naka, Y.: Management of engineering standards for plant maintenance based on business process model. In: Proceedings of the 20th European Symposium on Computer Aided Process Engineering, Ischia, Italy, pp. 1363–1368. 6–9 June 2010
6. Shimada, Y., Kitajima, T., Fuchino, T., Takeda, K.: Disaster management based on business process model through the plant lifecycle. In: Approaches to Managing Disaster - Assessing Hazards, Emergencies and Disaster Impacts, pp. 19–40. InTech (2012)

Disaster Recovery Framework for e-Learning Environment Using Private Cloud Collaboration and Emergency Alerts

Satoshi Togawa[1(✉)] and Kazuhide Kanenishi[2]

[1] Faculty of Management and Information Science,
Shikoku Univeristy, Tokushima, Japan
doors@shikoku-u.ac.jp
[2] Center for University Extention,
The University of Tokushima, Tokushima, Japan
marukin@cue.tokushima-u.ac.jp

Abstract. In this research, we have built a framework of disaster recovery such as against earthquake, tsunami disaster and a heavy floods for e-Learning environment. Especially, our proposed framework is based on private cloud collaboration. We build a prototype system based on IaaS architecture, and this prototype system is constructed by several private cloud fabrics on each site such as several universities. These private cloud fabric; that is handled almost like same block device. For LMS (Learning Management System) to work, we need to boot up virtual machines which installed LMS. The virtual disk images of each virtual machines are stored into the distributed storage system. The distributed storage system will be able to keep running as a large block device. We can control the virtual machine's status and virtual machines positioning on the private cloud fabrics by the private cloud collaboration controller related with the emergency alert via smart phone. We think that our private cloud collaboration framework can continue working for e-Learning environment under the post-disaster situation. In this paper, we show our private cloud collaboration framework. And, we show the experimental results on the prototype system.

Keywords: Private cloud collaboration · Disaster recovery · E-Learning · Disaster alert notification

1 Introduction

On March 11, 2011, a major earthquake attacked to Eastern Japan. Especially, the east coast of Eastern Japan was severely damaged by the tsunami attacking. In Shikoku area including our universities in Western Japan, it is predicted that Nankai earthquake will happen in the near future. There is an interval theory that occurs every 100 to 150 years on the Pacific side in Western Japan. It is expected to have Nankai earthquake in the next 30 years, and its occurrence rate is between 70 % and 80 %. We have to prepare the disaster for the major earthquake.

In addition, we have a lot of bad experiences which is the record rainfall in a short period last few years. There are not uncommon story which the huge flood is caused by

© Springer International Publishing Switzerland 2015
S. Yamamoto (Ed.): HIMI 2015, Part II, LNCS 9173, pp. 588–596, 2015.
DOI: 10.1007/978-3-319-20618-9_58

a short period rainfall. Especially, we had the heavy record rainfall and heavy floods, it attacked to Western Japan area at August 2014. We had heavy damage by these disaster. It is no longer special for us to suffer from disasters very often. We think the preparing for the disaster including these heavy floods is very important for keeping our life, also it is very important for the information system's field.

On the other hand, the informatization of educational environment on universities is rapidly progressed by evolutional information technology in Japan. Current education environment cannot be realized without educational assistance system, such as LMS (Learning Management System), learning ePortfolio, teaching ePortfolio and so on. The learning history of students is stored by these educational assistance system. The fact is that awareness of the importance of learning data such as learning histories and teaching histories. The assistance systems are important same as learning data. Today's educational environment on universities depends on educational assistance system with information technology infrastructure. If the educational assistance system with students learning history is lost by natural disasters, we think it become equivalent to lost sustainability for educational activity.

In addition, an integrated authentication framework of inter-cloud is used to share the course materials. For example, Shibboleth Federations such as GakuNin [1] is used to authenticate other organization's user for sharing the course materials within consortium of universities. Today's universities educational activity cannot continue smoothly without those learning data and assistance system.

We can find applications for constructing information system infrastructure by the private cloud for academic field such as Yokoyama's study [2]. The target of these study is to provide massively parallel computing such as Apache Hadoop environment [3]. Their aims are to provide effective use of computer hardware resources, and providing a centralized control of computer hardware resources. It is different purpose for disaster recovery and the reduction of damage by large-scale disasters.

In this research, we have built a framework of disaster recovery from large-scale disaster such as earthquake, tsunami and huge floods for e-Learning environment. We build the private cloud computing fabrics and these inter-cloud environment, and our target is to build the private cloud collaboration framework. This private cloud environment and private cloud collaboration framework are constructed from any private cloud fabrics with the distributed storage system into several organizations such as universities. The Learning Management System such as Moodle [4] build on several private cloud fabrics. Each VM (Virtual Machine) has a LMS and the related data with a SQL database. General IaaS (Infrastructure as a Service) platform such as Linux KVM (Kernel-based Virtual Machine) [5] has a live-migration function with network shared storage and Virtual Machine Manager [6]. General network shared storage is constructed by iSCSI, NFS and usual network attached storage system. These network shared storage systems are bound to any physical storages on the each organizations. Therefore, it is difficult to do the live-migration of VMs between inter-organizations.

Our prototype platform is built with distributed storage system and KVM based IaaS architecture on a lot of usual server machines with network interfaces. It is able to handle many VMs including LMS and the data with enough redundancy. And, this prototype platform will operate inter-organizations. Thus, our prototype platform will be able to operate integrative each organization's private cloud fabric. If one organization's e-Learning environment on the private fabric is lost by some disaster, it will be able to keep running same environment on other organizations environment. In addition, our prototype platform can get emergency earthquake alert by smartphone via cell-phone carrier in Japan. Japanese cell-phone carrier is able to send emergency alert message when major earthquake generated cooperating with Japan Meteorological Agency. Our prototype platform make live-migration function when earthquake alert grasped.

In this paper, we propose a private cloud collaboration framework between private cloud fabrics on several organizations, and we show a configuration of the prototype system. And, we show the results of experimental use and examine these results. Finally, we describe future study and conclusions.

2 Assisting the Disaster Recovery for e-Learning Environment

In this section, we describe the private cloud collaboration framework of e-Learning environment. Especially, the purpose of this framework is a disaster recovery for LMS such as Moodle, and to keep running LMS and related data.

Figure 1 shows a framework of disaster recovery assistance for the e-Learning environment. Each organization such as university has each private cloud fabric. Each private cloud fabric has several server hardware at least four machines to get enough fabric's redundancy, and network connections between several server hardware. Each server hardware does not independent other server hardware on the private cloud fabric.

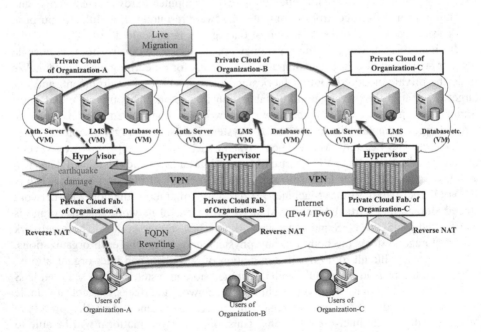

Fig. 1. Framework of disaster recovery assistance

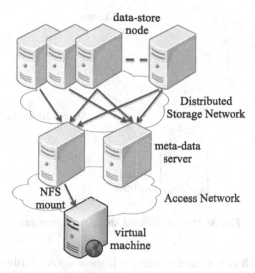

Fig. 2. Hybrid distributed storage architecture

They provide computing resources and data store resources via VMs, their resources are changed adaptively by the request from the administrators. Each VM which exists on the private cloud fabric is generated from the resources in the private cloud fabric, it is able to process any function such as authentication, and LMS function on the VM. In addition, Each VM can migrate between other private cloud fabrics, and it is able to continue to keep processing.A live migration function needs a shared file system to do the VM's migration. The product of Sheepdog Project [7] is applied to our framework. Sheepdog system is a distributed storage application optimized to QEMU and KVM hypervisor. Our proposed framework builds by KVM hypervisor, and Sheepdog distributed storage system provides highly available block level storage volumes. It can be attached to QEMU based VMs, it can be used to boot disk image for the VMs. Sheepdog distributed storage cluster does not have controller or meta-data servers such as any Storage Area Network (SAN) based storage system or other distributed storage system.

Figure 2 shows an architecture of hybrid distributed storage. This architecture has meta-data servers. The meta-data servers manage the meta-data information for split chunk data which is stored on the several data-store node. And, meta-data servers export the mount point using POSIX API such as NFS for virtual machine image. When the chunked data store to several data-store node, meta-data information which stored meta-data server is updated by stored chunk data. However, meta-data server become a single point of failure. All virtual machines can't access the VM image file and users data when the meta-data information is lost. We think this problem is very strict.

Figure 3 shows an architecture of pure distributed storage. The pure distributed storage system does not have metadata on the organized nodes. When the VM wants to get some data from distributed storage system, the consistent hashing method is used for searching target data from stored nodes of distributed storage system. The distributed storage system which is based on Sheepdog product does not have the single point of failure. Because, Sheepdog has a fully symmetric architecture. This architecture does not

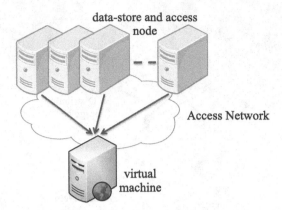

Fig. 3. Pure distributed storage architecture

have central node such as a meta-data server. If some server hardware which compose Sheepdog cluster, it has small risk to lost the VM image file and history data.

In addition, we think each VM image is able to find other organization's private cloud fabric. Because, Sheepdog based distributed storage system is constructed integrally on the several organization's private cloud fabrics. It can be able to reboot the VMs on other organization's private fabric under the disaster situation. Where possible, the VMs which are running on the several organizations move to riskless other private cloud fabric, and keep running the VMs.

Each private cloud fabric of several organizations has private cloud collaboration controller. A private cloud collaboration controller is constructed from customized smartphone and Libvirt Virtualization Toolkit [8]. Today's general smartphone has a function which catch the disaster alert notification. The disaster alert notification is delivered by mobile phone network using ETWS (Earthquake and Tsunami Warning System) message [9]. Our customized smartphone passes alert notification to the private cloud controller when the smartphone received ETWS messages. The private cloud controller which received alert notification makes live-migration command for controlled VMs.

However, if VMs migrate between several private cloud fabrics in working condition, it is not true that each organization's users can use several services. The hostname which is used to access the services, it must be rewrite to the previous organization's FQDN (Fully Qualified Domain Name). Generally, the users of organization-A want to access own LMS, they use the FQDN of organization-A. When the VM of organization-A is under controlled by the private cloud fabric of organization-B, that VM's FQDN has to provide the hostname related to organization-A. This function must operate at the same time as the live migration function.

We applied a reverse network address translation technology (reverse NAT) to keep users connectivity. The VMs which are providing LMS services migrate between several private cloud fabrics. These private cloud fabrics are deployed to inside of reverse NAT, and these are deployed same Layer2 segment under the L2VPN technology. When the VM migrate from one private cloud fabric to other private cloud fabric, the reverse NAT gets the migration status. The reverse NAT which is accepted the migration status can to rebuild DNS host entry.

As a result, we think we can assist to provide this inter-cloud framework against the disasters for e-Learning environment.

3 System Configuration

We show the configuration of proposed prototype system in Fig. 4. This is a prototype system configuration of proposed framework.

This system has four components and two internal networks. The first one of the components is the node cluster. This is a core component of our prototype system. They are constructed by eight node hardware as shown by node1 to node8. The cluster which is constructed from node1 to node4 is placed same private cloud fabric. And the other cluster which is constructed from node5 to node8 is placed same private cloud fabric. These private cloud fabrics are placed different organization physically. These private cloud fabrics are connected with L2VPN such as EtherIP technology. And the IPsec technology is used to make a secure tunnel connection for L2VPN. As a result, both private cloud fabrics are organized same cluster logically.

This node hardware which is organized for private cloud fabric is based on Intel architecture with three network interfaces. Each node has the function of KVM hypervisor, virtualization API and Sheepdog distributed storage API. Each node can be used for the VM execution infrastructure, and it is also to use the composing element of Sheepdog

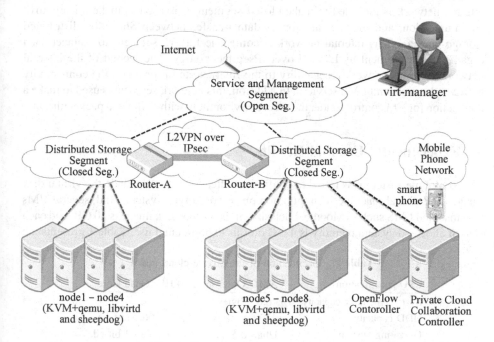

Fig. 4. Prototype system configuration

distributed storage system. As a result, it is realized sharing the hardware to use VM executing infrastructure, and it is implemented a reliability and a scalability of the storage.

The second one of the components is a Software Defined Network (SDN) controller based on OpenFlow [10] architecture. These servers which compose the VM execution infrastructure have the function of OpenFlow switch based on Open vSwitch [11]. This function is used for making optimum path dynamically, and it is also used for integrating several distributed storage.

The third one of the components is the Virtual Machine Manager. An administration interface for VM's administrator is provided by virt-manager. This function is used for management several VMs by VM's administrator on this prototype system. The virt-manager uses Libvirt Virtualization Toolkit to make VM's management functions. Libvirt Virtualization Toolkit supports any hypervisor such as KVM/QEMU, Xen, VMware ESX and so on. Any hypervisor functions are abstracted by Libvirt functions, VM's management application is able to make control the VM's status.

The fourth one of the components is the private cloud collaboration controller. This cloud controller has functions, there are catching earthquake alert notification via smartphone, and making live-migration command for target node machines. And the private cloud collaboration controller has each VMs status on private cloud fabrics, it was caught from Libvirt Virtualization Toolkit and Virtual Machine Manager. When the private cloud collaboration controller makes live-migration command to target VMs, it was planned adaptively based on managed VMs status. As a result, any alert system of earthquake will control VMs live-migration and saving the learning history via Libvirt interface on this prototype system.

On the other hands, our prototype system has two internal networks. The one of the internal network is provided to make closed segment, it is used to make a keep-alive communication, and making the storage data transfer between Sheepdog distributed storage clusters. This internal network become one Layer2 segment to connect each organization's segment by L2VPN over IPsec technology. The second of the internal network provides network reachability to the Internet, and it provides the connectivity between the users and LMS services. In addition, this network segment is used to make a connection for VM controls under the secure environment with optimized packet filtering.

4   Experimental Use and Results

This prototype system was tested to confirm its effectiveness. We made the virtual disk images and virtual machines configuration on our prototype system. And, several VMs was installed LMS such as Moodle. Each size of the virtual disk image is 20 GB, and each size of allocated system memory is 4 GB on this experimental use. Table 1 presents the

Table 1. Specification of the private cloud nodes

CPU specification	AMD Opteron 3250 HE (Quad Core)
System memory capacity	16.0 Gbytes
HDD capacity	250 Gbytes with SATA600 interface
Operating system	Ubuntu Server 14.04.1 LTS 64 bit ed.

node hardware specification for the private cloud fabrics, and OpenFlow controller and private cloud collaboration controller specification are presented in Table 2.

Table 2. Specification of openflow controller and private cloud collaboration controller

CPU specification	Intel Xeon E3-1230 3.2 GHz (Quad Core)
System memory capacity	16.0 Gbytes
HDD capacity	250 Gbytes with SATA600 interface
Operating system	Ubuntu Server 14.04.1 LTS 64 bit ed.

The prototype of the private cloud fabrics are constructed by eight node machines, and each node has 250 Gbytes capacity HDD. The total amount of physical HDD capacity is about 2.0 Tbytes. Each clustered node uses about 4 Gbytes capacities for the hypervisor function with an operating system. We think this amount is ignorable small capacity. However, the distributed storage system has triple redundancy for this test. As a result, we can use about 700 Gbytes storage capacity with enough redundancy. The total capacity of the distributed storage system can extend to add other node servers, exchange to larger HDDs, and taking both solutions. We can take enough scalability and redundancy by this distributed storage system.

We tried to do a live-migration in our prototype system. We make the test with two cases. One of the cases is to do live-migration in the same private cloud fabric. This case is targeted making live-migration in an organization. Other case is to do live-migration between private cloud fabrics. This case is targeted making live-migration inter-organization.

Table 3 shows the time of live-migration for experimental trial. We used the operate VM's live-migration by the interface of Virtual Machine Manager. The time of live-migration for same private cloud fabric is needed 23.8 s. The time of live-migration for inter-private cloud fabrics is needed 24.6 s. We think that both experimental times is enough live-migration time for a disaster reduction of provided VMs. And, we could get a complete successful result with active condition.

Table 3. Time of live migration

From node1 to node2 (same private cloud)	23.8 s
From node1 to node5 (inter private cloud)	24.6 s

In addition, the live-migration of these experimental use is operated by private cloud collaboration controller, and this live-migration function was triggered by customized Android based smartphone. We think this experimental use is pretty good, the time requirement for VMs migrating was a short period. However, the results were getting under the initial condition. The VM which are made heavy use of LMS has large size of virtual disk image. Therefore, the time of live-migration will needed more than initial condition. We think we have to make the experimental use under the actual condition.

In the real situation, we think we will use an emergency notification of the disaster from any mobile communication carrier such as NTT DoCoMo, KDDI and Softbank via their smart phones. The custom application program is installed to any smartphone such as Android platform and iPhone platform. If we can get the information of emergency notifications via smartphone with near field communication method such as USB interface, Bluetooth communication method and so on, we will be able to make a trigger of VMs live-migration with more precision.

5 Conclusion

In this paper, we proposed a framework of disaster recovery for e-Learning environment. Especially, we described an assistance to use our proposed framework, and we show the importance of an against the earthquake and tsunami disaster for e-Learning environment. We built the prototype system based on our proposed framework, and we described a system configuration of the prototype system. And, we shown the results of experimental use and examine.For the future, we have a plan to implement the function of getting earthquake notification from other smartphone such as iOS based smartphone. And we will try to test the cloud computing orchestration framework such as OpenStack and CloudStack. And, we will try to experiment confirming its effectiveness under the inter-organization environment with multipoint organizations.

Acknowledgement. This work was supported by JSPS KAKENHI Grant Number 25350333.

References

1. GakuNin Official Web site. http://www.gakunin.jp/
2. Yokoyama, S., et al.: A proposal of academic community cloud architecture and its evaluation. IPSJ J. **54**(2), 688–698 (2013)
3. Apache Hadoop Official Web site. http://Hadoop.apache.org/
4. Moodle Official Web site. http://moodle.org/
5. Linux KVM Official Web site. http://www.linux-kvm.org/
6. Virtual Machine Manager Official Web Site. http://virt-manager.org/
7. Sheepdog Project Web Site. http://www.orsg.net/sheepdog/
8. Libvirt Virtualization Toolkit Web Site. http://libvirt.org/
9. GPP Specification detail: Earthquake and Tsunami Warning System (ETWS). http://www.3gpp.org/DynaReport/23828.htm
10. OpenFlow Web Site. http://www.openflow.org/
11. Open vSwitch Web Site. http://openvswitch.org/

Information and Interaction
for in Novel Advanced Environments

Study About Creation of *"Maai"* Involving Intention Using Rhythm Controller

Development of *Maai* Creating Agent and Interaction Experiments Between Human and Agent

Shiroh Itai[(✉)] and Yoshiyuki Miwa

Faculty of Science and Engineering, Waseda University, Tokyo, Japan
itai@fuji.waseda.jp, miwa@waseda.jp

Abstract. In this paper, we developed a *"Maai"* creating agent that predicts human's intention from the changes in his/her controller manipulation method (i.e., relationship between controller input and avatar motion) of a rhythm controller. And, we examined whether the human's intention is reflected in the controller manipulation method in the creation of *Maai* involving the human's intention. From results, we showed that the human's intention to create *Maai* with the opponent leads to the potential for changes in the human's controller manipulation method. Furthermore, we showed that such an intention of a human as to whether he/she intends to maintain or collapse *Maai* is expressed in his/her controller manipulation method. Consequently, our research shows that an unconscious process plays a role in the creation of *Maai* involving the human's intention.

Keywords: *Maai* · Embodiment · Intention · Agent · Unconscious process

1 Introduction

A human, within a complex environment, is capable of performing spontaneous actions that suit the situation and maintains an appropriate distance ("Maai") from another person nearby. The Japanese concept of Maai is closely related to interpersonal distance, which is determined by individual feelings. Anthropologist E.T. Hall's proxemics [1] suggests that such distances are produced in response to social and physiological relationships, surroundings, and so on. To study such Maai, it is insufficient to consider action as only externally expressed motion. We must also consider the mental and embodied functions that create that action. However, how the mental and embodied functions work is generally very difficult to observe from the outside.

By including both mental and embodied functions in our input interface, we believe that we have solved this problem of *Maai* when operating avatars in virtual space. Furthermore, our past research has included the development of a "rhythm controller" [2–4] that has the following two characteristics.

1. The rhythmic operation of the rhythm controller precedes the avatar motion.
2. There is no one-to-one mapping between the controller input and avatar movement.

S. Yamamoto (Ed.): HIMI 2015, Part II, LNCS 9173, pp. 599–609, 2015.
DOI: 10.1007/978-3-319-20618-9_59

Characteristic 1 enables handling of an avatar as if it was a part of one's own body. As a result, it becomes possible for an operator of the controller to create *Maai* with the other person on the display screen through an embodied interaction. Because of characteristic 2, we believe that the mental and embodied functions are reflected in the controller manipulation method (i.e., relationship between controller input and avatar motion). With this premise, we examine the controller manipulation method when two human test subjects improvizationally create *Maai* with their opponents using the rhythm controller. Our research [5–7] revealed the following:

- When the constant *Maai* is maintained, a human test subject did not change his/her controller manipulation method, and this method was same and consistent across two human test subjects.
- In the "*Kendo*" (Japanese fencing) match through avatars, the controller manipulation method when *Maai* is maintained differs from when *Maai* is collapsed.

The feature of *Maai* in the *Kendo* match is that humans intentionally collapse *Maai* and create new *Maai*, whereas *Maai* discussed in proxemics is desired to be maintained [8]. These results indicate that the intention of a human as to whether he/she intends to maintain or collapse *Maai* may be reflected in his/her controller manipulation method.

In this paper, as the first step towards addressing the issue described above, we examine whether a human's intention is reflected in the controller manipulation method in the creation of *Maai* involving the human's intention. Specifically, we conduct experiments where a human test subject (i.e., human operator) and an agent that controls its avatar in such a way as to maintain a constant distant from a human avatar create *Maai*, and examine the difference of the human's controller manipulation method depending on whether the human has an intention to create *Maai*. Additionally, if the intention of a human as to whether he/she intends to maintain or collapse *Maai* is reflected in his/her controller manipulation method, we believe that the agent that predicts intentions of a human operator from the changes in his/her controller manipulation method will beat him/her in the *Kendo* match. Therefore, we develop a *Maai* creating agent for achieving this, and conduct experiments where this agent and a human operator play *kendo* matches.

2   Rhythm Controller

Here, we describe the rhythm controller and a method to examine the controller manipulation method (i.e., relationship between the controller input and avatar motion) when an operator creates avatar motion using the rhythm controller. When a zero-cross point is created on the controller waveform, as shown in Fig. 1, the controller waveform between zero-cross points up to two points prior to this incidence was integrated; thus, the integrated value (ΔS) is used as a velocity output value for the next zero-cross point to operate the avatar. This ΔS, which is the area of a one-cycle wave form of the rhythm controller, is primarily determined by the difference in the cycle (i.e., interval between neighboring zero-cross points, ΔT) and the difference in the amplitude (ΔA). Consequently, avatar velocity V can be expressed in the following form:

$$V(t_n \sim t_{n+1}) = \int_{t_{n-2}}^{t_n} s(t)dt$$

$$= |S_n| - |S_{n-1}|$$

t_n : n th zero crossing time
$s(t)$: Angle of controller lever
S_n : Integrated value of angle of controller lever
A_n : Amplitude of controller waveform
T_n : Half cycle of controller waveform

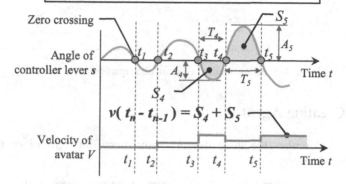

Fig. 1. Transformation rule of rhythm controller

$$V = k \cdot \Delta S = f(\Delta T, \Delta A) \tag{1}$$

In this regard, the operator can independently change both the cycle and amplitude of the rhythm controller waveform with freedom, which means that the operator can also freely changes the relationship between the two. Consequently, the operator can temporally (dynamically) change not only the avatar velocity but also the function f that is equal to the relationship between the controller input and avatar motion—in other words, the controller manipulation method. Note that the operator can determine function f independently of avatar velocity V. In this study, in order to examine function f (i.e., controller manipulation method), $(\Delta T, \Delta A, V)$ was plotted in a three-dimensional (3D) scatter plot when the zero-cross point was created on the controller waveform (Fig. 2). Furthermore, we use principal component analysis to reduce ΔT and ΔA to one principal component, which is then used as the explanatory variables in a regression analysis by which we are able to estimate function f; the dependent variable in the regression analysis is V. The parameters for determining the linear regression lines in the 3D space obtained from our analysis are the azimuth angle θ and the polar angle ϕ. θ is the variable representing a relationship between ΔT and ΔA. And, ϕ is the variable representing a relationship between V and variables affecting V other than ΔT and ΔA. However, because it is empirically demonstrated that the controller waveform created by a (human) operator is approximated by sine waves, V is determined by only ΔT and ΔA. In other words, ϕ does not change. In this paper, therefore, the differences between the linear regression lines (i.e., differences in the controller manipulation method) are evaluated using the azimuth angle θ.

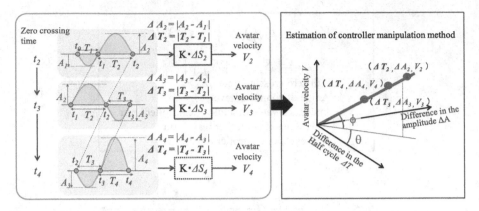

Fig. 2. Estimation method of controller manipulation method

3 *Maai* Creating Agent

The following describes the three design requirements for a *Maai* creating agent developed in this paper.

- The *Maai* creating agent uses Eq. (1) to control the movement of its avatar and to create and maintains an appropriate distance (*Maai*) from the avatar controlled by a (human) controller operator.
- In the same manner as with a (human) operator, the *Maai* creating agent generates a sound at the zero crossing point of the controller waveform.
- The *Maai* creating agent evaluates the controller manipulation method of a (human) operator in real-time, and from the changes in the human's controller manipulation method, predicts the intention of the (human) operator and creates avatar movements.

In order to satisfy the above design requirements, we developed a *Maai* creating agent (Fig. 3) with four operation modes as described below.

- Record human's controller manipulation method while moving forward and backward in a predetermined manner (stationary operation mode)
- Using the *Maai* creating model by Aizawa [9], maintain an appropriate distance (*Maai*) from the avatar controlled by a (human) operator by creating avatar movements (*Maai* operation mode)
- Retreat when the avatar controlled by a (human) operator approached the avatar controlled by the agent using the human's controller manipulation method associated with collapsing *Maai* (avoidance operation mode)
- Advance and swing a sword at the avatar controlled by a (human) operator when the avatar controlled by a (human) operator approached the avatar controlled by the agent using the human's controller manipulation method associated with maintaining *Maai* (attack operation mode)

In the *kendo* match experiments to be described later in this paper, the *Maai* creating agent first runs in stationary operation mode and then starts playing *kendo* matches

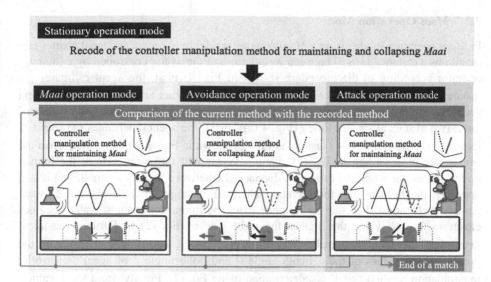

Fig. 3. *Maai* creating agent

against an avatar controlled by a (human) operator. While in a *kendo* match, the agent operates in one of other three modes other than stationary operation mode. The details of these four operation modes are explained below.

3.1 Stationary Operation Mode

In stationary operation mode, the agent records the human's controller manipulation method in the following manner. First, a (human) operator moves its avatar while maintaining a constant distance (*Maai*) from the agent's avatar that moves forward and backward in a predetermined manner. During this time interval, for each frame (frame rate of 50 [fps]), the azimuth angle θ of the human's controller manipulation method is calculated from ΔT and ΔA data of the (human) operator in the most recent 0.5 [s] interval using the least-squares method. Then, the maximum θ_{max}, minimum θ_{min} and standard deviation θ_{SD} is calculated for the θ value for 1 [s] interval. When the value of θ_{SD} becomes below 0.1, the human's controller manipulation method are considered stable, and the corresponding θ_{max} and θ_{min} are recorded as the human's controller manipulation method associated with maintaining *Maai*.

Next, the (human) operator, after maintaining a distance (*Maai*) from the agent's avatar moving back and forth in a predetermined manner, collapses the distance (*Maai*), approaches and swings his sword at agent's avatar at the timing of his choice. At this time, the azimuth angle θ_c of the human's controller manipulation method is calculated, using the least-squares method, from ΔT and ΔA data of the (human) operator in the 1 [s] immediately before approaching the agent's avatar. Then, the value of θ_c is recorded as the human's controller manipulation method associated with collapsing *Maai*.

3.2 *Maai* Operation Mode

In *Maai* operation mode, using a *Maai* creating model by Aizawa, the agent creates and maintains a distance (*Maai*) between its aviator and the avatar controlled by a (human) operator according to the procedure shown in Fig. 4. First, the agent estimates the distance ΔX between human operator's and agent's avatars at time $t + \hat{T}$ of the next zero crossing point of the agent's controller waveform from the positions and speeds of these two avatars at current time t (Fig. 4 (a)). Next, the agent determines the speed of its avatar ($\hat{V}_{com}$) at time $t + \hat{T}$ using the Eq. (2) shown in Fig. 4 (b). Note that, when the avatar moves according to Eq. (2), agent's avatar will move away from the human operator's avatar when the estimated distance ΔX between avatars is small, and it will approach the human operator's avatar, when ΔX is large. Therefore, agent's avatar adjusts its location such that its distance from the human operator's avatar becomes closer to the ΔX value that makes the right side of Eq. (2) 0. Further, the agent determines the agent's controller waveform $\hat{\Delta T}$, $\hat{\Delta A}$, $\hat{T}$, and $\hat{A}$ (Fig. 4 (c)) from the predetermined values of the azimuth angle θ and polar angle ϕ of agent's controller manipulation method and $\hat{V}_{com}$ determined using Eq. (2). Finally, from these values, using the method shown in Fig. 4, the agent generates its controller waveform for the time interval from t to $t + \hat{T}$. Note that, in *Maai* operation mode, the agents calculates, for each frame, the azimuth angle θ_r of the human's controller manipulation method, using the least-squares method, from ΔT and ΔA data of the human operator in the most recent 0.1 [s] interval. Based on this calculated azimuth angle value θ_r, the agent

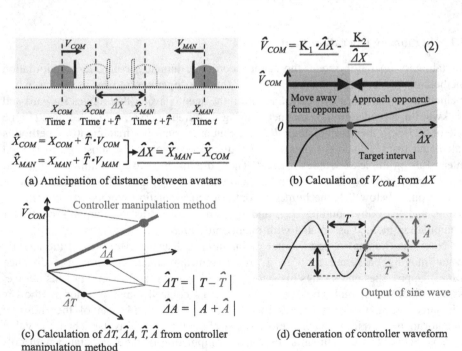

(a) Anticipation of distance between avatars

(b) Calculation of V_{COM} from ΔX

(c) Calculation of $\hat{\Delta T}$, $\hat{\Delta A}$, $\hat{T}$, $\hat{A}$ from controller manipulation method

(d) Generation of controller waveform

Fig. 4. *Maai* operation mode

determines whether to transition to avoidance operation mode or attack operation mode. This is discussed in more detail below.

3.3   Avoidance Operation Mode

In this paper, the agent assumes that the human operator intends to collapse *Maai*, when the azimuth angle θ_r of the human's controller manipulation method is within the range of $\theta_c \pm 1.5$ [deg], and when the human operator's avatar moves forward. In this case, agent's avatar transitions to avoidance operation mode and retreats to the outside of the *kendo* match field (i.e., outside of the display screen) at avatar's maximum speed V_{max} that the human controller operator can achieve using the rhythm controller. Note that, in the *kendo* match between the agent and the human operator, if the human controller operator strikes agent's avatar with his/her sword, the agent assumes that the human operator changed his/her controller manipulation method associated with collapsing *Maai* and updates the value of θ_c to the value used in this case.

3.4   Attack Operation Mode

In this paper, the agent considers that it is likely to succeed in striking the human operator's avatar with its sword, when human operator intends to maintain *Maai* with the distance between avatars small. Consequently, when these four conditions are all satisfied, the agent transitions to attack operation mode, advances its avatar at the maximum speed V_{max} and swings its sword.

A)   The value of θ_r lies between θ_{max} and θ_{min}.
B)   The human avatar is moving forward.
C)   The distance between agent's and human avatars is within 300 (the size of the *kendo* match field is 1000).
D)   8 [s] or more has passed since agent's moving from avoidance operation mode to *Maai* operation mode.

Note that condition D) is introduced to prevent frequent transition to attack operation mode.

4   Experiment Results

Through the use of a *Maai* creating agent developed in this study, we researched the difference of the controller manipulation method depending on whether humans have an intention to create *Maai*. First, we investigated the movement of agent's avatar when the human operator freely controls its avatar without considering that he/she attempts to maintain an appropriate distance (*Maai*) from agent's avatar that only operates in *Maai* operation mode. The results showed that the cross-correlation coefficient of the changes in agent's and human avatar positions was 0.98 with a delay time of 21 [ms] (Fig. 5(a)). From this, we conclude that it was possible for the agent in *Maai* operation mode to synchronize the movement of its avatar to that of the human avatar. Note that, in this

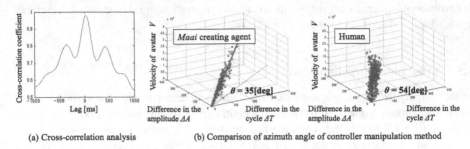

(a) Cross-correlation analysis   (b) Comparison of azimuth angle of controller manipulation method

Fig. 5. Results of experiment between human and agent

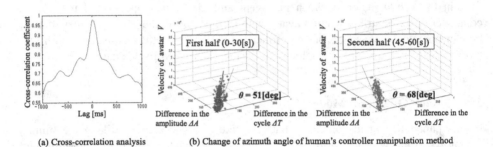

(a) Cross-correlation analysis   (b) Change of azimuth angle of human's controller manipulation method

Fig. 6. Results of cooperative move experiment between human and agent

experiment, when the azimuth angle of agent's controller manipulation method was initially set to 35 [deg], a value that is different from the initial azimuth angle of the human's controller manipulation method (54 [deg]), the azimuth angle of the human's controller manipulation method keeps 54 [deg], and two azimuth angle values never converged to the single common value (Fig. 5(b)).

Next, we instructed the human operator to move his/her avatar freely while creating constant *Maai* with agent's avatar and conducted an experiment to investigate inter-actions between the human operator and the agent that only operates in *Maai* operation mode. In the experiments, the azimuth angle of the agent's controller manipulation method changed from 50 [deg] in the first 30 [s] of the experiment to 70 [deg] in the second 30 [s]. The results showed that the cross-correlation coefficient of the changes in agent's and human avatar positions was 0.98 with a delay time of 15 [ms] (Fig. 6(a)). This result shows that agent and human operator create the synchronized motion between mutual avatars before as well as after experiment. In addition, from examining the azimuth of the human's controller manipulation method, we confirmed that the human operator adjusted the azimuth angle of his/her controller manipulation method to match that of the agent's controller manipulation method, resulting in different azimuth angles between the first and the second half of the experiment (Fig. 6 (b)).

Next, we conducted experiments where a *Maai* creating agent and a human operator played 20 *kendo* matches. The human test subjects were all proficient with rhythm controller operations and skilled in *kendo* matches using the controller. Further, in the experiments, for all agent operation modes, the azimuth angle of the agent's

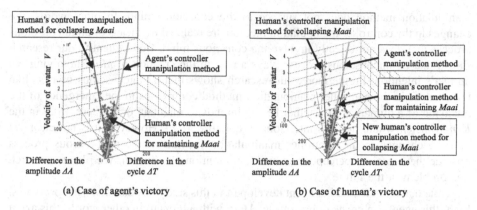

(a) Case of agent's victory   (b) Case of human's victory

Fig. 7. Results of *Kendo* match between human and agent

controller manipulation method was set to the average azimuth value (48 [deg]) of five human test subjects when they were maintaining *Maai*. In the experiments, the human test subjects were found to continue to lose a *kendo* match, and this was not only because the agent was able to predict the intention of the human test subjects to collapse *Maai* and successfully avoided being hit by the sword, but also because the human test subjects were completely unable to avoid agent's sword. For the first time in the ninth *kendo* match, the human test subject was finally able to create new controller manipulation method that were different from θ_c recorded in stationary operation mode and won the match over the agent (Fig. 7(b)). However, winning percentage of the human test subjects was only 20 [%].

5 Discussions

Results in Fig. 5 in the previous section show that when a human test subject had no intention of maintaining *Maai* with his opponent (agent), he/she did not adjust his/her controller manipulation method to match those of the opponent (agent), even if the avatars' movements were synchronized. On the other hand, when a human test subject had intention of maintaining *Maai* with his opponent (agent), he/she adjusted his/her controller manipulation method to match those of the opponent (agent), even if the opponent (agent) changed its controller manipulation method in the middle of the experiment (Fig. 6). These results show that the human's intention to create *Maai* with the opponent leads to the potential for changes in the human's controller manipulation method. Furthermore, a human test subject played *kendo* matches against a *Maai* creating agent that predicts the intension of a human test subject. We observed that the winning percentage of the agent reached 80 [%]. Human test subjects who competed against the agent commented that "the agent successfully retreated as soon as I started thinking of narrowing *Maai* to agent's avatar" and "the agent seized a chance to attack and beat me". These results indicate that the intention of a human as to whether he/she intends to maintain or collapse *Maai* is reflected in his/her controller manipulation method. In a creation of an avatar movement using the rhythm controller, the controller manipulation method does not surface to the conscious mind. In other words, the changes in the controller manipulation method are realized by means of an unconscious process that does not directly involve the conscious mind. Consequently, our research shows that an unconscious process plays a role in the creation of *Maai* involving the human's intention. Furthermore, our research shows that an unconscious process like the changes in the controller manipulation method contributes to the emergence of the intension of a human as to whether he/she intends to maintain or collapse *Maai* in the *Kendo* match where humans intentionally collapse *Maai*. However, it is not clear yet that the changes in the controller manipulation method as the unconscious process precede the conscious perception of such an intention of a human. We plan to research this problem in the future.

Note that a *Maai* creating agent developed in this study has the following problems. First, this agent can create only constant *Maai* with a human. In other words, this agent cannot create various *Maai* like the *kendo* match between humans. Results of our previous studies [6] show that entrainment [10–12] in multiple cycles is created in rhythm controller waveform of human operators when *Maai* is improvisationally created between two avatars in a *Kendo* match. However, a controller waveform of this agent does not change through the interaction with human operators. Furthermore, the controller manipulation method of this agent does not change in the *Kendo* match. Therefore, this agent cannot realize the emergence of the new controller manipulation method as shown in Fig. 7. We plan to study a way to solve the above-mentioned problems.

6 Summary

In our research, we developed a *Maai* creating agent that predicts human's intention from the changes in human's controller manipulation method (i.e., relationship between controller input and avatar motion) of a rhythm controller and determines its movement accordingly. And, we examined whether the human's intention is reflected in the controller manipulation method in the creation of *Maai* involving the human's intention. From results, we showed that the human's intention to create *Maai* with the opponent leads to the potential for changes in the human's controller manipulation method. Furthermore, we demonstrated that the agent can predict intentions of a human operator as to whether he/she intends to maintain or collapse *Maai* from the changes in his/her controller manipulation method. In other words, we showed that such an intention of a human is expressed in his/her controller manipulation method. Consequently, our research shows that an unconscious process plays a role in the creation of *Maai* involving the human's intention.

Acknowledgments. This study was partially supported by the Project Research "Principal of emergence for empathetic "*Ba*" and its applicability to communication technology" by RISE Waseda University, "Artifacts/Scenario/Human Institute" of Waseda University, and JSPS Grant-in-Aid for Young Scientists (B) Number 26870659. Especially the authors appreciate Prof. Yoji Aizawa for their valuable discussion and suggestion about our research. The authors also appreciate our graduate students, Kazutaka Sudo, Kazuki Fukusima for their cooperation for developing the system and conducting experiments.

References

1. Hall, E.T.: The Hidden Dimension. Garden City, New York (1966)
2. Itai, S., Kudo, A., Miwa, Y., Aizawa, Y.: Creation and co-share of timing in an actual communication. In: Proceedings. of the 2002 IEEE International Conference on Systems, Man and Cy-bernetics, CD-ROM (2002)
3. Itai, S., Miwa, Y.: Co-Existing communication using a robot as your agent. In: Proceedings of the 2004 IEEE/RSJ International Conference on Intelligent Robots and Systems, pp.1218-1225 (2004)
4. Itai, S., Miwa, Y.: Creation and co-share of "Maai" by the interface employing the embodiment. In: Proceedings of the 2004 IEEE International Workshop on Robot and Human Inter-active Communication, pp.193-198 (2004)
5. Itai, S., Yasui, T., Miwa, Y.: Soft Interface with the Ambiguity Creation of the Action by Avatar Controller Inducing the Embodiment. In: Yamamoto, S. (ed.) HCI 2014, Part II. LNCS, vol. 8522, pp. 413–422. Springer, Heidelberg (2014)
6. Itai, S., Miwa, Y.: Soft entrainment: co-emergence of "Maai" and entrainment by rhythm controller. In: Fukuda, S. (ed.) Emotional Engineering, vol. 3, pp. 73–92. Springer, Switzerland (2014)
7. Itai, S., Miwa, Y.: Soft interface - study on ambiguity of action utilizing rhythm controller. ASTE Spec. Issue 10(3), (2015).CD-ROM
8. Minami, H. (ed.): Study of Ma. Kodansha, Tokyo (1983)
9. Aizawa, Y.: pers. comm. (2002)
10. Condon, W.S., Sander, L.S.: Neonate movement is synchronized with adult speech. Science 183, 99–101 (1974)
11. Kendon, A.: Movement coordination in social interaction: some examples described. Acta Psychol. 32, 101–125 (1970)
12. Webb, J.T.: Interview synchrony: an investigation of two speech rate measures in an automated standardized interview. In: Pope, B., Siegman, A.W. (eds.) Studies in Dyadic Communication, pp. 115–133. Pergamon, New York (1972)

Designing the Embodied Shadow Media Using Virtual Three-Dimensional Space

Yusuke Kajita[1](✉), Takuto Takahashi[1], Yoshiyuki Miwa[2],
and Shiroh Itai[2]

[1] Undergraduate School of Creative Science and Engineering,
Waseda University, Tokyo, Japan
yozoral080@suou.waseda.jp, chobby75@akane.waseda.jp
[2] Faculty of Science and Engineering, Waseda University, Tokyo, Japan
miwa@waseda.jp, itai@fuji.waseda.jp

Abstract. In this paper, we discuss media technology that enables the emergence of bodily expressions. We paid attention to the difference between body and shadow movements, so we developed the system which generates the shadow media using skeleton information which is able to express the posture of person simply. To realize the system, we use virtual three-dimensional space and three-dimensional human model. By dividing the system processes into every software programs and creating the method to connect these programs, we got prospects of success for cloudization of the shadow media system. From our experimental results, we discovered that the system is able to be used for the research of bodily sensations, the emergence of bodily expressions, and supports of co-creative expressions.

Keywords: Communication · Co-creation · Expression · Shadow media · Skeleton information · Virtual three-dimensional space

1 Introduction

The authors have focused on the shadow, which has an inseparable relationship with the body, and researched a shadow media system that supports co-creative expressions. A major feature of this system is that by presenting shadows of varying shapes and colors (hereafter called "shadow media"), which have been artificially generated from a person's feet, the system encourages the creation of bodily expressions through the creation of a gap between the body and the shadow [1–3]. In addition, we demonstrated that presenting the shadow of a person at a geographically separated location in the space of another allows communication with a sense of coexistence between remote locations [4]. We then performed research that utilizes the features of these types of shadow media to support the sharing of shadow media and the co-creative expressions between remote locations [5].

However, we found the following two problems in the existing system, which generates shadows by processing images of the body itself obtained using thermo cameras and other devices (Fig. 1(a)). First, because the system deals with two-dimensional images, shadow media movements are limited to two-dimensional

S. Yamamoto (Ed.): HIMI 2015, Part II, LNCS 9173, pp. 610–621, 2015.
DOI: 10.1007/978-3-319-20618-9_60

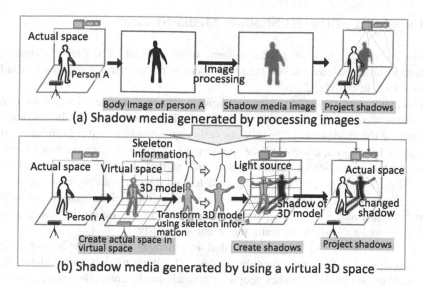

Fig. 1. Existing shadow media and shadow media using virtual 3D space

operations. Second, it is difficult to modify the shadow media separately for individual body parts.

On the other hand, in the study of Computer Graphics, there are researchers who have reproduced a three-dimensional (3D) model from the body of a person, and operated the 3D model using the data of a skeleton structure [6–9]. In addition, there are ongoing researches on real-time generation technology of a 3D shadow model created in virtual space [10].

In this study, the authors propose and develop a new shadow media system that uses a virtual 3D space and skeleton information to allow for the generation of shadow media, the design of movements for generated shadow media, and the mutual transmission of shadow media between multiple points (Fig. 1(b)). To accomplish this, this system uses a method that creates a 3D model of a person's body that is then used to generate the shadow. By allowing the 3D model to be controlled with skeleton information, the system can control the position, pose, and movement of the shadow media in 3D. Moreover, we implement shadow media communication that uses skeleton information, which uses less data compared to image data.

By utilizing virtual 3D space and skeleton information, this system not only solves the two problems listed above but also opens the possibility of realizing shadow media robotization or shadow media expression space design as well as multi-point shadow system communication and cloud integration. In other words, this system is expected not only to support co-creative expressions, but also serve a crucial role as a platform for utilizing shadow media in a variety of fields such as rehabilitation and amusement.

In this paper, we explain the details of the system for generating shadow media using a virtual 3D space and skeleton information (hereafter called "the 3D Shadow Media System") and introduce an actual example of shadow media generated using this system.

2 Capability of the 3D Shadow Media System

Developing the 3D Shadow Media System which consist of virtual 3D space and skeleton information could allow the researchers to realize various designs of shadow media shown in the Fig. 2.

The application of skeleton structure information will enable a local operation of the shadow media. With the skeleton structure, a local movement can be produced in each arm of the shadow (Fig. 2(a)). It also allows the shadow to flip from left to right (Fig. 2(b)). In addition, controlling the movements of the shadow media piece-by-piece allows for the generation of shadow media such as that in which the body becomes a spring (Fig. 2(c)). Then, by combining past logged data of walking movements with current skeleton information, we can separate the movement of the shadow media from the person and make it walk separately (Fig. 2(d)). In the future, it should also be possible to make the shadow media move autonomously.

The major feature of this study is that it generates shadow media not through human images, but through a combination of 3D human models and skeleton information. Thus, 3D models of other people or animals can be controlled using one's own skeleton information. In other words, the system can replace one's own shadow with those of other people or animals (Fig. 2(e)). In addition, because the shadow media is generated in a virtual 3D space, it can freely change the number and position of virtual light sources used with the shadow media (Fig. 2(f)) as well as display the shadows of virtual objects placed within the virtual space (Fig. 2(g)). With the introduction of a physics engine into the virtual space, it can also move shadow media in environments that differ from the actual space, such as a weightless space (Fig. 2(h)). This means that this system allows for the free design of the shadow media expression space.

Also, since this study generates shadow media from skeleton information, it implements shadow media communication by transmitting only skeleton information. Due to the fact that skeleton information requires far smaller amounts of data in comparison to image data, this allows us to increase communication speed and implement communication between multiple points, allowing shadow media from a variety of people to be shared among multiple points (Fig. 2(i)). Moreover, if we

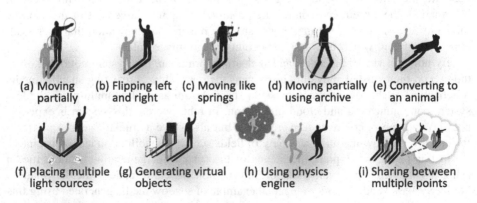

(a) Moving partially (b) Flipping left and right (c) Moving like springs (d) Moving partially using archive (e) Converting to an animal

(f) Placing multiple light sources (g) Generating virtual objects (h) Using physics engine (i) Sharing between multiple points

Fig. 2. Capability of the 3D shadow media system

construct a shadow database that collects and stores 3D models, accessing this database would allow for the creation of arbitrary shadow media of people registered in the database from skeleton information. This means that the series of shadow media generation processes can be stored in the cloud.

3   Development of the 3D Shadow Media System

In this study, we prepared, "model data", a 3D model of a person with skeleton information built into it in advance. In other words, by performing as much of the processing required to map skeleton information to 3D models beforehand, we ensured the real-time property of the shadow media generation process. Based on this, in this study we developed a shadow media system composed of the six construction steps given below (Fig. 3).

1. Create a virtual space
2. Obtain human skeleton information
3. Create model data
4. Operate on skeleton information (skeleton controller)
5. Deform model data using skeleton information
6. Generate and display the shadow media images

Steps 1 and 3 are performed beforehand, and steps 2 and 4 through 6 are performed in real time. The following describes the methodology of how to realize a communication of skeleton information among these processes.

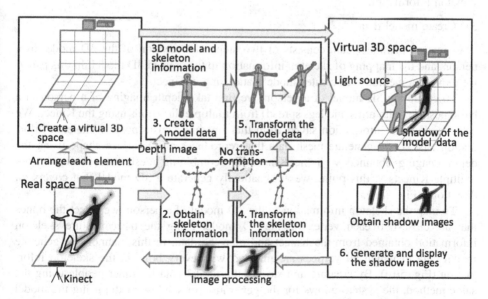

Fig. 3. Shadow media generation process using the virtual 3D space

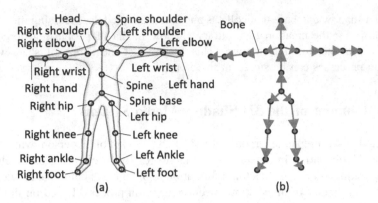

Fig. 4. Skeleton information and the direction of the vectors (bones)

1) Create a virtual space

Place the elements that compose the shadow media system, such as the apparatus used to measure physical images and skeleton information (such as a Kinect), the screen, and projector within the virtual space. These elements are placed in the virtual space using the same coordinates and dimensions of those in the actual space.

2) Obtain human skeleton information

We use Microsoft Kinect or NaturalPoint OptiTrack to obtain skeleton information. The obtained data, showing major positions of human skeleton [11] (Fig. 4(a)), is utilized to create vectors (bones) indicated in the Fig. 4(b). This has been used as skeleton information.

3) Create model data

The creation of model data consists of two steps: the creation of the 3D model of a person, and the mapping of skeleton information to the created 3D model. In this paper, we explain a method that creates model data using a Kinect.

To create the 3D model of a person, we first take depth imaging of a person in a basic posture (with arms and legs spread) from multiple directions using the Kinect. We call the skeleton information saved from that imaging "basic posture skeleton information". Next, we generate mesh data that reproduces a 3D surface shape using the depth imaging obtained with the Kinect. By combining mesh data obtained from multiple Kinects at this point, we automatically generate a 3D model that covers all directions (Fig. 5(a)).

To map the skeleton information to the 3D model of a person, we select the bones that are closest to each vertex on the 3D model using the basic posture skeleton information obtained from the Kinect and map the data. In this manner, we generate model data in which all vertices are mapped with every bone in the skeleton information (Fig. 5(b)). By creating and storing the model data for other people using the same method, the system allows for the generation of shadow media using the model data from many people. It also allows one to generate shadow media for objects other

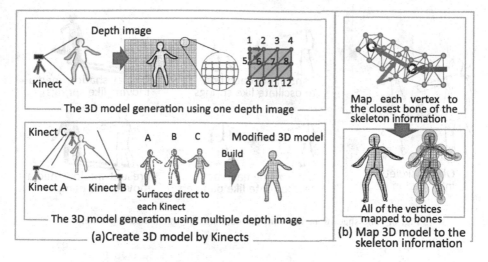

Fig. 5. Automatic generation of the 3D model using the kinect

than humans by creating models for subjects such as animals, which have different skeletons from humans, by mapping the bones.

4) Operate on skeleton information (Skeleton Controller)

In this study, we implement deformation of individual parts of the skeleton information through performing the following operations, either independently or in tandem, on arbitrary bones within the skeleton information.

– Vary the time of the final positional coordinates of bones using an arbitrary function
– Apply a transformation matrix to bone vectors for rotation or size manipulation

In addition, the ends of all bones in the current skeleton information and the skeleton information processed a frame earlier are connected to one another by springs and dampers. This system allows the skeleton to oscillate or attenuate in reaction to human body movements. (See the Fig. 6.)

5) Deform model data using skeleton information

To deform the shadow media by operating on the skeleton information using the skeleton controller, we must modify the pose of the 3D model of a person. The processing method is explained below. First, using the skeleton information bones of the 3D model created in 3) and the skeleton information bones operated on by the skeleton controller, we calculate a transformation matrix for each respective bone. Next, we use a transformation matrix corresponding to the bone mapped to each vertex in model data in 3) to transform coordinates. Modifying the vertices that compose the 3D model in this fashion, the 3D model is deformed to the skeleton information pose operated on by the skeleton controller as shown in Fig. 7.

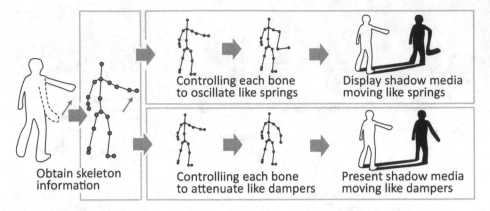

Fig. 6. The shadow media with the oscillated or attenuated movements

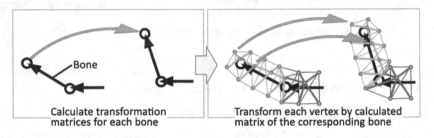

Fig. 7. The transformation of the model data using skeleton information

6) Generate and display the shadow media image

In this system, we use virtual light sources placed at arbitrary points in the virtual space, the 3D model generated in 5), and a screen to generate shadows of 3D models on a screen in the virtual space (Fig. 8(a)). Specifically, we first create projection images of the 3D model from the positions of the virtual light sources. Next, we cut rectangles of the projection image where the projection range of the projector (a quadrangular pyramid) and screen intersect (the "projection surface"). Finally, we map the projection image cut from the projection surface to the projection surface. As a result, a black 3D model image is projected in the correct position. Obtaining that shadow image as a projection image as seen from the position of the projector allows for the generation of a shadow image as projected from the projector in actual space (Fig. 8(b)).

Finally, we perform media processing such as modifications to color and shape on the created shadow image. This image is called the shadow media image, and is displayed using the projector.

7) Communication of the skeleton information

In this study, we are aiming at cloudizing the shadow media system by dividing the above-mentioned 1 through 6 processes of shadow generation and by building connections among the processes via IP communication technology. The following is the description of its outline.

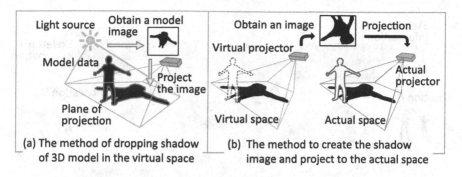

Fig. 8. Generate and project the shadow media image

First, we have dividend the work of shadow media generation into three processes: obtaining skeleton information, operating the information and applying the information to model data to generate shadow media.

So as to realize data communications among those three processes, we have developed a server software to achieve a multi-point P2P communication via TURN (Traversal Using Relay NAT) [12] methods, an encoder that is able to define data structure freely. A series of systems used in this study have been named CIPC (Central Inter-process Communication). With data buffer prepared in the server, these systems enable a one-on-multi people communication among the processes. This feature separates CIPC from the conventional TURN methods.

The above mentioned steps have allowed us to divide the shadow media processes, achieve arbitrary P2P communications among the divided processes and have prospects of success for cloudization of the shadow media system. The Fig. 9 shows the shadow media system developed in this study.

4   Utilization of the 3D Shadow Media System

4.1   The Shadow Media using the Skeleton Controller

Fig. 10 shows examples of using the skeleton controller to modify parts of the shadow media individually. Fig. 10(a) shows shadow media with periodic motion (2[s] period) added to the movement of the hips. Fig. 10(b) shows shadow media with an arm deformed to bend unnaturally. In this fashion, the system allows the projection of shadow media in poses that humans could not normally achieve. In addition, Fig. 11 shows shadow media in which the person's movements oscillate like a spring, and shadow media in which movements are attenuated, being displayed. As a result, participants who experienced shadow media being oscillated reported feeling a sensation of being pulled. At the same time, participants who experienced shadow media being attenuated reported feeling as though they were in a heavy space. These results demonstrate the possibility of using the system to control shadow media movement to evoke transformations in physical sensations.

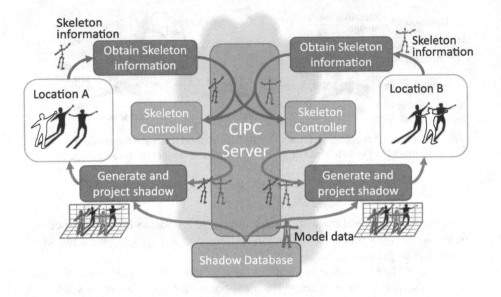

Fig. 9. The structure of the new shadow media system

(a) The shadow media with periodic
motion around the spine base

(b) The shadow media with the
unnaturally bended arms

Fig. 10. Every part of the shadow media modified individually

(a) The shadow media moving like
springs

(b) The shadow media moving like
dampers

Fig. 11. The shadow media moving like springs and dampers

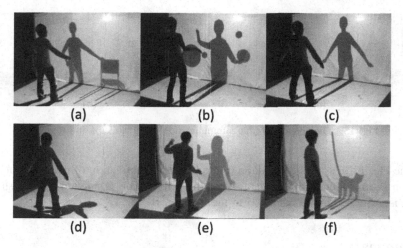

Fig. 12. The shadow media using the virtual 3D space

4.2   The Shadow Media using the Virtual 3D Space

Fig. 12 shows examples of virtual objects that do not exist within the actual space being placed in the virtual 3D space, and their shadows being displayed. In Fig. 12(a), the shadow of a 3D model mimicking the shape of a chair is projected in the actual space. In Fig. 12(b), multiple spherical objects are floated in the air of the virtual space, and their shadows are projected in the actual space. This system also allows for modification of the positions of virtual light sources for the shadow media. In Fig. 12(c), the virtual light source is positioned at eye-level front and center with respect to the screen. In contrast, in Fig. 12(d) the virtual light source is placed above the person's head. In addition, this system also allows switching the shadow of the person for the shadows of other people or animals. In Fig. 12(e), shadow media created using female model data is displayed for a male. In Fig. 12(f), shadow media created by applying the 3D model of a cat to a person is displayed. Those results demonstrate that the utilization of the inseparability between the shadow media and human body allows various articles to be positioned in a space where a person exists while relating those items to the person. By using the inseparability, a person can be transformed into another person or being: an adult, a child or an animal. Moreover, the outcome shows that the relation between human body and shadow can be changed in a various way through spatial or temporal operation of the virtual light source.

4.3   The Shadow Media Communication using CIPC

We have carried out a shadow media communication between remote locations by conducting the following processes; transmitting skeleton information mutually between geographically remote locations then utilizing the transmitted data to generate shadow media at each location (Fig. 13(a)).

Fig. 13. The shadow media communication using skeleton information

The Fig. 13(b) shows application of the skeleton information of male person at the location A to a female model data. After the information is applied to it, a shadow media is generated and transmitted to the location B.

5   Summary

In this study, we proposed and developed a system for generating shadow media using a virtual 3D space and skeleton information. Specifically, we developed a skeleton controller capable of operating on skeleton information and constructed a system that automatically generates and deforms 3D models of people and projects shadows generated in a virtual 3D space in an actual space. As a result, the system can freely control the pose of the shadow media as well as the movements of individual parts of the shadow. Moreover, the system displays the shadows of other people or animals as one's own shadow media, modifies the position of virtual light sources for the shadow media, and displays shadow media for objects that do not exist in the actual space. By the effects of the inseparability between the human shadow and body and of the bodily wholeness observed in the human shadow, this system enables creation of a media space of expression, different from C-Ged one, and generation of a new shadow media or shadow media expression space. In future work, we would like to utilize this system as a platform for media systems that support collaborative expression.

Acknowledgments. This study was partially supported by JSPS Grant-in-Aid for Scientific Research (B) Number 26280131, the Project Research "Principal of emergence for empathetic "Ba" and its applicability to communication technology" by RISE Waseda University, and "Artifacts/Scenario/Human Institute" of Waseda University.

References

1. Miwa, Y.: Co-creative expression and support for communicability. J. Soc. Instrum. Control Eng. **51**(11), 1016–1022 (2012)
2. Miwa, Y., Itai, S., Watanabe, T., Nishi, H.: Shadow awareness: enhancing theater space through the mutual projection of images on a connective slit-screen, leonardo. J. Int. Soc. Arts Sci. Technol. **44**(4), 325–333 (2011)

3. Hayashi, N., Miwa, Y., Itai, S., Nish, H.: Bodily expression media by dual domain design of shadow. In: Yamamoto, S. (ed.) HCI 2013, Part III. LNCS, vol. 8018, pp. 195–202. Springer, Heidelberg (2013)
4. Miwa, Y., Ishibiki, C.: Shadow communication: system for embodied interaction with remote partners. In: Proceeding of the CSCW 2004, pp. 467-476 (2004)
5. Miwa, Y., Nishide, A., Hayashi, N., Itai, S., Nishi, H.: Co-creative bodily expression through remote shadow media system. In: Yamamoto, S. (ed.) HCI 2014, Part II. LNCS, vol. 8522, pp. 445–454. Springer, Heidelberg (2014)
6. Kakadiaris, I.A., Metaxas, D.: 3D human body model acquisition from multiple views. In: Proceedings of the Fifth International Conference on Computer Vision, pp. 618-623. IEEE (1995)
7. Tong, J., Zhou, J., Liu, L., Pan, Z., Yan, H.: Scanning 3d full human bodies using kinects. IEEE Trans. Visual. Comput. Graphics 18(4), 643–650 (2012)
8. Aitpayev, K., Gaber, J.: Creation of 3D human avatar using kinect. Asian Trans. Fundam. Electron. Commun. Multimedia 1(5), 12–24 (2012)
9. Chadwick, J.E., Haumann, D.R., Parent, R.E.: Layered construction for deformable animated characters. In: ACM Siggraph Computer Graphics, vol. 23(3), pp. 243-252. ACM (1989)
10. Lake, A.T., Marshall, C.S.: Generating a shadow for a three-dimensional model. U.S. Patent No. 6,906,724 (2005)
11. Webb, J., Ashley, J.: Beginning Kinect Programming with the Microsoft Kinect SDK. Apress, New York (2012)
12. Mahy, R., Matthews, P., Rosenberg, J.: Traversal using relays around Nat (turn): Relay extensions to session traversal utilities for Nat (stun). Internet Request for Comments (2010)

Kick Extraction for Reducing Uncertainty in RoboCup Logs

Tomoharu Nakashima[1](✉), Satoshi Mifune[1], Jordan Henrio[1],
Oliver Obst[2], Peter Wang[2], and Mikhail Prokopenko[3]

[1] Osaka Prefecture University, Gakuen-Cho 1-1, Naka-Ku, Sakai, Osaka, Japan
tomoharu.nakashima@kis.osakafu-u.ac.jp,
{satoshi.mifune,jordan.henrio}@cs.osakafu-u.ac.jp
[2] CSIRO Computational Informatics, Epping, NSW 1710, Australia
{oliver.obst,peter.wang}@csiro.au
[3] The University of Sydney, Darlington, NSW 2006, Australia
mikhail.prokopenko@sydney.edu.au

Abstract. The effectiveness of using log information in RoboCup soccer simulation 2D league is shown in this paper. Although it is not possible to exactly know a strategy that a team is taking, that strategy is well represented by how the players in the team kick during games. Extracted kicks such as passes and dribbles form a kick distribution, which hopefully represent the team' strategy. In order to show the usefulness of the kick distribution, a series of computational experiments are conducted where the uncertainty in predicting the game results is reduced by grouping the games based on the kick distributions.

Keywords: RoboCup · Feature extraction · Strategy analysis · Clustering · Earth Mover's Distance (EMD)

1 Introduction

RoboCup [1], especially RoboCup soccer simulation, is meant to be a research platform for various fields. Artificial intelligence is one of the important research fields. There have been several number of works where AI techniques were applied to RoboCup soccer simulation. For example, Riedmiller et al. [2] presented neural-network approaches for reinforcement learning that were successfully implemented in his RoboCup soccer simulation 2D team. Budden and Prokopenko [3] proposed a method that impvoved the precision of localization using particle filter. Nakashima et al. [4] proposed an evolutionary approach where offensive strategies evolved based on the game scores and the history of the teams' game results.

While the above mentioned works concern the learning of the soccer players, there are other aspects of RoboCup research including Naruse's work on the strategy analysis in set plays for the small robot league. This work used log files that are produced after games finish. It is intuitively possible that log information of soccer games provides useful and important insight for improving soccer teams. It can also be used to analyze the trend of the competitions over years. For example, Gabel and Riedmiller [5]

© Springer International Publishing Switzerland 2015
S. Yamamoto (Ed.): HIMI 2015, Part II, LNCS 9173, pp. 622–633, 2015.
DOI: 10.1007/978-3-319-20618-9_61

presented the analysis on the trend over the ten years of competitions as well as quantitative evaluation of team strategies. Abreu et al. [6] used log information in order to compare the robotic soccer and the human soccer, showing the similarity and dissimilarity between them. However, there are only a few works of extracting useful knowledge for improving teams from log information. In the RoboCup soccer simulation 2D league, log information is compiled in log files, which have all information on finished games such as the position of players and the ball, the actions made by players, and the communication between players plus coaches. Although there is a need for obtaining useful knowledge from those log files, effective methods have not been proposed yet. There are mainly two difficulties in dealing with log information. One is that it is unknown what kind of information to use. The other is that even if such information is successfully obtained it is still unknown how to use it.

This work proposes one solution to the first difficulty: which kind of information is useful in log files. Among the various kind of possibility, kicks are selected as the focus in this paper. Kicks in this paper include dribbles and passes only and intercepted ball kicks and clearing kicks are not considered. The purpose of this work is to show the possibility of mining log files for useful knowledge on games. A series of computational experiments are conducted to show that uncertainty in predicting the game results is reduced by the clustering of kick distributions.

2 Kick Distribution

2.1 Log Files

A game in RoboCup soccer simulation 2D is conducted in computers. All the field information is managed by a computer process called a soccer server. It maintains the position and velocity of players and the ball, players' stamina, and it also handles the message communication between by players plus coaches. The next status of players and the ball is also calculated by the soccer server based on the actions made by the players. The information on the current status is sent from the soccer server via the UDP protocol. The actions available for players are body-turn, dash, and kick. The players must determine the direction and strength of those actions. Besides kick and dash, communication action can also be performed such as say, point, and neck-turn. All those actions are recorded as log information and dumped in log files after games are finished.

2.2 Kick Extraction

Dribbles and passes are extracted as kicks from log information in this paper. A dribble is defined as more than one subsequent kicks by the same player. A pass is defined as two subsequent kicks by different players from the same team. All dribbles and passes are extracted from the log files along with the distance between the two kicking points. There is no threshold in the distance for the kick extraction. Those kicks that brought the ball out of the bounds or intercepted (i.e., unsuccessful) passes by opponent teams are not extracted in this paper.

A distance between the subsequent kicks is also recorded as well as the position of the first kick. Figure 1 shows the results of kick extraction from the log file of a game between opuSCOM vs UvA_Trilearn. In this figure, the position of the red poles indicates the place of the ball where players have kicked it, and the height shows the distance that the ball traveled until the next kick. A set of extracted kicks from one single game is called a kick distribution in this paper.

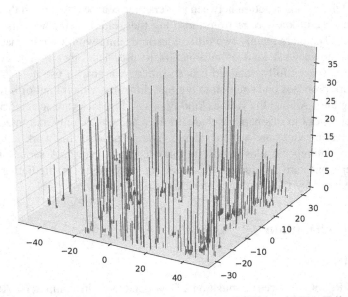

Fig. 1. Extracted kicks from a game between opuSCOM and UVA_Trilearn

Each extracted kick is not separately dealt with in this paper, but whole the extracted kicks are treated as one pattern of the game. Thus, the extracted kicks form its distribution as in Fig. 1. Three types of kick distributions are generated from a single game: One is based on the extracted kicks by the right team, and another kick distribution is based on the kicks from the left team. The third kick distribution generated from a game log file is the combined distribution of the two (i.e., right and left) where all the extracted kicks regardless of the sides are brought into one single distribution.

3   Clustering Kick Distributions

3.1   Distance Measure Between Two Kick Distributions

A distance represents a similarity between two objects. An object is assumed to be represented by a real-valued vector in most of the cases. It is generally assumed in clustering research that all vectors have the same dimensionality so that the similarity measure is calculated easily such as Euclidean distance, cosine similarity, and Manhattan distance. Our interest in this paper is in the similarity between kick distributions that are generated by extracting kicks from log files. As the number of kicks in the kick distributions are different each other, it is highly likely that those well-known similarity measures cannot be used as it is. Instead, this paper employs Earth Movers Distance (EMD) as the similarity measure between kick distributions. EMD allows to calculate the distance between two vectors with different dimensionalities. It also allows a weight in each element of the vectors. Calculation of an EMD between two vectors with weights is done by formulating it as a transportation problem of a resource from one supplying group of cities to another demanding group of cities.

This paper calculates the distance between two kick distributions by taking an element kick with a kick distance in one kick distribution as a supplying place with available resource and also by taking an element kick in the other kick distribution as a demanding with a necessary amount of the resource.

3.2 Agglomerative Hierarchical Clustering

Among a number of clustering method, agglomerative hierarchical clustering algorithm is employed in this paper. Let us say there are N kick distributions $d_1, d_2, \ldots, d_N$ to be grouped by the clustering method. The following is the procedure of the agglomerative hierarchical clustering:

Step 1. Let each kick distribution form a cluster.
Step 2. Calculate the EMD between any pairs of clusters. The distance between two clusters is defined by the average over any pairs of the cluster elements.
Step 3. Group the nearest two clusters and make them a new cluster.
Step 4. Repeat Step 2. and Step 3. until all the kick distribution belong to one single cluster.

4 Experiments

4.1 Experimental Settings

In order to see if it is possible to reduce the uncertainty in predicting the results, a number of games were conducted to produce log files. Three teams are selected in the computational experiments of this paper: Gliders2014, HELIOS2014, and WrightEagle2014, which participated in the 2014 RoboCup competition.

Table 1 shows the game results after performing about ten games per opponent team. The teams that are used as opponent teams in Table 1 also participated in the RoboCup 2014 competition (Cyrus, Oxsy, UFSJ2D, and YuShan). The table also shows the uncertainty to predict the game results without knowing the opponent team name. The uncertainty is measured by the information entropy based on the number of win/lose games.

Table 1. Game results of the three teams

Team name	Win	Lose	Total games	Uncertainty
Gliders2014	29	24	53	0.99357
Helios2014	30	20	50	0.97095
WrightEagle2014	42	15	57	0.83147

The reason why the number of total games is different among the three teams is that some game matches did not finish properly for some technical problems that may be only solved by the developers of the teams. Thus, the total number of the games in the fourth column of Table 1. It is seen from Table 1 that Team WrightEagle has the lowest uncertainty since it won the most of the games. Gliders2014 has the highest uncertainty since the numbers of wins and losses are closest to each other.

4.2   Clustering Results

The uncertainty reducing process consists of the following steps: Obtaining log files, extracting kicks, and applying the hierarchical clustering. The clustering process was applied to the extracted kicks for the kick distributions obtained in Subsection 4.1. As there are three sets of kick distributions (teams of interest, their opponents, both mixed), there are nine (three times three) sets of kick distributions for the three teams. The clustering results are shown in Figs. 2, 3, 4, 5, 6, 7, 8, 9, and 10. In these figures, the forks in higher level shows that the merger of two clusters occurred in the latter process of the clustering. Thus, if three clusters are to be used from the clustering results, three higher vertical lines should be used as the corresponding three clusters.

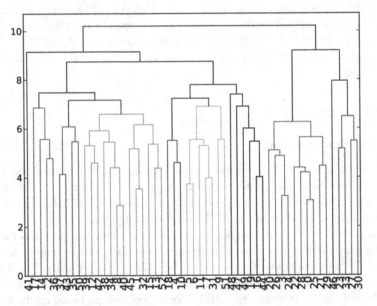

Fig. 2. Clustering results for kick distributions of Gliders2014

4.3   Discussions

In order to show the reduction in the uncertainty of game results, the entropy measure is calculated for each clustering results with different numbers of clusters. Tables 2, 3, 4, 5, 6, 7, 8, 9, and 10 show the uncertainty in the game results.

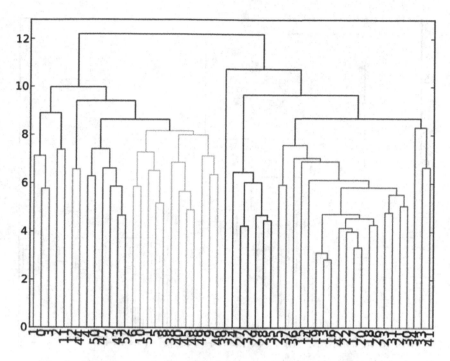

Fig. 3. Clustering results for kick distributions of Gliders2014's opponents

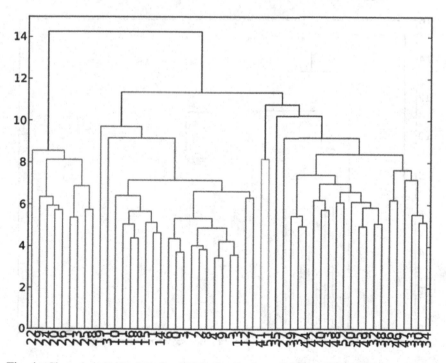

Fig. 4. Clustering results for mixed kick distributions of Gliders2014 and its opponents

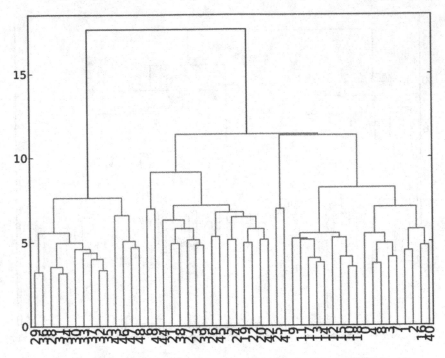

Fig. 5. Clustering results for kick distributions of HELIOS2014

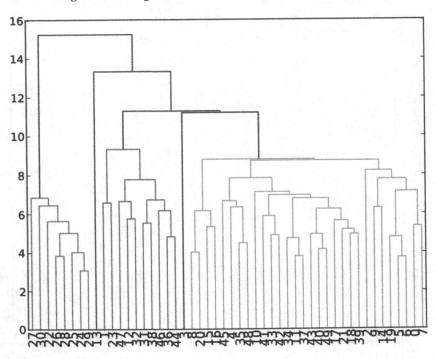

Fig. 6. Clustering results fior kick distributions of HELIOS2014's opponents

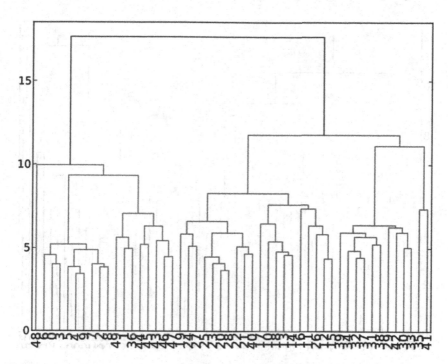

Fig. 7. Clustering results for mixed kick distributions of HELIOS2014 and its opponents

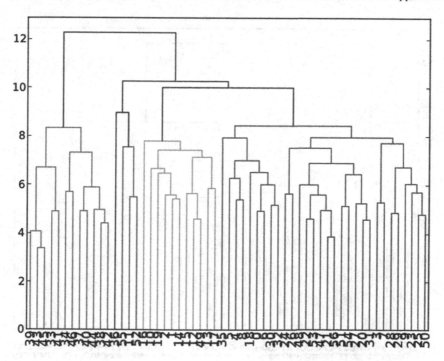

Fig. 8. Clustering results for kick distributions of WrightEagle2014

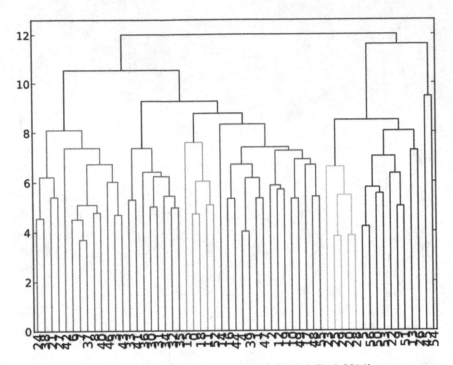

Fig. 9. Clustering results fior kick distributions of WrightEagle2014's opponents

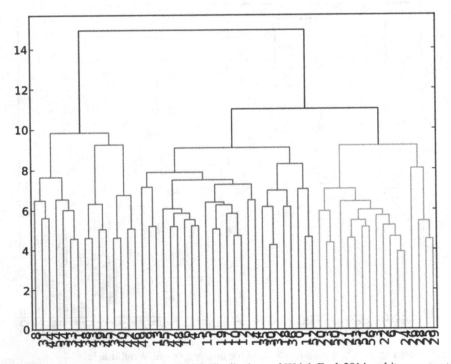

Fig. 10. Clustering results for mixed kick distributions of WrightEagle2014 and its opponents

Table 2. Uncertainty in game results for Gliders2014

# of clusters	Cluster 1 (Win/lose)		Cluster 2		Cluster 3		Cluster 4		Cluster 5		Entropy
3	17	21	8	2	4	1					0.915559
4	1	0	16	21	8	2	4	1			0.893208
5	1	0	10	11	6	10	8	2	4	1	0.888028

Table 3. Uncertainty in game results for Gliders2014's opponent

# of clusters	Cluster 1 (Win/lose)		Cluster 2		Cluster 3		Cluster 4		Cluster 5		Entropy
3	8	17	0	1	21	6					0.815907
4	1	4	7	13	0	1	21	6			0.809897
5	1	4	7	13	0	1	5	1	16	5	0.807928

Table 4. Uncertainty in game results for mixed Gliders2014 and its opponents

# of clusters	Cluster 1 (Win/lose)		Cluster 2		Cluster 3		Cluster 4		Cluster 5		Entropy
3	9	0	8	13	12	11					0.813237
4	9	0	8	13	2	0	10	11			0.775445
5	9	0	8	13	2	0	0	1	10	10	0.757225

Table 5. Uncertainty in game results for HELIOS2014

# of clusters	Cluster 1 (Win/lose)		Cluster 2		Cluster 3		Cluster 4		Cluster 5		Entropy
3	10	4	10	6	10	10					0.947093
4	10	4	10	6	2	0	8	10			0.90388
5	10	4	0	2	10	4	2	0	8	10	0.840135

Table 6. Uncertainty in game results for HELIOS2014's opponent

# of clusters	Cluster 1 (Win/lose)		Cluster 2		Cluster 3		Cluster 4		Cluster 5		Entropy
3	8	0	0	1	22	19					0.81683
4	8	0	0	1	8	2	14	17			0.760191
5	8	0	0	1	8	2	0	1	14	16	0.742461

Table 7. Uncertainty in game results for mixed HELIOS2014 and its opponents

# of clusters	Cluster 1 (Win/lose)		Cluster 2		Cluster 3		Cluster 4		Cluster 5		Entropy
3	6	12	15	5	9	3					0.849804
4	6	12	15	5	7	3	2	0			0.831356
5	0	1	6	11	15	5	7	3	2	0	0.819236

Table 8. Uncertainty in game results for WrightEagle

# of clusters	Cluster 1 (Win/lose)		Cluster 2		Cluster 3		Cluster 4		Cluster 5		Entropy
3	11	1	2	2	29	12					0.784639
4	11	1	2	2	4	7	25	5			0.681908
5	11	1	1	0	1	2	4	7	25	5	0.660064

Table 9. Uncertainty in game results for WrightEagle2014's opponent

# of clusters	Cluster 1 (Win/lose)		Cluster 2		Cluster 3		Cluster 4		Cluster 5		Entropy
3	28	13	12	2	2	0					0.793533
4	11	2	17	11	12	2	2	0			0.761416
5	11	2	17	11	12	2	1	0	1	0	0.761416

Table 10. Uncertainty in game results for mixed WrightEagle2014 and its opponents

# of clusters	Cluster 1 (Win/lose)		Cluster 2		Cluster 3		Cluster 4		Cluster 5		Entropy
3	14	1	14	11	14	3					0.727528
4	7	0	7	1	14	11	14	3			0.710828
5	7	0	3	1	4	0	14	11	14	3	0.69147

From these tables, it is seen that the uncertainty is reduced by clustering the kick distribution for any sets of kick distributions. Especially, mixing kick distributions of both teams in a game reduce the uncertainty the most for Gliders2014 and WrightEagle. This clustering results may provide useful information. For example, they can be further used for the analysis of ongoing games by the coach and for deciding whether a team changes its strategy if it is losing with a high possibility.

5   Conclusions

This paper presented the possible use of log files in the prediction of games. Kicks distribution is the focus of the research as a single kick itself is not enough to obtain useful information on the strategy of teams. This paper used hierarchical agglomerative clustering to generate the grouping of kick distributions. One difficulty was to measure the similarity between two distributions due to the difference in the number of kicks. In order to overcome this issue, EMD was used. An EMD between two kick distribution is calculated by taking a kick position as the position of the place of supply/demand, and the kick distance as the quantity of the supply/demand in that place. A series of computational experiments were conducted and the results of the experiments showed that the uncertainty in the game prediction from kick distribution was reduced by the clustering results.

As this is the beginning of the research work, the next step is to further improve the reduction rate of the uncertainty. The results of this study can also be used in the actually prediction task of games. This is another future research. Another future works are to see if there are more useful features that can be extracted from log files.

References

1. Kitano, H., Minoru, A., Kuniyoshi, Y., Noda, I., Osawa, E., Matsubara, H.: RoboCup: a challenge problem for AI. AI Mag. **18**(1), 73–85 (1997)
2. Riedmiller, M., Gabel, T., Hafner, R., Lange, S.: Reinforcement learning for robot soccer. Auton. Robots **27**(1), 55–74 (2009)
3. Budden, D., Prokopenko, M.: Improved particle filtering for Pseudo-uniform belief distributions in robot localisation. In: Behnke, S., Veloso, M., Visser, A., Xiong, R. (eds.) RoboCup 2013. LNCS, vol. 8371, pp. 385–395. Springer, Heidelberg (2014)
4. Nakashima, T., Ishibuchi, H., Takatani, M., Nii, M.: The effect of using match history on the evolution of RoboCup soccer team strategies. In: The 2006 IEEE Symposium on Computational Intelligence and Games, pp. 60–66. IEEE (2006)
5. Gabel, T., Riedmiller, M.: On progress in RoboCup: the simulation league showcase. In: Ruiz-del-Solar, J. (ed.) RoboCup 2010. LNCS, vol. 6556, pp. 36–47. Springer, Heidelberg (2010)
6. Abreu, P., Moreira, J., Costa, I., Castelão, D., Reis, L., Garganta, J.: Human versus virtual robotics soccer a technical analysis. Eur. J. Sport Sci. **12**(1), 26–35 (2011)

Virtual Bogie: Exhibition System to Understand Mechanism of Bogie with Digital Display Case

Tomohiro Tanikawa[✉], Hirosi Ohara, Ryo Kiyama, Takuji Narumi, and Michitaka Hirose

Graduate School of Information Science and Technology, The University of Tokyo, 7-3-1 Hongo, Bunkyo-ku, Tokyo, Japan
{tani,ohara,rkiyama,narumi, hirose}@cyber.t.u-tokyo.ac.jp

Abstract. We aim to construct a digital display case system that effectively conveys background information about an exhibited object, and introduce our system into museum exhibition rooms. In this paper, we present a digital display case system that enables viewers to interact with an exhibited artifact in a manner that conveys its dynamic mechanism more easily than conventional approaches. Based on a field trial at a museum, we report visitors' observations, reviews from museum curators, and a detailed evaluation and discussion of the system.

Keywords: Digital display case · Digital museum · Dynamic mechanism · Virtual reality

1 Introduction

In recent years, museums have demonstrated increasing interest in the use of digital technologies to provide supplementary background information about the exhibits within their exhibitions. The conventional approach to do so has been the placement of static displays, such as panels with text and figures, near the exhibited objects to convey relevant information. However, because the exhibit and the panel are often detached, this is an ineffective and problematic way to help visitors connect to the exhibit and its information. In particular, it is difficult for visitors to understand the dynamic mechanism of an exhibited artifact based on static information displayed on a panel. For example, in order to convey the dynamic mechanism of railway bogies, the Railway Museum of Saitama, Japan has been exhibiting authentic railway bogies alongside descriptions of figures, captions, cut models, and other materials intended to show visitors their mechanism of action (Fig. 1). However, the museum argues that it has been difficult to understand the mechanism of a real moving bogie because it cannot be shown in the static descriptions. On the other hand, a video that describes the mechanism is not always effective. Because it is a non-interactive system, most visitors simply pass by without watching the video to the end. Thus, an interactive exhibition system provides an effective way for visitors to interact with exhibitions and more easily comprehend dynamic mechanisms.

© Springer International Publishing Switzerland 2015
S. Yamamoto (Ed.): HIMI 2015, Part II, LNCS 9173, pp. 634–645, 2015.
DOI: 10.1007/978-3-319-20618-9_62

Fig. 1. Exhibition of the railway bogie

The goal of our project is to construct a digital display case system that enables museums to effectively convey background information about exhibits in an exhibition using digital technology and virtual exhibits. While previous studies [1, 2] have examined static exhibits, this study focuses on exhibits with dynamic characteristics such as their mechanisms. The purpose is the development of an exhibition system that assists visitors to understand these mechanisms. In this study, we chose the railway bogie as an example and implemented a digital display case system with which visitors can interact. We conducted a field trial of the system in the Railway Museum and received reviews of the system and exhibition from the curators of the museum.

2 Related Works

Several examples of digital technology have been introduced in museums. One of the most popular technologies is the museum theater. A number of studies have been conducted on gallery talks in theaters [3]. A museum theater can use images to convey a variety of information about the theme of the exhibition to visitors in an effective manner. However, it is difficult to connect the contents in a museum theater to exhibits in the exhibition room, because museum theaters are located away from the exhibition room, beyond separation walls.

Several studies have been conducted on exhibition systems that superimpose images on exhibits. One of them is an exhibition system with a head-mounted display (HMD) [4]. However, wearable systems such as HMDs are problematic when introduced into permanent exhibitions because they are difficult for museum staff to manage. Virtual Showcase [5] can be cited as another example. This system superimposes images on exhibits using a half mirror and allows multiple users to observe and interact with the augmented information in the display. Exfloasion [6] extends this concept, enabling presentation of floating images with different depths by constructing the imaging surface of two layers and placing half mirrors both back and forth. These exhibition systems can effectively present information by superimposing it on the exhibit. However, it is difficult to convey dynamic information such as mechanisms since the exhibit to be stored in the system is static.

Other studies have examined systems that enable user interaction through the use of virtual exhibits or touch-enabled systems. Wakita et al. reported a system that allows direct interaction with the virtual fabric using a space interface device for artificial reality (SPIDAR) haptic force display that presents force on the basis of data measured with a laser range scanner [7]. However, the systems above are designed to realize the experience of touching static exhibits and, to the extent of the authors' knowledge, there are very few systems for exhibitions that allow users to manipulate the exhibit itself in order to easily understand its dynamic mechanism.

On the other hand, virtual experiment platforms have been designed and developed for students to understand the mechanism of motion systems in recent years [8]. Fan et al. [9] developed a system for students to perform motion experiments of mechanisms and to understand the composition of the mechanism and its motion principle through simulation.

The development of digital mock-up (DMU) technology and related studies is popular in the modern manufacturing industry [10, 11]. DMU technology enables the design of products and the simulation of their behavior. Therefore, it is possible to improve the quality of products, reduce production costs, and shorten development periods. It is reasonable to infer that visitors can understand the dynamic mechanism of exhibits more easily by applying DMU technology to exhibition systems.

3   Implementation

The purpose of this study is to construct an exhibition system that effectively conveys the dynamic mechanism of an exhibited artifact using digital technology. An interactive exhibition system provides an effective way for visitors to interact with exhibits and to see how the mechanism works, thereby conveying the related information. The use of a digital display case system that displays virtual exhibits is an effective method to achieve this purpose. Therefore, we constructed a system as described in the following sections.

3.1   Digital Display Case System

We constructed a digital display case system composed of three three-dimensional (3D) displays in the shape of a box. The reason we chose the shape of a three-sided display case was that the appearance of the system would resemble a display case that could be introduced seamlessly in place of conventional display cases in museums. To view the exhibit, a user wears a pair of 3D glasses with a Polhemus sensor, which measures the orientation and rotation of the receptor using magnetic fields generated by the transmitter. Based on the point of view measured by this sensor, the system calculates images to display. This enables the user to view an exhibit from many angles as if it were inside the case (Fig. 2).

We will describe the components from which the digital display case system is constructed. The computer that controls the system is a workstation with an Intel Xeon 3.33 GHz CPU. The workstation is connected to NVIDIA Quadro Plex 2200 D2 that

Fig. 2. Digital Display Case system

Fig. 3. Components of Digital Display Case for interaction

synchronizes output to the screen with three 40″ 3D displays. The sensor attached to the 3D glasses is Polhemus 3SPACE ISOTRAKII. The controller was used to operate exhibits in the digital display case (Fig. 3). Dynamic computation to operate the system was performed by the Open Dynamics Engine (ODE) [12], a physics engine. In addition, the system runs at 30 fps.

3.2   Contents to Understand the Mechanism of Railway Bogie

We propose an approach for magnifying flexure of components interactively in a digital display case system (DDCS) [1], to provide an understanding of exhibit mechanisms. Because actual flexure of real components is too little to find by users, our system show changed parts and convey mechanism to users by magnifying that flexure (Fig. 4).

A. The mechanism of the railway bogie (DT46)

The mechanism of the railway bogie described in this paper is a hollow shaft parallel Cardin drive system as shown in Fig. 6. The bogie needs to suppress vibration in order to prevent vibration up and down the body when it is running on a rail.

In previous system [12], we showed 0 series Shinkansen's bogie in the DDCS (Fig. 5). It has axle and bolster springs. It also has flexible joints consisting of an

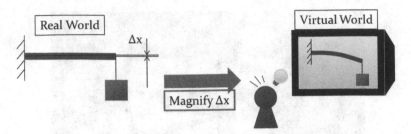

Fig. 4. Concept to provide understanding by magnifying Δx

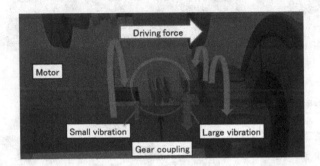

Fig. 5. Mechanism of the railway bogie (0 series Shinkansen)

annular gear, external gears, a spring, and so forth. The role of flexible joints is to transmit driving force from the motor to the wheels and to prevent vibration from being transmitted to the motor. Owing to this joint, trains can remain stable while running.

In this study, we choose hollow shaft parallel Cardin driving devices of DT46 which is popularly used bogie mechanism in Japanese commuter train. This mechanism have features that the motor shaft is a hollow shaft (pipe-like axis) and that shaft include another shaft to transfer driving force to gears and wheels as shown in Fig. 6. When misalignment between motor shaft and gear shaft are occurred while running, this system keep to transfer driving force to gears and wheels by bending flexural plate and declining gear shaft (Fig. 7). In order to convey such a complicated mechanism, the exhibition system requires functionality that enables visitors to interact with the exhibit and see how the mechanism works visually. Therefore, we implemented the system to allow the visitor to operate the railway bogie with acceleration or deceleration. In addition, this system possesses a function to make its parts transparent in six steps as shown in Fig. 5, so that visitors can see both the outside and the inside. Using these functions, visitors can observe the hidden parts of the mechanism as if the railway bogie was real and running.

In this system, the railway bogie in the digital display case is designed to run on a rail defined by a sine curve. In addition, the amplitude of the rail is defined to be larger than an actual rail since it is necessary to distend the mechanical movement of the bogie in order to convey the mechanism to visitors (Fig. 8). When the railway bogie runs above a certain speed, users are unable to see it run because the speed is too fast and the

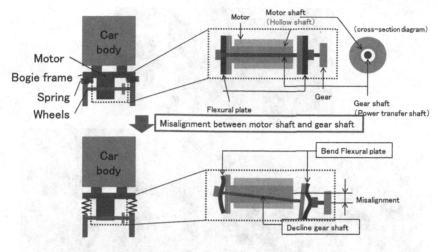

Fig. 6. Mechanism of hollow shaft parallel Cardan drive system (DT46)

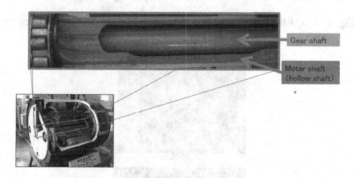

Fig. 7. Real exhibit of the railway bogie (DT46)

gears and wheels do not appear to rotate. Therefore, we assigned a different color to parts of the gears and wheels. This makes it possible to perceive that the railway bogie is running at high speed.

An interface for museum exhibitions needs to be sufficiently easy such that anyone is able to operate it. Therefore, to operate the railway bogie, we used the controller shown in Fig. 3, which is mainly used for operating trains. Using the controller, acceleration and braking can be performed by manipulating the lever. Furthermore, it is possible to change reproduction speed, the mode of flexure plate (Fig. 9) and the transparency (Fig. 10) by pressing each of two buttons and the mode by pressing each of the other buttons (Fig. 11).

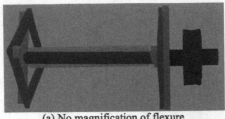

(a) No magnification of flexure

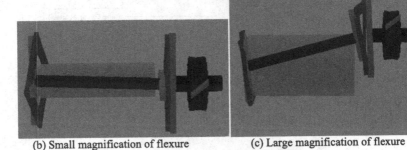

(b) Small magnification of flexure   (c) Large magnification of flexure

Fig. 8 Magnification of flexure to present understanding of mechanism

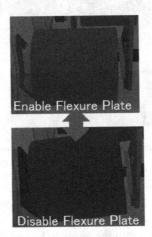

Enable Flexure Plate

Disable Flexure Plate

Fig. 9. Mode of flexure plate

4 Exhibition and User Study

4.1 Exhibition of the DDCS with the Level of Abstraction Switching

We exhibited the DDCS with the proposed level of abstraction switching method at the Railway Museum

The exhibition period was 14 days (January 8–13, 15–20, 26, 2014) and was open from 10:00 to 18:00. At the time of the exhibition, one or two docents assigned to explain the system generally remained near the digital display case (Fig. 12).

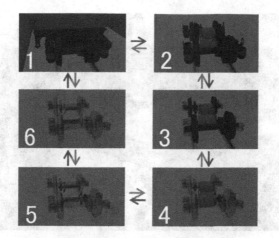

Fig. 10. Step-step transparency

Fig. 11. Typical view of proposed contents (enable flexure plate, transparency mode 5)

4.2   User Study for Evaluating the Effectiveness of Magnification

We performed a user study to evaluate the effectiveness of the interactive switching method for the level of magnification as an approach to provide a deeper under-standing of exhibits' mechanisms. We exhibited two types of interactive model, switching the method every other day. The first method enabled the visitor to switch the level of abstraction (with abstract switching condition). In this condition, the users could abstract the model shown in the DDCS step by step. Figure 8 illustrates each step and the pattern of level of abstraction switching with the abstract switching condition. The second method enabled the visitor to switch only the transparency of the parts that are unrelated to the principle of the mechanism (without abstract switching condition). This method was used in the previous study [3]. In this condition, the visitor could

Fig. 12. Exhibition of the DDCS at the Railway Museum

Table 1. Quiz to investigate user's understanding of mechanism

Q1	Allingment between the hollow shaft adn gear shaft in cross-section diagram
Q2	Allignment between the both flexure plates of gear shaft
Q3	Shape of the flexture plates (static secne)
Q4	Shape of the flexture plates (with misallignment between motor and gear shaft)
Q5	Atitude of gear shaft (with misallignment between motor and gear shaft)

switch the model between 1 and 2 in Fig. 8. We asked the visitors to take a brief quiz on the mechanism of the pendulum bogie to determine their comprehension. Each cooperating visitor took the quiz twice, before and after experiencing the sys-tem. We compared how the percentage of questions answered correctly increased after trying the system between conditions. We prepared two types of quiz; one with sixteen questions for adults, and another with sixteen questions for children. This is because the difficulty of the quiz related to abstract concepts depends on age. Based on the one for adults, we simplified the quiz for children (Table 1 and Fig. 13).

4.3 Results and Discussion

Figure 14 shows the average and standard deviation of the percentage of questions answered correctly under each condition. The number of cooperating adults was 10 for "small magnification" condition, and 8 for "large magnification" condition.

We used the student's paired t-test for the percentage of questions answered correctly by each participant in "before-experience" and "after-experience" conditions. This test revealed that there is a significant difference between the percentages of question Q2 answered correctly when the adults tried the test with the small

Q5.モータと歯車がずれたとき、歯車の軸はどうなっているかな？

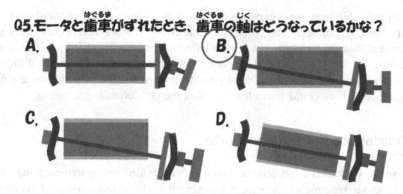

Fig. 13. Actual question to konw user's understanding of Q5

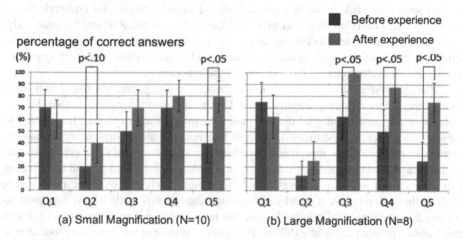

Fig. 14. Percentage of Questions Answered Correctly under each condition (Average and Standard Deviation).

magnification (p < 0.05). This test revealed that there is a significant difference between the percentage of questions Q3 and Q4 answered correctly when the adults tried the test with the large magnification ($p < 0.05$). The test also revealed that a significant difference between the percentages of question Q5 answered correctly when children tried the test with both small and large magnification condition ($p < 0.05$). There was no significant difference between the percentages of other questions answered correctly. These Q2, Q3, Q4 and Q5 are question to investigate user's understanding of function of flexure plates. These results indicate that the proposed method can provide a deeper understanding of the complicated mechanisms of hollow shaft parallel Cardin driving devices.

We asked participants to fill in a questionnaire with a seven-point rating scale and free descriptions after they experienced the exhibition. Almost all participants answer that they understand well and increase their interests about mechanism.

After the exhibition, we received a review of the system from the standpoint of the Railway Museum curators. The curators evaluated the visitors' reactions as very good, and reported that the exhibition was very effective in helping visitors understand the mechanism. On the other hand, they pointed out that they felt it was too difficult for visitors who were not familiar with physics to understand the principle of the mechanism, although they could grasp the way that the pendulum bogie works.

5   Conclusion and Future Works

In this study, we aimed to propose and construct an exhibition system enabling visitors to understand a dynamic mechanism of an exhibited artifact using a digital display case system that effectively conveyed background information about the exhibit. We chose a railway bogie as an exhibit with dynamic mechanisms and constructed the exhibition system such that visitors could interact with the railway bogie and comprehend its mechanism and function. We also exhibited this system at the Railway Museum. The usefulness of this system to convey the dynamic mechanism of exhibits was demonstrated in the reactions and opinions of visitors who had experienced it, in questionnaires, and in evaluations by the curators of the museum.

After the system was exhibited in a museum for this paper, we found that there were some points requiring improvement. During the exhibition, one or two docents were generally near the digital display case system and they explained the system to viewers. However, it is difficult to ensure that docents are always near the case in permanent exhibitions in museums. Therefore, we need to modify the system so that visitors are able to experience it intuitively and understand the background information that the museum wishes to convey about the exhibit, such as a dynamic mechanism, even if there is no docent nearby. Moreover, though this system was designed to convey the mechanism of railway bogies, we must improve it to convey other railway mechanisms or other types of exhibits. To do that, we believe it is necessary to examine the technique in this paper in more detail. Moreover, the system should be improved for experience by multiple users, as the current system cannot display an appropriate image for this situation.

We intend to introduce the digital display case system into permanent exhibitions in museums, and then to improve the system. In response to this exhibition, we learned that there are some points that should be taken into consideration if we intend to introduce the system into a museum. One point is that it is necessary for museums to make this system easier to manage. Moreover, we must adapt the system in consideration of the environment of the museum.

Acknowledgment. This research is supported by publicly-offered project "Mixed Reality Digital Museum" of Ministry of Education, Culture, Sports, Science and Technology (MEXT) of Japan. The authors would like to thank all the members of our project. Especially curators from the Railway Museum.

References

1. Kajinami, T., Hayashi, O., Narumi, T., Tanikawa, T., Hirose, M.: Digital Display Case: Museum exhibition system to convey background information about exhibits. In: Proceedings of Virtual Systems and Multimedia (VSMM) 2010, pp. 230–233, October 2010
2. Kajinami, T., Narumi, T., Tanikawa, T., Hirose, M.: Digital display case using non-contact head tracking. In: Shumaker, R. (ed.) Virtual and Mixed Reality, HCII 2011, Part I. LNCS, vol. 6773, pp. 250–259. Springer, Heidelberg (2011)
3. Tanikawa, T., Ando, M., Yoshida, K., Kuzuoka, H., Hirose, M.: Virtual gallery talk in museum exhibition. In: Proceedings of ICAT 2004, pp. 369– 376 (2004)
4. Kondo, T., Manabe, M., Arita-Kikutani, H., Mishima, Y.: Practical uses of mixed reality exhibition at the national museum of nature and science in Tokyo. In: Joint Virtual Reality Conference of EGVE - ICAT - EuroVR, December 2009
5. Bimber, O., Encarnacao, L.M., Schmalstieg, D.: The virtual showcase as a new platform for augmented reality digital storytelling. In: Proceedings of the Workshop on Virtual Environments 2003, vol. 39, pp. 87–95 (2003)
6. Nakashima, T., Wada, T., Naemura, T.: Exfloasion: multi-layered floating vision system for mixed reality exhibition. In: 2010 16th International Conference on Virtual Systems and Multimedia (VSMM), pp. 95–98, October 2010
7. Wakita, W., Akahane, K., Isshiki, M., Tanaka, H.T.: A texture-based direct-touch interaction system for 3d woven cultural property exhibition. In: Koch, R., Huang, F. (eds.) ACCV 2010 Workshops, Part II. LNCS, vol. 6469, pp. 324–333. Springer, Heidelberg (2011)
8. Fritzson, P., Engelson, V.: Modelica – a unified object-oriented language for system modeling and simulation. In: Jul, E. (ed.) ECOOP 1998. LNCS, vol. 1445, pp. 67–90. Springer, Heidelberg (1998)
9. Fan, X., Zhang, X., Cheng, H., Ma, Y., He, Q.: A virtual experiment platform for mechanism motion cognitive learning. In: Shumaker, R. (ed.) Virtual and Mixed Reality, Part II, HCII 2011. LNCS, vol. 6774, pp. 20–29. Springer, Heidelberg (2011)
10. Gomes de Sa, A., Zachmann, G.: Virtual reality as a tool for verification of assembly and maintenance processes. Comput. Graph. 23(3), 389–403 (1999)
11. Xin, X., Gangfeng, T., Xuexun, G., Menghua, C.: The study of automobile chassis design and development based on Digital Mock-Up. In: 2011 International Conference on Electric Information and Control Engineering (ICEICE), pp. 2814–2817, April 2011
12. Kiyama, R., Kajinami, T., Ueta, M., Narumi, T., Tanikawa, T., Hirose, M.: Digital display case to convey dynamic mechanisms of exhibits. In: The 18th International Conference on Virtual Systems and Multimedia, pp. 299–306 (2012)
13. Open Dynamics Engine. http://www.ode.org
14. Sreng, J., Bergez, F., Legarrec, J., Lecuyer, A., Andriot, C.: Using an event-based approach to improve the multimodal rendering of 6DOF virtual contact. In: Virtual Reality Software and Technology - VRST, pp. 165–173 (2007)

Fortune Air: An Interactive Fortune Telling System Using Vortex Air Cannon

Ryoko Ueoka[1(✉)] and Naoto Kamiyama[2]

[1] Faculty of Design, Kyushu University, Fukuoka, Japan
r-ueoka@design.kyushu-u.ac.jp
[2] Graduate School of Design, Kyushu University, Fukuoka, Japan
naoto.k70@gmail.com

Abstract. In Japan, people visit shrines in order to pray for good fortune. By determining our fortune, we draw fortune telling paper slips called Omikuji. Omikuji contains predictions ranging from daikichi ("great good luck") to daikyo ("great bad luck") As a novel interactive fortune telling system, we propose "Fortune Air". By generating the adequate pattern of vortex rings with the smoke of the incense aroma according to a prayer's interaction, visual, olfactory and tactile feedback is realized. As a first step of this interactive system, we implemented a prototype of fortune air. For generating the pattern of vortex air rings, we use two air cannons placed side by side. Vortex rings shot by each air cannon make various patterns of air such as merging or repelling. We define four patterns of vortex rings and adapt them as special meaning of couple matching fortune telling system. In this paper we performed two basic experiments to determine the parameters of controlling the pattern of double vortex rings. From the results, we confirmed that distance of air cannons and combination of value of air pressure will increase the probability to generate a designated pattern though it is difficult to control all of the patterns of vortex air rings under everyday environment. Finally we made a fortune air system to evaluate the performance.

Keywords: Interactive air media · Vortex ring · Air cannon

1 Introduction

In Japan, people visit shrines in order to pray for good fortune. By determining our fortune, we draw fortune telling paper slips called Omikuji. Omikuji contains predictions ranging from daikichi ("great good luck") to daikyo ("great bad luck") As a novel interactive fortune telling system, we propose "Fortune Air". By generating the adequate pattern of vortex rings with the smoke of the incense aroma according to a prayer's interaction, visual, olfactory and tactile feedback is realized. In this paper as a first step of this interactive system, we implemented a prototype of air fortune. A user is able to see a fortune generated by two vortex rings according to his choice of a fortune stick. For generating the pattern of vortex air rings, we use two air cannons placed side by side. And vortex rings shot by each air cannon make various patterns of air such as merging or repelling. We define four patterns of vortex rings and adapt them as special meaning of

S. Yamamoto (Ed.): HIMI 2015, Part II, LNCS 9173, pp. 646–656, 2015.
DOI: 10.1007/978-3-319-20618-9_63

couple matching fortune telling system. In this paper we performed two basic experiments to determine the parameters of controlling the pattern of double vortex rings. From the results, we confirmed that distance of air cannons and combination of value of air pressure will increase the probability to generate a designated pattern though it is difficult to control all of the patterns of vortex air rings under everyday environment. Finally we made a fortune air system to evaluate the performance.

2 Related Studies

2.1 Air Media

Generally, vortex ring is generated by a moderate size hole being punched out on one of the faces of a cardboard box, and the side of the box is struck, creating a mass of air that travels linearly while holding its shape. In other words, a vortex air cannon requires a container that has a circular hole, and can be easily built if there is a device to rapidly push the air out [1]. Vortex rings are also highly studied physically, and stability conditions and speed control can be designed according to the well known principles. In our previous research [2], we developed a small air pressured facial tactile display to generate another sensation for theater environment. By applying our previous knowledge, we developed two small air cannons placed side by side to control patterns of vortex ring for this research. As for interactive media system while being unobtrusive, air pressure is used for haptic interface. Suzuki et al. used air jet to give force feedback to improve realistic sensation when interacting with virtual object as an unobtrusive haptic display [3]. Sodhi et al. also developed a compact air pressured tactile display called aireal to give a haptic sensation on CG object to a game playing user in real world [4]. And as an unobtrusive aroma transmitter, vortex ring is used for an olfactory display transmitting aroma far to a targeting user while not diffusing it around the space [5]. In this research, we try to develop to control and create the pattern of vortex rings for physical message. This message is mainly existing visually but in the future the pattern will be used for multi sensory display integrating olfactory and haptic functions.

2.2 Ritual-Related Interactive Interface Design in HCI

In HCI field, we have often seen an interface to enhance the traditional rituals technically. ThanatoFenestra [6] is an interactive altar to change and control the photos of the deceased by a candlelight's movement and burning aroma (a metaphor of incense sticks), which are used for ritual in front of altar to pray for the deceased. This proposed system enhances interaction with the deceased. Our proposed system is not an replacement of an altar for family deceased but for public use. A prayer companion [7] was proposed as a design study for supporting prayers' life by providing RSS news feeds as a resource to the prayer activity to the cloistered nuns. This proposed system is an interface to provide updated news as a resource of the prayer activity for rather technically handicapped people such as cloistered nuns or elderly people. Our proposed device is not providing any social affairs but substitute a fortune telling written by text to a fortune telling predicted by air.

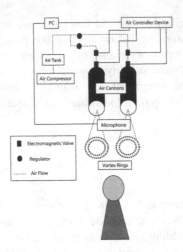

Fig. 1. Fortune air system outline

3 Fortune Air System Scheme

3.1 System Outline

Figure 1 shows system outline of the fortune air prototype. Two parallel air cannons generate two vortex rings by controlling four electromagnetic valves. Two electromagnetic valves are implemented in one air cannon. The one electromagnetic valve flows the compressed air to air container unit of the air cannon. And another valve flows the compressed air from the air container when to generate vortex ring. On and off of these valves are controlled by PC and arduino. Our hypothesis is that by controlling pressure value contained in the air container of each air cannon will change a behavior of two vortex rings.

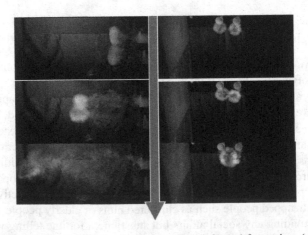

Fig. 2. Merging of vortex rings: side view (left) and front view (right)

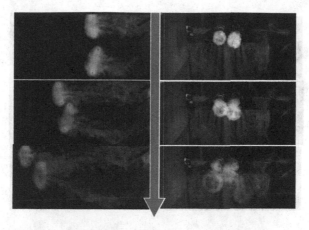

Fig. 3. Rebound of vortex rings: side view (left) and front view (right)

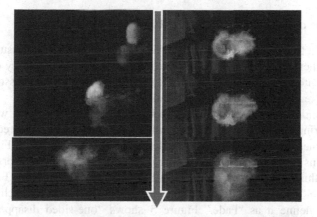

Fig. 4. Disappearance of vortex rings: side view (left) and front view (right)

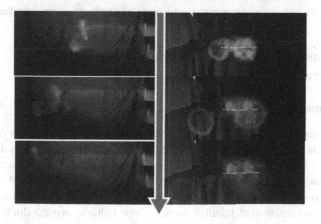

Fig. 5. One-sided disappearance of vortex rings: side view (left) and front view (right)

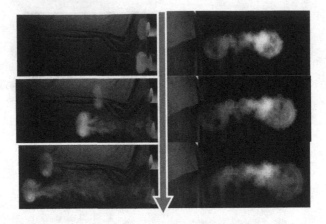

Fig. 6. No interference of vortex rings: side view (left) and front view (right)

3.2   Patterns of Translational Vortex Rings and Their Messages

It is known that translational movement of two vortex rings causes pressure decrease in between and then vortex rings approach each other. We did preliminary experiment to observe the patterns of translational vortex rings by changing air pressure value. We found that there are five patterns of translational vortex rings.

Figure 2 shows "merging." This is a merging of two vortex rings, which makes a large vortex ring. This proceeds slowly while straining in every direction. As this pattern combines two rings into one, we define it as "Good match." Figure 3 shows "rebound." This is a rebound of two vortex rings and each ring goes forward opposite direction. As this pattern acts repulsively, we define it as "Bad match." Figure 4 shows "disappearance." Two vortex rings disappear as they closely approach and rebound strongly. We define it as "Fade." Figure 5 shows "one-sided disappearance." One vortex ring out of two disappears as they closely approach and rebound.

We define it as "One-sided fade." Figure 6 shows "no interference." There is no interference between two vortex rings and each of them goes straight forward.

4   Preliminary Experiment to Evaluate Probability of Controlling Vortex Rings

4.1   Experiment 1

The five patterns of vortex rings we observed need to be controlled in order to make fortune air system. A pattern which is generated by two vortex rings is determined by three factors according to the previous researches [8]. Three factors are impulse volume, distance between air cannons and speed of vortex rings. Adequate interference of two vortex rings will occur by controlling the three factors. In order to observe how two controlled parallel vortex rings behave, we conducted the experiment. Figure 7 shows an air cannon we made for the experiment. A tank contains

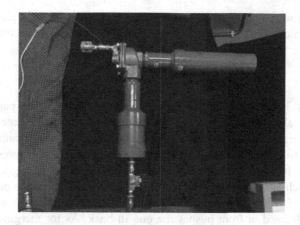

Fig. 7. Air cannon prototype

compressed air flowed from air compressor tank. Released diaphragm valve evolves compressed air and pushed air passes through a cannon with round surface, which swirls air and generate a vortex ring. From our previous research, we determined the parameter of the adequate length of a tube as 40.0 cm, which generates a vortex ring stably. And a diameter of the tube is 7.0 cm and volume of the air tank is 1077 cm3 [8]. For controlling the air flow, we used the diaphragm valve(VXFA23) manufactured by SMC. We found quite an amount of leaks of air with one of the valves. So we repaired it with rubber ring to prevent leaks. This may be impossible to transmit same value of air pressure from two air cannons, but we proceeded the preliminary experiment to observe the pattern.

Instead of controlling impulse volume and speed of air, we control value of air pressure. We tested with five kinds of pressure value; 0.04,0.055,0.07,0.085,0.1[MPa]. As for the distance parameter, we tested three kinds of distance of air cannons;

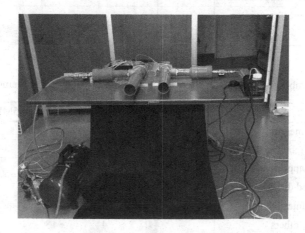

Fig. 8. Experiment settings

14.0,17.5,21.0 [cm]. We did 20 trials of each 15 kinds of settings and observed the pattern of generated vortex rings. Figure 8 shows the experiment settings.

4.2 Result

Tables 1, 2, and 3 show numbers of generated vortex ring of each pattern with controlled pressure value of each distance of air cannons. The result indicates that there is a tendency of generated pattern according to the distance of two air cannons as well as pressure value. But "no interference" appears comparatively high pressure with any distance. This is because vertical force of each vortex ring is stronger than the horizontal force which attracts each vortex ring. One-sided disappearance occurs under the condition of 0.055 MPa and wider distance (21.0 cm). The distance is adequate so that the vortex ring located in front pushes the one in back. As for merging and rebound, they often occur under the condition of 0.04 MPa without the relations to distance condition. This is because the horizontal force is balanced each other. The relative speed of each vortex must affect the generation of either pattern. As for the migration, two vortex rings approach with the same speed, which causes to generate a big vortex ring. As for the rebound, two vortex rings approach with a slightly different speed. As two vortex rings hit unevenly, no migration but rebound occurs instead.

The experiment confirms that slight difference of speed of two vortex rings determine the pattern of vortex rings.

Table 1. Numbers of generated patterns of vortex ring with 14.0 diameter cannons

14.0cm	0.04MPa	0.055MPa	0.07MPa	0.085MPa	0.1MPa
merging	10	3			
rebound	7	1			
disappearance	3	15			
one-sided disappearance		1			
no interference					
others			20	20	20

Table 2. Numbers of generated patterns of vortex ring with 17.5 cm diameter cannons

17.5cm	0.04MPa	0.055MPa	0.07MPa	0.085MPa	0.1MPa
merging	14	5			
rebound	6	2	2		
disappearance		8			
one-sided disappearance		1			
no interference				20	20
others		4	18		

Table 3. Numbers of generated patterns of vortex ring with 21 cm diameter cannons

21cm	0.04MPa	0.055MPa	0.07MPa	0.085MPa	0.1MPa
merging	5				
rebound	3	9			
disappearance	1				
one-sided disappearance		5			
no interference		1	18	20	20
others	11	5	2	0	0

5 Experiment to Define the Configuration of Air Pressure to Increase the Probability of Generation of the Designated Pattern of Vortex Rings

5.1 Experiment 2

From the previous experiment, we confirmed that the difference of speed affects the generated pattern of double vortex rings, especially merging and rebound. So as the next step, we executed an experiment to evaluate if it is possible to generate an intended pattern of vortex rings. In this experiment, we observe the pattern of vortex rings by changing the air pressure of each air cannon. In order to execute the experiment, we made new air cannons as Fig. 9 shows. Main change of the device was that we changed diaphragm valve of air cannon (VXZ260), which has less leak of air than the previous one. From the previous experiment, we determined the distance of two air cannons as 17.5 cm. This is because it was observed four patterns except for one-sided fade evenly rather than other two conditions. We also fixed the air pressure of one air cannon as 0.045 MPa. And we evaluated how the generated pattern changed among five kinds of air pressure; 0.04, 0.043, 0.045, 0.047, 0.05 MPa. We did 50 trials of each condition.

Fig. 9. Revised air cannons

5.2 Result

Table 4 shows the result of the experiment. Though we could not control the generated pattern exactly from controlling the level of air pressure but we found a tendency of generated pattern by combination of air pressure. Five kinds of patterns were able to be generated among the combination of either air pressure. Especially among three kinds of air pressure; 0.043, 0.045, 0.047 MPa, each merging, disappearance and rebound condition was observed one-third probability. From the result, we found the range of air pressures which are likely to generate merging, disappearance or rebound and no interference is highly generated by 0.04 MPa. And among the range of air pressure we tried, there were little generation of the pattern of "one-sided fade." It concludes that four patterns of two vortex rings are likely to be controlled by changing the combination of air pressure.

Table 4. Numbers of generated patterns of vortex ring

	0.04MPa	0.043MPa	0.045MPa	0.047MPa	0.05MPa
merging	2	4	17	25	2
rebound	6	17	21	2	16
disappearance	14	20	8	22	23
one-sided disappearance	1	3	4	1	1
no interference	26	6	0	0	8
others	1	0	0	0	0

6 Fortune Air Prototype System

We made a prototype system of air fortune especially for love matching. This interactive system tells four types of fortune by the pattern of vortex rings, good matching, bad matching, disappearance and no interference. Prototype system is shown in Fig. 10. A user pulls out one of stick fortunes, which was implemented different type of resistor in each stick. By putting the picked stick on the plate which has two conductive poles, the regulator changes its value of output voltage, which determines 7 air pressure value from the range of 0.04 to 0.05 [MPa] shot by an air cannon. The selected value of air pressure probably determines the pattern of vortex rings. Figure 11 shows stick fortunes and a plate.

The flow of the user interface is as follows;

a. A user pulls one of the stick fortunes and put it on the plate.
b. He does two bows and two claps and one bow performance, which is a traditional pray style at shrine in Japan and the system detects the sound of two claps and vortex rings are shot by air cannons.

This prototype system was demonstrated on February 28th 2014 at the conference site. About a hundred participants tried a fortune air and enjoyed the generated pattern of

Fig. 10. Fortune air prototype: front view (left) and side view (right)

Fig. 11. Stick fortunes and a plate

vortex rings. Though it is difficult precisely control the pattern, we confirmed that this system is effective to enjoy the probability of the generated pattern as an entertainment system.

7   Conclusions and Future Works

In order to propose a novel interactive system called fortune air, we implemented a prototype of fortune air as a first step. For generating the pattern of vortex air rings, we use two air cannons placed side by side and vortex rings shot by each air cannon make various patterns of air such as merging air ring or repelling air ring. We define four patterns of vortex rings and adapt them as special meaning of couple matching fortune telling in order to make the interaction. In this paper we performed a basic experiment to determine the parameters of controlling the pattern of double vortex rings and implemented the system for evaluating system performance of generating these patterns. And we tested its performance by demonstrating at the conference. We confirmed that it would be possible to make interactive fortune telling system by vortex rings. We will implement a camera tracking system to track the pattern of vortex rings so that the system will detect the pattern automatically.

Acknowledgement. This work was supported by JSPS KAKENHI Grant Number 25350016.

References

1. Tsushiro, H., Yabe, A., Yoshizawa, Y., Sasamoto, A., Bai, B., Imamura, H., Kieda, K.: Mechanism of cut and connection phenomenon of two vortex rings. NAGARE: J. Jpn Soc. Fluid Mech. **17**(4), 279–287 (1998)
2. Hashiguchi, S., Omori, N., Yamamoto, S., Ueoka, R., Takeda, T.: Application to the 3D theater using a air pressured facial tactile display. In: Proceedings of ADADA (Asia Digital Art and Design Association) International Conference 2012, pp. 118–121 (2012)
3. Suzuki, Y., Kobayashi, M., Ishibashi, S.: Design of force feedback utilizing air pressure toward untethered human interface. In: Extended Abstracts of CHI2002, pp. 808–809, April 2002
4. Sodhi, R., Poupyrev, I., Glisson, M., Israr, A.: AIREAL: Interactive Tactile Experiences in Free Air. ACM Trans. Graph. (TOG) Siggraph Conf. Proc. **34**((4)(134)), 10 (2013)
5. Yu, J., Yanagida, Y., Kawato, S., Tetsutani, N.: Air cannon design for projection-based olfactory display. In: Proceedings of ICAT 2003 (The 13th International Conference on Artificial Reality and Telexistence), pp. 136–142 (2003)
6. Uriu, D., Okude, N.: ThanatoFenestra: photographic family altar supporting a ritual to pray for the deceased. In: Proceedings of the 8th ACM Conference on Designing Interactive Systems, pp. 422–425 (2010)
7. Gaver, W., Blythe, M., Boucher, A., Jarvis, N., Bowers, J., Wright P.: The prayer companion openness and specificity, materiality and spirituality. In: Proceedings of the SIGCHI Conference on Human Factors in Computing Systems, pp. 2055–2064 (2010)
8. Hashiguchi, S., Takamori, F., Ueoka, R., Takeda, T.: Design and evaluation of vortex air cannon for air pressured facial tactile display. Trans. Hum. Interface Soc. **14**(1–4), 375–382 (2012)

Development of the Horror Emotion
Amplification System by Means
of Biofeedback Method

Ryoko Ueoka[✉] and Kouya Ishigaki

Department of Design Kyushu University, 4-9-1 Shiobaru Minami-Ku Fukuoka,
Fukuoka 8158540, Japan
r-ueoka@design.kyushu-u.ac.jp,
k.ishigaki.654@s.kyushu-u.ac.jp

Abstract. Current 3D digital film gives us a more realistic sensation. However there is still some problem that keeps us away from immersing the horror contents. In order to find an effective way to amplify horror emotion to viewers, we propose cross modal display system to enhance horror emotion. As a first step, we developed a pseudo heart beat feedback system to give vibrotactile feedback. We made a locker-type 3d movie watching environment while generating heart beat-like vibration on the sole of the foot. We conducted the experiment to view the horror movie with the system. In this experiment, we gave two types of pseudo heart beat vibration. One is to raise heart beat vibration by referring a user's heart rate real time. Other is to raise heart beat vibration in a stepwise manner up to predetermined heart rate value. We evaluated which method is effective to raise viewer's real heartbeat.

Keywords: Vibrotactile feedback · Horror emotion · Pseudo heartbeat · Biofeedback · Synchronization

1 Introduction

Current 3D digital film gives us a more realistic sensation. However there is still some problem that keeps us away from immersing the horror contents. In order to find an effective way to amplify horror emotion to viewers, we propose cross modal display system to enhance horror emotion. As a first step, we developed a pseudo heartbeat feedback system to give vibrotactile feedback. In concrete, we made a locker-type 3d movie environment while generating heartbeat-like vibration on the sole of the foot. We conducted the experiment to view the horror movie with the system. In this experiment, we propose two methods to generate pseudo heart beat vibration. One is to raise heartbeat vibration by referring a user's heart rate real time. Another one is to raise heartbeat vibration in a stepwise manner up to predetermined heart rate value. We evaluated whether our proposed system effects to change viewers' real heart rate and analyzed which type of method is effective to change its real heart rate by comparing ration of synchronization.

© Springer International Publishing Switzerland 2015
S. Yamamoto (Ed.): HIMI 2015, Part II, LNCS 9173, pp. 657–665, 2015.
DOI: 10.1007/978-3-319-20618-9_64

2 Related Works

2.1 Cross Modal Stimuli and Emotion

As for utilizing crossmodal effect for emotion amplification, Furukawa et al. proposed the system to control piloerection on the forearm artificially to generate the feeling of surprise while playing audio or watching movie [1, 2]. Coen et al. conducted an experiment to evaluate a link between negative emotional state and abnormal visceral sensation from the point of brain processing [3]. As experimental settings, they compared brain process of a subject listening to emotionally negative music with artificially giving stimuli into its distal esophagus and concluded that outer stimuli into esophagus amplifies negative emotion.

2.2 Biofeedback and Emotion

Ohkura et al. clarified the relationship between emotional feeling such as surprising or exciting feeling and change of biological signals such as ECG (electrocardiogram), SPA (skin potential activity) to derive the Kansei model to evaluate emotional state objectively. [4] One of their researches described that the fearful feeling was influenced by change of visual stimuli by evaluating the raise of heart rate [5].

The interactive art work called "Empathetic heartbeat" generates empathetic feeling by watching movies while hearing its own heartbeat being amplified through the stethoscope on its chest [6]. To overlay heartbeat coming from its own body is effective to imagine other people's emotion in the movie and is immersed in a story.

These previous research and work suggest that emotion and biosignal are well related and thus biofeedback will be effective to change its emotional state from outer stimuli. Our previous research also concluded that watching horror movie in a closed space raised heart rate significantly rather than watching it in an open space [7] (Fig. 1).

Based on these findings, we developed a cross modal system to experience horror movie with vibrotactile feedback of pseudo heartbeat simulated by its own heart rate in a closed box. We evaluated if there is emotional change by watching the horror movie with the system. In this paper, we evaluated if vibrotactile feedback of pseudo heartbeat draws real heart beat faster.

Fig. 1. Horror movie capture image

2.3 Synchronization Phenomena

Synchronization phenomena is an interacting elements existing in the world. For example if a large number of fireflies gather around a single tree, they will eventually start to flash at the same time creating a bright flashing light. Similarly we experience in a concert halls a large number of hand claps sound separately but synchronize eventually. This synchronization phenomena is mathematically defined with so called the Kuramoto model [8]. This model is defined as the Eq. 1.

$$\frac{d\phi i}{dt} = \omega_i + \frac{K}{N}\sum_{j=1}^{N} \sin(\phi_i - \phi_j)$$ (1)

where a population N coupled phase oscillators in i is φ_i and its variable velocity is φ_j having natural frequencies ω_i distributed with a given probability density K of dt. We adapt this model to evaluate the effectiveness pseudo heartbeat frequency to change real heartbeat frequency. We calculate the rate of synchronization between the pseudo heartbeat frequency and its real heartbeat frequency in order to evaluate the effectiveness of these two biological rhythm.

3 Horror Emotion Amplification System

We developed a prototype horror emotion amplification system. The system configuration is shown as Fig. 2. The system simulates a locker box with peeping holes on the front panel with paralyzed film. This is a same design with our previous research in [7]. By peeping a hole, a person watches 3D movie without wearing a paralyzed glasses. With our new prototype system, we added a vibrotactile display on the bottom in order to give feedback of real/pseudo heartbeat. As Fig. 3 shows, we implemented a subwoofer (Buttkicker BKA-113-C) under 50 cm(w) × 50 cm(d) × 20 cm(h) wood plate. By standing on it, a user feels generated heartbeat through bottom of feet. We expect echoing its own heartbeat produces as if he were locked in a closed area. We developed monitoring application which records its interval time of heart beat, edits heart beat timing and outputs vibration of edited heart beat through the vibrotactile display while capturing his heart rate with a photodiode heart rate sensor real time. Figure 4 shows a captured display of the monitoring application.

Figure 5 shows an overall system we implemented. 2 m × 6 m silver screen and vinyl pipes' screen frame are constructed with four persons at site. Two rear projectors are set on the back of the screen for 3d projection.

Figure 6 shows a locker-like box. The size of the box is 50 cm × 50 cm × 200 cm. One person is able to stand inside a box while peeping holes in front for watching a 3d movie played on the silver screen outside. A person's heart rate is captured on the

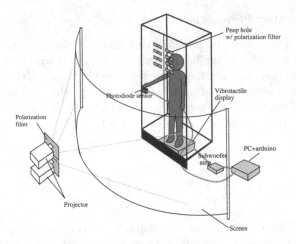

Fig. 2. System diagram

Fig. 3. Vibrotactile feedback system bottom (left), front (right)

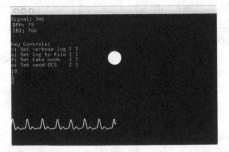

Fig. 4. Monitoring display of heart rate

middle finger of right hand by a photodiode sensor (Fig. 6 top right). A frequency pattern of interval of heart beat is generated according to the captured heart rate and sent to vibrotactile display (Fig. 6 bottom right).

Fig. 5. Experiment Setting

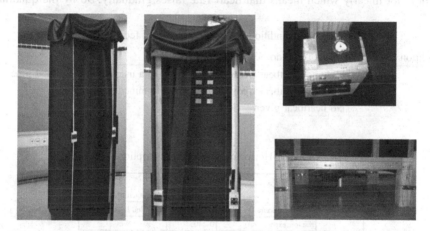

Fig. 6. Locker-like box and its attachments (photodiode sensor (top right), subwoofer speaker (bottom right))

4   Pseudo Biofeedback Experiment

The purpose of the experiment is to evaluate if the system amplifies horror experience and to analyze two methods of generating pseudo heartbeat is effective to change the frequency of real heart rate and evaluate which is more effective. In this paper we used rate of synchronization between real heart rate and pseudo heart rate to compare the effectiveness between two proposed conditions.

Horror movie we used for the experiment was the same one in the previous research [7]. The scene of the movie was categorized into 14 scenes. We followed the categories and displayed real and pseudo heart rate calculated by two conditions.

The conditions to generate pseudo heart rate is described as follows.

The first one is to raise pseudo heart rate interactively adapting a subject's heart rate real time. The second one is to raise pseudo heart rate in a stepwise manner up to the predetermined heart rate. As a control condition, no vibriotactile stimulus was given to one third of the total subjects. Table 1 shows fluctuation conditions and Table 2 shows conditions given in each categorized scene.

As the previous finding in [7], the maximum raised heart rate of subject's heart rate is 20 bpm larger than mean heart rate while it watches about 120 s' highlight of the same horror movie in a closed locker in the upright position. We concluded that this number is biologically boundary of fluctuation of heart rate for 120 s as a human being in the upright position. So we fixed the maximum increase of pseudo heart rate is 20 bpm larger than mean heart rate of each subject. So if a subject's mean heart rate is 70 bpm, we did not raise pseudo heart rate more than 90 bpm.

Pseudo heart rate (*fBPM*) is calculated by Eq. 2. Elapsed time after giving vibrotactile stimulus is defined as Δt. Average heart rate at rest is defined as *aBPM*. The subtraction of average heart rate for 10 s of each subject and generated pseudo heart rate is defined as *dif*. Also we simulate the raise of heart rate is similar to quadratic function not linearly which means that heart rate raises gradually. So by the quadratic

Table 1. Conditions of pseudo heartbeat feedback

Condition No.	Type of pseudo heart beat
1	Vary its heartbeat frequency adapting to a user's heart rate real time
2	Vary its heartbeat frequency by predetermined value
3	No heartbeat given

Table 2. Horror movie scene description

Scene No.	Scene	Time(sec)	Vibrotactile heart beat condition 1	condition 2
1	rest (pre experimemt)	0-240	None	
2	pre locker vibration	241-293		
3	a subject's locker vibration	294-312	real heart beat	
4	a friend being dragged into a locker	335-342		
5	zombie appeared	356-414		
6	another friend is killed	415-427		
7	zombie approched (disappeared to left direction)	429-456		
8	locker vibration from left side	457-463	Vary its heart beat frequency adapting to a user's heart rate real time	Vary its heart beat frequency by predetermined value
9	zombie murmured	464-472		
10	zombie close-up	476-481		
11	rest (1-30s)	481-514		
12	rest (31-60s)	515-544		
13	rest (61-90s)	545-574		
14	rest (91-120s)	575-604	None	

function $20 = a120(sec)^2$, we led coefficient a as 720. Dif is ignored when to calculate the pseudo heart rate of condition 2.

$$fBPM = 60000 \times (\frac{720}{\Delta t(\sec)^2 + 720 \times \alpha BPM}) - dif \tag{2}$$

30 university students (male 17 female 13) participated the experiment and each 10 subjects did the experiment with one of the conditions. The experiment was conducted one by one in a darkroom. A subject entered a box and stood still while looking at point of gaze on the screen for four minutes. We recorded the heart rate of this four minutes as rest time and the mean heart rate was calculated to determine maximum value of raising heart rate. After the four-minute rest time, the horror movie was played as well as vibrotactile stimulus was displayed. The first 101 s from the scene 2 to 4, real heart rate of each subject was used to generate vibrotactile stimuls in order to get accustomed to the stimulus on the foot. From scene 5 to 10, the pseudo heart rate was calculated to generate vibrotactile stimulus. After the movie, subject stood still for two minutes to record heart rate as after rest.

5 Result

Figure 7 shows ratio indicator of mean heart rate of each scene and mean heart rate of rest time. From scene 5 (zombie appeared), pseudo heartbeat was displayed by the vibrotactile display. And the highlight of the movie was scene 10 (zombie close-up). We did not find any change of heart rate in all conditions when the movie started. However in condition 1, from scene 6 (another friend is killed) heart rate raised gradually and during the hightlight scene the heart rate raised maximum value during the movie was played. Also after the movie the heart rate still kept increasing. The maximum value of all scenes was scene 12 (rest(31–60 s)). In condition 2, scene 7 (zombie approched) was maximum heart rate during the movie not the highlight scene. And the maximum value of all scenes was scene 11 (rest (− 30 s)). In condition 3, the highlight scene was the maximum value of the heart rate of all scenes but right after the highlight, heart rate declined.

We also analyzed rate of synchronization of condition 1 and 2 in order to evaluate which method effects to change real heart rate. Kuramoto order parameter was calculated by Eq. 3. This parameter affects the strength of binding of real and pseudo heart rate. The phase of heart rate ($HFrequency = \theta$) was calculated by Eq. 4. Inter-beat interval is defined as IBI as well as fake inter-beat interval ($fIBI$) and based on last 128 $(f)IBIs$, mean $\overline{(f)IBI}$ was calculated.

$$SyncRatio = \frac{1}{2}\left|\sum e\hat{\imath}\theta\right| \tag{3}$$

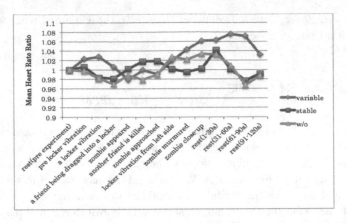

Fig. 7. Mean heart rate ratio

$$HFrequency = \frac{2\pi \times IBI_i}{\overline{IBI}} \tag{4}$$

Figure 8 shows mean rate of synchronization of each scene. If the rate is close to 1.0, rate of synchronization between real and pseudo heart rate is linked, which indicates that vibrotactile stimulus effects real heart rate.

Rate of synchronization in condition 1 is larger than that in condition 2. We applied t-test and there is significant difference in scene 8 ($p < 0.05$), scene 10 ($p < 0.01$) and scene 11 ($p < 0.01$). Even though there is no significant difference, scene 6, 7 and 9 also tend to be different ($p < 0.1$). This indicates to raise pseudo heart rate interactively adapting to real heart rate and feedback vibrotactile stimulus to a subject effects to change real heart rate more than another method.

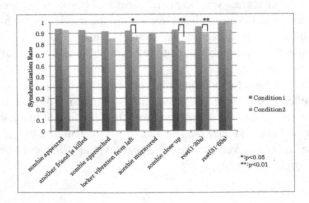

Fig. 8. Rate of synchronization of each scene of condition 1 and 2

6 Discussion and Future Works

As a first step of the research, we developed a pseudo heartbeat feedback system to give vibrotactile feedback. In concrete, we made a locker-type 3d movie environment while generating heart beat-like vibration on the sole of the foot. We conducted the experiment with the system. In this experiment, we gave two types of pseudo heart beat vibration. One is to raise heart beat vibration by referring a user's heart rate real time. Another one is to raise heartbeat vibration in a stepwise manner up to predetermined heart rate value.

We evaluated whether our proposed system effects to change viewers' real heart rate and analyzed which type of method is effective.

In conclusion we found

(1) By giving vibrotactile feedback, it is likely to give afterglow of horror experience.
(2) By generating pseudo heart rate synchronizing user's heart rate real time, it is more effective to change one's real heart rate.

From these results, it is possible to control one's horror emotion with the combination of audiovisual and vibrotactile feedback. In this experiment, in order to find an effective method to use vibrotactile feedback as crossmodal stimuli, we hypothesized the raise of heart rate is similar to quadratic function. But it is still not clear this method is adequate to simulate raise of heart rate. Now we are interested in adapt Kuramoto synchronization model to simulate heart rate by referring a user's heart rate real time. In future work we plan to adapt Kuramoto synchronization model to generate pseudo heart rate and analyze its effect. Also we will add olfactory stimuli in addition to visual and vibrotactile stimulus to evaluate which combination of crossmodal stimulus is effective to amplify the horror emotion.

References

1. Furukawa, S., et al.: Facilitating a surprised feeling by artificial control of piloerection on the forearm. In: 3rd Augmented Human International Conference, Article No. 8 (2012)
2. Furukawa, S., et al.: Chilly chair: facilitation an emotional feeling with artificial piloerection. In: ACM SIGGRAPH 2012 Emerging Technologies, Article No. 5 (2012)
3. Coen, S.J., et al.: Negative mood affects brain processing of visceral sensation. J. Gastroenterol. **137**(1), 253–261 (2009)
4. Harada, Y., et al.: Content evaluation of exciting feeling by using biosignals. Adv. Hum. Factors Ergon. **2014**, 488–493 (2014)
5. Kakegawa, Y., et al.: Development and evaluation of an exciting interactive system utilizing biological signals (The second report). In: 53th Jido Seigyo Rengo Koenkai, pp. 618–621 (2010) (Japanese)
6. Empathetic heartbeat. http://www.junji.org/eh/. Accessed 13 February 2015
7. Omori, N., Tsutsui, M., Ueoka, R.: A method of viewing 3D horror contents for amplifying horror experience. In: Yamamoto, S. (ed.) HCI 2013, Part III. LNCS, vol. 8018, pp. 228–237. Springer, Heidelberg (2013)
8. Acebron, J.A., et al.: The kuramoto model: a simple paradigm for synchronization phenomena. Rev. Mod. Phys. **77**(1), 137–185 (2005)

Application of the Locomotion Interface Using Anthropomorphic Finger Motion

Yusuke Ujitoko[(⊠)] and Koichi Hirota

The University of Tokyo, Tokyo 113-8656, Japan
yusuke.ujitoko@gmail.com, k-hirota@k.u-tokyo.ac.jp

Abstract. This paper describes new applications of a locomotion interface that uses fingers instead of legs. With this device, users let two fingers "stand" or "walk" on a ball floating on water. The first-person perspective presented to the user is updated according to the state of the ball. The aim is to make users feel virtually present by means of the synchrony between their vision and the haptic information from their fingers. The difficulty of controlling of the ball with fingers lets users subjectively experience an unsteady foothold. The proposed system is structured to be space saving and cost effective compared to an ordinary full-body motion simulator and is thus suitable for museum exhibitions.

Keywords: Locomotion · Finger motion · Multimodality · Ground instability

1 Introduction

In our ordinary lives, we often feel like sharing our own experience with others; on the other hand, we would like to experience what others have experienced. During a trip, for example, we would like to tell others about the rural landscape, the surrounding historical environment, or the emotional ups and downs by seeing them. We can summarize the above as the feeling of "being there," which can never be communicated by mere images or videos. Digital information technologies that measure, record, and preserve experiences have been developed recently. Wearable wide-angle cameras such as GoPro have become commonplace, making the recording of an individual experience easily possible. Therefore, a means of displaying archived information to users has attracted increasing attention. What is the best way to experience what others have experienced as our own experience?

The sensation of walking plays a key role in the subjective feeling of presence or the sensation of being in one place, even when one is physically situated in another place [1]. It has been reported that the extent to which a locomotion technique resembles its real-world counterpart has a positive effect on the sensation of presence [2, 3]. There have been two directions in research on locomotion: the development of wide-area trackers so that users can actually walk about and the development of body-active surrogates for walking, e.g., a treadmill and walking-in-place [4–6]. Both ideas are straightforward and have the advantage of possibly providing direct haptic feedback to the user's legs. If achieved, they would be the most natural locomotion system. However, the devices or systems tend to be large and complicated because of the need to support full-body motion. Therefore, we cannot always feasibly construct these

© Springer International Publishing Switzerland 2015
S. Yamamoto (Ed.): HIMI 2015, Part II, LNCS 9173, pp. 666–674, 2015.
DOI: 10.1007/978-3-319-20618-9_65

full-body simulators. Another method for operating a virtual body is to use fingers as an input system instead of legs. For example, finger motions that mimic leg movements can be used for operating bipedal walking robots [7] and navigational tasks [8]. In this method, the physical motion is scaled down, and consequently, physical body fatigue should be reduced, as compared with that incurred by full-body locomotion techniques. We tested the occurrence of the sense of body ownership in our last study [9]. Our preliminary results suggested that the synchrony between the first-person perspective, which is a key component of human self-consciousness, and proprioceptive information was able to induce body ownership over a virtual avatar's invisible legs. This body ownership causes users to interpret the haptic stimulation through their fingers as deriving from the avatar's legs.

This paper describes new applications of a locomotion interface that uses fingers. With this interface, users let their two fingers "stand" or "walk" on a ball floating on water. The first-person perspective provided to the user is updated according to the state of the ball. Users have two main modes of feedback: the first-person perspective and the haptic information from their fingers. The method used in this study was the same as our last study [9]. The aim of this study is to make users feel as if they exist in a virtual world by means of the synchrony between their vision and the haptic information.

After making some prototype systems and conducting informal tests, we found that the floating ball had an interesting feature when interacting with human fingers. It is difficult to control the floating ball with two fingers in the desired manner. We tried to take advantage of this difficulty to allow users to experience an unsteady foothold experientially. When do we feel an unsteady foothold? An earthquake is an obvious case when people cannot maintain their posture. People are also likely to stagger on a suspension bridge or boat. Playground equipment, e.g., a swing or a unicycle, can make people have a fun balancing posture and enjoy unsteadiness. If we imagine these scenes, we can readily grasp how people feel the unsteady ground. In other words, when we would like to create these scenes virtually, an unsteady feeling on the ground is indispensable for presence. To generate an unsteady foothold, the ground needs to be shaken mechanically. When using anthropomorphic finger motion as input, the system can be structured in a space-saving and cost-effective way compared to an ordinary full-body simulator and is thus suitable for museum exhibitions. We adopted this method and tried to make users feel an unsteady foothold in two scenes.

2 Related Work

Walking in a virtual world is a fundamental task that virtual-reality technologies should be able to accomplish. Providing the ability to walk through virtual scenes is of great importance for many applications such as training, architectural visits, tourism, entertainment, games, and rehabilitation. Over the years, a large number of technical approaches have been proposed and investigated. Most of these addressed the locomotion interface that supports human leg motions themselves [4, 5]. Full-body locomotion using these interfaces is able to facilitate the acquisition of spatial knowledge of an environment and results in better navigation in the virtual environment than using common input devices [10]. However, there is a problem for practical use: entire devices supporting full-body motions tend to be large and complicated. Instead of simulating full-body locomotion, several interaction techniques using a full-body metaphor have been presented [3, 11, 12]. These met the demands to avoid user collision with real-world obstacles. However, these metaphor techniques are lacking in terms of kinesthetic feedback.

Another method for realizing locomotion is to use fingers instead of legs. This takes advantage of the structural similarities between fingers and legs. Users operate their fingers as if walking or running. For example, two fingers were used to mimic leg movements for generating the full-body motion of animation characters [13] or operating bipedal walking robots [7]. The advantage of this approach is the possibility of scaling down the device or environments around the fingers. We studied whether the tactile stimulation on the user's fingers can be felt as a tactile experience on the sole of a virtual avatar. We proved that the synchrony between the first-person perspective of the avatar as presented by a monitor and the proprioceptive information together with the motor activity of the user's fingers are able to induce an illusory feeling that is equivalent to a sense of ownership over the invisible avatar's legs [9]. Under this condition, the ground under the virtual avatar's foot is felt through the user's fingertip. The plasticity of the tactile perception using an anthropomorphic finger motion interface was also investigated. The experimental results suggested that the participants interpreted the tactile sensation on the basis of the difference in scale between fingers and legs. The tactile size perception was proportional to the avatar's body (foot) size.

There has been another approach based on the "walking-in-place" technique. The finger walking in place (FWIP) method was proposed in [8, 14]. In this method, users can move forward or backward and rotate in a virtual world as a users' fingers slide on a multitouch sensitive surface. In terms of spatial-knowledge acquisition (e.g., spatial relationships and features), the FWIP results exhibited a better performance than a rate-based translation and turning system (i.e., joystick) during maze navigation tasks.

A locomotion interface using fingers has some restrictions such as those on the translational or rotational direction due to the limitations of the wrist and is not suitable for long-term use because of fatigue. On the other hand, it has the advantage of spatial acquisition and is suitable for situations in which users cannot use their legs or for paraplegics.

3   Prototype

When using finger motions as an interface, users remain at the same physical position. Therefore, an interface based on an actual walking motion is not suitable because of space restrictions. Solutions to these restrictions consider the physical constraints on the user's movement in one of two ways. One is the development of a finger-walking simulator such as treadmills [4, 5] or the Virtusphere [15]. Another solution is so-called walking-in-place techniques, which enable the user to navigate in virtual environments by walking in place. Generally, the latter metaphor techniques are lacking in kinesthetic feedback. Therefore, we adopted the finger-walking simulator. A prototype is illustrated in Fig. 1. We made this by referring to the Virtusphere [15]. However, the entire system was scaled down and simply structured with consumer goods.

Fig. 1. Prototype

When the user's fingers "walk" on the plastic ball and rotate it, the optical mouse under the plastic ball tracks the rotation. This device enables users unlimited walking in the same physical space. There are two aspects of this device that need to be improved. First, considerable friction is generated between the plastic ball and the three ball casters, which made users feel an awkward contact force while walking. Second, it is difficult to give users some force feedback. For precise tracking, the distance between the ball and the optical mouse should be strictly controlled. Therefore, it is impossible to translate the ball and provide the fingers with force feedback.

4 Proposed System

4.1 Concept

Smooth movement of the surface and force feedback would make users feel a sub-jective feeling of presence. Considering these points, we tried to improve the device through trial and error and finally, had the idea of using a ball floating on water. The water replaced the ball casters as the support for the ball and led to smooth rotation of the ball. The force due to the buoyancy was experienced by the user's fingers. We aim to make users feel a ground instability via their fingers due to the difficulty of con-trolling the ball. Haptic and visual feedback was provided to the user from the floating ball as a result of the user's finger input, and these two types of sensory information would be integrated. We expect that illusory body ownership over the avatar in the virtual world would be induced if users do not feel a discrepancy between the haptic feedback to the fingers and the visual information.

4.2 System Configuration

Figure 2 shows a system diagram of the proposed system. The system comprises three parts: a user who experiences the content, a ball that plays a role in haptic input/output, and a server that projects the visual world. The system provides the user with visual and haptic information. We make use of a ball floating on water for haptic input/output. Fingers contact the ball and interact with it, and the ball is freely in extra motion.

The state of the ball was tracked by a PlayStation Move (PS Move) that is fixed inside the ball. The PS Move is able to obtain values from an accelerometer, a gyroscope, and a magnetometer. These values are sent to a server via Bluetooth 2.0 wireless radio communication. The server updates the graphical perspective as new values are obtained and projects a new perspective.

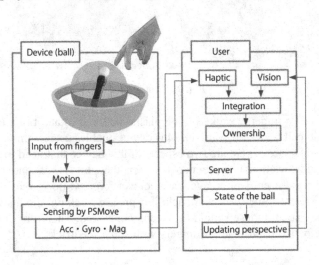

Fig. 2. System diagram

5   Application

Informal user tests showed that it was difficult to control the ball with two fingers. The force users apply to the ball makes it unsteady as a result of the interaction between the ball and the water. For example, in order to keep the ball at a constant position, users apply force to the ball. As users push the ball into the water, the buoyancy increases. We prepared a semispherical container filled with water so that the reaction force constantly arises, no matter which direction the ball is pushed (Fig. 3).

With this system, we developed two scenes. One is to walk down a mountain on a rainy day. The other is to stand on a small boat.

5.1   Walking Down a Mountain on a Rainy Day

The aim of this application is to induce the feeling of actually walking down a mountain trail in a user with their own feet. Users are asked to "walk" on the ball floating on water with two fingers while watching a first-person video of a person walking down a mountain on a rainy day. The video was taken on Trail 6 at Mt. Takao, which is the most dangerous trail course on the mountain. The cameraman captured video by holding a GoPro camera near his eyes. The avatar in the video pays attention to the muddy ground and wet rockface and looks down at the ground – the cameraman's foot is in the video (Fig. 4).

Fig. 3. Device overview

Fig. 4. First-person perspective while walking down the trail

In order to induce the feeling of "being there" and actually walking down a mountain trail with their own feet, we did three things. The first was to relate the rotating speed of the ball according to finger motion to the playback speed of the first-person video. The PS Move inside the ball measures the rotation of the horizontal axis to the users. The measured rotation determines the playback speed. The walking speed of the cameraman was not completely, but to some extent, constant. If the users rotate the ball faster, the avatar in the video moves faster. If the ball is rotated slowly, the avatar correspondingly moves slowly. The avatar in the video not only goes forward but also backward by means of reverse playback. Whether the avatar goes forward or backward depends on the direction of rotation of the floating ball. Second, we made full use of force feedback to the user's fingers. We aimed at making users interpret the reaction force resulting from a pushed ball as an impact of a sole while stepping down the mountain trail. Third, the difficulty of controlling of a ball with fingers increases in time with the relative unsteadiness of the steps while walking down the rainy rocky trail. The effects of these three points are expected to make users experience the video subjectively.

5.2 Standing on a Small Boat

The aim of this application was to induce a feeling in users of standing on a boat with their own feet. Users are asked to "stand" on the ball and keep it steady with two fingers while watching a first-person perspective of a virtual avatar over a small boat floating on the water. The graphical perspective was rendered by Unity (Fig. 5). In this application, the floating ball in the real world corresponds to the small boat in the virtual environment.

Fig. 5. First-person perspective from the boat

A weight was fixed to the bottom sphere inside the ball. The ball does not easily rotate and becomes steady because of the weight. The PS Move measured the values, and the orientation of the ball was calculated from them. The orientation of the ball determines the orientation of the first-person perspective of the virtual avatar. Maintaining a ball at a constant position resembles the sensation of maintaining balance on the boat with two legs. We aimed to make users feel the ground instability from the fingers.

6 Exhibition in a Public Space

We demonstrated our applications at a public media art exhibition on campus (Fig. 6). The number of people who tried out these applications was over 500.

We found that the ways in which users moved their fingers were different from person to person. We obtained feedback from the visitors about these applications.

Fig. 6. The visitors experienced the applications

For the application of walking down the trail, most feedback indicated that the synchronous playback of the video with a user's finger motion made users feel as if they were actually going forward with their legs, even though the footsteps of the person in the video were not completely synchronous. When users rotated the ball, the fingers got wet and some reported that the wet fingers had an important effect on being immersed in the rainy scene in the video.

As for the application of standing on a boat, we received following feedback. It was difficult to maintain balance with two fingers. The rotation of the viewpoint made users feel that they were in the virtual world. There were reports that the feeling of the ground instability was much stronger when operating the ball with fingers than when just watching someone operate the device. This indicated that the application had the effect of enhancing presence.

7   Conclusion

This paper described a new application of a locomotion interface that uses fingers instead of legs. With this device, users let their two fingers "stand" or "walk" on a ball floating on water. The first-person perspective presented to the user updated according to the state of the ball. The aim was to make users feel that they are "there" by means of the synchrony between their vision and the haptic information from their fingers. The difficulty in controlling of the ball with their fingers lets users experience an unsteady foothold subjectively. The proposed system was structured to be space saving and far more cost effective than an ordinary full-body motion simulator and is thus suitable for museum exhibitions.

References

1. Witmer, B.G., Singer, M.J.: Measuring presence in virtual environments: a presence questionnaire. Presence: Teleoperators Virtual Environ. **7**, 225–240 (1998)

2. Slater, M., Usoh, M., Steed, A.: Taking steps: the influence of a walking technique on presence in virtual reality. ACM Trans. Comput.-Human Interact. **7**, 225–240 (1995)
3. Usoh, M., et al.: Walking > walking-in-place > flying, in virtual environments. In: SIGGRAPH 1999 Proceedings of the 26th Annual Conference on Computer Graphics and Interactive Techniques, pp. 359–364 (1999). doi:10.1145/311535.311589
4. Darken, R., Cockayne, W., Carmein, D.: The omni-directional treadmill: a locomotion device for virtual worlds. In: ACM Symposium on User Interface Software and Technology, pp. 213–221 (1997). doi:10.1145/263407.263550
5. Iwata, H.: Torus treadmill: realizing locomotion in VEs. IEEE Comput. Graph. Appl. **19**, 30–35 (1999)
6. Slater, M., Steed, A., Usoh, M.: The virtual treadmill: a naturalistic metaphor for navigation in immersive virtual environments. In: Göbel, M. (ed.) Virtual Environments 1995. Eurographics, pp. 135–148. Springer, Vienna (1995). doi:10.1007/978-3-7091-9433-1_12
7. Fernando, C.L., et al.: An operating method for a bipedal walking robot for entertainment. In: ACM SIGGRAPH ASIA 2009 Art Gallery & Emerging Technologies: Adaptation 79, ACM (2009). doi:10.1145/1665137.1665198
8. Kim, J.-S., Gračanin, D., Matković, K., Quek, F.: Finger walking in place (FWIP): a traveling technique in virtual environments. In: Butz, A., Fisher, B., Kruger, A., Olivier, P., Christie, M. (eds.) Smart Graphics. LNCS, vol. 5166, pp. 58–69. Springer, Heidelberg (2008)
9. Ujitoko, Y., Hirota, K.: Interpretation of tactile sensation using an anthropomorphic finger motion interface to operate a virtual avatar. In: 2014 24th International Conference on Artificial Reality and Telexistence (ICAT) (2014). doi:10.1109/ICAT.2013.6728900
10. Waller, D., Loomis, J.M., Haun, D.B.M.: Body-based senses enhance knowledge of directions in large-scale environments. Psychon. Bull. Rev. **11**, 157–163 (2004)
11. Razzaque, S., Kohn, Z., Whitton, M.C.: Redirected walking. In: Proceedings of the EUROGRAPHICS, pp. 289–294 (2001)
12. Williams, B., Narasimham, G.: Updating orientation in large virtual environments using scaled translational gain. In: Proceedings of the 3rd Symposium on Applied Perception in Graphics and Visualization, vol. 1, pp. 21–29 (2006)
13. Lockwood, N., Singh, K.: Finger walking: motion editing with contact-based hand performance. In: Proceedings of the ACM SIGGRAPH/Eurographics Symposium on Computer Animation, pp. 43–52 (Eurographics Association, 2012)
14. Kim, J.-S., Gračanin, D., Matković, K., Quek, F.: The effects of finger-walking in place (fwip) for spatial knowledge acquisition in virtual environments. In: Taylor, R., Boulanger, P., Krüger, A., Olivier, P. (eds.) Smart Graphics. LNCS, vol. 6133, pp. 56–67. Springer, Heidelberg (2010)
15. Medina, E., Fruland, R., Weghorst, S.: Virtusphere: walking in a human size vr "hamster ball". Proc. Human Factors Ergon. Soc. Annu. Meet. **52**, 2102–2106 (2008)

Considering a New Nanbu Fuurin Design that Play a Healing Sound – Including Innovations in Appearance and Texture, and Continually Improving–

Ying Zhang[1(✉)] and Takamitsu Tanaka[2]

[1] Graduate School of Engineering, Iwate University,
4-3-5 Ueda, Morioka, Iwate, Japan
pinkywing.z@gmail.com
[2] Iwate University, 2-18-33 Ueda, Morioka, Iwate, Japan
taktak@iwate-u.ac.jp

Abstract. This study concerns the design of Japanese traditional wind chimes, called *Nanbu Fuurin* in Japanese. The purpose of this study is to pass on and carry forward this traditional craft, while also giving it a new modern element. In order to, relieve pressures from life, work, study, disaster occurrences, the designers give the well-known *Nanbu Fuurin* a design of texture to improve people's emotions and offer feelings of treatment visually.

Keywords: Nanbu Fuurin · Healing · Texture design

1 Introduction

1.1 History of *Nanbu Fuurin*

Nanbu Fuurin [1] is a traditional Japanese wind chime that is made from Nanbu ironware (Fig. 1). This specific wind chime is offered in an original Nanbu ironware bronze colors. Japanese people typically use it *Nanbu Fuurin* as a garden ornament and it is typically hung it from the eaves of their homes during the summer time. It has the shape of a bell with the clapper in the middle of the chime. *Nanbu Fuurin* originated from Southern ironware called *Nanbu Tekki*, this is a traditional craft of Iwate Prefecture, Japan. Traditional craft refers to the revitalization of traditional healing. The traditional craft industry is based on relevant law, and is formed after years of art and technology inheritance in a particular region [2]. "*Nanbu Fuurin* is an award-winning traditional craft, first recognized by the Minister of Economy, Trade and Industry in 1975 [3], and is made from an important kind of southern iron (Fig. 2) [4]." *Nanbu Tekki* (Southern ironware) is using a 400-year-old technique developed in Japan's Iwate Prefecture.

Nanbu Fuurin are hand-cast out of southern ironware. They have a unique texture that exhibits the Japanese "Wabi-sabi (A not deliberately prominent decoration and appearance, emphasis on material things Imperfect, rustic, and to experience the test of time beauty.) [5]" aesthetic, and are cast in different shapes, each with a

© Springer International Publishing Switzerland 2015
S. Yamamoto (Ed.): HIMI 2015, Part II, LNCS 9173, pp. 675–684, 2015.
DOI: 10.1007/978-3-319-20618-9_66

Fig. 1. Japanese wind chime *Nanbu Fuurin* (Color figure online)

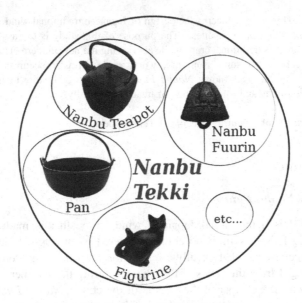

Fig. 2. Types of *Nanbu Tekki*

different timbre. The sound is so exquisite that Nanbu Fuurin are the local people's favorite decoration. They have also been selected as one of a hundred distinctive objects that create the "Sound Landscape of Japan" [6].

1.2   Nanbu Fuurin New Demand for Healing

In addition, *Nanbu Fuurin* is one of Japan's most popular export products. Japan is a country in which natural disasters such as tsunamis and earthquakes frequently occur. When an earthquake struck Japan on March 11th, 2011, many buildings collapsed;

Fig. 3. *Suzumushi*(bell cricket)

many people lost their homes and had to move into temporary housing provided by the Japanese government. Even worse, many of the victims suffered from Post-Traumatic Stress Disorder (PTSD) [7]. To ease and treat this condition, Xue et al. (2002) identified that the sound of the *Suzumushi* (bell cricket) (Fig. 3), which has a wide population distribution throughout Asia, can provide relief from the symptoms of PTSD [8]. *Suzumushi* sound like a bell is named .When hearing this sound, prove that the arrival of autumn [9]. Our team therefore proposed a plan to design a new type of Nanbu Fuurin with a sound resembling that of the *Suzumush*. Focusing on artistic considerations (designing and developing the *Nanbu Fuurin*), this time we will focus on the part of texture design.

2   Current Design Practices

2.1   Current Conditions and Problems in Nanbu Fuurin Texture

Most Nanbu Fuurin patterns currently on the market are drawn from traditional patterns, the natural landscape, and local customs and practices [4]. Widely used patterns include the following: (1) *Arare* (hail) pattern. This pattern, which originated in the Edo period, is still in used and is very popular (Fig. 4). Consumers consider the Arare pattern the southern unique pattern. (2) Animal patterns. Nanbu Fuurin use patterns of animals such as turtles, insects, and owls (Fig. 5). Since ancient times, people have lived closely with animals. (3) Plant patterns. South central iron casting researchers typically use flower patterns. The most common is the cherry blossom, followed by the chrysanthemum (Fig. 6). The most patterns in traditional crafts are derived from natural scenery or local customs. These traditional textures make people feel comfortable and satisfy domestic consumers. For the international market, however, new designs should be added reflecting foreign consumers' preferences, values, lifestyles, and backgrounds. This full paper will explore this issue in detail.

And with regard to color, traditional Nanbu Fuurin mainly uses the original bronze colors of *Nanbu Tekki*. However, these dull colors do not have a positive

Fig. 4. Arare pattern

Fig. 5. Animal pattern

Fig. 6. Plant pattern

therapeutic effect. Surveys have shown that they can actually make consumers feel bored or frightened, especially on dark nights. It is therefore necessary to combine color psychology and user surveys to make better selections in the development and deployment of colors.

2.2 Our Previous Design Practices

The author proposed according to the physical calculation, studies of the Related Virtual Display of *Nanbu Fuurin*, aims to show virtual simulations through the

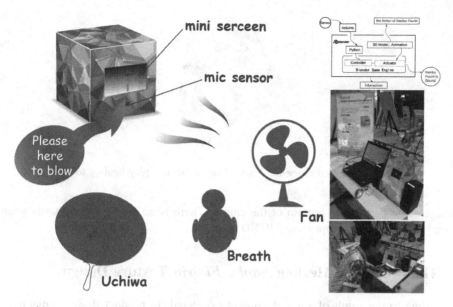

Fig. 7. How to play the Summer breeze box

combination of art and technology, and to model the charm and sound of the *Nanbu Fuurin*. Do the "Summer breeze box" of the toy box (Fig. 7). The "Summer breeze box" uses a sensor to detect a virtual wind, and measures the amplitude change of the *Nanbu Fuurin*'s swing according to the strength of the wind. The box connects user input to the sensor using Python, Arduino, and Blender; Blender generates an animation and simulates the sound of the *Nanbu Fuurin*. Although the simulation has shown that the sound and the movement of *Nanbu Fuurin* swings with the breeze following the strength of the wind that made by user [16]. However the simulated model of *Nanbu Fuurin* still lack of a unique design appearance features such as texture, and pattern which leads to the fascination of *Nanbu Fuurin*. Therefore, on this paper we will improve the apparel design of *Nanbu Fuurin*.

2.3 Healing *Nanbu Fuurin*: Research into Bell Cricket Wind Chimes

The new *Nanbu Fuurin* designs be modeled. It is necessary to identify a shape that not only sounds like a bell cricket, but also looks beautiful, providing enjoyment to people who see it. Cognitive modeling is not generally used to create wind chimes. At present, *Nanbu Fuurin* are generally shaped to resemble temple bells. All of these wind chimes are designed by experienced professional craftsmen. However, there is no research into the connection between shape and timbre.

So far, according to Nagata, Y.'s current research, studies have identified the bell cricket's sound frequency range: 4–4.5 kHz. When the iron piece inside the Nanbu Fuurin hits the swinging bell, it sounds similar to the bell cricket, but not exactly the same. To achieve precisely the same sound, the new design of Nanbu Fuurin must

Fig. 8. Proposed shape for *Nanbu Fuurin* that can play healing tones

change some part of the bottom of the chime. There is no single shape that is guaranteed to relieve the symptoms of PTSD (Fig. 8).

3   The Propose of Healing *Nanbu Fuurin* Texture Design

According to the result of some document expressed, in product design semantic is influence mood role [17]. so, this paper a relieve stress healing *nanbu fuurin* design should be considered as the following points:

(1) The affinity. For example, people often want to close to a soft and lovely animal doll. Or the other things with affinity, such as beautiful plants, cute little animal, delicious food and so on. While these things with affinity have several basic characteristics, such as simple, lovely, kind, harmless. For their shapes, they often have parts of circular or arc, and the sharp appearance should be avoided [18].

(2) The feeling of calm. Following Color Theory in Design (2008), the color selection use for product design will be effect people emotion and image [10]. For instance, Blue color give the feeling of calmness and refreshing [13]. Green color give the feeling of natural, relieve stress and heal help [14]. Light pink color give the feeling of tenderness, kindness and comforting feeling [15]. Moreover, from the color combinations and brightness of color can be created the calmness and relaxing atmosphere to effect the psychology healing for people [10].

(3) The feeling of happiness. A pleasant atmosphere will make people feel comfortable and relax. Like a image of playing with a child, the happy atmosphere can infect people feeling. Thence, the design with childlike and naive also can bring people pleasure [19].

(4) The positive visual. For alleviate the pressure, it is also important that let people relieve from the negative, and stressful. For example, rainbow has been hailed as a symbol of good luck and happiness in many places of the world. When you are feeling down, if you see the rainbow, you will feel happy, and mood will become clear and positive. As the analysis of rainbow color, the rainbow colors include most of colors in

the hue ring. However, the unity of hue's shade and level, make rainbow have the sense of balance and stability, and the atmosphere of lively, bright, happy and upward [10]. The healing *Nanbu Fuurin* also will be designed by these points in the visual.

3.1 Improvement to Texture Design Based on the Element of a Lucky Green Clover

Design A (Hope Type): A green clover deign is used, representing luck and happiness, to make the consumer feel relaxed, calm, and refreshed, and it provides an environment that fosters sober judgment (Fig. 9). Green symbolizes peace and health. Clovers are arranged in a smooth spiral pattern. Elegant pattern arrangements allow a person to feel relaxed, alleviating psychological pressure.

3.2 Improvement to Texture Design Based on a Lively Circus Atmosphere

Design B (Joy Type): This idea from the circus. When at the circus, people enjoy in joyful atmosphere. The designers use a pink-to-blue gradient. Pink provides a warm feeling, then slowly combines with blue to encourage reflection, thus easing pressure (Fig. 10). To avoid sharp angles, triangular circus flags are changed into a rounded design, avoiding stimulation that can bring on emotional instability.

3.3 Improvement to Texture Design Based on Kenji Miyazawa's Fairy Tales

Design C (Fantasy Type): A railroad motif with colored line drawings of train wheels is used as the design element, based on the "Ginga Tetsudō no Yoru (Night on the

lucky green clover

Fig. 9. Design A: Hope Type (Color figure online)

Fig. 10. Design B: Joy Type (Color figure online)

Galactic Railroad)" fairy tale by the famous writer Kenji Miyazawa, born in Japan's Iwate Prefecture [11] (Fig. 11). Gorgeous colors are reminiscent of the masters from the fairy tale fantasy, causing people to temporarily forget their pain, sadness, and pressure, and brighten their moods.

3.4 Improvements to Texture Design Based on Japanese Ukiyo-E

Design D (Retro Type): The famous Japanese Ukiyo-e piece "The Great Wave off Kanagawa" is chosen as an element of this abstract design, reminiscent of Japan's traditional Se-gaiha patterns [12] (Fig. 12). Bright colors are chosen to evoke a summer seaside atmosphere. The lively patterns and bright colors that also alleviate psychological pressure.

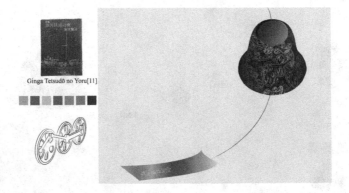

Fig. 11. Design C: Fantasy Type (Color figure online)

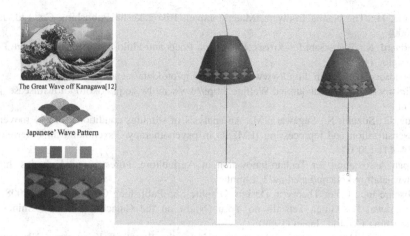

The Great Wave off Kanagawa[12]

Japanese' Wave Pattern

Fig. 12. Design D: Retro Type (Color figure online)

4   Conclusion and Future Research

Our design involves great innovation while continuing to retain the same basic shape and user impressions. It may be challenging for consumers who have used only traditional *Nanbu Fuurin*, and for the craftspeople who make them. However, once we have conquered the difficulties and made stylish new Fuurin with all of the characteristics mentioned above, our design will represent not only the perfect combination of traditional techniques with modern science and technology, but also it will make an innovative leap for the traditional production process. During post-disaster reconstruction, this project could provide a template that expresses humanity, using design to better serve the community.

Plans for future research: (1) We will make a questionnaire survey for Japanese users at home and international users abroad, aimed at improving the texture design of healing *Nanbu Fuurin*. (2) We will explore and design more *Nanbu Fuurin* models that can play healing sounds. We have therefore produced a 3D model using 3D software, importing the sound of the bell cricket, and simulating its demonstration.

Acknowledgement.   We express our gratitude to Associate Professor Nagata, Y. for his advice and technical support on Nanbu Fuurin sound, which allowed this research to be carried out smoothly.

References

1. IWACHU. http://iwachu.co.jp/
2. METI Tohoku Home Page. http://www.tohoku.meti.go.jp/s_cyusyo/densan-ver3/html/top_1.html
3. Tanaka, T.: Practice of design development for japanese traditional crafts technology in the nanbu-tekki. J. Soc. Art Educ. Univ. **41**, 159–164 (2009)

4. Horie, H.: The Nanbu Ironware, Materia Japan. Rikogakusha Publishing Co. Ltd, Japan (2000)
5. Leonard, K.: Wabi-Sabi for Artists, Designers, Poets and Philosophers. Stone Bridge Press, Berkeley (1994)
6. Soundscapes of Japan. http://www-gis2.nies.go.jp/oto/data/scene/info011.html
7. Ministry of Health, Labour and Welfare. http://www.mhlw.go.jp/kokoro/know/disease_ptsd.html
8. Xue, C., Suzuki, K., Sugawara, M.: An analysis of stimulus conditions for eye movement desensitization and reprocessing (EMDR) in psychotherapy. Psycholohie in Osterreich **5**, 434–441 (2002)
9. Japan Association for Techno-innovation in Agriculture, Forestry and Fisheries. https://www.jataff.jp/konchu/breeding/2_1.html
10. Obscure Inc.: Color Theory in Design. Graphic-Sha Publishing Co. Ltd, Japan (2008)
11. Miyazawa, K.: Ginga Tetsudō no Yoru (Night on the Galactic Railroad). Shinchosha Publishing Co. Ltd, Japan (1989)
12. Katsushika, H.: Kanagawa-oki nami-ura (Under the Wave off Kanagawa). Nishimuraya Yohachi (Eijudô), Japan (1831)
13. Blue color. http://psychology.about.com/od/sensationandperception/a/color_blue.htm
14. Green color. http://psychology.about.com/od/sensationandperception/a/color_green.htm
15. Light pink color. http://www.empower-yourself-with-color-psychology.com/color-pink.html
16. Zhang, Y.: According to the Physical Calculation: Studies of the Related Virtual Display of Nanbu Fuurin, Japan (2003)
17. Xu, S.H., Ma, Y.J.: Emotional Design of Product, The new western theoretical version, vol.11, pp. 223–224 (2007)
18. Zhang, J.Y., Gan J.: Research on Emotional Design of Pressure Relieving Product, Packaging Engineering (2011)
19. Wu, T., Qie, X.J.: A Survey on the influence from child-fun design style of groen-up's mind. Art Des. **9**, 222–223 (2010)

Author Index

Printed in the United States
By Bookmasters